Guide and Index to the Texas Adjutant General Service Records

1836–1935

Volume 1

Cumulative Index

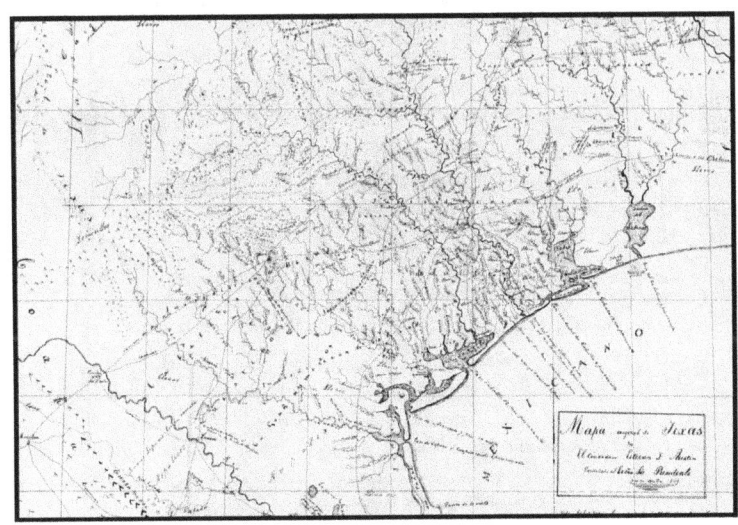

By Anthony Black
and the Texas State Archives

Edited by Robert de Berardinis

HERITAGE BOOKS
2009

HERITAGE BOOKS
AN IMPRINT OF HERITAGE BOOKS, INC.

Books, CDs, and more—Worldwide

For our listing of thousands of titles see our website
at
www.HeritageBooks.com

Published 2009 by
HERITAGE BOOKS, INC.
Publishing Division
100 Railroad Ave. #104
Westminster, Maryland 21157

Copyright © 2009 Robert de Berardinis

Other Heritage Books by Robert de Berardinis:

Guide and Index to Texas Confederate Pension Application and Payment Records, 1899–1979; Volume 1: A–D
Anthony Black, Robert de Berardinis and the TSLAC Staff, Edited by Robert de Berardinis

Guide and Index to Texas Confederate Pension Application and Payment Records, 1899–1979; Volume 2: E–M
Anthony Black, Robert de Berardinis and the TSLAC Staff, Edited by Robert de Berardinis

Guide and Index to Texas Confederate Pension Application and Payment Records, 1899–1979; Volume 3: N–Z
Anthony Black, Robert de Berardinis and the TSLAC Staff, Edited by Robert de Berardinis

Guide and Index to the Republic of Texas Donation Voucher Files, 1879–1887, and Confederate Script Voucher Files, 1881–1883, in the Texas General Land Office
Texas General Land Office, Edited by Robert de Berardinis

Guide and Index to the Texas Adjutant General Service Records, 1836–1935; Volume 1: Cumulative Index
Anthony Black and the Texas State Archives, Edited by Robert de Berardinis

Guide and Index to the Texas Adjutant General Service Records, 1836–1935; Volume 2: Separate Indexes
Anthony Black and the Texas State Archives, Edited by Robert de Berardinis

Guide and Index to the Texas Confederate Audited Civil and Military Claims, 1861–1865
Texas State Archives, Edited by Robert de Berardinis

Guide and Indexes to the Conserved and Microfilmed Harris County, Texas Records of Oaths and Allegiance, Declarations of Intent, and Final Naturalizations, 1886–1906
Robert de Berardinis

Cover illustration is a detail from the 76 cm x 64 cm map of Texas, "*Mapa original de Texas*," drawn by Stephen F. Austin ca. 1829 for the President of Mexico. It is map number 0917 from the Texas State Archives and reproduced with permission from the Texas State Archives.

All rights reserved. No part of this book may be reproduced or transmitted in any form or by any means, electronic or mechanical, including photocopying, recording or by any information storage and retrieval system without written permission from the author, except for the inclusion of brief quotations in a review.

International Standard Book Numbers
Paperbound: 978-0-7884-4765-5
Clothbound: 978-0-7884-8169-7

Table of Contents

Contents to Volume 1: Cumulative Index iv

Introduction v

Guide to the Service Records 1

    Separate Index to the Army of the Rep. of Texas 19

    Separate Index to the Navy of the Rep. of Texas 32

    Separate Index to the Mounted Volunteers 41

    Separate Index to the Minute Men 45

    Separate Index to the Texas State Troops 47

    Separate Index to the Confederate States Army 52

    Separate Index to the State Police 54

    Separate Index to the Frontier Forces 62

    Separate Index to the Frontier Battalion 70

    Separate Index to the Volunteer Guard 96

    Separate Index to the United States Volunteers 136

    Separate Index to the Regular Rangers 176

    Separate Index to the Special Rangers 189

    Separate Index to the Loyalty Rangers 227

    Separate Index to the Railroad Rangers 232

Contents to Volume 2

Contents to Volume 1: Cumulative Index iv

Introduction v

Guide to the Service Records 1

    Separate Index to the Army of the Rep. of Texas 19

    Separate Index to the Navy of the Rep. of Texas 32

    Separate Index to the Mounted Volunteers 41

    Separate Index to the Minute Men 45

    Separate Index to the Texas State Troops 47

    Separate Index to the Confederate States Army 52

    Separate Index to the State Police 54

    Separate Index to the Frontier Forces 62

    Separate Index to the Frontier Battalion 70

    Separate Index to the Volunteer Guard 96

    Separate Index to the United States Volunteers 136

    Separate Index to the Regular Rangers 176

    Separate Index to the Special Rangers 189

    Separate Index to the Loyalty Rangers 227

    Separate Index to the Railroad Rangers 231

Introduction

The term "service record" brings to the twenty-first century researcher's mind a folder stuffed with documents, promotions, awards, orders to transfer, pay records, etc. Of course it would be headed by a printed form with the highlights of service written on it. Unfortunately, most of the service records prior to the Frontier Forces and Frontier Battalions consist of documents that give evidence for service, but are not a printed form with the highlights of service written on it. The underlying documents are available online and on microfilm. They are available online at the Texas State Archives web site at:

<http://www2.tsl.state.tx.us/trail/ServiceSearch.jsp!>.

Microfilm is available through the Texas State Library and Archives Commission or at Clayton Library (Houston).

1. *Service Records of the Army of the Republic of Texas, 1836–1845,*
2. *Service Records of the Navy of the Republic of Texas, 1836–1845,*
3. *Service Records of the Mounted Volunteers, 1854–1861,*
4. *Service Records of the Minute Men, 1855–1862, 1872–1874,*
5. *Service Records of the Texas State Troops, 1861–1865,*
6. *Service Records of the Confederate States Army, 1861–1865,*
7. *Service Records of the State Police, 1870–1871,*
8. *Service Records of the Frontier Forces, 1870–1871,*
9. *Service Records of the Frontier Battalion, 1874–1901,*
10. *Service Records of the Texas Volunteer Guard, 1881–1903,*
11. *Service Records of the United States Volunteers, 1898,*
12. *Service Records of the Regular Rangers, 1855–1861, 1901–1935,*
13. *Service Records of the Special Rangers, 1916–1934,*
14. *Service Records of the Loyalty Rangers, 1918,* and
15. *Service Records of the Railroad Rangers, 1922–1935.*

In using the "All Branches" index, the family name of the veteran is given first. The usage of the index compilers at the Texas State Archives is to generally put "von" and "de" after the family name and put "Van" and "La" in front of the family name. The next field is the branch of service. The last field gives the box "call" number that held the documents at the time of indexing.

Researchers should keep in mind, especially with nineteenth century records, that the absence of an individual from these records does not mean he did not serve. It is important to check the other source materials listed in the "**Related Materials**" section of the finding aid. To aid researchers for service of individuals either in the Republic or state of Texas, the following records should be consulted:

At the Texas State Archives

1. Departmental Correspondence, 1846–1943, (Adj. Gen. Dept.),[1]

---

[1] The correspondence from 1846 through 1860 was microfilmed as *Correspondence of the Texas Adjutant General, 1846–61* (microfilm edition; Austin: Clayton Library Friends, 2006). The Correspondence and Letter Books from 1861 through 1865 was microfilmed as *Civil War Correspondence of the Texas Adjutant General, 1861–65* (microfilm edition; Austin: CLF, 2006). The correspondence from 1865 through 1877 was microfilmed as *Reconstruction Correspondence of the Texas Adjutant General, 1865–77* (microfilm edition; Austin: CLF, 2006). The Indexes to Letters Received and Registers of Letters Received, but not the Letterpress Books from 1870 through 1883 were microfilmed as *Indexes to the Registers of Letters Received*

At the Texas State Archives, Continued

2. Texas Revolution Military Rolls, 1835–1836, (Adj. Gen. Dept.),
3. United States Volunteers Military Rolls, 1835–1837, 1842, (Adj. Gen. Dept.),
4. Army of the Republic Military Rolls, 1836–1842, (Adj. Gen. Dept.),
5. Republic of Texas Militia Military Rolls, 1836–1845, (Adj. Gen. Dept.),
6. Republic of Texas Minute Men Military Rolls, 1841–1842, (Adj. Gen. Dept.),
7. Campaigns of 1842 Military Rolls, 1842, (Adj. Gen. Dept.),
8. Republic of Texas Navy Military Rolls, 1835–1846, (Adj. Gen. Dept.),
9. Copies of Military Rolls, 1838–1839, 1842, (Adj. Gen. Dept.),[2]
10. Army Papers, 1835–1846, (Adj. Gen. Dept.),[3]
11. Navy Papers, 1835–1855, (Adj. Gen. Dept.),[4]
12. Republic Ranger Records, 1839–1846, (Adj. Gen. Dept.),[5]
13. Republic of Texas Claims, 1835–1860, (Comptroller's Office),[6]
14. Warrant Registers/Memoranda of Drafts (Republic of Texas), 1836–1846, (Comptroller's Office),[7]
15. Texas General Warrant Registers and Their Index, 1846–1885, (Comptroller's Office),[8]
16. Registers and Indexes of Republic of Texas Public Debt Claims, 1848–1861, (Comptroller's Office),[9]
17. Pre-Civil War Ranger Records, 1846–1862, (Adj. Gen. Dept.),[10]
18. Texas Rangers (pre-Civil War) Military Rolls, 1846–1861, (Adj. Gen. Dept.),[11]
19. Civil War Military Rolls, 1855, 1861–1865, (Adj. Gen. Dept.),
20. Civil War Records, 1855, 1860–1866, (Adj. Gen. Dept.),
21. Army of the United States Military Rolls, 1860–1861, 1864–1865, (Adj. Gen. Dept.),

---

by the Texas Adjutant General, 1870–83 (microfilm edition; Houston: CLF, 2005) and *Registers of Letters Received by the Texas Adjutant General, 1870–83* (microfilm edition; Houston: CLF, 2005), respectively. This is followed by the series *Early Modern Correspondence of the Texas Adjutant General, 1877–83* (microfilm edition; Austin: CLF, 2006).

[2] Nos. 2–9 were microfilmed as *Military Rolls of the Republic of Texas, 1835–46* (microfilm edition; Austin: CLF, 2004).

[3] These were microfilmed as *Republic of Texas Army Papers, 1835–46* (microfilm edition; Austin: CLF, 2005).

[4] These were microfilmed as *Republic of Texas Navy Papers, 1835–55* (microfilm edition; Austin: CLF, 2004).

[5] These were microfilmed as *Records of the Texas Rangers of the Republic of Texas, 1839–46* (microfilm edition; Austin: CLF, 2005).

[6] The index and original claim files have been digitized and published online at the Texas State Archives' web site.

[7] These were microfilmed as *Warrant Registers/Memoranda of Drafts (Republic of Texas), 1836–46.* (microfilm edition; Austin: CLF, 2004).

[8] These were microfilmed as *Texas General Warrant Registers and Their Index, 1846–85* (microfilm edition; Houston: CLF, 2004).

[9] These were microfilmed as *Registers and Indexes of Republic of Texas Public Debt Claims, 1848–61.* (microfilm edition; Austin: CLF, 2004).

[10] These were microfilmed as *Ante-Bellum Records of the Texas Rangers, 1846–62* (microfilm edition; Austin: CLF, 2005).

[11] These were microfilmed as *Ante-Bellum Military Rolls of the Texas Rangers, 1846–61* (microfilm edition; Austin: CLF, 2004).

At the Texas State Archives, **Continued**

22. Special Appropriations Ledgers: Other, 1860–1865, 1879, 1881–1885, 1897–1909, (Comptroller's Office),[12]
23. Register of Military Vouchers and Warrants (and Civil Warrants Drawn on Military Appropriations), 1862–1865, (Treasurer's Office),[13]
24. Confederate Pension Application Records, 1899–1979, with Index (Comptroller's Office),[14]
25. Confederate Pension Payments Volumes, 1899–1905, 1909–1910, 1915–1966, with Indexes (Comptroller's Office),[15]
26. Confederate Audited Civil Claims, with Index (Comptroller's Office),
27. Confederate Audited Military Claims, with Index (Comptroller's Office),[16]
28. Indigent Confederate Families, 1863–1865, with Index (Comptroller's Office),[17]
29. Records of Sam Houston, 1824–1862, (Governor's Office),[18]
30. Records of Edward Clark, 1861, (Governor's Office),[19]
31. Records of Francis R. Lubbock, 1861–1881, (Governor's Office),[20]
32. Records of Pendleton Murrah, 1863–1865, (Governor's Office),[21]
33. Strays Collection, State Military Board Strays, 1860–1864, (Military Board),

---

[12] These were microfilmed as Special Appropriation Ledgers for the Frontier Defense of Texas, 1861–65, 1879 (microfilm edition; Houston: CLF, 2005).

[13] These were microfilmed as *Civil War Register of Military Vouchers and Warrants, 1862–65* (Houston: CLF, 2005). There is no finding aid or index to this unprocessed volume.

[14] The Confederate Pension Applications, No. 20, were microfilmed by the Genealogical Society of Utah. This microfilm set is obsolete. These are currently being digitized for online publication at the website of the Texas State Archives. A new index to replace the online index is available in print, for which, see Note 15 below.

[15] These were microfilmed with a new index. Currently, information from the mortuary warrants and pay stubs is being included in the funded pension application folders and being digitized by the Texas State Archives. The payment series, except for the early payment stubs, was microfilmed as *Confederate Pension Warrant Registers and Stubs, 1950–55* (microfilm edition; Houston: CLF, 2005)., and *Texas Confederate Mortuary Warrant Registers, 1917–66*, (microfilm edition; Houston: CLF, 2005). There is a comprehensive guide to all of the pension records with a corrected index to the online index by this author, *Guide & Index to Texas Confederate Pension Application and Payment Records, 1899–1979* (Westminster, Md.: Heritage Books, 2008).

[16] An index and guide to both Nos. 22 and 23 is available in print as *Guide and Index to the Texas Confederate Audited Civil and Military Claims, 1861–1865* (Westminster, Md.: Heritage Books, 2008).

[17] These were microfilmed as *Indigent Confederate Families, 1863–65* (microfilm edition; Austin: CLF, 2006). An index is available online and by Robert de Berardinis.

[18] Only the *Executive Record Books of Appointments*, etc. made by President and Governor Houston have been microfilmed already by the Texas State Archives. This is just a small part of this collection.

[19] Only the *Executive Record Books of Appointments*, etc. made by Governor Clark have been microfilmed already by the Texas State Archives. This is just a small part of this collection.

[20] Only the *Executive Record Books of Appointments*, etc. made by Governor Lubbock have been microfilmed already by the Texas State Archives. This is just a small part of this collection.

[21] Only the *Executive Record Books of Appointments*, etc. made by Governor Murrah have been microfilmed already by the Texas State Archives. This is just a small part of this collection.

At the Texas State Archives, Continued

34. Texas State Military Board Records, 1861–1865, 1955, (Military Board),[22]
35. Applications for Special Pardons for Former Texas Confederates, 1865–1867, (Adj. Gen. Dept.),
36. Minute Men Military Rolls, 1865–1866, (Adj. Gen. Dept.),
37. 5th Military District/District of Texas Records, 1865–1870, (Adj. Gen. Dept.),[23]
38. Parker and Wise County Minute Men Records, 1865–1866, (Adj. Gen. Dept.),
39. Minute Men Records, 1872–1877, (Adj. Gen. Dept.),[24]
40. General Orders, 1870–1912, Reconstruction and Ranger Records (Adj. Gen. Dept.),[25]
41. Special Orders, 1870–1897, Reconstruction and Ranger Records (Adj. Gen. Dept.),[26]
42. Special Orders, 1897–1901, Ranger Records (Adj. Gen. Dept.),
43. Frontier Forces Military Rolls, 1870–1874, (Adj. Gen. Dept.),[27]
44. Frontier Forces Records, 1870–1874, (Adj. Gen. Dept.),[28]
45. Texas State Police Military Rolls, 1870–1873, (Adj. Gen. Dept.),[29]
46. State Police Records, 1870–1873, (Adj. Gen. Dept.),[30]
47. State Guard Military Rolls, 1870–1872, (Adj. Gen. Dept.),
48. Provisional State Troops Military Rolls, 1871, (Adj. Gen. Dept.),
49. Militia Military Rolls, 1874–1877, (Adj. Gen. Dept.),
50. Texas Rangers Military Rolls, 1873–1874, (Adj. Gen. Dept.),[31]
51. Reserve Militia Military Rolls, 1870–1873, (Adj. Gen. Dept.),
52. State Guard and Reserve Militia Records, 1870–1873, (Adj. Gen. Dept.),[32]
53. Special State Troops Military Rolls, 1876–1880, (Adj. Gen. Dept.),
54. Special Force Military Rolls, 1880–1881, (Adj. Gen. Dept.),
55. Special State Troops/Special Force Records, 1874–1881, (Adj. Gen. Dept.),[33]
56. Frontier Battalion Military Rolls, 1874–1901, (Adj. Gen. Dept.),

---

[22] These last two collections are unprocessed, not microfilmed, and without finding aids.

[23] These were microfilmed as *Military Records of Texas Reconstruction, 1865–70* (microfilm edition; Austin: CLF, 2006).

[24] These were microfilmed as *Texas Minute Men Records during Reconstruction, 1865–77* (microfilm edition; Austin: CLF, 2006).

[25] These were microfilmed as *General Orders of the Texas Adjutant General, 1870–1912* (microfilm edition; Houston: CLF, 2005).

[26] These were microfilmed as *Special Orders of the Texas Adjutant General, 1870–97* (microfilm edition; Houston: CLF, 2005).

[27] These were microfilmed as *Military Rolls of the Frontier Forces of Texas, 1870–74* (microfilm edition; Austin: CLF, 2006).

[28] These were microfilmed as *Records of the Frontier Forces of the State of Texas, 1870–74* (microfilm edition; Houston: CLF, 2005).

[29] These were microfilmed as *Military Rolls of the Texas State Police, 1870–73* (microfilm edition; Austin: CLF, 2005).

[30] These were microfilmed as *Records of the Texas State Police During Reconstruction, 1870–73* (microfilm edition; Austin: CLF, 2005).

[31] Nos. 46–49 were microfilmed as Military Rolls of the State Guard, Provisional Troops, Militia, and Texas Rangers, 1870–1877 (microfilm edition; Austin: CLF, 2005).

[32] These were microfilmed as *Records of the Texas State Guard and Reserve Militia, 1870–74* (microfilm edition; Houston: CLF, 2005).

[33] Nos. 53–55 were microfilmed as *Military Records & Rolls of the Texas State Troops and the Special Force, 1874–81* (microfilm edition; Houston: CLF, 2005).

At the Texas State Archives, Continued

57. Frontier Battalion Records, 1874–1901, (Adj. Gen. Dept.),
58. Ranger Force Records, 1901–1962, (Adj. Gen. Dept.),
59. Transcripts and Notes, 1852–1975, (Adj. Gen. Dept.),
60. Records of State Claims against the United States, 1871–1890, (Adj. Gen. Dept.),
61. Records Concerning Federal Ranger Pensions, 1908–1932, (Adj. Gen. Dept.),
62. Ranger Reminiscences, 1937, (Adj. Gen. Dept.),
63. Ranger Force Military Rolls, 1901–1910, 1913–1914, (Adj. Gen. Dept.),
64. Texas Volunteer Guard Records, 1874–1904, (Adj. Gen. Dept.),
65. Texas Volunteers (Spanish-American War) Records, 1898–1904, (Adj. Gen. Dept.),
66. Texas Volunteer Guard Military Rolls, 1880–1903, (Adj. Gen. Dept.),
67. Spanish-American War Military Rolls, 1898–1899, 1901, (Adj. Gen. Dept.),
68. Texas National Guard Records, 1902–1931, 1939, 1941–1945, 1950 (Adj. Gen. Dept.),
69. Texas National Guard Military Rolls, 1902–1913, 1915, 1917, 1935, (Adj. Gen. Dept.),

At the Texas General Land Office[34]

70. Republic of Texas Donation Vouchers, 1879–1887,[35]
71. Confederate Scrip Vouchers, 1881–1883,[36]

Indexes in the Reading Room of the Texas State Archives

1. Index to the Military Rolls of the Navy of the Republic of Texas, 1836–46, (Adj. Gen. Dept.), "Index by Sailor's Name,"
2. Index to the Military Rolls of the Navy of the Republic of Texas, 1836–46, (Adj. Gen. Dept.), "Index by Ship's Name,"
3. Index to Civil War Military Rolls: Alphabetical List and by County, (Adj. Gen. Dept.), "Confederate Captains/County File,"
4. Index to Civil War Military Rolls by Organizational Units, (Adj. Gen. Dept.), "Battalion, Regiment, Brigade File,"
5. Index to Texas Rangers, 1836–1880, (Adj. Gen. Dept.), "Texas Ranger Rolls Card File," and
6. Index to Memorials and Petitions of the Republic & State of Texas, 1836–1937, (Texas Legislature), "Memorials & Petitions Card File."[37]

General Bibliographies

1. Beers, Henry Putney. *Spanish & Mexican Records of the American Southwest: A Bibliographical Guide to Archive & Manuscript Sources.* Tucson: University of Arizona Press, 1979.
2. Beers, Henry Putney. *Guide to the Archives of the Government of the Confederate States of America.* Washington: National Archives, 1968.

---

[34] There is a printed index and guide to both of these filmed collections, Texas General Land Office, *Guide and Index to the Republic of Texas Donation Voucher Files, 1879–1887, and Confederate Scrip Voucher Files, 1881–1883, in the Texas General Land Office*, Robert de Berardinis, ed., (Westminster, Md.: Heritage Books, 2008).

[35] These were microfilmed as *The Republic of Texas Donation Voucher Files, 1879–1887* (microfilm edition; Austin: CLF, 2003).

[36] These were microfilmed as *Confederate Scrip Voucher Files, 1881–1883*, (microfilm edition; Austin: CLF, 2003).

[37] All but No. 4 were microfilmed by the title listed above.

3. Cummins, Light Townsend, and Alvin R. Bailey, Jr. *A Guide to the History of Texas.* New York: Greenwood Press, 1988.
4. Munden, Kenneth W., and Henry Putney Beers. *Guide to Federal Archives Relating to the Civil War.* Washington: National Archives, 1962.

Microfilm from the U.S. National Archives[38]

Republic of Texas

1. T151, *Despatches From U.S. Consuls in Galveston, Texas, 1832–1846,*
2. T153, *Despatches From U.S. Consuls in Texas, 1825–1845,*
3. T728, *Despatches From U.S. Ministers to Texas, 1836–1845,* and
4. T809, *Notes From the Texan Legation in the United States to the Department of State, 1836-1845.*

Mexican War

5. M278, *Compiled Service Records of Volunteer Soldiers Who Served During the Mexican War in Organizations From the State of Texas.*

Confederate Service Records and Their Indexes

6. M227, *Index to Compiled Service Records of Confederate Soldiers Who Served in Organizations from the State of Texas,*
7. M253, *Consolidated Index to Compiled Service Records of Confederate Soldiers,*
8. M258, *Compiled Service Records of Confederate Soldiers Who Served in Organizations Raised Directly by the Confederate Government,*
9. M260, *Records Relating to Confederate Naval and Marine Personnel,*
10. M323, *Compiled Service Records of Confederate Soldiers Who Served in Organizations From the State of Texas,*
11. M331, *Compiled Service Records of Confederate Generals and Staff Officers, and Nonregimental Enlisted Men,*
12. M347, *Unfiled Papers and Slips Belonging in Confederate Compiled Service Records.*
13. M818, *Index to Compiled Service Records of Confederate Soldiers Who Served in Organizations Raised Directly by the Confederate Government and of Confederate Generals and Staff Officers and Nonregimental Enlisted Men,*
14. M861, *Compiled Records Showing Service of Military Units in Confederate Organizations,* and
15. T456, *Reference File Relating to Confederate Medical Officers.*

Confederate Records Relating to Texas

16. M119, *Letters Sent by Lt. Col. G.H. Hill, Commander of the Confederate Ordnance Works at Tyler, Texas, 1864–1865,*
17. P2227, *Austin Confederate Court Dockets. 1862–1864,* and
18. P2228, *Galveston Confederate Court Dockets, 1861–1865.*

General Confederate Records

19. M410, *Index to the Letters Received by the Confederate Adjutant and Inspector General and by the Confederate Quartermaster General, 1861–1865,*

---

[38] It is easier to list current microfilm titles than all of the records available, for which, see [National Archives and Records Administration], *Guide to Federal Records in the National Archives of the United States*, 3 vols. (Washington, DC : NARA, G.P.O., 1998).

Microfilm from the U.S. National Archives, **Continued**

20. M437, *Letters Received by the Confederate Secretary of War, 1861–1865,*
21. M469, *Letters Received by the Confederate Quartermaster General, 1861–1865,*
22. M474, *Letters Received by the Confederate Adjutant and Inspector General, 1861–1865,*
23. M499, *Letters Received by the Confederate Secretary of the Treasury, 1861–1865,*
24. M500, *Letters Sent by the Confederate Secretary of the Treasury, 1861, 1864–1865, 1861–1865,*
25. M522, *Letters Sent by the Confederate Secretary of War, 1861–1865,*
26. M523, *Letters Sent by the Confederate Secretary of War to the President, 1861–1865,*
27. M524, *Telegrams Sent by the Confederate Secretary of War, 1861–1865,*
28. M618, *Telegrams Received by the Confederate Secretary of War, 1861–1865,*
29. M627, *Letters and Telegrams Sent by the Confederate Adjutant and Inspector General, 1861–1865,*
30. M628, *Letters and Telegrams Sent by the Engineer Bureau of the Confederate War Department, 1861–1864,*
31. M836, *Confederate States Army Casualties: Lists and Narrative Reports, 1861–1865,*
32. M900, *Letters and Telegrams Sent by the Confederate Quartermaster General, 1861–1865,*
33. M901, *General Orders and Circulars of the Confederate War Department, 1861–1865,*
34. M909, *Papers Pertaining to Vessels of or Involved With the Confederate States of America: 'Vessel Papers,'*
35. M935, *Inspection Reports and Related Records Received by the Inspection Branch in the Confederate Adjutant and Inspector General's Office,*
36. M1091, *Subject File of the Confederate States Navy, 1861–1865,*
37. T1025, *Correspondence and Reports of the Confederate Treasury Department, 1861–1865,* and
38. T1129, *Records of the Cotton Bureau of the Trans–Mississippi Department of the Confederate War Department, 1862–1865.*

Union Records Pertaining to Confederates

M345, *Union Provost Marshal's File of Papers Relating to Individual Civilians,*
M416, *Union Provost Marshal's File of Papers Relating to Two or More Civilians,*
M598, *Selected Records of the War Department Relating to Confederate Prisoners of War, 1861–1865,*
M621, *Reports and Decisions of the Provost Marshal General, 1863–1866,*
M918, *Register of Confederate Soldiers, Sailors, and Citizens Who Died in Federal Prisons and Military Hospitals in the North, 1861–1865,* and
M1163, *Historical Reports of the State Acting Assistant Provost Marshal General and District Provost Marshals, 1865.*

General Civil War Records

M262, *Official Records of the Union and Confederate Armies, 1861–1865,*
M275, *Official Records of the Union and Confederate Navies, 1861–1865,*
M823, *Official Battle Lists of the Civil War, 1861–1865,*
M1036, *Military Operations of the Civil War: A Guide Index to the Official Records of the Union and Confederate Armies, Volume 1, 1861–1865,*

Microfilm from the U.S. National Archives, **Continued**

M1546, *Petitions Submitted to the U.S. Senate for the Removal of Political Disabilities of Former Confederate Officeholders, 1869–1877,*

M1815, *Military Operations of the Civil War: A Guide Index to the Official Records of the Union and Confederate Armies, Volumes 2–5, 1860–1865*, and

P2282, *Correspondence of Military Commands Utilized in 'The War of the Rebellion: A Compilation of the Official Records of the Union and Confederate Armies. 1861–1865, 1862–1866.*

Union Soldiers from Texas in the Civil War

M402, *Compiled Service Records of Volunteer Union Soldiers Who Served in Organizations From the State of Texas.*

Reconstruction Era Records

M1165, *Letters Sent by the Department of Texas and the Fifth Military District, 1856–1858, 1865–1870,*

M1193, *Registers of Letters Received and Letters Received of the Department of Texas, the District of Texas, and the 5th Military District, 1865–1870,*

M821, *Records of the Assistant Commissioner for the State of Texas, Bureau of Refugees, Freedmen, and Abandoned Lands, 1865–1869,*

M1188, *Correspondence of the Office of Civil Affairs of the District of Texas, the 5th Military District, and the Department of Texas, 1867–1870,*

M1189, *Headquarters Records of Fort Stockton, Texas, 1867–1886,*

M1114, *Letters Sent by Headquarters, Department of Texas, 1870–1898,* and

M1449, *Letters Received by the Department of Justice From the State of Texas, 1871–1884.*

Modern Records

P2209, *Minutes of the U.S. District Court for the Western District of Texas, Austin Division, 1851–1915,* and

M1381, *Headquarters Records of the District of the Pecos, 1878–1881.*

The Editor

Bill Clemons birthday, my brother in law,
a descendent of James Austin Clemons,
General Sam Houston's saddle boy at San Jacinto
October 3

This book is dedicated to
Mary Smith Fay, CG, FASG,

Teacher, Friend, and Yenta.

One of God's finer angels.

Texas Adjutant General's Department Service Records, 1836–1845, 1854–1865, 1870–1935

These records consist of a variety of types of documents, including enlistment certificates, discharge certificates, certificates of appointment, applications, descriptive lists, warrants of authority, oaths of service, affidavits of service, paymaster's certificates, final statements, vouchers, receipts, powers of attorney, copies of orders and special orders, clothing charts, and correspondence and memoranda to and from state and federal military and pension authorities. They comprise the service records (sometimes artificially constructed) for members of the various military, militia, and ranger organizations which have served in Texas, 1836–45, 1854–65, 1870–1935. *They do not, however, represent all of the persons who have served in these organizations.*

Agency History

On November 13, 1835, the Consultation created the office of Adjutant General, as one of five heads of departments under the Commander–in–Chief of the Texian Army (the other offices being Inspector General, Quartermaster General, Surgeon General, and Paymaster General). On December 20, 1836, the 1st Congress passed "an Act to organize and fix the Military establishment of the Republic of Texas," which in addition to the aforementioned bureaus, created a Commissary General of Subsistence, a Commissary General of Purchases, and a Colonel of Ordnance, all of whom answered to the Secretary of War. On December 18, 1837, Congress passed—and later passed again over President Sam Houston's veto—an act making the Adjutant General a position elected by the Congress; the first man so elected was Hugh McLeod. This arrangement lasted less than two years, however, with subsequent Adjutant Generals—beginning with McLeod on January 30, 1839—being appointed by the President. Congress combined the offices of Adjutant General and Inspector General on January 28, 1840, and technically abolished this position on January 18, 1841. Yet Peter Hansborough Bell served as Adjutant General of Militia soon thereafter; and in legislation of February 1842, there is a reference to an Acting Adjutant General.

The Texas Navy at first operated under a separate Secretary of the Navy, appointed by the President as authorized by an act of Congress approved October 25, 1836. On January 18, 1841, Congress abolished this office and created a Naval Bureau under the Secretary of War and Marines. Of course, the end of the Republic in 1846 meant the end of the Texas Navy as well.

Whereas under the Republic the Adjutant General was subservient to the Secretary of War, under statehood the position was elevated to that of head of all military departments. After annexation, the 1st Legislature provided for an Adjutant General to be appointed by the Governor, in "an Act to organize the Militia of the State of Texas" (April 21, 1846). The duties which fell to the Adjutant General included:

> The issuance of all military orders;
> The maintenance of records of appointments,
> Promotions,
> Resignations,
> Deaths,
> Commissions, etc.;
> The receipt of monthly and annual returns,
> Muster rolls from the various military units;
> The keeping of the records of general courts martial;
> Recruitment and enrollment of Rangers and militiamen; and now,

Guide to Texas Adjutant General Service Records

Issuing all bounty and donation land warrants for military service to the Republic.

This last duty was assumed by the Commissioner of Claims, pursuant to an Act of the legislature passed August 1, 1856. The office of the Adjutant General had been the victim of apparent arson in October 1855—allegedly by persons engaged in land certificate fraud. The position of Adjutant General was itself reestablished by the Militia Law of February 14, 1860, by which act he also assumed the duties of Quartermaster General and Ordnance Officer of the State.

With the Civil War came the reorganization of the office, an act of December 25, 1861 creating an Adjutant and Inspector General, who would also serve as Quartermaster and Commissary General, and Ordnance Officer. Oversight of the 33 Brigades of the Texas State Troops plus the Frontier Regiment fell to this office, just as later Adjutant Generals would split their time between the Militia and the Rangers (whatever the prevailing terminology). The demands of the Confederate States Army, often conflicting with the needs and desires of the State of Texas, would affect the entire period of the War.

During the Congressional phase of Reconstruction, the military affairs of the State of Texas, and many aspects of civil government, were controlled by the commander of the District of Texas (1866–68), or of the 5th Military District (1868–70). Within months of Texas' readmission to the Union under Radical Republican Governor Edmund J. Davis (1870), the Legislature created the Frontier Forces (June 13), the State Guard and Reserve Militia (June 24), and the State Police (July 1), all of which were commanded by a newly restored state Adjutant General. On November 25, 1871, the Legislature added a fifth organization, the Minute Men. The first Adjutant General so appointed, James Davidson, absconded with over $37,000 of state funds in 1872. The State Guard and Reserve Militia were merged into a simple state militia on March 19, 1873, and the State Police force was abolished April 22, 1873.

The place of the Frontier Forces was taken in 1873 and 1874 by the Rangers and the Frontier Men, and finally by the Frontier Battalion, organized by an act passed April 10, 1874. At about the same time one can date the evolution of the Texas Volunteer Guard as the definitive militia organization for the state. On July 22, 1876, "an Act to suppress lawlessness and crime in certain parts of the state" authorized the creation of the Special State Troops, commanded first by Captain Leander McNelly and subsequently by Captain J. L. Hall. In the last year of the operation of this Special Force (1880–81), it was commanded by Captain Thomas L. Oglesby.

The Spanish–American War (1898) saw the nationalization of the Texas Volunteer Guard, which was organized into four regiments of infantry and one of cavalry, and designated the Texas Volunteers. After the war they were de–nationalized, and reorganized on April 1, 1903 as the Texas National Guard. On August 5, 1917, the Texas National Guard was drafted into federal service, forming the 36th Division, which was to be mobilized during World War II as well.

The Frontier Battalion was reorganized as the Ranger Force by an act of the Legislature on March 29, 1901. From time to time this regular force was supplemented by specially commissioned Special Rangers, Railroad Rangers, Cattlemen's Association Rangers, and Loyalty Rangers. Finally, on August 10, 1935, the Ranger Force was transferred to the Texas Department of Public Safety.

Scope and Contents of the Records

These records consist of a variety of types of documents, including enlistment certificates, discharge certificates, certificates of appointment, applications, descriptive lists, warrants of authority, oaths of service, affidavits of service, paymaster's certificates, final statements, vouchers, receipts, powers of attorney, copies of orders and special orders, clothing

Guide to Texas Adjutant General Service Records

charts, and correspondence and memoranda to and from state and federal military and pension authorities. They comprise the service records (sometimes artificially constructed) for members of the various military, militia, and ranger organizations which have served in Texas, 1836–45, 1854–65, 1870–1935. They do *not,* however, represent *all* of the persons who have served in these organizations.

Within each military organization, files are arranged alphabetically by the name of the person. Access, however, is through an alphabetical union list that gives the name, the two– or three–letter code indicating the military organization, and the box number. This union list is available at Clayton Library published as Robert de Berardinis, ed., *The Official CLF Guide to the Indexes of the Service Records of the Republic and State of Texas, 1836–1929* (Houston: Clayton Library Friends, 2005) or in two binders in the State Archives' search room, as well as online at <http://www.tsl.state.tx.us/arc/service/index.html>.

Organization

These records are organized into 16 series:
>Army of the Republic Service Records, 1836–45,
>Navy of the Republic Service Records, 1836–45,
>Mounted Volunteers Service Records, 1854–61,
>Minute Men Service Records, 1855–62, 1872–74,
>Texas State Troops Service Records, 1861–65,
>Confederate States Army Service Records, 1861–65,
>State Police Service Records, 1870–71,
>Frontier Forces Service Records, 1870–71,
>Frontier Battalion Service Records, 1874–1901,
>Texas Volunteer Guard Service Records, 1881–1903,
>United States Volunteers (Spanish–American War) Service Records, 1898,
>Regular Rangers Service Records, 1855–61, 1901–35,
>Special Rangers Service Records, 1916–34,
>Loyalty Rangers Service Records, 1918,
>Railroad Rangers Service Records, 1922–35, and
>Texas National Guard Service Records, 1901–[ca. 1929]

Restrictions on Access

Texas National Guard service records contain medical information certified by an examining surgeon, constituting "a record of the identity, diagnosis, evaluation, or treatment of a patient by a physician..." (V.T.C.A., Occupations Code, §159.002(b) and (d)). The medical information is confidential for 100 years from the date of its creation. All other records are unrestricted.

No folder listing of Texas National Guard service records has been made available for the State Archives search room, and these individuals are not listed in the alphabetical union index.

Restrictions on Use

When necessary, Texas National Guard service records will be redacted to comply with the Occupations Code (medical records).

Related Material

The following materials are offered as possible sources of further information on the agencies and subjects covered by the records. The listing is not exhaustive.

Guide to Texas Adjutant General Service Records

Texas State Archives

In addition to the records listed, portions of many 19th and 20th century governors' records concern the Adjutant General's Department and related matters. Search governors' finding aids for rangers, militia, volunteer guard, national guard, or other similar terms.

[Editor's note: Please consult Introduction for those items below which are available in print or on microfilm.]

Texas Comptroller's Office, Republic of Texas Claims, 1835–[ca. 1900], 259 reels of 35mm microfilm. [Index available at <http://www.tsl.state.tx.us/arc/repClaims/index.html>]

Texas Comptroller's Office, Registers and Indexes of Public Debt Claims, 1848–1863, 1866–1867, 1871–1873

Texas Comptroller's Office, Republic Pension Indexes, 1870–1920

Texas Comptroller's Office, Civil War Claims, Audited Military Claims (Texas State Troops), 1861–1865, [often erroneously referred to as "Confederate" Military Claims, Index available edited by Robert de Berardinis, photcopies of claims are available]

Texas Comptroller's Office, Confederate Pension Records, 1899–1979 (available on Family History Library microfilm. This microfilm is obsolete as documents were added to folders after microfilming, contact TSLAC for photocopies of folders)

Texas Comptroller's Office, Texas Ranger Pensions, 1917–1938, 1959–1990

Texas Comptroller's Office, Registers of Letters Received, 1846–1899

Texas Comptroller's Office, Outgoing Letters (letterpress books), 1860–1921

Texas Comptroller's Office, General Warrant Department, Outgoing Correspondence, 1901–1913

Texas Comptroller's Office, Warrant Clerks Transmittal Books (Form 76): General Warrants, 1887–1909

Texas Comptroller's Office, Unprocessed Records Primarily Relating to County Officials, 1835–1944

Texas Adjutant General's Department, Departmental Correspondence, 1846–1943 (microfilmed to 1883)

Texas Adjutant General's Department, Army Papers, 1835–1846

Texas Adjutant General's Department, Navy Papers, 1835–1847, 1852, 1855

Texas Adjutant General's Department, Military Rolls, 1835–1915, 1917, 1935, Undated (to

Texas Adjutant General's Department, Civil War Records, 1855, 1860–1866, Undated

Texas Adjutant General's Department, Reconstruction Records, 1865–1873, Undated

Texas Adjutant General's Department, Texas Volunteer Guard Records, 1874–1904, Undated

Texas Adjutant General's Department, Texas Volunteers (Spanish–American War) Records, 1898–1904

Texas Adjutant General's Department, Texas National Guard Records, 1902–1931, 1939, 1941–1945, 1950, Undated

Texas Adjutant General's Department, Ranger Records, 1839–1975, Undated

Manuscript Collections, Declaration for Survivor's Pension—Indian Wars. (This collection consists of photocopies of 435 Pension applications found in the National Archives.)

Publications

Stephens, Robert W., comp., *Texas Ranger Indian War Pensions*. Quanah, Texas: Nortex Press, 1975.

White, Virgil D., comp., *Index to Indian Wars Pension Files, 1892–1926*, 2 volumes. Waynesboro, Tennessee: The National Historical Publishing Company, 1987.

Guide to Texas Adjutant General Service Records

Accession Information

These records were transferred to the Texas State Archives by the Texas Adjutant General's Department (and probably by other state offices as well) on February 21, 1934, and on various unknown dates.

Army of the Republic Service Records, 1836–1845

These records consist of enlistment and discharge papers, plus affidavits of service, pay and claim vouchers. They comprise the service records of the Army of the Republic, 1836–45. There are approximately 1,368 files. A typical enlistment record contains the following information:

City and date,
Name of the enlistee,
Place of birth,
Age,
Height,
Complexion,
Color of eyes and hair,
Profession, and
Term of enlistment.

After an oath "that I will bear true Faith and Allegiance to the Republic of Texas, and that I will serve her faithfully and honestly against all her Enemies and Opposers whomsover; and that I will observe and obey the Orders of the President of the Republic of Texas, and the Orders of the Officers appointed over me, according to the Rules and Articles of War" is the signature of the enlistee and of the official taking the oath.

Enabling legislation for the Army of the Republic has five components:

1. Act to raise a regular army (November 24, 1835, calling for 1,120 men),
2. Act for establishing rules and articles for government of the armies of the Republic of Texas (November 21, 1836),
3. Joint Resolution authorizing the President to reorganize the army (November 30, 1836),
4. Act to organize and fix the military establishment of the Republic of Texas [besides volunteers and mounted rifle corps and militia] (December 20, 1836, which authorized four regiments of infantry, with ten companies per regiment, one regiment of cavalry, and one regiment of artillery), and
5. Joint resolution for the relief of soldiers composing the late 1st Regiment of Infantry [which had been disbanded sometime after February 5, 1840] (December 10, 1841).

Arrangement

These records are arranged alphabetically by name of the individual. More precise access, however, is through an alphabetical union list that gives the name of the individual, the two– or three–letter code indicating the military organization, and the box number. This union list is available at Clayton Library published as Robert de Berardinis, ed., *Guide and Index to the Texas Adjutant General Service Records, 1836–1935* (Westminster, Md.: Heritage Books, 2008) or in two binders in the State Archives' search room, as well as online at <http://www.tsl.state.tx.us/arc/service/index.html>.

Guide to Texas Adjutant General Service Records
Army of the Republic Service Records, 1836–1845

Box
401-001 thru 401-012   Army of the Republic Service Records, 1836–1845

Navy of the Republic Service Records, 1836–1845

These records consist of copies of receipts, usually narrow strips of paper, constituting proof of payment for services. They comprise (rather artificially) the service records of the Navy of the Republic, 1836–1845. There are approximately 895 files. A typical voucher gives the place (often a ship) and date, with a statement such as "Rec'd from A. Hurd, Purser of Navy, twenty dollars as bounty for entering the naval service of the Republic of Texas." Signatures of the enlistee and a witness follow.

Arrangement

These records are arranged alphabetically by name of the individual. More precise access, however, is through an alphabetical union list that gives the name of the individual, the two– or three–letter code indicating the military organization, and the box number. This union list is available at Clayton Library published as Robert de Berardinis, ed., *Guide and Index to the Texas Adjutant General Service Records, 1836–1935* (Westminster, Md.: Heritage Books, 2008) or in two binders in the State Archives' search room, as well as online at <http://www.tsl.state.tx.us/arc/service/index.html>.

Navy of the Republic Service Records, 1836–1845

Box
401-013 thru 401-027   Navy of the Republic Service Records, 1836–1845

Mounted Volunteers Service Records, 1854–1861

These records consist of paymaster's certificates, assignments of powers of attorney, and affidavits of service. They comprise the service records of the Mounted Volunteers, 1854–1861. There are approximately 375 files. A typical affidavit of service gives the following information:
  County,
  Name,
  Rank,
  Name of Captain,
  Place and date of mustering into service,
  Place and date of discharge,
  Length of service,
  Name of appointed agent and attorney,
  Signature of the volunteer discharged,
  The witness, and
  The official taking the affidavit.

Arrangement

These records are arranged alphabetically by name of the individual. More precise access, however, is through an alphabetical union list that gives the name of the individual, the two– or three–letter code indicating the military organization, and the box number. This union list is available at Clayton Library published as Robert de Berardinis, ed., *Guide and Index to the Texas Adjutant General Service Records, 1836–1935* (Westminster, Md.: Heritage Books, 2008) or in two binders in the State Archives' search room, as well as online at <http://www.tsl.state.tx.us/arc/service/index.html>.

Guide to Texas Adjutant General Service Records
Mounted Volunteers Service Records, 1854–1861

Box
401-028 thru 401-031　　　　　　　　Mounted Volunteers Service Records, 1854–1861

Minute Men Service Records, 1855–1862, 1872–1874

These records consist of powers of attorney and letters from the Adjutant General regarding service. They comprise, somewhat artificially, the service records of Minute Men, 1855–1862 and 1872–1874. There are approximately 76 files. A typical power of attorney gives the following information:
>Name of minute man,
>Rank,
>Captain,
>Company (e.g., Lampasas County Minute Men),
>Dates of mustering in and out,
>Date of power of attorney, and
>Signatures.

Arrangement

These records are arranged alphabetically by name of the individual. More precise access, however, is through an alphabetical union list that gives the name of the individual, the two- or three-letter code indicating the military organization, and the box number. This union list is available at Clayton Library published as Robert de Berardinis, ed., *Guide and Index to the Texas Adjutant General Service Records, 1836–1935* (Westminster, Md.: Heritage Books, 2008) or in two binders in the State Archives' search room, as well as online at <http://www.tsl.state.tx.us/arc/service/index.html>.

Minute Men Service Records, 1855–1862, 1872–1874

Box
401-032　　　　　　　　Minute Men Service Records, 1855–1862, 1872–1874

Texas State Troops Service Records, 1861–1865

These records consist of discharge papers; copies of orders, extracts of special orders, etc.; and copies of Adjutant General correspondence regarding service. They comprise the service records of Texas State Troops, 1861–1865. There are approximately 482 files. A typical discharge includes the following information:
>Name,
>Rank,
>Captain,
>Company,
>Regiment,
>Mustering officer,
>Place and date of mustering in,
>Term of service, and
>Reason for discharge.

This is followed by dates and dollar amounts due the soldier:
>For pay,
>For use of horse,

Guide to Texas Adjutant General Service Records

For use of arms,
For pay for traveling from place of discharge to mustering-in location, and
For clothing.

Then this is followed by the amount the soldier owes to the State of Texas for clothing furnished him in kind, and the contract price of the ration. These discharges end with the place, date, and signature of the commanding officer.

Arrangement

These records are arranged alphabetically by name of the individual. More precise access, however, is through an alphabetical union list that gives the name of the individual, the two– or three–letter code indicating the military organization, and the box number. This union list is available at Clayton Library published as Robert de Berardinis, ed., *Guide and Index to the Texas Adjutant General Service Records, 1836–1935* (Westminster, Md.: Heritage Books, 2008) or in two binders in the State Archives' search room, as well as online at <http://www.tsl.state.tx.us/arc/service/index.html>.

Texas State Troops Service Records, 1861–1865

Box
401-033 thru 401-038   Texas State Troops Service Records, 1861–1865

Confederate States Army Service Records, 1861–1865

These records consist of copies of correspondence from the U.S. War Department to the Adjutant General of Texas, confirming service in the Confederate States Army, plus other supporting documentation. They comprise (rather artificially) the service records of some of the soldiers in the Confederate States Army in Texas, 1861–65. There are approximately 204 files. A typical item of correspondence from the War Department would read as following: "The records show that one B.F. Price (not born as Ben F. Price) Corporal, Company C, 23rd Regt. Texas Cavalry, Confederate States Army, enlisted July 1, (year not shown) at Clarksville, for 3 years. The muster roll for January and February, 1864, only roll on file, shows him absent, on detached service since February 3. No later record of him has been found."

Arrangement

These records are arranged alphabetically by name of the individual. More precise access, however, is through an alphabetical union list that gives the name of the individual, the two– or three–letter code indicating the military organization, and the box number. This union list is available at Clayton Library published as Robert de Berardinis, ed., *Guide and Index to the Texas Adjutant General Service Records, 1836–1935* (Westminster, Md.: Heritage Books, 2008) or in two binders in the State Archives' search room, as well as online at <http://www.tsl.state.tx.us/arc/service/index.html>.

Related Material

The following materials are offered as possible sources of further information on the agencies and subjects covered by the records. The listing is not exhaustive.

Texas State Archives
Texas Comptroller's Office, Confederate Pension Application Records, 1899–1979.

Confederate States Army Service Records, 1861–1865

Box
401-039 thru 401-040   Confederate States Army Service Records, 1861–1865

Guide to Texas Adjutant General Service Records
State Police Service Records, 1870–1871

These records consist of certificates of appointment, pay vouchers, and subvouchers. They comprise the service records of the State Police, 1870–1871. There are approximately 872 files. A typical certificate of appointment gives the following information:
- Name of Governor (Edmund J. Davis),
- Name of policeman,
- Rank, and
- Date.

They are countersigned by the Secretary of State. Pay vouchers and sub–vouchers give dates, pay per month, total pay, name, rank, and district. They also contain signatures of the Chief of State Police and the policeman himself.

Arrangement

These records are arranged alphabetically by name of the individual. More precise access, however, is through an alphabetical union list that gives the name of the individual, the two– or three–letter code indicating the military organization, and the box number. This union list is available at Clayton Library published as Robert de Berardinis, ed., *Guide and Index to the Texas Adjutant General Service Records, 1836–1935* (Westminster, Md.: Heritage Books, 2008) or in two binders in the State Archives' search room, as well as online at <http://www.tsl.state.tx.us/arc/service/index.html>.

State Police Service Records, 1870–1871

Box
401-041 thru 401-050   State Police Service Records, 1870–1871

Frontier Forces Service Records, 1870–1871

These records consist of copies of final statements whose originals were filed in the Comptroller's office of the State of Texas. They comprise the service records of the Frontier Forces, 1870–71. There are approximately 798 files. A typical final statement gives the following information:
- Name,
- Rank,
- Captain,
- Company,
- Birthplace,
- Age,
- Height,
- Complexion,
- Eye and hair color,
- Occupation,
- Place and date mustered into service,
- Term of service,
- Reason of discharge (Special Order Number),
- Inclusive dates for which pay is due, and
- Account of debts (including one Winchester carbine).

The place and date of discharge are followed by the signatures of the company commander and the Adjutant General.

Guide to Texas Adjutant General Service Records

Arrangement

These records are arranged alphabetically by name of the individual. More precise access, however, is through an alphabetical union list that gives the name of the individual, the two- or three-letter code indicating the military organization, and the box number. This union list is available at Clayton Library published as Robert de Berardinis, ed., *Guide and Index to the Texas Adjutant General Service Records, 1836–1935* (Westminster, Md.: Heritage Books, 2008) or in two binders in the State Archives' search room, as well as online at <http://www.tsl.state.tx.us/arc/service/index.html>.

Frontier Forces Service Records, 1870–1871

Box

401-132 thru 401-140   Frontier Forces Service Records, 1870–1871

Frontier Battalion Service Records, 1874–1901

These records consist of discharge certificates and descriptive lists. They comprise the service records of the Frontier Battalion, 1874–1901. There are approximately 2,916 files. A typical discharge certificate gives the following information:

    Date,
    Name,
    Rank,
    Name of company commander,
    Letter of company,
    Date of muster,
    Name of last officer paying him,
    Final date of last pay,
    Date to which pay is still due him,
    Amount due, and
    Amounts and reasons of indebtedness.

The descriptive list was "for identification, will be kept in possession of the Ranger to whom it refers, and will be exhibited as a warrant of his authority." A typical descriptive list gives the following information:

    Name,
    Rank,
    Company designation,
    Age, height,
    Color of hair and complexion,
    Place of birth,
    Occupation,
    When and where enlisted, and
    By whom.

The end of the list gives place and date and is signed by the company commander.

Arrangement

These records are arranged alphabetically by name of the individual. More precise access, however, is through an alphabetical union list that gives the name of the individual, the two- or three-letter code indicating the military organization, and the box number. This union list is available at Clayton Library published as Robert de Berardinis, ed., *Guide and Index to the Texas Adjutant General Service Records, 1836–1935* (Westminster, Md.: Heritage Books, 2008) or in two binders in the State Archives' search room, as well as online at <http://www.tsl.state.tx.us/arc/service/index.html>.

Related Material
The following materials are offered as possible sources of further information on the agencies and subjects covered by the records. The listing is not exhaustive.

Texas State Archives
Texas Comptroller's Office, Texas Ranger Pensions, 1917–1938, 1959–1990 (bulk 1959–1990),

Manuscript Collections
Declaration for Survivor's Pension—Indian Wars, (This collection consists of photocopies of 435 pension applications found in the National Archives.)

Publications
Stephens, Robert W., comp., *Texas Ranger Indian War Pensions*. Quanah, Tex.: Nortex Press, 1975.

White, Virgil D., comp., *Index to Indian Wars Pension Files, 1892–1926*, 2 Vols. Waynesboro, Tenn.: The National Historical Publishing Co., 1987.

Frontier Battalion Service Records, 1874–1901

Box
401-141 thru 401-178　　　　　　　　Frontier Battalion Service Records, 1874–1901

Texas Volunteer Guard Service Records, 1881–1903

These records consist of enlistment certificates, applications and descriptive lists, discharge certificates, and clothing charts. They comprise the service records of the Texas Volunteer Guard, 1881–1903. There are approximately 4,414 files. A typical enlistment certificate/application and descriptive list gives the following information:

  Date,
  Name of enlistee,
  Name of captain,
  Designation of company,
  Age,
  Weight,
  Height,
  Color of hair and eyes,
  Complexion,
  Place of birth, and
  Occupation

The applicant then signs an oath. Some of the earlier certificates give only name, place of birth, age, occupation, date, and signature. A typical discharge certificate gives the following information:

  Name,
  Rank,
  Company,
  Regiment,
  Date of enlistment,
  Birthplace,
  Age at enlistment,
  Height,
  Complexion,

Guide to Texas Adjutant General Service Records

Color of eyes and hair,
Occupation, and
Reason for discharge.

The reason for discharge may also include dishonorable discharges, e.g. "nonpayment of dues and non–attendance at drill". A typical clothing chart gives all appropriate sizes for coat, overcoat, vest, and pants. It then gives "peculiarities...so far as it will assist in making a good fit" (e.g., stooping shoulders, stands erect, sloping shoulders, square shoulders, height, weight, age).

Arrangement

These records are arranged alphabetically by name of the individual. More precise access, however, is through an alphabetical union list that gives the name of the individual, the two– or three–letter code indicating the military organization, and the box number. This union list is available at Clayton Library published as Robert de Berardinis, ed., *Guide and Index to the Texas Adjutant General Service Records, 1836–1935* (Westminster, Md.: Heritage Books, 2008) or in two binders in the State Archives' search room, as well as online at <http://www.tsl.state.tx.us/arc/service/index.html>.

Texas Volunteer Guard Service Records, 1881–1903

Box
401-179 thru 401-218   Texas Volunteer Guard Service Records, 1881–1903

United States Volunteers (Spanish–American War) Service Records, 1898

These records consist of receipts for pay owed for service in Texas prior to mustering into U.S. service in the Spanish–American War, voucher affidavits, oaths of enlistment, receipts for Texas service for Volunteers killed in action, and claim vouchers for service in the Texas Volunteers prior to rejection by a U.S. Medical Examiner. They comprise the service records of the United States Volunteers (Spanish–American War), 1898. There are approximately 4,400 files. A typical affidavit gives the following information:

Name,
Rank,
Company,
Regiment,
Place and date of assembly,
Place and date of rendezvous,
Date mustered into U.S. service,
Signature, and
Date of affidavit.

Attached to the affidavit is usually a receipt for pay from date of assembly/rendezvous to date of muster.

Arrangement

These records are arranged alphabetically by name of the individual. More precise access, however, is through an alphabetical union list that gives the name of the individual, the two– or three–letter code indicating the military organization, and the box number. This union list is available at Clayton Library published as Robert de Berardinis, ed., *Guide and Index to the Texas Adjutant General Service Records, 1836–1935* (Westminster, Md.: Heritage Books, 2008) or in two binders in the State Archives' search room, as well as online at <http://www.tsl.state.tx.us/arc/service/index.html>.

Guide to Texas Adjutant General Service Records
United States Volunteers (Spanish–American War) Service Records, 1898

Box
401-219 thru 401-256   United States Volunteers (Spanish–American War) Service Records, 1898

Regular Rangers Service Records, 1855–1861, 1901–1935

These records consist of memoranda from the Adjutant General of Texas to the U.S. Commissioner of Pensions regarding records of service in the Indian Wars, 1855–1861; and enlistment/oath of service/description forms, and warrants of authority/descriptive lists relating to service in the Ranger Force, 1901–1935. They comprise the service records of the Texas Rangers, 1855–1861 and the Ranger Force, 1901–1935. There are approximately 1,407 files. A typical memorandum to the federal Commissioner of Pensions gives the following information:

- Name on muster roll,
- Designation (rank and company),
- Name of commanding officer,
- Dates of service,
- Campaigns,
- Personal description,
- Age,
- Occupation,
- Place of birth, and
- Tracing of signature.

A typical Oath of Service for the Ranger Force gives the Ranger's:

- Signature to the oath,
- Place and date of the oath,
- Age,
- Height,
- Weight,
- Hair,
- Eyes,
- Complexion,
- Where born,
- Occupation,
- Letter designation of company,
- Value of horse, and
- By whom enlisted.

The later forms, "Warrant of Authority and Descriptive List," and "Enlistment, Oath of Service, and Description," give all of the previous details, plus residence address. In addition, the enlistment certificate gives marital status, and previous service.

Arrangement

These records are arranged alphabetically by name of the individual. More precise access, however, is through an alphabetical union list that gives the name of the individual, the two– or three–letter code indicating the military organization, and the box number. This union list is available at Clayton Library published as Robert de Berardinis, ed., *Guide and Index to the Texas Adjutant General Service Records, 1836–1935* (Westminster, Md.: Heritage Books, 2008) or in two binders in the State Archives' search room, as well as online at <http://www.tsl.state.tx.us/arc/service/index.html>.

Guide to Texas Adjutant General Service Records
Regular Rangers Service Records, 1855–1861, 1901–1935

Box
401-051 thru 401-065   Regular Rangers Service Records, 1855–1861, 1901–1935

Special Rangers Service Records, 1916–1934

These records consist of two kinds of forms: "enlistment, oath of service and description," and "warrant of authority and descriptive list." They comprise the service records of the Special Rangers, 1916–1934. There are approximately 4,161 files. A typical enlistment, oath of service and description form gives the following information:

Name,
Place of birth,
Age,
Occupation,
Date of enlistment,
Signature,
Date of oath,
Height,
Complexion,
Color of eyes and hair,
Weight,
Residence,
Marital status, and
Previous service.

A typical warrant of authority and descriptive list gives:

Name,
Rank,
Age,
Birth place,
Height,
Weight,
Hair,
Eyes,
Complexion,
Occupation,
Residence,
Where and when enlisted,
By whom enlisted, and
An expiration date for the warrant.

Arrangement

These records are arranged alphabetically by name of the individual. More precise access, however, is through an alphabetical union list that gives the name of the individual, the two– or three–letter code indicating the military organization, and the box number. This union list is available at Clayton Library published as Robert de Berardinis, ed., *Guide and Index to the Texas Adjutant General Service Records, 1836–1935* (Westminster, Md.: Heritage Books, 2008) or in two binders in the State Archives' search room, as well as online at <http://www.tsl.state.tx.us/arc/service/index.html>.

Guide to Texas Adjutant General Service Records
Special Rangers Service Records, 1916–1934

Box
401-066 thru 401-110   Special Rangers Service Records, 1916–1934

Loyalty Rangers Service Records, 1918

These records consist of "enlistment, oath of service and description" forms. They comprise the service records of the Loyalty Rangers, 1918. There are approximately 486 files. A typical enlistment, oath of service and description gives the following information:

    Name,
    Place of birth,
    Age,
    Occupation,
    Date of enlistment,
    Signature,
    Date of oath,
    Height,
    Complexion,
    Color of eyes and hair,
    Residence,
    Marital status, and
    Previous service.

Arrangement

These records are arranged alphabetically by name of the individual. More precise access, however, is through an alphabetical union list that gives the name of the individual, the two– or three–letter code indicating the military organization, and the box number. This union list is available at Clayton Library published as Robert de Berardinis, ed., *Guide and Index to the Texas Adjutant General Service Records, 1836–1935* (Westminster, Md.: Heritage Books, 2008) or in two binders in the State Archives' search room, as well as online at <http://www.tsl.state.tx.us/arc/service/index.html>.

Loyalty Rangers Service Records, 1918

Box
401-127 thru 401-131   Loyalty Rangers Service Records, 1918

Railroad Rangers Service Records, 1922–1935

These records consist of two kinds of forms: "enlistment, oath of service and description," and "warrant of authority and descriptive list." They comprise the service records of the Railroad Rangers, 1922–1935. There are approximately 1,081 files. A typical enlistment, oath of service and description form gives the following information:

    Name,
    Place of birth,
    Age,
    Occupation,
    Date of enlistment,
    Signature,
    Date of oath,
    Height,

Guide to Texas Adjutant General Service Records

        Complexion,
        Color of eyes and hair,
        Weight,
        Residence,
        Marital status, and
        Previous service.

A typical warrant of authority and descriptive list gives:
        Name,
        Rank,
        Age,
        Birth place,
        Height,
        Hair,
        Eyes,
        Complexion,
        Occupation,
        Residence,
        Where and when enlisted, and
        By whom enlisted.

Arrangement

These records are arranged alphabetically by name of the individual. More precise access, however, is through an alphabetical union list that gives the name of the individual, the two– or three–letter code indicating the military organization, and the box number. This union list is available at Clayton Library published as Robert de Berardinis, ed., *Guide and Index to the Texas Adjutant General Service Records, 1836–1935* (Westminster, Md.: Heritage Books, 2008) or in two binders in the State Archives' search room, as well as online at <http://www.tsl.state.tx.us/arc/service/index.html>.

Railroad Rangers Service Records, 1922–1935

Box
401-111 thru 401-126   Railroad Rangers Service Records, 1922–1935

Texas National Guard Service Records, 1901–[ca. 1929]

These records consist of "enlistment, description and physical examination" forms (or "description, physical record and enlistment" and other variants), oaths of office for officers of the Texas National Guard, extracts from service records, and memoranda to the Adjutant General concerning service records. They comprise the service records of the Texas National Guard, 1901–[ca. 1929]. There are approximately 11,750 files. The typical description and enlistment portion of the form gives the following information:

        Company,
        Regiment,
        Name,
        Place of birth,
        Age,
        Occupation,
        Date of enlistment,
        Signature,
        Date of oath,

Guide to Texas Adjutant General Service Records

    Name of recruiting officer,
    Height,
    Complexion,
    Eyes,
    Hair,
    Previous military or naval service, and
    Grade or rank.

Some forms also give marital status, residence address, and telephone number. The physical examination/record portion of the form gives some combination of the following:

    Figure and general appearance,
    Weight,
    Height,
    Vision,
    Hearing,
    Chest and contained organs,
    Size of chest in inches (expiration and inspiration),
    Mobility,
    Abdomen and contained organs,
    Genital–urinary apparatus,
    Upper extremities,
    Lower extremities,
    Skin,
    Piles,
    Rheumatism,
    Varicose veins,
    Varicocele,
    Coughs,
    Hernia,
    Feet,
    Previous sickness,
    Heart,
    Teeth,
    Personal marks, and
    Remarks.

These are all certified by an examining surgeon. Consent in case of minor is given by the parent or guardian.

Arrangement

These records are arranged alphabetically by name of the individual.

Restrictions on Access

These records contain medical information certified by an examining surgeon, constituting "a record of the identity, diagnosis, evaluation, or treatment of a patient by a physician". (V.T.C.A., Occupations Code, §159.002(b) and (d)). The medical information is confidential for 100 years from the date of its creation.

No folder listing has been made available for the State Archives search room, and these individuals are not listed in the alphabetical union index.

Guide to Texas Adjutant General Service Records
Restrictions on Use

When necessary, Texas National Guard service records will be redacted to comply with the Occupations Code (medical records). Only the physical examination/physical record portion of the service record form will need to be redacted.

Texas National Guard Service Records, 1901–[ca. 1929]

Box
401-257 thru 401-380B   Texas National Guard Service Records, 1901–[ca. 1929]

Description by Archives staff at unknown dates and Tony Black for the Texas State Archives, August 2000, from TARO (Texas Archival Resources Online).

Code to Service Branches in Index

ARM	Army of the Republic
CSA	Confederate States Army
FB	Frontier Battalion
FF	Frontier Forces
LR	Loyalty Rangers
MM	Minute Men
MV	Mounted Volunteers
NAV	Navy of the Republic
RR	Regular Rangers
RRR	Railroad Rangers
SP	State Police
SR	Special Rangers
TST	Texas State Troops
TVG	Texas Volunteer Guard
USV	United States Volunteers, Spanish-American War

Index to Service Records—All Branches

Aake, Charles	ARM	401-1	Adam, George B.	TVG	401-179
Aaron, Calvin Jackson	CSA	401-39	Adam, George Emile	TVG	401-179
Aaron, J. H.	TVG	401-179	Adam, Joseph	ARM	401-1
Abbott, A. C.	RRR	401-111	Adams, A. J.	SR	401-66
Abbott, B.	SR	401-66	Adams, A. J.	FB	401-141
Abbott, B. P.	LR	401-127	Adams, A. M.	RR	401-51
Abbott, Elisha G.	USV	401-219	Adams, A. S.	FB	401-141
Abbott, W. J.	SR	401-66	Adams, A. Semones	TVG	401-179
Abdill, Wade H.	TVG	401-179	Adams, Albert J.	USV	401-219
Abel, Hector V.	TVG	401-179	Adams, Aquilla	TST	401-33
Abel, John	ARM	401-1	Adams, B. W.	SR	401-66
Abel, Joseph S.	ARM	401-1	Adams, Benjamin F.	ARM	401-1
Abell, Benjamin	NAV	401-13	Adams, C. D.	SR	401-66
Abell, Benjamin H.	ARM	401-1	Adams, Chas.	TVG	401-179
Abell, T. J.	RR	401-51	Adams, Christopher C.	USV	401-219
Abell, Z.	FB	401-141	Adams, Claude A.	USV	401-219
Abercrombie, J. W.	FF	401-132	Adams, Columbus William	SR	401-66
Abercrombie, Wiley A.	ARM	401-1	Adams, E. O.	SR	401-66
Aberly, William	ARM	401-1	Adams, F. M.	TST	401-33
Abernathy, Harvey A.	USV	401-219	Adams, G. W.	TST	401-33
Abernathy, R. H.	SR	401-66	Adams, George	SR	401-66
Abernathy, R. H.	LR	401-127	Adams, George M.	SR	401-66
Abernathy, Tom	SR	401-66	Adams, Harold W.	RR	401-51
Abernathy, W. Gib	RR	401-51	Adams, Henderson L.	TST	401-33
Abernathy, William R.	USV	401-219	Adams, Henry	TVG	401-179
Abernethy, W. Douglas	USV	401-219	Adams, Isaac	ARM	401-1
Abington, Chas. R.	USV	401-219	Adams, J. B.	SR	401-66
Able, Levi	SP	401-41	Adams, James	ARM	401-1
Able, PeteR	ARM	401-1	Adams, James A.	FB	401-141
Abney, A. A.	TVG	401-179	Adams, Jefferson	ARM	401-1
Abney, Glenn M.	RR	401-51	Adams, Jefferson C.	USV	401-219
Abney, Glenn M.	SR	401-66	Adams, Joe	SR	401-66
Abney, Harry	TVG	401-179	Adams, John	FB	401-141
Abney, J. B.	RRR	401-111	Adams, John F.	SR	401-66
Abney, Paul C.	TVG	401-179	Adams, John Q.	ARM	401-1
Abram, Samuel S.	TVG	401-179	Adams, John W.	RRR	401-111
Abrams, W. W.	FB	401-141	Adams, John W.	SR	401-66
Absher, John A.	TVG	401-179	Adams, John W.	FB	401-141
Achilles, Henry F.	USV	401-219	Adams, Jones Q.	SR	401-66
Acker, A. W.	RRR	401-111	Adams, L. C.	RR	401-51
Acker, PhiliP	LR	401-127	Adams, Lewis J.	TVG	401-179
Acker, Walter, Jr.	SR	401-66	Adams, M. A.	SR	401-66
Ackerman, D. Verplanck	ARM	401-1	Adams, Nathan F.	RRR	401-111
Ackerman, P. A.	ARM	401-1	Adams, P. G.	TST	401-33
Aclars, Barnard	ARM	401-1	Adams, R. K.	SR	401-66
Acosta, Deonicio	RR	401-51	Adams, Rich H.	TST	401-33
Acree, Eli Jefferson	USV	401-219	Adams, Roy	RR	401-51
Acres, Charles	RRR	401-111	Adams, S. J.	FB	401-141
Adair, Andrew M.	ARM	401-1	Adams, Thos. N.	USV	401-219
Adair, E.	TVG	401-179	Adams, Tom	SR	401-66
Adair, J. T.	FB	401-141	Adams, Tom, Jr.	SR	401-66
Adair, William	NAV	401-13	Adams, W. E.	TVG	401-179
Adam, Anton	USV	401-219	Adams, W. H.	SR	401-66
Adam, D.	TVG	401-179	Adams, Wherry B.	ARM	401-1

Index to Texas Adjutant General Service Records—All Service Branches

Name	Branch	Record
Adams, William	TST	401-33
Adams, William	ARM	401-1
Adams, William C.	MV	401-28
Adams, Wilson	SP	401-41
Adamson, George R.	FB	401-141
Adamson, H. L.	TVG	401-179
Adamson, W. S.	SR	401-66
Addington, D. L.	TVG	401-179
Addington, King	USV	401-219
Addington, O. J.	TVG	401-179
Addington, T.	FB	401-141
Addison, A. K.	SR	401-66
Addison, A. S.	RR	401-51
Addison, A. S.	SR	401-66
Addison, James	ARM	401-1
Addison, Nathaniel	ARM	401-1
Addison, R. M.	TVG	401-179
Addy, John	ARM	401-1
Aderhold, F. B.	SR	401-66
Adkins, J. D.	USV	401-219
Adkins, Thos. R.	USV	401-219
Adkinson, F.	FB	401-141
Adkisson, J. F.	TVG	401-179
Adkisson, John F.	TVG	401-179
Agnew, Charles M.	USV	401-219
Agnew, Jarvis	ARM	401-1
Aguilo, J. B.	TVG	401-179
Ahr, L.	FB	401-141
Ahunbeck, Chas. C.	USV	401-219
Aiken, Charles Robert	USV	401-219
Aikens, Charles E.	MV	401-28
Aikens, J. S.	RR	401-51
Ainsworth, W. H.	TVG	401-179
Aira, Hampton	USV	401-219
Aitken, George T.	SR	401-66
Aitken, Oliver C.	USV	401-219
Ake, G. W.	RR	401-51
Akens, J. S.	SR	401-66
Akers, Walter S.	USV	401-219
Akin, A.	NAV	401-13
Akin, Boon	TVG	401-179
Akin, John B.	USV	401-219
Akin, Nick	SR	401-66
Akin, William	ARM	401-1
Akles, Hezekiah B.	ARM	401-1
Albert, Charles	NAV	401-13
Albert, Robert L.	USV	401-219
Albin, G. L.	SR	401-66
Albin, Gould	RR	401-51
Albrich, William	SP	401-41
Albright, Conrad, Jr.	SR	401-66
Albright, Fletcher W.	RR	401-51
Albright, Guy H.	SR	401-66
Albright, Jacob B.	USV	401-219
Albright, Robert M.	USV	401-219
Alcantar, C. P.	TVG	401-179
Alcorn, Wesley W.	TVG	401-179
Alderede, Isidro	FF	401-132
Alderete, B.	SR	401-66
Alderete, M. C.	SP	401-41
Alderman, Marvin R.	ARM	401-1
Alderman, Stanberry	SR	401-66
Alderman, Stanberry	LR	401-127
Alders, Bernice Oran	RRR	401-111
Alders, Ellis Roland	RRR	401-111
Alderson, Blair	TVG	401-179
Alderson, Geo. E.	USV	401-219
Alderson, Henry	ARM	401-1
Alderson, Louie I.	TVG	401-179
Alderson, William F.	FB	401-141
Aldonado, S.	FF	401-132
Aldrich, G. R.	TVG	401-179
Aldrich, J. W.	RR	401-51
Aldrich, J. W.	SR	401-66
Aldridge, J. C.	RR	401-51
Alexander, A. A.	SR	401-66
Alexander, A. C.	FB	401-141
Alexander, Albert	ARM	401-1
Alexander, Almerile M.	CSA	401-39
Alexander, B. F.	TVG	401-179
Alexander, C. W.	MV	401-28
Alexander, Charles H., Jr.	SR	401-66
Alexander, Curtis R.	USV	401-219
Alexander, Daniel	ARM	401-1
Alexander, E. M.	SP	401-41
Alexander, Franklin	RR	401-51
Alexander, Fred	SP	401-41
Alexander, George L.	TST	401-33
Alexander, George M.	TST	401-33
Alexander, Guy	TVG	401-179
Alexander, H. H.	RRR	401-111
Alexander, H. M.	SR	401-66
Alexander, J. B.	CSA	401-39
Alexander, J. B.	ARM	401-1
Alexander, J. M.	MM	401-32
Alexander, J. R.	RRR	401-111
Alexander, J. W.	ARM	401-1
Alexander, James	ARM	401-1
Alexander, James F.	TST	401-33
Alexander, John M.	TVG	401-179
Alexander, Joseph	RR	401-51
Alexander, Joseph	SP	401-41
Alexander, L. R.	TVG	401-179
Alexander, Lyman C.	TVG	401-179
Alexander, R. C.	FF	401-132
Alexander, S. S.	USV	401-219
Alexander, Simon	SP	401-41
Alexander, T. H.	FB	401-141
Alexander, W. E.	TVG	401-179
Alexander, W. J.	CSA	401-39
Alexander, W. J.	TST	401-33
Alexander, W. L.	RRR	401-111

Index to Texas Adjutant General Service Records—All Service Branches

Name	Branch	Record
Alexander, W. N.	RR	401-51
Alexander, W. W.	SR	401-66
Alford, I. B.	SR	401-66
Alford, J. T.	USV	401-219
Alford, Julius C.	CSA	401-39
Alford, Starley F.	RRR	401-111
Alford, Steve	RRR	401-111
Alford, Winfield	ARM	401-1
Allala, Jesus	FF	401-132
Allan, C. J.	SR	401-66
Allard, George W.	TST	401-33
Allbright, J. J.	TVG	401-179
Allbright, Jim J.	SR	401-66
Allbright, L.	TVG	401-179
Allcorn, James	ARM	401-1
Allday, William D.	RR	401-51
Allee, A. W.	SR	401-66
Allee, A. Y.	SR	401-66
Allee, J. C.	SR	401-66
Allen, A. J.	FB	401-141
Allen, B. B.	CSA	401-39
Allen, B. K.	TVG	401-179
Allen, Bunk	TVG	401-179
Allen, C.	ARM	401-1
Allen, C. H.	FB	401-141
Allen, C. J.	LR	401-127
Allen, C. T.	FB	401-141
Allen, Charles B.	USV	401-219
Allen, Charles T.	FB	401-141
Allen, Chas.	TVG	401-179
Allen, Clement	ARM	401-1
Allen, Corrie A.	USV	401-219
Allen, Dory	USV	401-219
Allen, Dwyer L.	TVG	401-179
Allen, E. T.	SP	401-41
Allen, Ed	FB	401-141
Allen, Ernest W.	SR	401-66
Allen, F. T.	NAV	401-13
Allen, Frank	FB	401-141
Allen, Frank C.	TVG	401-179
Allen, G. H.	NAV	401-13
Allen, G. H.	FB	401-141
Allen, G. M.	RR	401-51
Allen, George	ARM	401-1
Allen, George S.	TVG	401-179
Allen, Guss	USV	401-219
Allen, H.	FB	401-141
Allen, H. A.	ARM	401-1
Allen, Hugh	TST	401-33
Allen, Hugh	RR	401-51
Allen, J. B.	FB	401-141
Allen, J. B.	TVG	401-179
Allen, J. Campbell, Jr.	TVG	401-179
Allen, J. D.	TVG	401-179
Allen, J. L.	FB	401-141
Allen, J. O.	FB	401-141
Allen, James	ARM	401-1
Allen, James C.	ARM	401-1
Allen, James E.	ARM	401-1
Allen, John	NAV	401-13
Allen, John	ARM	401-1
Allen, John D.	USV	401-219
Allen, John H.	NAV	401-13
Allen, John M.	USV	401-219
Allen, Jules V.	SR	401-66
Allen, Luther M.	USV	401-219
Allen, Martin	ARM	401-1
Allen, Nathan	NAV	401-13
Allen, Neil	SR	401-66
Allen, Paul	TVG	401-179
Allen, Pleasant T.	FB	401-141
Allen, R. E. L.	SR	401-66
Allen, R. F.	TVG	401-179
Allen, R. T. P.	TST	401-33
Allen, Richard L.	TVG	401-179
Allen, Robert	RR	401-51
Allen, Robert D.	CSA	401-39
Allen, Robert J.	TVG	401-179
Allen, S. P.	TST	401-33
Allen, Sam M.	SR	401-66
Allen, Samuel W.	ARM	401-1
Allen, Sid	SR	401-66
Allen, Sidney J.	USV	401-219
Allen, T. D.	ARM	401-1
Allen, T. S.	FB	401-141
Allen, Thomas T.	NAV	401-13
Allen, Thomas W.	RRR	401-111
Allen, Thos. E.	USV	401-219
Allen, Tom B.	TVG	401-179
Allen, Virgil W.	RRR	401-111
Allen, W. C.	RR	401-51
Allen, W. F.	SR	401-66
Allen, W. Howard, Jr.	USV	401-219
Allen, W. T.	FB	401-141
Allen, Wilbur P.	SR	401-66
Allen, William	ARM	401-1
Allen, William	ARM	401-1
Allen, William B.	USV	401-219
Allen, William Henry	NAV	401-13
Allen, William I.	SR	401-66
Allen, William W.	USV	401-219
Allender, U. S.	TVG	401-179
Alley, D. N.	TVG	401-179
Alley, Elick A.	USV	401-219
Alley, J. M.	TVG	401-179
Alley, Marvin	USV	401-219
Alley, Powell	RR	401-51
Alley, Robert F.	SR	401-66
Alley, Thomas	ARM	401-1
Alley, William T.	RR	401-51
Allgood, James D.	RRR	401-111
Allingworth, J.	TVG	401-179

Index to Texas Adjutant General Service Records—All Service Branches

Allison, C. L. .... SR 401-66
Allison, James .... ARM 401-1
Allison, Sidney .... TVG 401-179
Allison, W. D. .... SR 401-66
Allison, W. D. .... FB 401-141
Allison, W. L. .... FB 401-141
Allison, William .... ARM 401-1
Allman, Ambrus Foster .... RR 401-51
Allmond, Howard .... TVG 401-179
Ally, John .... ARM 401-1
Almond, John W. .... FB 401-141
Alquest, Joseph W. .... USV 401-219
Alsabrook, Will .... SR 401-66
Alsabrook, Will .... LR 401-127
Alsobrook, Will M. .... RR 401-51
Alston, James .... ARM 401-1
Alston, Jewell E. .... TVG 401-179
Alston, W. T. .... FB 401-141
Alsup, John .... RR 401-51
Alsworth, Willett .... TVG 401-179
Altizer, O. B. .... RRR 401-111
Alton, William H. .... SR 401-66
Alvey, Richard Walker .... USV 401-219
Alvis, E. .... TVG 401-179
Amacker, M. M. .... SP 401-41
Amason, Hiram .... SP 401-41
Amerito, Frank .... FF 401-132
Ames, Dudley .... SR 401-66
Ames, Joseph .... ARM 401-1
Ames, L. .... SR 401-66
Ames, L. .... LR 401-127
Amey, E. J. .... SR 401-66
Amitt, Louis .... FF 401-132
Ammann, Albert .... TST 401-33
Amon, Albert .... FF 401-132
Amonett, W. L. .... SR 401-66
Amsler, Edward, Jr. .... TVG 401-179
Amsley, S. M. .... FB 401-141
Amthor, G. M. .... TVG 401-179
Analla, Christobal .... FF 401-132
Analla, F. .... FF 401-132
Andele, Joe .... FB 401-141
Anderhill, Morris D. .... NAV 401-13
Anders, J. L. .... SR 401-66
Anders, Joseph Lee .... RR 401-51
Anderson, A. J. .... MV 401-28
Anderson, A. S. .... USV 401-219
Anderson, Alvin P. .... MM 401-32
Anderson, Alvin S. .... USV 401-219
Anderson, Andrew .... USV 401-219
Anderson, Andrew L. .... USV 401-219
Anderson, Archie A. .... USV 401-219
Anderson, Archie L., Jr. .... TVG 401-179
Anderson, Arnold .... USV 401-219
Anderson, Arthur C. .... RRR 401-111
Anderson, B. H. .... FB 401-141
Anderson, B. J. .... TVG 401-179
Anderson, C. Harper .... TVG 401-179
Anderson, Calvin .... SP 401-41
Anderson, Calvin Vance .... TVG 401-179
Anderson, Carl A. .... TVG 401-179
Anderson, Charles .... NAV 401-13
Anderson, Charles G. .... SR 401-66
Anderson, Charles S. .... ARM 401-1
Anderson, Chas. W. .... USV 401-219
Anderson, D. C. .... TVG 401-179
Anderson, David .... RR 401-51
Anderson, E. M. .... SP 401-41
Anderson, E. P. .... FB 401-141
Anderson, E. P., Jr. .... TVG 401-179
Anderson, E. P., Jr. .... USV 401-219
Anderson, Frank M. .... USV 401-219
Anderson, G. B. .... SR 401-66
Anderson, G. W. .... RRR 401-111
Anderson, George D. .... TVG 401-179
Anderson, Henry Newton .... TVG 401-179
Anderson, Herbert H. .... SR 401-66
Anderson, Houston .... FB 401-141
Anderson, Hugh .... ARM 401-1
Anderson, Ira .... SR 401-66
Anderson, J. E. .... TST 401-33
Anderson, J. P. .... USV 401-219
Anderson, J. W. .... SR 401-66
Anderson, James .... NAV 401-13
Anderson, Jno. A. .... USV 401-219
Anderson, John .... NAV 401-13
Anderson, John .... ARM 401-1
Anderson, John N. .... FB 401-141
Anderson, Jonathan .... ARM 401-1
Anderson, Leon M. .... TVG 401-179
Anderson, Magnus J. .... USV 401-219
Anderson, Matthew .... ARM 401-1
Anderson, Ottis Allen .... SR 401-66
Anderson, Porter .... USV 401-219
Anderson, R. .... FB 401-141
Anderson, R. G. .... SR 401-66
Anderson, R. T. .... FB 401-141
Anderson, Robert L. .... RRR 401-111
Anderson, Robert L. .... USV 401-219
Anderson, Robert S. .... USV 401-219
Anderson, Robt. .... TVG 401-179
Anderson, S. R. .... SR 401-66
Anderson, Samuel J., Jr. .... USV 401-219
Anderson, Thomas P. .... NAV 401-13
Anderson, Thomas P. .... ARM 401-1
Anderson, W. A. .... FB 401-141
Anderson, W. D. .... FB 401-141
Anderson, Will P. .... USV 401-219
Anderson, William .... SR 401-66
Anderson, William .... USV 401-219
Anderson, William Bernard .... RRR 401-111
Anderson, William C. .... MM 401-32

Index to Texas Adjutant General Service Records—All Service Branches

Anderson, William H. ....SP............401-41
Anderson, William T. ....USV.........401-219
Anding, A. F. ....SR............401-66
Andlauer, George A. ....SR............401-66
Andreas, Ben ....FF............401-132
Andrew, George ....SR............401-66
Andrew, William ....ARM........401-1
Andrewartha, Ernest ....TVG.........401-179
Andrews, Edwin B. ....USV.........401-219
Andrews, Eugene L. ....USV.........401-219
Andrews, Frank ....FB............401-141
Andrews, G. R. ....SP............401-41
Andrews, Geo. M. ....TVG.........401-179
Andrews, H. B. ....FB............401-141
Andrews, John G. ....USV.........401-219
Andrews, Leroy ....TVG.........401-179
Andrews, M. B. ....SR............401-66
Andrews, Moise..........................USV.........401-219
Andrews, Philip ....NAV........401-13
Andrews, Sam G. ....SR............401-66
Andrews, T. C. ....TVG.........401-179
Andrews, T. E. ....TVG.........401-179
Andrews, Vernon.......................SR............401-66
Andrews, W. R. ....RRR........401-111
Andrews, W. W. ....RRR........401-111
Andrews, Walter William..........RR...........401-51
Andrick, August ....TVG.........401-179
Andrus, E. P. ....TVG.........401-179
Andrus, W. M. ....TVG.........401-179
Angell, C. Roy, Rev. ....SR............401-66
Angell, Cecil..............................TVG.........401-179
Angelo, Joe D. ....SR............401-66
Angle, Charles T.......................RRR........401-111
Angler, J. C. ....SP............401-41
Anglin, A. ....FB............401-141
Anglin, Albert............................TVG.........401-179
Anglin, Everett ....SR............401-66
Anglin, Everett ....LR............401-127
Anglin, W. B. ....FB............401-141
Anglum, Frank ....FB............401-141
Angus, Eugene P. ....TVG.........401-179
Annable, Benjamin ....NAV........401-13
Annia, Frank M. ....USV.........401-219
Annis, John...............................MV..........401-28
Ansley, S. M. ....FB............401-141
Anstead, Frank P. ....USV.........401-219
Anthony, Clyde B. ....USV.........401-219
Anthony, Howard H. ....USV.........401-219
Anthony, Mark ....USV.........401-219
Anthony, T. C. ....TVG.........401-179
Antilley, H. P. ....MV..........401-28
Anton, Joseph Robert ....SR............401-66
Antonio, Estavan ....FF............401-132
Apel, Hiram ....SR............401-66
Apodaca, Antonio.....................RR...........401-51
Apodaca, Reyes ....FB............401-141

Appleby, Bate L. ....USV.........401-219
Appleby, John A. ....SR............401-66
Applegate, Edward J. ....USV.........401-219
Applegate, William B. ....USV.........401-219
Appleman, John.......................NAV........401-13
Appleton, William H. ....ARM........401-1
Applewhite, J. E. ....USV.........401-219
Applewhite, J. H. ....FB............401-141
Applewhite, Scott ....TVG.........401-179
Applewhite, T. D. ....USV.........401-219
Applewhite, Will ....TVG.........401-179
Appling, B. S. ....TVG.........401-179
Appling, John ....SR............401-66
Aramboa, N. ....FF............401-132
Arbough, J. A. ....FF............401-132
Arbs, Winifred........................TVG.........401-179
Arbuckle, Alex ....SP............401-41
Arbuckle, Clarence ....TVG.........401-179
Arbuckle, J. D. ....FB............401-141
Arbury, John L. ....USV.........401-219
Arcambal, Charles L. ....NAV........401-13
Arce, Martiniano....................FB............401-141
Archer, Chas. E. ....TVG.........401-179
Archer, Geo. W........................USV.........401-219
Archer, J. ....TVG.........401-179
Archer, J. F. ....SR............401-66
Archer, Linton P. ....RR...........401-51
Archer, Osceola ....USV.........401-219
Archer, William ....ARM........401-1
Archer, William ....FF............401-132
Archibald, William P..............SR............401-66
Ard, James C. ....USV.........401-219
Ardis, Louis E. ....SR............401-66
Arga, W. P. ....TVG.........401-179
Argent, A. ....SP............401-41
Arhelger, Max.........................USV.........401-219
Arias, Gabino.........................FF............401-132
Arias, Julian...........................SP............401-41
Arispe, Leon ....RR...........401-51
Arispe, Thomas......................FB............401-141
Arle, Hartinian ....FB............401-141
Arledge, W. E. ....TVG.........401-179
Armor, William L. ....NAV........401-13
Armour, Haskell J. ....TVG.........401-179
Arms, William S. ....SR............401-66
Armstrong, A. E. ....SR............401-66
Armstrong, Alonzo L. ....USV.........401-219
Armstrong, C. E. ....RRR........401-111
Armstrong, C. E. ....USV.........401-219
Armstrong, E. H. ....SR............401-66
Armstrong, E. P. ....SP............401-41
Armstrong, George ....SP............401-41
Armstrong, J. T. ....FB............401-141
Armstrong, James L............SP............401-41
Armstrong, Jno. B................TVG.........401-179
Armstrong, John ....ARM........401-1

23

Index to Texas Adjutant General Service Records—All Service Branches

Armstrong, John B. ....FB 401-141
Armstrong, John L. ....USV 401-219
Armstrong, Joseph.............................USV 401-219
Armstrong, Louis L. ....SR 401-66
Armstrong, Noah................................FB 401-141
Armstrong, Pat M. ....SR 401-66
Armstrong, R. H. ....FB 401-141
Armstrong, Robert..............................ARM 401-1
Armstrong, S. A. ....SR 401-66
Armstrong, T. D. ....RR............401-51
Armstrong, William ....USV 401-219
Armstrong, William S. ....ARM 401-1
Armstrong, William T. ....RRR 401-111
Arnel, M. ....SP 401-41
Arnett, A. H. ....FB 401-141
Arnett, J. C. ....SR 401-67
Arnett, Lon ....FB 401-141
Arnim, A.C..RR............401-51
Arnim, A. C. ....SR 401-67
Arnold, Alfred.....................................USV 401-219
Arnold, B. H. ....TVG 401-179
Arnold, Benjamin F............................SR 401-67
Arnold, Bob...TVG 401-179
Arnold, Charles H. ....RR............401-51
Arnold, Claude G. ....TVG 401-179
Arnold, Clay W. ....USV 401-219
Arnold, Earl...SR 401-67
Arnold, Edwin....................................USV 401-219
Arnold, Ernest, Jr. ....TVG 401-179
Arnold, H. L. ....SR 401-67
Arnold, Herman H. ....TVG 401-179
Arnold, J. L. ....SR 401-67
Arnold, J. L. ....TVG 401-179
Arnold, James L. ....USV 401-219
Arnold, James Rufus ....RRR 401-111
Arnold, Jas. P. ....TVG 401-179
Arnold, Joe ....TVG 401-179
Arnold, L. ....TVG 401-179
Arnold, L. T. ....SP 401-41
Arnold, Neal.......................................SR 401-67
Arnold, S. A. ....FF 401-132
Arnold, S. S. ....FF 401-132
Arnold, Samuel G..............................ARM 401-1
Arnold, W. E. ....TVG 401-180
Arnold, W. N. ....RRR 401-111
Arnold, William H. ....TST 401-33
Arnoldi, E. R. ....TVG 401-180
Aron, Leon A. ....TVG 401-180
Aronson, Max....................................TVG 401-180
Arp, Rufus ....SR 401-67
Arrington, G. W. ....FB 401-141
Arrington, George W. ....SR 401-67
Arrington, J. M. ....SR 401-67
Arrington, M. L. ....SR 401-67
Arrington, M. L. ....LR 401-127
Arriola, Thomas ....MV 401-28

Arrollas, Jesus ....FF............401-132
Artee, James R. ....USV 401-219
Arthur, W. L. ....SR 401-67
Arto, William ....TVG 401-180
Arvim [?], Henry G. ....USV 401-219
Arwark, John ....SP 401-41
Arwine, Daniel ....SP 401-41
Asbell, Tilder J. ....USV 401-219
Asbury, Hugh Seward ....TVG 401-180
Asbury, John T. ....RR............401-51
Asbury, John T. ....SR 401-67
Asbury, Rome ....SR 401-67
Ascarate, Frank M. ....RR............401-51
Aschner, Irvin H. ....SR 401-67
Ashabran, Jefferson...........................ARM 401-1
Ashburn, H. T. ....FB 401-141
Ashby, J. C. ....TVG 401-180
Ashby, James M. ....ARM 401-1
Ashby, W. R. ....RRR 401-111
Ashe, John B. ....TVG 401-180
Asher, John G....................................ARM 401-1
Asher, Johnnie H. ....RR............401-51
Asher, L. T. ....RRR 401-111
Asher, W. E. ....USV 401-219
Ashley, Alto A. ....USV 401-219
Ashley, Bennie Eugen......................USV 401-219
Ashley, Jim. ....RRR 401-111
Ashley, John......................................TVG 401-180
Ashley, L. B. ....USV 401-219
Ashley, Rubin F. ....USV 401-219
Ashworth, Samuel L. ....USV 401-220
Ashworth, Sub...................................USV 401-220
Askew, G. J. ....TVG 401-180
Askew, R. G. ....RR............401-51
Askew, W. A. ....TVG 401-180
Askey, W. H. ....SR 401-67
Askey, W. H. ....LR 401-127
Atchley, John J. ....TVG 401-180
Atchley, John J. ....USV 401-220
Aten, C. G. ....SR 401-67
Aten, C. G. ....LR 401-127
Aten, C. G. ....FB 401-141
Aten, E. D..FB 401-141
Aten, Ira ....FB 401-141
Ater, Allen C. ....RRR 401-111
Ater, Guy...SR 401-67
Atkins, Geo. P. ....USV 401-220
Atkins, J. W. ....SR 401-67
Atkins, L. F. ....TVG 401-180
Atkins, P. B. ....SP............401-41
Atkins, Robert ....MV 401-28
Atkins, Rufus U................................TVG 401-180
Atkins, T. B. ....FB 401-141
Atkins, Thomas E. ....USV 401-220
Atkinson, Francis ....TST 401-33
Atkinson, H. A. ....USV 401-220

Index to Texas Adjutant General Service Records—All Service Branches

Name	Branch	Record
Atkinson, H. P.	TVG	401-180
Atkinson, Henry R.	TVG	401-180
Atkinson, J. V.	FB	401-142
Atkinson, Jethro	TST	401-33
Atkinson, John G.	SP	401-41
Atkinson, Richard H.	TVG	401-180
Atkinson, Richard Lee	RRR	401-111
Atkinson, Robt. W.	TVG	401-180
Atkinson, Samuel C.	ARM	401-1
Atkinson, Thomas S.	FB	401-142
Atlee, Edwin A., Jr.	USV	401-220
Attal, ToM	SR	401-67
Attman, Thomas	MV	401-28
Attoway, James W.	RR	401-51
Attwell, Sam B.	SR	401-67
Atwell, James	USV	401-220
Atwell, U. S.	SR	401-67
Atwood, Arch	TVG	401-180
Atwood, Dick	TVG	401-180
Atwood, Dick S.	USV	401-220
Atwood, H.	TVG	401-180
Atwood, J. W.	TVG	401-180
Atwood, James W.	USV	401-220
Aue, Max	MV	401-28
Augustin, Antonio	FF	401-132
Augustine, Robert	MV	401-28
Aule, Joseph H.	NAV	401-13
Aultman, Anton	TVG	401-180
Aultman, H. O.	RR	401-51
Austin, Alexander R.	ARM	401-1
Austin, Charles A.	TVG	401-180
Austin, Charles S.	NAV	401-13
Austin, Clarence G.	USV	401-220
Austin, Eddie	TVG	401-180
Austin, George Y.	USV	401-220
Austin, James	RR	401-51
Austin, John H.	SR	401-67
Austin, John W.	USV	401-220
Austin, Roy G.	RRR	401-111
Austin, V. E.	SR	401-67
Austin, V. E.	LR	401-127
Austin, William	SP	401-41
Authis, Lee D.	USV	401-220
Author, G. M.	USV	401-220
Autin, Jori D.	USV	401-220
Autrey, George	TVG	401-180
Autrey, Max M.	SR	401-67
Autrey, Samuel E.	USV	401-220
Autrey, W. C.	SR	401-67
Autrey, Z. F.	FF	401-132
Avant, A. M.	SR	401-67
Avant, B. F.	FF	401-132
Avant, Durham	MV	401-28
Avant, Homer Hoyl	RRR	401-111
Avant, James	MV	401-28
Avary, J. C.	TVG	401-180
Aveilhe, J. B.	SR	401-67
Avent, A. S.	TVG	401-180
Avent, L. F.	FB	401-142
Avery, C. N.	SR	401-67
Avery, P. G.	FB	401-142
Avery, W. A.	FB	401-142
Avery, W. M.	FB	401-142
Aves, Henry D.	TVG	401-180
Avila, Gregorio	SR	401-67
Avriett, Edd	RR	401-51
Avriett, Hall	RR	401-51
Aycock, K.	FB	401-142
Aydelott, J. M.	SR	401-67
Ayers, D. T.	TVG	401-180
Ayers, Frank	FB	401-142
Ayers, T. L.	NAV	401-13
Aylett, Percy	USV	401-220
Aynesworth, A. F.	SP	401-41
Aynesworth, G. L.	SP	401-41
Aynesworth, I. H.	MM	401-32
Aynesworth, W. P.	USV	401-220
Ayres, George	ARM	401-1
Ayres, John B.	USV	401-220
Ayres, R. O.	SR	401-67
Baar, Leon F.	RR	401-51
Babb, Fred O.	TVG	401-180
Babb, J. T.	FB	401-142
Babb, James Robert	SR	401-67
Babb, John S.	SP	401-41
Babb, Tom G.	TVG	401-180
Babcock, Howard E.	TVG	401-180
Babeman, Duprey	TVG	401-180
Babeman, Duprey	USV	401-220
Babin, A. D.	ARM	401-1
Bacchus, G.	TST	401-33
Bache, R.	NAV	401-13
Bacher, Peter	USV	401-220
Bachman, J. B.	RRR	401-111
Backus, E. E.	TVG	401-180
Backus, M.	TVG	401-180
Bacon, Arthur J.	RRR	401-111
Bacon, Chas.	USV	401-220
Bacon, E. C.	SR	401-67
Bacon, Jesse	FF	401-132
Bacon, Thos. S.	USV	401-220
Bacon, Tyrce G.	ARM	401-1
Bader, Emil	FF	401-132
Bader, Fred	SP	401-41
Bader, Gus	USV	401-220
Badger, Al H.	SR	401-67
Badger, Frank J.	TVG	401-180
Badger, Frank J.	USV	401-220
Badrum, Charles	ARM	401-1
Baernstein, Sol	TVG	401-180
Bagby, Geo. H.	USV	401-220
Bagby, W. H.	SP	401-41

Index to Texas Adjutant General Service Records—All Service Branches

Name	Branch	Record
Baggett, Edward	TVG	401-180
Baggett, J. A.	FB	401-142
Baggett, William T.	USV	401-220
Bagley, E. W.	RRR	401-111
Bagley, Morgan	TST	401-33
Bagnall, Fred R.	TVG	401-180
Bagwell, W. H.	FB	401-142
Bagwill, Joel Harley	TVG	401-180
Bahr, Jack August	SR	401-67
Baiby, Isaac	ARM	401-1
Bail, Arthur	USV	401-220
Bailes, Tom O.	FB	401-142
Bailey, A. A.	USV	401-220
Bailey, Arthur	TVG	401-180
Bailey, Charles Anson	USV	401-220
Bailey, Charles H.	RR	401-51
Bailey, Chas.	USV	401-220
Bailey, Chas. L.	FB	401-142
Bailey, F. A.	TVG	401-180
Bailey, F. W.	TVG	401-180
Bailey, Frank T.	SR	401-67
Bailey, Harry M.	SR	401-67
Bailey, Henry P.	SR	401-67
Bailey, J. B.	NAV	401-13
Bailey, J. R.	SR	401-67
Bailey, J. W.	SR	401-67
Bailey, J. W.	USV	401-220
Bailey, James	USV	401-220
Bailey, Jefferson D.	USV	401-220
Bailey, Jesse	TVG	401-180
Bailey, Jno. H.	TVG	401-180
Bailey, John M.	TVG	401-180
Bailey, K. H.	SR	401-67
Bailey, L. H.	TVG	401-180
Bailey, Marvin E.	RR	401-51
Bailey, Oliver D.	USV	401-220
Bailey, Pittrer A.	USV	401-220
Bailey, Robert L.	RRR	401-111
Bailey, Stonewall	TVG	401-180
Bailey, Thomas J.	USV	401-220
Bailey, Thos. R.	FB	401-142
Bailey, V. Horace	TVG	401-180
Bailey, W. C.	FB	401-142
Bailey, William L.	USV	401-220
Bailiff, Forest L.	USV	401-220
Baillio, F. B.	TVG	401-180
Bain, James E.	USV	401-220
Bain, L. E.	USV	401-220
Bain, Robert	SR	401-67
Baine, Patrick M.	USV	401-220
Baines, Victor L.	USV	401-220
Baines, William M.	FB	401-142
Bains, W. W.	SP	401-41
Baird, A. W.	USV	401-220
Baird, C. C.	FB	401-142
Baird, Deward C.	SR	401-67
Baird, Earl H.	USV	401-220
Baird, F. S.	FB	401-142
Baird, H. E.	SR	401-67
Baird, H. M.	TVG	401-180
Baird, James E.	MM	401-32
Baird, Jos.	ARM	401-1
Baird, Milton C.	RR	401-51
Baird, P. C.	FB	401-142
Baird, R. C.	SR	401-67
Baird, Robt. A.	USV	401-220
Baird, S. M.	TST	401-33
Baird, W. W.	TVG	401-180
Baker, A. H.	SP	401-41
Baker, A. Y.	RR	401-51
Baker, A. Y.	FB	401-142
Baker, Alfred R.	RR	401-51
Baker, Alfred Randolph	RR	401-51
Baker, Andrew Hugh	TVG	401-180
Baker, Arthur G.	USV	401-220
Baker, B. F.	RRR	401-111
Baker, Brainard H.	USV	401-220
Baker, C. A.	TVG	401-180
Baker, C. M.	RRR	401-111
Baker, Charles	FF	401-132
Baker, Chas. A.	USV	401-220
Baker, Chell M.	RR	401-51
Baker, D. P.	FF	401-132
Baker, D. P.	SP	401-41
Baker, Dan	TVG	401-180
Baker, Elma	TVG	401-180
Baker, Emmett L.	TVG	401-180
Baker, F. S.	RRR	401-111
Baker, Felix	USV	401-220
Baker, Fenton J.	SR	401-67
Baker, Frank P.	RR	401-51
Baker, Frank P.	SR	401-67
Baker, G. C., Jr.	TVG	401-180
Baker, Geo. W.	USV	401-220
Baker, George	NAV	401-13
Baker, George A.	TST	401-33
Baker, George S.	USV	401-220
Baker, George W.	FB	401-142
Baker, H. H.	FB	401-142
Baker, H. T.	SR	401-67
Baker, Hardie	TVG	401-180
Baker, Henry	FF	401-132
Baker, Henry	FB	401-142
Baker, Hiram C.	USV	401-220
Baker, Isaac Chas.	USV	401-220
Baker, Isaac W., Jr.	TVG	401-180
Baker, J.	RR	401-51
Baker, J. E.	RR	401-51
Baker, J. H.	RR	401-51
Baker, J. H.	FB	401-142
Baker, J. M.	FB	401-142
Baker, J. S.	FB	401-142

Index to Texas Adjutant General Service Records—All Service Branches

Baker, James P. ....TST 401-33
Baker, James W. ....FB............401-142
Baker, Jefferson T. ....SR............401-67
Baker, John H. ....NAV.........401-13
Baker, Jonathan H. ....TST 401-33
Baker, Joseph Eugene......................RR............401-51
Baker, Jules J. ....RR............401-51
Baker, Jules J. ....RRR 401-111
Baker, L. K. ....RR............401-51
Baker, L. L...RRR 401-111
Baker, Leon ....SR............401-67
Baker, Leonard T..............................USV 401-220
Baker, Lonnie ....USV 401-220
Baker, M. B. ....SR............401-67
Baker, M. J. ....TST 401-33
Baker, Milton A.................................SP............401-41
Baker, O. D. ....FB............401-142
Baker, O. G. ....TVG 401-180
Baker, Ollie L. ....TVG 401-180
Baker, Omer R. ....RR............401-51
Baker, Omer R. ....SR............401-67
Baker, Oscar ....TVG 401-180
Baker, R. D. ....SR............401-67
Baker, R. J. ....SR............401-67
Baker, Robert....................................ARM 401-1
Baker, Roy H. ....SR............401-67
Baker, Theodore B............................SR............401-67
Baker, Thos. G. ....USV 401-220
Baker, Tom ....SR............401-67
Baker, W. B. ....SR............401-67
Baker, W. R. ....FF 401-132
Baker, W. S. ....SR............401-67
Baker, W. W. ....FB............401-142
Baker, Walter E. ....USV 401-220
Baker, William H...............................SP............401-41
Baker, William R...............................USV 401-220
Balch, G. Y. ....NAV.........401-13
Balclay, Abariste ....FF 401-132
Balcomb, T. ....FB............401-142
Baldeschuiler, M. F. ....FB............401-142
Baldwin, B. ....TVG 401-180
Baldwin, B. C. ....RR............401-51
Baldwin, Berk C. ....RR............401-51
Baldwin, Bird F. ....USV 401-220
Baldwin, Edward B. ....SR............401-67
Baldwin, Edwin I...............................USV 401-220
Baldwin, Frank ....SR............401-67
Baldwin, G. Frank ....SR............401-67
Baldwin, George F............................SR............401-67
Baldwin, J. H. ....SP............401-41
Baldwin, John S................................USV 401-220
Baldwin, Leo ....RR............401-51
Bales, Douglas L. ....SR............401-67
Bales, S. B. ....TST 401-33
Ball, A. ....TVG 401-180
Ball, A. T. ....USV 401-220
Ball, Carlos B. ....MM 401-32
Ball, Chas. R. ....USV 401-220
Ball, Chester B. ....USV 401-220
Ball, E. C. ....TVG 401-180
Ball, E. G. ....TVG 401-180
Ball, Elisha ....ARM 401-1
Ball, George......................................MM 401-32
Ball, Glenn..SR............401-67
Ball, J. K. ....FB............401-142
Ball, James.......................................ARM 401-1
Ball, James W. ....USV 401-220
Ball, Joe D. ....SR............401-67
Ball, Larkin ....MV 401-28
Ball, M. L. ....FB............401-142
Ball, Prentis E. ....SR............401-67
Ball, Taylor.......................................LR 401-127
Ball, W. D. ....TVG 401-180
Ballantine, George W. ....SP............401-41
Ballard, Benjamin G. ....USV 401-220
Ballard, Blan.....................................NAV.........401-13
Ballard, Claude ....SR............401-67
Ballard, J. L. ....SR............401-67
Ballard, John....................................SP............401-41
Ballard, John Houston ....SR............401-67
Ballard, Lawson C. ....TVG 401-180
Ballard, Luke ....TVG 401-180
Ballard, R. A. ....TVG 401-180
Ballard, Ray R. ....RR...........401-51
Ballentyne, J. M. ....FB............401-142
Ballew, Hugh C. ....USV 401-220
Ballew, Hugh Clyde ....TVG 401-180
Ballew, Thomas B. ....SR............401-67
Ballinger, Silvanno ....USV 401-220
Balser, John ....NAV.........401-13
Bames, Perry M. ....MV 401-28
Bames, Richard D............................TST 401-33
Band, C. S. ....TVG 401-180
Bandy, John ....TST 401-33
Bandy, Thomas................................TST 401-33
Bane, James R. ....USV 401-220
Bangoes, Mateas.............................MV 401-28
Banister, John Randolph................FB............401-142
Banister, Neill H. ....SR............401-67
Banister, William L. ....FB............401-142
Banks, A. F. ....SR............401-67
Banks, Charles ....ARM 401-1
Banks, John ....FB............401-142
Banks, Vincent ....ARM 401-1
Bankston, John ....SR............401-67
Banner, Roland R. ....USV 401-220
Bannerman, E. ....FB............401-142
Bantia, Jesse ....RR............401-51
Barada, G..FF 401-132
Barak, Paul ....USV 401-220
Barbee, A. O. ....NAV.........401-13
Barbee, James G. ....MV 401-28

Index to Texas Adjutant General Service Records—All Service Branches

Name	Branch	Record
Barbee, John	TVG	401-180
Barbee, Joseph	USV	401-220
Barbee, L. C.	USV	401-220
Barbee, Willis M.	RR	401-51
Barber, A. A.	FB	401-142
Barber, G. G.	TVG	401-180
Barber, H. E.	USV	401-220
Barber, J. H.	FB	401-142
Barber, J. W.	FB	401-142
Barber, John E.	LR	401-127
Barberie, Arthur	USV	401-220
Barcena, Primitivo	SP	401-41
Barclay, Pvt.	TST	401-33
Barclay, Samuel D.	MV	401-28
Barclay, Will W.	TVG	401-180
Barclay, William A.	MV	401-28
Barcus, George W.	USV	401-220
Barder, Aaron	RR	401-51
Barder, S. A.	RRR	401-111
Bardwell, C. P.	FB	401-142
Barefoot, F. S.	FB	401-142
Barfield, W. B.	TVG	401-180
Bargsley, John	RRR	401-111
Bargsley, John L.	RR	401-51
Bargsley, John L.	FB	401-142
Bargsley, W. M.	SR	401-67
Barho, Will H.	TVG	401-180
Barineau, Sam H.	TVG	401-180
Barker, A. C.	RR	401-51
Barker, A. C.	SR	401-67
Barker, B. R.	RRR	401-111
Barker, Ben M.	SR	401-67
Barker, Charles	SP	401-41
Barker, D. S.	SR	401-67
Barker, D. S.	FB	401-142
Barker, Denny W.	SR	401-67
Barker, George E.	SR	401-67
Barker, J. G.	USV	401-220
Barker, William	ARM	401-1
Barker, William	ARM	401-1
Barker, William H.	USV	401-220
Barkley, J. D.	RR	401-51
Barkley, J. D.	RRR	401-111
Barkley, James M.	LR	401-127
Barkow, Gus	RRR	401-111
Barkow, Gus P. H.	SR	401-67
Barksdale, Claud C.	SR	401-67
Barler, W. L.	RR	401-51
Barlow, Albert B.	TVG	401-180
Barlow, J. H.	RRR	401-111
Barnard, A. A.	TVG	401-180
Barnard, J. B. F.	NAV	401-13
Barnes, A. M.	RRR	401-111
Barnes, E. A.	SR	401-67
Barnes, Edward A.	RRR	401-111
Barnes, George W.	SR	401-67
Barnes, George W.	USV	401-220
Barnes, H. E.	RRR	401-111
Barnes, Hughie E.	USV	401-220
Barnes, J. F.	SR	401-67
Barnes, J. W.	RRR	401-111
Barnes, J. W.	SR	401-67
Barnes, James D.	RRR	401-111
Barnes, James W.	TST	401-33
Barnes, Jno. B.	USV	401-220
Barnes, W. F.	TVG	401-180
Barnes, W. F.	USV	401-220
Barnes, William H.	USV	401-220
Barnett, Andrew	SP	401-41
Barnett, Dewitt T.	RR	401-51
Barnett, E. L.	RR	401-51
Barnett, Frank	SR	401-67
Barnett, Graham	SR	401-67
Barnett, Gramison (Granson)	SP	401-41
Barnett, H. P.	TVG	401-180
Barnett, J. C.	SR	401-67
Barnett, J. G.	RR	401-51
Barnett, Jas. A.	USV	401-220
Barnett, John	USV	401-220
Barnett, John J.	FB	401-142
Barnett, Joseph R.	SR	401-67
Barnett, L. B.	RR	401-51
Barnett, L. D.	TVG	401-180
Barnett, Othias	ARM	401-1
Barnett, S. E.	SR	401-67
Barnett, Thomas	NAV	401-13
Barnett, William F.	MV	401-28
Barnett, William T.	USV	401-220
Barney, John	NAV	401-13
Barnhart, Charles M.	SR	401-67
Barnhart, Horace Chilton	SR	401-67
Barnhart, J. M.	CSA	401-39
Barnhart, O. F.	USV	401-220
Barnhill, P. C.	TST	401-33
Barnhill, Pink	SR	401-67
Barnhill, Pinkney L.	RR	401-51
Barnhill, Pinkney L.	FB	401-142
Barnom, D. E.	TVG	401-180
Barnum, B. P.	TVG	401-180
Baron, Gilbert L.	USV	401-220
Barr, Ed W.	SR	401-67
Barr, Robert	FF	401-132
Barrager, B. A.	RRR	401-111
Barrera, Jesus	FF	401-132
Barrett, A. T.	SR	401-67
Barrett, C. H.	FF	401-132
Barrett, G. W.	SR	401-67
Barrett, George	FB	401-142
Barrett, H. S.	RRR	401-111
Barrett, James	ARM	401-1
Barrett, James	TVG	401-180
Barrett, Oscar	TVG	401-180

Index to Texas Adjutant General Service Records—All Service Branches

Name	Branch	Record
Barrett, R. J.	SR	401-67
Barrett, William F.	USV	401-220
Barrick, David M.	USV	401-220
Barrientes, Abel G.	SR	401-67
Barrier, M. E.	USV	401-220
Barringer, J. C.	FB	401-142
Barrington, Gus	SR	401-67
Barrington, Thad	TVG	401-180
Barron, Alonza Mellvine	TVG	401-180
Barron, Charlie	SR	401-67
Barron, J. F.	FB	401-142
Barron, Julian E.	USV	401-220
Barrow, A. B.	RR	401-51
Barrow, A. B.	SR	401-67
Barry, A. P.	FB	401-142
Barry, Desmond Albert	SR	401-67
Barry, J. F.	SR	401-67
Barry, James W.	USV	401-220
Barry, John	NAV	401-13
Barry, Tom K.	TVG	401-180
Barry, William	ARM	401-1
Bartee, J. W.	RRR	401-111
Bartell, Cary	TVG	401-180
Bartell, Sam E.	RR	401-51
Barter, C. M.	SR	401-67
Barter, S. J.	RRR	401-111
Barthelimi, Francis	NAV	401-13
Barthet, F.	ARM	401-2
Bartholomew, Charles	FB	401-142
Bartholomew, G. N.	FB	401-142
Bartholomew, Joseph	FB	401-142
Bartle, N. E.	TVG	401-180
Bartlett, C. E.	FB	401-142
Bartlett, Charles	NAV	401-13
Bartlett, E. J.	FB	401-142
Bartlett, Jno. T., Jr.	TVG	401-180
Bartlett, L. E.	TVG	401-180
Bartlett, Ned	TVG	401-180
Bartlett, Oscar	TVG	401-180
Bartlett, Reuel G.	USV	401-220
Bartlett, Thomas Edward	SR	401-68
Bartlett, Will D.	TVG	401-180
Bartlett, Will D.	USV	401-220
Bartley, Arthur	TVG	401-180
Bartlow, J. H.	FB	401-142
Barton, C. S.	SR	401-68
Barton, Charles	FB	401-142
Barton, D. C.	TVG	401-180
Barton, E. J.	TVG	401-180
Barton, Early	USV	401-220
Barton, Emmett	TVG	401-180
Barton, Frank E.	USV	401-220
Barton, J.	FB	401-142
Barton, J. L.	USV	401-220
Barton, John	NAV	401-13
Barton, John J.	SR	401-68
Barton, L. C.	SR	401-68
Barton, O. M.	USV	401-220
Barton, P. E.	LR	401-127
Barton, Riley	FB	401-142
Barton, Stafford P.	USV	401-220
Barton, Stephen T.	TVG	401-180
Barton, T. H.	TVG	401-180
Barton, Thomas D.	TVG	401-180
Barton, W.	FB	401-142
Barton, Will H.	USV	401-220
Barton, William	NAV	401-13
Basham, T. J.	FB	401-142
Basinger, H. L.	SR	401-68
Baskett, Chas. L.	USV	401-220
Basore, Warren	SR	401-68
Basques, Moses	FF	401-132
Bass, Albert F.	USV	401-220
Bass, Alonzo T.	TST	401-33
Bass, J. Leland	TVG	401-180
Bass, Joseph H.	USV	401-220
Bass, R. M.	SR	401-68
Bass, Richard A.	RRR	401-111
Bass, Robert Lee	RRR	401-111
Bass, W. E.	TVG	401-180
Bass, Walter	TVG	401-180
Bassett, B. H.	TST	401-33
Bassett, J. C.	TVG	401-181
Bassett, Samuel	FF	401-132
Bassett, W. F.	TVG	401-181
Bastian, Henry	SP	401-41
Batcheller, Hugh	ARM	401-2
Batchelor, F. M.	TST	401-33
Batchelor, Lemon B.	TST	401-33
Bateman, Charles S.	USV	401-220
Bateman, Logan W.	USV	401-220
Bates, Albert F.	RRR	401-111
Bates, Andrew	FF	401-132
Bates, Arthur	FB	401-142
Bates, B. L.	RRR	401-111
Bates, Bert E.	TVG	401-181
Bates, Carroll	RR	401-51
Bates, Clyde A.	USV	401-220
Bates, David	SR	401-68
Bates, E. A.	FF	401-132
Bates, Elmer E.	USV	401-221
Bates, Felix	TST	401-33
Bates, Gerald	TVG	401-181
Bates, H. C.	USV	401-221
Bates, Hal	TVG	401-181
Bates, J. H.	FB	401-142
Bates, J. R.	RR	401-51
Bates, L.	FB	401-142
Bates, L. E.	SR	401-68
Bates, L. H.	SR	401-68
Bates, L. H.	FB	401-142
Bates, Lawrence	FB	401-142

Index to Texas Adjutant General Service Records—All Service Branches

Name	Branch	Record
Bates, Michael	ARM	401-2
Bates, Richard Roy	RRR	401-111
Bates, S. B.	RR	401-51
Bates, Sam	RR	401-51
Bates, Samuel O.	USV	401-221
Bates, T. L.	TVG	401-181
Bates, W. B.	FB	401-142
Bates, W. F.	RR	401-51
Bates, W. L.	FB	401-142
Bates, W. W.	FB	401-142
Bates, Walter	TVG	401-181
Bates, Wharton	FB	401-142
Bates, Wilson	RR	401-51
Bates, Winfred F.	RR	401-51
Batsell, Chas.	TVG	401-181
Batsell, J. M.	SR	401-68
Batte, R. L., Jr.	SR	401-68
Battey, W. C.	FB	401-143
Battis, George	USV	401-221
Battiste, Jos. F.	USV	401-221
Battle, Oliver L.	USV	401-221
Battle, Waddey W.	TVG	401-181
Battot, Christian	FF	401-132
Battot, John	FF	401-132
Batts, Walter B.	USV	401-221
Baty, Arthur P.	USV	401-221
Baty, W. E.	SR	401-68
Bauchelle, William E.	TST	401-33
Bauchette, James	NAV	401-13
Bauchman, Oscar	SR	401-68
Bauer, A. C.	TVG	401-181
Bauer, Jakob	TVG	401-181
Bauer, Will	TVG	401-181
Bauer, William, Jr.	TVG	401-181
Bauerfeind, J. W.	TVG	401-181
Baugh, F. A.	RR	401-52
Baugh, W. W.	TVG	401-181
Baughman, Abraham	USV	401-221
Baughn, R. H.	SR	401-68
Bauhetta, Thomas	NAV	401-13
Baumann, Peter, Jr.	TVG	401-181
Baumbach, E. J.	TVG	401-181
Baumberger, Charles	SR	401-68
Baumgarten, J. H.	SR	401-68
Baurgeois, William A.	USV	401-221
Baurland, C. P.	FF	401-132
Baushell, August	TVG	401-181
Baviesclusky, Edward	ARM	401-2
Bawcom, Newton C.	MV	401-28
Bawcone, J. C.	SP	401-41
Baxter, J. N.	SR	401-68
Baxter, J. W.	FB	401-143
Baxter, Oliver H.	TVG	401-181
Baxter, Otho	USV	401-221
Bay, R. Milton	USV	401-221
Bayker, A. R.	RR	401-52
Bayless, Geo. C.	TVG	401-181
Baylor, Albert Searcy	LR	401-127
Baylor, George W.	FB	401-143
Baylor, George W., Jr.	FB	401-143
Baylor, H. W.	SR	401-68
Baylor, J. W.	FB	401-143
Baylor, John R.	MV	401-28
Baylor, S. J.	FB	401-143
Bazer, J. L.	USV	401-221
Beach, D. Morey	TVG	401-181
Beach, H. A.	TVG	401-181
Beach, W. C.	RR	401-52
Beadles, W. W.	FF	401-132
Beakley, G. W.	FB	401-143
Beakley, J. C.	SR	401-68
Beakley, John	SP	401-41
Beakley, Wright	SP	401-41
Beal, N. R.	TVG	401-181
Beal, W. C.	FB	401-143
Beale, Thomas W.	ARM	401-2
Beall, Charles	RR	401-52
Beall, Charles	SR	401-68
Beall, Charley P.	RR	401-52
Beall, Horace	ARM	401-2
Beall, Jerome B.	MV	401-28
Beall, John B.	USV	401-221
Beall, T. D.	RR	401-52
Beall, W. E.	RR	401-52
Beall, W. O.	SR	401-68
Beam, E.	FF	401-132
Beam, Jesse	FF	401-132
Beaman, Charles	SP	401-41
Beamer, G. H.	NAV	401-13
Bean, Edward M.	RR	401-52
Bean, Gilbert C.	TVG	401-181
Bean, Isaac	ARM	401-2
Bean, J. B.	RR	401-52
Bean, J. M.	RR	401-52
Bean, Joseph C.	RR	401-52
Bean, Milton	RR	401-52
Bean, Sam H.	SR	401-68
Bean, W. E.	TVG	401-181
Bean, William	USV	401-221
Beane, John C.	FF	401-132
Bear	ARM	401-2
Beard, A. G.	RR	401-52
Beard, Burnie	TVG	401-181
Beard, C. C.	FB	401-143
Beard, J. T.	TVG	401-181
Beard, James S.	TVG	401-181
Beard, Oliver Caliway	RRR	401-112
Beard, Rube Simonton	LR	401-127
Beard, Rube Simonton	SR	401-68
Bearon, William	SP	401-41
Beasley, Allen	SR	401-68
Beasley, C. S.	RR	401-52

Index to Texas Adjutant General Service Records—All Service Branches

Name	Branch	Record
Beasley, C. S.	SR	401-68
Beasley, Doak S.	USV	401-221
Beasley, H. W. A.	RRR	401-112
Beasley, H. W. Allen	RR	401-52
Beasley, James M.	LR	401-127
Beasley, Sam D.	USV	401-221
Beasley, Talmage B.	USV	401-221
Beatts, William	NAV	401-13
Beatty, David	ARM	401-2
Beatty, George	NAV	401-13
Beaty, Geo. S.	FB	401-143
Beaty, George W.	USV	401-221
Beaty, R. E.	RR	401-52
Beaty, R. E.	SR	401-68
Beaty, Russell W.	USV	401-221
Beaty, Washington	ARM	401-2
Beaty, Wilbur O.	TVG	401-181
Beauchamp, Douglas	SR	401-68
Beauchamp, Gerald Downing	SR	401-68
Beauchamp, James E.	USV	401-221
Beauman, M. E.	FB	401-143
Beaumier, George	TVG	401-181
Beaumier, O. L.	RR	401-52
Beaumont, Frank	FB	401-143
Beaumont, W. P.	FB	401-143
Beavens, Christopher Conway	TVG	401-181
Beavens, Phil R.	TVG	401-181
Beavers, Homer	USV	401-221
Beavers, Washington L.	MM	401-32
Beavert, L. P.	FF	401-132
Becher, Paul	USV	401-221
Bechon, William	NAV	401-13
Beck, Albert J.	TVG	401-181
Beck, J. C.	SP	401-41
Beck, J. W. E. H.	SR	401-68
Beck, James L.	USV	401-221
Beck, John	FF	401-132
Beck, John C.	LR	401-127
Beck, Joseph	MM	401-32
Beck, O. Edgar	TVG	401-181
Becker, Alvin L.	SR	401-68
Becker, Arthur E.	TVG	401-181
Becker, Carl	USV	401-221
Becker, Francis C.	SR	401-68
Becker, Otto	FF	401-132
Beckett, Oscar R.	USV	401-221
Beckett, Stafford E.	RR	401-52
Beckham, C. A.	SR	401-68
Beckham, Charles M.	RRR	401-112
Beckham, Clifford G.	RR	401-52
Beckham, J. M.	FB	401-143
Beckham, L. E.	TVG	401-181
Beckham, Robt. H.	USV	401-221
Beckhnsen, Fred	TVG	401-181
Beckman, A. M.	FF	401-132
Becknell, William	ARM	401-2
Beckner, Charles M.	USV	401-221
Beckway, Frank J.	TVG	401-181
Beckwith, A. J.	TVG	401-181
Beckwith, Ed L.	USV	401-221
Beckworth, Robert E. L.	USV	401-221
Becton, E. P.	SR	401-68
Bedell, B. E.	SP	401-41
Bedell, William A., Jr.	SR	401-68
Bedford, G. E.	SR	401-68
Bee, Anderson	TVG	401-181
Bee, Carlos	TVG	401-181
Bee, H. P.	USV	401-221
Bee, Hamilton P.	TST	401-33
Beebee, David P.	USV	401-221
Beechly, Bertie W.	USV	401-221
Beechly, John L.	USV	401-221
Beehn, Chas. A.	TVG	401-181
Beers, Frank E.	USV	401-221
Beeson, Horace Watz	RRR	401-112
Beeton, William	NAV	401-13
Beezley, C. W.	SR	401-68
Behrens, A. F.	TVG	401-181
Beidler, Dorsey	TVG	401-181
Beinhaner, Julius	USV	401-221
Beissner, Fred L.	USV	401-221
Beitiger, Lorenzo	FF	401-132
Belcher, Harvey	SR	401-68
Belcher, W. W.	RR	401-52
Belcher, W. W.	RRR	401-112
Belcher, W. W.	SR	401-68
Belden, Samuel A., Jr.	USV	401-221
Belden, W. A.	SR	401-68
Belfi, Charles	USV	401-221
Belitzer, Max	TVG	401-181
Belk, Lee W.	TVG	401-181
Bell, Alexander	ARM	401-2
Bell, Bryan	SR	401-68
Bell, C. L.	RR	401-52
Bell, C. S.	SP	401-41
Bell, D. P.	SR	401-68
Bell, D. P.	TVG	401-181
Bell, E. A.	FB	401-143
Bell, Edward Dudley	TVG	401-181
Bell, Eugene	FB	401-143
Bell, Farley S.	FB	401-143
Bell, Frank W.	TVG	401-181
Bell, G.	SP	401-41
Bell, G. W.	FB	401-143
Bell, George Whitis	SR	401-68
Bell, Irvin	MM	401-32
Bell, Ivan C.	SR	401-68
Bell, J. M.	FB	401-143
Bell, James M.	USV	401-221
Bell, Joe A.	TVG	401-181
Bell, John E.	USV	401-221
Bell, John R.	USV	401-221

Index to Texas Adjutant General Service Records—All Service Branches

Name	Branch	Number
Bell, Joseph N.	USV	401-221
Bell, Joseph V.	SR	401-68
Bell, Joseph W.	FB	401-143
Bell, Lee	SR	401-68
Bell, Meatlow J.	USV	401-221
Bell, O. L.	FB	401-143
Bell, R. W.	FB	401-143
Bell, Richard	TVG	401-181
Bell, Robert R.	USV	401-221
Bell, Robert S.	MM	401-32
Bell, Sie	RR	401-52
Bell, Stephen	ARM	401-2
Bell, T. W.	SR	401-68
Bell, Thomas	NAV	401-13
Bell, Thomas A.	MV	401-28
Bell, Thos. H.	USV	401-221
Bell, Tyree L.	SR	401-68
Bell, W. A.	TVG	401-181
Bell, W. H.	RRR	401-112
Bell, W. R.	RRR	401-112
Bell, Walter E.	USV	401-221
Bell, William	ARM	401-2
Bell, William D.	USV	401-221
Bell, William S.	CSA	401-39
Bell, Zachariah T.	TVG	401-181
Bella, Henry	NAV	401-13
Bellah, J. L.	TVG	401-181
Bellamy, Oscar	SR	401-68
Bellemy, Raymond	RR	401-52
Beller, Henry	NAV	401-13
Bellinger, Carnot	TVG	401-181
Bellinger, William K.	USV	401-221
Bellmont, L. T.	SR	401-68
Bellows, William J.	TVG	401-181
Beman, C. S.	FB	401-143
Benavides, Refugio	FF	401-132
Benbow, James R.	TST	401-33
Bencini, Jas. A.	USV	401-221
Bendall, Adolph	ARM	401-2
Bendel, Henry W.	SR	401-68
Bendetti, George	RRR	401-112
Bendozo, Bentino	FF	401-132
Bendy, Henry W.	TST	401-33
Bendy, Thomas A.	FB	401-143
Benedict, Charles R.	ARM	401-2
Benedict, O.	TST	401-33
Benefiel, Lawrence	FB	401-143
Benefiel, S. E.	RR	401-52
Benefield, Ben	TVG	401-181
Benevides, C.	FB	401-143
Benevides, Patricio	FF	401-132
Beng, Hermann	TVG	401-181
Benge, T. F.	SR	401-68
Benge, T. F.	LR	401-127
Benites, Antonio	ARM	401-2
Benjamin, D. G.	TVG	401-181
Benjamin, Edward B.	USV	401-221
Benjamin, Jacob F.	TVG	401-181
Benner, Andrew	ARM	401-2
Benner, William H.	USV	401-221
Bennett, A. E.	RR	401-52
Bennett, A. E.	RRR	401-112
Bennett, Albert Earest	SR	401-68
Bennett, D. A.	TVG	401-181
Bennett, Daniel R.	USV	401-221
Bennett, F.	FF	401-132
Bennett, F. W.	TVG	401-181
Bennett, Frederick	NAV	401-13
Bennett, Frederick W.	USV	401-221
Bennett, George	ARM	401-2
Bennett, Granville	RR	401-52
Bennett, J.	TVG	401-181
Bennett, J. A. N.	SP	401-41
Bennett, J. E.	SR	401-68
Bennett, J. W.	SR	401-68
Bennett, Joe E.	SR	401-68
Bennett, John A.	TVG	401-181
Bennett, John C.	TVG	401-181
Bennett, John G.	USV	401-221
Bennett, John H. M.	TVG	401-181
Bennett, Johnathan H.	ARM	401-2
Bennett, Jordon W.	RR	401-52
Bennett, L. E.	NAV	401-13
Bennett, O. H.	SP	401-41
Bennett, R. O.	RR	401-52
Bennett, Robert L.	TVG	401-181
Bennett, S.	FF	401-132
Bennett, T. C.	RR	401-52
Bennett, W. Edwin	TVG	401-181
Bennett, William P.	RR	401-52
Bennis, J. G.	SR	401-68
Benoit, Frank	USV	401-221
Benson, F. L.	LR	401-127
Benson, George	TST	401-33
Benson, James	FF	401-132
Benson, Roy H.	LR	401-127
Benson, T. H.	FB	401-143
Benson, Thomas	FF	401-132
Benson, W. W.	LR	401-127
Benson, W. W.	SR	401-68
Benson, Walter	USV	401-221
Benson, William	ARM	401-2
Bent, George W.	TVG	401-181
Bentinck, George Clifford	SR	401-68
Bentley, Clyde L.	RR	401-52
Bentley, Ellis B.	TVG	401-181
Bentley, J. W.	TVG	401-181
Bentley, W. F.	FB	401-143
Bentley, W. V.	RR	401-52
Benton, Lee C.	USV	401-221
Benton, Nat	FB	401-143
Bentz, D. D.	FB	401-143

Index to Texas Adjutant General Service Records—All Service Branches

Name	Branch	Record
Bentz, Nicholas	USV	401-221
Berchelmann, Adolph, Dr.	SR	401-68
Berdwell, E. C.	TVG	401-181
Berge, H. Zum	FF	401-132
Bergen, Joseph	ARM	401-2
Bergen, Timothy	ARM	401-2
Bergin, Joe L.	SR	401-68
Beringer, Chas.	TVG	401-181
Beringer, O. A.	TVG	401-181
Berlocher, S.	TVG	401-181
Berman, Paul P.	USV	401-221
Bernard, J. B. F.	NAV	401-13
Bernard, Leonard	TVG	401-181
Berndt, Herman C.	USV	401-221
Bernhaner, Julius	TVG	401-181
Bernhardt, Arthur H.	USV	401-221
Bernheim, Lucien	TVG	401-181
Berning, John H.	TVG	401-181
Bernowsky, W.	NAV	401-13
Berrey, L. C.	SR	401-68
Berry, Andrew	TST	401-33
Berry, Andrew J.	SR	401-68
Berry, B. M.	FF	401-132
Berry, C. S.	TVG	401-181
Berry, Eugene Allen	TVG	401-181
Berry, Franklin	MV	401-28
Berry, H. C.	FB	401-143
Berry, H. V.	SR	401-68
Berry, Holly T.	USV	401-221
Berry, J. A.	FB	401-143
Berry, J. T.	SR	401-68
Berry, John A.	USV	401-221
Berry, John F.	SP	401-41
Berry, John M.	USV	401-221
Berry, John W.	ARM	401-2
Berry, Silas N.	SR	401-68
Berry, Thomas A.	TVG	401-181
Berry, Victor	FB	401-143
Berry, W. J.	FB	401-143
Berry, W. M.	TVG	401-181
Berry, Wesley B.	USV	401-221
Berry, Will	TVG	401-181
Berryman, A. B.	CSA	401-39
Berryman, I. M.	TST	401-33
Berryman, O. G.	RRR	401-112
Bersham, William	FB	401-143
Bertling, Otto	TVG	401-181
Bertram, Joseph S.	USV	401-221
Bertram, R.	TST	401-33
Bertrand, William A.	TVG	401-181
Berwick, Bab	SR	401-68
Besh, B. F.	FB	401-143
Bess, Lemuel A.	TVG	401-181
Besse, W. A.	TVG	401-181
Besserer, William	SP	401-41
Best, Ernest	SR	401-68
Best, Ernest, Jr.	SR	401-68
Betancourt, M. Z.	USV	401-221
Bethea, Cade	USV	401-221
Bethune, William D.	USV	401-221
Bettinger, F. A.	NAV	401-13
Bettis, A. R.	SR	401-68
Bettis, B.	SR	401-68
Bettis, James Moore	USV	401-221
Bettis, W. D.	TVG	401-181
Bettran, Pepe	TST	401-33
Betts, C. S.	NAV	401-13
Betzel, W. F.	TVG	401-181
Beucanan, James	NAV	401-13
Beucher, James	NAV	401-13
Beveridge, John Lewis	TVG	401-181
Beverley, A. J.	RR	401-52
Beverly, A. F.	SR	401-68
Beverly, Bob	SR	401-68
Beverly, Claude Horace	SR	401-68
Beverly, Robert E.	USV	401-221
Beverly, T. H.	RR	401-52
Bevers, S.	FB	401-143
Bevers, W. E.	RRR	401-112
Beversdolph, August	MV	401-28
Bevill, W. H.	RR	401-52
Bevins, Jeremiah	ARM	401-2
Bewley, Homer	TVG	401-181
Beyer, Robert Chapman	SR	401-68
Beyley, W. M.	USV	401-221
Bibb, Robt. T.	TVG	401-181
Biberstein, H. R., von	FF	401-132
Biberstein, R.	MV	401-28
Bible, Hugh	TVG	401-181
Bible, Hugh	USV	401-221
Bickham, J. C.	TVG	401-181
Bickle, J. E.	USV	401-221
Bickler, George W.	SR	401-68
Bickley, Jackie	SR	401-68
Biddie, James	TST	401-33
Biddy, James	FF	401-132
Bidena, Charles	TVG	401-181
Bieberstein, Edgar	TVG	401-181
Biehn, Harry	RRR	401-112
Bierbower, Charles G.	USV	401-221
Bierbower, Richard C.	USV	401-221
Bierce, Frank M.	TVG	401-181
Bierchwale, Charles	FB	401-143
Bierschwale, Conrad	FB	401-143
Bieze, T. H.	SR	401-68
Bigar, IsoM	SP	401-41
Bigford, George	FB	401-143
Biggar, James H.	TVG	401-181
Bigger, William	NAV	401-13
Biggers, Eugene M.	USV	401-221
Biggers, S. W.	MM	401-32
Biggers, Virgil R.	USV	401-221

Index to Texas Adjutant General Service Records—All Service Branches

Name	Branch	Record
Biggers, William H.	USV	401-221
Biggerstaff, Jack	RRR	401-112
Biggio, C. C.	TVG	401-181
Biggio, William J.	TVG	401-181
Biggio, William Joseph	SR	401-68
Biggs, A. A.	SR	401-68
Biggs, Carl	USV	401-221
Biggs, G. S.	USV	401-221
Biggs, K. D.	TVG	401-181
Biggs, K. D.	USV	401-221
Biggs, Norman	USV	401-221
Biggs, Orien M.	SR	401-68
Bigley, Jessie M.	USV	401-221
Bigum, Martin	USV	401-221
Bilber, John	ARM	401-2
Bilberry, E. M.	RR	401-52
Bilberry, W. M.	TVG	401-181
Billegos, Silvero	FF	401-132
Billereal, Nives	FF	401-132
Billings, D. D.	LR	401-127
Billings, W. C.	SR	401-68
Billingsley, J. P.	SR	401-68
Billingsley, James F.	USV	401-221
Billingsley, Sam J.	MV	401-28
Billingsley, W. B.	SP	401-41
Billingsly, A. W.	SR	401-68
Billingsly, Albert W.	RR	401-52
Billingsly, W.	USV	401-221
Billo, John	FF	401-132
Bills, B. C.	RR	401-52
Bills, Joe	SP	401-41
Bills, L. C.	RR	401-52
Bills, L. C.	SR	401-68
Bills, Lee C.	RRR	401-112
Billups, Stanley N.	USV	401-221
Bims, Paul W.	USV	401-221
Binford, C. B.	LR	401-127
Binford, Gene B.	LR	401-127
Binford, John	FB	401-143
Binford, W. T.	SR	401-68
Binge, George H.	USV	401-221
Bingham, Alexander	USV	401-221
Bingham, C. C.	MM	401-32
Bingham, Charles T.	LR	401-127
Bingham, Geo. R.	FB	401-143
Bingham, Isaac G.	USV	401-221
Bingham, John H.	MV	401-28
Binnings, H. L.	SR	401-68
Binnion, J. B.	RR	401-52
Binyon, Jim	TVG	401-181
Bippert, Alfred E.	USV	401-221
Bippert, John	FB	401-143
Bird, G. H.	FB	401-143
Bird, J. C.	FB	401-143
Bird, J. T.	FB	401-143
Bird, J. W.	LR	401-127
Bird, James	ARM	401-2
Bird, Joe D.	FB	401-143
Bird, John L.	USV	401-221
Bird, O. L.	RRR	401-112
Bird, Peter	TST	401-33
Bird, Robert A.	TVG	401-181
Bird, Robert L.	USV	401-221
Birdsell, L.	SP	401-41
Birdson, C. B.	USV	401-221
Birdwell, George	ARM	401-2
Birdwell, John	FB	401-143
Birdwell, Preston K.	USV	401-221
Birdwell, Zachariah	ARM	401-2
Birge, N. A., Jr.	USV	401-221
Birgson, Bert	TVG	401-181
Birmingham, Ed	SP	401-41
Birmingham, George	TVG	401-181
Birmingham, Giles Clark	RRR	401-112
Birmingham, W. D.	FB	401-143
Biry, Joseph	FF	401-132
Bisbee, Ira	ARM	401-2
Biscailuz, Eugene W.	SR	401-68
Biscarro, Innocente	FF	401-132
Bishop, Earl	TVG	401-181
Bishop, H. N.	SR	401-68
Bishop, Harris M.	USV	401-221
Bishop, Homet	RRR	401-112
Bishop, J. D.	FB	401-143
Bishop, J. R.	FB	401-143
Bishop, James H.	USV	401-221
Bishop, Joe	TVG	401-181
Bishop, L. P.	RR	401-52
Bishop, Leo H.	SR	401-68
Bishop, Leo Henderson	RR	401-52
Bishop, Paul Herndon	RRR	401-112
Bishop, T. S.	SR	401-68
Bisland, Edmond M.	USV	401-221
Bissell, George	SR	401-68
Biter, C. A.	TVG	401-181
Bitter, Joseph	FF	401-132
Bittle, Percy B.	TVG	401-181
Bittle, W. A.	TVG	401-181
Bittner, Fred	USV	401-221
Bivins, Richard E.	USV	401-221
Bixley, John B.	TVG	401-182
Bizot, Francis C.	USV	401-221
Bizot, Lawrence E.	USV	401-221
Black, Augustus L.	LR	401-127
Black, Charles Jack	TVG	401-182
Black, CleM	SP	401-41
Black, E. M.	LR	401-127
Black, Edward B.	SR	401-68
Black, Edward Butler	RRR	401-112
Black, Frank	RR	401-52
Black, Frank A.	RR	401-52
Black, George B.	FB	401-143

Index to Texas Adjutant General Service Records—All Service Branches

Name	Branch	Record
Black, George H.	SR	401-68
Black, Haller William	RRR	401-112
Black, Ike	TVG	401-182
Black, Joe M.	TVG	401-182
Black, John	NAV	401-13
Black, John H.	USV	401-221
Black, M. J.	FB	401-143
Black, R. F.	TST	401-33
Black, W. B.	FB	401-143
Black, W. B.	TVG	401-182
Black, W. J.	CSA	401-39
Black, W. W.	SP	401-41
Black, Walter M.	TVG	401-182
Black, William L.	USV	401-221
Black, William S.	ARM	401-2
Blackburn, David E.	USV	401-221
Blackburn, Dick	TVG	401-182
Blackburn, F. B.	TVG	401-182
Blackburn, Geo. M.	USV	401-222
Blackburn, J. M.	RRR	401-112
Blackburn, John W.	USV	401-222
Blackburn, M. W.	RR	401-52
Blackburn, Ralph J.	TVG	401-182
Blackburn, Richard C.	USV	401-222
Blackburn, W. L.	USV	401-222
Blackburn, Will	TVG	401-182
Blackford, George	FB	401-143
Blackman, Ben F.	SR	401-68
Blackman, John	ARM	401-2
Blackman, Newt S.	TVG	401-182
Blackmon, Jas. M.	USV	401-222
Blackmon, Paul Jones	TVG	401-182
Blackmon, W. D.	RR	401-52
Blackmore, Willard	ARM	401-2
Blackney, Tom	FB	401-143
Blackshare, W. E.	FB	401-143
Blacksher, W. R.	SP	401-41
Blackwell, C. J.	RRR	401-112
Blackwell, C. J.	SR	401-68
Blackwell, Charles J.	RR	401-52
Blackwell, Charles J.	SR	401-68
Blackwell, Clell M.	RR	401-52
Blackwell, Cole Y.	RRR	401-112
Blackwell, J. H.	TST	401-33
Blackwell, J. M.	FF	401-132
Blackwell, J. W.	FB	401-143
Blackwell, J. Milton	LR	401-127
Blackwell, James S.	TVG	401-182
Blackwell, Jesse T.	TST	401-33
Blackwell, S. C.	RR	401-52
Blackwell, Samuel Clay	RR	401-52
Blackwell, W. B.	TVG	401-182
Blackwell, W. C. C.	FB	401-143
Blackwell, William B.	USV	401-222
Blackwell, William T.	TVG	401-182
Blain, John	SR	401-68
Blaine, Edward J.	TVG	401-182
Blaine, Edward J.	USV	401-222
Blaine, Frank Edward	TVG	401-182
Blaine, John E.	SR	401-68
Blaine, Samuel H.	USV	401-222
Blair, A. J.	FB	401-143
Blair, J. B.	RRR	401-112
Blair, J. C.	SR	401-68
Blair, J. E.	FB	401-143
Blair, J. J.	FB	401-143
Blair, James C.	FB	401-143
Blair, Jesse	RR	401-52
Blair, John	RR	401-52
Blair, Joseph Edward	RRR	401-112
Blair, Paul	SR	401-68
Blair, Paul H.	RRR	401-112
Blair, Samuel	NAV	401-13
Blair, W. J.	FB	401-143
Blair, W. T.	LR	401-127
Blake, Cabeen	TVG	401-182
Blake, Geo. Wm.	TVG	401-182
Blake, J. S.	TVG	401-182
Blakeley, Tom M.	SP	401-41
Blakely, Bassett	TVG	401-182
Blakely, T. C.	TVG	401-182
Blakeney, T. J.	TVG	401-182
Blakeslee, Morton F.	SR	401-68
Blakney, Pete	SR	401-68
Blalock, Bishop M.	RRR	401-112
Blalock, F. M.	TVG	401-182
Blalock, Jeff	FB	401-143
Blalock, Sidney F.	MV	401-28
Blalock, W. F.	SR	401-68
Blalock, W. H.	USV	401-222
Blanchard, Ben	FB	401-143
Blanchard, E.	USV	401-222
Blanchette, Claud D.	USV	401-222
Bland, Jeff	FB	401-143
Bland, Joseph L.	USV	401-222
Bland, R. S.	TVG	401-182
Blandin, Jno. G.	USV	401-222
Blanding, Douglas	TVG	401-182
Blanding, R. P.	TVG	401-182
Blankenship, C. K.	RRR	401-112
Blankenship, Samuel	USV	401-222
Blanton, John	FB	401-143
Blanton, W. H.	CSA	401-39
Blardone, William C.	USV	401-222
Blassingame, Easley R.	USV	401-222
Bledsoe, Flem. G.	FB	401-143
Bledsoe, R. R.	RR	401-52
Bledsoe, Roy R.	USV	401-222
Bleker, Edward B.	USV	401-222
Bleker, Edward G.	TVG	401-182
Blevins, Charles A. "Sunny"	SR	401-68
Blevins, G. W.	MV	401-28

Index to Texas Adjutant General Service Records—All Service Branches

Name	Branch	Record
Blevins, John H.	MM	401-32
Blevins, W. C.	FB	401-143
Blocker, A. P.	SR	401-68
Blocker, A. P.	FB	401-143
Blocker, D. W.	FB	401-143
Blocker, Frank Harwood	TVG	401-182
Blocker, Preston	TVG	401-182
Blocker, R. C.	RR	401-52
Blocker, W. W.	SR	401-68
Blocker, Webster	TVG	401-182
Blocker, Webster	USV	401-222
Blom, T.	NAV	401-13
Blomer, Henry	TVG	401-182
Blomer, Henry	USV	401-222
Blood, C. D.	SP	401-41
Bloom, William	ARM	401-2
Bloomer, Aaron	FB	401-143
Bloor, Alfred W.	USV	401-222
Bloor, Alfred Wainwright	TVG	401-182
Blottin, Paul	TVG	401-182
Blount, J. F.	TVG	401-182
Blount, Percy	TVG	401-182
Bloxom, John, Jr.	RR	401-52
Bloxom, Will H.	TVG	401-182
Blucher, John F.	USV	401-222
Blucher, Oliver A.	USV	401-222
Blucher, Richard P.	USV	401-222
Bludworth, B. L.	CSA	401-39
Blum, A. J.	FB	401-143
Blum, A. O.	TVG	401-182
Blum, Henry	SR	401-68
Blum, Ike	TVG	401-182
Blum, J. C.	CSA	401-39
Blum, John E.	USV	401-222
Blum, Joseph	CSA	401-39
Blumentritt, Louis	SP	401-41
Blundell, John	MV	401-28
Bly, George	FB	401-143
Bly, Ira	FB	401-143
Blythe, Edward A.	TVG	401-182
Blythe, Joseph	FF	401-132
Blythe, Robert L.	TVG	401-182
Board, Edgar M.	USV	401-222
Boardman, Joseph E.	USV	401-222
Boatwright, J. S.	SR	401-69
Boaz, Edgar	FB	401-143
Bob, T.	SR	401-69
Bobbitt, O. E.	SR	401-69
Bobo, W. A.	FB	401-143
Bock, Chick E.	SR	401-69
Bockelman, Fred	SR	401-69
Bockem, W. P.	SR	401-69
Bocklet, S.	TVG	401-182
Bocoman, J. P.	USV	401-222
Boddie, Jack	RRR	401-112
Boden, O. B.	TVG	401-182
Bodiford, John C.	USV	401-222
Bodine, Sid	SR	401-69
Bodwell, C. P.	FB	401-143
Boehlest, N.	TVG	401-182
Boehme, Arwin	MM	401-32
Boekelman, Louis F.	USV	401-222
Boerner, Fred	MM	401-32
Boettcher, Chas. F.	USV	401-222
Boeving, Chas. A.	USV	401-222
Bogart, Samuel	RR	401-52
Boger, Horace L.	TVG	401-182
Bogess, G. S.	MV	401-28
Boggess, A. A.	TVG	401-182
Boggs, A. D.	TVG	401-182
Boggs, George E.	LR	401-127
Boggs, R. J.	FB	401-143
Boggs, Thomas H.	USV	401-222
Boggs, Waller K.	SR	401-69
Bogue, William	NAV	401-14
Bogusch, Robert C.	TVG	401-182
Bohan, Barnard	ARM	401-2
Bohanen, W. M.	FB	401-143
Bohannon, Henry	USV	401-222
Bohannon, Robert Chilton	TVG	401-182
Bohart, Charles	RR	401-52
Bohart, Charles	SR	401-69
Bohl, Ambrose	FF	401-132
Bohls, A. W.	SR	401-69
Bohls, Frank	FF	401-132
Bohon, James L.	RRR	401-112
Bohz, John	MV	401-28
Boice, Josiah	FB	401-143
Boid, Elbert	SP	401-41
Boison, Henrick	ARM	401-2
Bokemeyer, Julius	TVG	401-182
Bokemeyer, W. H.	TVG	401-182
Boker, J. M.	FB	401-144
Boker, John H.	NAV	401-14
Boldridge, B. F.	SP	401-41
Bolen, Edward	ARM	401-2
Boles, Abel	RR	401-52
Boles, J. Ross	SR	401-69
Boles, Joseph	RR	401-52
Bolick, J. H.	TVG	401-182
Bolick, T. H.	TVG	401-182
Bolin, J. W.	TVG	401-182
Bolland, John W.	FB	401-144
Bolling, Egmont	MV	401-28
Bolster, Henry A.	USV	401-222
Bolt, John C.	SP	401-41
Bolton, F.	FB	401-144
Bolton, James H.	TVG	401-182
Bolton, T. D.	TVG	401-182
Bolton, William	ARM	401-2
Boman, Charles	FF	401-132
Bomar, J. L.	FB	401-144

Index to Texas Adjutant General Service Records—All Service Branches

Name	Branch	Record
Bomar, R. L.	SR	401-69
Bomar, Richard M.	MV	401-28
Bomar, Spencer E.	USV	401-222
Bomefeld, I. A.	SP	401-41
Bond, Charles	TST	401-33
Bond, Henry	ARM	401-2
Bond, John H.	SR	401-69
Bond, Joseph F.	SP	401-41
Bond, Morton B. A.	USV	401-222
Bond, Richard D.	USV	401-222
Bond, Thomas A.	SR	401-69
Bond, Virgil A.	SP	401-41
Bonds, F. W.	RRR	401-112
Bonds, H. S.	TVG	401-182
Bonds, Olin C.	RRR	401-112
Bondy, Celestian	NAV	401-14
Bone, Rob L.	USV	401-222
Bone, Samuel Bernard	TVG	401-182
Boner, Joseph	MV	401-28
Bonn, Richard	TVG	401-182
Bonnard, Alexander	ARM	401-2
Bonner, Frank L.	TVG	401-182
Bonner, Guy	TVG	401-182
Bonner, J. S.	SR	401-69
Bonner, John S.	LR	401-127
Bonner, John Thomas	TVG	401-182
Bonner, M. H.	RRR	401-112
Bonner, S. A.	SR	401-69
Bonner, T. H.	TVG	401-182
Bonnet, J. W.	SP	401-41
Bonnet, R. J.	TVG	401-182
Bonnet, W. A.	TVG	401-182
Bonnet, William	SP	401-41
Booker, Ferdinand	ARM	401-2
Booker, Ferdinand C.	ARM	401-2
Booker, W. H.	TST	401-33
Bookman, A. W.	SP	401-41
Bookser, Edward	TVG	401-182
Boon, J. T.	TVG	401-182
Boone, Alfred	RRR	401-112
Boone, Alfred	SR	401-69
Boone, B. C.	SP	401-41
Boone, Daniel T.	TST	401-33
Boone, Gordon	TVG	401-182
Boone, H. H.	TVG	401-182
Boone, Henry T.	TVG	401-182
Boone, Hood	TVG	401-182
Boone, Hood	USV	401-222
Boone, John	RRR	401-112
Boone, Lemuel P.	RR	401-52
Boone, Lovell	TVG	401-182
Boone, M. A.	USV	401-222
Boone, T. R. "Dan"	SR	401-69
Boone, Walter	TVG	401-182
Boost, Jacob	ARM	401-2
Booth, C. H., Jr.	SR	401-69
Booth, Edgar	TVG	401-182
Booth, Edwin	SR	401-69
Booth, Edwin A.	USV	401-222
Booth, Ernest	USV	401-222
Booth, Frederick A.	USV	401-222
Booth, George M.	TVG	401-182
Booth, Joseph Gean	TVG	401-182
Booth, R. E.	RRR	401-112
Booth, W. V.	SR	401-69
Boothe, C. S.	SR	401-69
Boothe, C. W.	SR	401-69
Boothe, Carl	SR	401-69
Boothe, F. H.	LR	401-127
Boothe, George R.	SR	401-69
Boothe, Joseph E.	MV	401-28
Boothe, R. E., Sr.	SR	401-69
Boothe, William N.	TST	401-33
Booton, Kirtley	USV	401-222
Boozer, Joe N.	USV	401-222
Boozer, Odis	TVG	401-182
Boozman, Frank	USV	401-222
Bordages, Asa C.	USV	401-222
Bordeaux, Jim	RRR	401-112
Borden, Howard D.	USV	401-222
Borders, Bert	USV	401-222
Borders, John V.	USV	401-222
Bordley, Matthias	ARM	401-2
Boreing, J. W.	FB	401-144
Boren, A. E.	FB	401-144
Boren, J. M.	LR	401-127
Borglund, Gutzon	SR	401-69
Borhaz, Charles	SP	401-41
Boring, D. H.	TVG	401-182
Boring, J. W.	USV	401-222
Boring, Joseph A.	USV	401-222
Borman, John H.	USV	401-222
Borow, Frank M.	USV	401-222
Borroum, J. S.	SR	401-69
Bossy, Frank	USV	401-222
Bostic, George	TVG	401-182
Bostick, John H.	SP	401-41
Boswell, G. W.	RRR	401-112
Bottcher, Herman	USV	401-222
Bottenhouse, C.	FF	401-132
Bouey, Henry W.	USV	401-222
Boulden, C. E.	FB	401-144
Boulte, C. A.	TVG	401-182
Boultenhouse, C.	FF	401-132
Boulware, H. W.	TVG	401-182
Bounds, Edgar W.	USV	401-222
Bounds, J. E.	SR	401-69
Bourgoeis, J. B.	MV	401-28
Bourland, Dewhart Lee, Jr.	USV	401-222
Bourland, James	TST	401-33
Bourne, Daniel	ARM	401-2
Bourne, Thomas	ARM	401-2

Index to Texas Adjutant General Service Records—All Service Branches

Name	Branch	Record
Boutwell, E. M.	SR	401-69
Bovey, Henry W.	TVG	401-182
Bowden, Charles F.	SR	401-69
Bowden, Lemuel	FB	401-144
Bowen, B. C.	TVG	401-182
Bowen, D. H.	FB	401-144
Bowen, Frank	TVG	401-182
Bowen, John	NAV	401-14
Bowen, Milton L.	SR	401-69
Bowen, Tom F.	USV	401-222
Bowen, William	ARM	401-2
Bowen, William F.	FF	401-132
Bowens, Turner	TVG	401-182
Bower, George L.	USV	401-222
Bower, James Rowzee	SR	401-69
Bower, Thurston	SR	401-69
Bower, William S.	TVG	401-182
Bowers, Fred W.	RRR	401-112
Bowers, Geo. W.	TVG	401-182
Bowers, I. D.	TVG	401-182
Bowers, Marshall	TVG	401-182
Bowers, Winn	SP	401-41
Bowers, William	ARM	401-2
Bowers, Yates	USV	401-222
Bowie, D. M.	FF	401-132
Bowie, W. A.	TVG	401-182
Bowles, David C.	FB	401-144
Bowles, Eugene Ogden	TVG	401-182
Bowles, F. E.	SR	401-69
Bowles, G.	TST	401-33
Bowles, J. B.	TVG	401-182
Bowles, Jack L.	RRR	401-112
Bowles, W. E.	TVG	401-182
Bowling, W. A.	TVG	401-182
Bowman, Augustus	ARM	401-2
Bowman, J. T.	SR	401-69
Bowman, J. T.	LR	401-127
Bowman, Joseph	USV	401-222
Bowman, Ohio C.	USV	401-222
Bowman, S. C.	FB	401-144
Bowman, W. D.	RRR	401-112
Bowman, W. P.	SR	401-69
Bown, Fred K.	FF	401-132
Bown, Frederick	SP	401-41
Bowyer, G. W.	FB	401-144
Bowyer, J. George	TVG	401-182
Bowyer, Robert M.	USV	401-222
Bowyer, W. K.	USV	401-222
Box, James E.	ARM	401-2
Box, L. H.	CSA	401-39
Box, Zula R.	USV	401-222
Boxley, A. D.	TVG	401-183
Boxley, L. D.	LR	401-127
Boyd, A.	FB	401-144
Boyd, Allen S.	USV	401-222
Boyd, Andrew	NAV	401-14
Boyd, Cecil	RR	401-52
Boyd, Dim	TVG	401-183
Boyd, Elbert L.	USV	401-222
Boyd, G. L.	FB	401-144
Boyd, Henry A.	TVG	401-183
Boyd, Hugh DeP.	USV	401-222
Boyd, J. J.	RRR	401-112
Boyd, J. J.	FB	401-144
Boyd, J. L.	RRR	401-112
Boyd, J. L.	SR	401-69
Boyd, James	TVG	401-183
Boyd, James V.	USV	401-222
Boyd, John B.	RRR	401-112
Boyd, John G.	TST	401-33
Boyd, John H.	FB	401-144
Boyd, Lynn A.	SR	401-69
Boyd, R. A.	RR	401-52
Boyd, Robert A.	RR	401-52
Boyd, Samuel R.	TVG	401-183
Boyd, Theodore	USV	401-222
Boyd, W. A.	SR	401-69
Boyd, W. E.	USV	401-222
Boyd, W. R.	SR	401-69
Boyd, W. R.	TVG	401-183
Boyd, W. T.	SP	401-42
Boyd, Will T.	FF	401-132
Boyer, Chas. W.	USV	401-222
Boyer, D. T.	USV	401-222
Boyett, Dorsey H.	TVG	401-183
Boyett, Dorsey H.	USV	401-222
Boykin, F. M.	FB	401-144
Boykin, Melvin F.	RR	401-52
Boylan, James D.	NAV	401-14
Boyle, Emery B.	USV	401-222
Boyle, James	ARM	401-2
Boyle, John	FB	401-144
Boyle, W. W.	SR	401-69
Boyles, Clarence S.	TVG	401-183
Boyles, John	FB	401-144
Boynton, Alexander	SR	401-69
Boynton, G. S.	SP	401-42
Boynton, Lyman J.	USV	401-222
Boynton, O. P.	LR	401-127
Boysen, B. C.	SR	401-69
Bozarth, E. L.	TVG	401-183
Bozarth, J. J.	SP	401-42
Bozarth, J. T.	SP	401-42
Bozarth, W. J.	TVG	401-183
Boze, Charles L.	USV	401-222
Bozer, J. L.	USV	401-222
Braband, August	TVG	401-183
Bracewell, James A.	RR	401-52
Bracewell, James A.	SR	401-69
Brack, Arthur J.	TVG	401-183
Bracken, B. C.	USV	401-222
Bracken, E. C.	TVG	401-183

Index to Texas Adjutant General Service Records—All Service Branches

Name	Branch	Record
Bracken, John W.	FB	401-144
Brackney, Mahon A.	USV	401-222
Bradberry, J. M.	FB	401-144
Braden, Edward	TST	401-33
Braden, J. M.	FB	401-144
Bradfield, York	TVG	401-183
Bradford, C. A.	SR	401-69
Bradford, Gramille R.	TVG	401-183
Bradford, J. P.	TVG	401-183
Bradford, R. J.	FB	401-144
Bradford, Robert	NAV	401-14
Bradley, Aaron	USV	401-222
Bradley, Abraham	ARM	401-2
Bradley, F. H.	SP	401-42
Bradley, J. W.	USV	401-222
Bradley, Joe W., Jr.	SR	401-69
Bradley, John	SP	401-42
Bradley, Michael	ARM	401-2
Bradley, P. B.	TVG	401-183
Bradley, Q. O.	TVG	401-183
Bradley, Robert	SR	401-69
Bradley, Urb	USV	401-222
Bradley, W. C.	FB	401-144
Bradley, Walter L.	USV	401-222
Bradshaw, Harry	TVG	401-183
Bradshaw, Humberg	TVG	401-183
Bradshaw, Jackson	MV	401-28
Bradshaw, James C.	USV	401-222
Bradshaw, James H.	USV	401-222
Brady, Charles	FB	401-144
Brady, E. W.	SP	401-42
Brady, Francis	ARM	401-2
Brady, Frank T.	SR	401-69
Brady, H. P.	SR	401-69
Brady, Henry Elmore	USV	401-222
Brady, Hubert P.	RR	401-52
Brady, John W.	USV	401-222
Brady, Terrance	ARM	401-2
Brady, Th.	SP	401-42
Brady, Thomas	NAV	401-14
Brady, Tom G.	RR	401-52
Brady, Zode	USV	401-222
Brahan, R. W.	SR	401-69
Brame, Charles E.	ARM	401-2
Bramham, J. C.	FB	401-144
Bramlitt, Richard E.	TVG	401-183
Branard, G. A., Jr.	TVG	401-183
Branch, P. B., Jr.	SR	401-69
Branch, W. C.	SR	401-69
Branch, W. E.	TVG	401-183
Branch, William E.	USV	401-222
Branchle, Karl	USV	401-222
Brandis, Charles	TST	401-33
Brandon, Daniel	USV	401-222
Brandon, Robert	USV	401-222
Brandt, Christian	FF	401-132
Brandt, G. P.	TVG	401-183
Brandt, Russell W.	SR	401-69
Branham, A. W.	TVG	401-183
Brannan, George E.	SR	401-69
Brannard, Henry	TVG	401-183
Brannig, Ike	TVG	401-183
Brannon, Joe	FB	401-144
Brannon, V. J.	FB	401-144
Brannum, William T.	NAV	401-14
Branom, Curt	LR	401-127
Branom, Jeff	SR	401-69
Branom, Joe H.	RR	401-52
Bransom, G. W.	CSA	401-39
Brant, R. P.	USV	401-222
Brantley, Dennis	TVG	401-183
Brantley, John L.	SP	401-42
Brantley, John P.	SP	401-42
Brantley, R. C.	SR	401-69
Brantly, C. B.	USV	401-222
Brantly, G. A.	SP	401-42
Branton, W. E.	SR	401-69
Branum, George W.	FB	401-144
Branum, W. D.	TVG	401-183
Branum, William D.	RRR	401-112
Braselton, W. M.	RR	401-52
Braselton, Walter	RR	401-52
Brashear, S. H.	TVG	401-183
Brashear, William C.	NAV	401-14
Brasher, B. E.	RR	401-52
Brasher, B. E.	SR	401-69
Brasher, George E.	USV	401-222
Brasher, I. H. L.	ARM	401-2
Brasher, S. C.	TVG	401-183
Brasher, William C.	SR	401-69
Brass, Gus M., Jr.	USV	401-222
Bratton, J. O.	RR	401-52
Bratton, J. O.	SR	401-69
Braubach, Phillipp	MV	401-28
Braun, W.	TVG	401-183
Brauner, Otto	SR	401-69
Brawner, Thornton	ARM	401-2
Bray, Isaie	TST	401-33
Bray, John L.	ARM	401-2
Brayson, Thomas	NAV	401-14
Brazele, Jefferson	RR	401-52
Brazelton, William L.	SR	401-69
Braziel, J. N.	LR	401-127
Breaker, J. W. H.	FF	401-132
Breazeale, R. F.	TVG	401-183
Brecher, Edgar A.	SR	401-69
Breddin, Gustav	TVG	401-183
Bredt, Carl	SR	401-69
Bredwell, W. C.	FB	401-144
Breeding, E. L.	FB	401-144
Breeding, John	ARM	401-2
Breeding, Marvin Thomas	RRR	401-112

Index to Texas Adjutant General Service Records—All Service Branches

Breeding, Webb S. .... TVG 401-183
Breedlove, James D. .... SR 401-69
Breedlove, Wallace O. .... USV 401-222
Breedlove, Wallace Ogden........... TVG 401-183
Brehmer, Fred .... FB 401-144
Brehmer, Fritz .... FB 401-144
Brehmer, Oscar C. .... LR 401-127
Bremond, Walter, Jr. .... SR 401-69
Brenan, William A. .... USV 401-222
Brennan, James .... ARM 401-2
Brennan, James .... FB 401-144
Brennan, Robert L. .... USV 401-222
Brenner, Stanislaus.................... ARM 401-2
Brent, James .... NAV 401-14
Brentano, C. B. .... SP 401-42
Brett, Hugh .... FB 401-144
Brewer, E. A. .... TVG 401-183
Brewer, E. J. .... RRR 401-112
Brewer, J. D. .... SR 401-69
Brewer, J. Z. .... USV 401-222
Brewer, W. J. .... MV 401-28
Brewer, William E. .... TVG 401-183
Brewerton, Edwin .... NAV 401-14
Brewington, Walt .... TVG 401-183
Brewster, C. H. .... FB 401-144
Brewster, Dwight C. .... TVG 401-183
Brewster, J. M. .... FB 401-144
Brewster, Joseph William .... USV 401-222
Brewster, W. Henry.................... NAV 401-14
Brey, Oscar................................ ARM 401-2
Breyer, A. .... TVG 401-183
Briant, Paul H. .... USV 401-222
Brice, Donald .... USV 401-222
Brice, Tenville L. .... USV 401-222
Bridenhal, David .... CSA 401-39
Bridge, H. J. M. .... FB 401-144
Bridge, Joe H. .... SR 401-69
Bridge, M. V. .... FB 401-144
Bridge, W. E. .... MV 401-28
Bridgeman, James .... ARM 401-2
Bridgers, Henry .... TVG 401-183
Bridges, Arthur A....................... USV 401-222
Bridges, H. S. .... TVG 401-183
Bridges, Jack .... FB 401-144
Bridges, Joseph C....................... TVG 401-183
Bridges, Joseph C....................... USV 401-222
Bridges, M. T. .... FF 401-132
Bridges, M. V. .... SP 401-42
Bridges, Pierce .... TVG 401-183
Bridgforth, J. W. .... USV 401-222
Bridgwater, Thos. A.................... USV 401-222
Bridie, Jesse Claude .... RRR 401-112
Bridwell, William C. .... FB 401-144
Brigance, A. F. .... FB 401-144
Brigance, W. H. .... SR 401-69
Brigg, Ferdinand W. .... USV 401-222

Briggs, Edward W. .... SP 401-42
Briggs, Elias .... RR 401-52
Briggs, Gaskell W. .... TVG 401-183
Briggs, J. W. .... USV 401-222
Briggs, Jas. E. .... USV 401-222
Briggs, L. F. .... USV 401-222
Briggs, William G. .... FB 401-144
Bright, Demps L. .... TVG 401-183
Bright, I. F. .... SR 401-69
Brightman, Oswell Oliver .... LR 401-127
Brightwell, Chris C. .... USV 401-222
Brigman, Leroy .... SR 401-69
Brigman, M. A. .... LR 401-127
Brigman, Martin A. .... RRR 401-112
Brim, Jefferson K. .... SR 401-69
Brine, J. O. .... TVG 401-183
Brinegar, Willie Dale .... SR 401-69
Brinkerhoff, Herbert G................ USV 401-222
Brinkley, W. M. .... SR 401-69
Brinkmann, Frank N................... SR 401-69
Brinkmeyer, J. E. .... SR 401-69
Brinsmade, Allen C. .... TVG 401-183
Brisbin, A. W. .... SR 401-69
Briscoe, Birdsall P. .... USV 401-222
Briscoe, Dolph .... RR 401-52
Briscoe, Dolph .... SR 401-69
Briscoe, G. C. .... TVG 401-183
Briscoe, Ira J. .... USV 401-223
Briscoe, J. D. .... RRR 401-112
Briscoe, Payne .... SR 401-69
Briscoe, Thomas M. .... FB 401-144
Brister, William .... MV 401-28
Bristol, J. .... TVG 401-183
Bristol, William M. .... TVG 401-183
Brite, Charles .... FF 401-132
Brite, Charles E. .... SR 401-69
Brite, John William .... SR 401-69
Britnet, W. W. .... FF 401-132
Brito, S. A. .... FB 401-144
Britton, Benjamin .... TST 401-33
Britton, Ed................................. FB 401-144
Britton, J. L. .... TVG 401-183
Britton, J. M. .... FB 401-144
Britton, J. W. .... RR 401-52
Britzmann, Ernest W. .... USV 401-223
Broaddus, James Andrew .... TVG 401-183
Broadstreet, Ernest B. .... USV 401-223
Broadwater, G. B. .... FB 401-144
Broadwell, Franklin B. .... USV 401-223
Brock, Fred................................ USV 401-223
Brock, Frederick........................ USV 401-223
Brockner, John .... ARM 401-2
Brockner, William .... ARM 401-2
Brodbeck, George .... MV 401-28
Broert, Owen............................. TVG 401-183
Broeshe, E. R. .... TVG 401-183

Index to Texas Adjutant General Service Records—All Service Branches

Name	Branch	Number
Bromley, Tolbert T.	USV	401-223
Bronnum, Merril	ARM	401-2
Bronough, John C.	NAV	401-14
Brook, W. B.	USV	401-223
Brooke, Bennett	USV	401-223
Brookfield, William C.	ARM	401-2
Brooks, B. L.	TVG	401-183
Brooks, Ben Hill, Jr.	LR	401-127
Brooks, C. J.	USV	401-223
Brooks, C. M.	RR	401-52
Brooks, C. M.	RRR	401-112
Brooks, C. N.	SR	401-69
Brooks, E. T.	SR	401-69
Brooks, Fred	TVG	401-183
Brooks, G. W., Jr.	TVG	401-183
Brooks, J. A.	RR	401-52
Brooks, J. A.	FB	401-144
Brooks, James T., Jr.	USV	401-223
Brooks, Joeb., Capt.	SR	401-69
Brooks, Joe B.	RR	401-52
Brooks, John J.	FB	401-144
Brooks, Joshua M.	USV	401-223
Brooks, Oden R.	USV	401-223
Brooks, Robert A.	USV	401-223
Brooks, Rupert	TVG	401-183
Brooks, Sam Raymond	SR	401-69
Brooks, Theron	SR	401-69
Brooks, W. A., Jr.	SR	401-69
Brooks, Washington L.	USV	401-223
Brooks, William	NAV	401-14
Brooks, William T.	TVG	401-183
Brookshire, R. M.	SR	401-69
Brookshire, Samuel	MM	401-32
Broom, Joseph M.	NAV	401-14
Broome, C. L.	FB	401-144
Broome, C. W.	TVG	401-183
Brophy, Frank	FB	401-144
Brophy, J. E.	SR	401-69
Brossard, Francis X.	ARM	401-2
Brotzer, Curt	FF	401-132
Brotzer, Richard	MV	401-28
Brounson, Uriel S.	ARM	401-2
Broussard, J. D.	SR	401-69
Broussard, John J.	USV	401-223
Brown, A.	FB	401-144
Brown, A. C.	SP	401-42
Brown, A. W.	RR	401-52
Brown, Albert G.	TST	401-33
Brown, Andres	FF	401-132
Brown, Archie	FB	401-144
Brown, B. H.	TVG	401-183
Brown, Baylor B.	SR	401-69
Brown, Benjamin S.	ARM	401-2
Brown, C.	TST	401-33
Brown, C. B.	TVG	401-183
Brown, C. F.	FB	401-144
Brown, C. P.	RR	401-52
Brown, C. W.	TVG	401-183
Brown, Charles	ARM	401-2
Brown, Charles	FF	401-132
Brown, Charles B.	RR	401-52
Brown, Charles Edward	USV	401-223
Brown, Charley	SP	401-42
Brown, Clarence E. R.	USV	401-223
Brown, Clifton A.	USV	401-223
Brown, Collins C.	USV	401-223
Brown, Creed C.	USV	401-223
Brown, D. B.	CSA	401-39
Brown, E. C.	SR	401-69
Brown, E. W.	SR	401-69
Brown, Edward	USV	401-223
Brown, Edward F.	USV	401-223
Brown, Elias N.	USV	401-223
Brown, Ellis	USV	401-223
Brown, F. Watts	TVG	401-183
Brown, Frank G.	USV	401-223
Brown, Frank, Jr.	TVG	401-183
Brown, Fredrick	USV	401-223
Brown, G. C.	SR	401-69
Brown, George	NAV	401-14
Brown, George C.	RR	401-52
Brown, George E.	LR	401-127
Brown, George M.	FB	401-144
Brown, George P.	FB	401-144
Brown, George R.	USV	401-223
Brown, George W.	TVG	401-183
Brown, George W.	USV	401-223
Brown, Gratz	FB	401-144
Brown, H. Alvin	TVG	401-183
Brown, H. J.	FB	401-144
Brown, H. R.	FF	401-132
Brown, Harry	FF	401-132
Brown, Harry P.	SR	401-69
Brown, Heinrick	ARM	401-2
Brown, Henry	CSA	401-39
Brown, Henry	NAV	401-14
Brown, Henry	MV	401-28
Brown, Henry	TVG	401-183
Brown, Henry C.	USV	401-223
Brown, Herbert Fredrick	TVG	401-183
Brown, Horace M.	USV	401-223
Brown, Howell C.	FB	401-144
Brown, Hugh	ARM	401-2
Brown, Hunter P.	TVG	401-183
Brown, J. A.	RRR	401-112
Brown, J. A.	SR	401-69
Brown, J. A.	TVG	401-183
Brown, J. Aynes	SR	401-69
Brown, J. B.	FB	401-144
Brown, J. E.	RRR	401-112
Brown, J. Eugene	SR	401-69
Brown, J. G.	FB	401-144

Index to Texas Adjutant General Service Records—All Service Branches

Name	Branch	Page
Brown, J. M.	FB	401-144
Brown, J. M.	TVG	401-183
Brown, J. O.	FB	401-144
Brown, J. S.	FB	401-144
Brown, J. W.	FF	401-132
Brown, James	NAV	401-14
Brown, James	TST	401-33
Brown, James	ARM	401-2
Brown, James	FF	401-132
Brown, James	RRR	401-112
Brown, James A.	RR	401-52
Brown, James A.	SR	401-70
Brown, James E.	RRR	401-112
Brown, James L.	FB	401-144
Brown, James M.	SP	401-42
Brown, James M.	TVG	401-183
Brown, James W.	ARM	401-2
Brown, Jeff	TVG	401-183
Brown, Jep	MM	401-32
Brown, Jeremiah	NAV	401-14
Brown, Jerry A.	SR	401-70
Brown, Jim	FB	401-144
Brown, Jim J.	TVG	401-183
Brown, John	NAV	401-14
Brown, John	ARM	401-2
Brown, John	ARM	401-2
Brown, John	ARM	401-2
Brown, John D.	TST	401-33
Brown, John E.	USV	401-223
Brown, John G.	FB	401-144
Brown, John H.	USV	401-223
Brown, Jordan A.	USV	401-223
Brown, Joseph	USV	401-223
Brown, L. B.	TVG	401-183
Brown, L. C.	SR	401-70
Brown, Lanie B.	USV	401-223
Brown, Lee B.	USV	401-223
Brown, Lee C.	TVG	401-183
Brown, Loyd T.	SR	401-70
Brown, N. J.	FB	401-144
Brown, Neill	TST	401-33
Brown, Nickolas	FB	401-144
Brown, Nolan Odis	RRR	401-112
Brown, O. J.	RRR	401-112
Brown, Paul R. J.	TVG	401-183
Brown, Perry D.	RRR	401-112
Brown, Pollie D.	TVG	401-183
Brown, R. C.	SP	401-42
Brown, R. G.	TVG	401-183
Brown, Richard	ARM	401-2
Brown, Richmond N.	USV	401-223
Brown, Robert D.	RR	401-52
Brown, Robert E.	TVG	401-183
Brown, Robert W.	USV	401-223
Brown, S. L.	SR	401-70
Brown, S. L.	TVG	401-183
Brown, Septimus W.	ARM	401-2
Brown, Sherwood	TVG	401-183
Brown, Sy	TVG	401-183
Brown, T. H., Jr.	TVG	401-183
Brown, T. I.	TVG	401-183
Brown, T. T.	SR	401-70
Brown, Thomas	NAV	401-14
Brown, Thomas J.	SP	401-42
Brown, W. D.	TVG	401-183
Brown, W. Dorsey	TVG	401-183
Brown, W. H.	FB	401-145
Brown, W. M.	TVG	401-183
Brown, W. R.	TVG	401-183
Brown, W. W.	SR	401-70
Brown, Wayman E.	USV	401-223
Brown, Wiley G.	SR	401-70
Brown, William	NAV	401-14
Brown, William	ARM	401-2
Brown, William	ARM	401-2
Brown, William	SP	401-42
Brown, William H.	ARM	401-2
Brown, William S.	ARM	401-2
Brown, Willie	TVG	401-183
Brown, Willis D.	USV	401-223
Browncomb, F. E.	RRR	401-112
Browne, George P., Jr.	USV	401-223
Browne, H. M.	SP	401-42
Browne, James	USV	401-223
Browne, Joseph	USV	401-223
Browne, Langston	USV	401-223
Browne, Thomas W.	USV	401-223
Brownell, Joe	TVG	401-183
Brownfield, A. R.	LR	401-127
Browning, Carl T.	TVG	401-183
Browning, Charles	SR	401-70
Browning, George W.	NAV	401-14
Browning, James T.	SP	401-42
Browning, R. M.	FB	401-145
Brownlee, Houghton	SR	401-70
Brownlee, William R.	TVG	401-183
Brownlee, William R.	USV	401-223
Brownlow, Joseph B.	USV	401-223
Brownrigg, Malcolm	USV	401-223
Broyles, A. J.	FB	401-145
Broyles, Andrew	FB	401-145
Broyles, Geo.	TVG	401-183
Bruce, Charles Fenton Werner	USV	401-223
Bruce, Claude H.	TVG	401-183
Bruce, R. H.	TVG	401-183
Bruce, W. E.	SP	401-42
Brucks, Henry	FF	401-132
Brugniens, John	ARM	401-2
Bruker, Raymond	ARM	401-2
Brumby, Robt. H.	USV	401-223
Brundidge, James W.	TVG	401-183
Brunds, Frederick	ARM	401-2

Index to Texas Adjutant General Service Records—All Service Branches

Name	Branch	Record
Bruni, Louis Henry	SR	401-70
Brunkenhoefer, Fred	TVG	401-184
Brunkenhoefer, Fred	USV	401-223
Brunner, Cole K.	RR	401-52
Brunner, John, Jr.	TVG	401-184
Brunow, George F.	TVG	401-184
Bruns, Albert	MV	401-28
Brunson, Glen S.	SR	401-70
Brush, D. R.	FB	401-145
Brush, Oliver Grant, Capt.	SR	401-70
Brush, William B.	TVG	401-184
Bruster, A. A.	FB	401-145
Bruton, James W.	FB	401-145
Bruton, W. T.	LR	401-127
Bryan, C. E.	SR	401-70
Bryan, Chas. O.	TVG	401-184
Bryan, Chester	TVG	401-184
Bryan, Edward W.	USV	401-223
Bryan, Fred A.	SR	401-70
Bryan, Henry H.	USV	401-223
Bryan, J. W.	SR	401-70
Bryan, James D.	SP	401-42
Bryan, James R.	USV	401-223
Bryan, L. B.	SR	401-70
Bryan, Leo O.	TVG	401-184
Bryan, R. A.	FB	401-145
Bryan, Romulus L.	USV	401-223
Bryan, Tyler	TVG	401-184
Bryan, Willis B.	TVG	401-184
Bryan, Willis B.	USV	401-223
Bryant, Andrew J.	NAV	401-14
Bryant, Charles	NAV	401-14
Bryant, Clevie	TVG	401-184
Bryant, Ed	SR	401-70
Bryant, George W.	FF	401-132
Bryant, George W.	FB	401-145
Bryant, I. E.	RRR	401-112
Bryant, J. R.	TVG	401-184
Bryant, J. T.	TVG	401-184
Bryant, Oscar W.	SR	401-70
Bryant, R. E.	RR	401-52
Bryant, R. E.	FB	401-145
Bryant, Tom	SR	401-70
Bryant, Waldo E.	USV	401-223
Bryant, William J.	USV	401-223
Bryarly, R. S.	TVG	401-184
Bryarly, Joe L.	USV	401-223
Bryce, J. W.	SR	401-70
Bryden, Charles	TVG	401-184
Bryden, E. J.	TVG	401-184
Brydon, James	ARM	401-2
Brymer, Joseph Carl	USV	401-223
Bryson, L. G.	TVG	401-184
Bryson, S. S.	TVG	401-184
Bryson, W.	TVG	401-184
Buch, Fritz	TVG	401-184
Buchanan, A. A.	FB	401-145
Buchanan, Alexander	TVG	401-184
Buchanan, Arthur H.	TVG	401-184
Buchanan, Frank J.	USV	401-223
Buchanan, George A.	TST	401-33
Buchanan, George S.	SR	401-70
Buchanan, H. N.	USV	401-223
Buchanan, J. B.	RR	401-52
Buchanan, J. B.	SR	401-70
Buchanan, James	NAV	401-14
Buchanan, James C.	USV	401-223
Buchanan, John	MV	401-28
Buchanan, M. B.	SR	401-70
Buchanan, Michael	MV	401-28
Buchanan, William Y.	FB	401-145
Buchele, Frederick	ARM	401-2
Buchetti, Robert B.	USV	401-223
Buchholz, F. F. "Jack"	SR	401-70
Buck, A. O.	TVG	401-184
Buck, B. B.	USV	401-223
Buck, Eugene	SR	401-70
Buck, George E.	FB	401-145
Buck, J. M.	MV	401-28
Buck, Louis W.	TVG	401-184
Buck, O. H.	TVG	401-184
Buckelew, P. W.	SP	401-42
Buckes, Earl	TVG	401-184
Buckingham, William B.	USV	401-223
Buckler, Henry	ARM	401-2
Buckler, J. A.	TVG	401-184
Buckley, Cornelius	TVG	401-184
Buckley, Timothy	ARM	401-2
Bucklin, J. H.	SR	401-70
Buckner, Murrell S.	TVG	401-184
Buckner, W.	FB	401-145
Buehring, W., Jr.	TVG	401-184
Buell, Allen	TVG	401-184
Buell, Allen	USV	401-223
Buell, J. L.	SP	401-42
Buest, George	TVG	401-184
Buffington, T. P.	TVG	401-184
Bugg, Robert C.	ARM	401-2
Bugg, William A.	USV	401-223
Bugg, Z. P.	MV	401-28
Bugnor, P. L.	TST	401-33
Buhler, Frank S.	TVG	401-184
Buhler, George A.	TVG	401-184
Buhse, Hermann	TVG	401-184
Builand, Stephen	USV	401-223
Bujac, Etienne de P.	TVG	401-184
Bull, Buster	SR	401-70
Bull, W. C.	SR	401-70
Bullard, A. T.	RR	401-52
Bullard, Alfred T.	SR	401-70
Bullard, Claude	USV	401-223
Bulloch, Smiley H.	USV	401-223

Index to Texas Adjutant General Service Records—All Service Branches

Name	Branch	Record
Bumbrey, J. M.	TVG	401-184
Bumgardener, W.	FB	401-145
Bunce, Sidney E.	SR	401-70
Bunch, David F.	FB	401-145
Bunch, Thomas J.	USV	401-223
Bundy, John C.	FB	401-145
Bundy, Mark P.	USV	401-223
Bundy, Z. T.	FB	401-145
Bunkley, W. N.	TVG	401-184
Bunn, T. A.	FB	401-145
Bunner, George C.	NAV	401-14
Bunting, Daniel	NAV	401-14
Buquoi, P. L.	ARM	401-2
Burch, Cecil J.	SR	401-70
Burch, George	TVG	401-184
Burch, George	USV	401-223
Burch, Henry	TST	401-33
Burch, J. B.	FB	401-145
Burch, Samuel L.	USV	401-223
Burch, Walter L.	USV	401-223
Burchain, William	FB	401-145
Burchard, Amasa F.	TVG	401-184
Burchard, Phinea, Jr.	USV	401-223
Burchard, R. M.	TVG	401-184
Burchard, Reaves L.	USV	401-223
Burchard, William F.	USV	401-223
Burckle, C. G.	ARM	401-2
Burdett, Robert Lee	RR	401-52
Burditt, J. H.	TVG	401-184
Burditt, J. H.	USV	401-223
Burell, Robert L.	RR	401-52
Burell, Robert L.	SR	401-70
Buresh, Frank	TVG	401-184
Burford, Frank	USV	401-223
Burford, Freeman W.	SR	401-70
Burford, W. E.	RR	401-52
Burford, W. E.	RRR	401-112
Burford, W. W.	RRR	401-112
Burger, G. G.	TVG	401-184
Burger, William B.	TVG	401-184
Burges, Alfred R.	USV	401-223
Burges, Sterrett	TVG	401-184
Burges, Tom C.	TVG	401-184
Burgess, A. S.	TST	401-33
Burgess, Charles	ARM	401-2
Burgess, John	NAV	401-14
Burgess, Walter J.	USV	401-223
Burgess, Willie	TVG	401-184
Burgheim, Clarence A.	USV	401-223
Burk, Robert H.	TVG	401-184
Burk, Thomas M.	MV	401-28
Burke, C. A.	TVG	401-184
Burke, Charles A.	SP	401-42
Burke, Conrad	NAV	401-14
Burke, David N.	NAV	401-14
Burke, Edmond	USV	401-223
Burke, Frank J.	SR	401-70
Burke, Frank W.	SR	401-70
Burke, George C.	USV	401-223
Burke, J. D.	NAV	401-14
Burke, J. J.	FB	401-145
Burke, Jack R.	TVG	401-184
Burke, Jack R.	USV	401-223
Burke, James	NAV	401-14
Burke, James	ARM	401-2
Burke, John	TST	401-33
Burke, K. P.	SR	401-70
Burke, Pleasant E.	TVG	401-184
Burke, Richard	ARM	401-2
Burke, Robert J.	USV	401-223
Burke, Ross E.	USV	401-223
Burke, W. B.	SR	401-70
Burke, Wilbur H.	USV	401-223
Burke, William	SP	401-42
Burkett, G. W., Jr.	TVG	401-184
Burkhalter, David R.	USV	401-223
Burkhalter, J. F.	TVG	401-184
Burkhardt, John H.	USV	401-223
Burkhart, Alex C.	SP	401-42
Burkhead, Joseph	USV	401-223
Burks, Ira G.	TVG	401-184
Burks, J. H.	RRR	401-112
Burks, R. F.	SR	401-70
Burks, Vegie	USV	401-223
Burks, Willie Hopkins	RRR	401-112
Burlage, John	TST	401-33
Burleson, A. B.	SP	401-42
Burleson, A. S.	TVG	401-184
Burleson, Aaron	FF	401-132
Burleson, Clarence	SR	401-70
Burleson, Corley	TVG	401-184
Burleson, D. C.	MV	401-28
Burleson, Ed	TST	401-33
Burleson, H. E.	USV	401-223
Burleson, J.	FF	401-132
Burleson, J. W.	FB	401-145
Burleson, Jeff B.	USV	401-223
Burleson, M. T.	RRR	401-112
Burleson, Oliver	TVG	401-184
Burleson, S. M.	SR	401-70
Burleson, S. M.	SR	401-70
Burleson, Stephen M.	RR	401-52
Burleson, William M.	TVG	401-184
Burmingham, D. W.	TVG	401-184
Burmingham, J. T.	TVG	401-184
Burmingham, William D.	TVG	401-184
Burnam, J. H.	TVG	401-184
Burnett, Daniel	RR	401-53
Burnett, Finis A.	RRR	401-112
Burnett, James	MM	401-32
Burnett, John M.	USV	401-223
Burnett, William C.	FB	401-145

Index to Texas Adjutant General Service Records—All Service Branches

Name	Branch	Number
Burnett, William J.	FB	401-145
Burnette, Charles	USV	401-223
Burney, Charles	NAV	401-14
Burney, J. E.	FB	401-145
Burney, J. G.	FB	401-145
Burney, J. H.	FB	401-145
Burney, John M.	RR	401-53
Burney, R. H.	FB	401-145
Burney, Robert H.	USV	401-223
Burney, William R.	RR	401-53
Burnham, Edward	TVG	401-184
Burnham, G. H.	SR	401-70
Burnitt, Fred G.	USV	401-223
Burns, Arthur	ARM	401-2
Burns, Columbus	TST	401-33
Burns, Cyrus E.	LR	401-127
Burns, D. B.	RR	401-53
Burns, Elijah H.	ARM	401-2
Burns, F. C.	TVG	401-184
Burns, Frank	FB	401-145
Burns, Frank C.	USV	401-223
Burns, J.	FB	401-145
Burns, James M.	SR	401-70
Burns, John E.	TVG	401-184
Burns, John P., Jr.	LR	401-127
Burns, L. T.	SR	401-70
Burns, Michael	ARM	401-2
Burns, Michel	NAV	401-14
Burns, Oscar	FB	401-145
Burns, Patrick J.	USV	401-223
Burns, Perry S.	TVG	401-184
Burns, Peter	SP	401-42
Burns, Simon	MV	401-28
Burns, T. A.	SP	401-42
Burns, T. W.	SP	401-42
Burns, Uvalde, Jr.	TVG	401-184
Burr, B. F.	FB	401-145
Burr, Eldo H.	USV	401-223
Burr, J. K.	FB	401-145
Burrage, Richard W.	USV	401-223
Burrel, Ben	FF	401-132
Burrel, Joe	FF	401-132
Burress, Louis A.	USV	401-223
Burris, Benjamin F.	FB	401-145
Burris, Claude Clinton	LR	401-127
Burris, D.	RRR	401-112
Burris, G. A.	FB	401-145
Burris, J. A.	FB	401-145
Burris, Sedlie	TVG	401-184
Burris, Thomas A.	USV	401-223
Burris, Thomas R.	USV	401-223
Burris, Walter J.	USV	401-223
Burroughs, J. M.	USV	401-223
Burroughs, James M.	TVG	401-184
Burroughs, Jim	SR	401-70
Burroughs, John J., Jr.	TVG	401-184
Burroughs, P. M.	SR	401-70
Burrow, G. O.	RR	401-53
Burrow, George O.	SR	401-70
Burrow, George W.	USV	401-223
Bursh, Gasper	ARM	401-2
Burst, Eran	ARM	401-2
Burt, A. B.	TVG	401-184
Burt, C. W.	FB	401-145
Burt, James Ross	ARM	401-2
Burt, L.	TVG	401-184
Burton, Ed	SR	401-70
Burton, J. N.	FB	401-145
Burton, John	FB	401-145
Burton, M.	RR	401-53
Burton, M.	SR	401-70
Burton, M. H.	USV	401-223
Burton, Musgrove	USV	401-223
Burton, Nathaniel, Jr.	USV	401-223
Burton, R. L.	RRR	401-112
Burton, T.	FB	401-145
Burton, Walter H.	TVG	401-184
Burton, William	ARM	401-2
Burtrand, William U.	USV	401-223
Burwell, C. B.	RR	401-53
Burwell, Charles B., Jr.	SR	401-70
Burwell, W. M.	RRR	401-112
Burwell, W. M.	FB	401-145
Busby, C. C.	SR	401-70
Busby, C. V.	SP	401-42
Busby, Nathan	SP	401-42
Busby, Sam L., Col.	SR	401-70
Busch, Carl G.	SR	401-70
Busch, Louis A.	SP	401-42
Busch, M. A.	USV	401-223
Buschicks, Hugo	SP	401-42
Buser, F. Henry	TVG	401-184
Bush, Andrew J., Jr.	USV	401-223
Bush, Granville H.	USV	401-223
Bush, Harvey G.	USV	401-223
Bush, Julius A.	TST	401-33
Bush, Richard A.	SR	401-70
Bush, William	FF	401-132
Bushey, Alf	FB	401-145
Bushnell, Lawrence R.	USV	401-223
Bushnick, Frank H.	TVG	401-184
Bushong, George E.	RR	401-53
Busi, Silvio H.	TVG	401-184
Busk, Robert	TVG	401-184
Bussa, Henry F.	USV	401-223
Buster, Adolphus O.	USV	401-223
Buster, Arthur L.	RR	401-53
Buster, Arthur L.	SR	401-70
Buster, Earl	RR	401-53
Buster, J. E.	LR	401-127
Buster, William A.	FB	401-145
Bustillo, Secillio	FF	401-132

Index to Texas Adjutant General Service Records—All Service Branches

Name	Branch	Record
Butcher, Arthur J.	USV	401-223
Butcher, Carroll M.	SR	401-70
Butler, Carl	SR	401-70
Butler, Carl	USV	401-223
Butler, Clark E.	SR	401-70
Butler, E. A.	TVG	401-184
Butler, Edward R.	NAV	401-14
Butler, F. M.	FB	401-145
Butler, Frank	FB	401-145
Butler, Fred	TVG	401-184
Butler, Galvin E.	TVG	401-184
Butler, Galvin E.	USV	401-223
Butler, Henry A.	TVG	401-184
Butler, J. B.	RRR	401-112
Butler, J. D.	TVG	401-184
Butler, J. W.	SR	401-70
Butler, James C.	USV	401-223
Butler, John	SP	401-42
Butler, John F.	ARM	401-2
Butler, Leander G.	SP	401-42
Butler, M. N.	RR	401-53
Butler, O. T.	USV	401-223
Butler, P. B.	FB	401-145
Butler, R. F.	TVG	401-184
Butler, R. R.	SR	401-70
Butler, Richard	NAV	401-14
Butler, Richard N.	RR	401-53
Butler, S. C.	SR	401-70
Butler, Sidney	SR	401-70
Butler, Stephen F.	USV	401-223
Butler, T. B.	RR	401-53
Butler, T. B., Jr.	SR	401-70
Butler, Thomas B.	RRR	401-112
Butler, Thomas B.	SR	401-70
Butler, W.	NAV	401-14
Butler, W. B.	RR	401-53
Butler, W. E.	USV	401-223
Butler, W. T.	USV	401-223
Butler, W. Z.	FB	401-145
Butler, William	CSA	401-39
Butler, William G.	TST	401-33
Butridge, W. N.	USV	401-224
Butterfield, F. L.	TVG	401-184
Butterworth, R. H.	FB	401-145
Buttery, Thomas G.	TVG	401-184
Buttery, Thomas G.	USV	401-224
Buttery, William P.	TVG	401-184
Buttles, Frank	USV	401-224
Buttrill, Clyde	SR	401-70
Butts, Charles	ARM	401-2
Butts, I. W.	FB	401-145
Buvens, I.	FF	401-132
Buvens, William G.	RRR	401-112
Buzley, C. W.	SR	401-70
Byars, Frank P.	USV	401-224
Byars, W. S.	RR	401-53
Bybee, S. M.	RRR	401-112
Byers, Daniel W.	FB	401-145
Byers, J. R.	FB	401-145
Byfield, William	FF	401-132
Byington, William H.	TVG	401-184
Byler, Rufus	MV	401-28
Bynum, E. B., Jr.	SR	401-70
Bynum, Martin L.	USV	401-224
Bynum, R. S.	SR	401-70
Bynum, Thomas P.	CSA	401-39
Byrd, A. B.	RRR	401-112
Byrd, Abraham S.	USV	401-224
Byrd, C.	FB	401-145
Byrd, Harvey Lee	SR	401-70
Byrd, J. A.	FB	401-145
Byrd, John T.	USV	401-224
Byrd, Louis	USV	401-224
Byrd, S. J.	SR	401-70
Byrd, Sam	USV	401-224
Byrd, Stephen J.	RR	401-53
Byrd, Steve J.	SR	401-70
Byrne, James	SR	401-70
Byrnes, Julien Morgan	TVG	401-184
Byrney, Charles	NAV	401-14
Byron, Cornelius	TST	401-33
Byron, J. A.	FB	401-145
Cabaniss, Harry C.	TVG	401-184
Cabarser, Christofer	SP	401-42
Cabiness, R. H., Jr.	USV	401-224
Cable, G. E.	SR	401-70
Cabot, John A.	TST	401-33
Caddell, G. W.	FB	401-145
Cade, Peter	ARM	401-2
Cadena, Alexander	SR	401-70
Cadena, Merejilda	FF	401-132
Cage, Albert G., Jr.	TVG	401-184
Cage, James C.	USV	401-224
Cage, John M.	USV	401-224
Cage, Marcus T.	USV	401-224
Cagle, T. J.	TVG	401-184
Cahill, J. E.	TVG	401-184
Cahill, John W.	CSA	401-39
Cahill, M. H.	RRR	401-113
Cahn, A.	TVG	401-184
Cahoon, Harry N.	USV	401-224
Cailloux, John F.	SR	401-70
Cain, Charles	RRR	401-113
Cain, D. C.	SR	401-70
Cain, G. C.	TVG	401-184
Cain, J. A.	RRR	401-113
Cain, J. A.	SR	401-70
Cain, James Jacob	SR	401-70
Cain, John J.	RR	401-53
Cain, John Jacob	TVG	401-185
Cain, Robert R.	USV	401-224
Cain, S. P.	USV	401-224

Index to Texas Adjutant General Service Records—All Service Branches

Name	Branch	Record
Caldwell, Ballard	TVG	401-185
Caldwell, C. O.	TVG	401-185
Caldwell, Dee	FB	401-145
Caldwell, E. F.	FF	401-132
Caldwell, Ed B.	FF	401-132
Caldwell, George E.	TVG	401-185
Caldwell, H. G.	SR	401-70
Caldwell, Harry J.	USV	401-224
Caldwell, Lemuel	ARM	401-2
Caldwell, O. T.	TVG	401-185
Caldwell, Virgial Lee	RRR	401-113
Caldwell, William	ARM	401-2
Cale, George W., Jr.	SR	401-70
Cale, T. L.	NAV	401-14
Calenga, Ramon	FF	401-132
Calhoun, Clem	SR	401-70
Calhoun, George C.	USV	401-224
Calhoun, Harrold S.	USV	401-224
Calhoun, J. C.	ARM	401-2
Calhoun, J. C.	TVG	401-185
Calhoun, J. J.	TVG	401-185
Calhoun, Lewis	ARM	401-2
Calias, Cordelius	ARM	401-2
Calk, W. C.	USV	401-224
Call, D.	TVG	401-185
Callaghan, T. H.	CSA	401-39
Callahan, Jeremiah	USV	401-224
Callahan, John R.	FB	401-145
Callahan, R. E.	SR	401-70
Callahan, S. J.	FB	401-145
Callahan, Wesley H.	FF	401-133
Callan, J. J.	RR	401-53
Callan, J. J.	FB	401-145
Callan, James, Jr.	RRR	401-113
Callan, Leo A.	SR	401-70
Callan, M. M.	CSA	401-39
Callard, Richard	NAV	401-14
Callaugh, J. T.	FF	401-133
Callaway, Christopher C.	USV	401-224
Callaway, Earl	SR	401-70
Callaway, I. N.	USV	401-224
Callaway, Jewett S.	USV	401-224
Callaway, Milton A.	SR	401-70
Callaway, W. D.	FB	401-145
Callaway, Walter P.	FB	401-145
Callaway, William B.	TVG	401-185
Callicott, William C.	FB	401-145
Calliham, K. C.	USV	401-224
Callingham, George R.	USV	401-224
Calliott, Charles	NAV	401-14
Calliott, Charles	ARM	401-2
Callis, Joe	FB	401-145
Callis, W. E.	FB	401-145
Calloway, Walter P.	FB	401-145
Calvert, Clarence Lee	SR	401-70
Calvert, Collin	TVG	401-185
Calvert, D. P.	SR	401-70
Calvert, George V.	ARM	401-2
Calvert, James	ARM	401-2
Calvert, James	TVG	401-185
Calvert, W. W.	USV	401-224
Calvin, Noel	TVG	401-185
Calvit, Joe	SR	401-70
Cambeilh, Paul	TVG	401-185
Cameron, Benjamin F.	USV	401-224
Cameron, Jeremiah	MV	401-28
Cameron, John M.	FB	401-145
Cameron, L. R.	SP	401-42
Cameron, Leon	TVG	401-185
Cameron, Robert	ARM	401-2
Cameron, William H.	NAV	401-14
Cammack, H. C.	FB	401-145
Cammack, Morgan	FB	401-145
Cammell, A. J.	FF	401-133
Cammeron, Augustus	ARM	401-2
Camp, A. H.	FB	401-145
Camp, B. T.	FB	401-145
Camp, Charles	SR	401-70
Camp, Charles L.	USV	401-224
Camp, Harry Leroy	TVG	401-185
Camp, John F.	MV	401-28
Camp, Lee Gordon	TVG	401-185
Campbell, A.	FB	401-145
Campbell, A. H.	TVG	401-185
Campbell, Alexander	ARM	401-2
Campbell, Alexander	FB	401-145
Campbell, Alexander	USV	401-224
Campbell, Alva C.	USV	401-224
Campbell, Angus	NAV	401-14
Campbell, Bob	TVG	401-185
Campbell, Charles K.	SR	401-70
Campbell, Charles M.	TVG	401-185
Campbell, Clarence L.	SR	401-70
Campbell, Clyde W.	TVG	401-185
Campbell, Colin	SP	401-42
Campbell, D. W.	RRR	401-113
Campbell, D. W.	SR	401-70
Campbell, E.	FB	401-145
Campbell, E. L.	TVG	401-185
Campbell, Evan S.	ARM	401-2
Campbell, F. D.	FB	401-145
Campbell, F. E.	USV	401-224
Campbell, F. L.	FB	401-145
Campbell, F. R.	SR	401-70
Campbell, G. W.	CSA	401-39
Campbell, G. W.	FB	401-145
Campbell, George B.	CSA	401-39
Campbell, George C.	USV	401-224
Campbell, George W.	SP	401-42
Campbell, Guy	USV	401-224
Campbell, J. T.	FB	401-145
Campbell, J. W.	TVG	401-185

Index to Texas Adjutant General Service Records—All Service Branches

Name	Branch	Record
Campbell, James	MV	401-28
Campbell, James M.	TVG	401-185
Campbell, Jas., Jr.	TVG	401-185
Campbell, JiM	TVG	401-185
Campbell, Joe	TVG	401-185
Campbell, John	ARM	401-2
Campbell, John A.	RRR	401-113
Campbell, L. F.	FB	401-145
Campbell, Lloyd	USV	401-224
Campbell, Lucius M.	TVG	401-185
Campbell, Michael	ARM	401-2
Campbell, N. G.	TVG	401-185
Campbell, O. W.	RRR	401-113
Campbell, R. A.	TVG	401-185
Campbell, R. N.	USV	401-224
Campbell, Robt. W.	USV	401-224
Campbell, S.	TVG	401-185
Campbell, Squire	ARM	401-2
Campbell, T. M.	TVG	401-185
Campbell, Thomas H.	TVG	401-185
Campbell, W. E.	FB	401-145
Campbell, William	ARM	401-2
Campbell, William	ARM	401-2
Campbell, William	ARM	401-2
Campbell, William	TVG	401-185
Campbell, Zannie V.	USV	401-224
Campbell, Zollie K.	RR	401-53
Campton, Joe	USV	401-224
Camron, J. H.	FB	401-146
Canada, Henry	TVG	401-185
Canady, C. W.	RRR	401-113
Canahan, Dennis	ARM	401-3
Canales, A. T.	SR	401-70
Canales, A. T.	LR	401-127
Candena, Merejilda	FF	401-133
Candler, John	FF	401-133
Cane, Louis Franklin	TVG	401-185
Canfield, H. D.	FB	401-146
Canfield, John	ARM	401-3
Canfield, W. P.	TVG	401-185
Canfield, W. S.	SP	401-42
Cannedy, D. D.	SP	401-42
Cannedy, G. L.	FB	401-146
Cannon, Albert J.	USV	401-224
Cannon, Barney	ARM	401-3
Cannon, Guy R.	TVG	401-185
Cannon, John James	USV	401-224
Cannon, Melville A.	USV	401-224
Cannon, Rufus	ARM	401-3
Cannon, Rupert	TVG	401-185
Cannon, Thomas	ARM	401-3
Cano, E.	SP	401-42
Cano, Encarnacion	FF	401-133
Canon, Edward F.	USV	401-224
Canon, George	SP	401-42
Canter, Joshua	ARM	401-3
Canterbury, Claude	USV	401-224
Cantley, C. L.	FB	401-146
Cantrel, Miles	FF	401-133
Cantrell, C. C.	SR	401-70
Cantrell, H. C.	FB	401-146
Cantrell, R. A.	SR	401-70
Cantrell, W. H.	SR	401-70
Cantrell, William	SR	401-70
Cantrell, William, Jr.	SR	401-70
Cantu, Miguel	FB	401-146
Cantwell, J. T., Jr.	TVG	401-185
Capehart, C. C.	SR	401-71
Capers, E. P.	TVG	401-185
Capp, Harvy	RR	401-53
Cappick, John	NAV	401-14
Capps, Harvey	ARM	401-3
Capps, W. B.	ARM	401-3
Capron, James T.	TST	401-33
Capur, R. L.	TVG	401-185
Caraway, Richard A. B.	USV	401-224
Card, J. A.	TVG	401-185
Carden, Joseph W.	USV	401-224
Carder, Claude	USV	401-224
Cardwell, A.	FB	401-146
Cardwell, A. M.	FB	401-146
Cardwell, F. H.	FB	401-146
Cardwell, O. D.	RR	401-53
Cardwell, O. D.	SR	401-71
Cardwell, P. A.	RR	401-53
Careton, William	FB	401-146
Carey, Laurence	USV	401-224
Carey, Thomas	RR	401-53
Cargile, Dan H.	USV	401-224
Cargile, Lee	RR	401-53
Cargile, Lee	SR	401-71
Cargill, Eugene A.	USV	401-224
Cargill, Walter S.	USV	401-224
Carhart, Henry	ARM	401-3
Cariker, Jesse L.	SR	401-71
Carington, F. A.	FB	401-146
Carl, William	RR	401-53
Carleton, Bob	RR	401-53
Carleton, Bob	SR	401-71
Carlile, Henry	RRR	401-113
Carlin, Daniel	ARM	401-3
Carlin, Thomas	TVG	401-185
Carlisle, C. C.	SP	401-42
Carlisle, C. H., Jr.	TVG	401-185
Carlisle, J. N.	SR	401-71
Carlisle, O. H.	SR	401-71
Carlisle, O. H.	TVG	401-185
Carlock, Oscar L.	USV	401-224
Carlock, W. H.	SR	401-71
Carlos, Ralphael	NAV	401-14
Carloss, Thos. C.	USV	401-224
Carlson, F. A.	SR	401-71

Index to Texas Adjutant General Service Records—All Service Branches

Name	Branch	Record
Carlton, D. H.	SR	401-71
Carlton, J. S.	TVG	401-185
Carlton, Oswald Snider	SR	401-71
Carmaday, D. R.	TVG	401-185
Carmay, Chas. C.	USV	401-224
Carmichael, Dix	SR	401-71
Carmichael, F. P.	FB	401-146
Carmichael, Horace H.	SR	401-71
Carmichael, Joseph N.	USV	401-224
Carnahan, John	TVG	401-185
Carnahan, John	USV	401-224
Carnal, E. B.	FB	401-146
Carnal, K. C.	FB	401-146
Carnal, William L.	USV	401-224
Carnell, E.	FB	401-146
Carnes, Herff A.	RR	401-53
Carnes, J. P.	SR	401-71
Carnes, John	MM	401-32
Carnes, Q. B.	RR	401-53
Carnett, L. O.	SR	401-71
Carnett, Roy James	SR	401-71
Carney, Charles L.	USV	401-224
Carnutte, Robert H.	LR	401-127
Carodine, Isaac	ARM	401-3
Carolan, Edward Henry	SR	401-71
Carolan, Patrick	ARM	401-3
Caroline, Tarance	ARM	401-3
Caroll, Robert	SP	401-42
Carothers, G. S.	SR	401-71
Carothers, Grover	SR	401-71
Carothers, Sam Western	USV	401-224
Carothers, William C.	TVG	401-185
Carpenter, D. H.	RRR	401-113
Carpenter, D. H.	SR	401-71
Carpenter, E. P.	SR	401-71
Carpenter, Leonard I.	USV	401-224
Carpenter, S. J.	RR	401-53
Carpenter, William	TVG	401-185
Carr, Anthony	USV	401-224
Carr, B. F.	ARM	401-3
Carr, Charles C.	RRR	401-113
Carr, Chas. H.	USV	401-224
Carr, Chas. R.	USV	401-224
Carr, J. A.	TVG	401-185
Carr, J. K.	TVG	401-185
Carr, James A.	SP	401-42
Carr, James C.	CSA	401-39
Carr, John	FB	401-146
Carr, R. J.	CSA	401-39
Carr, W. W.	TVG	401-185
Carr, William D.	RR	401-53
Carreon, Jose T.	SP	401-42
Carrico, M. W.	SR	401-71
Carrigan, J. W.	USV	401-224
Carrington, L. D.	RRR	401-113
Carrington, W. D.	USV	401-224
Carroll, A. C.	SR	401-71
Carroll, A. D.	SP	401-42
Carroll, A. H.	TST	401-33
Carroll, Abner M.	CSA	401-39
Carroll, Benajah Harvey, Jr.	USV	401-224
Carroll, Berry	TVG	401-185
Carroll, C. C.	USV	401-224
Carroll, E. E.	SR	401-71
Carroll, E. J.	TVG	401-185
Carroll, Ed. A., Jr.	LR	401-127
Carroll, Ed. A., Jr.	SR	401-71
Carroll, H. D. G.	TVG	401-185
Carroll, H. R., Jr.	SR	401-71
Carroll, J. D.	LR	401-127
Carroll, J. D.	SR	401-71
Carroll, J. F.	FB	401-146
Carroll, J. H.	USV	401-224
Carroll, James Douglas	USV	401-224
Carroll, James F.	USV	401-224
Carroll, John	ARM	401-3
Carroll, John J.	SR	401-71
Carroll, William Granville	RRR	401-113
Carruthers, F. W., Jr.	TVG	401-185
Carskadden, O. L.	FB	401-146
Carsner, Henry Davies	TVG	401-185
Carson, C. L.	RR	401-53
Carson, D. Thomas	FB	401-146
Carson, F. L.	SR	401-71
Carson, J. B.	TVG	401-185
Carson, R. L.	SR	401-71
Carson, Thomas	SP	401-42
Carson, Thomas F.	TVG	401-185
Carson, Thomas J.	MM	401-32
Carson, Tom	FB	401-146
Carson, William C.	TVG	401-185
Carta, C. A.	RR	401-53
Carta, John	RR	401-53
Carter, A. G.	USV	401-224
Carter, Arthur	SR	401-71
Carter, Arthur	LR	401-127
Carter, Ben F.	FB	401-146
Carter, Bob C.	USV	401-224
Carter, Bracton Cleve	USV	401-224
Carter, Edmund Barney	RRR	401-113
Carter, Edward L.	USV	401-224
Carter, F. M.	FB	401-146
Carter, Geo. Mitchell	TVG	401-185
Carter, Henry A.	MV	401-28
Carter, Henry F.	SR	401-71
Carter, J. D.	USV	401-224
Carter, J. E.	FB	401-146
Carter, J. H.	FB	401-146
Carter, J. M.	FB	401-146
Carter, J. T.	SR	401-71
Carter, James	USV	401-224
Carter, Jim	RR	401-53

Index to Texas Adjutant General Service Records—All Service Branches

Name	Branch	Record
Carter, Jim	RRR	401-113
Carter, Joe D.	TVG	401-185
Carter, John	TVG	401-185
Carter, John Q. A.	SP	401-42
Carter, John Roe	TVG	401-185
Carter, Joseph	FF	401-133
Carter, L. B.	RR	401-53
Carter, Leonard B.	RR	401-53
Carter, Oliver J.	TVG	401-185
Carter, P. S.	FB	401-146
Carter, R. C.	RR	401-53
Carter, R. G.	RRR	401-113
Carter, Reuben	SP	401-42
Carter, S. L.	SR	401-71
Carter, T. M.	LR	401-127
Carter, T. M.	SR	401-71
Carter, Thomas	MV	401-28
Carter, W. D.	TVG	401-185
Carter, W. Y.	FB	401-146
Carter, William H.	USV	401-224
Cartier, John A.	USV	401-224
Cartledge, C. H.	FB	401-146
Cartwright, A. B.	FB	401-146
Cartwright, A. I.	SR	401-71
Cartwright, C. A.	FB	401-146
Cartwright, George Washington	ARM	401-3
Cartwright, L. F.	FB	401-146
Cartwright, O. V.	TVG	401-185
Cartwright, T. J.	FB	401-146
Cartwright, W. C.	FB	401-146
Cartwright, W. L.	FB	401-146
Caruth, W. W., Jr.	SR	401-71
Caruthers, L. B.	FB	401-146
Caruthers, W. H. C.	FB	401-146
Caruthers, William	FF	401-133
Carver, Duke	SR	401-71
Carver, Egbert P.	MV	401-28
Carver, G. W.	RRR	401-113
Carver, I.	FB	401-146
Carver, P. S.	RR	401-53
Carver, Samuel B.	ARM	401-3
Carver, Wayne	RRR	401-113
Casanova, J. J.	SP	401-42
Casarez, Jose O.	TVG	401-185
Casas, Cristobal	SP	401-42
Casbeer, J. R.	TVG	401-185
Case, Fred	USV	401-224
Case, H. Leroy	USV	401-224
Case, John	FB	401-146
Casey, Daniel E.	USV	401-224
Casey, Eli	MV	401-28
Casey, George	SR	401-71
Casey, James T.	TVG	401-185
Casey, R. C.	SR	401-71
Casey, Thomas	ARM	401-3
Casey, William	ARM	401-3
Casey, William	MV	401-28
Cash, A. A.	TVG	401-185
Cash, T. L.	TVG	401-185
Cash, Thomas A.	RR	401-53
Cash, W. C.	LR	401-127
Cash, W. C.	SR	401-71
Cash, Webb	TVG	401-185
Cashion, Flanoy	SR	401-71
Cashion, James A.	MV	401-28
Casimir, Louis S.	TVG	401-185
Casimir, Louis S.	USV	401-224
Cask, Thomas D.	ARM	401-3
Caskey, Charles D.	USV	401-224
Casley, Lewis	NAV	401-14
Cason, R. L.	LR	401-127
Caspary, Charles Lee, Jr.	TVG	401-185
Cass, Edwin C.	USV	401-224
Cass, Jesse L.	USV	401-224
Cass, Mack	NAV	401-14
Cass, R. E.	SR	401-71
Cass, R. N.	USV	401-224
Cassaday, F. M.	MV	401-28
Cassady, John	ARM	401-3
Cassels, Albert Edward	SR	401-71
Cassels, Benjamin E.	RRR	401-113
Cassic, Charles M.	USV	401-224
Cassiday, John	FF	401-133
Cassidy, Andrew	ARM	401-3
Cassidy, E. N.	SR	401-71
Cassin, Robert A.	NAV	401-14
Cassity, Willom	TVG	401-185
Casstems, Charley	USV	401-224
Castello, Ricardo	FF	401-133
Castello, Richard	SP	401-42
Castillo, Cisto	FF	401-133
Castillo, Eleno	USV	401-224
Castin, Robert	RR	401-53
Castleberry, R. E. L.	TVG	401-185
Castoloa, Michael	ARM	401-3
Caston, E. H. D.	USV	401-224
Caston, William	FF	401-133
Castro, C.	FB	401-146
Castro, Orlando	MV	401-28
Castrow, A. V.	SR	401-71
Caswell, C. B.	SP	401-42
Caswell, D. H.	SR	401-71
Catchings, J. W.	RRR	401-113
Caterson, Hugh H., Jr.	SR	401-71
Cates, J. J.	USV	401-224
Cates, M. L.	TVG	401-185
Cates, Roy	SR	401-71
Cates, Wesley	FB	401-146
Cates, William J.	USV	401-224
Cates, William S.	TVG	401-185
Cathey, Fred W.	USV	401-224
Cathey, M. E.	RR	401-53

Index to Texas Adjutant General Service Records—All Service Branches

Cathey, W. J. ....RR 401-53
Catlin, J. H. ....SP 401-42
Cato, Elmer ....RRR 401-113
Catt, Isaac ....ARM 401-3
Caudle, Loyd ....RRR 401-113
Causey, Henry T. ....RRR 401-113
Causey, Henry T. ....SR 401-71
Causey, T. N. ....SR 401-71
Causey, T. N. ....LR 401-127
Cavallo, Pedro ....SP 401-42
Cavanagh, James ....ARM 401-3
Cavaness, Mathew ....MM 401-32
Cavannah, William ....ARM 401-3
Cave, J. H. ....FB 401-146
Cave, W. D. ....USV 401-224
Caven, David B. ....USV 401-224
Caven, William ....USV 401-224
Cavender, Cecil L. ....SR 401-71
Cavender, Perry ....RR 401-53
Cavendish, Thom. C. ....TST 401-33
Caver, Lee ....USV 401-224
Caves, Jas. J. ....TVG 401-185
Cavin, Henry C. ....FB 401-146
Cavin, W. T. ....FB 401-146
Cavin, William ....FB 401-146
Caviness, Joel F. ....MV 401-28
Cavitt, J. F. ....SR 401-71
Cavitt, J. F. ....LR 401-127
Cavvatt, John ....ARM 401-3
Cawthon, Herbert ....USV 401-224
Cawthon, James W. ....RR 401-53
Cayce, J. B. ....SR 401-71
Cazares, Cleofas ....TVG 401-185
Cazell, Gabriel F. ....USV 401-224
Cecil, James H. ....USV 401-224
Cecil, Joseph ....ARM 401-3
Cecil, Samuel ....USV 401-224
Celvero, Jesus ....FF 401-133
Center, W. H. ....FF 401-133
Cepna, Walter G. ....MV 401-28
Cersas, Bartoto ....FF 401-133
Cervin, August ....SR 401-71
Cesares, Jose ....FF 401-133
Cessna, Green K. ....SP 401-42
Cestrunk, Robert ....FF 401-133
Chaddick, William T. ....USV 401-224
Chadick, I. S. ....RR 401-53
Chadick, W. D. ....LR 401-127
Chadoin, Alonzo D. ....MV 401-28
Chadwick, Robert Alvin, Jr. ....TVG 401-185
Chaffe, James Aylmen ....TVG 401-185
Chaffin, Emmett F. ....USV 401-224
Chaffin, Jas. R. ....USV 401-224
Chaffin, John ....ARM 401-3
Chaffin, W. L. ....FB 401-146
Chalaupka, Wenzel A. ....TVG 401-185

Chalick, W. D. ....SR 401-71
Chalmers, Tom G. ....FB 401-146
Chamberlain, B. ....FF 401-133
Chamberlain, George A. ....SR 401-71
Chamberlain, George E. ....SR 401-71
Chamberlain, James D. ....USV 401-224
Chamberlain, Urial T. ....FB 401-146
Chambers, C. M. ....USV 401-224
Chambers, Chas. M. ....USV 401-224
Chambers, Claud V. ....USV 401-224
Chambers, Daniel ....USV 401-224
Chambers, James Floyd ....SR 401-71
Chambers, John ....FF 401-133
Chambers, W. F. ....SR 401-71
Chambers, W. F. ....USV 401-224
Chamblin, Wyatt ....RRR 401-113
Champion, A. ....FB 401-146
Champion, G. W. ....FB 401-146
Champion, James M. ....MV 401-28
Champion, Marcus G. ....TVG 401-185
Champion, N. ....TVG 401-185
Champion, P. S. ....FB 401-146
Champion, T. E. ....USV 401-224
Champlain, John ....ARM 401-3
Chance, J. W. ....TVG 401-185
Chancellor, Freddie L. ....USV 401-224
Chancellor, J. T. ....SR 401-71
Chancellor, Jos. T. ....USV 401-224
Chandler, Alfred ....CSA 401-39
Chandler, G. L. ....USV 401-224
Chandler, H. I. ....RRR 401-113
Chandler, H. I. ....SR 401-71
Chandler, J. S. ....SR 401-71
Chandler, W. H., Jr. ....SR 401-71
Chandler, Ward ....SR 401-71
Chandler, William B. ....RRR 401-113
Chandler, William E. ....RRR 401-113
Chaney, Henry ....RRR 401-113
Chaney, R. A. ....FB 401-146
Chapa, Frank L. ....SR 401-71
Chapel, Jacob ....NAV 401-14
Chapel, Jacob ....ARM 401-3
Chapelle, Jean ....ARM 401-3
Chapin, A. W. ....RR 401-53
Chapin, Dwight D. ....SR 401-71
Chaplin, James ....ARM 401-3
Chapman, Adam B. ....FB 401-146
Chapman, Ambrose M. ....USV 401-224
Chapman, Ambrose Monroe ....TVG 401-185
Chapman, Frank ....FB 401-146
Chapman, G. W. ....RRR 401-113
Chapman, George W. ....RR 401-53
Chapman, George W. ....RRR 401-113
Chapman, George Wallace ......RR 401-53
Chapman, J. S. ....SP 401-42
Chapman, Leicester Charles ....SR 401-71

Index to Texas Adjutant General Service Records—All Service Branches

Name	Branch	Record
Chapman, McNeil	TVG	401-185
Chapman, McNeil	USV	401-224
Chapman, Paul	SR	401-71
Chapman, S. J.	CSA	401-39
Chapman, T. J.	TVG	401-186
Chapman, W. A.	TVG	401-186
Chapman, William J.	MV	401-28
Chapman, Willie H.	SR	401-71
Chappell, James H.	USV	401-225
Chappell, Jessy P.	USV	401-225
Chappell, W. T.	TVG	401-186
Charles, H. R.	SR	401-71
Charles, W. S.	SR	401-71
Charlsworth, John R.	USV	401-225
Charlton, Conde N.	USV	401-225
Charninsky, Isadore	SR	401-71
Charo, Cecilio	FB	401-146
Chase, Archibald	NAV	401-14
Chase, Charles H.	ARM	401-3
Chase, Jerome B.	USV	401-225
Chase, W. R.	TST	401-33
Chastain, Claud P.	USV	401-225
Chastain, J. F.	SR	401-71
Chastain, M. B.	FB	401-146
Chastain, R. B.	RRR	401-113
Chastain, Richard B.	RR	401-53
Chastain, Richard B.	FB	401-146
Chastain, T. S.	FB	401-146
Chatham, Lee	TVG	401-186
Chatham, Lee	USV	401-225
Chatham, Willie L.	USV	401-225
Chatman, Edward C.	USV	401-225
Chavez, Macedonio	FF	401-133
Chavez, Dubijen	FF	401-133
Chavez, Geo. A.	USV	401-225
Chavez, S. T.	RR	401-53
Chavice, Sevanno	FF	401-133
Chavlein, Claude	ARM	401-3
Cheatham, J. A.	FB	401-146
Cheatham, Monah R.	FB	401-146
Cheely, J. M.	USV	401-225
Cheitmer, W. L.	TVG	401-186
Chenault, L., Jr.	TVG	401-186
Cheney, Keller	SR	401-71
Cheney, Willard Ervin	RRR	401-113
Chenneville, John	FB	401-146
Cherico, Felix	SR	401-71
Cherico, J. I., Dr.	SR	401-71
Cherry, Noah	MV	401-28
Cherry, R. L.	SR	401-71
Cherry, W. C.	TVG	401-186
Cherry, Wes	SP	401-42
Cherry, Wilber	ARM	401-3
Cherry, William P.	MM	401-32
Cherryhome, H. S.	CSA	401-39
Cherryhomes, Thomas Roy	SR	401-71
Cherryhomes, Thomas Roy	LR	401-127
Chesher, A. L.	FB	401-146
Cheshier, C. N.	TVG	401-186
Cheshire, Clayton H., Lt.	SR	401-72
Chesser, W. S.	FF	401-133
Chessher, J. P.	RR	401-53
Chesshers, James	ARM	401-3
Chesshir, Ollie B.	RR	401-53
Chesshir, Ollie Burnett	RRR	401-113
Chesshir, Sam P.	RR	401-53
Chester, Eldon M.	TVG	401-186
Chevaillier, C. F., Jr.	TVG	401-186
Chevallier, Charles	ARM	401-3
Chew, Jas. H.	TVG	401-186
Chilcutt, John	USV	401-225
Childers, George P.	USV	401-225
Childers, Homer William	TVG	401-186
Childers, J. C.	SR	401-72
Childers, J. D., Jr.	SR	401-72
Childers, John N.	ARM	401-3
Childers, Milas A.	SR	401-72
Childers, P. A.	SR	401-72
Childers, Preston A.	SR	401-72
Childers, S. B.	FB	401-146
Childress, George W.	SR	401-72
Childress, Oscar R.	USV	401-225
Childress, Tom	FB	401-146
Childress, William A.	TVG	401-186
Childress, William B.	USV	401-225
Childs, Joseph H.	USV	401-225
Chiles, Dabney	USV	401-225
Chiles, James	USV	401-225
Chiles, James A.	USV	401-225
Chilton, Ben W.	TVG	401-186
Chilton, Hugh	LR	401-127
Chilton, P. H.	SR	401-72
Chilton, P. H.	FB	401-146
Chilton, T. H.	TVG	401-186
Chinn, G. K.	FB	401-146
Chinn, H. W.	FB	401-146
Chinn, R. Holmes	NAV	401-14
Chipman, H.	FB	401-146
Chisholm, George	USV	401-225
Chism, A. O.	RR	401-53
Chism, William	ARM	401-3
Chisman, Francis T.	NAV	401-14
Chisolin, J. O.	TVG	401-186
Chisolm, Robert	TVG	401-186
Chisum, Alonzo	USV	401-225
Chisum, John S.	TST	401-33
Chisum, Toney C.	SR	401-72
Chiton, Hugh	SR	401-72
Chitwood, James T.	USV	401-225
Chitwood, Roy D.	SR	401-72
Chitwood, William H.	USV	401-225
Chivers, William B.	USV	401-225

Index to Texas Adjutant General Service Records—All Service Branches

Name	Branch	Record
Chlebowski, Frank	USV	401-225
Choat, Gabriel	RR	401-53
Choat, William	MV	401-28
Choate, D. B.	SR	401-72
Choate, D. Boone	LR	401-127
Choate, S. B.	RRR	401-113
Choate, W. M.	FB	401-146
Choate, William G.	RRR	401-113
Chollar, George E.	USV	401-225
Chrisman, J. H.	FF	401-133
Chrisman, W. C.	SR	401-72
Chrisman, W. M.	SR	401-72
Chrisman, William J.	USV	401-225
Christal, Peter M.	USV	401-225
Christensen, Robert B.	USV	401-225
Christenson, C. A.	TVG	401-186
Christian, A. H.	FB	401-146
Christian, Carl	USV	401-225
Christian, Clark F.	SR	401-72
Christian, G. L.	TVG	401-186
Christian, Greenup	ARM	401-3
Christian, J. A.	TVG	401-186
Christian, L. E.	TVG	401-186
Christian, Wiley	USV	401-225
Christian, William G.	TVG	401-186
Christian, Winter W.	TVG	401-186
Christie, A. B.	SR	401-72
Christie, B. V.	SR	401-72
Christie, Eugene	SR	401-72
Christmas, T. E.	SR	401-72
Christophel, Charles	FF	401-133
Christopher, Rufus A.	TVG	401-186
Christopher, W. H.	TVG	401-186
Chrystall, John	FF	401-133
Chsehier, Caspar L.	USV	401-225
Chubbuck, J. F.	RR	401-53
Chullzkey, Reese	TVG	401-186
Chunn, W. E.	SR	401-72
Church, Edwin H., Jr.	USV	401-225
Church, Francis H.	SP	401-42
Church, Ralph	FB	401-146
Churchwell, John	TVG	401-186
Churvi, George M.	USV	401-225
Chute, Richard	FB	401-146
Chuyler, George	ARM	401-3
Cincera, L. T.	SR	401-72
Cinnamon, Nathan	TVG	401-186
Cisco, W. J.	FF	401-133
Claflin, W. S.	USV	401-225
Clagett, H.	MV	401-28
Clagett, Howard B.	TVG	401-186
Claiborne, W. H.	RR	401-53
Claman, William F.	USV	401-225
Clampitt, Nathan W.	USV	401-225
Clancey, C. L.	NAV	401-14
Clanton, Newman H.	TST	401-33
Clardy, Joseph	USV	401-225
Clardy, U. P.	SP	401-42
Clark, A. J.	TST	401-33
Clark, Albert P.	USV	401-225
Clark, B. C.	RRR	401-113
Clark, B. C.	TVG	401-186
Clark, B. F.	RR	401-53
Clark, Bailey W.	SR	401-72
Clark, Basil, Jr.	TVG	401-186
Clark, C. E.	SR	401-72
Clark, C. M.	TVG	401-186
Clark, Carroll S.	USV	401-225
Clark, Charles	FF	401-133
Clark, Charles	USV	401-225
Clark, Charles C.	USV	401-225
Clark, Clardie P.	SR	401-72
Clark, Coke	USV	401-225
Clark, David	USV	401-225
Clark, E. E.	FF	401-133
Clark, Edward	SR	401-72
Clark, Edwin S.	TVG	401-186
Clark, Edwin S.	USV	401-225
Clark, Francis M.	FF	401-133
Clark, Frank B.	SR	401-72
Clark, Frank R.	SR	401-72
Clark, G. H.	TVG	401-186
Clark, G. W.	FB	401-146
Clark, George W.	SR	401-72
Clark, George W.	LR	401-127
Clark, H. D.	SR	401-72
Clark, H. E.	RRR	401-113
Clark, Harvey R.	RR	401-53
Clark, Hawkins	ARM	401-3
Clark, Hosea L.	USV	401-225
Clark, I. M.	USV	401-225
Clark, J. E.	CSA	401-39
Clark, J. G.	TVG	401-186
Clark, J. T.	CSA	401-39
Clark, James A.	USV	401-225
Clark, James P.	NAV	401-14
Clark, Jeff	USV	401-225
Clark, John	NAV	401-14
Clark, John	TVG	401-186
Clark, John Franklin	RRR	401-113
Clark, John M.	USV	401-225
Clark, John T., Jr.	USV	401-225
Clark, John W.	SR	401-72
Clark, Joseph B.	RR	401-53
Clark, Joseph H.	ARM	401-3
Clark, Judson J.	USV	401-225
Clark, Leonard K.	USV	401-225
Clark, Marcus H.	SR	401-72
Clark, Noah C.	RRR	401-113
Clark, Noble	SR	401-72
Clark, P. J. W.	FB	401-146
Clark, Peter	NAV	401-14

Index to Texas Adjutant General Service Records—All Service Branches

Name	Branch	Record
Clark, R. B.	TVG	401-186
Clark, R. M.	NAV	401-14
Clark, Ray M.	SR	401-72
Clark, Robert G.	TVG	401-186
Clark, S. R.	FB	401-146
Clark, Thom. W.	FB	401-146
Clark, Thomas D.	ARM	401-3
Clark, Tom B.	SR	401-72
Clark, V. H.	SR	401-72
Clark, W.	FB	401-146
Clark, W. E.	FB	401-146
Clark, W. S.	TVG	401-186
Clark, W. T.	TVG	401-186
Clark, Wallace L.	USV	401-225
Clark, Walter H.	TVG	401-186
Clark, William D.	MV	401-28
Clark, William S.	USV	401-225
Clark, William W.	ARM	401-3
Clark, Wright	SP	401-42
Clarke, C. W.	FB	401-146
Clarke, Chas. W.	FB	401-146
Clarke, Frank	TVG	401-186
Clarke, J. M.	FB	401-146
Clarke, James Stewart	USV	401-225
Clarke, John S.	TST	401-33
Clarke, P. S.	FB	401-146
Clarke, R.	SR	401-72
Clarke, Rufugio	LR	401-127
Clarke, William P.	USV	401-225
Clarkson, William	SR	401-72
Clary, Thomas	ARM	401-3
Clavin, Geo. A.	TVG	401-186
Clavin, Geo. A.	USV	401-225
Clawson, Henry W.	NAV	401-14
Clay, F. A.	TVG	401-186
Clay, J. Edwin	USV	401-225
Clay, James M.	NAV	401-14
Clay, William S.	USV	401-225
Claybourn, Wayne	TVG	401-186
Claybourne, Seawell	TVG	401-186
Claybrook, J. H.	SR	401-72
Claybrook, J. H.	LR	401-127
Clayhorn, Rufus	USV	401-225
Claypool, Clinton	TVG	401-186
Claypool, Cooper	TVG	401-186
Claypool, Henry C.	TVG	401-186
Clayton, Edwin S.	TVG	401-186
Clayton, Irvin	USV	401-225
Clayton, J. R.	USV	401-225
Clayton, Jess T.	USV	401-225
Clayton, Jos. M.	TST	401-33
Clayton, R. M.	FB	401-146
Clayton, Turner	TVG	401-186
Claywell, Samuel A.	USV	401-225
Cleary, J. G.	TST	401-33
Cleaveland, Charles	ARM	401-3
Clegg, Ira T.	USV	401-225
Clegg, John H.	TVG	401-186
Clem, Curtis E.	SR	401-72
Clemens, EgaR	TVG	401-186
Clemens, Jesse J.	TST	401-34
Clement, Frank J., Jr.	SR	401-72
Clement, J. B.	NAV	401-14
Clement, W. Connell	SR	401-72
Clements, Andy F.	RRR	401-113
Clements, James K. P.	TST	401-34
Clements, R. H.	NAV	401-14
Clements, Roger E.	USV	401-225
Clements, S. M.	RRR	401-113
Clements, William	ARM	401-3
Clements, William	FB	401-147
Clemmons, O. D.	USV	401-225
Clemons, J. E.	RRR	401-113
Clemons, J. E.	TVG	401-186
Clemow, Frank J.	TVG	401-186
Clendenen, Albert	SR	401-72
Clendenin, W. H.	SR	401-72
Clendenin, W. H.	LR	401-127
Cleveland, C. A.	SR	401-72
Cleveland, C. D.	TVG	401-186
Cleveland, Larkin	FF	401-133
Cleveland, Leroy	RR	401-53
Cleveland, William D., Jr.	TVG	401-186
Cleveland, William John	RRR	401-113
Clewis, Lewis	SP	401-42
Click, Elridge S.	MV	401-28
Click, W. L.	TVG	401-186
Clifford, C. A.	TVG	401-186
Clifford, Forshey N.	TVG	401-186
Clifford, Munson H.	TVG	401-186
Clift, James T.	MV	401-28
Clift, W. H.	FB	401-147
Clifton, J. T.	FB	401-147
Clifton, Thomas	ARM	401-3
Clifton, W. J.	FB	401-147
Clifton, W. T.	FB	401-147
Cline, Ira W.	RR	401-53
Cline, L. L.	SR	401-72
Cline, L. S.	SR	401-72
Cline, Mack	TVG	401-186
Cline, W. B.	SR	401-72
Cline, W. H.	FF	401-133
Clinton, John	NAV	401-14
Clinton, John	SP	401-42
Clinton, Lawrence	TST	401-34
Clinton, Paul	FB	401-147
Cload, J. H.	TVG	401-186
Clonts, B. M.	TVG	401-186
Clopton, J. C.	SR	401-72
Clopton, J. C.	USV	401-225
Clopton, Mortimer L., Jr.	USV	401-225
Clopton, William A.	USV	401-225

Index to Texas Adjutant General Service Records—All Service Branches

Name	Branch	Record
Clopton, William M.	MV	401-28
Close, E. S.	MV	401-28
Close, Will S.	USV	401-225
Cloud, A. L.	RRR	401-113
Cloud, A. L.	SR	401-72
Cloud, J. C.	LR	401-127
Cloud, John E.	USV	401-225
Cloud, L. E.	RRR	401-113
Cloud, William G.	USV	401-225
Clough, E. L., Capt.	SR	401-72
Clough, Judson	SP	401-42
Clouse, A. W.	USV	401-225
Clousintzer, E. A.	SR	401-72
Cloyes, A. J.	FB	401-147
Cluck, Frederick E.	USV	401-225
Clymer, Eugene	TVG	401-186
Clymer, W. E.	TVG	401-186
Coalson, S. D.	FB	401-147
Cobb, S. S.	FF	401-133
Cobb, Dent N.	SR	401-72
Cobb, E. H.	FF	401-133
Cobb, Henry A.	NAV	401-15
Cobb, J. E.	SR	401-72
Cobb, Percy	TVG	401-186
Cobb, T. E.	SR	401-72
Cobb, T. S.	TVG	401-186
Cobb, W. C.	SR	401-72
Cobberley, Willard E.	USV	401-225
Cobble, John F.	TVG	401-186
Cobbs, T. D.	TVG	401-186
Cobeau, John B.	NAV	401-15
Coburn, H. D., Col.	SR	401-72
Cocca, Giuseppe	SR	401-72
Cochran, Chas. F.	RRR	401-114
Cochran, J. H.	USV	401-225
Cochran, J. L.	SR	401-72
Cochran, Joe T.	FB	401-147
Cochran, John W.	LR	401-127
Cochran, John W.	SR	401-72
Cochran, John W.	USV	401-225
Cochran, Richard	NAV	401-15
Cochran, Richard	ARM	401-3
Cochran, W. H.	TST	401-34
Cocke, Richard	TVG	401-186
Cocke, Richard	USV	401-225
Cocke, William T.	NAV	401-15
Cockrell, William W.	TVG	401-186
Cockrell, William W.	USV	401-225
Cockrill, Oscar E.	USV	401-225
Code, Philip	ARM	401-3
Cody, George P.	RR	401-53
Coffall, David M.	USV	401-225
Coffee, A. B.	SR	401-72
Coffee, A. B.	FB	401-147
Coffee, James	TST	401-34
Coffee, W.	LR	401-127
Coffee, W.	SR	401-72
Coffee, Walter D.	SR	401-72
Coffee, Walter Douglas	LR	401-127
Coffey, Benjamin	CSA	401-39
Coffey, Carl Delmer	RRR	401-114
Coffey, H. H.	SP	401-42
Coffey, Homer Sales	USV	401-225
Coffey, John S.	SP	401-42
Coffey, Thomas J.	SP	401-42
Coffield, H. B.	CSA	401-39
Coffield, John	FF	401-133
Coffin, A. L.	SR	401-72
Coffin, A. L.	TVG	401-186
Coffman, W. W.	RRR	401-114
Cogdell, D. M.	SR	401-72
Cogdell, D. M.	LR	401-127
Cogdell, Earl	SR	401-72
Cogdill, C. O.	USV	401-225
Coggill, George	ARM	401-3
Coggin, A. J.	RR	401-53
Coggin, H. I.	SR	401-72
Coggins, Edward L.	USV	401-225
Coggins, T. J.	FB	401-147
Coghill, James E.	ARM	401-3
Cohen, Harry H.	SR	401-72
Cohen, Ike	TVG	401-186
Cohen, Isaac	USV	401-225
Cohen, Louis	USV	401-225
Cohen, Louis B.	USV	401-225
Cohen, Robt. I., Jr.	SR	401-72
Cohen, Sam	SR	401-72
Cohn, Simon	SR	401-72
Coke, William	FF	401-133
Coker, A. M.	TVG	401-186
Coker, JiM	SR	401-72
Coker, Joe	USV	401-225
Coker, L. B.	SR	401-72
Coker, L. B.	LR	401-127
Coker, L. T.	RR	401-53
Coker, R. A.	LR	401-127
Coker, R. A.	SR	401-72
Coker, S. W.	TVG	401-186
Colbath, A.	FB	401-147
Colbaugh, John	FF	401-133
Colbert, James A.	TVG	401-186
Colbert, T. R.	SR	401-72
Colburn, E.	FB	401-147
Colby, Conrad F.	USV	401-225
Coldwell, Neal	FB	401-147
Cole, Allen	RR	401-53
Cole, C. B.	FB	401-147
Cole, C. H.	FB	401-147
Cole, Elmer	SR	401-72
Cole, H. P.	FB	401-147
Cole, J. P.	LR	401-127
Cole, J. P.	SR	401-72

Index to Texas Adjutant General Service Records—All Service Branches

Name	Branch	Record
Cole, James R.	RRR	401-114
Cole, John A.	TVG	401-186
Cole, L. L.	LR	401-127
Cole, L. L.	SR	401-72
Cole, O. H.	RRR	401-114
Cole, Ross Robert	SR	401-72
Cole, S. R.	RR	401-53
Cole, T. J.	RRR	401-114
Cole, Thomas J.	RR	401-53
Cole, Thomas L.	NAV	401-15
Cole, W.	TST	401-34
Cole, W. F.	FB	401-147
Cole, William	NAV	401-15
Coleman, A. D.	SR	401-72
Coleman, Andrew	SP	401-42
Coleman, Andrew J.	USV	401-225
Coleman, C. F.	RRR	401-114
Coleman, Charlie R.	USV	401-225
Coleman, Chas. H.	USV	401-225
Coleman, Chas. P.	TVG	401-186
Coleman, Dan	RR	401-53
Coleman, Dan	RRR	401-114
Coleman, Dan	FB	401-147
Coleman, E. E.	SR	401-72
Coleman, Edd	FB	401-147
Coleman, Ell	FB	401-147
Coleman, Henry	FF	401-133
Coleman, Henry	SR	401-72
Coleman, I. W.	RR	401-53
Coleman, J. Wood	RR	401-53
Coleman, John	ARM	401-3
Coleman, L. B.	FB	401-147
Coleman, M.	SR	401-72
Coleman, M.	LR	401-127
Coleman, Pat	FB	401-147
Coleman, Richard Llewellyn	TVG	401-186
Coleman, Richard Llewellyn	USV	401-225
Coleman, S. R.	TVG	401-186
Coleman, S. T.	FB	401-147
Coleman, T. A.	SR	401-72
Coleman, T. A.	TVG	401-186
Coleman, Thomas A	SR	401-72
Coleman, Tom	LR	401-127
Coleman, Tom	SR	401-72
Coleman, William	NAV	401-15
Coleman, Y. O.	TVG	401-186
Colemere, J. H.	TVG	401-186
Coleson, George W.	USV	401-225
Colgate, William A.	USV	401-225
Collaton, James	TST	401-34
Collery, Willy	ARM	401-3
Colley, E. M.	RR	401-53
Colley, E. M.	RRR	401-114
Colley, Eugene G.	FB	401-147
Colley, G. W.	RR	401-53
Colley, J. H.	RRR	401-114
Collicott, W. M.	FB	401-147
Collier, Crocket	FF	401-133
Collier, Frank	TVG	401-186
Collier, Hardee W.	SR	401-72
Collier, J. L.	FB	401-147
Collier, Lewie H.	USV	401-225
Collier, Percy H.	TVG	401-186
Collier, Richard	FB	401-147
Collier, Thomas	USV	401-225
Collier, W. W.	FB	401-147
Collier, William	SR	401-72
Collins, A. G.	FB	401-147
Collins, Alby D.	SR	401-72
Collins, Alex	NAV	401-15
Collins, Amos	TVG	401-186
Collins, Benjamin F.	USV	401-225
Collins, Buck	SR	401-72
Collins, Charles M.	FB	401-147
Collins, Charley F.	USV	401-225
Collins, D. S.	RRR	401-114
Collins, E.	USV	401-225
Collins, E. I.	LR	401-127
Collins, Eck	RRR	401-114
Collins, Edward	NAV	401-15
Collins, Frank	USV	401-225
Collins, George	FB	401-147
Collins, Harry W.	RR	401-53
Collins, J.	SP	401-42
Collins, J. F.	FB	401-147
Collins, J. Percy	TVG	401-186
Collins, J. W.	TVG	401-186
Collins, James	NAV	401-15
Collins, Jim	SR	401-72
Collins, Neil	TVG	401-186
Collins, Peter	NAV	401-15
Collins, R. L.	SR	401-72
Collins, Richard E.	USV	401-225
Collins, Roy R.	SR	401-72
Collins, Royal R.	RRR	401-114
Collins, Thomas D.	TVG	401-186
Collins, Tom	TVG	401-186
Collins, W.	FB	401-147
Collins, W. C.	FB	401-147
Collins, W. W.	FB	401-147
Collins, Walter	SR	401-72
Collister, George B.	ARM	401-3
Collons, E. I.	SR	401-72
Collor, E. George	NAV	401-15
Collum, J. S.	FB	401-147
Colly, E. G.	FB	401-147
Collyns, Cecil B.	SR	401-72
Colp, C. J.	SR	401-72
Colquitt, R. M.	SR	401-72
Colquitt, W. Homer	SR	401-72
Colquitt, Will K.	SR	401-72
Colston, OliveR	TVG	401-186

Index to Texas Adjutant General Service Records—All Service Branches

Name	Branch	Page
Colter, Thaddeus	FF	401-133
Columbia, J. L.	FB	401-147
Colvert, Carl Lee	SR	401-73
Colvin, Garland Greenberry	TVG	401-186
Combs, L.	FB	401-147
Comegys, Cornelius G.	TVG	401-186
Comegys, Cornelius G.	USV	401-225
Comerio, Frank C.	SR	401-73
Comestock, James C.	ARM	401-3
Commons, Marion	USV	401-225
Compere, E. S.	TVG	401-186
Compere, M. H.	TVG	401-186
Compton, Arthur Michael	SR	401-73
Compton, Bruce	TVG	401-186
Compton, Edward A.	SR	401-73
Compton, Joseph J.	SR	401-73
Compton, S. L.	RRR	401-114
Compton, T. D.	TVG	401-187
Comstock, Theo B.	FB	401-147
Comwall, Richard O., Jr.	USV	401-225
Conains, F. A.	SR	401-73
Conaway, A. N.	FF	401-133
Conaway, William B.	USV	401-225
Conden, William	ARM	401-3
Condon, William	NAV	401-15
Cone, W. T.	SR	401-73
Cone, William D.	TVG	401-187
Cone, William Thomas	RRR	401-114
Conerly, T. P.	TVG	401-187
Conger, H. E.	SR	401-73
Conger, Thomas E.	TVG	401-187
Conger, Thomas E.	USV	401-225
Conkey, C. R.	SR	401-73
Conlan, Peter	ARM	401-3
Conley, Fountain S.	ARM	401-3
Conley, George	ARM	401-3
Conley, J. T.	RR	401-53
Conley, James	SP	401-42
Conley, M. J.	TVG	401-187
Conley, S. B.	TST	401-34
Conlin, William P.	FB	401-147
Conly, John	ARM	401-3
Conly, Pete F.	ARM	401-3
Conn, Hugh E.	FB	401-147
Connally, Graham	RRR	401-114
Connally, Graham	SR	401-73
Connally, L. H.	FB	401-147
Connally, Tom T.	TVG	401-187
Connally, Tomas	RR	401-53
Connally, William	FB	401-147
Connally, William	TVG	401-187
Connell, Edward F.	FB	401-147
Connell, J.	RR	401-53
Connell, J. G.	FB	401-147
Connell, James	TVG	401-187
Connell, John	NAV	401-15
Connell, John H., Jr.	USV	401-225
Connell, W. J.	SR	401-73
Connell, Wilmer Jennings	RRR	401-114
Connelly, James	SP	401-42
Conner, George	FB	401-147
Conner, J. A.	SR	401-73
Conner, J. F.	LR	401-127
Conner, T. E.	SR	401-73
Conner, W. M.	TVG	401-187
Conner, W. Max	LR	401-127
Connolly, Dan T.	USV	401-226
Connolly, James	FF	401-133
Connolly, Thomas W.	USV	401-226
Connor, C. R.	FB	401-147
Connor, George	SR	401-73
Connor, George W. "Buck"	RR	401-53
Connor, John R.	ARM	401-3
Connor, William	ARM	401-3
Connor, William E.	NAV	401-15
Connoway, William B.	TST	401-34
Conrad, Gwynne, Capt.	SR	401-73
Conrad, J. Z.	TVG	401-187
Conrad, M.	FB	401-147
Conrad, Samuel L.	FB	401-147
Conrad, T.	FB	401-147
Conro, L. R.	SR	401-73
Conro, L. R.	LR	401-127
Consalus, John J.	FB	401-147
Contat, Robert L.	RRR	401-114
Converse, Walter C.	NAV	401-15
Convill, Thomas	NAV	401-15
Conway, Bennie	TVG	401-187
Cook. L. W.	SR	401-73
Cook, Ben	USV	401-226
Cook, Ben H.	TVG	401-187
Cook, Benj. P.	USV	401-226
Cook, C. C.	SP	401-42
Cook, Charles	SR	401-73
Cook, Charles	LR	401-127
Cook, Charles G.	USV	401-226
Cook, Claude E.	TVG	401-187
Cook, Ed A.	USV	401-226
Cook, Enoch	FB	401-147
Cook, Eugene A.	USV	401-226
Cook, Fred	USV	401-226
Cook, Fred W.	USV	401-226
Cook, Frederick	NAV	401-15
Cook, Geo. P.	USV	401-226
Cook, George J.	FB	401-147
Cook, Herbert	TVG	401-187
Cook, J. E.	TST	401-34
Cook, J. L.	RR	401-53
Cook, John	TVG	401-187
Cook, John Cliff	RR	401-53
Cook, John F.	RRR	401-114
Cook, L. J.	SR	401-73

Index to Texas Adjutant General Service Records—All Service Branches

Name	Branch	Record
Cook, L. J.	SR	401-73
Cook, Lewis H.	FB	401-147
Cook, Paul	FB	401-147
Cook, Peter	NAV	401-15
Cook, T. H.	RR	401-53
Cook, T. T.	FB	401-147
Cook, Thomas H.	SR	401-73
Cook, Thomas Hugh	RRR	401-114
Cook, W. A.	FB	401-147
Cook, W. F.	FF	401-133
Cook, W. Thomas	TST	401-34
Cook, Walter C.	USV	401-226
Cooke, David R.	USV	401-226
Cooke, George H.	RRR	401-114
Cooke, Gordon L.	TVG	401-187
Cooke, John Howard	TVG	401-187
Cooke, Lorenzo N.	TVG	401-187
Cooke, Mortimer M.	TVG	401-187
Cooke, T. P.	FB	401-147
Cooke, W. G.	ARM	401-3
Cooke, William Q.	TVG	401-187
Cooker, Thos.	ARM	401-3
Cooksey, C. B.	FB	401-147
Cooksey, Tom L.	SR	401-73
Cooksey, William F.	FB	401-148
Cooley, F. L.	TVG	401-187
Cooley, W. S.	FB	401-148
Cooley, William F.	USV	401-226
Coon, George R.	USV	401-226
Coon, Robert P.	USV	401-226
Cooper I.	RR	401-53
Cooper, A. J.	TVG	401-187
Cooper, Alfred M.	ARM	401-3
Cooper, Alvin J.	USV	401-226
Cooper, B. Frank	TVG	401-187
Cooper, C. H.	FB	401-148
Cooper, E.	TVG	401-187
Cooper, Edward	ARM	401-3
Cooper, Ernest L.	TVG	401-187
Cooper, Frank	TVG	401-187
Cooper, G. T.	SR	401-73
Cooper, H. H.	TVG	401-187
Cooper, H. L.	TVG	401-187
Cooper, Herbert Newton	SR	401-73
Cooper, Homer T.	USV	401-226
Cooper, Hugh Jackson	RRR	401-114
Cooper, J. B.	TVG	401-187
Cooper, J. M.	RR	401-53
Cooper, James P.	ARM	401-3
Cooper, Jim	FF	401-133
Cooper, John	ARM	401-3
Cooper, John A.	SR	401-73
Cooper, John A.	LR	401-127
Cooper, Joseph W.	USV	401-226
Cooper, Lee O.	USV	401-226
Cooper, Lester Lee	TVG	401-187
Cooper, M. C.	TVG	401-187
Cooper, Marion	TVG	401-187
Cooper, Price	FB	401-148
Cooper, Robert M.	USV	401-226
Cooper, Saint Cloud	TVG	401-187
Cooper, Santiago	FB	401-148
Cooper, Thomas	SP	401-42
Cooper, Thomas E.	RRR	401-114
Cooper, William	SP	401-43
Cooper, William Eugene	RRR	401-114
Coopwood, B. F.	FF	401-133
Coopwood, J. D.	FB	401-148
Coopwood, W. W.	USV	401-226
Coorpender, Robt. B.	RR	401-53
Coots, George	RR	401-53
Cope, Clifton	USV	401-226
Cope, J. A.	TVG	401-187
Cope, Tom	FB	401-148
Cope, W. D.	RR	401-53
Cope, W. D.	SR	401-73
Cope, William J.	USV	401-226
Copeland, Dan	CSA	401-39
Copeland, F. R.	RRR	401-114
Copeland, J. E.	TVG	401-187
Copeland, J. O.	FB	401-148
Copeland, Jess D.	USV	401-226
Copeland, John M.	TVG	401-187
Copeland, Joseph W.	USV	401-226
Copeland, Will	TVG	401-187
Copelin, Dewey C.	RRR	401-114
Copell, Harry H.	TVG	401-187
Coplan, Edward	FB	401-148
Copland, F. F.	FB	401-148
Copons, Jasper M.	USV	401-226
Coppedge, Albert A.	RRR	401-114
Coppedge, J. P.	TVG	401-187
Coquat, Julius	ARM	401-3
Coray, F. M.	SR	401-73
Corbet, James H.	USV	401-226
Corder, B. T.	SR	401-73
Corder, R. E.	RRR	401-114
Corder, Thomas	RR	401-53
Corder, W. A.	ARM	401-3
Cordera, Rafael	FB	401-148
Corkill, ErnesT	SR	401-73
Corlen, Rosendo	FB	401-148
Corley, Dott	USV	401-226
Corley, Elton I.	SR	401-73
Corley, G. Walter	SR	401-73
Corley, Lane	TVG	401-187
Corn, G. H.	SR	401-73
Corn, Joseph N.	FB	401-148
Corn, Lee B.	FB	401-148
Cornelius, James F.	SR	401-73
Cornell, G. H.	TVG	401-187
Cornell, James	NAV	401-15

Index to Texas Adjutant General Service Records—All Service Branches

Name	Branch	Record
Corner, Benj. C.	USV	401-226
Cornett, R. M.	SR	401-73
Cornett, R. M.	LR	401-127
Cornitius, O. M.	TVG	401-187
Cornwell, George E.	FB	401-148
Corper, Owen T.	USV	401-226
Cortes, W. F.	TVG	401-187
Corts, James T.	USV	401-226
Corwin, J. C.	SR	401-73
Cory, John	USV	401-226
Cory, Kirk C.	TVG	401-187
Cosby, G. M.	SR	401-73
Cosby, Hugh Edwin	SR	401-73
Cosgrove, F. J.	TVG	401-187
Cosgrove, James A.	TVG	401-187
Cosgrove, Thomas	TVG	401-187
Cosgrove, William	TST	401-34
Cosmos, John	FB	401-148
Cosson, Pierre	NAV	401-15
Costello, James	USV	401-226
Costello, Joe	TVG	401-187
Costelo, James	ARM	401-3
Costen, William G.	FB	401-148
Costley, AlberT	FB	401-148
Costley, S. L.	FB	401-148
Cotrel, William E.	USV	401-226
Cottingham, A. C.	FF	401-133
Cottingham, J. H.	RRR	401-114
Cottingham, J. P., Jr.	RRR	401-114
Cottingham, T. O.	FF	401-133
Cottingham, W. E.	FF	401-133
Cottingham, Wesley P.	USV	401-226
Cotton, Anderson	SP	401-43
Cotton, B. W.	SR	401-73
Cotton, C. H.	FB	401-148
Cotton, Clyde Henry	RRR	401-114
Cotton, D. N.	SR	401-73
Cotton, Enoch George	NAV	401-15
Cotton, J. M.	FB	401-148
Cotton, Thomas M.	MM	401-32
Cottrell, J. M.	USV	401-226
Cottrell, J. W.	FB	401-148
Cotulla, Ed	FB	401-148
Cotulla, Simon	SR	401-73
Cotulla, Simon	LR	401-127
Couch, A. P.	SR	401-73
Couch, Andrew J.	MV	401-28
Couch, Jesse G.	USV	401-226
Couch, Key	USV	401-226
Couch, Leslie	USV	401-226
Couch, Patrick H.	USV	401-226
Couillard, Antoine	SP	401-43
Couk, George W.	USV	401-226
Could, J. C.	SR	401-73
Couley, ToM	TVG	401-187
Coulter, J. J., Jr.	USV	401-226
Coulter, John	NAV	401-15
Counahan, Dennis	NAV	401-15
Cound, George H.	RRR	401-114
Courtney, J. L.	RRR	401-114
Courtney, Sam	TVG	401-187
Cousins, F. A.	LR	401-127
Coutier, Jesse	USV	401-226
Coutler, George	TVG	401-187
Covert, Frank M., Jr.	SR	401-73
Covey, J. E.	SR	401-73
Covey, J. E.	LR	401-127
Covey, L. G.	TVG	401-187
Covington, C. W.	FB	401-148
Covington, D. E.	RR	401-53
Covington, D. E.	RRR	401-114
Covington, D. E.	SR	401-73
Covington, R. D.	TVG	401-187
Covington, T. E.	SR	401-73
Covington, T. W.	FB	401-148
Covington, W. B.	MV	401-28
Cowan, B. F.	SR	401-73
Cowan, Hugh	TVG	401-187
Cowan, I. M.	TST	401-34
Cowan, J. D.	FB	401-148
Cowden, G. D.	SR	401-73
Cowden, J. D.	FB	401-148
Cowden, Jax M.	LR	401-127
Cowdey, Jax M.	SR	401-73
Cowell, J. B.	TVG	401-187
Cowen, Bee	SR	401-73
Cowles, John E.	FB	401-148
Cowlfield, Ed	TVG	401-187
Cowling, James	SP	401-43
Cowsert, Gully	SR	401-73
Cox, A. F.	FF	401-133
Cox, A. H.	TST	401-34
Cox, A. H.	FF	401-133
Cox, A. W.	FF	401-133
Cox, B. F.	FB	401-148
Cox, Bates	SR	401-73
Cox, Bates	LR	401-127
Cox, Ben	FB	401-148
Cox, Ben G.	FB	401-148
Cox, Ben L.	SR	401-73
Cox, Benjamin L.	USV	401-226
Cox, Billy	FF	401-133
Cox, Bowen	TVG	401-187
Cox, Charles S.	RR	401-53
Cox, Charley E.	USV	401-226
Cox, Cornelius	NAV	401-15
Cox, D. W.	RR	401-53
Cox, Dee W.	RR	401-53
Cox, Dee W.	RRR	401-114
Cox, E. A.	USV	401-226
Cox, Eddie	SR	401-73
Cox, Edgar M.	USV	401-226

Index to Texas Adjutant General Service Records—All Service Branches

Name	Branch	Record
Cox, Edward	ARM	401-3
Cox, Euclid W.	RRR	401-114
Cox, Eugene	TVG	401-187
Cox, Frank	SP	401-43
Cox, G. F.	SR	401-73
Cox, H. B.	TVG	401-187
Cox, Harris R.	USV	401-226
Cox, Hugh	FF	401-133
Cox, J. H.	SR	401-73
Cox, J. W.	SP	401-43
Cox, James H.	USV	401-226
Cox, James S.	USV	401-226
Cox, John Richard	RRR	401-114
Cox, L. M.	SR	401-73
Cox, L. Wade	SR	401-73
Cox, Lewis	TVG	401-187
Cox, Luther A.	TVG	401-187
Cox, Marshall	FB	401-148
Cox, Robert A.	USV	401-226
Cox, Roy	SR	401-73
Cox, Roy W.	SR	401-73
Cox, S. V.	RRR	401-114
Cox, Silas Vernon	SR	401-73
Cox, T. F.	TVG	401-187
Cox, Talbot	SP	401-43
Cox, Thomas R.	TST	401-34
Cox, Thos. W.	USV	401-226
Cox, Volney	TVG	401-187
Cox, W. A.	TVG	401-187
Cox, W. E.	TVG	401-187
Cox, W. H.	TVG	401-187
Cox, W. P., Sr.	SR	401-73
Cox, Walker	SR	401-73
Cox, WalkeR	LR	401-127
Cox, Walter Ains	USV	401-226
Cox, Whit Allen	TVG	401-187
Cox, William C.	TVG	401-187
Coy, Dillard	SR	401-73
Coy, Frank	FB	401-148
Coy, Frederick S.	USV	401-226
Coy, J. S.	FB	401-148
Coy, Paulin S.	FB	401-148
Coyle, M. G.	FB	401-148
Coyle, Masterson	RRR	401-114
Coyle, William P., Jr.	TVG	401-187
Cozby, Bascom	USV	401-226
Cozine, Louis N.	SR	401-73
Crabb, A. A.	TVG	401-187
Crabtree, John R. C.	USV	401-226
Crabtree, Lewis C.	USV	401-226
Craddock, A. H.	SR	401-73
Craddock, E. L.	SR	401-73
Craddock, Horace M.	TVG	401-187
Craddock, W. E.	TVG	401-187
Craft, Lee Pinkney	RRR	401-114
Craft, PeteR	ARM	401-3
Craft, R. C.	SR	401-73
Craft, W. A.	FB	401-148
Craft, William Bentford	SR	401-73
Craft, William Bentford	LR	401-127
Crager, W. M.	SR	401-73
Crager, W. M.	LR	401-127
Cragg, Howard	RR	401-54
Craig, Alvin	USV	401-226
Craig, D. H.	SR	401-73
Craig, J. B.	FB	401-148
Craig, J. F.	TVG	401-187
Craig, O. M.	TVG	401-187
Craig, Walter A.	SR	401-73
Craig, Weems	SR	401-73
Craige, Jerome Western	USV	401-226
Craighead, C. A.	SR	401-73
Craighead, Pat	RR	401-54
Crain, J. A.	SR	401-73
Crain, J. E.	TVG	401-187
Crain, James G.	RR	401-54
Crain, T. F.	FB	401-148
Crain, W. H.	TVG	401-187
Crain, William N.	USV	401-226
Cramer, Theodore E.	SP	401-43
Crandall, Arthur L.	TVG	401-187
Crandall, Jay F.	USV	401-226
Crane, Charles	FF	401-133
Crane, James P.	TVG	401-187
Crane, John W.	USV	401-226
Crane, Mike	USV	401-226
Crane, W. R.	SR	401-73
Crangle, William C.	NAV	401-15
Crank, Albert A.	USV	401-226
Crank, William H., Jr.	TVG	401-187
Cranz, G. E.	TVG	401-187
Crapper, John	USV	401-226
Crasso, Adolph	TVG	401-187
Craven, Chas.	TVG	401-187
Craven, F. A.	RR	401-54
Craven, John E.	TVG	401-187
Craven, W. K.	TVG	401-187
Cravey, Fletcher	RRR	401-114
Cravey, Fletcher	SR	401-73
Cravey, James	SR	401-73
Cravy, Charles	FF	401-133
Crawford, A. C.	TVG	401-187
Crawford, Aaron	ARM	401-3
Crawford, Alexander	ARM	401-3
Crawford, Charles M.	SR	401-73
Crawford, D. B.	SR	401-73
Crawford, E. C.	TVG	401-187
Crawford, Geo. B.	USV	401-226
Crawford, H. C.	TVG	401-187
Crawford, J. B.	TVG	401-187
Crawford, J. D.	RR	401-54
Crawford, James L.	TST	401-34

Index to Texas Adjutant General Service Records—All Service Branches

Name	Branch	Record
Crawford, James W.	USV	401-226
Crawford, John	TVG	401-187
Crawford, John A.	ARM	401-3
Crawford, John W.	USV	401-226
Crawford, Joseph D.	RRR	401-114
Crawford, Pete	SR	401-73
Crawford, R. C.	FB	401-148
Crawford, Sam	FB	401-148
Crawford, Tobe	RRR	401-114
Crawford, W. H.	TVG	401-187
Crawford, W. J.	SR	401-73
Crawford, William	NAV	401-15
Crawford, William H.	TST	401-34
Crawford, William Lockhart	RRR	401-114
Crawleigh, A. F.	USV	401-226
Crawson, A. W.	FB	401-148
Creary, E.	SP	401-43
Creecy, D. C.	NAV	401-15
Creecy, Joseph Rice	NAV	401-15
Creekmore, S. K.	FB	401-148
Creel, Grady	SR	401-73
Creel, J. A.	FB	401-148
Creemer, Jeff	SR	401-73
Creery, James A	NAV	401-15
Creighton, Clyde H.	SR	401-73
Creighton, William	NAV	401-15
Cremer, Joseph G.	USV	401-226
Cremor, Cornelius	NAV	401-15
Crenshaw, A. F.	TVG	401-187
Crenshaw, Acy B.	MV	401-28
Crenshaw, Hugh C.	USV	401-226
Crenshaw, Jerry G.	USV	401-226
Cress, W. D.	TST	401-34
Crews, J. F.	FB	401-148
Crews, T. W.	SR	401-73
Crews, Thomas C.	FF	401-133
Crim, J. Malcolm	SR	401-73
Crim, L. N.	SR	401-73
Cringle, Thos.	ARM	401-3
Crisman, J. H.	TVG	401-187
Crisp, Downing H.	NAV	401-15
Crisp, John W.	USV	401-226
Crisp, M. S.	TVG	401-187
Crist, H.	FB	401-148
Criswell, Lewis	TVG	401-188
Crittenden, Dennis L.	SR	401-73
Crittenden, F. C.	RR	401-54
Crittenden, W. R.	LR	401-127
Crixell, Louis M.	SR	401-73
Crockett, C. A.	TVG	401-188
Crockett, George B.	USV	401-226
Crockett, J. E.	RR	401-54
Crockett, J. E.	SR	401-73
Crockett, James J.	USV	401-226
Crockett, Quinn M.	USV	401-226
Crockett, W. M.	USV	401-226
Croft, Ewell Lee	SR	401-73
Croittendon, W. R.	SR	401-73
Croker, Raphael	NAV	401-15
Cromeans, Jackson	TST	401-34
Cromeans, Thomas	TST	401-34
Cromwell, George L.	FF	401-133
Cromwell, R.	FB	401-148
Cronan, Thomas Winter	USV	401-226
Cronin, P. H.	TVG	401-188
Cronin, Phillip	TST	401-34
Croom, J. R.	TVG	401-188
Cropper, Elisha G.	ARM	401-3
Cropper, John	TVG	401-188
Crosbee, John A.	ARM	401-3
Crosby, E. H.	SR	401-73
Crosby, Edmand F.	USV	401-226
Crosby, Edmund P.	NAV	401-15
Crosby, John	TVG	401-188
Crosby, W. S.	SP	401-43
Crosland, D. E.	TST	401-34
Cross, Antonio	TST	401-34
Cross, C. S.	USV	401-226
Cross, G. D.	FB	401-148
Cross, H. D.	RR	401-54
Cross, H. D.	RR	401-54
Cross, Harry	SR	401-74
Cross, Haywood	SP	401-43
Cross, Joe J.	LR	401-127
Cross, Joe J.	SR	401-74
Cross, L. B.	TVG	401-188
Cross, R. A.	SR	401-74
Cross, W. M.	TVG	401-188
Cross, W. P.	SR	401-74
Crossett, J. E.	TVG	401-188
Crossman, A.	NAV	401-15
Crosson, John	RR	401-54
Crosson, John	SR	401-74
Crosson, Thomas C.	SR	401-74
Crotty, John	USV	401-226
Crow, Emmett M.	RR	401-54
Crow, EzrA	SR	401-74
Crow, J. D.	SR	401-74
Crow, John Furman	RR	401-54
Crow, W. S.	SR	401-74
Crow, William P.	USV	401-226
Crowan, James	ARM	401-3
Crowder, J. A.	SP	401-43
Crowder, Jim	SR	401-74
Crowder, Ray F.	SR	401-74
Crowder, T. S.	FB	401-148
Crowel, John	ARM	401-3
Crowell, D. C.	FB	401-148
Crowell, J. C.	USV	401-226
Crown, John F.	RRR	401-114
Crowson, T. J.	SP	401-43
Crowthers, G. W.	FB	401-148

Index to Texas Adjutant General Service Records—All Service Branches

Name	Branch	Record
Croxton, A. L.	TVG	401-188
Crum, Geo. L.	TVG	401-188
Crump, E. H.	MV	401-28
Crump, Edd	TVG	401-188
Crump, Jno. S.	MV	401-28
Crump, S. B.	FB	401-148
Crump, W. D.	TVG	401-188
Crumpler, Henry	SR	401-74
Crumpton, C. B.	RRR	401-114
Crunch, W. C.	TVG	401-188
Crunk, Chester	SR	401-74
Crunk, W. B.	SR	401-74
Crutcher, Sam H.	TVG	401-188
Crutcher, T. E.	USV	401-226
Crutchfield, D. M.	FB	401-148
Crutchfield, R.	FB	401-148
Cubine, William E.	TVG	401-188
Cubley, K. A.	USV	401-226
Cudd, David J.	TST	401-34
Cude, Asa W.	USV	401-226
Cude, W. H.	RRR	401-114
Cuellar, Francisco	SP	401-43
Cuellar, LenA	FB	401-148
Cuenod, A. H.	TVG	401-188
Culberson, J. Samuel	MM	401-32
Culbson, S. J.	TVG	401-188
Cule, David Miles	ARM	401-3
Cullen, Clement L.	RRR	401-114
Cullen, G. W.	TVG	401-188
Cullen, J. R.	TVG	401-188
Cullen, R. F.	TVG	401-188
Cullinan, J.	TVG	401-188
Cullinan, Michael P.	SR	401-74
Cullman, James	ARM	401-3
Culp, Fielding R.	NAV	401-15
Culp, G. C.	RRR	401-114
Culp, George C.	RR	401-54
Culp, William C.	SR	401-74
Culpeper, H.	TVG	401-188
Culpepper, Cornelius V.	SR	401-74
Culpepper, Dan	TVG	401-188
Culpepper, F. M.	USV	401-226
Culpepper, S.	FB	401-148
Culwell, A. L.	SR	401-74
Culwell, J. C.	FB	401-148
Culwell, J. J.	SR	401-74
Culwell, J. W.	TVG	401-188
Culworth, Robt. H.	SR	401-74
Cumby, William	TVG	401-188
Cummings, A. P.	RR	401-54
Cummings, C. N.	SR	401-74
Cummings, Cyrus	NAV	401-15
Cummings, L. S.	FB	401-148
Cummings, Royal E.	TVG	401-188
Cummings, S. M.	FB	401-148
Cummings, S. T.	TVG	401-188
Cummins, Robert Marcus	RRR	401-114
Cuney, P. M.	SP	401-43
Cunliffe, Paul	TVG	401-188
Cunningham, Aaron W.	RR	401-54
Cunningham, Alfred Boyd	RRR	401-114
Cunningham, D. H.	SR	401-74
Cunningham, David H.	TST	401-34
Cunningham, Edward H., Dr.	SR	401-74
Cunningham, F. M.	TST	401-34
Cunningham, Floyd F.	USV	401-226
Cunningham, Geo. S.	USV	401-226
Cunningham, H. A.	USV	401-226
Cunningham, H. H.	SR	401-74
Cunningham, I. R.	RR	401-54
Cunningham, J. F.	SR	401-74
Cunningham, James	NAV	401-15
Cunningham, James	FB	401-148
Cunningham, K. F.	RR	401-54
Cunningham, Kin F.	USV	401-226
Cunningham, L. C.	USV	401-226
Cunningham, Melville	USV	401-226
Cunningham, P. A.	SR	401-74
Cunningham, Richard T.	TST	401-34
Cunningham, Robert L.	TVG	401-188
Cunningham, Robt. R.	TVG	401-188
Cunningham, Solomon M.	TVG	401-188
Cunningham, T. B.	SR	401-74
Cunningham, T. M.	LR	401-127
Cunningham, T. M.	SR	401-74
Cunningham, W.	SR	401-74
Cunningham, W. J.	SR	401-74
Cunningham, W. P.	RR	401-54
Cunningham, William	ARM	401-3
Cunningham, William S.	USV	401-226
Cupp, John D.	FB	401-148
Cupples, C. T.	RR	401-54
Curd, Creed P.	SR	401-74
Cureton, Calvin M.	USV	401-226
Cureton, J. J.	TST	401-34
Curham, Wilson R.	TVG	401-188
Curlee, James B.	TVG	401-188
Curneal, Patrick T.	ARM	401-3
Curnutt, Lon	RRR	401-114
Curnutte, Robert H.	SR	401-74
Curran, Patrick	TST	401-34
Curran, William	SP	401-43
Currie, H. C.	FB	401-148
Curry, Benjamin F.	USV	401-226
Curry, C. B.	RR	401-54
Curry, J. L.	FB	401-148
Curry, John	FB	401-148
Curry, N. A.	FB	401-149
Curry, P. W.	TVG	401-188
Curry, SaM	NAV	401-15
Curry, Thomas	NAV	401-15
Curry, W. A.	FB	401-149

Index to Texas Adjutant General Service Records—All Service Branches

Name	Branch	Record
Curtin, James	ARM	401-3
Curtis, Charles C.	TVG	401-188
Curtis, F. H.	SR	401-74
Curtis, J. O.	TVG	401-188
Curtis, J. R.	SR	401-74
Curtis, J. S.	TVG	401-188
Curtis, James	ARM	401-3
Curtis, Leno V.	TST	401-34
Curtis, Nathaniel	NAV	401-15
Curtis, Thos. B.	USV	401-227
Curtright, Nat S.	SR	401-74
Cusack, Francis	SP	401-43
Cushing, A. C.	TVG	401-188
Cushing, E. B.	TVG	401-188
Cushman, Charles A.	NAV	401-15
Cushney, W. H.	FF	401-133
Custard, Walter	FF	401-133
Custer, Ed	RR	401-54
Custer, Ed	SR	401-74
Cutbirth, G. C.	RRR	401-114
Cuthbertson, Robt.	USV	401-227
Cutler, Clark	TVG	401-188
Cutler, Thomas	NAV	401-15
Cutter, John B.	USV	401-227
Dabbs, Charles G.	TVG	401-188
Dabgier, John	NAV	401-15
Dabney, Benjamin H.	USV	401-227
Dabney, Charles	ARM	401-3
Dabney, Guy	SR	401-74
Dabney, John	ARM	401-3
Dacamara, H.	TVG	401-188
Dackus, Henry	NAV	401-15
Daffan, L. A.	TVG	401-188
Daffin, E. J.	TVG	401-188
Daggett, C. B.	USV	401-227
Daggett, Lorenzo D.	USV	401-227
Dagley, F. H.	FB	401-149
Dagnal, J. D.	TVG	401-188
Dahlberg, Gus	USV	401-227
Dahlesh, Edward A.	USV	401-227
Dahlin, Chas.	TVG	401-188
Dailey, Jno. P.	USV	401-227
Dailey, John	NAV	401-15
Dailey, R. E.	SR	401-74
Daily, Michael	ARM	401-3
Daily, William	ARM	401-3
Dake, Lewis R.	NAV	401-15
Dake, Louis W.	NAV	401-15
Dale, Elijah V.	ARM	401-3
Dale, George	USV	401-227
Dale, M. K.	TVG	401-188
Dale, Samuel W.	USV	401-227
Daley, Harry A.	SR	401-74
Daley, Watson	TVG	401-188
Dalkowitz, Morris	SR	401-74
Dallmeyer, W.	TVG	401-188
Dalrymple, William C.	MM	401-32
Dalrymple, William C.	MV	401-28
Dalrymple, William T.	TVG	401-188
Dalton, Dennis	ARM	401-3
Dalton, J. W.	TVG	401-188
Dalton, Jeremiah M.	USV	401-227
Dalton, John	ARM	401-3
Dalton, John Edward	RRR	401-114
Dalton, O. B.	FF	401-133
Dalton, William I.	USV	401-227
Daly, Cornelius	ARM	401-3
Daly, J. E.	TVG	401-188
Dalzell, George A.	FB	401-149
Damon, B. F.	TVG	401-188
Damon, H. F.	FB	401-149
Damon, H. G.	FB	401-149
Damon, J. M.	TVG	401-188
Damon, M. A.	SP	401-43
Dampier, O. M.	FB	401-149
Dana, Nelson	FB	401-149
Dance, R.	FB	401-149
Dandall, Frank	USV	401-227
Dane, W. B.	TVG	401-188
Danforth, Tom	USV	401-227
Daniel, Charlie H.	TVG	401-188
Daniel, Edwin A.	USV	401-227
Daniel, Ernest N.	TVG	401-188
Daniel, Frank A.	USV	401-227
Daniel, J. H.	FB	401-149
Daniel, J. J.	FB	401-149
Daniel, J. P.	FB	401-149
Daniel, Travis V.	SR	401-74
Daniel, W. S.	TVG	401-188
Daniels, David F.	RR	401-54
Daniels, Harry	USV	401-227
Daniels, John H.	RRR	401-114
Daniels, M. R.	FB	401-149
Daniels, Marcellus	FB	401-149
Dann, J. G.	NAV	401-15
Dannel, Harvey H.	RRR	401-114
Dannelley, John L.	SR	401-74
Dannelley, W. A.	SR	401-74
Danner, Will	TVG	401-188
Darby, Henry R.	TVG	401-188
Darby, Isaac	TVG	401-188
Darby, J. P.	SR	401-74
Darby, J. S.	RR	401-54
Darcy, Samuel I.	RR	401-54
Darden, N. M.	USV	401-227
Darden, Ross	USV	401-227
Dare, James D.	TVG	401-188
Darlington, Claude	RR	401-54
Darnaby, L. L.	SR	401-74
Darnell, A. H.	TVG	401-188
Darnell, Mercer Claude	RRR	401-114
Darnell, William	FB	401-149

Index to Texas Adjutant General Service Records—All Service Branches

Name	Branch	Page
Darsey, R. C.	FB	401-149
Darst, E. H.	TVG	401-188
Dart, Richard	TVG	401-188
Darwin, R. E.	RRR	401-114
Dashiell, Geo. R.	TVG	401-188
Dashiell, Geo. R.	USV	401-227
Dashiell, J. Y.	TST	401-34
Dashiell, Walter R.	USV	401-227
Daugherty, Bryan	USV	401-227
Daugherty, Chas.	TVG	401-188
Daugherty, D. D.	TVG	401-188
Daugherty, Edward	FB	401-149
Daugherty, J. M.	TVG	401-188
Daugherty, Jack H.	USV	401-227
Daugherty, John R.	MV	401-28
Daugherty, Joseph R.	TVG	401-188
Daugherty, W. H.	TVG	401-188
Daugherty, William	RRR	401-114
Daugherty, William F.	USV	401-227
Daugherty, William H.	USV	401-227
Daughny, Andrew J.	TST	401-34
Daughtre, C. W.	TVG	401-188
Daum, Adam	TVG	401-188
Dauphin, John Thomas	RRR	401-114
Dauphin, W. D.	RRR	401-114
Dausin, William	USV	401-227
Davenport, A. H. S.	FB	401-149
Davenport, E. M.	RR	401-54
Davenport, F. R.	SR	401-74
Davenport, Joe E.	SR	401-74
Davenport, John M.	MV	401-28
Davenport, Leslie	RRR	401-114
Davenport, Richard W.	TVG	401-188
Davenport, Thorn E.	MV	401-28
Davey, M. A.	TVG	401-188
David, Davis	SR	401-74
David, Eugene W.	SR	401-74
David, Lewis A.	RRR	401-114
David, Loyd A.	RR	401-54
David, W. C.	FB	401-149
Davidson, C. E.	USV	401-227
Davidson, Hugh	FF	401-133
Davidson, Hugh	SP	401-43
Davidson, Isaaiah	ARM	401-3
Davidson, J. R.	TVG	401-188
Davidson, James	SP	401-43
Davidson, Louis S.	SR	401-74
Davidson, O. E.	SR	401-74
Davidson, Peter	ARM	401-3
Davidson, Richard S.	USV	401-227
Davidson, Thomas J.	RR	401-54
Davidson, Thomas R.	SR	401-74
Davies, John	NAV	401-15
Davies, Luther	LR	401-128
Davis, A. G.	USV	401-227
Davis, A. H.	RR	401-54
Davis, A. T.	TVG	401-188
Davis, Albert	MV	401-28
Davis, Alexander	USV	401-227
Davis, Alexander B.	MV	401-28
Davis, Andrew	NAV	401-15
Davis, Augustus	ARM	401-3
Davis, B.	FB	401-149
Davis, Ben Joe	TVG	401-188
Davis, Ben M.	FB	401-149
Davis, Britton	SR	401-74
Davis, Burnham	NAV	401-15
Davis, C. B.	TVG	401-188
Davis, C. M.	RRR	401-114
Davis, C. M.	SR	401-74
Davis, CaleB	NAV	401-15
Davis, Charles	NAV	401-15
Davis, Charles	NAV	401-15
Davis, Charles	SR	401-74
Davis, Charles	TVG	401-188
Davis, Charles	USV	401-227
Davis, Charles A.	TVG	401-188
Davis, Charles Albert	USV	401-227
Davis, Charles N.	RR	401-54
Davis, Chas. E.	TVG	401-188
Davis, David	NAV	401-15
Davis, David	ARM	401-3
Davis, Deck	TVG	401-188
Davis, Deck	USV	401-227
Davis, E. F.	SR	401-74
Davis, E. F.	LR	401-128
Davis, E. T.	SR	401-74
Davis, Ernest	TVG	401-188
Davis, F. L.	SR	401-74
Davis, G. C.	SR	401-74
Davis, G. W.	ARM	401-3
Davis, George	FF	401-133
Davis, George	SP	401-43
Davis, George K.	SR	401-74
Davis, George K.	USV	401-227
Davis, George W.	USV	401-227
Davis, Gould	RR	401-54
Davis, Gould	SR	401-74
Davis, H. J.	TST	401-34
Davis, Henry	NAV	401-15
Davis, Henry C.	ARM	401-3
Davis, Herbert J.	TVG	401-188
Davis, Hillsman	SR	401-74
Davis, Howard E.	SR	401-74
Davis, Ira D.	TVG	401-188
Davis, J. A.	RRR	401-114
Davis, J. B.	SR	401-74
Davis, J. C.	RR	401-54
Davis, J. F.	FB	401-149
Davis, J. Frank	SR	401-74
Davis, J. G.	FB	401-149
Davis, J. H.	FB	401-149

Index to Texas Adjutant General Service Records—All Service Branches

Name	Branch	Page
Davis, J. K.	USV	401-227
Davis, J. L.	FB	401-149
Davis, J. L.	FB	401-149
Davis, J. L.	FB	401-149
Davis, J. M.	SR	401-74
Davis, J. N.	FB	401-149
Davis, J. R.	SR	401-74
Davis, J. S.	FB	401-149
Davis, J. W.	USV	401-227
Davis, Jack	SR	401-74
Davis, James	TST	401-34
Davis, James	ARM	401-3
Davis, James	SP	401-43
Davis, James E.	SR	401-74
Davis, James Lee	TVG	401-188
Davis, Jeferson	TST	401-34
Davis, Joe	TVG	401-188
Davis, Joe P.	TVG	401-188
Davis, John	NAV	401-15
Davis, John	ARM	401-3
Davis, John	FF	401-133
Davis, John A.	NAV	401-15
Davis, John C.	TVG	401-188
Davis, John F.	USV	401-227
Davis, John H.	RR	401-54
Davis, John H., Sr.	SR	401-74
Davis, John H., Sr.	LR	401-128
Davis, John P.	ARM	401-3
Davis, John W.	TVG	401-188
Davis, Joseph H.	USV	401-227
Davis, Joseph J.	TST	401-34
Davis, L.	RR	401-54
Davis, L.	FB	401-149
Davis, L. E.	SR	401-74
Davis, L. L.	TVG	401-188
Davis, Lawrence	SR	401-74
Davis, Leo B.	TST	401-34
Davis, Leslie C.	USV	401-227
Davis, Levi	RR	401-54
Davis, Lloyd	TVG	401-188
Davis, Louis E.	TVG	401-189
Davis, Luther	SR	401-74
Davis, M.	FB	401-149
Davis, M. B.	FB	401-149
Davis, M. D.	FB	401-149
Davis, M. L.	SR	401-74
Davis, Mack	USV	401-227
Davis, Martin	RRR	401-114
Davis, Martin B.	TVG	401-189
Davis, O. B.	SR	401-74
Davis, O. T.	SR	401-74
Davis, Oscar	NAV	401-15
Davis, Otis	TVG	401-189
Davis, Price B.	USV	401-227
Davis, R. E.	TVG	401-189
Davis, R. I.	USV	401-227
Davis, R. J.	FB	401-149
Davis, R. L.	SP	401-43
Davis, R. S.	FB	401-149
Davis, R. W.	TST	401-34
Davis, Reuben	RRR	401-114
Davis, Robert	MV	401-29
Davis, Robert O.	RRR	401-114
Davis, S. G.	USV	401-227
Davis, S. W.	SP	401-43
Davis, S. W.	SR	401-74
Davis, Sam J.	USV	401-227
Davis, Stanley G.	SR	401-74
Davis, T. J.	SP	401-43
Davis, Theodore	USV	401-227
Davis, Thos. H.	TVG	401-189
Davis, Thos. H.	USV	401-227
Davis, Thos. J.	FB	401-149
Davis, Tom	TVG	401-189
Davis, Uel L.	USV	401-227
Davis, W. A.	FB	401-149
Davis, W. B.	RR	401-54
Davis, W. B.	SR	401-74
Davis, W. E.	TVG	401-189
Davis, W. L.	TVG	401-189
Davis, W. O.	RR	401-54
Davis, W. O.	SR	401-74
Davis, W. P.	FB	401-149
Davis, W. W.	SP	401-43
Davis, Wayne C., Jr.	SR	401-74
Davis, Will W.	RR	401-54
Davis, William	TST	401-34
Davis, William	ARM	401-3
Davis, William	SR	401-74
Davis, William D.	SR	401-74
Davis, William D.	USV	401-227
Davis, William H.	TVG	401-189
Davis, William H.	USV	401-227
Davis, William P., Jr.	TVG	401-189
Davis, William T.	FF	401-133
Davis, William W.	TVG	401-189
Davis, Willie	TVG	401-189
Davis, Willie G.	TVG	401-189
Davis, Wooten	SR	401-74
Davison, Claude	USV	401-227
Davisson, C. W.	TVG	401-189
Davoren, Ed. J.	TVG	401-189
Davy, John	ARM	401-3
Daws, A. C.	SR	401-74
Daws, A. C.	LR	401-128
Dawson, C. M.	TVG	401-189
Dawson, Ira J.	TVG	401-189
Dawson, J. C.	SR	401-74
Dawson, J. C.	LR	401-128
Dawson, Joseph E.	USV	401-227
Dawson, R. D.	SR	401-74
Dawson, Robert	FB	401-149

Index to Texas Adjutant General Service Records—All Service Branches

Name	Branch	Record
Day, A. R.	SR	401-74
Day, E. H.	FB	401-149
Day, Earl E.	SR	401-74
Day, Elisha L., Jr.	TVG	401-189
Day, Frank E.	LR	401-128
Day, Frank E.	SR	401-74
Day, H. M.	FB	401-149
Day, Henry S.	ARM	401-4
Day, James P.	FB	401-149
Day, Jesse L.	TVG	401-189
Day, John	NAV	401-15
Day, John	ARM	401-4
Day, John T.	SR	401-74
Day, Kenny S.	ARM	401-4
Day, W. W.	TVG	401-189
De La Garza, Miguel	LR	401-128
De La Garza, Miguel	SR	401-75
De Mullos, Carlos	RR	401-54
Deadmore, John C.	ARM	401-4
Deale, Thomas	NAV	401-16
Dean, C.	FB	401-149
Dean, Chas. B.	USV	401-227
Dean, D.	RRR	401-115
Dean, E. R.	TVG	401-189
Dean, Ed	RRR	401-115
Dean, George W.	USV	401-227
Dean, John M.	SR	401-74
Dean, Jno. M.	LR	401-128
Dean, William	ARM	401-4
Dean, William F.	TVG	401-189
Deans, Lee Roy	TVG	401-189
Dear, Arthur William	TVG	401-189
Dear, Arthur William	USV	401-227
Dear, Dan	SR	401-74
Dearborn, Monroe H.	NAV	401-16
Dearing, Ellsworth E.	USV	401-227
Dearing, James C.	NAV	401-16
Dearinger, S.	TVG	401-189
DeArman, J. T.	TVG	401-189
Deason, R. F.	USV	401-227
Deason, Robert	USV	401-227
Deaton, A. C.	FB	401-149
Deaton, E. S.	TVG	401-189
Deaton, Geo. W.	TVG	401-189
Deaton, William F.	USV	401-227
Deats, Arnold E.	TVG	401-189
Deats, Arnold E.	USV	401-227
Deats, F. G.	TVG	401-189
Deaver, Joseph J.	FB	401-149
DeBard, J. D.	TVG	401-189
Debogory, Eugene, Col.	SR	401-74
Debolt, E. B.	SR	401-74
DeBona, Joe	TVG	401-189
Debord, John H.	RR	401-54
Debrant, George	ARM	401-4
DeChanlonger, Auguste	ARM	401-4
Dechman, E. S.	TVG	401-189
Decker, Arnold H.	SR	401-75
Decker, Benjamin	ARM	401-4
Decker, Charles	FF	401-133
Decker, Charles M.	SR	401-75
Decker, Davis E.	TVG	401-189
Decker, Joseph Lawrence	RRR	401-115
Decker, Lafayette	USV	401-227
Deckman, Al	SR	401-75
DeCorchva, S. D.	TVG	401-189
Dederick, Peter	NAV	401-16
Dee, Ebb	FB	401-149
Deecan, W. B.	LR	401-128
Deel, R. K.	FB	401-149
Deel, T. T.	FB	401-149
Deel, Tip	FB	401-149
Deen, A. B.	TVG	401-189
Deen, Irwin J.	TVG	401-189
Deer, John A.	USV	401-227
Dees, M. A.	SR	401-75
Dees, M. A.	LR	401-128
Dees, Robert B.	USV	401-227
Deetz, Charles	TVG	401-189
Deffenbough, Frank	TVG	401-189
Degaish, Bady	SR	401-75
Degen, Louis W.	USV	401-227
DeGermer, Albert	ARM	401-4
Deggs, C. L.	FB	401-149
Deggs, T. W.	FB	401-149
Degraftenreid, J. T.	SR	401-75
DeGrazier, J. L.	TVG	401-189
Degrazier, John L.	SR	401-75
DeGuire, A. W., Rev.	SR	401-75
DeHay, Lee R.	TVG	401-189
Dehnke, Chas. A.	FB	401-149
Deibert, Glen Townsend	SR	401-75
Deison, James L.	TVG	401-189
DeJarnette, Frank W.	FB	401-149
DeJarnette, Mumford	FB	401-149
DeJarnette, N. B.	FB	401-149
DeLacy, N. L.	TVG	401-189
DeLafosse, Roy E.	SR	401-75
Delamater, Harris Howard	TVG	401-189
Delamere, Isaac	ARM	401-4
DeLamoriniere, J. C.	TVG	401-189
DeLane, Alfred	USV	401-227
DeLaney, Anderson	FB	401-149
Delaney, Henry	MM	401-32
DeLaney, Pleasant K.	FB	401-149
Delaney, W.	TVG	401-189
Delaney, W. M.	TVG	401-189
Delany, H. E.	FB	401-149
DeLatimer, Walter	TVG	401-189
Delemeter, John	FF	401-133
DeLesderniers, Stafford G.	TVG	401-189
Delfraisse, L. E.	FB	401-149

Index to Texas Adjutant General Service Records—All Service Branches

Name	Branch	Record
Delfs, Jno. H.	TVG	401-189
Delgado, Frederick	TVG	401-189
Delgado, Marcello	SP	401-43
Delgado, Martin	ARM	401-4
Delgado, VictoR	SP	401-43
Delhomme, L. E.	TVG	401-189
Delling, M. G.	RR	401-54
Delos Santos, Sidney	SR	401-75
Demoney, Otis A.	USV	401-227
Demontel, Charles	TST	401-34
Denalsano, W. L.	SR	401-75
DeNalsano, Walt Leon	TVG	401-189
Denalsone, W. L.	RR	401-54
Denbo, Bruce E.	TVG	401-189
Denbo, John W.	USV	401-227
Dendy, James W.	TVG	401-189
Denen, Thos.	TVG	401-189
Denham, Arthur H.	USV	401-227
Denison, Frank, Jr.	RR	401-54
Denison, Frank, Jr.	SR	401-75
Denison, James B.	USV	401-227
Denison, John	ARM	401-4
Denman, C. C.	RR	401-54
Denman, F. G.	TVG	401-189
Denman, Henry	USV	401-227
Denman, J. H.	TVG	401-189
Denman, L. L.	FB	401-149
Denman, Thos. Lamar	TVG	401-189
Denning, W. J.	TVG	401-189
Dennis, J. J.	TST	401-34
Dennis, James	FB	401-149
Dennis, Lewis N.	USV	401-227
Dennis, Robert E.	USV	401-227
Dennis, W. J.	TVG	401-189
Dennis, William L.	USV	401-227
Denny, B. A.	TVG	401-189
Denny, D. B.	SR	401-75
Denny, J. J.	SR	401-75
Denny, J. R.	SR	401-75
Denny, Thomas	ARM	401-4
Denny, X. A.	TVG	401-189
Dension, Frank	TVG	401-189
Denson, B. F.	SR	401-75
Denson, B. H.	USV	401-227
Denson, Benjamin H.	TVG	401-189
Denson, H. H.	SR	401-75
Denson, Harvey	TST	401-34
Denson, Harvey	MV	401-29
Denson, J. B.	USV	401-227
Denson, L. M.	SR	401-75
Denson, Rush	SR	401-75
Dent, Geo. L.	TVG	401-189
Denton, Ashley F.	USV	401-227
Denton, J. M.	SR	401-75
Denton, J. M.	FB	401-149
Denton, Jacob	ARM	401-4
Denton, John Whitney	CSA	401-39
Derden, J. B.	SR	401-75
Derden, William I.	USV	401-227
Dereil, John	NAV	401-16
Derrett, Dunn	USV	401-227
Derrick, George	CSA	401-39
Derrick, Thomas	TVG	401-189
Derrick, William T.	FB	401-149
Derrman, L. L.	FB	401-149
Derrough, Harry H.	USV	401-227
Derryberry, N. C.	RR	401-54
Derson, W. G.	TVG	401-189
Derwin, Patrick	ARM	401-4
Desbignes, Joseph	ARM	401-4
DeSeil, John	NAV	401-16
Deshozo, E. C.	TVG	401-189
Desmoineaux, Charles	ARM	401-4
Desmond, Edward	SP	401-43
Desmond, Patrick W.	USV	401-227
Despain, Duncan L.	SR	401-75
Detemple, T. H.	RRR	401-115
Deterz, H.	NAV	401-16
Devall, Sam S., Capt.	SR	401-75
Devenger, Henry F.	RR	401-54
Devens, Fry	USV	401-227
Dever, Raymond A.	USV	401-227
Deverine, George D.	ARM	401-4
Devinney, Thomas A.	TST	401-34
Dewalt, L. C.	SR	401-75
Dewalt, T. B.	SR	401-75
Deware, C. A.	SR	401-75
Dewees, Joseph Wilson	MM	401-32
DeWeese, Oscar S.	USV	401-227
Dewitt, Howard C.	RRR	401-115
Dewitt, Howard C.	TVG	401-189
Dewitt, J. R.	TVG	401-189
Dewoody, T. V.	FB	401-149
Dewssen, Alexander	TVG	401-189
Dexter, A. N.	FB	401-149
Dexter, John F.	SR	401-75
DeZeal, John	NAV	401-16
Dial, Jack	RR	401-54
Dial, Jack	SR	401-75
Dial, James L.	RR	401-54
Dial, James L.	RRR	401-115
Dial, William	ARM	401-4
Dial, William Angelo	RR	401-54
Dial, William Angelo	RRR	401-115
Dial, William Angelo	SR	401-75
Diamond, ClifF	SR	401-75
Diamond, John	ARM	401-4
Dibrell, C. M.	FB	401-149
Dibrell, J. W.	USV	401-227
Dibrell, James W.	USV	401-227
Dibrell, John L.	RR	401-54
Dickard, Luke	SR	401-75

Index to Texas Adjutant General Service Records—All Service Branches

Name	Branch	Record
Dicken, Geo.	USV	401-227
Dicken, Robert S.	USV	401-227
Dickens, Howard	SR	401-75
Dickens, Thomas E.	MV	401-29
Dickens, William M.	SR	401-75
Dickenson, J. L.	SR	401-75
Dickenson, O. W.	TVG	401-189
Dickerson, Floyd	SR	401-75
Dickerson, George W.	SR	401-75
Dickerson, Oscar W.	SR	401-75
Dickerson, William A.	TVG	401-189
Dickeson, D. A.	SR	401-75
Dickey, Clate	TVG	401-189
Dickey, John W.	CSA	401-39
Dickey, Walter	TVG	401-189
Dickie, James T.	USV	401-227
Dickinson, Alonzo	CSA	401-39
Dickinson, Charles H.	FB	401-149
Dickinson, John	NAV	401-16
Dickinson, Morgan W.	TVG	401-189
Dickson, A. E.	TVG	401-189
Dickson, C. C.	USV	401-227
Dickson, Dan	TVG	401-189
Dickson, David C.	TVG	401-189
Dickson, Grover C.	TVG	401-189
Dickson, H. A.	SR	401-75
Dickson, J. J.	TVG	401-189
Dickson, John	TST	401-34
Dickson, John	FF	401-133
Dickson, R. A.	TVG	401-189
Dickson, R. H.	TST	401-34
Dickson, Richard L.	TVG	401-189
Dickson, Robert W.	TVG	401-189
Dickson, Robert W.	USV	401-227
Dickson, Samuel W.	USV	401-227
Dickson, William	ARM	401-4
Dickson, William O.	TVG	401-189
Diehl, Anton	USV	401-227
Diehl, Joseph W.	USV	401-227
Dielon, James C.	USV	401-227
Diemer, Brick P.	USV	401-228
Diener, Chas. F.	USV	401-228
Dies, Jack	USV	401-228
Dies, Martin	USV	401-228
Dieter, John Geo.	USV	401-228
Dietz, Jephthah W.	USV	401-228
Dietz, Joe W.	USV	401-228
Digges, J. D.	SR	401-75
Digges, John D.	RRR	401-115
Diggins, Cornelius	ARM	401-4
Digman, D. T. W.	RR	401-54
Dignowity, A. M.	SP	401-43
Dikes, James L.	SR	401-75
Dikes, Mark W.	ARM	401-4
Dilbeck, John L.	USV	401-228
Dill, H. L.	RRR	401-115
Dill, H. L.	SR	401-75
Dillaha, Tom L.	TVG	401-189
Dillard, A.	FB	401-150
Dillard, E. P.	RR	401-54
Dillard, J. L.	TVG	401-189
Dillard, Pinckney D.	TST	401-34
Dillard, Terry Moorman	RRR	401-115
Dillard, William E.	USV	401-228
Dilliard, I. L.	TVG	401-189
Dillo, John	FB	401-150
Dillon, A. C.	SP	401-43
Dillon, Geo. H.	USV	401-228
Dillon, John Martin	TVG	401-189
Dillon, Pat H.	SR	401-75
Dillon, Thomas H.	TVG	401-189
Diltz, John	USV	401-228
Dilworth, J. C.	RR	401-54
Dilworth, J. C.	RRR	401-115
Dilworth, W. P.	USV	401-228
Dimmick, Alvin	ARM	401-4
Dinkins, I. H.	CSA	401-39
Dinwiddie, John	ARM	401-4
Dinwiddie, S. T.	SR	401-75
Dinwiddie, S. T.	LR	401-128
Dippel, William	TVG	401-189
Dirks, Otto L.	RRR	401-115
Dirks, William B.	USV	401-228
Disler [Dissler ?], John	SR	401-75
Dismore, James	NAV	401-16
Dismukes, Thomas	USV	401-228
Ditto, John	FB	401-150
Ditto, John H.	SR	401-75
Dix, Chas. S.	USV	401-228
Dix, Ford	FB	401-150
Dix, Horatio	ARM	401-4
Dix, Wright C.	USV	401-228
Dixon, Henry D.	TVG	401-189
Dixon, J. S.	RRR	401-115
Dixon, James Arthur	TVG	401-189
Dixon, John	USV	401-228
Dixon, Norman K.	SR	401-75
Dixon, Randolph	TVG	401-189
Doak, Curtis M.	TVG	401-189
Doan, Joseph	ARM	401-4
Doane, Alonzo B.	USV	401-228
Doaty, R. E.	FB	401-150
Dobbins, E. E.	TVG	401-189
Dobbins, Paul	TVG	401-189
Dobbins, Roy A.	SR	401-75
Dobbs, G. H.	FB	401-150
Dobbs, N.	USV	401-228
Dobbs, Thomas	ARM	401-4
Dobkins, Alex	TVG	401-189
Doby, L. G.	TVG	401-190
Dodd, Aaron C.	NAV	401-16
Dodd, Curtis	TST	401-34

Index to Texas Adjutant General Service Records—All Service Branches

Name	Branch	Record
Dodd, Edmund C.	USV	401-228
Dodd, J. C.	SR	401-75
Dodd, J. H.	RRR	401-115
Dodd, James	TST	401-34
Dodge, F. J.	FB	401-150
Dodge, Lawrence E.	USV	401-228
Dodson, F. E.	SR	401-75
Dodson, J. D.	TVG	401-190
Dodson, Tim	FB	401-150
Doherty, Anthony O.	TST	401-34
Doherty, B. C.	TVG	401-190
Doherty, John	NAV	401-16
Doherty, Michael	ARM	401-4
Doherty, Patrick	ARM	401-4
Dohl, Valentine	FF	401-133
Dolan, Pat	FB	401-150
Dolan, T. P.	FB	401-150
Dolbin, Reese Conklin	SR	401-75
Dolch, Louis	TST	401-34
Dolf, H. W.	SR	401-75
Dolin, Frank A.	TVG	401-190
Dollahite, J. B.	FB	401-150
Dollahite, J. C.	FF	401-133
Dollarhide, J. R.	FB	401-150
Dollins, C. C.	USV	401-228
Domingo, Lawrence B.	TVG	401-190
Donagan, Thomas	ARM	401-4
Donahoe, Henry	SP	401-43
Donald, Guy D.	TVG	401-190
Donald, Guy D.	USV	401-228
Donald, John A.	TVG	401-190
Donaldson, Amos	ARM	401-4
Donaldson, John L.	SR	401-75
Donaldson, Sam M.	SR	401-75
Donaldson, Suel	RRR	401-115
Donally, Cyrus	NAV	401-16
Donalson, Thos. D.	TVG	401-190
Donavin, Danl	ARM	401-4
Donegan, A. Y.	TVG	401-190
Donegan, J. B.	FB	401-150
Donelley, Ed	FB	401-150
Donley, John C.	NAV	401-16
Donnaly, N.	FB	401-150
Donnell, M. O.	FB	401-150
Donnell, Sylvester Henry	TVG	401-190
Donnell, Tom O.	FB	401-150
Donnelley, Dillon C.	USV	401-228
Donnelly, H. A.	FB	401-150
Donnelly, Leo E.	TVG	401-190
Donnelly, Martin	SP	401-43
Donoghue, Thomas	SP	401-43
Donoho, Marcus B.	USV	401-228
Donoho, Robert	SP	401-43
Donoho, Robert E.	TVG	401-190
Donoho, Robert E.	USV	401-228
Donohoe, Thos. J.	TVG	401-190
Donohoo, Charles	SR	401-75
Donovan, Bartholomew	SP	401-43
Donovan, Henry J.	SP	401-43
Donovan, John J.	FB	401-150
Donovan, Oscar	USV	401-228
Donovan, Timothy K.	MV	401-29
Doolan, James	USV	401-228
Dooley, G. L.	RR	401-54
Dooley, J. H.	RRR	401-115
Dooley, John H.	LR	401-128
Dooley, Jno. H.	SR	401-75
Dooley, Joseph Josephus	RRR	401-115
Dooley, Michael E.	USV	401-228
Dooley, Patrick E.	USV	401-228
Dooley, W. B.	TVG	401-190
Doolin, Barlett	ARM	401-4
Doolittle, G. M.	FB	401-150
Doorly, Michael	NAV	401-16
Dorado, Ramon	FF	401-133
Doran, Felix, Jr.	SR	401-75
Doran, John	ARM	401-4
Doran, Robt. B.	FB	401-150
Doran, T. H.	SP	401-43
Doran, W. R.	FB	401-150
Dorbandt, Virgil A.	SR	401-75
Dore, H. A.	TVG	401-190
Dorey, Fletcher	NAV	401-16
Dorfman, Sam Y.	SR	401-75
Dorman, C. E.	USV	401-228
Dorman, John K.	SP	401-43
Dornblaser, Owen F.	TVG	401-190
Dorrity, J. T.	TVG	401-190
Dorsey, C. W.	RR	401-54
Dorsey, Herman Edward	RRR	401-115
Dorsey, R. C.	FB	401-150
Dortch, Cliff	TVG	401-190
Dotson, Louis	TVG	401-190
Dott, Jack	SR	401-75
Doubt, Daniel	ARM	401-4
Dougerty, Edward F.	TVG	401-190
Dougharty, James	ARM	401-4
Dougherty, George F.	USV	401-228
Dougherty, James	FB	401-150
Dougherty, Marcellus, Jr.	RR	401-54
Dougherty, Marcellus, Jr.	SR	401-75
Dougherty, Patrick	NAV	401-16
Dougherty, S. K.	USV	401-228
Dougherty, S. O.	FF	401-133
Dougherty, Thomas	NAV	401-16
Dougherty, W. S.	FB	401-150
Doughty, A. C.	FB	401-150
Doughty, Frank	TVG	401-190
Douglas, Geo. T.	FB	401-150
Douglas, Henry	ARM	401-4
Douglas, Jack	SR	401-75
Douglas, O. W.	TVG	401-190

Index to Texas Adjutant General Service Records—All Service Branches

Name	Branch	Record
Douglas, W. C.	TVG	401-190
Douglas, Y. E.	FB	401-150
Douglass, E. F.	TVG	401-190
Douglass, Ebb H.	USV	401-228
Douglass, J. H.	TVG	401-190
Douglass, Nathan	SP	401-43
Douglass, R. E.	CSA	401-39
Douglass, V.	RRR	401-115
Douglass, W. B.	TVG	401-190
Douglass, W. C.	TVG	401-190
Douglass, W. W.	USV	401-228
Douglass, Will	TVG	401-190
Douthit, Jules A.	USV	401-228
Dove, Andrew	TST	401-34
Dowd, Louis H.	TVG	401-190
Dowdell, Louis A., Jr.	TVG	401-190
Dowdy, J. F.	RR	401-54
Dowdy, J. F.	SR	401-75
Dowdy, James L.	TVG	401-190
Dowe, James W.	SR	401-75
Dowe, Luke	FB	401-150
Dowe, O. C.	RR	401-54
Dowe, O. C.	SR	401-75
Dowe, O. C.	SR	401-75
Dowe, William	NAV	401-16
Dowell, John	TVG	401-190
Dowell, Maurice H.	TVG	401-190
Dowell, S. G.	TVG	401-190
Dowlen, Cornell H.	TVG	401-190
Dowler, R. B.	TVG	401-190
Dowler, Ralph B.	RRR	401-115
Downes, Orral	NAV	401-16
Downey, Herbert Cecil	RRR	401-115
Downey, John	SP	401-43
Downey, William	NAV	401-16
Downing, S. M.	SR	401-75
Downing, S. M.	LR	401-128
Downing, William W.	TVG	401-190
Downs, J. B.	SR	401-75
Downs, John B.	TVG	401-190
Downs, Sie	TVG	401-190
Downs, W. F.	TVG	401-190
Doxey, T. A.	TVG	401-190
Doyle, Dennis	NAV	401-16
Doyle, Hugh	SP	401-43
Doyle, W. E.	FB	401-150
Doyle, William JacoB	SR	401-75
Doyle, Winchester	ARM	401-4
Dozer, F. A.	ARM	401-4
Dozier, Robt. H.	USV	401-228
Dozier, T. E.	FB	401-150
Draffin, R. L.	TVG	401-190
Drake, C. J.	TVG	401-190
Drake, Henry	NAV	401-16
Drake, James M.	USV	401-228
Drake, John M.	TVG	401-190
Drake, John R.	SR	401-75
Drake, Millard O.	RR	401-54
Drake, N. F.	FB	401-150
Drake, N. S.	MV	401-29
Drake, Ralph L.	USV	401-228
Drake, Sam	SP	401-43
Drake, W. E.	SP	401-43
Drake, W. M. G.	USV	401-228
Drake, William	TVG	401-190
Draper, Asa	SR	401-75
Draper, Clarence E.	USV	401-228
Draper, E. M.	TVG	401-190
Draper, Harvey W.	SR	401-75
Draper, J. C.	SR	401-75
Draper, John	SR	401-75
Draper, John C.	SR	401-75
Draper, W. H.	TVG	401-190
Drawbridge, William	NAV	401-16
Drees, Fred, Rev.	SR	401-75
Drennan, John Elbert	SR	401-75
Drennan, Robert Franklin	TVG	401-190
Drennan, T. L.	TVG	401-190
Drennan, W. H.	USV	401-228
Dresler, John J.	USV	401-228
Drew, Archie	TVG	401-190
Drew, Octavius Clifton, Jr.	TVG	401-190
Drew, Octavius Clifton, Jr.	USV	401-228
Drew, W. M.	FF	401-133
Drewry, S. A.	TVG	401-190
Dreyer, Herbert	TVG	401-190
Drinkard, G. T.	TVG	401-190
Drips, Samuel W.	NAV	401-16
Driscoll, Ed	TVG	401-190
Driskile, W. M.	TVG	401-190
Driskill, E. D.	RR	401-54
Driskill, E. D.	SR	401-75
Driskill, John A.	SR	401-75
Driskill, William Rufus	MV	401-29
Driver, Levi A.	USV	401-228
Droddy, S. A.	SR	401-75
Droddy, S. A.	LR	401-128
Dromgoole, Orin	SR	401-75
Drozd, J. H.	SR	401-75
Druesedon, Karl L.	USV	401-228
Drugan, James	ARM	401-4
Drum, R. A.	TVG	401-190
Drummond, W. J.	TVG	401-190
Drummond, William	FF	401-133
Drury, Ross	TVG	401-190
Dubell, Tom	TVG	401-190
Dubignow, Joseph	NAV	401-16
DuBois, Abraham E.	NAV	401-16
Dubois, ElishA	ARM	401-4
Dubois, Louis	ARM	401-4
Dubose, Ben B.	RR	401-54
Dubose, C. B.	FB	401-150

Index to Texas Adjutant General Service Records—All Service Branches

Name	Branch	Record
Dubose, E. M.	RR	401-54
Dubose, E. M.	SR	401-75
Dubose, Edwin M.	SR	401-75
Dubose, Edwin M.	FB	401-150
Dubose, Friendly	FF	401-133
Dubose, H. G.	FB	401-150
DuBose, James M.	TVG	401-190
Dubose, Matthew E.	SR	401-75
DuChamp, Charles R. V.	USV	401-228
Duchesno, Modesti	ARM	401-4
Duckworth, Edwin	USV	401-228
Duckworth, F. M.	FB	401-150
Duckworth, T. N.	TVG	401-190
Duckworth, Thom. N.	FB	401-150
Dudley, H. L.	USV	401-228
Dudley, John Lee	TST	401-34
Dudley, John Lee	SR	401-75
Dudley, Raymond M.	SR	401-75
Duerler, Louis	FF	401-133
Duerler, Louis	FF	401-133
Duff, Charles A.	USV	401-228
Duff, Lee	TVG	401-190
Duff, R. C.	TVG	401-190
Duff, Will A.	TVG	401-190
Duffan, J.	TVG	401-190
Duffy, John	USV	401-228
Duffy, Marcus M.	FF	401-133
Duffy, Marcus M.	FF	401-133
Duffy, Thomas P.	FB	401-150
Duffy, William	USV	401-228
Dugan, George	RRR	401-115
Dugan, John	RR	401-54
Dugat, Charles W.	ARM	401-4
Dugey, E. G.	TVG	401-190
Duggan, E. R.	SR	401-75
Duggan, E. T.	SR	401-75
Duggan, Edward, Jr.	USV	401-228
Duggan, Randolf Freeman	USV	401-228
Duggan, Randolph Freeman	TVG	401-190
Dugger, Samuel Newton	RRR	401-115
Dugger, W. C., Jr.	TVG	401-190
Duke, E. A.	TVG	401-190
Duke, E. P.	SP	401-43
Duke, R. E.	SR	401-75
Duke, S. A.	USV	401-228
Duke, Wheeler	SR	401-75
Dukes, James Andrews	TST	401-34
Dulany, H. H.	FB	401-150
Dulany, Nelson	TST	401-34
Dulin, William P.	USV	401-228
Dumas, J. D.	RR	401-54
Dumas, Thomas	TVG	401-190
Dumas, Thomas B.	USV	401-228
Dumas, V. J.	USV	401-228
Dumas, Vern	SR	401-75
Dumble, Davey H.	TVG	401-190
Dumble, Davey H.	USV	401-228
Dumble, F. W.	FB	401-150
Dumble, F. W.	TVG	401-190
Dumler, Chas. A.	TVG	401-190
Dunagan, T. M., Jr.	RR	401-54
Dunaway, J. D.	RR	401-54
Dunaway, W. E.	TVG	401-190
Dunaway, William E.	USV	401-228
Dunbar, Luther L.	NAV	401-16
Dunbar, Posey	TVG	401-190
Dunbar, R. A.	USV	401-228
Dunbar, Richard B., Col.	SR	401-75
Dunbar, Sam	SR	401-75
Dunbury, William	ARM	401-4
Duncan, C. D.	SR	401-76
Duncan, G. M.	USV	401-228
Duncan, J.	FB	401-150
Duncan, J. B.	SR	401-76
Duncan, J. B.	LR	401-128
Duncan, J. E.	SR	401-76
Duncan, J. R.	FB	401-150
Duncan, James	NAV	401-16
Duncan, Jno. O.	USV	401-228
Duncan, John W.	USV	401-228
Duncan, Lawrence	RRR	401-115
Duncan, Lee	USV	401-228
Duncan, Presley	USV	401-228
Duncan, Robt. M.	TST	401-34
Duncan, Samuel H.	RR	401-54
Duncan, TurneR	SP	401-43
Duncan, Virgil H.	USV	401-228
Duncan, Virgil M.	SR	401-76
Duncan, W. E.	RR	401-54
Duncan, W. K.	RR	401-54
Duncan, W. T.	SR	401-76
Duncan, W. T.	SR	401-76
Dungan, H. H.	SR	401-76
Dunham, Robt.	TVG	401-190
Dunham, Sylvanus	ARM	401-4
Dunham, W. C.	SR	401-76
Dunkin, Amos S.	MV	401-29
Dunklin, Franc M.	RR	401-54
Dunlap, Forrest	RRR	401-115
Dunlap, Frank B.	USV	401-228
Dunlap, Guy K.	USV	401-228
Dunlap, J. F.	RRR	401-115
Dunlap, M. L.	SR	401-76
Dunlap, Robert C.	USV	401-228
Dunlap, Thomas M.	USV	401-228
Dunlap, W. W.	TVG	401-190
Dunlap, William H.	SP	401-43
Dunlap, William W.	TST	401-34
Dunlavy, William	ARM	401-4
Dunman, J. E.	RR	401-54
Dunman, James E.	RRR	401-115
Dunman, Rex E.	SR	401-76

Index to Texas Adjutant General Service Records—All Service Branches

Name	Branch	Record
Dunman, W. H.	FB	401-150
Dunn, Alonzo B.	USV	401-228
Dunn, C. E.	TVG	401-190
Dunn, Ed	NAV	401-16
Dunn, Edward	ARM	401-4
Dunn, George	SP	401-43
Dunn, George B.	SR	401-76
Dunn, George B.	LR	401-128
Dunn, Glen	SR	401-76
Dunn, Grover Cleveland	SR	401-76
Dunn, J. B.	SR	401-76
Dunn, J. B.	LR	401-128
Dunn, J. C.	RRR	401-115
Dunn, J. F.	FB	401-150
Dunn, Jacob G.	NAV	401-16
Dunn, James	RRR	401-115
Dunn, James P.	FF	401-133
Dunn, John	FF	401-133
Dunn, John A.	MV	401-29
Dunn, John M.	FB	401-150
Dunn, L. E.	SP	401-43
Dunn, Matt	FF	401-133
Dunn, Michael	ARM	401-4
Dunn, Mike	FB	401-150
Dunn, Nicholas	FB	401-150
Dunn, Nicolas	USV	401-228
Dunn, R. F.	TVG	401-190
Dunn, Robert L.	USV	401-228
Dunn, Thomas H.	FB	401-150
Dunn, Tracy B.	TVG	401-190
Dunn, W. B.	FB	401-150
Dunn, William	RR	401-54
Dunn, William S.	TVG	401-190
Dunnam, B. B.	TVG	401-190
Dunnaway, J. D.	RR	401-54
Dunnigan, R. L.	USV	401-228
Dunning, James	ARM	401-4
Dunning, Lewis	ARM	401-4
Dunovin, John	NAV	401-16
Dunton, Alfred K.	ARM	401-4
Dunwoody, Quincy C.	USV	401-228
Dupree, Abe E.	TVG	401-190
Dupree, Daniel B.	MV	401-29
Dupree, Earle	TVG	401-190
Dupree, F. G.	CSA	401-39
Dupriest, C. W.	FB	401-150
Dupriest, M.	FB	401-150
Dupuy, Thomas M.	USV	401-228
Duque, Blas	FF	401-133
Duran, Asceano	FB	401-150
Duran, Joe E.	RRR	401-115
Duran, Santos	RR	401-54
Duran, Santos	FF	401-133
Durand, Augustus	FB	401-150
Durbin, J. W.	FB	401-150
Durbin, Will	FB	401-150
Duren, George A.	TVG	401-190
Durfee, A. G.	USV	401-228
Durham, Charles	TVG	401-190
Durham, G. P.	FB	401-150
Durham, George P., Jr.	SR	401-76
Durham, George, Jr.	RR	401-54
Durham, H. M.	TVG	401-190
Durham, Harbo N.	USV	401-228
Durham, Paul	FF	401-133
Durham, T. O.	TVG	401-190
Durham, W. R.	USV	401-228
Durham, W. S.	SP	401-43
Durham, Walter A.	SR	401-76
Duringer, W. A.	TVG	401-190
Durnett, Sam	TVG	401-190
Durrett, Edward	USV	401-228
Durrett, T. H.	SP	401-43
Durst, J. B.	SR	401-76
Durst, James H.	ARM	401-4
Durst, Jno. J.	USV	401-228
Durst, S. O.	RRR	401-115
Durst, Sterling O.	RR	401-54
Dustin, V. G.	SR	401-76
Dustin, Vyvian Glenroy	LR	401-128
Dutcher, Alfred	ARM	401-4
Dutcher, Ch. L.	TST	401-34
Dutoit, William E.	USV	401-228
Duty, Milton T.	RR	401-54
Duty, R. P.	FB	401-150
Duval, Louis	ARM	401-4
DuVall, William P.	TVG	401-191
Dwiggins, William A.	ARM	401-4
Dwight, Mel J.	RRR	401-115
Dwire, John M.	SP	401-43
Dwyer, Charles G.	USV	401-228
Dwyer, Geo. James	TVG	401-191
Dyches, P. F.	RR	401-54
Dyches, P. F.	SR	401-76
Dycus, Charlie T.	LR	401-128
Dye, Clyde L.	RR	401-54
Dye, J. K. P.	SP	401-43
Dye, John	RR	401-54
Dyer, A. J.	TVG	401-191
Dyer, Albert F.	NAV	401-16
Dyer, Alf. S., Jr.	TVG	401-191
Dyer, Benjamin	NAV	401-16
Dyer, C. F.	RRR	401-115
Dyer, D. H.	ARM	401-4
Dyer, Ora E.	USV	401-228
Dyer, Oree	TVG	401-191
Dyer, W. A.	TVG	401-191
Eades, John S.	RR	401-54
Eads, Gano	FB	401-150
Eads, James T.	RR	401-54
Eads, Ralph	SR	401-76
Eager, G. E.	RRR	401-115

Index to Texas Adjutant General Service Records—All Service Branches

Name	Branch	Record
Eagle, W. H.	FB	401-150
Eagleshum, WilliaM	ARM	401-4
Eaker, Amos K.	MM	401-32
Eakin, J. C.	SR	401-76
Eakin, W. S.	SR	401-76
Eakins, A. G.	FB	401-150
Eakins, T. E.	FB	401-150
Eales, James	ARM	401-4
Eanes, C. R.	FB	401-150
Eanes, D. W.	FB	401-150
Eanes, H. L.	RR	401-54
Eanes, H. L.	FF	401-133
Eanes, Robt. H	FB	401-150
Eanes, W. H.	FB	401-150
Earhart, J. B.	TST	401-34
Earle, Isham H.	RR	401-54
Earle, John H.	FB	401-150
Earle, Roland Arthur	SR	401-76
Earley, B. F.	SP	401-43
Early, Stephen T.	SR	401-76
Early, W. N.	SR	401-76
Early, W. N.	LR	401-128
Earnest, D. P.	SR	401-76
Earnest, D. P.	LR	401-128
Earnest, Dave	FB	401-150
Earnest, Frank B.	USV	401-228
Earnest, J. D.	FB	401-150
Earnest, John W.	SP	401-43
Earp, V. Earl	SR	401-76
Earps, John	RR	401-54
Easley, A. C.	TVG	401-191
Easley, Chester A.	USV	401-228
Easley, Edwin S.	USV	401-228
Easley, Oda L.	USV	401-228
Easley, T. C.	TVG	401-191
Easley, Walter S.	USV	401-228
Eason, Ed P.	SR	401-76
Eason, Ed P.	LR	401-128
Eason, J. I.	SR	401-76
Eason, William L.	USV	401-228
East, Arthur Lee	SR	401-76
East, James W	RRR	401-115
East, Roy E.	SR	401-76
East, T. T.	SR	401-76
East, Tom T.	SR	401-76
Easter, J. F.	SR	401-76
Easter, J. F.	LR	401-128
Easterling, A. C.	SR	401-76
Easterwood, William Edward, Jr.	SR	401-76
Eastin, Ed	FB	401-150
Eastman, B. F.	RR	401-54
Easton, Evan S.	USV	401-228
Easton, John C.	USV	401-228
Easton, T. B.	TVG	401-191
Eastwood, Lewis H.	ARM	401-4
Eaton, Alen W.	USV	401-228
Eaton, Allen	ARM	401-4
Eaton, Alvin	ARM	401-4
Eaton, G. W.	TST	401-34
Eaton, James H.	USV	401-228
Eaton, T. B.	FB	401-150
Eaton, T. J.	FF	401-133
Eaves, Jack	SR	401-76
Eaves, L. A.	SR	401-76
Eayrs, John	NAV	401-16
Eberly, Edward S.	TVG	401-191
Ecard, Edward	ARM	401-4
Eccleston, H. D.	TVG	401-191
Echabod, Esphan	FB	401-150
Echols, Basil L.	USV	401-228
Echols, George	TVG	401-191
Echols, James E.	USV	401-228
Eckard, Alfred	FF	401-133
Eckenroth, Charles J.	USV	401-228
Eckert, L. W.	SR	401-76
Eckhardt, Charles L.	SR	401-76
Eckhardt, O. L.	SR	401-76
Eckhardt, Robert J.	SR	401-76
Eckles, Andrew B.	MV	401-29
Eckman, Nicholas Branch	TVG	401-191
Ector, Matthew Duncan	TST	401-34
Eddleman, James F.	USV	401-228
Eddleman, R. R.	RRR	401-115
Edds, Henry	SR	401-76
Edds, J. J.	RR	401-54
Edds, John J.	RR	401-54
Eddy, L. W.	ARM	401-4
Eden, Isaac Newman	RRR	401-115
Edens, R. A.	TVG	401-191
Edgar, Edward R.	USV	401-228
Edgar, John	ARM	401-4
Edgar, John	FF	401-133
Edgar, John	SP	401-43
Edgar, Josiah R.	ARM	401-4
Edge, C. L.	SR	401-76
Edge, G. W.	FB	401-150
Edge, Henry C.	RR	401-54
Edge, Victor B.	TVG	401-191
Edington, C. L.	FB	401-150
Edington, J. F.	SR	401-76
Edmiston, Fred W., Capt.	SR	401-76
Edmiston, T. R.	SR	401-76
Edmonds, J. C.	USV	401-228
Edmonds, Newton C.	USV	401-228
Edmonds, W. F.	TVG	401-191
Edmondson, A. L.	RRR	401-115
Edmondson, W. Frank	SR	401-76
Edmondson, Walter	TVG	401-191
Edmonson, James E.	ARM	401-4
Edmundson, John K.	SR	401-76
Edrington, L. M.	TVG	401-191
Eduy, Ben	TVG	401-191

Index to Texas Adjutant General Service Records—All Service Branches

Name	Branch	Page
Edwards, ____ Pvt.	RR	401-54
Edwards, AlberT	USV	401-228
Edwards, ArthuR	ARM	401-4
Edwards, B. E.	SR	401-76
Edwards, Charley W., Jr.	TVG	401-191
Edwards, D. M.	FB	401-150
Edwards, D. W.	FF	401-133
Edwards, Dan V.	USV	401-228
Edwards, E. M.	TVG	401-191
Edwards, Eddie	TVG	401-191
Edwards, Edward C.	USV	401-228
Edwards, Ellinger R.	RRR	401-115
Edwards, Entler S.	SR	401-76
Edwards, F. F.	FB	401-151
Edwards, George E.	TVG	401-191
Edwards, H. B.	SR	401-76
Edwards, H. L.	SP	401-43
Edwards, H. L.	TVG	401-191
Edwards, Haynie E.	SR	401-76
Edwards, Henry	ARM	401-4
Edwards, Henry H.	SR	401-76
Edwards, J. L.	USV	401-228
Edwards, James C.	CSA	401-39
Edwards, James F.	USV	401-228
Edwards, Joe	TVG	401-191
Edwards, John R.	USV	401-228
Edwards, Julien E.	SP	401-43
Edwards, L. W.	RR	401-54
Edwards, L. W.	ARM	401-4
Edwards, M. M.	SR	401-76
Edwards, M. W.	TVG	401-191
Edwards, P. F.	ARM	401-4
Edwards, Pete	FB	401-151
Edwards, Roswell	TVG	401-191
Edwards, S.	FB	401-151
Edwards, S. G.	TVG	401-191
Edwards, S. V.	FB	401-151
Edwards, S. V.	LR	401-128
Edwards, Samuel	SP	401-43
Edwards, Samuel V.	SR	401-76
Edwards, T. A.	USV	401-228
Edwards, Thom. J.	RR	401-54
Edwards, W. O.	FB	401-151
Edwards, W. R.	SR	401-76
Edwards, W. W.	SR	401-76
Edwards, W. W.	TVG	401-191
Edwards, W. W.	LR	401-128
Edwards, Walter R.	RRR	401-115
Edwards, William	NAV	401-16
Edwards, William	TST	401-34
Edwards, William	RR	401-54
Eeds, James	SP	401-43
Egan, Andrew	ARM	401-4
Egan, Patrick	USV	401-228
Egan, Richard J.	TST	401-34
Egbert, Dock	TVG	401-191
Egbert, E. M.	TVG	401-191
Egerton, Samuel	NAV	401-16
Ehlers, Martin F.	TVG	401-191
Eicke, Oscar J.	TVG	401-191
Eickenroht, Reno A.	RR	401-54
Eicker, Kraft	TVG	401-191
Eidman, Hugh B.	SR	401-76
Eidman, Hugh B.	LR	401-128
Eilermann, John H.	ARM	401-4
Eilers, F. W.	TVG	401-191
Eilers, M. L.	SR	401-76
Eitelman, Mike G.	USV	401-228
Eitt, WilliaM	USV	401-228
Ekdahl, S. N.	SR	401-76
Elder, S. M.	SR	401-76
Elder, William F.	SP	401-43
Eldred, Henry T.	TVG	401-191
Eldred, W. W.	FB	401-151
Eldridge, Frank	TVG	401-191
Eldridge, Frank	USV	401-229
Eldridge, J. L.	FB	401-151
Eldridge, John T.	RR	401-54
Elgin, A. W.	SP	401-43
Elgin, James H.	RRR	401-115
Elgin, John B.	MV	401-29
Elhmed, E.	USV	401-229
Elias, Viciente	FF	401-133
Elkin, W. B.	TVG	401-191
Elkins, Allen R.	USV	401-229
Elkins, E. F.	TVG	401-191
Elkins, H. D.	RR	401-54
Elkins, John M.	MM	401-32
Elkins, R. S.	SP	401-43
Elkins, S. P.	FF	401-133
Eller, Levi A.	USV	401-229
Ellett, Innes	SP	401-43
Ellie, B. S.	SR	401-76
Ellington, F. M.	SR	401-76
Ellington, F. M.	LR	401-128
Ellington, G. E.	USV	401-229
Ellington, G. W.	FB	401-151
Ellington, J. M.	SP	401-43
Ellington, W. E.	TVG	401-191
Elliot, C. H.	FB	401-151
Elliot, Jesse	ARM	401-4
Elliot, W. A.	FB	401-151
Elliott, A. E.	USV	401-229
Elliott, Andrew P.	USV	401-229
Elliott, Carroll O.	TVG	401-191
Elliott, Carroll O.	USV	401-229
Elliott, H. B.	MV	401-29
Elliott, H. E.	SR	401-76
Elliott, H. K.	TVG	401-191
Elliott, H. W.	FB	401-151
Elliott, Howard E.	SR	401-76
Elliott, J. B.	TVG	401-191

Index to Texas Adjutant General Service Records—All Service Branches

Name	Branch	Page
Elliott, J. T.	SR	401-76
Elliott, James A.	USV	401-229
Elliott, Jno. B.	TVG	401-191
Elliott, John	SR	401-76
Elliott, John	SR	401-76
Elliott, John I.	MM	401-32
Elliott, Lloyd G.	SR	401-76
Elliott, Loyd G.	RRR	401-115
Elliott, M. W.	FB	401-151
Elliott, R. H.	SP	401-43
Elliott, Robert	RRR	401-115
Elliott, Sanferd E.	USV	401-229
Elliott, Titus C.	USV	401-229
Elliott, W. C.	SR	401-76
Elliott, W. H.	TST	401-34
Elliott, William J.	SR	401-76
Elliott, William J.	LR	401-128
Elliott, Wyatt	NAV	401-16
Ellis, A. T.	TVG	401-191
Ellis, Ace	RR	401-54
Ellis, Ace	SR	401-76
Ellis, Benjamin S.	LR	401-128
Ellis, Billie Varner	TVG	401-191
Ellis, C. D.	FB	401-151
Ellis, Chalmers Hadley	RRR	401-115
Ellis, David S.	MV	401-29
Ellis, E. A.	SR	401-76
Ellis, E. E.	FB	401-151
Ellis, Ed W.	USV	401-229
Ellis, Emmette	TVG	401-191
Ellis, H. F.	SR	401-76
Ellis, H. L.	TVG	401-191
Ellis, Harry M.	TVG	401-191
Ellis, Hewey Gibbs	RRR	401-115
Ellis, J. K.	RRR	401-115
Ellis, James C.	USV	401-229
Ellis, James W.	USV	401-229
Ellis, Jim M.	RR	401-54
Ellis, Kurtz	TVG	401-191
Ellis, L. E.	RRR	401-115
Ellis, Louis	SR	401-76
Ellis, Mark L.	SR	401-76
Ellis, Odeen	SR	401-76
Ellis, R. G.	TVG	401-191
Ellis, T. D.	TVG	401-191
Ellis, T. W.	TVG	401-191
Ellis, Theodore H.	TVG	401-191
Ellis, Thomas A.	USV	401-229
Ellis, Thomas L.	USV	401-229
Ellis, W. D.	SR	401-76
Ellis, W. E.	FB	401-151
Ellis, W. R.	SR	401-76
Ellis, Waller H.	USV	401-229
Ellis, William	TVG	401-191
Ellis, Z. T.	FB	401-151
Ellison, Alonzo L.	USV	401-229
Ellison, Clifton T.	FB	401-151
Ellison, D. C.	RR	401-55
Ellison, J. W.	CSA	401-39
Ellison, J. W.	RR	401-55
Ellison, James M.	SR	401-76
Ellison, R. R.	RRR	401-115
Ellison, Ray	RRR	401-115
Ellison, Robert	FB	401-151
Ellison, Saml.	ARM	401-4
Ellison, Theophilus	ARM	401-4
Elliston, James B.	SR	401-76
Elliston, James S.	RRR	401-115
Elmore, G. M.	SR	401-76
Elmore, G. M.	LR	401-128
Elmore, John A.	FB	401-151
Elmore, Rush	SR	401-76
Elms, George Lee	RRR	401-115
Elms, Joe	TVG	401-191
Elolf, C. A.	TVG	401-191
Elolf, Fritz	USV	401-229
Elrod, Jess L.	SR	401-76
Elrod, Jesse Lee	LR	401-128
Elson, William M.	MV	401-29
Elston, C. N.	FB	401-151
Eltis, Seraphin	FB	401-151
Ely, Silas H.	USV	401-229
Emanuel, Chas. B.	TVG	401-191
Emanuel, Edgar	SP	401-43
Emanuel, Mark T.	USV	401-229
Embleton, R. V.	SR	401-76
Embry, Ura	SR	401-76
Emerson, Edward F.	USV	401-229
Emerson, George Noble	TVG	401-191
Emerson, Thos. D.	USV	401-229
Emery, Sam	FB	401-151
Emgard, Geo.	TVG	401-191
Emmerson, George	ARM	401-4
Emmert, Alonzo	USV	401-229
Emmett, William	NAV	401-16
Endel, M.	TVG	401-191
Endell, H.	TVG	401-191
Endom, Robert L.	USV	401-229
Engel, Geo. L.	USV	401-229
Engelhardt, Paul	FF	401-134
Engelhart, J. H.	TVG	401-191
Engelke, Charles J.	TVG	401-191
Engelking, C. P.	RR	401-55
Engelking, Lucas J.	RR	401-55
Engelman, Henry S.	USV	401-229
England, Andrew D.	TVG	401-191
England, Andrew D.	USV	401-229
Engle, Frederick	USV	401-229
Engler, Albert J.	USV	401-229
Engler, Julius Robert	ARM	401-4
English, Charles H.	USV	401-229
English, Ed	RRR	401-115

Index to Texas Adjutant General Service Records—All Service Branches

English, H. E. .... SR 401-76
English, Henry E. .... RR 401-55
English, J. M. .... SR 401-76
English, Jess T. .... SR 401-76
English, John W. .... TST 401-34
English, L. S. .... FB 401-151
English, Levi .... MV 401-29
English, William Lafayette .... RRR 401-115
Enhausen, Charles .... NAV 401-16
Ennis, Harry C. .... USV 401-229
Ennis, J. E. .... USV 401-229
Ennis, Walter Floyd .... TVG 401-191
Enochs, Graves Malcolm .... TVG 401-191
Enochs, J. H. .... SR 401-76
Enochs, O. F. .... FF 401-134
Enos, Theodore R. .... TVG 401-191
Ensley, Gilbert .... RRR 401-115
Ephraim, Sam .... USV 401-229
Epperson, R. H. .... SR 401-76
Epperson, W. S. .... FB 401-151
Eppes, C. L. .... FB 401-151
Epple, George L. .... SR 401-76
Epps, C. L. .... FB 401-151
Epps, Caro .... SR 401-76
Epps, John C. .... SR 401-76
Epps, Ned .... FB 401-151
Epstein, Louis .... TVG 401-191
Erarce, Francis .... NAV 401-16
Erby, William E. .... USV 401-229
Erisman, F. R., Sr. .... SR 401-76
Erisman, Fred .... SR 401-76
Ernandez, D. .... MV 401-29
Ernst, Augustus C. .... USV 401-229
Eron, A. .... SR 401-76
Erskine, F. P. G. .... RR 401-55
Erskine, Harry R. .... USV 401-229
Ervin, Thomas R. .... NAV 401-16
Erwin, A. .... TVG 401-191
Erwin, C. D. .... SR 401-77
Erwin, C. H. .... TVG 401-191
Erwin, Donald .... TVG 401-191
Erwin, G. W. .... USV 401-229
Erwin, J. H. .... RRR 401-115
Erwin, J. H. .... SR 401-77
Erwin, J. M. .... TVG 401-191
Erwin, Martin C. .... TVG 401-191
Erwin, O. R. .... FB 401-151
Erwin, W. H. .... TVG 401-191
Erwin, W. O. R. .... FB 401-151
Escajeda, Francisco .... TVG 401-191
Escamina, Pablo .... SP 401-43
Eskew, D. C. .... SR 401-77
Esparta, Eugene .... FF 401-134
Esquivel, John .... USV 401-229
Estabrook, William W. .... USV 401-229
Estapa, Leon .... SP 401-43
Estelle, Rhodes .... TVG 401-191
Estes, A. C. .... SR 401-77
Estes, Dillard .... SR 401-77
Estes, Edward .... SR 401-77
Estes, G. B. .... FB 401-151
Estes, George W. .... NAV 401-16
Estes, J. L. .... SR 401-77
Estes, James S. .... FF 401-134
Estes, John W. .... TVG 401-191
Estes, Lenard .... MM 401-32
Estes, Lewis Marion .... SR 401-77
Estes, Rankin .... USV 401-229
Estes, W. T. .... RRR 401-115
Estes, Wayne B., Jr. .... USV 401-229
Estrades, Andres .... FF 401-134
Esty, H. W. .... SR 401-77
Ethelton, Wayne .... USV 401-229
Etheredge, S. E. .... SR 401-77
Etheridge, Emmitte .... USV 401-229
Etheridge, Green B. .... TVG 401-191
Etheridge, Joe E. .... USV 401-229
Etheridge, John W. .... FB 401-151
Etie, Horace .... USV 401-229
Ettelson, C. L. .... SR 401-77
Etter, Gottlieb .... FF 401-134
Etter, JacoB .... MM 401-32
Etter, Will F. .... TVG 401-191
Eubank, March .... TVG 401-191
Eubanks, A. Hardy .... SR 401-77
Eubanks, Marian W. .... USV 401-229
Eubanks, Tom J. .... SR 401-77
Eubanks, William H. .... NAV 401-16
Evans, A. H. .... TVG 401-191
Evans, A. J. .... RR 401-55
Evans, A. J. .... SR 401-77
Evans, A. R. .... FB 401-151
Evans, Alfred D. .... FF 401-134
Evans, ArthuR .... SR 401-77
Evans, Augustus .... USV 401-229
Evans, B. H. .... RR 401-55
Evans, BoB .... SR 401-77
Evans, Charles Fred .... SR 401-77
Evans, Chas. .... TVG 401-191
Evans, Chas. D. .... TVG 401-191
Evans, CleM .... SR 401-77
Evans, D. F. .... TVG 401-191
Evans, Dewitt C. .... TST 401-34
Evans, Earnest R. .... USV 401-229
Evans, Ebb L. .... USV 401-229
Evans, Edward D. .... MV 401-29
Evans, Frederick .... USV 401-229
Evans, Guy H. .... TVG 401-191
Evans, H. A. .... TVG 401-191
Evans, H. C. .... CSA 401-39
Evans, Harold W. .... SR 401-77
Evans, Henry .... TST 401-34

Index to Texas Adjutant General Service Records—All Service Branches

Name	Branch	Record
Evans, Henry P.	USV	401-229
Evans, I.	SP	401-43
Evans, J.	FB	401-151
Evans, J. P.	RRR	401-115
Evans, J. R.	SR	401-77
Evans, J. R.	LR	401-128
Evans, James M.	ARM	401-4
Evans, James Rufus	TST	401-34
Evans, Joe B.	SR	401-77
Evans, John	FB	401-151
Evans, John W.	RR	401-55
Evans, John W.	SR	401-77
Evans, Jonathan	SP	401-43
Evans, Los	RRR	401-115
Evans, M. L.	CSA	401-39
Evans, Roger Q.	SR	401-77
Evans, S. H.	FB	401-151
Evans, Solomon H.	TVG	401-191
Evans, Thomas A.	MV	401-29
Evans, W. G.	TVG	401-191
Evans, W. L.	FB	401-151
Evans, W. T.	FB	401-151
Evans, Walter	ARM	401-4
Evans, Wilbur J.	TVG	401-191
Evans, William	NAV	401-16
Evans, William A.	USV	401-229
Evans, William E.	SP	401-43
Evans, William J.	FB	401-151
Evens, Hister	NAV	401-16
Evens, William T.	NAV	401-16
Everet, Samuel B.	RR	401-55
Everett, Carl B.	SR	401-77
Everett, F.	CSA	401-39
Everett, H. H.	USV	401-229
Everett, James	RR	401-55
Everett, M. W.	TVG	401-191
Everett, W. J., Jr.	RR	401-55
Everett, W. J., Jr.	SR	401-77
Everette, Will E.	FB	401-151
Everhart, S. V.	SP	401-43
Everheart, E. F.	SR	401-77
Everitt, Edward M.	TVG	401-191
Everitt, William N.	RRR	401-116
Everman, W. L.	TVG	401-191
Everman, W. L.	USV	401-229
Evers, George E.	SR	401-77
Evers, James R.	FF	401-134
Eversberg, Ernest H.	TVG	401-191
Eversberg, Max	TVG	401-191
Everton, Chas. F.	USV	401-229
Everton, M. T.	TVG	401-192
Everts, A. E.	TVG	401-192
Everts, Byron A., Jr.	TVG	401-192
Everts, Chester A.	SR	401-77
Eves, Edward	ARM	401-4
Evetts, Ed	FB	401-151
Evetts, J. H.	FB	401-151
Evetts, J. K.	RRR	401-116
Evetts, JiM	FB	401-151
Evetts, R. N.	RRR	401-116
Evetts, W. A.	FB	401-151
Evetts, W. E.	RRR	401-116
Ewald, C. F.	USV	401-229
Ewan, J. S.	FB	401-151
Ewing, C. C.	TVG	401-192
Ewing, Gregg	SR	401-77
Ewing, M. B.	SR	401-77
Ewing, M. B.	LR	401-128
Ewing, Robert B.	USV	401-229
Ewing, S. Finley	SR	401-77
Ewing, W. N.	FB	401-151
Ewing, William G.	USV	401-229
Ewit, Isidore	TVG	401-192
Eyck, E. Gen.	MV	401-29
Ezell, C. M.	RR	401-55
Ezell, C. M.	RRR	401-116
Ezell, Claude Clinton	SR	401-77
Ezell, H. G.	TVG	401-192
Ezell, P. B.	TVG	401-192
Ezelle, J. W.	SR	401-77
Ezelle, Jack W.	SR	401-77
Fadell, J. A.	SR	401-77
Fagan, Jno. F.	USV	401-229
Fagan, John	NAV	401-16
Fagan, John Frances	RR	401-55
Fagan, John Francis	SR	401-77
Fagan, John Francis	LR	401-128
Fagen, H. M.	FB	401-151
Faggard, Jas. E.	TVG	401-192
Fahlbusch, Basil C.	USV	401-229
Fahm, Cary	USV	401-229
Fahm, G. W.	TVG	401-192
Fahm, Jno. F.	USV	401-229
Fahm, Walton	TVG	401-192
Fahner, W. E.	SR	401-77
Fain, Joshua N.	USV	401-229
Fain, Mercer	MV	401-29
Fairbanks, John	RR	401-55
Fairchilds, Louis	TVG	401-192
Fairhurst, John	NAV	401-16
Fairley, Richard O.	TVG	401-192
Fakes, A. P.	TVG	401-192
Falcon, Alvino G.	FF	401-134
Falcon, Antonio G.	FF	401-134
Falcon, C. G.	FF	401-134
Falcon, Francisco	RR	401-55
Falkman, Andrews	NAV	401-16
Faller, Harold J.	SR	401-77
Falls, J. D.	SR	401-77
Falls, J. D.	LR	401-128
Falvy, John	SP	401-43
Fannesworth, G. H.	TVG	401-192

Index to Texas Adjutant General Service Records—All Service Branches

Name	Branch	Record
Fanning, Joe	FB	401-151
Fanning, Joseph T.	FF	401-134
Fanning, Martin W.	FB	401-151
Fanning, Michael	ARM	401-4
Farabee, Geo. E.	USV	401-229
Faris, Ellsworth E.	TVG	401-192
Faris, Thos. J.	RR	401-55
Farley, J. C.	SP	401-43
Farley, Joseph	ARM	401-4
Farley, Tom	FB	401-151
Farmer, James C.	RR	401-55
Farmer, Percy	RRR	401-116
Farmer, Robinson R.	SR	401-77
Farmer, W. E.	SR	401-77
Farnham, Francis	NAV	401-16
Farnham, Sidney	NAV	401-16
Farnsworth, Joseph E.	TVG	401-192
Farnsworth, OliveR	ARM	401-4
Farquhar, C. A.	TVG	401-192
Farquhar, F. M.	MM	401-32
Farquhar, Robert E.	USV	401-229
Farquhar, William B.	USV	401-229
Farr, E. F.	TVG	401-192
Farr, Rezin S., Jr.	USV	401-229
Farr, Thomas	TST	401-34
Farrall, James	ARM	401-4
Farrar, H. G.	RR	401-55
Farrar, Vertner V.	USV	401-229
Farrell, John E.	SR	401-77
Farrell, M.	FB	401-151
Farrell, Robert F.	SR	401-77
Farrington, Chas. B.	FB	401-151
Farris, J. H.	USV	401-229
Farris, Richard V.	USV	401-229
Farris, W. W.	TVG	401-192
Farrow, G. W.	FB	401-151
Farrow, George W.	SP	401-43
Farrow, J. H.	SR	401-77
Farrow, Samuel	ARM	401-4
Farrow, Thomas C.	USV	401-229
Fasselman, Will	TVG	401-192
Fathenee, Boss	TVG	401-192
Fatheree, I. N.	SR	401-77
Fatheree, Ira N.	RRR	401-116
Faubien, J. L.	RR	401-55
Faubion, Herbert E.	TVG	401-192
Faubion, J. E.	RR	401-55
Faubion, J. L.	RR	401-55
Faubion, J. L.	FB	401-151
Faubion, Jesse E.	TVG	401-192
Faubion, O. A.	TVG	401-192
Faubion, W. M.	SR	401-77
Faulk, James E.	SP	401-43
Faulk, Wesley	SP	401-43
Faulk, William L.	TVG	401-192
Faulk, William L., Jr.	TVG	401-192
Faulkner Tim L.	USV	401-229
Faulkner, A.	TVG	401-192
Faulkner, D. B.	FB	401-151
Faulkner, Edward	FB	401-151
Faulkner, L. B.	SR	401-77
Fauntleroy, J. B.	SP	401-43
Faust, Joseph	TVG	401-192
Faust, S. G.	SR	401-77
Faust, Walter	SR	401-77
Faust, Walter	TVG	401-192
Faust, Walter	LR	401-128
Fayssoux, C. I.	NAV	401-16
Feagan, Walter	TVG	401-192
Feagan, William Franklin	TVG	401-192
Feagan, William Franklin	USV	401-229
Feagin, J. D.	SR	401-77
Feagin, J. D.	LR	401-128
Featherston, C. H.	SR	401-77
Featherston, Merce	TVG	401-192
Featherstone, L. L.	TVG	401-192
Fechenbach, Leon L.	SR	401-77
Feddeman, J. M.	TVG	401-192
Fedder, Sam	TVG	401-192
Fedrick, Joseph F.	USV	401-229
Feegles, D. C.	SR	401-77
Fehl, George	ARM	401-4
Feigl, Fred	FB	401-151
Feigle, Martin	USV	401-229
Feild, Harry	SR	401-77
Feild, Harry	LR	401-128
Feist, Carl Gus	TVG	401-192
Felalla, Simion	FF	401-134
Fellbaum, Ernest S.	SR	401-77
Fellbaum, Lloyd	SR	401-77
Felps, Henry	RR	401-55
Felter, Charles R.	TVG	401-192
Felter, Frank	MV	401-29
Felton, William	ARM	401-4
Feltz, Jake B.	USV	401-229
Feltzer, Frank	MV	401-29
Felz, Jake	TVG	401-192
Fench, Henry	ARM	401-4
Fendley, J. M., Jr.	SR	401-77
Fenley, Ivy R.	RR	401-55
Fenley, Ivy R.	SR	401-77
Fenly, A. H.	FB	401-151
Fenn, Adolphus E.	USV	401-229
Fenn, Joe J.	RRR	401-116
Fennelle, Charlie	TVG	401-192
Fenner, Arthur	TVG	401-192
Fenner, Power R.	SR	401-77
Fenner, Powers	RRR	401-116
Ferand, John C.	NAV	401-16
Fergals, Ben	TVG	401-192
Ferguson, A. M.	MV	401-29
Ferguson, Alexander	SP	401-43

Index to Texas Adjutant General Service Records—All Service Branches

Ferguson, Chalmers ... USV ... 401-229
Ferguson, Chas. D. ... USV ... 401-229
Ferguson, David ... USV ... 401-229
Ferguson, David H. ... SR ... 401-77
Ferguson, H. B. ... SR ... 401-77
Ferguson, H. E. ... TVG ... 401-192
Ferguson, J. A. ... SP ... 401-43
Ferguson, J. E. ... SR ... 401-77
Ferguson, J. R. ... TVG ... 401-192
Ferguson, Jasper B. ... SR ... 401-77
Ferguson, Jasper N. ... RRR ... 401-116
Ferguson, Joe O. ... USV ... 401-229
Ferguson, John ... FF ... 401-134
Ferguson, John H. ... TVG ... 401-192
Ferguson, John H. ... USV ... 401-229
Ferguson, John M. ... USV ... 401-229
Ferguson, Joseph H. ... SR ... 401-77
Ferguson, M. A. ... RRR ... 401-116
Ferguson, Robert ... SP ... 401-43
Ferguson, Thomas ... FB ... 401-151
Ferguson, W. A. ... SR ... 401-77
Ferguson, W. A. ... LR ... 401-128
Ferguson, W. B. ... TVG ... 401-192
Ferguson, W. E. ... SR ... 401-77
Ferguson, Walter W. ... USV ... 401-229
Ferguson, William ... NAV ... 401-16
Ferguson, William ... ARM ... 401-4
Fernandez, E. A. ... TVG ... 401-192
Fernandez, Henry ... TVG ... 401-192
Fernando, Equilbeg ... FF ... 401-134
Ferrell, A. S. ... TVG ... 401-192
Ferrell, Arthur L. ... SR ... 401-77
Ferrell, H. C. ... TVG ... 401-192
Ferrell, J. L. ... SR ... 401-77
Ferrell, John A. ... USV ... 401-229
Ferrell, William ... TST ... 401-34
Ferrell, William P. ... USV ... 401-229
Ferrier, Bert E. ... SR ... 401-77
Ferris, A. G. ... SR ... 401-77
Ferris, Charles D. ... FB ... 401-151
Ferris, J. M. ... FB ... 401-151
Ferry, Louis ... FF ... 401-134
Fessler, Antonio ... FF ... 401-134
Fessmann, Fritz ... TVG ... 401-192
Feyden, Andrew ... ARM ... 401-4
Fichtenhaltz, Joe ... TVG ... 401-192
Fiedler, Jacob ... FB ... 401-151
Field, A. F. ... FB ... 401-151
Field, Andrew ... NAV ... 401-16
Field, George D. ... USV ... 401-229
Field, Ivine H. ... RR ... 401-55
Field, J. H. ... SR ... 401-77
Field, J. H. ... TVG ... 401-192
Field, John ... TST ... 401-34
Fielden, Clay M. ... SR ... 401-77
Fielder, Edward ... FB ... 401-151
Fielder, W. A. ... FF ... 401-134
Fields, A. E. ... USV ... 401-229
Fields, A. F. ... FB ... 401-151
Fields, Charles W. ... SR ... 401-77
Fields, Gilder H. ... TVG ... 401-192
Fields, Joe ... TVG ... 401-192
Fields, Lancie S. ... RRR ... 401-116
Fields, R. A. ... USV ... 401-229
Fields, W. L. ... USV ... 401-229
Fife, A. H. ... SR ... 401-77
Figures, C. H. ... FF ... 401-134
Files, R. C. ... FB ... 401-151
Filley, Ferd ... TVG ... 401-192
Fillmore, Harry E. ... USV ... 401-229
Finch, Alfonso ... USV ... 401-229
Finch, George E. ... RRR ... 401-116
Finch, Robert E., Jr. ... TVG ... 401-192
Finch, Thos. E. ... USV ... 401-229
Findley, C. D. ... SR ... 401-77
Findley, Oscar P. ... USV ... 401-229
Fine, H. E. ... RRR ... 401-116
Fine, Henry ... TVG ... 401-192
Fine, John, Jr. ... TVG ... 401-192
Fine, Julian B. ... RRR ... 401-116
Finely, E. F. ... SR ... 401-77
Fink, Abe ... TVG ... 401-192
Fink, E. M. ... FB ... 401-151
Fink, Richard G. ... TVG ... 401-192
Fink, Will C. ... TVG ... 401-192
Finklea, J. M. ... TVG ... 401-192
Finlan, James ... USV ... 401-229
Finley, Albert ... SR ... 401-77
Finley, Albert ... LR ... 401-128
Finley, Francis M. ... MM ... 401-32
Finley, I. N. ... SR ... 401-77
Finley, Lane ... SR ... 401-77
Finley, W. P. ... TVG ... 401-192
Finn, B. F. ... FB ... 401-151
Finn, Paul ... SR ... 401-77
Finney, John R. ... LR ... 401-128
Finney, John R. ... SR ... 401-77
Finnigan, John ... NAV ... 401-16
Finnin, Ed. ... CSA ... 401-39
Firmin, A. E. ... TVG ... 401-192
Firth, James ... NAV ... 401-16
Fischer, H. F. ... TVG ... 401-192
Fischer, Julius C. ... USV ... 401-230
Fischer, M. ... TVG ... 401-192
Fischer, Willie ... LR ... 401-128
Fish, Greenleaf ... ARM ... 401-4
Fisher, Armistead S. ... USV ... 401-230
Fisher, Beeman ... SR ... 401-77
Fisher, Clarence W. ... USV ... 401-230
Fisher, David F. ... TVG ... 401-192
Fisher, F. J. ... FB ... 401-151
Fisher, George W. ... TVG ... 401-192

Index to Texas Adjutant General Service Records—All Service Branches

Name	Branch	Ref
Fisher, Harry V.	SR	401-77
Fisher, Henry	SP	401-43
Fisher, Irving R.	TVG	401-192
Fisher, Joseph	FF	401-134
Fisher, L. C., Jr.	TVG	401-192
Fisher, R.	FB	401-151
Fisher, Rhoads	FB	401-151
Fisher, Rhodes	TST	401-34
Fisher, S. C.	TVG	401-192
Fisher, T. E.	SR	401-77
Fisher, Thomas L.	USV	401-230
Fisher, W. J.	FB	401-151
Fisher, Walter	TVG	401-192
Fisher, Willis	RR	401-55
Fisher, Willis	RRR	401-116
Fishman, Simon	TVG	401-192
Fisk, E. S.	FB	401-151
Fisk, G.	TVG	401-192
Fisk, John	FB	401-151
Fitch, D. E.	FB	401-151
Fitch, Thomas	RR	401-55
Fite, Robert B.	USV	401-230
Fithen, Taylor	SR	401-77
Fitsgerald, D. C.	TVG	401-192
Fitsgerald, James	USV	401-230
Fittger, CleM	TVG	401-192
Fitthian, W. E.	FB	401-151
Fitts, J. T.	USV	401-230
Fitz, Grady	RRR	401-116
Fitze, Charles B.	FB	401-151
Fitze, H. W.	TVG	401-192
Fitzgerald, C. A.	SR	401-77
Fitzgerald, Corea Aquilla	LR	401-128
Fitzgerald, Edward	ARM	401-4
Fitzgerald, J. M.	FF	401-134
Fitzgerald, John W.	MV	401-29
Fitzgerald, R. A.	RRR	401-116
Fitzgerald, Raymond	SR	401-77
Fitzgerald, S. M.	RR	401-55
Fitzgerald, W. C.	SR	401-77
Fitzgerlad, W. G.	SR	401-77
Fitzgerrald, Mays	USV	401-230
Fitzhugh, John T.	FB	401-151
Fitzmaurice, Edward M.	USV	401-230
Fitzpatrick, H. L.	SR	401-77
Fitzpatrick, William C.	USV	401-230
Fitzroy, Horatio	ARM	401-4
Fitzsimmons, Edward	NAV	401-16
Fitzsimmons, T. J.	TVG	401-192
Fitzsimmons, Tobe F.	USV	401-230
Fitzsimons, H. A.	SR	401-77
Fitzwater, Levi	ARM	401-4
Fitzwilliam, J.	FB	401-151
Flach, Louis E.	RR	401-55
Flagg, E. P.	FB	401-151
Flaherty, N. O.	TVG	401-192
Flake, Ethelo	TVG	401-192
Flanagan, C. R.	RRR	401-116
Flanagan, Edward E.	USV	401-230
Flanagan, G. W.	FB	401-151
Flanagan, M. Tracy	SR	401-77
Flanagan, R. J.	SR	401-77
Flaningan, Asa P.	USV	401-230
Flannegan, Thomas	NAV	401-16
Flannery, Isaac	NAV	401-16
Flatan, L. S., Jr.	TVG	401-192
Flatan, W. H.	TVG	401-192
Flateau, Louis Spencer, Jr.	TVG	401-192
Flato, Minnie Oliver	SR	401-77
Flechtner, Frederick	SR	401-77
Fleig, A. C.	USV	401-230
Fleming, Alex E.	USV	401-230
Fleming, Andrew J.	FB	401-151
Fleming, Angus	ARM	401-4
Fleming, B. P.	SP	401-43
Fleming, Clay F.	USV	401-230
Fleming, J. H.	SR	401-78
Fleming, M. H.	TVG	401-192
Fleming, Matthew	FB	401-151
Fleming, W. A.	RR	401-55
Flemming, Robert	ARM	401-4
Flenerndall, Jay	USV	401-230
Flenley, Peter	ARM	401-4
Fletcher, B. L.	USV	401-230
Fletcher, E. A.	LR	401-128
Fletcher, Emmett A.	SR	401-78
Fletcher, G. B.	SR	401-78
Fletcher, H. D.	SR	401-78
Fletcher, J. N.	FB	401-151
Fletcher, John D.	USV	401-230
Fletcher, Lloyd	SR	401-78
Fletcher, Ralph H.	USV	401-230
Fletcher, Robert R.	SR	401-78
Fletcher, Robert R.	LR	401-128
Fletcher, Theodore R.	USV	401-230
Fletcher, William B.	USV	401-230
Fletcher, William T.	USV	401-230
Fleurdelys, Zephir	ARM	401-4
Flewellen, E. A.	TVG	401-192
Flewellen, Hugh L.	TVG	401-192
Flewellen, W. L.	USV	401-230
Flick, Carl	TVG	401-192
Flinn, Joseph L.	USV	401-230
Flinn, Perry	ARM	401-4
Flint, B.	USV	401-230
Flint, Frank	SP	401-43
Flint, Joe L.	SR	401-78
Flint, John Y.	TST	401-34
Flippen, Malcolm	USV	401-230
Floeck, Julius	TVG	401-192
Flores, A. G.	SR	401-78
Flores, Claude	TVG	401-192

Index to Texas Adjutant General Service Records—All Service Branches

Name	Branch	Record
Flores, Felix	RR	401-55
Flores, Felix	SR	401-78
Flores, Mariano	FB	401-151
Flores, Ricardo	SP	401-43
Flores, Vincente	SP	401-43
Florey, Frank	SR	401-78
Florey, J. V.	SR	401-78
Florey, Jess	SR	401-78
Florey, John	ARM	401-4
Floro, V. E.	TVG	401-192
Flournoy, M. R.	SR	401-78
Flournoy, Melville C.	TVG	401-192
Flournoy, Melville C.	USV	401-230
Flowers, A. F.	TST	401-34
Flowers, Dennis	SR	401-78
Flowers, E. B.	SR	401-78
Flowers, J. L.	SR	401-78
Flowers, Martin O.	USV	401-230
Floyd, I. K., Capt.	SR	401-78
Floyd, J. W.	SR	401-78
Floyd, James Edward, Jr.	USV	401-230
Floyd, O. P.	SR	401-78
Floyd, Roy E.	SR	401-78
Floyd, SaM	RRR	401-116
Floyd, Thomas B.	USV	401-230
Floyd, Thos. S.	FB	401-151
Floyd, William E.	SR	401-78
Flukinger, Gus R.	SR	401-78
Flynn, H.	FF	401-134
Flynn, Thomas	FB	401-151
Flynn, Will F.	USV	401-230
Flynt, E. J.	FB	401-151
Flynt, J. P.	SR	401-78
Flynt, W. O.	FB	401-152
Flynt, W. Q.	FB	401-152
Fogg, John W.	ARM	401-4
Fogle, Naunon F.	TVG	401-192
Fogle, William P.	USV	401-230
Fogleman, H.	FB	401-152
Folbre, G. L.	SR	401-78
Foley, George P.	ARM	401-4
Foley, J. M.	SR	401-78
Foley, Thomas	FF	401-134
Folger, N. C. L.	NAV	401-16
Folick, Isaac	ARM	401-4
Follet, Robert	NAV	401-16
Follette, James E.	FF	401-134
Folts, Hon. William H.	SR	401-78
Folts, J. E.	FB	401-152
Folts, Thomas W.	SR	401-78
Folts, William H.	LR	401-128
Folwell, Jack	USV	401-230
Fondren, A. J.	TVG	401-192
Fondren, William A.	USV	401-230
Fones, R. Albert	USV	401-230
Fones, Solomon	ARM	401-4
Fontaine, John	NAV	401-16
Fontaine, Lawrence A. W.	TVG	401-192
Fook, Frank Keener	TVG	401-192
Fooshee, J. A.	USV	401-230
Foote, Emory	SP	401-43
Foote, Owen	ARM	401-4
Footman, John	ARM	401-4
Forbes, A. M.	TVG	401-192
Forbes, Geo. W.	FB	401-152
Forbes, J. R.	USV	401-230
Forbes, J. T.	USV	401-230
Forbes, L. P.	FB	401-152
Forbis, Tommy	SR	401-78
Ford, Dan	RRR	401-116
Ford, E. J.	FB	401-152
Ford, Edward C.	USV	401-230
Ford, Elgin	RR	401-55
Ford, Francis C.	TVG	401-192
Ford, Frank J.	USV	401-230
Ford, James B.	ARM	401-4
Ford, John C.	FB	401-152
Ford, John F., Dr.	SR	401-78
Ford, John S.	MV	401-29
Ford, L. L.	SR	401-78
Ford, Matthew	USV	401-230
Ford, Owen	RRR	401-116
Ford, Raymond G.	TVG	401-192
Ford, Thomas Cates	USV	401-230
Ford, W. B.	TVG	401-192
Ford, W. F.	FB	401-152
Ford, W. P.	TVG	401-192
Fordice, J.	FB	401-152
Fordyce, J.	FB	401-152
Fore, Thomas F.	USV	401-230
Forehand, B. D.	RRR	401-116
Forehand, Bill	RRR	401-116
Forehand, Boyd	SR	401-78
Forehand, R. B.	RRR	401-116
Forehand, T. B.	FF	401-134
Forehand, T. B.	FB	401-152
Foreman, A. J.	SP	401-43
Foreman, George A.	SR	401-78
Foreman, George R.	SP	401-43
Foreman, J. A.	TVG	401-192
Foreman, J. E.	SR	401-78
Foreman, John A.	RR	401-55
Foreman, Kenneth	SR	401-78
Foreman, Wallace	RR	401-55
Forester, Bruce R.	RRR	401-116
Forester, Louis	TVG	401-192
Forkner, G. T.	MV	401-29
Forman, Edgar	USV	401-230
Forman, Homer S.	USV	401-230
Former, O. J.	TVG	401-192
Forrest, Demps	TST	401-34
Forrest, Joseph A.	NAV	401-16

Index to Texas Adjutant General Service Records—All Service Branches

Name	Branch	Record
Forrest, Moreau	NAV	401-16
Forrest, W. Y.	SR	401-78
Forrest, W. Y.	LR	401-128
Forret, Zachariah	NAV	401-16
Forsgard, Edward F.	SR	401-78
Forsgard, Shirley C.	TVG	401-192
Forshay, Clifford G.	TVG	401-192
Forster, Robert	NAV	401-16
Forsyth, James, Jr.	TVG	401-192
Forsythe, James	ARM	401-5
Fort, Battle	MV	401-29
Fort, Geraldus A.	USV	401-230
Fort, Harry J.	TVG	401-193
Fort, John	MV	401-29
Fort, John M.	RR	401-55
Fort, L. A.	USV	401-230
Fortenberry, G. H.	RRR	401-116
Fortson, R. L.	TVG	401-193
Fortune, Louis A.	SR	401-78
Forwood, H. M.	TVG	401-193
Foscue, Garland B.	TVG	401-193
Fosel, Joseph H.	USV	401-230
Fosgate, Walter	ARM	401-5
Foshee, A. B.	SR	401-78
Foshee, W. F.	TVG	401-193
Fostel, Leonhard	FF	401-134
Foster, A. E.	FB	401-152
Foster, August	RRR	401-116
Foster, B. S.	FB	401-152
Foster, Buford	FF	401-134
Foster, C. C.	TVG	401-193
Foster, E. D.	SP	401-44
Foster, Frank	TVG	401-193
Foster, Geo. G.	TVG	401-193
Foster, Geo. W.	USV	401-230
Foster, George	NAV	401-16
Foster, George	FB	401-152
Foster, Homer	TVG	401-193
Foster, Hugh M.	TVG	401-193
Foster, Hugh M.	USV	401-230
Foster, J. W.	FB	401-152
Foster, James	NAV	401-16
Foster, Jesse G.	SR	401-78
Foster, Jim	TVG	401-193
Foster, John	NAV	401-16
Foster, John	ARM	401-5
Foster, John B.	TST	401-34
Foster, Mervin	TVG	401-193
Foster, RoberT	ARM	401-5
Foster, S. D.	USV	401-230
Foster, Samuel G.	FF	401-134
Foster, Theodore N.	CSA	401-39
Foster, W. B.	FB	401-152
Foster, W. P.	SR	401-78
Foster, William	SP	401-44
Foster, William D.	USV	401-230
Foster, William L.	TST	401-34
Fouke, Frank J.	USV	401-230
Fountain, J. L.	TVG	401-193
Fourny, Joe	TVG	401-193
Foushee, W. T.	FB	401-152
Foust, Harvey D.	RRR	401-116
Fouts, W. K.	TVG	401-193
Fouts, Weber H.	SR	401-78
Fowle, Henry	ARM	401-5
Fowler, A. T.	SR	401-78
Fowler, Aubrey	RRR	401-116
Fowler, C. C.	TVG	401-193
Fowler, Chas. A.	USV	401-230
Fowler, Clark	USV	401-230
Fowler, Claude	TVG	401-193
Fowler, E.	TVG	401-193
Fowler, Earl R.	TVG	401-193
Fowler, Earl R.	USV	401-230
Fowler, Eugene M.	USV	401-230
Fowler, F. V.	FB	401-152
Fowler, Godfrey R.	TVG	401-193
Fowler, Godfrey Rees	USV	401-230
Fowler, H.	RR	401-55
Fowler, Harrison E.	TVG	401-193
Fowler, I. J.	USV	401-230
Fowler, J. H.	SR	401-78
Fowler, J. K.	USV	401-230
Fowler, J. O.	USV	401-230
Fowler, James Knox	TVG	401-193
Fowler, Jessie E.	TVG	401-193
Fowler, John M.	ARM	401-5
Fowler, R. L.	SR	401-78
Fowler, Ralph J.	TVG	401-193
Fowler, Rex	RRR	401-116
Fowler, Richard	FF	401-134
Fowler, S. R.	TVG	401-193
Fowler, Wick	SR	401-78
Fowler, William Clarence	SR	401-78
Fowler, William R.	USV	401-230
Fowlkes, A. W.	SR	401-78
Fowlkes, John S.	USV	401-230
Fowlkes, Max. B.	SR	401-78
Fox, Frank	FF	401-134
Fox, Frank F.	USV	401-230
Fox, George C.	RRR	401-116
Fox, George Clarence	SR	401-78
Fox, Gustavus	MV	401-29
Fox, J. C.	RR	401-55
Fox, J. M.	RR	401-55
Fox, J. M.	MV	401-29
Fox, J. M.	SR	401-78
Fox, James Leslie	RR	401-55
Fox, Jay B.	SR	401-78
Fox, M. J., Jr.	TVG	401-193
Fox, Orren	MV	401-29
Fox, T. J. Oscar	TVG	401-193

Index to Texas Adjutant General Service Records—All Service Branches

Fox, W. A. ....TVG 401-193
Fox, W. W. ....FB............401-152
Foy, B. J. ....TVG 401-193
Foy, Glenn A. ....SR............401-78
Frahm, Cary...............................USV 401-230
Fraley, E. D. ....TVG 401-193
Frame, Jon S. ....FB............401-152
France, Thomas E. ....NAV........401-17
Francis, J. A. ....RR 401-55
Francis, J. B. ....SR............401-78
Francis, J. W. ....FB............401-152
Francis, John G. ....TVG 401-193
Francis, Louis ....ARM 401-5
Francis, Robert B. ....RRR 401-116
Francis, W. F. ....FB............401-152
Francis, William H. ....SR............401-78
Franco, Juan..............................TVG 401-193
Frank, A., Jr. ....USV 401-230
Frank, Isaac M. ....MV 401-29
Frankland, John ....ARM 401-5
Franklin, A. J. ....FB............401-152
Franklin, Anthony.....................NAV........401-17
Franklin, Arthur ....USV 401-230
Franklin, Benjamin ....NAV........401-17
Franklin, C. W. ....SR............401-78
Franklin, Carl J. ....USV 401-230
Franklin, Claude ....RR 401-55
Franklin, J. B. ....RR 401-55
Franklin, J. B. ....FB............401-152
Franklin, J. H. ....TVG 401-193
Franklin, James E. ....USV 401-230
Franklin, John ....ARM 401-5
Franklin, John ....SP 401-44
Franklin, Johon M. ....USV 401-230
Franklin, R. L. ....SR............401-78
Franklin, R. W. ....TVG 401-193
Franklin, S. J. ....TVG 401-193
Franklin, S. L. ....SR............401-78
Franklin, Thomas H. ....TVG 401-193
Franklin, Thomas H. ....USV 401-230
Franklin, W. ....CSA.........401-39
Franklin, W. C. ....USV 401-230
Franklin, William ....TST 401-34
Franklin, William ....USV 401-230
Franklin, William B. ....TVG 401-193
Franks, D. G. ....FB............401-152
Franks, Earl B. ....RR 401-55
Franks, Earl B. ....SR............401-78
Franks, F. ....MM 401-32
Franks, I. B. ....RRR 401-116
Franks, Ira B. ....SR............401-78
Franks, T. C. ....RR 401-55
Franks, Thomas B. ....MV 401-29
Franks, Tom C. ....RR 401-55
Franks, W. A. ....ARM 401-5
Franks, W. C. ....TVG 401-193
Fransal, A. ....FB............401-152
Franz, Arthur ....TVG 401-193
Frasch, G. ....TST 401-34
Fraser, Simon C. ....NAV........401-17
Frasure, H. C. ....TVG 401-193
Frayne, Thomas J. ....FB............401-152
Frazar, Martin F. ....USV 401-230
Frazer, Geo. A. ....FB............401-152
Frazier, Ben ....SR............401-78
Frazier, E. C. ....SR............401-78
Frazier, Earl B. ....SR............401-78
Frazier, Earl B. ....LR 401-128
Frazier, Geo. W. ....FB............401-152
Frazier, J. M., Jr. ....SR............401-78
Frazier, James ....TVG 401-193
Frazier, James M. ....FF 401-134
Frazier, Richard T. ....TVG 401-193
Frazier, Samuel ....FB............401-152
Frazier, Shiles B. ....USV 401-230
Frazier, W. P. ....FB............401-152
Frazior, E. ....SP 401-44
Freasier, E. M. ....RRR 401-116
Frederick, Harry A. ....TVG 401-193
Frederick, P. T. ....FB............401-152
Freeborn, Sterling D. ....TVG 401-193
Freedman, Sam ....TVG 401-193
Freeland, B. H. ....RRR 401-116
Freeland, Bide H. ....TVG 401-193
Freeman, C. T. ....CSA.........401-39
Freeman, Charles ....NAV........401-17
Freeman, Chas. W. ....USV 401-230
Freeman, F. J. ....FB............401-152
Freeman, F. L. ....FB............401-152
Freeman, F. M. ....RR 401-55
Freeman, F. S. ....TVG 401-193
Freeman, J. G. ....TVG 401-193
Freeman, J. H. ....SR............401-78
Freeman, J. W. ....TVG 401-193
Freeman, Jack ....SR............401-78
Freeman, Joseph B. ....RR 401-55
Freeman, O. B. ....SR............401-78
Freeman, Robert L. ....USV 401-230
Freeman, S. T. ....USV 401-230
Freeman, W. D. ....TVG 401-193
Freeman, W. W. ....FB............401-152
Freeman, William B. ....USV 401-230
French, A. H. ....SP 401-44
French, Chas. A. ....USV 401-230
French, D. F. ....TVG 401-193
French, Edward........................ARM 401-5
French, Geo. V. ....USV 401-230
French, Henry ....ARM 401-5
French, John M. ....USV 401-230
French, Marcellus ....MV 401-29
Frensal, August ....FB............401-152
Frey, Geo. W. A. ....TVG 401-193

Index to Texas Adjutant General Service Records—All Service Branches

Name	Branch	Record
Freye, C. E.	FF	401-134
Friddell, Paul	TVG	401-193
Fries, John P.	SP	401-44
Fripps, James	ARM	401-5
Frisby, Benjamin F.	MV	401-29
Frisby, Floyd L.	USV	401-230
Frischmeyer, Frank	RR	401-55
Frith, Henry	SP	401-44
Fritts, Jim	SR	401-78
Frittzs, Henry W.	SP	401-44
Fritze, William	FF	401-134
Frizzell, Ed	SR	401-78
Frizzell, Edd	RRR	401-116
Frizzell, Edward Milow	RRR	401-116
Frizzell, Sam	RRR	401-116
Frnka, Henry E.	SR	401-78
Fromme, Fritz	USV	401-230
Frommee, Otto	USV	401-230
Fronckiewier, John	NAV	401-17
Frost, Benjamin H.	CSA	401-39
Frost, Jack	SR	401-78
Frost, Roger	USV	401-230
Frost, Thomas C.	TST	401-35
Frost, Thos. W.	USV	401-230
Fry, F. P.	TVG	401-193
Fry, Hugh S.	SR	401-78
Fry, Lee T.	USV	401-230
Fryar, Thomas Vivian	TVG	401-193
Frye, Roy J.	SR	401-78
Frye, Roy J.	LR	401-128
Fryer, A. J.	FB	401-152
Fryer, J. H.	FB	401-152
Frymier, Ben F.	TVG	401-193
Fuchs, Ernest	FF	401-134
Fudge, Leroy	TST	401-35
Fuentes, Jose	FF	401-134
Fuerst, John	SR	401-78
Fuhrmann, August, Jr.	TVG	401-193
Fuhrmann, Charley	TVG	401-193
Fulbright, A. N.	CSA	401-39
Fulbright, C. H.	CSA	401-39
Fulbright, H. S.	CSA	401-39
Fulbright, James	CSA	401-39
Fulbright, Joe	RR	401-55
Fulbright, John	CSA	401-39
Fulbright, Martin A.	CSA	401-39
Fulbright, Peat	CSA	401-39
Fulbright, R. H.	CSA	401-39
Fulbright, William	CSA	401-39
Fulcher, Charles R.	SR	401-78
Fulcher, James	ARM	401-5
Fulcher, John	TVG	401-193
Fulcher, John T., Lt.	SR	401-78
Fulgham, J. W.	FB	401-152
Fulkes, J. A.	FB	401-152
Fulkes, Jack Allen	SR	401-78
Fuller, Alta T.	RRR	401-116
Fuller, Benjamin	ARM	401-5
Fuller, Charles F.	NAV	401-17
Fuller, Daniel	SP	401-44
Fuller, David	FB	401-152
Fuller, F. E.	TVG	401-193
Fuller, Jack	USV	401-230
Fuller, Joseph E.	TVG	401-193
Fuller, Lawrence T.	FB	401-152
Fuller, M. A.	SR	401-78
Fuller, M. A.	LR	401-128
Fuller, Morgan	SR	401-78
Fuller, N. N.	RRR	401-116
Fuller, Nathan N.	RR	401-55
Fuller, Nathan N.	SR	401-78
Fuller, R. J.	RR	401-55
Fuller, W. J.	USV	401-230
Fullerton, C. B.	FB	401-152
Fullerton, J. B.	RRR	401-116
Fullerton, J. W.	SR	401-78
Fulton, A. L.	FB	401-152
Fulton, Robt.	TVG	401-193
Fults, J. A. M.	RRR	401-116
Funk, Henry	USV	401-230
Funkhouser, Robert	SR	401-78
Funston, John W.	USV	401-230
Fuqua, Henry Earl	RR	401-55
Fuqua, Henry Earl	SR	401-78
Fuqua, J. H.	USV	401-230
Fuqua, W. H.	RR	401-55
Furbish, John	ARM	401-5
Furgerson, Alex	TVG	401-193
Furgeson, L.	FF	401-134
Furlong, W. H.	SR	401-78
Furlong, William Harrison	LR	401-128
Furman, E. E.	FB	401-152
Furman, William George	TVG	401-193
Fuss, G. A.	NAV	401-17
Fussell, Claud B.	SR	401-78
Fusselman, C. H.	FB	401-152
Futch, W. L.	SR	401-78
Futch, William Lee	RRR	401-116
Futral, W. B.	RRR	401-116
Futrell, Richard Lewis	SR	401-78
Gabbert, Blue	TVG	401-193
Gabbert, SheB	USV	401-230
Gabellmann, Frederick	ARM	401-5
Gaddis, Quillie Clayton	RRR	401-116
Gaddy, Ben F.	SR	401-79
Gaffers, William	FF	401-134
Gaffney, Harry M.	TVG	401-193
Gafford, Owen A.	USV	401-230
Gafford, William F.	USV	401-230
Gage, G. A.	SR	401-79
Gage, J. A.	USV	401-230
Gage, Monroe	TST	401-35

Index to Texas Adjutant General Service Records—All Service Branches

Gage, R. L. ....USV 401-230
Gahagan, William ....USV 401-230
Gahagan, William J. ....USV 401-230
Gainer, Charles S., Jr. ....SR 401-79
Gaines, AbnoR ....TVG 401-193
Gaines, C. M. ....SR 401-79
Gaines, C. M. ....LR 401-128
Gaines, D. Y. ....FB 401-152
Gaines, G. A. ....USV 401-230
Gaines, James F. ....TVG 401-193
Gaines, John Pierce ....SR 401-79
Gaines, R. P. ....TVG 401-193
Gaines, R. S. ....USV 401-230
Galbreath, J. W. ....RR 401-55
Gale, Henry ....NAV 401-17
Gale, John C. ....USV 401-230
Gale, Oliver P. ....ARM 401-5
Gales, Moses ....SP 401-44
Gallagher, B. B. ....FB 401-152
Gallagher, Charles M. ....NAV 401-17
Gallagher, Chas. ....FB 401-152
Gallagher, D. O. ....SR 401-79
Gallagher, David P. ....TVG 401-193
Gallagher, J. J. ....FB 401-152
Gallagher, J. S. ....TVG 401-193
Gallagher, Martin ....USV 401-230
Gallagher, N. A. ....SR 401-79
Gallaher, D. ....ARM 401-5
Gallaspy, W. ....RR 401-55
Gallot, George F. ....NAV 401-17
Galloway, Robert L. ....SR 401-79
Galloway, W. S. ....SR 401-79
Galloway, W. S. ....LR 401-128
Galny, Gus W. ....FB 401-152
Galvan, Rafael ....SR 401-79
Galyan, Thomas J. ....USV 401-230
Gambill, Jim T. ....RRR 401-116
Gambill, Seth ....USV 401-230
Gamble, J. D. ....SR 401-79
Gamble, J. D. ....LR 401-128
Gamble, S. A. ....FB 401-152
Gambrell, J. B. ....RRR 401-116
Gambrell, J. Hannon ....RRR 401-116
Gambrell, Rod D. ....SR 401-79
Gamel, Wilks B. ....USV 401-230
Gammill, T. W. ....TVG 401-193
Gammill, W. J. ....TVG 401-193
Gammon, John Lea ....TVG 401-193
Gammon, R. B. ....TVG 401-193
Gammon, William ....TVG 401-193
Gandrettr, Fredrick W. ....USV 401-230
Gandy, Amos ....NAV 401-17
Gann, James D. ....SP 401-44
Gann, W. N. ....SR 401-79
Gannaway, William R. ....RR 401-55
Gannels, A. ....FF 401-134
Ganney, I. N., Jr. ....MV 401-29
Gannon, W. ....TST 401-35
Gannon, William ....SP 401-44
Gant, Charles ....SR 401-79
Gant, J. F. ....TVG 401-193
Gantt, E. S. ....SP 401-44
Gantt, Sanford E. ....USV 401-230
Garbade, Henry ....TVG 401-193
Garcia, Amador E. ....SR 401-79
Garcia, Antonio ....FF 401-134
Garcia, Francisco ....FF 401-134
Garcia, G. N. ....FB 401-152
Garcia, Gregoria ....FF 401-134
Garcia, J. N. ....FB 401-152
Garcia, Jesus ....FF 401-134
Garcia, Leon ....SP 401-44
Garcia, M. ....FB 401-152
Garcia, Mariano ....FF 401-134
Garcia, Migvel ....FB 401-152
Garcia, Rafel ....RR 401-55
Garcia, Ramon ....FB 401-152
Garcia, Raphael ....FF 401-134
Garcia, Thomas ....FF 401-134
Gardien, W. L. ....SR 401-79
Gardien, W. L. ....TVG 401-193
Gardien, W. L. ....LR 401-128
Gardiner, Geo. T. ....USV 401-230
Gardiner, J. B. ....NAV 401-17
Gardner, C. A. ....SP 401-44
Gardner, Charles E. ....SR 401-79
Gardner, D. K. ....TVG 401-193
Gardner, Roy ....SR 401-79
Gardner, S. W. ....CSA 401-39
Gardner, T. A. ....SR 401-79
Gardner, Townsend ....ARM 401-5
Gardner, W. T. ....SR 401-79
Gardner, W. T. ....LR 401-128
Gardner, W. W. ....TVG 401-193
Gardner, Will N. ....USV 401-230
Garin, Dan ....USV 401-230
Garitty, Jas. ....TVG 401-193
Garland, Frank ....SP 401-44
Garland, Robert Frazier ....SR 401-79
Garland, S. J. M. ....TVG 401-193
Garland, Thomas Law ....SP 401-44
Garland, W. E. ....SP 401-44
Garleck, Henry Stow ....SR 401-79
Garlick, C. H. T. ....SR 401-79
Garlick, H. L. ....NAV 401-17
Garlick, H. StaR ....SR 401-79
Garlick, W. Fred ....RR 401-55
Garlock, Wilbert L. ....USV 401-230
Garner, C. E. ....USV 401-230
Garner, Chas. O. ....USV 401-230
Garner, Colus ....TVG 401-193
Garner, H. E. ....SR 401-79

Index to Texas Adjutant General Service Records—All Service Branches

Name	Branch	Record
Garner, Henry	USV	401-230
Garner, J. D.	FF	401-134
Garner, J. R.	RR	401-55
Garner, J. R.	SR	401-79
Garner, John	FF	401-134
Garner, Lon	SR	401-79
Garner, O. C.	SR	401-79
Garner, T. W.	RRR	401-116
Garner, Thomas	FB	401-152
Garner, Thomas J.	FF	401-134
Garner, William S.	MV	401-29
Garner, Winford Preston	RRR	401-116
Garnett, J. O.	TVG	401-193
Garrets, John	ARM	401-5
Garretson, A. J.	FF	401-134
Garrett, A. H.	SR	401-79
Garrett, A. H.	LR	401-128
Garrett, C. C.	SR	401-79
Garrett, C. C.	LR	401-128
Garrett, Donald W.	USV	401-231
Garrett, Felix J.	MV	401-29
Garrett, Henry	FB	401-152
Garrett, Henry M.	USV	401-231
Garrett, J. B.	SR	401-79
Garrett, J. F.	ARM	401-5
Garrett, James	NAV	401-17
Garrett, Joe A.	SR	401-79
Garrett, Joe A.	LR	401-128
Garrett, John M.	TVG	401-193
Garrett, Mansel	CSA	401-39
Garrett, Mansel	CSA	401-39
Garrett, O. H. P.	TVG	401-193
Garrett, Patrick F.	FB	401-152
Garrett, Robt. J.	RR	401-55
Garrett, Thos. E.	USV	401-231
Garrett, W. A.	TVG	401-193
Garrett, William	FB	401-152
Garrett, William W.	RRR	401-117
Garrett, Y. P.	SR	401-79
Garrettson, A. B.	FB	401-152
Garrick, Robert	NAV	401-17
Garrison, D. C.	SR	401-79
Garrison, G. K.	RR	401-55
Garrison, G. Kent	SR	401-79
Garrison, John F.	TVG	401-193
Garrison, Kent	SR	401-79
Garsa, Salome	FF	401-134
Gartlan, John	TVG	401-193
Gartman, H. J.	RRR	401-117
Garvey, L. C.	FB	401-152
Garvin, A. E.	RR	401-55
Garvin, A. E.	SR	401-79
Garvin, Jack A.	TVG	401-193
Gary, Hampson	TVG	401-193
Gary, Hampson	USV	401-231
Gary, HomeR	SR	401-79
Gary, J. W.	SR	401-79
Gary, Rodney	TVG	401-193
Garza, Christobal	SP	401-44
Garza, Eugene	USV	401-231
Garza, Francisco	FF	401-134
Garza, Juan	FF	401-134
Garza, Julio	SP	401-44
Garza, Lonnie	SR	401-79
Garza, Manuel	FF	401-134
Garza, Teodoro	FF	401-134
Garza, Wenceslan	FF	401-134
Gass, J. Fred	TVG	401-193
Gass, William T.	FB	401-152
Gastenberger, Jacob F.	NAV	401-17
Gaston, Lloyd U.	SR	401-79
Gaston, Robert K.	TVG	401-193
Gaston, Robert K.	USV	401-231
Gates, Carroll A.	SR	401-79
Gates, Frank S.	USV	401-231
Gates, G. A.	TVG	401-193
Gates, John Bell	TVG	401-193
Gates, Joseph D.	RR	401-55
Gates, N.	FB	401-152
Gates, Thomas	ARM	401-5
Gates, Thos. N.	USV	401-231
Gates, William	ARM	401-5
Gatewood, J. L.	SR	401-79
Gatliff, James	SP	401-44
Gatlin, James S.	FF	401-134
Gatlin, John G.	RR	401-55
Gatlin, Robt. P.	USV	401-231
Gatlin, T. G.	SP	401-44
Gattis, William G.	USV	401-231
Gatton, A. W.	TVG	401-193
Gatton, William O.	TVG	401-194
Gault, N. L.	SR	401-79
Gault, Robert T.	FF	401-134
Gauntt, Paul, Jr.	SR	401-79
Gauny, John N.	RR	401-55
Gause, Jerrie	TVG	401-194
Gaven, Nelson D.	TVG	401-194
Gavin, John	NAV	401-17
Gay, David	USV	401-231
Gay, Green D.	SR	401-79
Gaye, Peter	TVG	401-194
Gayle, J. M.	TVG	401-194
Gazette, Frank L.	SR	401-79
Gazley, T. J.	ARM	401-5
Gazzo, Giovanni	NAV	401-17
Gearhard, Frank E.	USV	401-231
Gearhart, William	SP	401-44
Gebhard, Lewis W.	RR	401-55
Gebhardt, Fred	RRR	401-117
Gebhart, Palin C.	TVG	401-194
Gee, Bert	RRR	401-117
Gee, James J.	USV	401-231

Index to Texas Adjutant General Service Records—All Service Branches

Name	Branch	Record
Gee, Virginius O.	TVG	401-194
Geen, Robert	TVG	401-194
Geers, Mack R.	USV	401-231
Gehnin, Alexander	USV	401-231
Geiger, Albert M.	USV	401-231
Geiger, John	MV	401-29
Geldmacher, Otto	USV	401-231
Gemoets, E. E.	SR	401-79
Gene, William	FF	401-134
Genity, John	RR	401-55
Gentry, Allen	RR	401-55
Gentry, F. P.	RRR	401-117
Gentry, G. N.	TST	401-35
Gentry, J. M.	RR	401-55
Gentry, James	USV	401-231
Gentry, Leroy	FF	401-134
Gentry, O. E.	RR	401-55
Gentry, Owens E.	SR	401-79
Gentry, Roley	MM	401-32
Gentry, S. N.	RRR	401-117
Gentry, William	CSA	401-39
Gentry, William James	RRR	401-117
Gentzen, Arthur E.	USV	401-231
Gentzen, Clarence	USV	401-231
George, A.	TST	401-35
George, A. P.	TVG	401-194
George, Charles	USV	401-231
George, D. F.	FB	401-152
George, Jacob F.	MV	401-29
George, James	NAV	401-17
George, Jess A.	USV	401-231
George, Joseph H.	USV	401-231
George, W. A., Jr.	TVG	401-194
George, William A.	RR	401-55
George, Willie	TVG	401-194
Gerbani, Gulius	NAV	401-17
Gerdes, Joseph	TVG	401-194
Geren, J. M.	FB	401-152
Geren, Jerry	FB	401-152
Gerhard, George	NAV	401-17
Gerhart, William	FF	401-134
Gerlach, Charles R.	USV	401-231
Gerland, Herman G.	USV	401-231
Germany, BoB	TVG	401-194
Germany, J. T.	FB	401-152
Geron, Frank C.	SR	401-79
Geron, Frank C.	LR	401-128
Gerrish, David A.	FB	401-152
Gerrish, Geo. H.	FB	401-152
Gerrish, M. E.	USV	401-231
Gerrity, Joe A.	SR	401-79
Gerron, Walter	SR	401-79
Gerth, Hugo K.	USV	401-231
Gettliff, James	FF	401-134
Ghent, Charles M.	USV	401-231
Ghent, Syd	USV	401-231
Gholson, A. G.	ARM	401-5
Gholson, Albert F.	RR	401-55
Gholson, Marion F.	TST	401-35
Gholson, Robert M.	USV	401-231
Gholson, Robert M.	USV	401-231
Gholson, T. R.	SR	401-79
Gibb, Robert L.	USV	401-231
Gibbens, J. E.	FB	401-152
Gibbens, James A.	FB	401-152
Gibbens, W. A.	FB	401-152
Gibbins, John D.	RR	401-55
Gibbons, Francis M.	FB	401-152
Gibbons, J. E.	NAV	401-17
Gibbons, James A.	FB	401-152
Gibbons, Robert W.	MV	401-29
Gibbs, Archie F.	USV	401-231
Gibbs, Dee	SR	401-79
Gibbs, George	TVG	401-194
Gibbs, George Stanley	TVG	401-194
Gibbs, H. G.	TVG	401-194
Gibbs, Henry A.	USV	401-231
Gibbs, J. H.	FB	401-152
Gibbs, J. M.	USV	401-231
Gibbs, Max	USV	401-231
Gibbs, W. M.	RRR	401-117
Gibler, Frank	SR	401-79
Gibs, Robert	NAV	401-17
Gibson, A. E.	SR	401-79
Gibson, A. M.	RRR	401-117
Gibson, Arthur B.	USV	401-231
Gibson, C. V.	SR	401-79
Gibson, Chas. C.	USV	401-231
Gibson, Daniel M.	FB	401-152
Gibson, F. M.	NAV	401-17
Gibson, George	RR	401-55
Gibson, George	SR	401-79
Gibson, Harry K.	USV	401-231
Gibson, J. Frank	SR	401-79
Gibson, J. Frank	LR	401-128
Gibson, J. GregG	RRR	401-117
Gibson, James	SR	401-79
Gibson, James B.	FB	401-152
Gibson, James G.	FB	401-152
Gibson, John	NAV	401-17
Gibson, N. M.	SR	401-79
Gibson, R. L.	FB	401-152
Gibson, Ruben	SP	401-44
Gibson, S. E.	SR	401-79
Gibson, Samuel L.	TST	401-35
Gibson, W. M.	FB	401-153
Gibson, W. S.	TVG	401-194
Gibson, William L.	USV	401-231
Giddens, Levi C.	TVG	401-194
Giddens, Wiley M.	USV	401-231
Giddings, Geo.	TVG	401-194
Giddings, Jas. A.	USV	401-231

Index to Texas Adjutant General Service Records—All Service Branches

Name	Branch	Record
Gideon, J. M.	SP	401-44
Giegerich, George	FB	401-153
Gies, Edward Chas.	USV	401-231
Giese, Adolph G.	TVG	401-194
Giesecke, H.	SR	401-79
Giesen, Ed W.	TVG	401-194
Giesenschlag, C.	SP	401-44
Giessler, William F.	FF	401-134
Giffers, William	SP	401-44
Giffin, C. W.	FB	401-153
Gifford, Isaac	NAV	401-17
Gilbert, Antonio	ARM	401-5
Gilbert, C.	FB	401-153
Gilbert, H. S.	TVG	401-194
Gilbert, John F.	SR	401-79
Gilbert, Lillian	SR	401-79
Gilbert, Phillip	SP	401-44
Gilbert, Phillip	USV	401-231
Gilbert, William	NAV	401-17
Gilbough, James M.	SR	401-79
Gilbreath, Charles H.	RRR	401-117
Gilbreath, Hugh	USV	401-231
Gilbreath, Malcom	NAV	401-17
Gildart, J. W.	RRR	401-117
Gildart, John B.	USV	401-231
Gildea, A. M.	FB	401-153
Gildea, C. A.	TVG	401-194
Gilder, A. W.	TVG	401-194
Gilder, J. L.	SP	401-44
Giles, B. F.	FB	401-153
Giles, B. Jeannette	SR	401-79
Giles, George W.	SR	401-79
Giles, Harry A.	TVG	401-194
Giles, Robert	NAV	401-17
Giles, Weldon A.	SR	401-79
Gilfillan, Calvin W.	SR	401-79
Gililland, J. K.	TVG	401-194
Gill, E.	FB	401-153
Gill, Richard	SR	401-79
Gill, S. L.	SR	401-79
Gill, S. L.	SR	401-79
Gill, Samuel L.	USV	401-231
Gill, William A.	FB	401-153
Gill, William D., Dr.	SR	401-79
Gilland, Maurice A.	USV	401-231
Gillar, Ernest	USV	401-231
Gillen, John	SR	401-79
Gillenwater, J. F.	USV	401-231
Gillespey, Joshua W.	NAV	401-17
Gillespie, Alexander	ARM	401-5
Gillespie, Bryson D.	USV	401-231
Gillespie, C.	FF	401-134
Gillespie, Charles	SP	401-44
Gillespie, D. W.	USV	401-231
Gillespie, J. G.	FB	401-153
Gillespie, J. P.	RR	401-55
Gillespie, J. T.	FB	401-153
Gillespie, J. W.	NAV	401-17
Gillespie, Preston H.	USV	401-231
Gillespie, Robert	NAV	401-17
Gillespie, Thom. P.	FB	401-153
Gillespie, Thomas	NAV	401-17
Gillett, Dick J.	FB	401-153
Gillett, E. T.	SR	401-79
Gillett, J. B.	FB	401-153
Gillett, James B.	SR	401-79
Gillett, James S.	MV	401-29
Gillett, Leonard T.	USV	401-231
Gillett, W. H.	USV	401-231
Gillette, Fred	SR	401-79
Gilley, James W.	TST	401-35
Gilley, Soloman G.	RR	401-55
Gilley, Thomas J.	FB	401-153
Gilley, WilliaM	ARM	401-5
Gillham, Art	SR	401-79
Gilliam, J. D.	SR	401-79
Gilliam, J. W.	TVG	401-194
Gilliam, James M.	USV	401-231
Gilliam, Richard H.	USV	401-231
Gilliam, William	RR	401-55
Gilliland, Carl	SR	401-79
Gilliland, Carl	LR	401-128
Gilliland, George	SR	401-79
Gilliland, Grenade Donaldson	RR	401-55
Gilliland, J. B.	SR	401-79
Gilliland, J. E.	LR	401-128
Gilliland, James	TVG	401-194
Gilliland, Robert E.	TVG	401-194
Gilliland, William	ARM	401-5
Gillis, John	FB	401-153
Gillman, O. F.	NAV	401-17
Gillock, Buford	FB	401-153
Gillon, John A.	RR	401-55
Gillon, John A.	SR	401-79
Gillson, William	SP	401-44
Gillum, F. C.	TVG	401-194
Gilmer, B. Bruister	TVG	401-194
Gilmer, J. W.	SR	401-79
Gilmore, J. H.	SR	401-79
Gilpin, George	TVG	401-194
Gilpin, John W.	SR	401-79
Gilpin, Ralph	NAV	401-17
Gilreath, J. D.	TVG	401-194
Gilreath, Munford	TVG	401-194
Gilreath, Munford	USV	401-231
Gimon, Milton E.	SR	401-79
Ginn, E. Y.	SR	401-79
Ginn, O. M.	SR	401-79
Ginsberg, Harry	SR	401-79
Gips, Manfred O.	SR	401-79
Gipson, F. C.	SR	401-79
Gipson, F. C.	LR	401-128

Index to Texas Adjutant General Service Records—All Service Branches

Name	Branch	Record
Girad, John F.	NAV	401-17
Girard, O. J.	USV	401-231
Girard, OliveR	TVG	401-194
Giraud, S. A.	USV	401-231
Gird, Benton B.	SR	401-79
Girdley, B. C.	SR	401-80
Girdley, B. C.	LR	401-128
Giroux, Joseph	SP	401-44
Girsewald, K.	FB	401-153
Girvin, Fitzhugh B.	USV	401-231
Givron, CasimiR	FF	401-134
Glascock, Lee	RR	401-55
Glascock, Lee	SR	401-80
Glasenapp, George V.	SP	401-44
Glasgow, W. H.	FF	401-134
Glass, Aubrey O.	TVG	401-194
Glass, C. C.	TVG	401-194
Glass, J. K.	FB	401-153
Glass, John Wates	FB	401-153
Glass, W. E.	TVG	401-194
Glass, WilliaM	TVG	401-194
Glasscock, C. B.	USV	401-231
Glasscock, C. G.	SR	401-80
Glasscock, Henry D.	RR	401-55
Glasscock, Mike E.	SR	401-80
Glasscock, Mike E., Jr.	SR	401-80
Gleason, George	FB	401-153
Glen, Andrew	ARM	401-5
Glenn W. L.	TVG	401-194
Glenn, Chas. I.	USV	401-231
Glenn, Harry	USV	401-231
Glenn, M. M.	FB	401-153
Glenn, William E.	NAV	401-17
Glick, George Alva	RRR	401-117
Glick, George Alvor	RR	401-55
Glicksman, M. D.	TVG	401-194
Glidden, Harry	SR	401-80
Glisson, A. B.	FB	401-153
Glitsch, Fritz W.	USV	401-231
Glohr, John	FF	401-134
Gloon, John	NAV	401-17
Glover, A. J.	TST	401-35
Glover, C. E.	SR	401-80
Glover, C. R.	TVG	401-194
Glover, Frank W.	TVG	401-194
Glover, George W.	USV	401-231
Glover, Homer T.	SR	401-80
Glover, Homer Thomas	SR	401-80
Glover, W. S.	SR	401-80
Goad, T. J.	SR	401-80
Goats, James A.	USV	401-231
Gobble, Charles	FB	401-153
Godbold, Harry E.	USV	401-231
Goddard, George E.	SR	401-80
Goddard, John D.	USV	401-231
Goddard, Kenneth E.	TVG	401-194
Godden, Benjamin	NAV	401-17
Godfree, C. H.	TVG	401-194
Godfrey, Augustus A.	USV	401-231
Godfrey, Douglas	SR	401-80
Godfrey, G. L.	TVG	401-194
Godfrey, James W.	USV	401-231
Godfrey, James W.	USV	401-231
Godley, Frank B.	TVG	401-194
Godsey, Frank W.	USV	401-231
Godshall, George W.	FB	401-153
Goebel, George	TVG	401-194
Goen, F. O.	RR	401-55
Goeth, Charles	TST	401-35
Goff, A. G.	SR	401-80
Goff, E. R.	FB	401-153
Goff, Louie S.	USV	401-231
Goff, T. J.	RR	401-55
Goff, Thomas J.	FB	401-153
Goforth, Laurence S.	RRR	401-117
Goggin, J. L.	FB	401-153
Goggin, William E.	TVG	401-194
Goins, William C.	SR	401-80
Golay, Travis L.	SR	401-80
Gold, Charles	NAV	401-17
Goldberg, Louis N.	SR	401-80
Golden, F. L.	FB	401-153
Golden, George	FF	401-134
Golden, George L.	USV	401-231
Golden, Spencer T.	TVG	401-194
Golden, Thomas W.	USV	401-231
Goldsmith, Albert	USV	401-231
Goldsmith, Ed S.	USV	401-231
Goldstein, Harry	SR	401-80
Goldthwaite, George	TST	401-35
Golightly, Thos. J.	ARM	401-5
Gollihar, Edward	USV	401-231
Golsan, H. L., Jr.	USV	401-231
Golsen, W. W.	FB	401-153
Goltomez, Abraham	ARM	401-5
Gombert, J. G.	SR	401-80
Gomez, Eusebia	FF	401-134
Gomez, Justo	FF	401-134
Gomez, Leonidas	FF	401-134
Gomez, Manuel	FF	401-134
Gomillion, R. L.	RRR	401-117
Gonsales, Terencino	FF	401-134
Gonzales, Antonio	FF	401-134
Gonzales, Juan	FF	401-134
Gonzales, Juan C.	SR	401-80
Gonzales, Santiago	FF	401-134
Gonzales, Theodore	FB	401-153
Gonzales, Willie	SR	401-80
Gonzalez, Juan C.	RR	401-55
Gonzalez, Juan C.	LR	401-128
Goobers, Andrew	USV	401-231
Gooch, Albert Rowland	SR	401-80

Index to Texas Adjutant General Service Records—All Service Branches

Name	Branch	Number
Gooch, John	TVG	401-194
Goodall, A. G.	NAV	401-17
Goodall, James P.	ARM	401-5
Goodall, James W.	ARM	401-5
Goode, Benjamin E.	SP	401-44
Goode, James L.	TVG	401-194
Goode, John W.	USV	401-231
Goode, RoberT	TST	401-35
Goodfellow, N. F.	FB	401-153
Goodfellow, Robert	RRR	401-117
Goodfellow, Robert	SR	401-80
Goodfellow, Robert	FB	401-153
Goodhue, J. W.	USV	401-231
Goodin, Jno. H.	TVG	401-194
Goodlet, Patrick	FF	401-134
Goodlett, J. B.	SR	401-80
Goodlett, J. B.	TVG	401-194
Goodlett, J. B.	LR	401-128
Goodloe, G. B.	RR	401-55
Goodloe, Gail Borden	SR	401-80
Goodloe, Winter	FB	401-153
Goodman, Abraham	USV	401-231
Goodman, Aronson	TVG	401-194
Goodman, Harry	TVG	401-194
Goodman, James R.	TVG	401-194
Goodman, Noton C.	USV	401-231
Goodman, Sam E.	USV	401-231
Goodner, F. M.	SP	401-44
Goodrich, A. T.	TVG	401-194
Goodrich, Horace G.	SR	401-80
Goodrich, John G.	USV	401-231
Goodrich, S. E.	RR	401-55
Goodsin, Edward	NAV	401-17
Goodson, Jesse W.	USV	401-231
Goodwin, ____	SR	401-80
Goodwin, Chas. C.	USV	401-231
Goodwin, D. A.	FB	401-153
Goodwin, Harry M.	TVG	401-194
Goodwin, Harry M.	USV	401-231
Goodwin, Henry H.	USV	401-231
Goodwin, J. F.	FB	401-153
Goodwin, John W.	USV	401-231
Goodwin, Leo, Jr.	SR	401-80
Goodwin, Mark L.	USV	401-231
Goodwin, O. W.	RR	401-55
Goodwin, P. W.	SP	401-44
Goodwin, Richard Lawrence	SR	401-80
Goodwin, William	SP	401-44
Goodwyn, F. E., Jr.	SR	401-80
Goodwyn, James Dobie	SR	401-80
Goody, George	ARM	401-5
Goodyear, Hartford	USV	401-231
Goolsbee, Herod	SP	401-44
Goolsby, Al J.	USV	401-231
Goolsby, John Arthur	RR	401-55
Gordon, Charles	TVG	401-194
Gordon, Daniel E.	USV	401-231
Gordon, David	TST	401-35
Gordon, George W.	TVG	401-194
Gordon, J. H.	FB	401-153
Gordon, J. H. "Jim"	SR	401-80
Gordon, John	TVG	401-194
Gordon, John F.	RR	401-55
Gordon, L. D.	TVG	401-194
Gordon, L. U.	SR	401-80
Gordon, William G.	USV	401-231
Gore, Andrew J.	MM	401-32
Gore, George	RRR	401-117
Gore, H.	FB	401-153
Gore, William	ARM	401-5
Gorham, W. M.	RR	401-55
Goring, Dick	FB	401-153
Gorman, John	NAV	401-17
Gorman, Johnson	ARM	401-5
Gorman, Patrick	NAV	401-17
Gorman, Patrick	ARM	401-5
Gormley, E. A.	SR	401-80
Gormos, Francisco	RR	401-55
Gosfield, William	FF	401-134
Goss, J. Fred	TVG	401-194
Goss, Robert G.	RR	401-55
Goss, Robert G.	SR	401-80
Gossett, Edward G.	TVG	401-194
Gossett, J. K.	SR	401-80
Gossett, J. S.	FB	401-153
Gossett, J. T.	SR	401-80
Gossett, J. W.	SR	401-80
Gossett, N. B.	TVG	401-194
Gossett, T. J.	FB	401-153
Gossett, W. S.	FB	401-153
Gossler, J. J.	SP	401-44
Goswick, Moses S.	RRR	401-117
Gouger, Henry E.	SR	401-80
Gouger, R. A.	SR	401-80
Gouger, Roland A.	RR	401-55
Gough, James W.	USV	401-231
Gould, Horatio	ARM	401-5
Gould, L.	FB	401-153
Gour, John C.	FF	401-134
Gourley, A.	FB	401-153
Gourley, D. W.	FB	401-153
Gourley, Grant	FB	401-153
Gowin, Lafayette	SR	401-80
Goynes, William W.	USV	401-231
Grace, Ben	USV	401-231
Grace, J. W.	FB	401-153
Grace, Patrick T.	ARM	401-5
Grace, Philip	USV	401-231
Grace, W. L.	SR	401-80
Grady, C. M.	FB	401-153
Grady, John W.	USV	401-231

Index to Texas Adjutant General Service Records—All Service Branches

Name	Branch	Record
Grady, T. J.	TVG	401-194
Graf, E. F.	SR	401-80
Grafton, Benton McAdams	SR	401-80
Grafton, James	ARM	401-5
Grafton, L.	TVG	401-194
Gragg, John	USV	401-231
Gragg, John G.	FF	401-134
Graham, A. F.	SR	401-80
Graham, A. H.	MV	401-29
Graham, A. W.	USV	401-231
Graham, Alexander G.	USV	401-231
Graham, Chas.	TVG	401-194
Graham, Daniel O.	USV	401-231
Graham, David L.	MV	401-29
Graham, E.	TVG	401-194
Graham, George	TVG	401-194
Graham, Hosea	RR	401-56
Graham, J. K.	NAV	401-17
Graham, James M.	USV	401-231
Graham, Joe M.	SR	401-80
Graham, John	RR	401-56
Graham, John B.	USV	401-231
Graham, Karl H.	USV	401-231
Graham, Marvin A.	USV	401-231
Graham, O. T.	TVG	401-194
Graham, S. T.	SP	401-44
Graham, Samuel	FB	401-153
Graham, W. B.	SR	401-80
Graham, Wade B.	LR	401-128
Grahame, James	FB	401-153
Gralen, August	MV	401-29
Gramm, Chas.	TVG	401-194
Gramm, John A.	TVG	401-194
Granbury, H. B.	RR	401-56
Grandy, Amos	NAV	401-17
Grandy, Amos	ARM	401-5
Granger, George W.	RRR	401-117
Granger, George W.	SR	401-80
Granger, Stanley C.	SR	401-80
Grant, A. C.	FB	401-153
Grant, Albert	FF	401-134
Grant, C. D.	FB	401-153
Grant, C. V.	TVG	401-194
Grant, Charles C.	TVG	401-194
Grant, Ed	TVG	401-194
Grant, Harrald D.	TVG	401-194
Grant, J. C.	FB	401-153
Grant, J. H.	TVG	401-194
Grant, J. S.	FB	401-153
Grant, John H.	USV	401-231
Grant, L. B.	USV	401-231
Grant, W. G.	FB	401-153
Grantham, Everett A.	TVG	401-194
Grantham, George H.	USV	401-231
Grantham, R.	CSA	401-39
Grantham, R. G.	SR	401-80
Grasberger, Joseph	USV	401-232
Grave, George	SP	401-44
Graves, C. E.	TVG	401-194
Graves, G. H.	TVG	401-194
Graves, George Shelton	SR	401-80
Graves, Hume	RR	401-56
Graves, J. C.	FB	401-153
Graves, J. N.	RRR	401-117
Graves, John W.	SR	401-80
Graves, Richard C.	FB	401-153
Graves, Richard S.	TVG	401-194
Graves, Theo.	TVG	401-194
Graves, W. E.	TVG	401-194
Gravett, Jas.	TVG	401-194
Gravett, L.	TVG	401-194
Gravett, William	TVG	401-194
Gravis, C. K.	SR	401-80
Gravis, Charles K.	LR	401-128
Gravis, John F.	FB	401-153
Graw, John A.	USV	401-232
Gray, Alfred G.	NAV	401-17
Gray, Andrew B.	NAV	401-17
Gray, B. O.	USV	401-232
Gray, Boon	TVG	401-194
Gray, C. R.	RR	401-56
Gray, Charles N.	SR	401-80
Gray, E. H.	TVG	401-194
Gray, Earl	USV	401-232
Gray, Edwin F.	NAV	401-17
Gray, George W.	RR	401-56
Gray, George W.	SR	401-80
Gray, Hardy	SP	401-44
Gray, Henry C.	FB	401-153
Gray, J. A.	TVG	401-194
Gray, J. F.	RRR	401-117
Gray, J. R.	TVG	401-194
Gray, J. W.	SR	401-80
Gray, J. W.	LR	401-128
Gray, James W.	ARM	401-5
Gray, Jerry	RR	401-56
Gray, Jerry	SR	401-80
Gray, Jerry Cope	SR	401-80
Gray, John D.	TST	401-35
Gray, John L.	USV	401-232
Gray, John M.	SR	401-80
Gray, John W.	USV	401-232
Gray, P. W.	CSA	401-39
Gray, Raymond	TVG	401-194
Gray, Thos. E.	USV	401-232
Gray, Tom R.	SR	401-80
Gray, W. H.	SR	401-80
Gray, W. H.	LR	401-128
Gray, W. K.	SR	401-80
Gray, William	ARM	401-5
Gray, William H.	TVG	401-194
Gray, William M.	FF	401-134

Index to Texas Adjutant General Service Records—All Service Branches

Name	Branch	Ref
Grayson, Frank	SP	401-44
Grayson, William	TVG	401-194
Grayson, William E.	TVG	401-194
Grayson, William E.	USV	401-232
Greathouse, Charles E.	TVG	401-194
Greathouse, Horace C.	RR	401-56
Greathouse, Robert B.	TVG	401-194
Grebe, Louis	TST	401-35
Green, A.	TVG	401-194
Green, A. E.	SR	401-80
Green, Amos E.	FB	401-153
Green, Benjamin F.	FF	401-134
Green, Boliver	SP	401-44
Green, C. C.	RR	401-56
Green, Charles W.	TST	401-35
Green, Charley	TVG	401-195
Green, Charlie	TVG	401-195
Green, Chas. L.	TVG	401-194
Green, Edd	FB	401-153
Green, Edward A.	USV	401-232
Green, Edward R.	NAV	401-17
Green, Elwood L.	TVG	401-195
Green, Eugene	TVG	401-195
Green, G. F.	FB	401-153
Green, George	USV	401-232
Green, George B.	FB	401-153
Green, George W.	SP	401-44
Green, Glen A.	SR	401-80
Green, Guy	TVG	401-195
Green, Guy	USV	401-232
Green, H.	TVG	401-195
Green, J. F.	FB	401-153
Green, J. M.	TVG	401-195
Green, J. P.	FB	401-153
Green, J. T.	USV	401-232
Green, J. W. B.	SR	401-80
Green, J. W. B.	LR	401-128
Green, Jacob	ARM	401-5
Green, James	SP	401-44
Green, Jesse A.	FF	401-134
Green, John	TST	401-35
Green, John	TVG	401-195
Green, John A., Jr.	TVG	401-195
Green, John F.	USV	401-232
Green, John G.	USV	401-232
Green, John W.	USV	401-232
Green, John W. B.	TVG	401-195
Green, John W. B.	USV	401-232
Green, Joseph T.	TVG	401-195
Green, R. A.	SR	401-80
Green, Robert A.	RRR	401-117
Green, Robt. B.	TVG	401-195
Green, T. E.	SP	401-44
Green, Thomas	TVG	401-195
Green, Thomas H.	FB	401-153
Green, Thomas J.	ARM	401-5
Green, W.	CSA	401-39
Green, W. C.	SR	401-80
Green, W. H.	FF	401-134
Green, W. M.	FB	401-153
Green, William	NAV	401-17
Green, William	FB	401-153
Green, William	TVG	401-195
Green, William J.	SR	401-80
Green, Willis	SP	401-44
Greenaway, Harry	MV	401-29
Greene, Carl	SR	401-80
Greene, Charles A.	USV	401-232
Greene, Chas. T.	USV	401-232
Greene, J. M.	TVG	401-195
Greene, J. P.	TVG	401-195
Greene, Robert M.	TVG	401-195
Greene, Rowan A.	USV	401-232
Greenert, Richard M.	USV	401-232
Greenrock, G. J.	TVG	401-195
Greenstreet, Wilber C.	TVG	401-195
Greenstreet, Wilber C.	USV	401-232
Greenwell, Samuel A., Jr.	TVG	401-195
Greenwood, Arch A.	SR	401-80
Greenwood, B. C.	FB	401-153
Greenwood, Samuel	NAV	401-17
Greer, C. B., Jr.	SR	401-80
Greer, D. C.	SR	401-80
Greer, D. C.	LR	401-128
Greer, Ed	TVG	401-195
Greer, G. B.	FB	401-153
Greer, Mike	TVG	401-195
Greer, O. H.	FB	401-153
Greer, Oscar	USV	401-232
Greer, Perry	FB	401-153
Greer, R. L.	USV	401-232
Greer, Robert L.	USV	401-232
Greer, Thomas J.	USV	401-232
Greer, W. J.	FB	401-153
Greer, William A.	USV	401-232
Greer, William H.	TST	401-35
Greer, William T.	USV	401-232
Gregg, E. M.	TVG	401-195
Gregg, John G.	FB	401-153
Gregg, Oliver H.	RR	401-56
Gregg, William	MV	401-29
Gregoire, Ambrose	ARM	401-5
Gregory, A. M.	SP	401-44
Gregory, Daniel L.	USV	401-232
Gregory, Eugene T.	USV	401-232
Gregory, Isac	MM	401-32
Gregory, J. C.	FB	401-153
Gregory, James F.	USV	401-232
Gregory, N.	FB	401-153
Grell, Fritz	TVG	401-195
Grenbaun, T. A.	SR	401-80
Gresham, James N.	TST	401-35

Index to Texas Adjutant General Service Records—All Service Branches

Name	Branch	Record
Grether, T.	NAV	401-17
Greve, Hans	USV	401-232
Grey, Alexander	NAV	401-17
Grey, John	USV	401-232
Grey, Thomas	ARM	401-5
Grey, William	FB	401-153
Gribble, A. T.	SR	401-80
Gribble, A. W.	SR	401-80
Gribble, William P.	USV	401-232
Grice, J. E.	TVG	401-195
Grier, J. Y.	TVG	401-195
Griffin, Cal	USV	401-232
Griffin, Charles	NAV	401-17
Griffin, E. B.	TVG	401-195
Griffin, Ed	TVG	401-195
Griffin, Edward O.	TVG	401-195
Griffin, F. M.	SP	401-44
Griffin, Frank S.	SR	401-80
Griffin, Fred E.	RR	401-56
Griffin, George L.	TVG	401-195
Griffin, Hugh L.	MM	401-32
Griffin, Ira B.	USV	401-232
Griffin, J. H.	FB	401-153
Griffin, James	ARM	401-5
Griffin, James P.	TVG	401-195
Griffin, K. W.	SR	401-80
Griffin, K. W.	LR	401-128
Griffin, Kay	USV	401-232
Griffin, M. A.	FB	401-153
Griffin, Ray	RR	401-56
Griffin, Ray	RRR	401-117
Griffin, Ray	SR	401-80
Griffin, Reuben R.	SR	401-80
Griffin, Royal A.	FB	401-153
Griffin, Sam H.	FB	401-153
Griffin, T. F.	SP	401-44
Griffin, Thomas	FB	401-153
Griffin, Thomas Dillard	USV	401-232
Griffin, Val	TVG	401-195
Griffin, W. C.	TVG	401-195
Griffin, W. H.	FB	401-153
Griffin, W. T.	FB	401-153
Griffin, William	FB	401-153
Griffin, William H.	FB	401-153
Griffis, John A.	TVG	401-195
Griffith, Crabb M.	USV	401-232
Griffith, E. R.	FB	401-153
Griffith, John E.	SR	401-80
Griffith, L. J.	FB	401-153
Griffith, Nicholas	ARM	401-5
Griffiths, T. W.	SR	401-80
Griffitts, H. W.	SR	401-80
Grigg, William	FF	401-134
Griggs, J. R.	SR	401-80
Grignon, A.	NAV	401-17
Grigsby, J. A.	RR	401-56
Grigsby, J. L.	SR	401-80
Grigsby, Luke M.	USV	401-232
Grigsby, Sid	USV	401-232
Grigsby, T. A.	SP	401-44
Grillet, A. M.	USV	401-232
Grillo, Joseph	USV	401-232
Grim, L. E.	TVG	401-195
Grimes, A. W.	FB	401-154
Grimes, Albert C.	FB	401-154
Grimes, Ben L.	TVG	401-195
Grimes, E. E.	TVG	401-195
Grimes, Frank	SR	401-80
Grimes, George M.	USV	401-232
Grimes, J. J.	SR	401-80
Grimes, J. J.	LR	401-128
Grimes, M. H.	SP	401-44
Grimes, Reid	TVG	401-195
Grimes, Robert H.	USV	401-232
Grimes, S. G.	RRR	401-117
Grimes, Samuel G.	USV	401-232
Grimes, W. B.	TVG	401-195
Grimes, W. T.	RR	401-56
Grimsinger, Aloys	FF	401-134
Grimsinger, Eugene	FF	401-134
Grimsley, William	ARM	401-5
Grindel, Albert	RR	401-56
Griner, Geo.	USV	401-232
Griner, John I.	USV	401-232
Griner, John Joseph	USV	401-232
Grinnage, S.	TVG	401-195
Grinnan, Mandly	USV	401-232
Grisham, Jesse W.	TVG	401-195
Grisham, W. J.	SR	401-80
Grisham, W. J.	LR	401-128
Grissom, Charles W.	SR	401-80
Griswald, T.	NAV	401-17
Griswell, John K.	TVG	401-195
Grizzard, L. A.	TVG	401-195
Grizzell, John H.	FB	401-154
Grober, Henry A.	TVG	401-195
Groce, Peter	ARM	401-5
Groce, W. W.	TST	401-35
Groce, Willie George	RRR	401-117
Grogan, John	USV	401-232
Gronso, W.	FB	401-154
Groos, Otto	USV	401-232
Gross, Abe	SR	401-81
Gross, Abe	TVG	401-195
Gross, Fred	NAV	401-17
Gross, Harry L.	RR	401-56
Gross, Henry C.	USV	401-232
Gross, John C.	FB	401-154
Gross, Leo	TVG	401-195
Grota, E. F.	SR	401-81
Grote, H.	TVG	401-195
Grover, James Edward	RR	401-56

Index to Texas Adjutant General Service Records—All Service Branches

Name	Branch	Record
Groves, H. B.	SR	401-81
Groves, W. H.	TVG	401-195
Groves, William R.	USV	401-232
Grow, William Paola	TVG	401-195
Gruetzner, Albert E.	SR	401-81
Grumble, William G.	CSA	401-39
Grumbles, Edward D.	CSA	401-39
Grumbly, W. M.	CSA	401-39
Grumdman, Otto	USV	401-232
Grundy, E. S.	TVG	401-195
Grush, H. L.	ARM	401-5
Grusham, James A.	TVG	401-195
Grylski, John	NAV	401-17
Guajardo, Santiago	FB	401-154
Gudenoge, Joseph T.	USV	401-232
Gueene, Rudolph, Jr.	TVG	401-195
Guerero, Alephos	FF	401-134
Guering, Robert	FF	401-134
Guerra, Hilario	FF	401-134
Guerra, Lino	FF	401-134
Guerra, Mathias	FF	401-134
Guerra, Pablo	TVG	401-195
Guerra, Rosalia	FF	401-134
Guerra, Thomas	TVG	401-195
Guerrero, Alejo	FB	401-154
Guessaz, O. C.	TVG	401-195
Guggenheim, Harry	SR	401-81
Guibourge, Claude	ARM	401-5
Guilford, H. Boyd	SR	401-81
Guillemean, W.	ARM	401-5
Guillemette, Louis	SR	401-81
Guin, Joseph H.	USV	401-232
Guinn, J. G.	TST	401-35
Guinn, Marvin E.	TVG	401-195
Guinn, R. A.	RRR	401-117
Gullahorn, Jack	TVG	401-195
Gulley, Barney	USV	401-232
Gulley, Robert L.	SR	401-81
Gullick, William H., Jr.	TVG	401-195
Gumm, Terry	RRR	401-117
Gunn, Elmer G.	SR	401-81
Gunn, Elmer G.	LR	401-128
Gunn [?], James	TVG	401-195
Gunn, Joe R.	USV	401-232
Gunn, Louis	USV	401-232
Gunn, W. E.	TVG	401-195
Gunning, J. H.	FF	401-134
Gunter, George E.	SR	401-81
Gunter, James A.	USV	401-232
Gunter, Mirt	TVG	401-195
Gunther, Otto	USV	401-232
Gunther, W. E.	SR	401-81
Gupton, G. D.	FB	401-154
Gurley, Geo. B.	TVG	401-195
Gurley, Jas. F.	TVG	401-195
Gusman, Manuel	FF	401-134
Gustafson, Oscar	RR	401-56
Gustafson, Oscar	SR	401-81
Gustafson, Walter L.	SR	401-81
Guthrie, Arthur F.	USV	401-232
Guthrie, Dan	FB	401-154
Guthrie, Jesse H.	TVG	401-195
Gutierrez, Agustin	TVG	401-195
Gutierrez, Angel	FF	401-134
Gutzeit, F. A.	RR	401-56
Guy, John F.	USV	401-232
Guynes, Charles O.	SR	401-81
Guynes, Luther Brown	RRR	401-117
Guynes, W. P., Jr.	SR	401-81
Guyness, E. E.	TVG	401-195
Guynn, J. W.	SR	401-81
Guyse, William H.	FB	401-154
Guzman, A. T.	FB	401-154
Guzman, Santiago	SR	401-81
Gwin, Phil	TVG	401-195
Gwynn, Frank G.	USV	401-232
Haag, Albert L.	TVG	401-195
Haas, Abraham	USV	401-232
Haas, Frederick	FF	401-134
Haas, Harry	USV	401-232
Haberle, Frank	FF	401-134
Haberlin, Gideon W.	USV	401-232
Haberstrot, T. D.	NAV	401-18
Haby, William	SR	401-81
Haby, William	LR	401-128
Hackett, Harry J.	USV	401-232
Hackett, James	ARM	401-5
Hackney, W. A.	USV	401-232
Hackworth, J. W.	SP	401-44
Hackworth, John W.	TVG	401-195
Hackworth, N. L.	TST	401-35
Hackworth, Stephen A.	SP	401-44
Hackworth, W. W.	MM	401-32
Hadden, J. H.	TVG	401-195
Haddon, Emmet P.	USV	401-232
Haden, Jno. F., Jr.	USV	401-232
Haden, W. B.	TVG	401-195
Haden, Wesley W.	TVG	401-195
Hadley, Robert	FB	401-154
Hadra, Frederick	TVG	401-195
Hadwin, James W.	ARM	401-5
Haeberly, John	FF	401-134
Haenche, Emil	USV	401-232
Hagan, Lon A.	TVG	401-195
Hagberg, Gosta	TVG	401-195
Hageman, Claude	USV	401-232
Hageman, E. R.	FB	401-154
Hageman, Ed	FB	401-154
Hagen, A.	FB	401-154
Hagen, Louis	FF	401-134
Hager, Dilworth S.	SR	401-81
Hagerman, E.	FB	401-154

Index to Texas Adjutant General Service Records—All Service Branches

Hagerty, William	NAV	401-18
Hagetstein, Henry	USV	401-232
Haggard, George	NAV	401-18
Hagins, W. J.	SR	401-81
Hagler, Bibb	USV	401-232
Hagler, C. H.	RR	401-56
Hagood, W. W.	SR	401-81
Hague, A. G.	TVG	401-195
Hahl, EarnsT	TVG	401-195
Hahn, Joseph	FF	401-134
Hahn, Willie	TVG	401-195
Haidusek, J. S.	USV	401-232
Haigler, B. F.	SR	401-81
Hail, Jules A.	USV	401-232
Hail, Thomas J.	MV	401-29
Haile, W. A.	TST	401-35
Haile, W. A.	USV	401-232
Hailey, Herschel T.	USV	401-232
Haines, D. T.	SR	401-81
Hairgrove, D. A.	TVG	401-195
Hairgrove, M. D. L.	TVG	401-195
Hairston, I. D.	TVG	401-195
Haislip, Calvin M.	USV	401-232
Hajny, Frank	TVG	401-195
Halarnnda, Neil	USV	401-232
Halastick, Ernest H.	USV	401-232
Halbert, Arthur	USV	401-232
Halbert, H. S.	RR	401-56
Halbert, Nathan	ARM	401-5
Halbert, T. H.	SR	401-81
Haldeman, Horace P.	TVG	401-195
Hale, A. C.	SR	401-81
Hale, Amon C.	RR	401-56
Hale, Charley L.	RR	401-56
Hale, Clarence	RRR	401-117
Hale, Eli Kirby	USV	401-232
Hale, George A.	SR	401-81
Hale, Grant	SR	401-81
Hale, Guy	SR	401-81
Hale, Howard B.	USV	401-232
Hale, J. M.	RR	401-56
Hale, James E.	NAV	401-18
Hale, James W.	USV	401-232
Hale, Joel N.	SR	401-81
Hale, John	USV	401-232
Hale, John W.	SP	401-44
Hale, Mason	NAV	401-18
Hale, T. J.	RR	401-56
Hale, W. D.	RR	401-56
Hale, W. F.	RR	401-56
Hale, W. F.	SR	401-81
Hale, W. F.	SR	401-81
Hale, W. F.	FB	401-154
Hale, W. J.	FB	401-154
Hale, Will	SR	401-81
Hale, Will	LR	401-128
Hales, Emett	SR	401-81
Haley, Ambrosel	TVG	401-195
Haley, Chas.	TVG	401-195
Haley, F. P.	USV	401-232
Haley, J. M.	SP	401-44
Haley, James	SP	401-44
Haley, John	NAV	401-18
Haley, John R.	FB	401-154
Haley, John W.	SP	401-44
Haley, P. D.	RR	401-56
Haley, P. D.	SR	401-81
Haley, Patrick Daniel	SR	401-81
Haley, Thomas	CSA	401-39
Haley, W. D.	TVG	401-195
Halff, Henry M.	USV	401-232
Halfin, Jacob	USV	401-232
Hall, A. M.	SR	401-81
Hall, Abner J.	USV	401-232
Hall, Alfred G.	USV	401-232
Hall, Archie S.	TVG	401-195
Hall, Asa D.	SR	401-81
Hall, B. H., Dr.	SR	401-81
Hall, Charles	NAV	401-18
Hall, Chesley L.	SR	401-81
Hall, Clarence C.	TVG	401-195
Hall, Claud	TVG	401-195
Hall, D. E., Jr.	TVG	401-195
Hall, E. G.	TVG	401-195
Hall, Egbert O.	USV	401-232
Hall, Florence C.	TVG	401-195
Hall, Frank S.	FB	401-154
Hall, G. A.	FB	401-154
Hall, George	NAV	401-18
Hall, George	ARM	401-5
Hall, George W.	TVG	401-195
Hall, H. C.	SR	401-81
Hall, Harvey	ARM	401-5
Hall, Horace C., M.D.	SR	401-81
Hall, Howard N.	RR	401-56
Hall, Irving	TVG	401-195
Hall, J. A.	TST	401-35
Hall, J. H.	SR	401-81
Hall, J. L.	SR	401-81
Hall, J. N., Jr.	USV	401-232
Hall, JacoB	NAV	401-18
Hall, James	NAV	401-18
Hall, James	ARM	401-5
Hall, James	ARM	401-5
Hall, James M.	RR	401-56
Hall, James M.	MV	401-29
Hall, James M.	TVG	401-195
Hall, Jas. W.	USV	401-232
Hall, Jerrey D.	RR	401-56
Hall, Jerry	SP	401-44
Hall, Jesse L.	FB	401-154
Hall, Jno. T.	TVG	401-195

Index to Texas Adjutant General Service Records—All Service Branches

Name	Branch	Record
Hall, Joe, Jr.	USV	401-232
Hall, John	NAV	401-18
Hall, John	TVG	401-195
Hall, John R.	NAV	401-18
Hall, Larry L.	RR	401-56
Hall, Max H.	TVG	401-195
Hall, Ollie	SR	401-81
Hall, Ollie	LR	401-128
Hall, Otis	ARM	401-5
Hall, R. T.	SR	401-81
Hall, Robt. R.	USV	401-232
Hall, Roy	TVG	401-195
Hall, Samuel	MV	401-29
Hall, Samuel H.	TVG	401-195
Hall, Samuel H.	USV	401-232
Hall, Thomas	ARM	401-5
Hall, Thomas T.	USV	401-232
Hall, Van	FB	401-154
Hall, W. D.	FB	401-154
Hall, W. P.	FB	401-154
Hall, W. T.	SP	401-44
Hall, William	NAV	401-18
Hall, William H.	SR	401-81
Hall, William K.	TVG	401-195
Hall, William Thomas	RR	401-56
Hallam, Joseph	MV	401-29
Hallebeke, Edd	RR	401-56
Halleck, Noah	NAV	401-18
Haller, A. F.	SR	401-81
Haller, August	FF	401-134
Haller, Paul	TST	401-35
Halley, John H.	TVG	401-195
Hallmark, R. C.	SR	401-81
Hallmark, W. P.	SR	401-81
Hallmark, W. P.	LR	401-128
Hallmark, William C.	ARM	401-5
Halloran, W. J.	SR	401-81
Halloway, H. E.	TVG	401-195
Halloway, Ije	USV	401-232
Hallum, John	USV	401-232
Halsted, S. T.	FB	401-154
Haltom, R. W.	TVG	401-195
Halton, George	ARM	401-5
Halverton, H. A.	FB	401-154
Ham, E. B.	SR	401-81
Ham, Ferdinand	ARM	401-5
Ham, J. A.	RRR	401-117
Haman, Louis E.	USV	401-232
Hamberlin, J. C.	TVG	401-195
Hamblen, W. P.	SR	401-81
Hambleton, B. E.	FB	401-154
Hambleton, B. P.	FB	401-154
Hambleton, William M.	MV	401-29
Hamburlin, J. C.	TVG	401-195
Hamby, Charles H.	RR	401-56
Hamell, John M.	USV	401-232
Hamer, C. P.	SR	401-81
Hamer, D. E.	RR	401-56
Hamer, D. E.	SR	401-81
Hamer, F. L.	SR	401-81
Hamer, Flavious L.	RR	401-56
Hamer, Frank A.	RR	401-56
Hamer, Harrison L.	RR	401-56
Hamer, Harrison L.	RRR	401-117
Hamer, Harrison L.	SR	401-81
Hames, Ira	FF	401-135
Hames, J. C.	FB	401-154
Hamill, Joseph	USV	401-232
Hamilton, A.	FF	401-135
Hamilton, A. S.	CSA	401-39
Hamilton, Amos	NAV	401-18
Hamilton, Austin T.	RR	401-56
Hamilton, C. H.	FB	401-154
Hamilton, C. R.	TVG	401-195
Hamilton, Carl E.	USV	401-232
Hamilton, D. T.	SR	401-81
Hamilton, Dick	SR	401-81
Hamilton, E. V.	TVG	401-195
Hamilton, Edward J.	TVG	401-195
Hamilton, ErnesT	SR	401-81
Hamilton, Ernest F.	SR	401-81
Hamilton, F. W.	FB	401-154
Hamilton, Frank	USV	401-232
Hamilton, Frank E.	TVG	401-195
Hamilton, Henry	NAV	401-18
Hamilton, Henry	SR	401-81
Hamilton, J. B.	TVG	401-195
Hamilton, J. D.	SR	401-81
Hamilton, J. D.	LR	401-128
Hamilton, J. E.	SR	401-81
Hamilton, J. E.	TVG	401-195
Hamilton, J. H.	LR	401-128
Hamilton, J. J.	TVG	401-195
Hamilton, James	NAV	401-18
Hamilton, Joseph B.	USV	401-232
Hamilton, N. J.	USV	401-232
Hamilton, Orange	FB	401-154
Hamilton, Richard M.	RR	401-56
Hamilton, Robert H.	FF	401-135
Hamilton, S. V.	FB	401-154
Hamilton, Thomas C.	TVG	401-195
Hamilton, W. B., Jr.	USV	401-232
Hamilton, W. T.	SR	401-81
Hamilton, W. Y.	TST	401-35
Hamilton, Wiley B.	MV	401-29
Hamilton, Wiley J.	MV	401-29
Hamilton, William B.	SR	401-81
Hamilton, Wilson C. L.	ARM	401-5
Hamm, Arthur B.	RR	401-56
Hamm, S. O.	RRR	401-117
Hammel, Otto	USV	401-232
Hammer, C. M.	TVG	401-195

Index to Texas Adjutant General Service Records—All Service Branches

Hammer, Geo.	FB	401-154	Hand, JacoB	FB	401-154
Hammer, S.	RRR	401-117	Hand, S. L.	RRR	401-117
Hammer, T. H.	FB	401-154	Hand, William M.	USV	401-233
Hammett, Augustus A.	USV	401-232	Handley, A. M.	FB	401-154
Hammett, Ed	RRR	401-117	Handley, Claud A.	RRR	401-117
Hammett, Robert C.	USV	401-232	Handley, E. J.	FB	401-154
Hammick, John A.	USV	401-232	Handlin, Thomas	NAV	401-18
Hammill, Henry	NAV	401-18	Handy, Roy	TVG	401-196
Hammock, Pierce	ARM	401-5	Hanekamp, Samuel	USV	401-233
Hammond, Alvin H.	USV	401-232	Haney, Jasper N., Jr.	USV	401-233
Hammond, E. A.	USV	401-232	Haney, John	SR	401-81
Hammond, E. C.	TVG	401-195	Hanger, Kenneth H.	RRR	401-117
Hammond, E. H.	RR	401-56	Hanigan, J. L.	RRR	401-117
Hammond, Frank	SR	401-81	Hankey, O. J.	FB	401-154
Hammond, Geo. W.	FB	401-154	Hanks, Benjamin F.	TVG	401-196
Hammond, George A.	TVG	401-195	Hanks, H. D.	TVG	401-196
Hammond, J. M.	TVG	401-195	Hanks, James S.	CSA	401-39
Hammond, John A.	TVG	401-195	Hanks, Joe P.	SR	401-81
Hammond, John S.	USV	401-232	Hanks, M. B.	RR	401-56
Hammond, Leroy	NAV	401-18	Hanks, M. B.	SR	401-81
Hammond, R. P.	USV	401-232	Hanks, M. F.	SP	401-44
Hammond, Will G.	TVG	401-195	Hanks, M. F.	USV	401-233
Hammonds, Alfred	TVG	401-195	Hanks, Raymond R.	USV	401-233
Hammong, E. H., Capt.	SR	401-81	Hanks, Rube M.	TVG	401-196
Hammons, T. M.	SR	401-81	Hanks, Rube M.	USV	401-233
Hamner, M. K.	RRR	401-117	Hanks, Wyatt	MV	401-29
Hamon, Ray L.	SR	401-81	Hanley, Thomas	TST	401-35
Hampil, Silas O.	TVG	401-196	Hanlin, John	ARM	401-5
Hampton, C. E.	TVG	401-196	Hanlon, William J.	USV	401-233
Hampton, E. G.	RR	401-56	Hanna, A. J.	SP	401-44
Hampton, E. G.	SR	401-81	Hanna, Alexander P.	TVG	401-196
Hampton, G. J.	RR	401-56	Hanna, C. C.	SR	401-81
Hampton, Homer H.	USV	401-232	Hanna, E. E.	SR	401-81
Hampton, J. H.	FB	401-154	Hanna, Ernest E.	RRR	401-117
Hampton, J. W.	FB	401-154	Hanna, Fred	SR	401-81
Hampton, R. G.	MV	401-29	Hanna, Joseph	RR	401-56
Hampton, W. B.	FB	401-154	Hanna, P. D.	SR	401-81
Hampton, William	FB	401-154	Hanna, Ross	TVG	401-196
Hamrick, George T.	SR	401-81	Hannagan, John	FF	401-135
Hamrick, James L.	USV	401-232	Hannah, Leon P.	RR	401-56
Hamvasy, EmeR	TVG	401-196	Hannahan, Jeremiah	ARM	401-5
Hancock, B. M.	TVG	401-196	Hannay, R. E.	SP	401-44
Hancock, Charles M.	USV	401-232	Hanney, W. M.	FB	401-154
Hancock, Curtis	TVG	401-196	Hannknche, Sg. C.	USV	401-233
Hancock, E. H.	SR	401-81	Hannon, John	ARM	401-5
Hancock, Ernest	TVG	401-196	Hannon, Martin E.	SR	401-81
Hancock, Eugene M.	USV	401-232	Hans, Gab	FF	401-135
Hancock, Geo. W.	USV	401-232	Hans, Justine	FF	401-135
Hancock, J. D.	FB	401-154	Hansen, Braxton B.	USV	401-233
Hancock, Jasper J.	TST	401-35	Hansen, Ernst C.	LR	401-128
Hancock, R. A.	TVG	401-196	Hansom, Harry	USV	401-233
Hancock, R. H.	TVG	401-196	Hanson, Bernard	TVG	401-196
Hancock, S. H.	USV	401-232	Hanson, C. J.	RR	401-56
Hancock, W. J.	SR	401-81	Hanson, Edward A.	NAV	401-18
Hancock, Will M.	USV	401-233	Hanson, Ernest C.	SR	401-81
Hancock, William T.	FB	401-154	Hanson, Howard	USV	401-233

Index to Texas Adjutant General Service Records—All Service Branches

Name	Branch	Record
Hanson, Jacob	SP	401-44
Hanson, M. M.	RRR	401-117
Hanson, William M.	RR	401-56
Hanway, Geo. W.	TVG	401-196
Happe, E. H.	SP	401-44
Haralson, Ike A.	USV	401-233
Haralson, J. C.	RR	401-56
Harbert, R. H.	TVG	401-196
Harbert, S. D.	FB	401-154
Harbison, Pelton Bruce	RR	401-56
Hardcastle, James	NAV	401-18
Hardee, Phill	FB	401-154
Hardeman, F. B.	SR	401-81
Hardeman, Harry J.	USV	401-233
Hardeman, William C.	TST	401-35
Harden, Jesse	NAV	401-18
Harden, John	TVG	401-196
Hardesty, Roy W.	RR	401-56
Hardie, J. Gunter	SR	401-81
Hardie, Spence	RRR	401-117
Hardie, Spence	TVG	401-196
Hardin, A. B.	SR	401-81
Hardin, A. H.	SR	401-81
Hardin, Aaron	TVG	401-196
Hardin, Allen	TVG	401-196
Hardin, Benj. F.	MV	401-29
Hardin, J. W.	TVG	401-196
Hardin, John Ernest	TVG	401-196
Hardin, Mike O.	RR	401-56
Hardin, P. C.	FB	401-154
Hardin, S. S.	FB	401-154
Hardin, W. G.	CSA	401-39
Harding, J. D.	MM	401-32
Harding, Joseph R.	FB	401-154
Harding, Thomas	ARM	401-5
Harding, William Arthur	RRR	401-117
Harding, William Arthur	SR	401-81
Hardman, J. W.	RRR	401-117
Hardman, John	NAV	401-18
Hardt, H. F.	TVG	401-196
Hardwicke, A. S.	TVG	401-196
Hardy, Addison R.	MV	401-29
Hardy, Gaston	FB	401-154
Hardy, Geo. W.	TVG	401-196
Hardy, Geo. W.	USV	401-233
Hardy, L. D.	SR	401-81
Hardy, S. M.	FB	401-154
Hardy, Sterling N.	FB	401-154
Hardy, William	NAV	401-18
Hare, John	ARM	401-5
Hare, L. R.	USV	401-233
Hare, Victor M.	TVG	401-196
Harger, John L.	USV	401-233
Hargett, Virgil A.	SR	401-82
Hargis, L. R.	SR	401-82
Hargis, Van D.	RR	401-56
Hargis, W. B.	SR	401-82
Hargis, W. B.	LR	401-128
Hargrave, Edward L.	NAV	401-18
Hargreaves, H. E.	FB	401-154
Hargrove, John	FB	401-154
Hargus, Peter B.	FB	401-154
Hargus, T. B.	FB	401-154
Hargus, Van D.	RR	401-56
Hargus, W. L.	FB	401-154
Harkey, J. D.	RR	401-56
Harkey, J. D.	SR	401-82
Harkey, J. D.	LR	401-128
Harkey, J. M.	FB	401-154
Harkey, O. K.	RRR	401-117
Harkins, C. C.	RRR	401-117
Harkreader, Samuel B.	USV	401-233
Harkrider, F. A.	TVG	401-196
Harkrider, R. E.	SR	401-82
Harlan, B. C.	FB	401-154
Harlan, Marvin A.	SR	401-82
Harlan, Samuel	FB	401-154
Harlan, Will	SP	401-44
Harle, Earl	TVG	401-196
Harle, M. E.	TVG	401-196
Harless, Ben F.	USV	401-233
Harleston, J. C.	ARM	401-5
Harley, Alex	SP	401-44
Harley, James A.	SR	401-82
Harley, John G.	USV	401-233
Harman, J. A.	CSA	401-39
Harman, W. C.	TVG	401-196
Harmon, Fred A.	TVG	401-196
Harmon, Hiram F.	TVG	401-196
Harmon, Kent	USV	401-233
Harmon, William	MV	401-29
Harmouth, Emil	FF	401-135
Harn, John F.	USV	401-233
Harn, S. D.	SP	401-44
Harned, Earnest M.	TVG	401-196
Harold, W. O.	TVG	401-196
Haroldson, C. L.	SR	401-82
Harper, Charles	TVG	401-196
Harper, Cole	FB	401-154
Harper, F. M.	FB	401-154
Harper, F. W.	TVG	401-196
Harper, Herman	SR	401-82
Harper, J. C.	SR	401-82
Harper, J. H.	SR	401-82
Harper, J. H.	LR	401-128
Harper, J. K.	TST	401-35
Harper, Jack P.	SR	401-82
Harper, Jim A.	SR	401-82
Harper, John	NAV	401-18
Harper, John	ARM	401-5
Harper, R. E.	TVG	401-196
Harper, R. L.	TVG	401-196

Index to Texas Adjutant General Service Records—All Service Branches

Name	Branch	Record
Harper, S. D.	TVG	401-196
Harper, Ulyses	TST	401-35
Harper, W. H.	SP	401-44
Harper, W. M.	TVG	401-196
Harper, Walter Marcellus	TVG	401-196
Harper, William J.	USV	401-233
Harpold, Herbert B.	USV	401-233
Harr, Jeptha	TST	401-35
Harrell, A. J.	CSA	401-39
Harrell, A. J.	TST	401-35
Harrell, David	TVG	401-196
Harrell, E. F.	RR	401-56
Harrell, E. W.	FB	401-154
Harrell, Edgar B.	RR	401-56
Harrell, Edward Hogan	SR	401-82
Harrell, Eugene Flowers	SR	401-82
Harrell, F. O.	TVG	401-196
Harrell, Francis O.	USV	401-233
Harrell, George	FB	401-154
Harrell, H.	FB	401-154
Harrell, J. M.	FF	401-135
Harrell, M. W.	LR	401-128
Harrell, Travis O.	FF	401-135
Harrell, William	MM	401-32
Harrigan, D. D.	SR	401-82
Harrington, C. H.	TVG	401-196
Harrington, Edlare E.	USV	401-233
Harrington, Edward B.	NAV	401-18
Harrington, John	NAV	401-18
Harrington, Lee	SR	401-82
Harrington, William E.	TVG	401-196
Harrington, William Edward	USV	401-233
Harris, A. A.	TST	401-35
Harris, A. G.	TVG	401-196
Harris, Andrew J.	RR	401-56
Harris, Ben A.	RRR	401-117
Harris, Boyce	RRR	401-117
Harris, C. E.	SR	401-82
Harris, Chas. M.	TVG	401-196
Harris, D. R.	RR	401-56
Harris, E. A.	TVG	401-196
Harris, Ed. H.	TVG	401-196
Harris, Elijah	RR	401-56
Harris, EscA	USV	401-233
Harris, F. A.	RRR	401-117
Harris, F. L.	FB	401-154
Harris, F. M.	TVG	401-196
Harris, Frank E.	USV	401-233
Harris, Frank W.	TVG	401-196
Harris, Fred T.	USV	401-233
Harris, G. A.	SR	401-82
Harris, George	FB	401-154
Harris, George W.	RR	401-56
Harris, Guy W.	RRR	401-117
Harris, H.	TVG	401-196
Harris, H. B.	SR	401-82
Harris, H. B.	LR	401-128
Harris, Homer D.	USV	401-233
Harris, I. A.	FB	401-154
Harris, Irwin C.	RR	401-56
Harris, Isaac	SP	401-44
Harris, J. C.	SP	401-44
Harris, J. C.	SR	401-82
Harris, J. D.	TVG	401-196
Harris, J. E.	SR	401-82
Harris, J. F.	SR	401-82
Harris, J. H.	SR	401-82
Harris, J. H.	FB	401-154
Harris, J. J.	TVG	401-196
Harris, J. T.	TVG	401-196
Harris, James	FB	401-154
Harris, James H.	USV	401-233
Harris, James W.	RR	401-56
Harris, Joe A.	FB	401-154
Harris, Joe A.	FB	401-154
Harris, John M.	RR	401-56
Harris, John M.	SR	401-82
Harris, John N.	TVG	401-196
Harris, John W.	RRR	401-117
Harris, John W.	SR	401-82
Harris, Linton A.	USV	401-233
Harris, Lon	LR	401-128
Harris, P. J.	SR	401-82
Harris, R. H.	FB	401-154
Harris, R. S.	RR	401-56
Harris, Richard C.	USV	401-233
Harris, Roy	SR	401-82
Harris, Sidney L.	SR	401-82
Harris, T. E.	RRR	401-117
Harris, T. H.	SR	401-82
Harris, T. J.	SR	401-82
Harris, T. M.	LR	401-128
Harris, Thomas S.	USV	401-233
Harris, Tupper	FB	401-154
Harris, W. J.	FB	401-155
Harris, W. R.	TVG	401-196
Harris, W. T.	TST	401-35
Harris, W. T.	FB	401-155
Harris, Will	SR	401-82
Harris, Will	LR	401-128
Harris, Willard W.	USV	401-233
Harris, William	NAV	401-18
Harris, William	ARM	401-5
Harris, William T.	SR	401-82
Harris, William W.	USV	401-233
Harrison, A. A.	FB	401-155
Harrison, Abraham	USV	401-233
Harrison, Albert O.	USV	401-233
Harrison, Arthur L.	USV	401-233
Harrison, Captain	SP	401-44
Harrison, E. M.	TVG	401-196
Harrison, Edward A.	NAV	401-18

Index to Texas Adjutant General Service Records—All Service Branches

Name	Branch	Record
Harrison, Frank P.	TVG	401-196
Harrison, Hulen M.	USV	401-233
Harrison, Ira A.	TST	401-35
Harrison, Isham	FB	401-155
Harrison, J. I.	RRR	401-117
Harrison, J. S.	TVG	401-196
Harrison, James C.	MV	401-29
Harrison, Jas. A.	TVG	401-196
Harrison, Jilson Paine	USV	401-233
Harrison, Nat	FB	401-155
Harrison, Oscar	TVG	401-196
Harrison, P. D.	TVG	401-196
Harrison, R. H., Dr.	SR	401-82
Harrison, Richard H.	FB	401-155
Harrison, Samuel A. M.	TVG	401-196
Harrison, T. D.	TST	401-35
Harrison, Thomas	ARM	401-5
Harrison, Thomas H.	USV	401-233
Harrison, W. D.	TVG	401-196
Harrison, W. F.	TVG	401-196
Harrison, Will E.	TVG	401-196
Harrison, William	MV	401-29
Harrison, William A.	USV	401-233
Harrod, J. F.	RR	401-56
Harrow, William	NAV	401-18
Harry, J. B.	FB	401-155
Harry, James	FB	401-155
Harry, R. D. W.	USV	401-233
Harry, Thomas C., Jr.	TVG	401-196
Hart, Alec (Alexander) T.	MV	401-29
Hart, Aron H.	MM	401-32
Hart, Benjamin	NAV	401-18
Hart, C. A.	TVG	401-196
Hart, E. H.	FB	401-155
Hart, H. W.	TVG	401-196
Hart, John S.	SR	401-82
Hart, L.	FB	401-155
Hart, R. D.	TVG	401-196
Hart, Sterling M.	TVG	401-196
Hart, Thos.	ARM	401-5
Hart, Virgil V.	USV	401-233
Hart, W. E.	SR	401-82
Hartal, W. L.	NAV	401-18
Harter, J. D.	FB	401-155
Hartgraves, Thomas D.	USV	401-233
Hartigan, J. S.	FB	401-155
Hartis, K. S.	TVG	401-196
Hartis, W. C.	TVG	401-196
Hartley, William	FB	401-155
Hartman, Harry	SR	401-82
Hartman, J. S.	FB	401-155
Hartman, W. D.	TVG	401-196
Hartmann, Conrad	TVG	401-196
Hartmann, Henry	ARM	401-5
Hartmann, Henry	FF	401-135
Hartsfield, Charles M.	USV	401-233
Hartsfield, John	RR	401-56
Hartson, H. L.	TVG	401-196
Hartsough, Jack B.	SR	401-82
Hartwell, Albert	SP	401-44
Hartz, H.	FB	401-155
Harvey, David	ARM	401-5
Harvey, J. J.	SR	401-82
Harvey, James W.	NAV	401-18
Harvey, Jess W.	SR	401-82
Harvey, Jess W.	LR	401-128
Harvey, Jesse	USV	401-233
Harvey, John M.	USV	401-233
Harvey, Leonard	FB	401-155
Harvey, Nehemiah	USV	401-233
Harvey, T. C.	FF	401-135
Harvey, Walter L.	TVG	401-196
Harvey, William	SR	401-82
Harvick, Ad	SR	401-82
Harvick, J. A.	SR	401-82
Harvie, Crawford	LR	401-128
Harvin, J. A.	SR	401-82
Harwell, J. C.	SR	401-82
Harwell, Jack	FB	401-155
Harwell, Oscar	SR	401-82
Harwood, Fred W.	FB	401-155
Harwood, G. E. W.	TST	401-35
Harwood, George W.	SR	401-82
Harwood, Joseph	SP	401-44
Harwood, R. H.	TVG	401-196
Hascall, Walter	USV	401-233
Hasdorff, William G.	SP	401-44
Haskell, J. D.	FB	401-155
Haskins, Henry	ARM	401-5
Haskins, M. T.	SP	401-44
Haskins, Robert F.	SP	401-44
Haskins, Thomas	ARM	401-5
Haslocher, Phillip	ARM	401-5
Hasroot, Augustus	FF	401-135
Hasroot, William	FF	401-135
Hassell, Jefferson W.	TVG	401-196
Hassell, Sam	RRR	401-117
Hastings, Arthur	SR	401-82
Hastings, Millard F.	FB	401-155
Hastings, O. L.	SR	401-82
Hasty, J. M.	SR	401-82
Hatchel, J. C.	SP	401-44
Hatcher, Hiram	FB	401-155
Hatcher, John B.	USV	401-233
Hatchitt, J. Byrd	USV	401-233
Hatchl, H. C.	TVG	401-196
Hatfield, James C.	USV	401-233
Hatfield, James N.	USV	401-233
Hatfield, W. M.	USV	401-233
Hatfield, William	ARM	401-5
Hathaway, C. L.	FB	401-155
Hathaway, Milton S.	USV	401-233

Index to Texas Adjutant General Service Records—All Service Branches

Hattox, C. T. ....FB............401-155
Hattwell, L., Jr. ....TVG........401-196
Haucenbury, Nehemiah ....ARM 401-5
Hauchins, Buhler W. ....USV 401-233
Hauck, John ....FF............401-135
Haughton, C. M. ....SR............401-82
Haughton, Charles M....................LR 401-128
Haughton, Hunter ....TVG 401-196
Hausaman, G. H. ....TVG 401-196
Hauscke, Hugo ....TVG 401-196
Hausenfluck, Thomas H. ....USV 401-233
Hauser, Sam J. ....TVG 401-196
Hausman, L. J. ....SR............401-82
Hausser, Albert ....SR............401-82
Hausser, William, Jr. ....TVG 401-196
Haux, Nicholas P. ....TVG 401-196
Haven, W. F. ....TVG 401-196
Havens, Daniel P. ....USV 401-233
Haver, Manz ....FF............401-135
Havis, William K. ....USV 401-233
Havlik, John Vincent ....TVG 401-196
Hawbacker, Samuel ....FB............401-155
Hawell, James J. ....USV 401-233
Hawes, Frank D. ....USV 401-233
Hawkins, Albert S. ....USV 401-233
Hawkins, Arl.................................SR............401-82
Hawkins, Charlie L.......................USV 401-233
Hawkins, Cleve D. ....SR............401-82
Hawkins, E. P. ....TVG 401-196
Hawkins, Geo. C. ....USV 401-233
Hawkins, George ....TVG 401-196
Hawkins, Henry w. ....TVG 401-196
Hawkins, Homer W. ....TVG 401-196
Hawkins, Homer W. ....USV 401-233
Hawkins, J. R................................USV 401-233
Hawkins, James B. ....FB............401-155
Hawkins, James D. ....USV 401-233
Hawkins, John A. ....SR............401-82
Hawkins, John H. ....USV 401-233
Hawkins, Joseph W. ....TVG 401-196
Hawkins, Joseph W. ....USV 401-233
Hawkins, R. ....USV 401-233
Hawkins, R. C...............................SR............401-82
Hawkins, Richard Crews..............RR 401-56
Hawkins, Sam...............................TVG 401-196
Hawkins, Smith ....ARM 401-5
Hawkins, T. T. ....RR 401-56
Hawkins, T. T. ....SR............401-82
Hawkins, Thomas ....SP 401-44
Hawkins, William ....FB............401-155
Hawks, Thomas Richard...............USV 401-233
Hawse, A. M. ....FB............401-155
Hawthorn, James ....NAV........401-18
Hawthorn, William L....................USV 401-233
Hawtof, E. Manuel ....SR............401-82
Hay, Andrew.................................ARM 401-5

Hay, G. C. ....SR............401-82
Hay, G. C. ....LR 401-128
Hay, J. Donald ....SR............401-82
Hay, L. ....FB............401-155
Hay, L. L. ....FB............401-155
Hay, Silas......................................MV 401-29
Hayden, Audie T. ....RR 401-56
Hayden, J. H. ....USV 401-233
Haye, John ....FF............401-135
Hayes, A. J. ....FF............401-135
Hayes, John L. ....USV 401-233
Hayes, N. J. ....FF............401-135
Hayes, Ralph R. ....USV 401-233
Hayes, Thos. P. ....TVG 401-196
Hayes, Travis ....SR............401-82
Hayes, Travis ....LR 401-128
Hayes, William Z. ....SR............401-82
Haygood, M. D. ....TVG 401-196
Haygood, Robert L. ....USV 401-233
Haygood, W. H. ....SR............401-82
Haylock, Henry L. ....MV 401-29
Haylon, Patrick ....ARM 401-5
Hayman, John...............................NAV........401-18
Haynes, Andrew W. ....TVG 401-196
Haynes, B. H.................................SR............401-82
Haynes, B. H.................................LR 401-128
Haynes, G. W................................ARM 401-5
Haynes, Joseph E..........................USV 401-233
Haynes, PeteR...............................SP 401-44
Haynes, R. A.................................FB............401-155
Haynes, W. H................................SR............401-82
Haynie, Charles R.........................SP 401-44
Haynie, George E. ....SP 401-44
Haynie, Herschel E.......................SR............401-82
Haynie, Tom.................................SR............401-82
Hays, H. L. ....FB............401-155
Hays, Henry..................................ARM 401-5
Hays, John ....FB............401-155
Hays, Richard S. ....USV 401-233
Hays, Robert Houston ....USV 401-233
Haysner, C. L. ....SR............401-82
Haysner, C. L. ....LR 401-128
Haywood, John C. ....FF............401-135
Haywood, Will J. ....FF............401-135
Hazelei, Peter................................ARM 401-5
Hazlett, E. B. ....SR............401-82
Hazlett, Walter ....SR............401-82
Hazlewood, James J.....................USV 401-233
Hazlewood, James L.....................USV 401-233
Hazlewood, John L.......................USV 401-233
Hazlewood, Sam...........................USV 401-233
Hazlitt, C. Y. ....SP 401-44
Head, Drew W. ....TVG 401-196
Head, John B. ....TVG 401-196
Head, John W. ....SP 401-44
Head, M. C. ....SR............401-82

Index to Texas Adjutant General Service Records—All Service Branches

Name	Branch	Record
Head, M. C.	LR	401-128
Head, R. M.	FB	401-155
Head, R. R.	RRR	401-117
Head, W. J.	TVG	401-197
Heafer, H. W.	USV	401-233
Heah, Henry B.	USV	401-233
Healy, P. Oliver	ARM	401-5
Heaney, A. G.	TVG	401-197
Heard, Georgia Catherine	SR	401-82
Heard, J. W.	SR	401-82
Heard, James I.	RR	401-56
Heard, James Ira	RR	401-56
Heard, Percy F.	SR	401-82
Heard, T. L.	RR	401-56
Heard, Thomas D.	FB	401-155
Heard, Wilson, Jr.	SR	401-82
Hearder, Stanley S.	USV	401-233
Hearldston, C. F.	USV	401-233
Hearn, Hicks	TVG	401-197
Hearn, J. D.	RRR	401-117
Hearn, J. P.	SR	401-82
Hearn, Richard Howard	SR	401-82
Hearn, Roy L.	RR	401-56
Hearne, Roy White	TVG	401-197
Hearne, Roy White	USV	401-233
Hearne, SelvA	TVG	401-197
Hearne, Wayne A.	TVG	401-197
Heartt, C. Walter	FB	401-155
Heath, G. A.	SR	401-82
Heath, J. H.	FF	401-135
Heath, J. J.	FB	401-155
Heath, Summer	USV	401-233
Heatherly, J. H.	FB	401-155
Heathington, E. W.	SR	401-82
Heaton, Harry W.	TVG	401-197
Heaton, Thomas	FF	401-135
Heaton, Thomas	SP	401-44
Heck, R. D.	SP	401-44
Hecker, George Harold	SR	401-82
Hedden, Charles M.	FB	401-155
Hedgecoke, Eugene	SR	401-82
Hedgecoke, Eugene	LR	401-128
Hedgepeth, J. R.	FF	401-135
Hedrick, Noey C.	USV	401-233
Hedroman, John	NAV	401-18
Heep, Mat S.	USV	401-233
Heffington, Ham	SR	401-82
Heffington, T. P.	FB	401-155
Heffter, H.	TST	401-35
Hefley, Jefferson Davis	SR	401-82
Heflin, Jno. W.	TVG	401-197
Heflin, Jno. W.	USV	401-233
Heflin, Marlin	FB	401-155
Heflin, Norman L.	USV	401-233
Hefner, Samuel D.	TVG	401-197
Heftmeyer, Emil	FF	401-135
Heibler, F. A.	FB	401-155
Heidelberg, Harry	TVG	401-197
Heifirm, John	FB	401-155
Heimann, Leon	TVG	401-197
Heine, Carl L.	USV	401-233
Heineman, Benjamin	FF	401-135
Heineman, John	FF	401-135
Heinemann, John	SP	401-44
Heinemann, William	FF	401-135
Heinen, John	SP	401-44
Heiner [Heinen], Henry	SP	401-44
Heinson, F. W.	SR	401-82
Heinz, E.	SP	401-44
Heisman, Dave	SR	401-82
Heitman, A. T.	USV	401-233
Heittner, Henry M.	TVG	401-197
Heller, Herman E.	SR	401-83
Helm, George A.	FB	401-155
Helm, Jack	SP	401-44
Helm, Joseph	NAV	401-18
Helm, Thos. A., Jr.	TVG	401-197
Helman, J. T.	TVG	401-197
Helms, J. J.	RRR	401-117
Helpinstill, J. B.	SR	401-83
Helsley, James	TVG	401-197
Helton, H. D.	LR	401-129
Hemme, Ed. F.	SR	401-83
Hemphill, A. B.	TST	401-35
Hemphill, B. F.	FB	401-155
Hemphill, Charles F.	SR	401-83
Hemphill, M. A.	TVG	401-197
Hemphill, S. G.	SP	401-44
Hemphill, Tillman	USV	401-233
Henckens, William	FF	401-135
Henderson, A. W.	ARM	401-6
Henderson, Alex	RRR	401-117
Henderson, Allen T.	USV	401-233
Henderson, Alvin	USV	401-233
Henderson, B. W.	SR	401-83
Henderson, Bennett Francis	MV	401-29
Henderson, Charles Moore	USV	401-233
Henderson, George	NAV	401-18
Henderson, Hal W.	USV	401-233
Henderson, Homer	RR	401-56
Henderson, J. E.	RRR	401-117
Henderson, J. S.	FB	401-155
Henderson, J. W.	MV	401-29
Henderson, J. W.	TVG	401-197
Henderson, James	ARM	401-6
Henderson, Jeff D.	TVG	401-197
Henderson, John	NAV	401-18
Henderson, John	ARM	401-6
Henderson, John	SP	401-44
Henderson, John F.	USV	401-233
Henderson, John S.	USV	401-233
Henderson, Joseph	FB	401-155

Index to Texas Adjutant General Service Records—All Service Branches

Name	Branch	Record
Henderson, L. K.	FB	401-155
Henderson, Leland	TVG	401-197
Henderson, R. L.	TVG	401-197
Henderson, Richard L.	USV	401-233
Henderson, Robert	MV	401-29
Henderson, Robt. Frank	USV	401-233
Henderson, Sam M.	USV	401-233
Henderson, W. B.	TVG	401-197
Henderson, Walter	TVG	401-197
Henderson, Will E.	USV	401-233
Henderson, William	FB	401-155
Henderson, William K.	USV	401-233
Hendrichson, H. C.	SR	401-83
Hendrick, Ben L. R.	TVG	401-197
Hendricks, A. K.	FB	401-155
Hendricks, E. B.	USV	401-233
Hendricks, Gus J.	CSA	401-39
Hendricks, T. A.	FF	401-135
Hendricks, William J.	RR	401-56
Hendrickson, B. W.	SR	401-83
Hendrix, Earl	SR	401-83
Hendrix, George A.	USV	401-234
Hendrix, H. E.	SR	401-83
Hendrix, Nelson	ARM	401-6
Hendrix, William T.	USV	401-234
Hendrixen, John L.	USV	401-234
Hendrixson, Rolen R.	USV	401-234
Hengy, Joseph	TVG	401-197
Henicke, H. G.	FB	401-155
Henigan, J. L.	RRR	401-117
Henkel, Chas.	TVG	401-197
Henley, Hugh M.	USV	401-234
Henley, R. S.	TVG	401-197
Henne, Herbert G.	SR	401-83
Henness, James	USV	401-234
Hennessey, Jack Francis, Jr.	RRR	401-117
Henrich, Steve	RR	401-56
Henrichson, H. C.	SR	401-83
Henrick, William	ARM	401-6
Henritty, James	USV	401-234
Henry, B. W.	TVG	401-197
Henry, D. F.	SR	401-83
Henry, D. F.	LR	401-129
Henry, Ed A	SP	401-45
Henry, George	FB	401-155
Henry, J. E.	FF	401-135
Henry, JacoB	FB	401-155
Henry, John	FB	401-155
Henry, John Quincy	SR	401-83
Henry, L.	FB	401-155
Henry, L. F.	TVG	401-197
Henry, L. W.	RR	401-56
Henry, Lewis	NAV	401-18
Henry, M. C.	TVG	401-197
Henry, Milton	USV	401-234
Henry, Robinson C.	USV	401-234
Henry, S. A.	FB	401-155
Henry, V. J.	TVG	401-197
Henry, William	SP	401-45
Henry, William R.	MV	401-29
Henshaw, N. E.	USV	401-234
Henshaw, W. S.	FB	401-155
Henslee, S. G.	TVG	401-197
Hensley, G. W.	RR	401-56
Hensley, H. H.	SR	401-83
Hensley, J. E.	RR	401-56
Hensley, J. H.	FB	401-155
Hensley, J. H.	FB	401-155
Hensley, John E.	RR	401-56
Hensley, L. J.	MM	401-32
Hensley, Lemuel J.	FB	401-155
Hensley, Luke	FB	401-155
Henson, A. L.	RR	401-56
Henson, C. W.	SR	401-83
Henson, John B.	TVG	401-197
Heppel, F. B.	SR	401-83
Heppel, Frank Barrett	RRR	401-117
Herald, George	FF	401-135
Herald, George	SR	401-83
Herbeck, H.	TVG	401-197
Herbeck, J.	TVG	401-197
Herbert, George R.	SR	401-83
Herbst, A. W.	RR	401-56
Herbst, A. W.	SR	401-83
Herera, Fermin	FF	401-135
Herera, Julian	FF	401-135
Herff, William L.	TVG	401-197
Hermant, J. H.	RR	401-56
Hermany, Edward G.	USV	401-234
Hern, George T.	RRR	401-117
Hernandez, Antonio	ARM	401-6
Hernandez, Carlos	FF	401-135
Hernandez, Eugene J.	USV	401-234
Hernandez, Manuel	ARM	401-6
Herndon, H. T.	TVG	401-197
Herndon, James	FB	401-155
Herndon, John	FB	401-155
Herndon, Lewis E.	USV	401-234
Herndon, Oliver P.	TVG	401-197
Herndon, Oliver P.	USV	401-234
Herndon, T. H.	FB	401-155
Herndon, Thos. T.	TVG	401-197
Herold, Charles	NAV	401-18
Herold, George	FB	401-155
Herold, William H.	TVG	401-197
Herr, A. W.	RRR	401-117
Herr, A. W.	SR	401-83
Herr, M. L.	FB	401-155
Herrage, Jackson	FB	401-155
Herre, Willis	USV	401-234
Herren, Arthur W.	TVG	401-197
Herrera, Jose	SR	401-83

Index to Texas Adjutant General Service Records—All Service Branches

Name	Branch	Record
Herriman, Clyde	USV	401-234
Herrin, Ike N.	FB	401-155
Herring, A. T.	TST	401-35
Herring, Chas. W.	USV	401-234
Herring, Curtis	TST	401-35
Herring, D. E.	TVG	401-197
Herring, Richard S.	USV	401-234
Herring, William W.	USV	401-234
Herrington, H. S.	TVG	401-197
Herrington, James	ARM	401-6
Herrmann, Gustav	FF	401-135
Herrmann, John L.	SR	401-83
Herron, Frank	FB	401-155
Herron, John	ARM	401-6
Herron, L. C.	FF	401-135
Herron, Nicholas	ARM	401-6
Herron, Samuel	FF	401-135
Hert, Frank	USV	401-234
Hervitt, IrA	TVG	401-197
Herzing, J. F.	RR	401-57
Hesber, J. H.	USV	401-234
Hess, Cliff	FB	401-155
Hess, Frank H.	USV	401-234
Hess, Fred A.	USV	401-234
Hess, Gattfred	TVG	401-197
Hess, J. L.	FB	401-155
Hess, James	TVG	401-197
Hess, John	FB	401-155
Hess, Otto	TVG	401-197
Hess, Reuben L.	USV	401-234
Hess, Roy R.	RRR	401-117
Hester, Braxton C.	TVG	401-197
Hester, Forest	SR	401-83
Hester, Frank M.	USV	401-234
Hester, J. G.	SR	401-83
Hester, James S.	FB	401-155
Hester, Patrick H.	USV	401-234
Hester, Thomas I.	SR	401-83
Hester, Thomas I.	LR	401-129
Hester, W. R. "Billie"	TST	401-35
Heth, William	ARM	401-6
Hetherly, John	FB	401-155
Heuchling, Friedrich	FF	401-135
Heuchling, Julius	FF	401-135
Heuermann, E. J.	RR	401-57
Heuermann, E. J.	SR	401-83
Hevermann, E. J.	RR	401-57
Hewell, A. G.	RRR	401-117
Hewett, Charles	TVG	401-197
Hewitt, Alfred M.	TST	401-35
Hewitt, Floyd Carl	TVG	401-197
Hewitt, J. R.	SR	401-83
Hewitt, James E.	USV	401-234
Hewitt, John H.	FB	401-155
Hewitt, Joseph E.	USV	401-234
Hey, Ben	SR	401-83
Heyer, George S.	SR	401-83
Heyman, Leo	SR	401-83
Heyser, E. S.	SR	401-83
Hibbert, Frank H.	SR	401-83
Hibbert, Frank H.	LR	401-129
Hibbs, Chas. B.	TVG	401-197
Hibler, F. A.	FB	401-155
Hickerson, James H.	SR	401-83
Hickerson, Wiley	ARM	401-6
Hickey, Benjamin	TVG	401-197
Hickey, Charles L.	TVG	401-197
Hickey, Ed L.	TVG	401-197
Hickey, Geo. C.	USV	401-234
Hickey, James	TST	401-35
Hickey, John	FB	401-155
Hickey, John B.	USV	401-234
Hickey, Louis	SR	401-83
Hickey, Patrick	ARM	401-6
Hickey, Richard T.	RR	401-57
Hickey, W. W.	TST	401-35
Hickkey, James	ARM	401-6
Hickman, C. C.	TVG	401-197
Hickman, Fred	RRR	401-118
Hickman, Fred	SR	401-83
Hickman, J. G.	USV	401-234
Hickman, T. R.	RR	401-57
Hickman, Thomas W.	USV	401-234
Hickman, Tom J.	FB	401-155
Hickman, Tom R.	RR	401-57
Hickman, Willett J.	SR	401-83
Hickox, J. H.	FB	401-155
Hickox, John E.	USV	401-234
Hicks, A. L.	SR	401-83
Hicks, Alexander Lincoln	LR	401-129
Hicks, Fabian L.	MV	401-29
Hicks, Henry	TVG	401-197
Hicks, J. M.	USV	401-234
Hicks, J. T.	TVG	401-197
Hicks, Jacob H.	USV	401-234
Hicks, Martin M.	USV	401-234
Hicks, N. B.	FB	401-155
Hicks, S. J.	SR	401-83
Hicks, Stonewall Jackson	LR	401-129
Hicks, William Carroll	RRR	401-118
Hiers, Charles F.	FB	401-155
Higginbotham, John Lucas	RRR	401-118
Higginbotham, William J.	SR	401-83
Higgins, David M.	TVG	401-197
Higgins, Elijah P.	FB	401-155
Higgins, PaT	SR	401-83
Higgins, Polk M.	USV	401-234
Higgins, William	TST	401-35
High, R. G.	TVG	401-197
Highfill, K. L.	RR	401-57
Highfill, K. L.	SR	401-83
Highsmith, F. C.	TVG	401-197

Index to Texas Adjutant General Service Records—All Service Branches

Name	Branch	Record
Highsmith, Thomas W.	USV	401-234
Hightower, C. E.	TVG	401-197
Hightower, J. T.	TVG	401-197
Hightower, L. V.	RR	401-57
Hightower, S. H.	TVG	401-197
Hightower, W. R.	RR	401-57
Hilbert, Henry	TVG	401-197
Hilburn, A. B.	RR	401-57
Hilburn, Earnest	SR	401-83
Hilburn, Ernest	SR	401-83
Hild, F. B.	SR	401-83
Hilkene, John H.	TVG	401-197
Hill, A. C.	FF	401-135
Hill, A. C.	SP	401-45
Hill, A. W.	RR	401-57
Hill, Arthur M.	TVG	401-197
Hill, Ben F.	TVG	401-197
Hill, C. W.	SR	401-83
Hill, Edward M.	TVG	401-197
Hill, Eli	MV	401-29
Hill, Emerson D.	USV	401-234
Hill, Ewing	USV	401-234
Hill, G. A.	TVG	401-197
Hill, G. W.	TST	401-35
Hill, George	SP	401-45
Hill, George H.	USV	401-234
Hill, George O.	RR	401-57
Hill, Gordon	RR	401-57
Hill, Gordon	SR	401-83
Hill, J.	TVG	401-197
Hill, J. Freeman	RRR	401-118
Hill, J. M.	FB	401-155
Hill, J. R.	TVG	401-197
Hill, J. R.	USV	401-234
Hill, James E.	RRR	401-118
Hill, Jesse J.	RR	401-57
Hill, John A.	SR	401-83
Hill, John C.	TVG	401-197
Hill, John H.	USV	401-234
Hill, John R.	USV	401-234
Hill, Joseph	NAV	401-18
Hill, Lon C.	SR	401-83
Hill, Loy	USV	401-234
Hill, Michael	FB	401-155
Hill, Milton	TVG	401-197
Hill, Pierre Bernard	RR	401-57
Hill, Raymond	TVG	401-197
Hill, RoberT	NAV	401-18
Hill, RoberT	FB	401-155
Hill, Robert P.	TVG	401-197
Hill, Rutherford E.	USV	401-234
Hill, S. V.	SR	401-83
Hill, Sam H.	SR	401-83
Hill, Sam Houston	SR	401-83
Hill, Samuel	TST	401-35
Hill, Thomas	NAV	401-18
Hill, Thomas H.	TVG	401-197
Hill, Thomas P.	USV	401-234
Hill, Thomas W.	USV	401-234
Hill, W. H.	SR	401-83
Hill, W. J.	RRR	401-118
Hill, W. L.	RRR	401-118
Hill, William C.	ARM	401-6
Hill, William Hickman	SR	401-83
Hill, William T.	USV	401-234
Hill, William Thomas	SR	401-83
Hillan, Anthony B.	USV	401-234
Hillboldt, W. F.	MV	401-29
Hillbolt, Frank W.	RR	401-57
Hille, J. S.	USV	401-234
Hilley, John G.	TVG	401-197
Hilliard, Claude A.	RR	401-57
Hilliard, John A.	TVG	401-197
Hilliard, W. L.	SR	401-83
Hilliard, Walter B.	TVG	401-197
Hilliard, Warren M.	USV	401-234
Hillier, John Wesley	USV	401-234
Hillmer, T. W.	SR	401-83
Hillyard, D. M.	SR	401-83
Hillyard, George W.	SP	401-45
Hillyer, T. S.	FB	401-155
Hilt, Henry	SP	401-45
Himmel, A.	FB	401-155
Hindle, Joseph	NAV	401-18
Hindman, George F.	USV	401-234
Hinds, Earl E.	SR	401-83
Hinds, Ernest	SR	401-83
Hinds, Fritz S.	SR	401-83
Hinds, James C.	FF	401-135
Hinemann, John	FF	401-135
Hines, Arthur	USV	401-234
Hines, Carlton	FB	401-156
Hines, Charlton	FB	401-156
Hines, D. J.	SR	401-83
Hines, Dan	RR	401-57
Hines, Daniel Jessie	RRR	401-118
Hines, J. E.	FB	401-156
Hines, Marcus W.	RR	401-57
Hines, O. S.	SR	401-83
Hines, R. E.	SR	401-83
Hines, R. E.	LR	401-129
Hines, W. H.	USV	401-234
Hinlay, Joseph	NAV	401-18
Hinnant, J. H.	RR	401-57
Hinner, Charles H.	NAV	401-18
Hinojosa, Daniel	RR	401-57
Hinojosa, Daniel	MV	401-29
Hinrichs, William	FF	401-135
Hinson, M. S.	RRR	401-118
Hinson, M. W.	RRR	401-118
Hinson, T. A.	TVG	401-197
Hinton, A. C.	NAV	401-18

Index to Texas Adjutant General Service Records—All Service Branches

Name	Branch	Record
Hinton, Albert P.	USV	401-234
Hinton, E. S.	RRR	401-118
Hinton, Monroe	RRR	401-118
Hinton, O. R.	TVG	401-197
Hinton, Sam	NAV	401-18
Hinton, William W.	ARM	401-6
Hinyard, Ben F.	USV	401-234
Hinyard, Rufus	MV	401-29
Hinzie, W. E.	SR	401-83
Hirsch, Arthur	TVG	401-197
Hirsch, Henry	TVG	401-197
Hirsch, Louis	TVG	401-197
Hirschfeld, Jake	TVG	401-197
Hirschfeld, Morris	TVG	401-197
Hitchcock, F.	TVG	401-197
Hitchcock, Ralph V.	SR	401-83
Hite, E. H.	SR	401-83
Hitt, John F.	SR	401-83
Hitt, John F.	LR	401-129
Hix, N. B.	FB	401-156
Hixson, M. K.	SR	401-83
Hoag, Louis S.	USV	401-234
Hobbs, Gabriel	SP	401-45
Hobbs, Paul A.	TVG	401-197
Hobdy, W. I.	SR	401-83
Hobgood, Charles B.	USV	401-234
Hobson, George W.	SP	401-45
Hobson, Lewis	SR	401-83
Hocker, John P.	USV	401-234
Hockwald, Henry	TVG	401-197
Hodel, Jacob	NAV	401-18
Hodge, A. J.	FF	401-135
Hodge, Archie D.	TVG	401-197
Hodge, D. G.	SR	401-83
Hodge, Frank Miller	USV	401-234
Hodge, Milton	MV	401-29
Hodge, Samuel B.	FF	401-135
Hodge, W. E.	RR	401-57
Hodge, W. T.	SR	401-83
Hodges, A. B.	RR	401-57
Hodges, A. B.	SR	401-83
Hodges, Arthur	TVG	401-197
Hodges, D. N.	FF	401-135
Hodges, Dee O.	USV	401-234
Hodges, Elmo	TVG	401-197
Hodges, Eugene C.	TVG	401-197
Hodges, Frank M.	TVG	401-197
Hodges, J. E.	SR	401-83
Hodges, John	TVG	401-197
Hodges, P. P.	SR	401-83
Hodges, Sam F.	TVG	401-197
Hodge(s), Thomas	SP	401-45
Hodges, Vera Candate	TVG	401-197
Hodges, W. H.	MM	401-32
Hodges, William H.	FB	401-156
Hodges, William S.	USV	401-234
Hodges, Willis	TVG	401-197
Hodges, Willis D.	USV	401-234
Hoehn, John M.	SP	401-45
Hoeny, Jack	TVG	401-197
Hoerster, Henry	SR	401-83
Hoes, E. B.	SR	401-83
Hoey, C. D.	RRR	401-118
Hoffar, Francis W.	FB	401-156
Hoffar, John N.	FB	401-156
Hoffer, Frank	FB	401-156
Hoffler, John	FB	401-156
Hoffman, Anton	SP	401-45
Hoffman, C.	TVG	401-197
Hoffman, John C.	RR	401-57
Hoffman, L. J.	SP	401-45
Hoffman, R. H.	SR	401-83
Hoffman, R. H., Hon.	SR	401-83
Hoffman, Rufus	USV	401-234
Hoffman, William	FF	401-135
Hoffman, William	FF	401-135
Hoffman, William	USV	401-234
Hoffman, William F.	USV	401-234
Hoffmann, John R.	USV	401-234
Hogan, Andrew	ARM	401-6
Hogan, F. L.	USV	401-234
Hogan, Frances	NAV	401-18
Hogan, Joseph W. B.	SR	401-83
Hogan, Micheal	SP	401-45
Hogan, Tom C.	USV	401-234
Hogan, William	ARM	401-6
Hoges, T. C.	SP	401-45
Hogg, Frank B.	USV	401-234
Hogg, Thomas E.	SR	401-83
Hogg, Tom	SR	401-83
Hoggatt, Lycurgus	ARM	401-6
Hoggett, L. S.	SR	401-83
Hogrefe, Henry	USV	401-234
Hogren, Samuel	RR	401-57
Hogue, C. C.	SR	401-83
Hogue, C. C.	LR	401-129
Hogue, Vernal L.	TVG	401-197
Hohenberger, William	FB	401-156
Hohmann, Christian	SP	401-45
Hoist, J. A.	TVG	401-198
Hoist, W. H.	TVG	401-198
Hoit, Kilburn	ARM	401-6
Hoke, John F.	USV	401-234
Holaday, Frank	SR	401-83
Holbein, John	USV	401-234
Holbert, James T.	SP	401-45
Holbert, William Claud	RRR	401-118
Holbin, Reuben	SR	401-83
Holbrook, H. G.	USV	401-234
Holbrook, Joseph Y.	USV	401-234
Holcomb, B. W.	CSA	401-39
Holcomb, Frank	TVG	401-198

Index to Texas Adjutant General Service Records—All Service Branches

Name	Branch	Record
Holcomb, Gus	TVG	401-198
Holcomb, H. S.	SR	401-83
Holcombe, James J.	ARM	401-6
Holdaway, John D.	FB	401-156
Holden, A.	FB	401-156
Holden, A. H.	FB	401-156
Holden, D. W.	FB	401-156
Holden, H. C.	RR	401-57
Holden, H. ClinT	SR	401-83
Holden, Hetsel Franklin	RRR	401-118
Holden, John	NAV	401-18
Holder, C. W.	SR	401-83
Holder, Heber L.	USV	401-234
Holder, James D.	USV	401-234
Holder, Joseph	USV	401-234
Holderby, J. B. H.	SR	401-83
Holderness, J. Ive	SR	401-83
Holdsworth, W. T.	USV	401-234
Holingsworth, W. D.	FF	401-135
Hollamon, Ferrell Exum	SR	401-83
Hollan, H. E.	SR	401-83
Hollan, J. G.	RR	401-57
Holland, A. L.	SR	401-83
Holland, Burton	TVG	401-198
Holland, Charles D.	SR	401-83
Holland, Christopher F.	USV	401-234
Holland, David	RR	401-57
Holland, Fred D.	RR	401-57
Holland, Frederick	USV	401-234
Holland, H. A.	FB	401-156
Holland, Harrison H.	TST	401-35
Holland, J. Grady	SR	401-83
Holland, J. Grady	LR	401-129
Holland, James S.	TVG	401-198
Holland, James S.	USV	401-234
Holland, Mitchel	TVG	401-198
Holland, Murray	SR	401-83
Holland, O. C.	SP	401-45
Holland, R. S.	USV	401-234
Holland, Robert J.	USV	401-234
Holland, S. M.	SP	401-45
Holland, Thornton	USV	401-234
Holland, W. J.	RR	401-57
Holland, W. J.	SR	401-83
Holland, W. R.	RR	401-57
Holland, Warner L.	TVG	401-198
Hollander, Everett E.	USV	401-234
Hollander, J. J. L.	SP	401-45
Hollebeke, Edd	RR	401-57
Holley, E. B.	RRR	401-118
Holley, Porter J.	CSA	401-39
Holley, Richard M.	USV	401-234
Holliday, Lucius	SP	401-45
Hollinger, E. B.	FB	401-156
Hollingsworth, L. R.	SR	401-83
Hollingsworth, M. W.	USV	401-234
Hollingsworth, Roby	TVG	401-198
Hollingsworth, Theo. G.	TVG	401-198
Hollingsworth, Wiley B.	USV	401-234
Hollis, Elbert H.	USV	401-234
Hollis, J. R.	RR	401-57
Hollis, James H.	FB	401-156
Hollis, Jesse	ARM	401-6
Hollis, John R.	RRR	401-118
Hollis, John Ransom	SR	401-83
Hollis, John Robert	RR	401-57
Hollis, L. W., Jr., MD	SR	401-83
Hollis, R. L.	RRR	401-118
Hollis, Thornton F.	CSA	401-39
Hollmig, Robert	FF	401-135
Holloman, F. E.	RR	401-57
Hollomon, W. O.	USV	401-234
Holloway, E. B.	TVG	401-198
Holloway, F. L.	FB	401-156
Holloway, F. M.	FB	401-156
Holloway, Felix	FF	401-135
Holloway, Harner M.	USV	401-234
Holloway, Jo D.	RR	401-57
Hollowell, J. C.	FB	401-156
Holman, E. M.	SR	401-83
Holman, H. C.	USV	401-234
Holman, James S.	ARM	401-6
Holman, Jesse R.	USV	401-234
Holman, John	RR	401-57
Holman, W. S.	USV	401-234
Holmes, C. H.	SR	401-83
Holmes, Frank	FF	401-135
Holmes, Frank H.	TVG	401-198
Holmes, Frank Marion	TVG	401-198
Holmes, John P.	FB	401-156
Holmes, John R.	TVG	401-198
Holmes, Lauret	USV	401-234
Holmes, N. H.	TVG	401-198
Holmes, Simon	ARM	401-6
Holmes, W. E.	RR	401-57
Holmes, W. E.	RRR	401-118
Holmes, Walter M.	LR	401-129
Holoday, Frank	RR	401-57
Holsey, Walter R.	USV	401-234
Holshouser, M. T.	RRR	401-118
Holstead, Richard T.	NAV	401-18
Holston, J. W.	FB	401-156
Holt, E. P.	FB	401-156
Holt, J. W.	FB	401-156
Holt, Joseph W.	MV	401-29
Holt, Tank	RR	401-57
Holt, Thad C.	TVG	401-198
Holtkamp, Otto A.	USV	401-234
Holton, Robert	TVG	401-198
Holtze, Augustus	NAV	401-18
Homan, Edward	NAV	401-18
Homan, John E.	USV	401-234

Index to Texas Adjutant General Service Records—All Service Branches

Name	Branch	Record
Homan, W. W.	TVG	401-198
Homeyer, Albert G.	TVG	401-198
Homuth, August	TVG	401-198
Hon, Alva M.	USV	401-234
Honea, Floyd R.	USV	401-234
Honea, James Arch	RRR	401-118
Honea, R. F.	RR	401-57
Honea, R. F.	SR	401-84
Honeycutt, L. D.	SR	401-84
Honre, A. A.	SR	401-84
Honse, Frank	RR	401-57
Honse, Frank	SR	401-84
Hood, A. F.	FB	401-156
Hood, Donald	ARM	401-6
Hood, Joe O.	SR	401-84
Hooker, L. D.	SR	401-84
Hooker, W. L.	FB	401-156
Hooks, D. A.	SR	401-84
Hooks, John H.	MV	401-29
Hooks, Thomas W.	SP	401-45
Hooper, James	ARM	401-6
Hooper, John	NAV	401-18
Hooper, R. B.	SR	401-84
Hooper, William	SP	401-45
Hoot, Thad	RRR	401-118
Hooten, J. B.	FB	401-156
Hooter, John H.	SR	401-84
Hoover, D. A.	USV	401-234
Hoover, John S.	TVG	401-198
Hoover, John S.	USV	401-234
Hoover, R. C., Sr.	SR	401-84
Hoover, Walter	TVG	401-198
Hoover, Walter	USV	401-234
Hope, EmmetT	RR	401-57
Hope, G. W.	SR	401-84
Hope, George	USV	401-234
Hope, L.	SR	401-84
Hope, L.	LR	401-129
Hopf, A. L.	SR	401-84
Hopkins, C. O.	SP	401-45
Hopkins, Charles E.	USV	401-234
Hopkins, E. C.	FB	401-156
Hopkins, George J.	SR	401-84
Hopkins, Hugh C.	USV	401-234
Hopkins, Lew D.	USV	401-234
Hopkins, Preston	RR	401-57
Hopkins, Robert H.	USV	401-234
Hopkins, W. B.	FB	401-156
Hopper, B. H.	RRR	401-118
Hopper, J. B.	FB	401-156
Hopper, J. C.	TVG	401-198
Hopper, T. A.	SR	401-84
Hopping, R. C.	SR	401-84
Hopson, Elton	TVG	401-198
Hopson, Joseph A. A.	USV	401-234
Hopson, Lee A.	USV	401-234
Hopson, P. H.	SR	401-84
Hopson, R. E.	USV	401-234
Hopson, W. T.	USV	401-234
Horan, John	ARM	401-6
Hord, Ed	SR	401-84
Hord, H. W.	SR	401-84
Hord, Homer D.	RRR	401-118
Hormon, H. N.	TVG	401-198
Horn, C. Camp	FB	401-156
Horn, E. W.	TVG	401-198
Horn, Edward N.	USV	401-235
Horn, John	ARM	401-6
Horne, Clark	TVG	401-198
Horne, E. S.	TVG	401-198
Horne, James E.	FB	401-156
Hornsbey, Collier C.	ARM	401-6
Hornsby, C. C.	ARM	401-6
Hornsby, Emory	RR	401-57
Hornsby, John W.	SR	401-84
Hornsby, W. W.	RR	401-57
Hornsby, W. W.	FB	401-156
Hornung, August	FF	401-135
Hornung, August	SP	401-45
Horny, Henry	FF	401-135
Horracks, Edward	SR	401-84
Horst, Paul	SR	401-84
Horton, B. S.	SR	401-84
Horton, C. A.	RRR	401-118
Horton, Charles Reid	SR	401-84
Horton, E.	NAV	401-18
Horton, Earl	RRR	401-118
Horton, F. C.	TVG	401-198
Horton, Frank	SR	401-84
Horton, Frank	TVG	401-198
Horton, Fred B.	SR	401-84
Horton, Fred B.	LR	401-129
Horton, Fred E.	SR	401-84
Horton, George N.	FB	401-156
Horton, Hal C.	SR	401-84
Horton, King W.	TVG	401-198
Horton, L. F.	RRR	401-118
Horton, William H.	RRR	401-118
Hosemann, Joseph	SP	401-45
Hosford, Fred	TVG	401-198
Hosford, Tom B.	TVG	401-198
Hoskins, Brice	TVG	401-198
Hoskins, Laurence W.	SR	401-84
Hossie, Thomas	ARM	401-6
Hosty, R. C.	USV	401-235
Hotchkiss, C. M.	USV	401-235
Hotchkiss, M. M.	TVG	401-198
Houchin, W. D.	SR	401-84
Houchins, J. F.	SR	401-84
Houchins, J. F.	LR	401-129
Hough, Claude	TVG	401-198
Hough, R. K.	FB	401-156

Index to Texas Adjutant General Service Records—All Service Branches

Name	Branch	Record
Houghton, Horace H.	ARM	401-6
Houghton, W. D.	ARM	401-6
Houk, Herman W.	USV	401-235
House, A. F.	FB	401-156
House, Charles L.	TVG	401-198
House, Edward M.	TVG	401-198
House, Frank	RRR	401-118
House, Joseph G.	TVG	401-198
House, R. E., M.D.	SR	401-84
House, R. J.	TVG	401-198
Houseton, A. G.	RRR	401-118
Houston, A. J.	TVG	401-198
Houston, A. L.	SR	401-84
Houston, A. W.	TVG	401-198
Houston, Edwin	SR	401-84
Houston, Edwin	LR	401-129
Houston, Forbes J.	TST	401-35
Houston, J. D.	FB	401-156
Houston, James	FF	401-135
Houston, James	SP	401-45
Houston, John	TVG	401-198
Houston, R. W.	TVG	401-198
Houston, Samuel, Jr.	CSA	401-39
Houston, T. J.	RRR	401-118
Houston, Tom A.	SR	401-84
Houston, Tom A.	LR	401-129
Houston, WalteR	ARM	401-6
Houston, William Sledge	RRR	401-118
Houy, William	FB	401-156
Houze, Henry	USV	401-235
Hovas, Turpin G.	USV	401-235
Howard, Annesley	MV	401-29
Howard, Buren D.	USV	401-235
Howard, Elmer F.	USV	401-235
Howard, G. W.	SP	401-45
Howard, Gaston S.	SR	401-84
Howard, George J.	SR	401-84
Howard, George W.	USV	401-235
Howard, H. L.	USV	401-235
Howard, Harry B.	USV	401-235
Howard, Henry B.	ARM	401-6
Howard, Jno. B.	LR	401-129
Howard, John B.	SR	401-84
Howard, John B.	TVG	401-198
Howard, John B.	USV	401-235
Howard, John I.	RRR	401-118
Howard, John S.	USV	401-235
Howard, John W.	FB	401-156
Howard, Jordan	TST	401-35
Howard, Joseph V.	TST	401-35
Howard, Leander G.	RR	401-57
Howard, Luke	NAV	401-18
Howard, Luke L.	USV	401-235
Howard, RheA	SR	401-84
Howard, Robert A.	USV	401-235
Howard, Thomas J.	TST	401-35
Howard, Van	USV	401-235
Howard, W. P.	TVG	401-198
Howard, WalteR	TVG	401-198
Howard, Walter D.	USV	401-235
Howard, Walter E.	USV	401-235
Howard, William	NAV	401-18
Howard, William B.	USV	401-235
Howe, Will A., Jr.	RRR	401-118
Howell, A. E.	SR	401-84
Howell, David	NAV	401-18
Howell, George	FF	401-135
Howell, George D.	FB	401-156
Howell, J. T.	MV	401-29
Howell, James J.	USV	401-235
Howell, James M.	SR	401-84
Howell, Jesse	TVG	401-198
Howell, John C.	TVG	401-198
Howell, John W.	USV	401-235
Howell, Mason	TVG	401-198
Howell, P. C.	TVG	401-198
Howell, T. H.	SR	401-84
Howell, Thomas	SP	401-45
Howell, W. Clifton	TVG	401-198
Howell, W. E.	TVG	401-198
Howell, Wallace N.	RR	401-57
Howerton, John E.	USV	401-235
Howeth, Cornelius H.	RR	401-57
Howison, Allan	SR	401-84
Howlett, Henry Lyman	TST	401-35
Howrey, C. W.	FB	401-156
Howry, Leonard	FB	401-156
Howze, J. W.	RRR	401-118
Hoy, Ben	SR	401-84
Hoyle, H. J.	SR	401-84
Hoyle, Josiah	NAV	401-18
Hoyt, C. G.	NAV	401-18
Hoyt, Guy A.	USV	401-235
Hoyt, L. D.	FB	401-156
Hoyt, Timothy	NAV	401-18
Hoyt, Timothy	ARM	401-6
Hoyte, Cornelius	NAV	401-18
Hrncir, Joe	SR	401-84
Hubbard, A. S.	TVG	401-198
Hubbard, Albert B.	USV	401-235
Hubbard, Golman	ARM	401-6
Hubbard, J. M.	SR	401-84
Hubbard, James M.	RRR	401-118
Hubbard, Thomas A.	TVG	401-198
Hubbell, Eddie	TVG	401-198
Hubert, C. C.	FB	401-156
Hubinger, Joseph E.	SR	401-84
Hucherson, Brant	TVG	401-198
Huchinson, George	TVG	401-198
Huckabay, Ben F.	TVG	401-198
Huckeba, S. E.	SR	401-84
Hudd, Edward	NAV	401-18

Index to Texas Adjutant General Service Records—All Service Branches

Name	Branch	Record
Huddle, John D.	TVG	401-198
Huddler, M. A.	SR	401-84
Huddleston, C. E.	RR	401-57
Huddleston, Clyde Eugene	SR	401-84
Huddleston, J. A.	SR	401-84
Huddleston, J. B.	USV	401-235
Huddleston, James P.	RR	401-57
Huddleston, L. L.	SR	401-84
Huddleston, Warner Lee	RRR	401-118
Hudgens, N. C.	TVG	401-198
Hudgins, W. F.	SR	401-84
Hudgins, W. O.	SR	401-84
Hudnall, Wade	SR	401-84
Hudson, Charles H.	USV	401-235
Hudson, D.	FB	401-156
Hudson, E. A.	USV	401-235
Hudson, Frank W.	USV	401-235
Hudson, H. H.	USV	401-235
Hudson, Herman J.	SR	401-84
Hudson, J. R.	SR	401-84
Hudson, Joe C.	FB	401-156
Hudson, JoshuA	ARM	401-6
Hudson, Louis L.	TVG	401-198
Hudson, R. B.	SP	401-45
Hudson, R. M.	RR	401-57
Hudson, Robert M.	USV	401-235
Hudson, Russell W.	RR	401-57
Hudson, Thom.	TVG	401-198
Hudson, W. E.	FF	401-135
Hudson, W. M.	USV	401-235
Hudson, W. W.	SR	401-84
Hudson, Wade H.	FF	401-135
Hudson, William	CSA	401-39
Hudson, William M.	NAV	401-18
Hudson, Willie	TVG	401-198
Hudson, Zachariah T.	SP	401-45
Huebel, Charles	ARM	401-6
Huebner, Frank L.	SP	401-45
Huehner, Albert H.	FB	401-156
Huelsbecke, Adolph	FF	401-135
Huettig, J. E.	TVG	401-198
Huey, James D.	USV	401-235
Huff, C. W.	FB	401-156
Huff, Charles C.	SR	401-84
Huff, Charles Chester	RRR	401-118
Huff, Claude	TVG	401-198
Huff, Lee	RRR	401-118
Huff, Lee	SR	401-84
Huff, Leslie N.	TVG	401-198
Huff, Nathan D.	USV	401-235
Huff, Stephen W.	TVG	401-198
Huff, William	NAV	401-18
Huff, William F.	USV	401-235
Huffaker, Charles	USV	401-235
Huffaker, D. Hunter	SR	401-84
Huffhines, Claude	TVG	401-198
Huffman, Benjamin F.	SP	401-45
Huffman, J. J.	RR	401-57
Huffman, James William	SR	401-84
Huffman, John M.	RR	401-57
Huffman, Riley	MM	401-32
Hufnagel, John	ARM	401-6
Huggett, Ira H. S.	TVG	401-198
Huggins, Sam H.	TVG	401-198
Hughes, Benjamin	ARM	401-6
Hughes, C. M.	SR	401-84
Hughes, Covey M.	LR	401-129
Hughes, Dan O.	TVG	401-198
Hughes, Edward	USV	401-235
Hughes, Emery H.	SR	401-84
Hughes, Esther	USV	401-235
Hughes, Everett	SR	401-84
Hughes, George F.	USV	401-235
Hughes, George M.	FB	401-156
Hughes, George S.	USV	401-235
Hughes, George W.	SR	401-84
Hughes, Howard R.	SR	401-84
Hughes, Hunter	TVG	401-198
Hughes, James	NAV	401-18
Hughes, James	ARM	401-6
Hughes, James	ARM	401-6
Hughes, James	USV	401-235
Hughes, James Clark	SR	401-84
Hughes, Jim	TVG	401-198
Hughes, John	RR	401-57
Hughes, John B.	MM	401-32
Hughes, John R.	RR	401-57
Hughes, John R.	FB	401-156
Hughes, L. H.	TVG	401-198
Hughes, L. R.	FB	401-156
Hughes, Michael	NAV	401-18
Hughes, Noah T.	USV	401-235
Hughes, Ollen Porter	SR	401-84
Hughes, P. H.	TVG	401-198
Hughes, R. L.	USV	401-235
Hughes, Robert	TVG	401-198
Hughes, Robert	USV	401-235
Hughes, T. P.	FF	401-135
Hughes, Thomas C.	USV	401-235
Hughes, Thomas Henry	RR	401-57
Hughes, W. C.	SR	401-84
Hughes, W. J.	TST	401-35
Hughes, W. P.	TST	401-35
Hughes, W. P.	FB	401-156
Hughes, W. S.	FB	401-156
Hughes, W. S.	FB	401-156
Hughes, William M.	USV	401-235
Hughes, William S.	NAV	401-18
Hulen, E. B.	RR	401-57
Hulen, Eugene B.	TVG	401-198
Hulen, John A.	RRR	401-118
Hulen, John A.	TVG	401-198

Index to Texas Adjutant General Service Records—All Service Branches

Name	Branch	Record
Hulen, John A.	USV	401-235
Hulin, W. H.	FB	401-156
Hull, A. S.	SR	401-84
Hull, C. F.	TVG	401-198
Hull, E. A.	TVG	401-198
Hull, James H.	SR	401-84
Hull, K. S.	RRR	401-118
Human, Charles	MV	401-29
Hume, Louis	TST	401-35
Hume, Thomas	FB	401-156
Hume, William	TVG	401-198
Humes, R. P.	SR	401-84
Humphrey, A. A.	SR	401-84
Humphrey, A. A.	LR	401-129
Humphrey, Ernest	SR	401-84
Humphrey, Herman	TVG	401-198
Humphrey, Louis A.	RRR	401-118
Humphrey, Manuel J.	TVG	401-198
Humphrey, Thomas D.	SR	401-84
Humphreys, A. Lowery	TVG	401-198
Humphreys, Ernest	SR	401-84
Humphreys, Fred	RR	401-57
Humphreys, Fred	SR	401-84
Humphreys, Herbert Sidney	RRR	401-118
Humphries, Otto	RR	401-57
Humphries, Otto	SR	401-84
Humrich, John	ARM	401-6
Humson, Edmond	NAV	401-18
Hundley, J. M.	TVG	401-198
Hune, Henry C.	SP	401-45
Hungerford, L. N.	RR	401-57
Hunnicut, J. R.	RR	401-57
Hunnicutt, J. D.	SR	401-84
Hunnicutt, J. R.	SR	401-84
Hunnicutt, M. P.	SP	401-45
Hunsaker, Roy	TVG	401-198
Hunt, A. A.	SR	401-84
Hunt, Albert G.	USV	401-235
Hunt, Charles	ARM	401-6
Hunt, E. L.	SR	401-84
Hunt, Edward L.	RRR	401-118
Hunt, Elijah C.	USV	401-235
Hunt, H. H.	SR	401-84
Hunt, J.	FB	401-156
Hunt, J. S.	USV	401-235
Hunt, John W.	SR	401-84
Hunt, John W.	LR	401-129
Hunt, Karl G.	SR	401-84
Hunt, Phil M.	TVG	401-198
Hunt, Phil M.	USV	401-235
Hunt, R. B.	USV	401-235
Hunt, R. E.	RR	401-57
Hunt, S. A.	RRR	401-118
Hunt, T. J.	RRR	401-118
Hunt, T. J.	SR	401-84
Hunt, W. C.	SR	401-84
Hunt, William H.	ARM	401-6
Hunt, William L.	ARM	401-6
Hunter, C. T.	RR	401-57
Hunter, Elbert C.	USV	401-235
Hunter, G. D.	TVG	401-198
Hunter, George D.	SR	401-85
Hunter, J. L.	SR	401-85
Hunter, James M.	FF	401-135
Hunter, James M.	USV	401-235
Hunter, James P.	RR	401-57
Hunter, Joe R.	SR	401-85
Hunter, John	SP	401-45
Hunter, John L.	FB	401-156
Hunter, John M.	SP	401-45
Hunter, John R.	TVG	401-198
Hunter, Oscar	USV	401-235
Hunter, Pat T.	USV	401-235
Hunter, R. G.	USV	401-235
Hunter, Samuel	ARM	401-6
Hunter, W. H.	MM	401-32
Hunter, W. L.	SP	401-45
Huntington, James M.	NAV	401-18
Hunton, G. P.	RR	401-57
Hunton, George P.	SR	401-85
Huntsman, U. S.	SR	401-85
Huntsucker, W. H.	SR	401-85
Huntsucker, W. H.	LR	401-129
Hurd, Arthur B.	USV	401-235
Hurd, James G.	NAV	401-18
Hurd, Norman	NAV	401-18
Hurd, W. R.	TVG	401-199
Hurd, William A.	NAV	401-18
Hurdle, Ben	USV	401-235
Hurdleston, C. H.	SR	401-85
Hurlburt, E. L.	SR	401-85
Hurley, P.[?] H.	SP	401-45
Hurley, Walter W.	USV	401-235
Hurley, William	SP	401-45
Hurley, William	TVG	401-199
Hurlock, M. A.	RRR	401-118
Hurnan, Charles	MV	401-29
Hurst, Cleveland C.	RR	401-57
Hurst, George B.	RR	401-57
Hurst, James	NAV	401-18
Hurst, William	MV	401-29
Hurt, A. H. D.	FB	401-156
Hurt, T. L.	FB	401-156
Hurtig, Henry John	TVG	401-199
Hurtth, Edward A.	USV	401-235
Huskey, L. C.	SR	401-85
Huskey, L. C.	LR	401-129
Husser, Charles H.	NAV	401-18
Husser, Joseph	FF	401-135
Hussey, A. G.	FB	401-156
Huston, Alexander	ARM	401-6
Huston, F. D.	TVG	401-199

Index to Texas Adjutant General Service Records—All Service Branches

Name	Branch	Record
Huston, James R.	USV	401-235
Huston, John	ARM	401-6
Hutch, E. M.	SP	401-45
Hutches, B. F.	TST	401-35
Hutcheson, W. C.	FB	401-156
Hutchings, George B.	USV	401-235
Hutchings, Henry	SR	401-85
Hutchings, Henry	TVG	401-199
Hutchings, R. L.	RRR	401-118
Hutchings, Thomas C.	USV	401-235
Hutchins, E. H.	USV	401-235
Hutchins, Spencer	TVG	401-199
Hutchinson, Andrew Calvin	TVG	401-199
Hutchinson, Andrew Calvin	USV	401-235
Hutchinson, Ben F.	USV	401-235
Hutchinson, Charles E.	USV	401-235
Hutchinson, Richard E.	USV	401-235
Hutchisen, George H.	SP	401-45
Hutchison, Clarence L.	USV	401-235
Hutchison, J. W.	SR	401-85
Hutchison, R. A.	FB	401-156
Hutchison, S. S.	FB	401-156
Hutchison, Sidney S.	RR	401-57
Hutchison, William S.	TVG	401-199
Hutchison, William S.	USV	401-235
Hutson, William Ferguson	USV	401-235
Hutt, Murray E.	SR	401-85
Hutto, Cecil	SR	401-85
Hutton, George Van	USV	401-235
Huvis, Benjamin	NAV	401-18
Hyams, Harry T.	SR	401-85
Hyatt, Perry Fred	USV	401-235
Hyatt, S. W.	SR	401-85
Hyatt, S. W.	LR	401-129
Hyde, Carlie	RR	401-57
Hyde, James A.	RR	401-57
Hyde, Wilmer J.	TVG	401-199
Hye, William	USV	401-235
Hyenck, Andrew B.	USV	401-235
Hyltin, Carl	RR	401-57
Hynes, Dominic	SP	401-45
Hynes, P. L.	RRR	401-118
Iglehart, David T., Jr.	SR	401-85
Iglehart, Thomas W.	USV	401-235
Ikard, B. D.	SR	401-85
Ikard, E. F.	FB	401-156
Ikard, S. R.	RR	401-57
Iles, Thomas	MV	401-29
Ilseng, Grant	SR	401-85
Iltis, Seraphine	FF	401-135
Imerarity, S. A.	TVG	401-199
Imhoff, Peter	TST	401-35
Inabirret, Felix W.	USV	401-235
Inabirret, Robert H.	USV	401-236
Ince, Henry Wilson	RRR	401-118
Ince, J. H. "Doc"	SR	401-85
Ince, Joseph Hugh	RRR	401-118
Infernaise, George A.	USV	401-236
Ingenhutt, Thomas	SP	401-45
Ingham, A. Y.	SR	401-85
Ingham, A. Y.	LR	401-129
Inglish, Jim N.	SR	401-85
Inglish, S. W.	TVG	401-199
Ingram, A. W.	FB	401-156
Ingram, Benjamin F.	TVG	401-199
Ingram, Dryden A.	USV	401-236
Ingram, George	SR	401-85
Ingram, Jesse N.	USV	401-236
Ingram, John	ARM	401-6
Ingram, L. E.	TVG	401-199
Ingram, R. V.	SR	401-85
Ingram, W. E.	MM	401-32
Ingram, W. J.	SP	401-45
Inman, James C.	FF	401-135
Insall, Cade	FB	401-156
Insall, Noel	SR	401-85
Ionak, Charles	FF	401-135
Irby, Loren E.	TVG	401-199
Irdstone, H. G.	TVG	401-199
Ireland, George	NAV	401-19
Ireson, James Wallace	TVG	401-199
Irion, J. L.	TST	401-35
Irish, B. M.	SP	401-45
Irons, John	FB	401-156
Irvin, Carroll	USV	401-236
Irvin, Driskill R.	SR	401-85
Irvin, John	NAV	401-19
Irvin, T. A.	RR	401-57
Irvin, T. A.	SR	401-85
Irvin, Thaddeus	ARM	401-6
Irvine, Edwin F.	USV	401-236
Irvine, Howard S.	USV	401-236
Irving, J.	FB	401-156
Irving, Joseph B.	FB	401-156
Irving, P. T.	TVG	401-199
Irving, Peyton	USV	401-236
Irving, Philip	TVG	401-199
Irving, R. J.	TST	401-35
Irwin, Charles	NAV	401-19
Irwin, Charles	ARM	401-6
Irwin, Chester	TVG	401-199
Irwin, Henry	ARM	401-6
Irwin, John Garland	SR	401-85
Irwin, L. S.	RR	401-57
Irwin, Russell D.	USV	401-236
Irwin, S. S.	SP	401-45
Irwin, T. K.	SR	401-85
Irwin, W. L.	RRR	401-118
Isaac, Charles	SR	401-85
Isaacs, Jefferson Davis	FB	401-156
Isaacs, Jno. C.	SR	401-85
Isaacs, John C.	LR	401-129

Index to Texas Adjutant General Service Records—All Service Branches

Name	Branch	Record
Isbell, Frank	TST	401-35
Isbell, Thomas	TST	401-35
Isbell, Tom P.	SR	401-85
Ish, W. A.	FB	401-156
Ish, William A.	SR	401-85
Isherwood, R. J.	TVG	401-199
Isom, George G.	USV	401-236
Israel, M. T.	FB	401-156
Itchingham, Arthur	ARM	401-6
Ives, G. A.	TVG	401-199
Ives, William B.	USV	401-236
Iveson, James W.	USV	401-236
Ivester, Horace	RRR	401-118
Ivey, C. L.	SR	401-85
Ivey, Charles A.	USV	401-236
Ivey, Curtis L.	LR	401-129
Ivey, J. F.	TVG	401-199
Ivey, J. H.	SR	401-85
Ivey, J. R.	FB	401-156
Ivie, Doc C.	USV	401-236
Ivy, A. I.	FB	401-156
Ivy, H. T.	USV	401-236
Ivy, Josh	SR	401-85
Ivy, Josh	LR	401-129
Izaguirre, Eduardo	SR	401-85
Izlien, Zephlin	ARM	401-6
Jack, Alvin N.	TVG	401-199
Jack, James	ARM	401-6
Jack, William C.	TVG	401-199
Jackman, Tom J.	RR	401-57
Jackson, Alfred	TVG	401-199
Jackson, B. H.	TVG	401-199
Jackson, C. C.	SR	401-85
Jackson, C. R.	FB	401-156
Jackson, Carl E.	USV	401-236
Jackson, Cecil	RR	401-57
Jackson, Dan W.	SR	401-85
Jackson, E. A.	USV	401-236
Jackson, E. P.	SR	401-85
Jackson, Edward A.	USV	401-236
Jackson, Edward Earl	RRR	401-119
Jackson, Ford	SR	401-85
Jackson, George	FF	401-135
Jackson, Harper	SP	401-45
Jackson, Henry	SP	401-45
Jackson, Henry	FB	401-156
Jackson, Herbert L.	USV	401-236
Jackson, Holly	USV	401-236
Jackson, Hugh	TVG	401-199
Jackson, J. B.	TVG	401-199
Jackson, J. J.	RR	401-57
Jackson, James A.	RRR	401-119
Jackson, Joe	SR	401-85
Jackson, John	RR	401-57
Jackson, John A.	SR	401-85
Jackson, John A.	USV	401-236
Jackson, L. R.	FB	401-157
Jackson, L. W.	SR	401-85
Jackson, Lyndon J.	RR	401-57
Jackson, O. C.	LR	401-129
Jackson, P. C.	FB	401-157
Jackson, P. C.	FB	401-157
Jackson, Robert Will	USV	401-236
Jackson, Rowland J.	USV	401-236
Jackson, Rube W.	USV	401-236
Jackson, Samuel A.	MV	401-29
Jackson, Samuel H.	TVG	401-199
Jackson, ScotT	USV	401-236
Jackson, Thomas S.	ARM	401-6
Jackson, V. L.	SR	401-85
Jackson, W. E.	SR	401-85
Jackson, W. G.	FB	401-157
Jackson, Walter	TVG	401-199
Jackson, Wilbur C.	USV	401-236
Jackson, Will E.	TVG	401-199
Jackson, William	ARM	401-6
Jackson, William	USV	401-236
Jackson, William D.	TVG	401-199
Jackson, William H.	USV	401-236
Jackson, William P.	MV	401-29
Jackson, Z. R.	FB	401-157
Jackson, Zebulon	FB	401-157
Jacob, F.	ARM	401-6
Jacob, Louie	TVG	401-199
Jacobs, Ike B.	TVG	401-199
Jacobs, J. C.	SR	401-85
Jacobs, John	RR	401-57
Jacobs, Terrell M., Capt.	SR	401-85
Jacobs, Thomas	NAV	401-19
Jacobs, William E.	USV	401-236
Jacobson, J. M.	SR	401-85
Jaeger, Edward	USV	401-236
Jager, Francis	ARM	401-6
Jaggi, James	TVG	401-199
Jainer, R. C.	TVG	401-199
Jalufka, James	USV	401-236
Jamail, Louis	SR	401-85
Jamar, Joe	SR	401-85
James, A. F.	FB	401-157
James, A. J.	TVG	401-199
James, C. B.	SR	401-85
James, D. L.	SR	401-85
James, D. R.	FB	401-157
James, Daniel	SP	401-45
James, E. P.	USV	401-236
James, F. W.	TVG	401-199
James, Gaines L.	TVG	401-199
James, Henry	SP	401-45
James, J. C.	MM	401-32
James, J. W.	FB	401-157
James, John V.	MV	401-29
James, John W.	SP	401-45

Index to Texas Adjutant General Service Records—All Service Branches

Name	Branch	Record
James, Michael	NAV	401-19
James, Philip	FB	401-157
James, R. H.	TVG	401-199
James, Robert C.	RRR	401-119
James, Robert N.	USV	401-236
James, S. A.	SR	401-85
James, S. A.	TVG	401-199
James, W. L.	TVG	401-199
James, Walter Edmond	RRR	401-119
James, Will C.	RR	401-57
James, William	NAV	401-19
James, William	FF	401-135
Jameson, L. C.	SR	401-85
Jameson, L. C.	LR	401-129
Jameson, Seaborn	RR	401-57
Jamison, J. A.	FB	401-157
Janak, Joe F.	SR	401-85
Janes, Oscar	TVG	401-199
Jannasch, C. R.	TVG	401-199
Jannasch, Fred E.	USV	401-236
Janner, Frank C.	USV	401-236
Jansen, JacoB	FF	401-135
January, Samuel A.	MV	401-29
Japhet, GustaV	TVG	401-199
Japlin, Charles V.	ARM	401-6
Jarmon, Steve W.	USV	401-236
Jarrard, Benson C.	USV	401-236
Jarrard, H. A.	TVG	401-199
Jarrel, E. F., Dr.	SR	401-85
Jarrell, C. A.	SR	401-85
Jarrell, Julius	TVG	401-199
Jarrett, Thad Johnson	SR	401-85
Jarrott, Marshall	USV	401-236
Jarvis, John	NAV	401-19
Jarvis, W. G.	TVG	401-199
Jarvis, William G.	USV	401-236
Jasper, C. P.	RRR	401-119
Jasper, M[unger]	SP	401-45
Jayne, Alvey E.	TVG	401-199
Jefcoat, A. M.	RRR	401-119
Jefferds, E. R.	FB	401-157
Jefferies, A. T.	SR	401-85
Jeffers, Floyd	RRR	401-119
Jeffers, William	SP	401-45
Jefferson, Frank	SR	401-85
Jefferson, Patrick	ARM	401-6
Jefferson, W. D.	FB	401-157
Jefferson, William D.	FB	401-157
Jeffery, Harry E.	USV	401-236
Jeffries, A. D.	TST	401-35
Jeffries, J. D.	SR	401-85
Jeffries, William	FF	401-135
Jeffry, S.	FB	401-157
Jekel, John	TVG	401-199
Jelkyl, Ross	ARM	401-6
Jemison, J. M.	SR	401-85
Jenkins, Albert Fletcher	TVG	401-199
Jenkins, Charles	FB	401-157
Jenkins, E. T.	SR	401-85
Jenkins, George W.	ARM	401-6
Jenkins, H. S.	TVG	401-199
Jenkins, Harry D.	USV	401-236
Jenkins, I. N.	FB	401-157
Jenkins, J. A.	USV	401-236
Jenkins, J. T.	TVG	401-199
Jenkins, Jack	TVG	401-199
Jenkins, Jesse William	TVG	401-199
Jenkins, Joe	RR	401-57
Jenkins, L. C.	FB	401-157
Jenkins, Lee	FB	401-157
Jenkins, N. L.	FB	401-157
Jenkins, R. Lee	SR	401-85
Jenkins, Rufus R.	FB	401-157
Jenkins, Sam	FB	401-157
Jenkins, T. E.	SR	401-85
Jenkins, W. L.	FB	401-157
Jenkins, W. R.	FB	401-157
Jenkins, W. W.	RR	401-57
Jenkins, William R.	USV	401-236
Jenkins, William V.	TST	401-35
Jenks, Horace V.	ARM	401-6
Jennings, A. A.	FF	401-135
Jennings, Clyde	RR	401-57
Jennings, Clyde	RRR	401-119
Jennings, David	ARM	401-6
Jennings, Dick B.	RRR	401-119
Jennings, E. E.	SR	401-85
Jennings, G. A.	SP	401-45
Jennings, H.	SP	401-45
Jennings, J. F.	SP	401-45
Jennings, J. T.	RRR	401-119
Jennings, John David	USV	401-236
Jennings, John Davis	TVG	401-199
Jennings, John M.	TST	401-35
Jennings, Josiah M.	USV	401-236
Jennings, N. A.	USV	401-236
Jennings, Oscar	TVG	401-199
Jennings, R. F.	SR	401-85
Jennings, R. S.	TST	401-35
Jennings, R. W.	TVG	401-199
Jennings, W. A.	TVG	401-199
Jennings, W. T.	FB	401-157
Jennings, Wade	USV	401-236
Jennings, Walter Bryant	RRR	401-119
Jensen, George	USV	401-236
Jenson, E. R.	FB	401-157
Jerden, Elmer	TVG	401-199
Jergins, Andrew T.	USV	401-236
Jergins, Jesse J.	TVG	401-199
Jernigan, Hubert	USV	401-236
Jernigan, John D.	TVG	401-199
Jernigan, L. F.	USV	401-236

Index to Texas Adjutant General Service Records—All Service Branches

Name	Branch	Record
Jernigan, N. M.	TVG	401-199
Jernison, Henry T.	TVG	401-199
Jerow, John	TST	401-35
Jerrells, George	FB	401-157
Jerrells, J.	FB	401-157
Jessee, Ira Ernest	RRR	401-119
Jessee, R. S.	TVG	401-199
Jessen, Adalbert	SP	401-45
Jester, L. L.	TVG	401-199
Jester, Sue M.	RR	401-57
Jeter, W. L.	SR	401-85
Jeterka, John	USV	401-236
Jett, J.	SR	401-85
Jett, W. P.	RR	401-58
Jetty, C. S.	TVG	401-199
Jewell, Arthur C., Capt.	SR	401-85
Jilek, Adolph A.	USV	401-236
Jimenes, Candelario	FF	401-135
John (an Indian)	ARM	401-6
Johnigan, F.	RRR	401-119
Johns, C. R.	FF	401-135
Johns, E.	NAV	401-19
Johns, Edward	NAV	401-19
Johns, Glover S.	SR	401-85
Johns, H. P.	RRR	401-119
Johns, Joseph	TVG	401-199
Johns, Lowell M.	USV	401-236
Johns, M. F.	FB	401-157
Johns, W. H.	FB	401-157
Johns, Watson	FB	401-157
Johns, William	TST	401-35
Johnsey, Virgil	TVG	401-199
Johnson, A. R.	TVG	401-199
Johnson, Adam R.	USV	401-236
Johnson, Adam R., Jr.	SR	401-85
Johnson, Albert	SR	401-85
Johnson, Albert	FB	401-157
Johnson, Alexander	ARM	401-6
Johnson, Alexander	SR	401-85
Johnson, Alf	FB	401-157
Johnson, Alfred	CSA	401-39
Johnson, Allen S.	RRR	401-119
Johnson, Amil	RR	401-58
Johnson, ArthuR	USV	401-236
Johnson, Arthur B.	TVG	401-199
Johnson, Arthur W.	USV	401-236
Johnson, Audrey	ARM	401-6
Johnson, B. F.	FB	401-157
Johnson, Ben	FB	401-157
Johnson, Benjamin	ARM	401-6
Johnson, Benjamin F.	USV	401-236
Johnson, Boss	TVG	401-199
Johnson, Burton Warren	TVG	401-199
Johnson, C. A.	FB	401-157
Johnson, C. C.	USV	401-236
Johnson, C. E.	FB	401-157
Johnson, C. H.	TVG	401-199
Johnson, C. M.	USV	401-236
Johnson, C. W.	FB	401-157
Johnson, Charles	TST	401-35
Johnson, Charles	TVG	401-199
Johnson, Charles A.	RRR	401-119
Johnson, Charles L.	USV	401-236
Johnson, Charles P.	TVG	401-199
Johnson, Charles W.	USV	401-236
Johnson, Charlie W.	RRR	401-119
Johnson, Claiborne	SP	401-45
Johnson, Clarence R.	RRR	401-119
Johnson, D. L.	SR	401-85
Johnson, D. R.	USV	401-236
Johnson, D. W.	FB	401-157
Johnson, Daniel W.	SR	401-85
Johnson, David	TVG	401-199
Johnson, Dewitt	USV	401-236
Johnson, E. A.	USV	401-236
Johnson, E. C.	FB	401-157
Johnson, E. E.	SR	401-85
Johnson, E. E.	TVG	401-199
Johnson, E. F.	SR	401-85
Johnson, ElaM	TVG	401-200
Johnson, Eli M.	MV	401-29
Johnson, Ervin	TVG	401-200
Johnson, Eugene	FB	401-157
Johnson, Eugene E.	TVG	401-200
Johnson, Eugene E.	TVG	401-200
Johnson, Floyd L.	TVG	401-200
Johnson, Francis	MM	401-32
Johnson, Francis	ARM	401-6
Johnson, Frank	TVG	401-200
Johnson, Frank N.	FB	401-157
Johnson, G. C.	SR	401-85
Johnson, G. H.	SR	401-85
Johnson, George	FB	401-157
Johnson, George A.	USV	401-236
Johnson, George E.	USV	401-236
Johnson, George H.	RR	401-58
Johnson, George Hugh	TVG	401-200
Johnson, George W.	TVG	401-200
Johnson, GilberT	FB	401-157
Johnson, Gus	TVG	401-200
Johnson, Gustaf William	USV	401-236
Johnson, H. L.	TVG	401-200
Johnson, Hadley	SR	401-85
Johnson, Harry	FB	401-157
Johnson, Harry Hubbard	SR	401-85
Johnson, Hayes Y.	USV	401-236
Johnson, Henry	NAV	401-19
Johnson, Henry	TVG	401-200
Johnson, I. M.	RRR	401-119
Johnson, I. P.	FB	401-157
Johnson, Ike	RRR	401-119
Johnson, Irwin	MV	401-29

Index to Texas Adjutant General Service Records—All Service Branches

Name	Branch	Record
Johnson, Isaac S.	USV	401-236
Johnson, J. A.	SP	401-45
Johnson, J. A.	FB	401-157
Johnson, J. F.	TVG	401-200
Johnson, J. H.	SR	401-85
Johnson, J. H.	LR	401-129
Johnson, J. J.	RRR	401-119
Johnson, J. N.	SR	401-85
Johnson, J. R.	FB	401-157
Johnson, J. W.	LR	401-129
Johnson, J. Willis, Jr.	SR	401-85
Johnson, James	NAV	401-19
Johnson, James	FB	401-157
Johnson, James L.	TVG	401-200
Johnson, James T.	USV	401-236
Johnson, Janis H.	USV	401-236
Johnson, Jewell	TVG	401-200
Johnson, Jim	FB	401-157
Johnson, Joe E.	TVG	401-200
Johnson, John	NAV	401-19
Johnson, John	MV	401-29
Johnson, John	MV	401-29
Johnson, John	FB	401-157
Johnson, John	FB	401-157
Johnson, John F.	USV	401-236
Johnson, John James	ARM	401-6
Johnson, John O.	FB	401-157
Johnson, John R.	ARM	401-6
Johnson, John Thomas	SR	401-85
Johnson, Joseph K.	SR	401-85
Johnson, Joseph V.	USV	401-236
Johnson, Julius R.	USV	401-236
Johnson, L. E.	SR	401-85
Johnson, L. E.	LR	401-129
Johnson, L. M.	SR	401-85
Johnson, L. M.	SR	401-85
Johnson, La Prade	USV	401-237
Johnson, Lee Roy	RRR	401-119
Johnson, Lee Roy	SR	401-85
Johnson, Levi	TVG	401-200
Johnson, Louis P.	USV	401-237
Johnson, Marcus H.	USV	401-237
Johnson, Marshall	RR	401-58
Johnson, Nathan	SP	401-45
Johnson, Nehemiah	TST	401-35
Johnson, Othor	SR	401-85
Johnson, P. G.	TVG	401-200
Johnson, Patrick	NAV	401-19
Johnson, Paul	TVG	401-200
Johnson, Phil G.	USV	401-237
Johnson, R. D.	SP	401-45
Johnson, R. H.	SR	401-85
Johnson, R. S.	FB	401-157
Johnson, Read	SR	401-85
Johnson, Robert	FB	401-157
Johnson, Robert D.	NAV	401-19
Johnson, Robert E.	SR	401-85
Johnson, Robert Earl	TVG	401-200
Johnson, Robert Earl	USV	401-237
Johnson, Robert H.	RR	401-58
Johnson, Robert L.	SR	401-85
Johnson, Roy M.	SR	401-86
Johnson, Rufus	SR	401-86
Johnson, S. W., Jr.	TVG	401-200
Johnson, Sam McL.	TVG	401-200
Johnson, T.	FB	401-157
Johnson, T. A.	TVG	401-200
Johnson, T. R.	FB	401-157
Johnson, Thes.	SP	401-45
Johnson, Thomas	NAV	401-19
Johnson, Thomas	RR	401-58
Johnson, Thomas	USV	401-237
Johnson, Thomas F.	ARM	401-6
Johnson, Thomas J.	SR	401-86
Johnson, Thomas L.	TVG	401-200
Johnson, Thomas R.	FB	401-157
Johnson, Tobe	USV	401-237
Johnson, Tom	SR	401-86
Johnson, W. A.	SP	401-45
Johnson, W. A.	SR	401-86
Johnson, W. B.	FB	401-157
Johnson, W. E.	SR	401-86
Johnson, W. F.	TVG	401-200
Johnson, W. G.	FB	401-157
Johnson, W. H.	SR	401-86
Johnson, W. I.	SR	401-86
Johnson, W. J.	SR	401-86
Johnson, W. J.	LR	401-129
Johnson, W. R.	SR	401-86
Johnson, W. S.	TVG	401-200
Johnson, William	CSA	401-39
Johnson, William	ARM	401-6
Johnson, William	TVG	401-200
Johnson, William A.	MM	401-32
Johnson, William H.	USV	401-237
Johnson, William Jasper	CSA	401-39
Johnson, William L.	USV	401-237
Johnson, William R.	RRR	401-119
Johnson, William T.	FB	401-157
Johnson, Willis	SR	401-86
Johnston, Andrew J.	USV	401-237
Johnston, B.	NAV	401-19
Johnston, Ben	TVG	401-200
Johnston, Charles E.	FB	401-157
Johnston, Floyd A.	TVG	401-200
Johnston, George	NAV	401-19
Johnston, H. L.	SR	401-86
Johnston, H. L. "Bud"	RR	401-58
Johnston, H. M.	RR	401-58
Johnston, Harvey C.	USV	401-237
Johnston, J. H.	FB	401-157
Johnston, J. M.	USV	401-237

Index to Texas Adjutant General Service Records—All Service Branches

Name	Branch	Record
Johnston, Jack T.	SR	401-86
Johnston, John	TST	401-35
Johnston, Lindley	ARM	401-6
Johnston, R. L.	TVG	401-200
Johnston, R. M.	TVG	401-200
Johnston, Robert M.	USV	401-237
Johnston, Roy W.	SR	401-86
Johnston, Sam C.	SR	401-86
Johnston, Samuel B.	USV	401-237
Johnston, T. K.	SR	401-86
Johnston, T. R.	FB	401-157
Johnston, W. F.	TVG	401-200
Johnston, Walter L.	SR	401-86
Johnston, William	USV	401-237
Johnston, William Scott	SR	401-86
Johnston, William Scott	LR	401-129
Joiner, H. S.	FB	401-157
Joiner, Henry H.	FF	401-135
Joiner, S. J.	RRR	401-119
Joline, Charles O.	FB	401-157
Jolly, David D.	SR	401-86
Jolly, James P.	FF	401-135
Jolly, Peter J.	USV	401-237
Jones, A.	TVG	401-200
Jones, A. C.	RRR	401-119
Jones, A. C.	SR	401-86
Jones, A. C.	TVG	401-200
Jones, A. F.	TVG	401-200
Jones, A. H.	FB	401-157
Jones, A. H.	FB	401-157
Jones, A. L.	FB	401-157
Jones, A. P.	USV	401-237
Jones, A. T.	SR	401-86
Jones, A. W.	RR	401-58
Jones, Albert E.	USV	401-237
Jones, Albert P.	USV	401-237
Jones, Albert R.	USV	401-237
Jones, Alex	TVG	401-200
Jones, Andrew	FF	401-135
Jones, Arthur	FB	401-157
Jones, Arthur H.	RRR	401-119
Jones, Aurelius H.	USV	401-237
Jones, B. H.	TVG	401-200
Jones, B. L.	FB	401-157
Jones, B. W.	USV	401-237
Jones, Burton	SP	401-45
Jones, Buster	RR	401-58
Jones, C. E.	TVG	401-200
Jones, C. L.	SR	401-86
Jones, C. R.	TVG	401-200
Jones, C. S.	FF	401-135
Jones, Caleb	MV	401-29
Jones, Charles	ARM	401-6
Jones, Charles E.	USV	401-237
Jones, Clifford B.	SR	401-86
Jones, Donald H.	SR	401-86
Jones, E. A.	TVG	401-200
Jones, E. B.	FB	401-158
Jones, E. E.	RRR	401-119
Jones, E. R.	TVG	401-200
Jones, E. Z.	SP	401-45
Jones, Edward	ARM	401-6
Jones, Edward S.	ARM	401-6
Jones, Elbert	RR	401-58
Jones, Elijah	USV	401-237
Jones, Elmus	USV	401-237
Jones, Emanuel	SP	401-45
Jones, Emmett	FB	401-158
Jones, Ernest L., Dr.	SR	401-86
Jones, F.	FB	401-158
Jones, Floyd	SR	401-86
Jones, Frank	FB	401-158
Jones, Frank M.	USV	401-237
Jones, Franklin	SP	401-45
Jones, Fred V.	SR	401-86
Jones, G. D.	RR	401-58
Jones, G. P.	SR	401-86
Jones, George A.	USV	401-237
Jones, George Lee	RR	401-58
Jones, George Lee	SR	401-86
Jones, George M.	USV	401-237
Jones, George S.	FB	401-158
Jones, George S. O.	USV	401-237
Jones, Gerald Allen	TVG	401-200
Jones, Gerry	FB	401-158
Jones, Guilford C.	USV	401-237
Jones, Gus	TVG	401-200
Jones, Gus T.	SR	401-86
Jones, Gustave	USV	401-237
Jones, Guy F.	TVG	401-200
Jones, H. M.	FB	401-158
Jones, H. M.	TVG	401-200
Jones, H. Worth	SR	401-86
Jones, Herbert M.	USV	401-237
Jones, Homer H.	SR	401-86
Jones, Hugh E.	USV	401-237
Jones, J. A.	FF	401-135
Jones, J. A.	FF	401-135
Jones, J. A.	TVG	401-200
Jones, J. C.	TVG	401-200
Jones, J. H.	TST	401-35
Jones, J. J.	FB	401-158
Jones, J. J.	TVG	401-200
Jones, J. L.	FB	401-158
Jones, J. M.	FB	401-158
Jones, J. M. W.	TVG	401-200
Jones, J. S.	TVG	401-200
Jones, J. W.	FB	401-158
Jones, J. W.	FB	401-158
Jones, James H.	RR	401-58
Jones, James R.	FF	401-135
Jones, Jesse	ARM	401-6

Index to Texas Adjutant General Service Records—All Service Branches

Name	Branch	Page
Jones, John	MM	401-32
Jones, John	ARM	401-6
Jones, John A.	RR	401-58
Jones, John B.	FB	401-158
Jones, John F.	USV	401-237
Jones, John I.	FB	401-158
Jones, John R.	RRR	401-119
Jones, John R.	SR	401-86
Jones, John R.	FB	401-158
Jones, John T.	FB	401-158
Jones, Kleber	FF	401-135
Jones, Leon	SR	401-86
Jones, Leon	FB	401-158
Jones, Leonard	TVG	401-200
Jones, Lester	SR	401-86
Jones, Lloyd D.	USV	401-237
Jones, Luther C.	RRR	401-119
Jones, M.	FB	401-158
Jones, M. H.	RR	401-58
Jones, M. L.	MV	401-29
Jones, M. R.	SR	401-86
Jones, M. V.	RR	401-58
Jones, Marcel	SR	401-86
Jones, Martin	ARM	401-6
Jones, Marvin F.	SR	401-86
Jones, N. B.	RR	401-58
Jones, N. B.	FB	401-158
Jones, N. J.	FB	401-158
Jones, N. J.	FB	401-158
Jones, N. P.	SP	401-45
Jones, Nat B.	RR	401-58
Jones, Nat B.	SR	401-86
Jones, Omer	RRR	401-119
Jones, Patrick	SP	401-45
Jones, Paul	SR	401-86
Jones, Paul	SR	401-86
Jones, Peter	ARM	401-6
Jones, Pinckney	FB	401-158
Jones, R.	FB	401-158
Jones, R. H.	RRR	401-119
Jones, R. R.	USV	401-237
Jones, R. S.	TVG	401-200
Jones, Raymond	USV	401-237
Jones, Relious M.	RR	401-58
Jones, Robert	SP	401-45
Jones, Robert E.	USV	401-237
Jones, Robert L.	USV	401-237
Jones, Rufus V. G.	TVG	401-200
Jones, S. R.	SR	401-86
Jones, Samuel H.	MM	401-32
Jones, Shelly	TVG	401-200
Jones, Shepherd	RR	401-58
Jones, Solomon	SP	401-45
Jones, Stephen H.	TVG	401-200
Jones, T. N.	TVG	401-200
Jones, T. O.	FF	401-135
Jones, T. R.	SR	401-86
Jones, T. S.	RR	401-58
Jones, T. S.	SR	401-86
Jones, T. W.	FB	401-158
Jones, Theodore	NAV	401-19
Jones, Thomas	ARM	401-6
Jones, Thomas	TVG	401-200
Jones, Tom B.	TVG	401-200
Jones, Verner	USV	401-237
Jones, W. B.	FB	401-158
Jones, W. B.	FB	401-158
Jones, W. C.	TVG	401-200
Jones, W. Clinton	RR	401-58
Jones, W. E.	SP	401-45
Jones, W. G.	TVG	401-200
Jones, W. H.	USV	401-237
Jones, W. K.	FF	401-135
Jones, W. K.	FB	401-158
Jones, W. N.	TVG	401-200
Jones, W. W.	FF	401-135
Jones, W. W.	FB	401-158
Jones, Wade W.	TVG	401-200
Jones, Walter F.	SR	401-86
Jones, Wes	TVG	401-200
Jones, Will	FB	401-158
Jones, Will C.	RR	401-58
Jones, William	NAV	401-19
Jones, William	ARM	401-6
Jones, William E.	TVG	401-200
Jones, William Frank	SR	401-86
Jones, William H.	SP	401-45
Jones, William J.	SR	401-86
Jones, William J.	LR	401-129
Jones, William T.	RR	401-58
Jones, Woodbury	NAV	401-19
Jones, Wordy	USV	401-237
Jonson, Perry F.	TVG	401-200
Jophnson, W. E.	SR	401-86
Joplin, J. L.	SR	401-86
Jordan, A. C.	LR	401-129
Jordan, A. D.	RR	401-58
Jordan, Aaron C.	SR	401-86
Jordan, Aaron H.	USV	401-237
Jordan, Charles O.	USV	401-237
Jordan, E. W.	FB	401-158
Jordan, Earnest C.	USV	401-237
Jordan, George R.	SR	401-86
Jordan, Horace	TVG	401-200
Jordan, Hugh N.	FB	401-158
Jordan, John	TVG	401-200
Jordan, John B.	USV	401-237
Jordan, S. B.	USV	401-237
Jordan, S. T.	FB	401-158
Jordan, S. W.	ARM	401-6
Jordan, Samuel	ARM	401-6
Jordan, T. E.	SR	401-86

Index to Texas Adjutant General Service Records—All Service Branches

Name	Branch	Record
Jordan, T. E.	LR	401-129
Jordan, Tink	TVG	401-200
Jordan, Wiley D.	RR	401-58
Jordan, William	NAV	401-19
Jorden, Thomas	ARM	401-6
Jordon, Harry Philip	TVG	401-200
Jorgenson, Edwin T.	SR	401-86
Joseph, Lee	SR	401-86
Joseph, Lee	LR	401-129
Joseph, Lewis L.	ARM	401-6
Josey, A.	TVG	401-200
Josey, John Paul	TVG	401-200
Josey, John R.	USV	401-237
Joslin, Benjamin N.	ARM	401-6
Joslyn, James B.	USV	401-237
Jourdan, Jeff B.	TVG	401-200
Jowell, J. H.	FB	401-158
Jowell, J. R. (Bud)	FB	401-158
Joy, C. W.	FB	401-158
Joy, Charles C.	TVG	401-200
Joyce, Martin O.	USV	401-237
Joyce, Robert F.	SP	401-45
Joyce, W. V.	TVG	401-200
Joyce, W. V.	USV	401-237
Judd, Amos F.	RRR	401-119
Judd, Michael H.	ARM	401-6
Judge, Walter H.	TVG	401-200
Judges, William	ARM	401-6
Judkins, Ben	RRR	401-119
Judkins, Howard	RRR	401-119
Judkins, Ralph	RRR	401-119
Judson, Daniel	NAV	401-19
Juhring, T. A.	SR	401-86
Julian, James L.	SR	401-86
Junck, Edward	TVG	401-201
Jung, Alfred M.	USV	401-237
Jung, Charles	SP	401-45
Jung, Charles	TVG	401-201
Jung, George	USV	401-237
Jungman, Peter	FB	401-158
Juninez, Hose Marion	NAV	401-19
Justice, Milton M.	ARM	401-6
Justis, Charley W.	USV	401-237
Justiss, A. N.	TVG	401-201
Justiss, T. F.	SR	401-86
Kaetnicy, John	FF	401-135
Kahen, Eugene	TVG	401-201
Kahlich, J. F.	USV	401-237
Kahn, M. C.	FB	401-158
Kaiding, August	USV	401-237
Kaigler, Willie D.	SR	401-86
Kainer, Armond	USV	401-237
Kaiser, Frank C.	FB	401-158
Kalen, C. B.	FB	401-158
Kamstra, L.	USV	401-237
Kanc, Daniel S.	USV	401-237
Kane, Henry	NAV	401-19
Kane, John W.	NAV	401-19
Kane, Thomas	ARM	401-6
Kania, H.	SR	401-86
Kantz, C.	NAV	401-19
Kanze, Thomas	NAV	401-19
Karcher, F.	TST	401-35
Karcher, Walter B.	TVG	401-201
Karm, John	FF	401-136
Karn, D. D.	SR	401-86
Karner, Fred S.	TVG	401-201
Karnes, Henry L.	SP	401-45
Karnes, Henry W.	ARM	401-6
Karns, H. S.	FF	401-136
Karotkin, A. L.	SR	401-86
Karotkin, Harry	SR	401-86
Kartzke, M. C.	TVG	401-201
Kastelaw, Paul	USV	401-237
Kastelka, August	USV	401-237
Kastrop, Edwin E.	TVG	401-201
Kattache, Clement	USV	401-237
Kattner, Otto	TVG	401-201
Kaufman, D. S.	TVG	401-201
Kaufman, Emil	TST	401-35
Kaufman, Gussie S.	USV	401-237
Kaump, Bernard	ARM	401-6
Kavanaugh, Frank	USV	401-237
Kavanaugh, Frank H.	USV	401-237
Kavanaugh, Malvin P.	TVG	401-201
Kaveneaugh, James	ARM	401-6
Kay, R. Rowland	SR	401-86
Keach, Eddie T.	USV	401-237
Keackworth, N. L.	TST	401-35
Keaghey, John S.	TVG	401-201
Keahey, Thomas E.	LR	401-129
Kearney, C.	FB	401-158
Kearney, James J.	TVG	401-201
Kearney, Martin W.	USV	401-237
Kearns, William	NAV	401-19
Keasler, Thomas B.	TVG	401-201
Keating, P. V.	SR	401-86
Keating, Paul W.	SP	401-45
Keating, Paul W.	FB	401-158
Keating, R. L.	TVG	401-201
Keating, Richard L.	USV	401-237
Keberer, JacoB	FB	401-158
Keck, Frank	LR	401-129
Keedy, Dwight B.	USV	401-237
Keeffe, John	ARM	401-6
Keel, C. B.	SP	401-45
Keel, Elmer R.	TVG	401-201
Keeler, Matthew	NAV	401-19
Keeler, Robert E.	USV	401-237
Keeley, F. P.	SR	401-86
Keeling, W. T.	TVG	401-201
Keen, W. H.	SR	401-86

Index to Texas Adjutant General Service Records—All Service Branches

Name	Branch	Record
Keenan, Charles L.	TVG	401-201
Keene, Henry	RR	401-58
Keener, A. S.	TVG	401-201
Keeran, C. A.	SR	401-86
Keeran, C. A.	FB	401-158
Keese, William A.	TST	401-35
Keesee, J. C.	SP	401-45
Keesee, Tom	SP	401-45
Keesee, William M.	MV	401-30
Keeton, James W.	FB	401-158
Keeton, James W.	TVG	401-201
Keeton, James W.	USV	401-237
Keeton, Silas Hare	USV	401-237
Kegans, H.	TVG	401-201
Kehl, Christian H.	USV	401-237
Kehoe, Thomas D.	TVG	401-201
Keilman, W. H.	USV	401-237
Keiser, PeteR	ARM	401-6
Keith, ArthuR	TVG	401-201
Keith, Byron D.	USV	401-237
Keith, Edwin E.	TVG	401-201
Keith, Eli	FB	401-158
Keith, Floyd C.	TVG	401-201
Keith, G. M.	MM	401-32
Keith, G. M.	FB	401-158
Keith, G. M.	FB	401-158
Keith, Homer H.	USV	401-237
Keith, J. L.	FB	401-158
Keith, Robert H.	USV	401-238
Keith, S.	TVG	401-201
Keith, S. P.	MM	401-32
Keith, T. E.	FB	401-158
Keith, W. H.	TVG	401-201
Keith, W. H. Harve	RR	401-58
Keith, W. O.	SR	401-86
Kell, RoberT	NAV	401-19
Kelleher, James	USV	401-238
Keller, A. N.	RRR	401-119
Keller, Charles	MV	401-30
Keller, J. C.	SR	401-86
Keller, Raymond	USV	401-238
Keller, Roger J.	USV	401-238
Kelley, Augusta Allen	RRR	401-119
Kelley, Frank A.	USV	401-238
Kelley, I. K.	SR	401-86
Kelley, J. H.	TVG	401-201
Kelley, John	NAV	401-19
Kelley, John	FB	401-158
Kelley, M. R.	SR	401-86
Kelley, Martin	SP	401-45
Kelley, R. H.	TVG	401-201
Kelley, W. E.	SR	401-86
Kelley, William	TST	401-35
Kelley, William	ARM	401-6
Kellie, Edward Irvin	TVG	401-201
Kellis, J. R.	LR	401-129
Kellner, Emil	SP	401-45
Kellogg, John B.	TST	401-35
Kellogg, Vonley S.	ARM	401-6
Kellum, J. T.	SR	401-86
Kellup, James	NAV	401-19
Kelly, A. B.	RRR	401-119
Kelly, A. B.	TVG	401-201
Kelly, Anzie B.	USV	401-238
Kelly, Benjamin F.	USV	401-238
Kelly, Charles P.	SR	401-86
Kelly, Charles R.	TVG	401-201
Kelly, Charles W.	USV	401-238
Kelly, Clarence Ferdenan	RRR	401-119
Kelly, Donald D.	USV	401-238
Kelly, E. D.	TVG	401-201
Kelly, E. L.	SR	401-86
Kelly, George W.	SR	401-86
Kelly, J. R.	TVG	401-201
Kelly, John H.	USV	401-238
Kelly, John S.	TVG	401-201
Kelly, John W.	RRR	401-119
Kelly, Kim	SP	401-45
Kelly, M. P.	ARM	401-6
Kelly, Martin	ARM	401-6
Kelly, Maurice	NAV	401-19
Kelly, Maurice	USV	401-238
Kelly, Maurice Parnell	TVG	401-201
Kelly, Michael	NAV	401-19
Kelly, Morris	NAV	401-19
Kelly, Nicholas	ARM	401-6
Kelly, O. B.	LR	401-129
Kelly, Patrick	MV	401-30
Kelly, R. H.	TVG	401-201
Kelly, R. J.	SR	401-86
Kelly, Ralph H.	USV	401-238
Kelly, Roy	SR	401-86
Kelly, T. B.	TVG	401-201
Kelly, Thomas J.	FF	401-136
Kelly, Tom	TVG	401-201
Kelly, W. J.	SR	401-86
Kelly, William	ARM	401-6
Kelly, William	ARM	401-6
Kelly, William	ARM	401-6
Kelly, William	SP	401-45
Kelly, William H.	USV	401-238
Kelly, William T.	FB	401-158
Kelly, William T.	USV	401-238
Kelm, Emil P.	USV	401-238
Kelsay, L. L.	RRR	401-119
Kelsey, Augustus W.	ARM	401-7
Kelsey, H. E.	SR	401-86
Kelsey, John	ARM	401-7
Kelso, A. A.	FF	401-136
Kelso, A. A.	SP	401-45
Kelso, Eber B.	SR	401-86
Kelso, John R.	FF	401-136

Index to Texas Adjutant General Service Records—All Service Branches

Name	Branch	Record
Kelso, John R.	SP	401-46
Kelso, L. R.	FB	401-158
Kelso, R. M.	TVG	401-201
Kelso, Sid	RR	401-58
Kelso, W. M.	RRR	401-119
Kelso, William M.	FF	401-136
Kelso, Winchester	TVG	401-201
Kemendo, S.	TVG	401-201
Kemp, B. E.	FB	401-158
Kemp, J. B.	TST	401-35
Kemp, J. H.	FB	401-158
Kemp, J. S.	FB	401-158
Kemp, John J.	USV	401-238
Kemp, John P.	RRR	401-119
Kemp, W. A.	TVG	401-201
Kemper, August	ARM	401-7
Kemper, E. P., Jr.	FB	401-158
Kemper, Harden N.	USV	401-238
Kempfer, John	SP	401-46
Kempner, Herbert, Jr.	SR	401-86
Kempner, R. Lee	LR	401-129
Kenah, Joseph	ARM	401-7
Kenan, Francis	ARM	401-7
Kendall, Douglas E.	USV	401-238
Kendall, Francis	TVG	401-201
Kendall, Oscar W.	USV	401-238
Kendall, Thomas C.	USV	401-238
Kendall, W. Y.	TVG	401-201
Kendall, WalteR	TVG	401-201
Kendrick, A. E.	SR	401-86
Kendrick, A. I.	SR	401-86
Kendrick, E. I.	USV	401-238
Kenedy, John G.	FB	401-158
Kenedy, John G., Jr.	SR	401-86
Kenedy, Patrick	SP	401-46
Keney, B. H.	RRR	401-119
Kennan, John	NAV	401-19
Kennard, James N.	MV	401-30
Kennard, John B.	USV	401-238
Kennedy, A. L.	RRR	401-119
Kennedy, A. L.	TVG	401-201
Kennedy, A. V.	SR	401-86
Kennedy, Alvis B.	TVG	401-201
Kennedy, Alvis B.	USV	401-238
Kennedy, Carl E.	SR	401-86
Kennedy, Charles Henry	RRR	401-119
Kennedy, Claude A.	TVG	401-201
Kennedy, D. E.	FB	401-158
Kennedy, David A.	TVG	401-201
Kennedy, David A.	USV	401-238
Kennedy, E. P.	NAV	401-19
Kennedy, H. C.	FB	401-158
Kennedy, J. B.	SR	401-86
Kennedy, John	TST	401-35
Kennedy, John, Jr.	FB	401-158
Kennedy, John, Jr.	TVG	401-201
Kennedy, Joseph	SP	401-46
Kennedy, Mac	SR	401-86
Kennedy, Mark T.	TVG	401-201
Kennedy, Paul	TVG	401-201
Kennedy, Paul L.	RRR	401-119
Kennedy, Roger B.	TVG	401-201
Kennedy, S. R.	LR	401-129
Kennedy, Thomas J.	RR	401-58
Kennedy, William G.	TST	401-35
Kennerly, John E.	RRR	401-119
Kenney, Charles T.	USV	401-238
Kenney, John	FB	401-159
Kenney, John	FB	401-159
Kenney, John J.	FB	401-159
Kenney, M. M.	TST	401-35
Kenney, Martin M.	TST	401-35
Kenney, Martin M.	FB	401-159
Kenney, ToM	TVG	401-201
Kenny, Henry	FF	401-136
Kenny, M.	FB	401-159
Kent, B.	FB	401-159
Kent, D. B.	TST	401-35
Kent, David	SP	401-46
Kent, Frank	FB	401-159
Kent, J.	MM	401-32
Keppler, Jacob	MV	401-30
Kerber, Charles	FF	401-136
Kerby, W. A.	SR	401-86
Kercheville, Mack	SR	401-86
Kern, C. V.	SR	401-86
Kern, Ernest M.	USV	401-238
Kernan, John	ARM	401-7
Kerr, Andrew P.	RR	401-58
Kerr, C. R.	RRR	401-119
Kerr, Charles	ARM	401-7
Kerr, Charles S.	USV	401-238
Kerr, Charlie	TVG	401-201
Kerr, H. B.	RRR	401-119
Kerr, Harry	USV	401-238
Kerr, Henry Neil	USV	401-238
Kerr, Henry Neil	USV	401-238
Kerr, J. D.	SR	401-87
Kerr, J. H.	RRR	401-119
Kerr, James Wade	USV	401-238
Kerr, Joseph Perry	RR	401-58
Kersee, Harry	TVG	401-201
Kersh, M. C.	USV	401-238
Kerst, Martin C.	USV	401-238
Kersten, Frederick	TVG	401-201
Kersten, Otto	USV	401-238
Kervin, John	ARM	401-7
Kesler, Henry	ARM	401-7
Kesterson, J. H.	TVG	401-201
Ketcham, Henry R.	TVG	401-201
Ketels, Hugo F.	TVG	401-201

Index to Texas Adjutant General Service Records—All Service Branches

Name	Branch	Record
Kethrer, Varras	MV	401-30
Ketner, WilliaM	TST	401-35
Kettache, Clement	TVG	401-201
Kettinger, J. A.	TVG	401-201
Key, Emmet M.	TVG	401-201
Key, J. G.	LR	401-129
Key, W. Homer	SR	401-87
Key, William A.	USV	401-238
Key, William L.	FB	401-159
Keyes, Louis	SR	401-87
Keysar, Amos	USV	401-238
Keyser, Ezra	MV	401-30
Keyser, Francis	FF	401-136
Keyser, William	NAV	401-19
Kezeler, Charles E.	FB	401-159
Kibbe, J. P.	CSA	401-39
Kibber, James L.	USV	401-238
Kibbey, Clarence H.	USV	401-238
Kidd, Clarence	USV	401-238
Kidd, George H.	ARM	401-7
Kidd, J. D.	USV	401-238
Kidstone, Charles	TVG	401-201
Kidwell, C. W.	TVG	401-201
Kiefer, E. H.	SR	401-87
Kiefer, Frederick William	TVG	401-201
Kieffer, Leo	USV	401-238
Kiel, Fritz	USV	401-238
Kienle, John	FF	401-136
Kier, Louie	SR	401-87
Kight, Roy	SR	401-87
Kilborn, O. E.	SR	401-87
Kilburn, Dale Gordan	USV	401-238
Kilcoyne, M. P.	RRR	401-119
Kilgore, Addison	FB	401-159
Kilgore, F. H.	LR	401-129
Kilgore, James E.	USV	401-238
Kilgore, Jasper B.	USV	401-238
Kilgore, John A.	USV	401-238
Kilgore, Manford D.	RRR	401-119
Kilgore, Willis L.	USV	401-238
Killebrew, George	TVG	401-201
Killen, John R.	USV	401-238
Killgo, John H.	SR	401-87
Killough, Sam B.	USV	401-238
Kilpatrick, Allen R.	USV	401-238
Kilpatrick, Groce R.	USV	401-238
Kilpatrick, Howard H.	USV	401-238
Kimball, Claude D.	USV	401-238
Kimbell, J. B.	FB	401-159
Kimbell, R. G.	FB	401-159
Kimberly, Clarence	USV	401-238
Kimberly, James	ARM	401-7
Kimble, William L.	TVG	401-201
Kimbrew, C. F.	FB	401-159
Kimbrough, Richard C.	USV	401-238
Kimes, D. M.	FB	401-159
Kimmons, Samuel A.	USV	401-238
Kinahan, John	FB	401-159
Kinahan, William	ARM	401-7
Kincaid, Drue R.	FB	401-159
Kincaide, Fred	USV	401-238
Kincannon, William D.	USV	401-238
Kincanon, Luther B.	USV	401-238
Kincheloe, W. A.	FB	401-159
Kinchen, Samuel C.	USV	401-238
Kinchloe, J.	MM	401-32
Kinder, L. S.	TVG	401-201
Kinehan, John	SP	401-46
King, A. A.	SR	401-87
King, Alfred	NAV	401-19
King, Alfred	ARM	401-7
King, Barrington	USV	401-238
King, Ben E.	SR	401-87
King, C. H.	SP	401-46
King, C. H.	SR	401-87
King, C. P. Engel	RR	401-58
King, Charles	FF	401-136
King, Charles E.	SP	401-46
King, Clarence W.	USV	401-238
King, Clark	TVG	401-201
King, Edmond M.	MV	401-30
King, Edward	FB	401-159
King, Edwin H.	TVG	401-201
King, G. B.	FB	401-159
King, George	FB	401-159
King, George B.	FB	401-159
King, George S.	USV	401-238
King, George W.	FB	401-159
King, Grover N.	SR	401-87
King, H. A.	SR	401-87
King, H. M.	USV	401-238
King, Harold A.	RR	401-58
King, J. A.	TVG	401-201
King, J. D.	USV	401-238
King, J. W.	FB	401-159
King, Jacob Luther	RRR	401-119
King, Jacob Luther	SR	401-87
King, James H.	USV	401-238
King, John	SR	401-87
King, John G., Jr.	ARM	401-7
King, John Henry	RRR	401-119
King, John L.	USV	401-238
King, John Willis	FB	401-159
King, Joseph	MV	401-30
King, Joseph	FB	401-159
King, Lud	USV	401-238
King, Michael M.	USV	401-238
King, N. G.	FB	401-159
King, Oliver Ralph	RRR	401-119
King, P. G.	FB	401-159
King, R. E.	RR	401-58
King, R. L.	TST	401-35

Index to Texas Adjutant General Service Records—All Service Branches

King, R. M. .... LR 401-129
King, Richard, Jr. .... LR 401-129
King, Robert Earl A. .... SR 401-87
King, Simpson .... SP 401-46
King, Stephen M. .... TVG 401-201
King, T. H. .... TVG 401-201
King, Thomas .... TVG 401-201
King, Thomas Sidney .... RRR 401-119
King, Tom .... TVG 401-201
King, Tom C. .... USV 401-238
King, W. D. .... TVG 401-201
King, W. H. .... FB 401-159
King, W. H. .... LR 401-129
King, W. L. .... TVG 401-201
King, W. L. .... TVG 401-202
King, W. W. .... RRR 401-119
King, W. W. .... FB 401-159
King, William .... RRR 401-119
King, William .... TVG 401-202
King, William .... TVG 401-202
King, William A. .... USV 401-238
King, William, Sr. .... SR 401-87
King, Willie .... TVG 401-202
King, Winton W. .... USV 401-238
Kingsbury, H. .... RR 401-58
Kingsbury, James R. .... FB 401-159
Kingsbury, R. H. .... FB 401-159
Kingsbury, R. H. .... FB 401-159
Kingsley, Charles T. .... FB 401-159
Kinkead, E. S. .... FB 401-159
Kinman, Otto .... SR 401-87
Kinnaman, A. L. .... SR 401-87
Kinne, Frank H. .... TVG 401-202
Kinne, Tempel .... TVG 401-202
Kinnell, E. P. .... NAV 401-19
Kinney, C. D. .... TVG 401-202
Kinney, Floyd M. .... USV 401-238
Kinney, Frank M. .... USV 401-238
Kinney, George H. .... SR 401-87
Kinney, John .... FB 401-159
Kinney, John J. .... FB 401-159
Kinney, Lamers .... TST 401-35
Kinney, Smith .... TVG 401-202
Kinney, W. C. .... TVG 401-202
Kinneymore, John C. P. .... ARM 401-7
Kinsey, Henry .... ARM 401-7
Kinsey, J. T. .... RR 401-58
Kinsey, John .... NAV 401-19
Kinslow, C. J. .... NAV 401-19
Kinsolving, E. L. .... TVG 401-202
Kintzing, M. R. .... NAV 401-19
Kipling, William .... FB 401-159
Kippenbrock, Oran .... TVG 401-202
Kipper, George W. .... SR 401-87
Kirby, Francis M. .... USV 401-238
Kirby, Glenn L. .... RRR 401-119

Kirby, Jared E. .... SP 401-46
Kirby, Jerimiah .... NAV 401-19
Kirby, Solomon E. .... USV 401-238
Kirby, W. H. .... SR 401-87
Kirby, William Hale .... RR 401-58
Kirchner, Carl .... FB 401-159
Kirchner, F. R. .... FF 401-136
Kirchner, F. R. .... SP 401-46
Kirk, A. M. .... SP 401-46
Kirk, Charles J. .... TVG 401-202
Kirk, Charles J. .... USV 401-238
Kirk, J. A. .... TVG 401-202
Kirk, J. M. .... SP 401-46
Kirk, James .... SP 401-46
Kirk, John .... ARM 401-7
Kirk, John R. .... FB 401-159
Kirk, Virgil .... TVG 401-202
Kirk, W. R. .... USV 401-238
Kirk, William .... RR 401-58
Kirkland, Banjamin .... USV 401-238
Kirkland, Edward .... ARM 401-7
Kirkland, Montie .... RR 401-58
Kirkland, P. J. .... FB 401-159
Kirkpatrick, Alonzo .... USV 401-238
Kirkpatrick, B. .... USV 401-238
Kirkpatrick, Hugh L. .... USV 401-238
Kirkpatrick, John A. .... FB 401-159
Kirkpatrick, Lee .... FB 401-159
Kirkpatrick, Robert .... TST 401-35
Kirkpatrick, W. R. .... RRR 401-119
Kirksey, A. J. .... FB 401-159
Kirksey, Isaac .... SP 401-46
Kirksey, James W. .... USV 401-238
Kirnan, David .... FF 401-136
Kirnan, Frank .... SP 401-46
Kirsch, Samuel E. .... USV 401-238
Kirtley, Marcus A. .... USV 401-238
Kisby, W. H. .... FB 401-159
Kisinger, George .... FF 401-136
Kissel, H. M. .... SR 401-87
Kissling, August .... USV 401-239
Kitchen, Curtis P. .... TVG 401-202
Kitchen, George .... USV 401-239
Kitchen, W. H. .... TVG 401-202
Kitchens, H. R. .... FB 401-159
Kite, R. E. Lee .... TVG 401-202
Kite, R. E. Lee .... USV 401-239
Kiulen, Charles A. .... TVG 401-202
Kivlen, Dan A. .... USV 401-239
Kizer, C. H. .... TVG 401-202
Kizer, E. J. .... TVG 401-202
Kizziar, William H. .... TVG 401-202
Klaerner, E. H. .... SR 401-87
Klalm, J. H. .... FB 401-159
Klappenberch, R. .... TST 401-35
Klaus, Ted C. .... RR 401-58

Index to Texas Adjutant General Service Records—All Service Branches

Name	Branch	Record
Klaus, Ted C.	MV	401-30
Klaus, Theo C.	RR	401-58
Kleberg, C.	RR	401-58
Kleberg, R. M.	RR	401-58
Kleberg, Robert J.	FB	401-159
Kleberg, Robert J., Jr.	RR	401-58
Kleffman, Robert F.	USV	401-239
Kleiber, Erskine	ARM	401-7
Kleid, Peter	FF	401-136
Kleid, Peter	SP	401-46
Klein, Arthur A.	USV	401-239
Klein, George C.	TVG	401-202
Klein, John	TVG	401-202
Klein, Otto	FF	401-136
Klein, W. D.	TVG	401-202
Klemann, Newton R.	RR	401-58
Kline, Morris	TVG	401-202
Klinger, Albert	RRR	401-119
Klinger, Walter J.	SR	401-87
Klockenhemper, Martin	USV	401-239
Klotz, F. R.	TVG	401-202
Klutts, Q. A.	SR	401-87
Knap, Samuel	NAV	401-19
Knapp, D. R.	TVG	401-202
Knapp, Frank B.	USV	401-239
Knauth, Paul	TVG	401-202
Knecht, August	USV	401-239
Kneitz, Joseph F.	SR	401-87
Kniaziewicz, J. E.	RRR	401-119
Knies, A. T.	SR	401-87
Knight, D. G.	RR	401-58
Knight, E. L.	FB	401-159
Knight, G. W.	MM	401-32
Knight, George	USV	401-239
Knight, Isaac D.	NAV	401-19
Knight, James M.	ARM	401-7
Knight, Joe B.	SR	401-87
Knight, John A.	MM	401-32
Knight, L. C.	FB	401-159
Knight, Lewis N.	MM	401-32
Knight, Louis R.	USV	401-239
Knight, Richard	NAV	401-19
Knight, W. E.	SR	401-87
Knighten, Homer	RRR	401-119
Knighten, Homer	SR	401-87
Knighten, Joseph E.	MV	401-30
Knightlinger, J. W.	RRR	401-119
Knillman, Charles A.	USV	401-239
Knoff, George M.	TVG	401-202
Knoll, Beauregard P.	TVG	401-202
Knoll, I. J.	TVG	401-202
Knoll, Lee G.	TVG	401-202
Knoll, Theodore H.	USV	401-239
Knopf, L. A.	TVG	401-202
Knoskey, Peter	FF	401-136
Knott, William H.	USV	401-239
Knowles, J. Troupe	FB	401-159
Knowles, James	ARM	401-7
Knowles, R. G.	SR	401-87
Knowlton, Minor	ARM	401-7
Known, John L.	SR	401-87
Knox, E. O.	SR	401-87
Knox, Elisha	USV	401-239
Knox, K. B.	SR	401-87
Knox, Leslie	TVG	401-202
Koch, Camille	TVG	401-202
Koch, Charles	TVG	401-202
Koch, Chris	TVG	401-202
Koch, Louis	NAV	401-19
Koch, Martin	SP	401-46
Koebig, Manfred	TVG	401-202
Koeler, Hermann	NAV	401-19
Koenig, Joe	USV	401-239
Koenning, W. P.	SR	401-87
Koger, Esten B.	SR	401-87
Kogler, George	SP	401-46
Kohn, E. A.	SR	401-87
Kohr, Joseph	FF	401-136
Kohr, Joseph	FF	401-136
Kohr, Joseph A.	SR	401-87
Kolb, Joseph L.	USV	401-239
Kolb, W. D.	USV	401-239
Kone, E. R.	TVG	401-202
Kone, S. R.	TST	401-35
Konger, E.	MM	401-32
Koon, James A.	SR	401-87
Koon, Thomas Earlton	RRR	401-119
Koon, William Henry	RR	401-58
Koonce, Jesse W.	USV	401-239
Koonsman, Martin N.	SR	401-87
Koonsman, Martin Nic	RR	401-58
Kopf, Charles Fredrick	TST	401-35
Korfleur, W.	NAV	401-19
Korioth, A.	TVG	401-202
Korn, Walter E.	RRR	401-119
Kornegay, C.	SR	401-87
Korst, George Edward	TVG	401-202
Korwin, George F.	SR	401-87
Koss, Joseph	USV	401-239
Kothmann, Elgin O.	SR	401-87
Kott, Edward	TVG	401-202
Kountr, Charles	NAV	401-19
Kowalski, B. L.	SR	401-87
Kraft, John E.	USV	401-239
Kratz, Hugo	SP	401-46
Kratz, R.	FB	401-159
Kratzer, Frederick	SP	401-46
Krause, A. L.	TVG	401-202
Krause, John D.	USV	401-239
Krause, Rudolph	SP	401-46
Krause, W. F.	SR	401-87

Index to Texas Adjutant General Service Records—All Service Branches

Name	Branch	Record
Krauskopf, E.	MV	401-30
Krauss, John Michel	ARM	401-7
Krautz, George	ARM	401-7
Krees, Frank J.	SR	401-87
Kreissle, John	TST	401-35
Krentzlin, Edward	TVG	401-202
Kretsinger, G. B.	TVG	401-202
Kretsinger, W. O.	TVG	401-202
Kretz, ScotT	TVG	401-202
Krichamer, Arnold H.	SR	401-87
Kriebaum, Adolph	FF	401-136
Kriegel, Emil F.	USV	401-239
Krieger, Adam	FF	401-136
Krieger, Adam	FB	401-159
Kries, Godfred	ARM	401-7
Kriger, Dave K.	USV	401-239
Kring, Joseph H.	SR	401-87
Kring, Kyle K.	RRR	401-119
Kritser, D. S.	SR	401-87
Krohn, I. H.	RR	401-58
Kroll, Ernest	SR	401-87
Kroll, Theodore H.	TVG	401-202
Kruegel, William	USV	401-239
Krueger, Albert	FF	401-136
Krum, J. A.	USV	401-239
Kuchler, Jacob	MV	401-30
Kuehne, E. B.	SR	401-87
Kuhlman, Daniel	USV	401-239
Kuhlman, William J.	USV	401-239
Kuhlmann, Ferd	FF	401-136
Kuhly, Charles	FB	401-159
Kuhn, Richard	USV	401-239
Kuhn, Yewell Preston	SR	401-87
Kulm, Joseph	SP	401-46
Kundig, John	NAV	401-19
Kuntz, Louis L.	USV	401-239
Kuykendall, J. B.	FB	401-159
Kuykendall, Samuel	FF	401-136
Kuykendall, Soloman	TVG	401-202
Kuykendall, W. H.	SR	401-87
Kyd, Thomas	ARM	401-7
Kyle, A. J.	TVG	401-202
Kyle, Alexander	TST	401-35
Kyle, C. C.	TVG	401-202
Kyle, D. C.	FB	401-159
Kyle, David W.	USV	401-239
Kyle, Ferg.	TST	401-36
Kyle, J. Allen	TVG	401-202
Kyle, J. Allen	TVG	401-202
Kyle, William	MV	401-30
Laas, August E.	LR	401-129
Laas, Charles H.	TVG	401-202
Labbaite, Edmund A.	SP	401-46
Labry, J. Taylor	TVG	401-202
Labuzan, Edwin W.	USV	401-239
Lacerme, John	FF	401-136
Lacey, Byron	TVG	401-202
Lacey, Elmer	TVG	401-202
Lacey, Irwin	SP	401-46
Lacey, J. B.	FF	401-136
Lackey, J. O.	USV	401-239
Lackey, John	ARM	401-7
Lackland, Scott B.	SR	401-87
Lacock, James K.	USV	401-239
LaCoste, Cyrus Hughes	TVG	401-202
Lacoste, J. B.	MV	401-30
Lacross, F.	FB	401-159
Lacy, Burton	USV	401-239
Lacy, F.	FB	401-159
Lacy, George J.	RR	401-58
Lacy, George J.	SR	401-87
Lacy, J. B.	TVG	401-202
Lacy, James T.	USV	401-239
Lacy, Joe L.	RR	401-58
Lacy, John	ARM	401-7
Lacy, John B.	FF	401-136
Lacy, M.	TVG	401-202
Lacy, McDonald	USV	401-239
Lacy, T. H.	SR	401-87
Lacy, Thomas M.	FF	401-136
Lacy, Will	FB	401-159
Ladd, Charles F. C.	SR	401-87
Laddy, William P.	ARM	401-7
LaDue, C. P.	FB	401-159
Lafitte, Joseph	ARM	401-7
LaFrance, P. C.	SP	401-46
LaGrange, Louis	FF	401-136
Lagrange, Pier	FB	401-159
Laird, H. F.	USV	401-239
Laird, J. C.	TVG	401-202
Laird, William L.	USV	401-239
Lake, George A.	USV	401-239
Lake, William E.	SR	401-87
Lake, William H.	TVG	401-202
Lally, Patrick	NAV	401-19
LaLonde, Samuel	USV	401-239
Lalter, John	NAV	401-19
Lamar, Charles	SP	401-46
Lamar, Troy	SR	401-87
Lamar, Will	SR	401-87
Lamb, Frederick W.	USV	401-239
Lamb, Hiram	RR	401-58
Lamb, Rufus H.	LR	401-129
Lamb, Thomas	SP	401-46
Lambdin, Robert B.	TST	401-36
Lambdin, W. McK.	USV	401-239
Lambert, Francis	NAV	401-19
Lambert, George W.	USV	401-239
Lambert, James W.	USV	401-239
Lambert, Madison C.	FB	401-159
Lambert, Will	FB	401-159
Lambeth, M. C.	FB	401-159

Index to Texas Adjutant General Service Records—All Service Branches

Name	Branch	Record
Lambkin, William S.	USV	401-239
Lambreth, John S.	TVG	401-202
Lambright, Matt	SR	401-87
Lamkin, George W.	TST	401-36
Lamkin, L. A. L.	TVG	401-202
Lamkin, L. D.	TVG	401-202
Lamkin, Lawrence	RRR	401-120
Lamkin, Lem	RR	401-58
Lamkin, Mortimer	TST	401-36
Lamkin, Robert Wadde	USV	401-239
Lamkin, Rom	SP	401-46
Lamkin, S. B.	TVG	401-202
Lammert, Adam	RR	401-58
Lamon, John	ARM	401-7
Lamon, Joseph	FF	401-136
Lamons, Richard P.	TVG	401-202
Lamont, John F.	USV	401-239
LaMoreaux, F. L.	TVG	401-202
Lamp, Edward D.	USV	401-239
Lampe, C. F.	USV	401-239
Lampert, George E.	NAV	401-19
Lancaster, F. B.	SP	401-46
Lancaster, F. H.	SR	401-87
Lancaster, J. K.	SR	401-87
Lancaster, S. B.	FB	401-159
Lance, Joseph	MV	401-30
Lance, William C.	USV	401-239
Land, C. G.	TVG	401-202
Land, W. A.	TVG	401-202
Landa, Harry	TVG	401-202
Landar, Charlie	SR	401-87
Landers, H. T.	FB	401-159
Landkuller, Henry	ARM	401-7
Landreth, Tom	USV	401-239
Landroz, C.	SP	401-46
Landrum, Hay T.	USV	401-239
Landrum, J. A.	SR	401-87
Landrum, William H.	USV	401-239
Lands, Jack "John"	SP	401-46
Lane, A. E.	SR	401-87
Lane, Addison	SP	401-46
Lane, D. A., Dr.	SR	401-87
Lane, E. D.	TST	401-36
Lane, F.	FB	401-159
Lane, F. M.	RR	401-58
Lane, Frank Andrew	FB	401-159
Lane, G. D.	RR	401-58
Lane, H. E.	USV	401-239
Lane, Hays W.	USV	401-239
Lane, J. C.	LR	401-129
Lane, Joe E.	TVG	401-202
Lane, Joe Y.	LR	401-129
Lane, John R.	USV	401-239
Lane, L. H.	TVG	401-202
Lane, Lewis A.	SP	401-46
Lane, S. E.	FB	401-159
Lane, Samuel M.	FB	401-159
Lane, Samuel W.	USV	401-239
Lane, T. J.	SP	401-46
Lane, Tarlton	FF	401-136
Lane, Van A.	FB	401-159
Lane, W. J.	FB	401-159
Lane, Walker J.	USV	401-239
Lane, Will R.	USV	401-239
Lane, William B.	TVG	401-202
Laneve, R. O.	SR	401-87
Laney, William	NAV	401-19
Laney, William	ARM	401-7
Lang, Ben S.	TVG	401-202
Lang, Benjamin	USV	401-239
Lang, Daniel H.	TVG	401-202
Lang, H. A.	RRR	401-120
Lang, J. R.	FF	401-136
Lang, Louis	USV	401-239
Lang, W. M. A.	TVG	401-202
Lang, W. R.	TVG	401-202
Lang, Willis L.	RR	401-58
Lange, Loui	USV	401-239
Lange, R. J.	FB	401-159
Langever, Charles E.	USV	401-239
Langford, Charles	TVG	401-202
Langford, Earl	RR	401-58
Langford, George	TVG	401-202
Langford, I. B.	SR	401-87
Langford, M. L.	RR	401-58
Langford, Mark L.	RR	401-58
Langford, W. S.	SR	401-87
Langham, C. L.	RRR	401-120
Langhammer, Charles	SP	401-46
Langhammer, E. G.	TVG	401-202
Langhlin, John	ARM	401-7
Langley, Edmund A.	SP	401-46
Langley, George W.	CSA	401-39
Langley, R. William	SR	401-87
Langram, R. M.	TVG	401-202
Langram, R. M.	USV	401-239
Langridge, James S.	USV	401-239
Langridge, William T.	USV	401-239
Langston, Boyd B.	RRR	401-120
Langston, C. L.	SR	401-87
Langston, Levi H.	USV	401-239
Langwell, Henry L., Sr.	SR	401-87
Lanham, Frank V.	SR	401-87
Lanier, Charlie Manlove	RRR	401-120
Lanier, G. T.	LR	401-129
Lanigan, Thomas	CSA	401-39
Lankford, John C.	USV	401-239
Lannes, Raymond J.	USV	401-239
Lanning, Harvey	NAV	401-19
Lansing, T. P.	NAV	401-19
Lansing, W.	NAV	401-19
Lanter, C. F.	FB	401-159

Index to Texas Adjutant General Service Records—All Service Branches

Name	Branch	Record
Lapowski, Nathan	TVG	401-202
Lapowski, Nathan	TVG	401-202
Larche, Marvin S.	USV	401-239
Lardner, William A.	FB	401-159
Larendon, George W.	TVG	401-202
Larg, George W.	MV	401-30
Large, Isham	RR	401-58
Largent, J. S.	LR	401-129
Largent, Tom G.	RR	401-58
Largent, Tom G.	SR	401-87
Largent, Tom J.	SR	401-87
Larkin, Barker	SR	401-87
Larkin, W. C.	SR	401-87
Larned, A. F. "Bud"	SR	401-87
Laro, Arthur E.	USV	401-239
Laroe, Dan	SR	401-87
Laroe, Ernest	SR	401-87
Laroque, Justinian	ARM	401-7
Larremore, Ed A.	SR	401-87
Larremore, George W.	FF	401-136
Larrimore, George	FB	401-159
Larry, D. F.	RRR	401-120
Larsen, William A.	RRR	401-120
Larson, Charles	FB	401-159
Larson, Fred A.	USV	401-239
LaRue, Doak	USV	401-239
Larue, Frank E.	SR	401-87
LaRue, Norton E.	TVG	401-202
Lasano, Gregorio	FF	401-136
Lasater, Byron	USV	401-239
Lasater, Joe E.	USV	401-239
Laseter, Lawrence	USV	401-239
Lasher, C.	FB	401-160
Lasley, J. P.	FB	401-160
Lassetter, William F.	TVG	401-202
Latchern [Latchem], John	SP	401-46
Latham, B. C.	TVG	401-202
Latham, F. H.	TVG	401-202
Latham, G. C.	RR	401-58
Latham, G. C.	SR	401-87
Latham, J. L.	FF	401-136
Latham, J. V.	FB	401-160
Latham, James	FF	401-136
Latham, John Barkley	SR	401-87
Latham, W. L.	USV	401-239
Lathen, Walker	TVG	401-202
Lathrop, Walter W.	USV	401-239
Latimer, Leslie C.	USV	401-239
Latimer, Travis	TVG	401-202
Latta, L.	RRR	401-120
Latta, Oscar	FB	401-160
Lattimore, D. E.	SR	401-87
Lauck, John H.	TVG	401-202
Lauderdale, C. W.	SR	401-87
Lauderdale, J. H.	TVG	401-202
Laughlin, G. Ernest	TVG	401-202
Laughlin, J. T.	RR	401-58
Laughlin, J. T.	RR	401-58
Lauraine, D. G.	TVG	401-202
Lauraine, Loye J.	SR	401-87
Laurence, C. H.	SP	401-46
Lauterstein, Lewis I.	SR	401-87
Lavoy, Frank Augusta	RRR	401-120
Lawhon, D. S.	TVG	401-202
Lawhon, George	FB	401-160
Lawhon, J. T.	FB	401-160
Lawhon, John W.	FB	401-160
Lawhon, W. A.	TVG	401-202
Lawhon, W. J.	FB	401-160
Lawhorn, J. D.	FB	401-160
Lawler, Hugh	ARM	401-7
Lawler, J. A.	FB	401-160
Lawless, B. L.	TST	401-36
Lawlor, J. W.	TVG	401-203
Lawrance, Henry C.	FF	401-136
Lawrence, Aubrey P.	USV	401-239
Lawrence, D.	FB	401-160
Lawrence, Dick	SR	401-87
Lawrence, Ernest	LR	401-129
Lawrence, Henry D.	USV	401-239
Lawrence, James	NAV	401-19
Lawrence, James	ARM	401-7
Lawrence, M. E.	SR	401-87
Lawrence, W. Dewey	SR	401-87
Lawrence, W. P.	TVG	401-203
Lawrence, Walter	USV	401-239
Lawry, Hugh F.	USV	401-239
Lawson, Andrew	ARM	401-7
Lawson, Charles A.	FB	401-160
Lawson, Elijah	TST	401-36
Lawson, Harry B.	USV	401-239
Lawson, Oscar	USV	401-239
Lawson, W. A.	USV	401-239
Lawther, P. W.	TVG	401-203
Lawton, A. L.	SR	401-87
Laxton, John	FB	401-160
Lay, A. J.	FB	401-160
Lay, David M.	RRR	401-120
Lay, J. W.	FB	401-160
Lay, Louis B.	FB	401-160
Lay, S. J.	FB	401-160
Lay, W. H.	RR	401-58
Laycock, Jesse D.	USV	401-239
Layman, T. N.	FB	401-160
Laymance, Tom I.	RR	401-58
Layne, A. J.	USV	401-239
Layne, George E.	RRR	401-120
Layne, George Edgar	SR	401-88
Layne, Hugh	SR	401-88
Layne, Hugh	LR	401-129
Layne, I. H.	TVG	401-203
Layne, Isaac N.	USV	401-239

Index to Texas Adjutant General Service Records—All Service Branches

Name	Branch	Page
Layne, J. R.	CSA	401-39
Layne, Willis	RRR	401-120
Layton, A. J.	RRR	401-120
Layton, Andrew	FB	401-160
Layton, Floyd	RR	401-58
Layton, Green B.	MV	401-30
Layton, Robert	FF	401-136
Layton, Rolly B.	USV	401-239
Layton, Samuel	NAV	401-19
Layton, William L.	FB	401-160
Lazenby, Walter H.	SR	401-88
Lea, H. D.	TVG	401-203
Lea, M. A.	MV	401-30
Lea, S. J.	TVG	401-203
Leach, Albert S.	TVG	401-203
Leach, Albert S.	USV	401-239
Leach, Donald B.	TVG	401-203
Leach, Frank W.	SR	401-88
Leach, G. M.	RRR	401-120
Leach, G. M.	SR	401-88
Leach, Harrold E.	TVG	401-203
Leach, Homer	FB	401-160
Leach, J. H.	RR	401-58
Leach, J. H.	RRR	401-120
Leach, J. H.	SR	401-88
Lead, H.	ARM	401-7
League, Charles H.	USV	401-239
Leahy, D. P.	RR	401-58
Leahy, D. P.	SR	401-88
Leahy, John	FB	401-160
Leahy, John	USV	401-239
Leak, W. C.	SR	401-88
Leakey, George	FB	401-160
Leakey, George P.	FB	401-160
Leal, Fluto	FF	401-136
Leal, Luciano	FB	401-160
Leary, John W.	USV	401-239
Leasman, Frederick Wm.	FF	401-136
Leasure, L. E.	FB	401-160
Leath, George Horace	SR	401-88
Leath, James A.	USV	401-239
Leath, William	TVG	401-203
Leatherman, D. M.	USV	401-239
Leavell, Charles H.	TVG	401-203
Leavell, Charles H.	USV	401-239
Leaverton, T. H.	LR	401-129
Leavy, Frank S.	FB	401-160
LeBarre, John F.	USV	401-239
LeBert, Loftus G.	TVG	401-203
LeBlanc, Arthur J.	LR	401-129
LeBrecht, Fred	TVG	401-203
LeCompte, Walter Nicles	RRR	401-120
Ledbetter, A. B.	CSA	401-39
Ledbetter, Andrew J.	CSA	401-39
Ledbetter, F. W.	SR	401-88
Ledbetter, F. W.	LR	401-129
Ledbetter, J. J.	RR	401-58
Ledbetter, J. J.	SR	401-88
Ledbetter, R. H.	SR	401-88
Ledbetter, W. H.	FB	401-160
Ledbetter, William H.	FB	401-160
Ledman, Thomas	FB	401-160
LeDoucrun, Charles	ARM	401-7
Lee, Abraham H.	TST	401-36
Lee, C. G.	SP	401-46
Lee, Charles E.	USV	401-239
Lee, D.	TVG	401-203
Lee, Ernest Calloway	TVG	401-203
Lee, Ernest Calloway	USV	401-239
Lee, Flint	LR	401-129
Lee, George	MV	401-30
Lee, George	SP	401-46
Lee, George W.	FF	401-136
Lee, H. G.	FB	401-160
Lee, H. M.	FB	401-160
Lee, H. P.	RRR	401-120
Lee, Isaac N.	FB	401-160
Lee, J. B.	TVG	401-203
Lee, James	MV	401-30
Lee, James B.	ARM	401-7
Lee, James W.	ARM	401-7
Lee, John Brown	ARM	401-7
Lee, John E.	RR	401-58
Lee, John S.	TVG	401-203
Lee, Leroy	SP	401-46
Lee, Lewis	TST	401-36
Lee, Lora M.	SR	401-88
Lee, M. E.	TVG	401-203
Lee, Marcellous P.	USV	401-239
Lee, Parmer E.	SR	401-88
Lee, R. E.	TVG	401-203
Lee, R. E.	USV	401-239
Lee, R. W.	ARM	401-7
Lee, Ralph D.	USV	401-239
Lee, Ray E.	SR	401-88
Lee, Richard Unett	TVG	401-203
Lee, Robert E.	SR	401-88
Lee, Roswell W.	ARM	401-7
Lee, Sam	SR	401-88
Lee, T. M.	SR	401-88
Lee, Task	TVG	401-203
Lee, Thomas B.	TVG	401-203
Lee, Walter T.	USV	401-239
Lee, Wellette	USV	401-239
Lee, William	USV	401-239
Lee, William A.	USV	401-239
Lee, William H.	TVG	401-203
Lee, William I.	USV	401-239
Lee, William M.	RR	401-58
Lee, William W.	USV	401-239
Lee, Willis	TVG	401-203
Leech, Richard Henry	NAV	401-20

Index to Texas Adjutant General Service Records—All Service Branches

Name	Branch	Record
Leecraft, A. N.	USV	401-239
Leeger, William	NAV	401-20
Leehan, Michael	FF	401-136
Leeman, Ray	SR	401-88
Leeman, W. B.	LR	401-129
Leeper, M. M.	FB	401-160
Leesman, F. Fred	FF	401-136
LeFebre, Adolph	ARM	401-7
Lefevers, J. M.	LR	401-129
Lefferty, Alexander L.	ARM	401-7
Leffler, Howard S.	TVG	401-203
Leffler, Howard S.	USV	401-239
Leftage, Henry	SP	401-46
Leftwich, C. J.	SR	401-88
Lege, Fred M., Jr.	SR	401-88
Lege, Frederick Merion	TVG	401-203
Lege, J.	TVG	401-203
Legg, George	ARM	401-7
Legler, E. B.	FF	401-136
Legrande, Edmond	ARM	401-7
Lehman, Julius	USV	401-239
Lehmann, C. F.	TVG	401-203
Lehmann, Max W.	TVG	401-203
Lehr, Fred P.	LR	401-129
Lehrson, W. E.	MV	401-30
Leib, Henry	FF	401-136
Leibe, Max	TVG	401-203
Leifeste, F. R.	SP	401-46
Leigh, J. S.	SR	401-88
Leigh, James	MV	401-30
Leigh, William A.	USV	401-239
Leigh, William M.	SR	401-88
Leight, J. S.	RRR	401-120
Leighton, Warren W.	TVG	401-203
Leitner, Lewis O.	USV	401-239
Leland, Brazan	NAV	401-20
Leman, D. A.	TVG	401-203
Lemann, John	ARM	401-7
Lemaster, William C.	USV	401-239
Leming, Paul W.	RRR	401-120
Lemley, T. J.	MM	401-32
Lemmons, Val	SP	401-46
Lemon, Ben	RRR	401-120
Lemond, W. R.	RRR	401-120
Lemons, James	FB	401-160
Lemons, Thomas	FB	401-160
Lemons, Thomas	FB	401-160
Lemoyne, W. O.	FB	401-160
Lenn, Peter	SP	401-46
Lennon, G. E.	USV	401-239
Lennon, Lewis H.	TVG	401-203
Lenoir, William Thomas	TVG	401-203
Lensing, A. L.	TVG	401-203
Lenz, E. R.	RR	401-58
Leon, E. H.	SR	401-88
Leonard, Harry	RRR	401-120
Leonard, Homer L.	SR	401-88
Leonard, M. T.	MM	401-32
Leonard, Martin	ARM	401-7
Leonard, Michael	ARM	401-7
Leonard, Miles P.	SR	401-88
Leonard, Patrick	SP	401-46
Leonard, Robert S.	USV	401-239
Leonard, W. E.	SR	401-88
Leonard, Will C.	USV	401-239
Leonardt, B. C.	SR	401-88
Leonhard, Martin L.	TVG	401-203
Leonhard, Martin L.	USV	401-239
Leopold, N.	TVG	401-203
Lepsise, Joseph	NAV	401-20
Lereilee, Desiree Emilee	ARM	401-7
Lerma, Francisco	FF	401-136
Leroy, F. P.	FB	401-160
Leslie, A. S.	RR	401-58
Leslie, Andrew Y.	LR	401-129
Leslie, Charles W.	USV	401-239
Leslie, John T.	USV	401-239
Leslie, Ziba	ARM	401-7
Lessing, W. D.	TVG	401-203
Lestarjette, Hal	USV	401-239
LeStourgeon, B. R.	USV	401-239
Lestrange, Richard	ARM	401-7
Lesueur, W. L.	RR	401-58
Letch, Christian	FF	401-136
Letchford, Isaac	ARM	401-7
Letts, James H.	SR	401-88
Letts, W. B.	SR	401-88
Leverett, H. W.	RRR	401-120
Leverett, J. S.	RR	401-58
Leverett, Joe	FB	401-160
Leverett, W. H.	TVG	401-203
Leverett, Z. T.	FF	401-136
Levering, Paul C.	LR	401-129
Leveritt, Hugh	MM	401-32
Leverson, Arthur	USV	401-239
Levey, J. G.	SR	401-88
Levey, Michael	ARM	401-7
Levi, Samuel	USV	401-239
Levisay, F. H.	TVG	401-203
Levisay, P. W.	FB	401-160
Levitt, Benjamin	ARM	401-7
Levitt, John J.	SP	401-46
Levy, Albert M.	NAV	401-20
Levy, Carl	TVG	401-203
Levy, Moses Albert	ARM	401-7
Levy, R. B.	TVG	401-203
Levy, Richard B.	USV	401-239
Levy, Sam	SR	401-88
Levy, W. M.	TVG	401-203
Levy, William Taylor	TVG	401-203
Lewellen, Riley D.	SR	401-88
Lewellin, W. C.	TVG	401-203

Index to Texas Adjutant General Service Records—All Service Branches

Lewis, A. D.	FF	401-136
Lewis, A. D.	FB	401-160
Lewis, A. Irvine	NAV	401-20
Lewis, A. L.	FF	401-136
Lewis, A. M.	FB	401-160
Lewis, A. S.	FF	401-136
Lewis, A. S.	TVG	401-203
Lewis, Alexander L.	RR	401-58
Lewis, Alonzo W.	USV	401-239
Lewis, Arthur	USV	401-240
Lewis, Bue. W.	USV	401-240
Lewis, Charles	NAV	401-20
Lewis, Charles	TVG	401-203
Lewis, Claud C.	USV	401-240
Lewis, Crawford B.	USV	401-240
Lewis, D. H.	SP	401-46
Lewis, Dan E.	RRR	401-120
Lewis, Daniel	ARM	401-7
Lewis, E. B.	TVG	401-203
Lewis, E. P.	SR	401-88
Lewis, Edward E.	USV	401-240
Lewis, H. W.	SR	401-88
Lewis, Harrison	FB	401-160
Lewis, Henry	USV	401-240
Lewis, J. B.	LR	401-129
Lewis, J. E.	LR	401-129
Lewis, J. F.	USV	401-240
Lewis, J. H.	FF	401-136
Lewis, J. L.	SR	401-88
Lewis, J. M.	TVG	401-203
Lewis, J. P.	FB	401-160
Lewis, Jacob H.	USV	401-240
Lewis, James J.	NAV	401-20
Lewis, James N.	USV	401-240
Lewis, Jepee J.	MM	401-32
Lewis, Joe W.	USV	401-240
Lewis, John	SP	401-46
Lewis, Joseph D.	USV	401-240
Lewis, L.	SP	401-46
Lewis, L. D.	TVG	401-203
Lewis, Moses	SP	401-46
Lewis, Myer A.	USV	401-240
Lewis, Nat	FB	401-160
Lewis, P. G.	FB	401-160
Lewis, Pat	RRR	401-120
Lewis, Robert B.	MV	401-30
Lewis, Robert C.	FB	401-160
Lewis, S.	FF	401-136
Lewis, Sam	TVG	401-203
Lewis, Stuart H.	USV	401-240
Lewis, Ted	RR	401-58
Lewis, Tom	USV	401-240
Lewis, Tom C.	FB	401-160
Lewis, Vivian S.	RRR	401-120
Lewis, W. C.	SR	401-88
Lewis, W. C.	FB	401-160
Lewis, W. R.	FB	401-160
Lewis, W. W.	SP	401-46
Lewis, W. W.	FB	401-160
Lewis, William	TST	401-36
Lewis, William C.	MV	401-30
Lewis, William E.	TVG	401-203
Lewis, William G.	NAV	401-20
Lewis, William H.	USV	401-240
Lewis, William W.	FB	401-160
Lewis, William X.	USV	401-240
Lewytte, D. D.	TVG	401-203
Lex, Conrad	MM	401-32
Libbe, Carl F.	USV	401-240
Libbe, Carl L.	TVG	401-203
Libbe, Theodore	TVG	401-203
Lichlyter, Frederick A.	FB	401-160
Lieb, Victor E.	SR	401-88
Lieberstein, Isaac	USV	401-240
Lieck, August	SP	401-46
Lieivenstone, Casper	ARM	401-7
Liggett, Oscar N.	TVG	401-203
Light, George E., Jr.	SR	401-88
Light, J. B.	SR	401-88
Light, John	FF	401-136
Light, John	FB	401-160
Light, Simon	USV	401-240
Lightfoot, George W.	SR	401-88
Lightfoot, W. J.	USV	401-240
Lightfoot, W. S.	USV	401-240
Lightfoot, William	FB	401-160
Lightner, W. M.	TVG	401-203
Ligon, D. L.	FB	401-160
Likens, Thos. M.	MV	401-30
Lile, John I.	USV	401-240
Lile, Lewis M.	RRR	401-120
Lilienthal, J. W.	TVG	401-203
Lilius, Thomas W.	USV	401-240
Lilley, E. C.	RRR	401-120
Lilley, Joseph	ARM	401-7
Liming, William F.	ARM	401-7
Lincecum, A. L.	SR	401-88
Lincicome, C. G.	RRR	401-120
Lind, Alex	USV	401-240
Linde, Knud W.	SR	401-88
Lindemann, Julius	TVG	401-203
Lindemann, O. A.	TVG	401-203
Lindenberg, Adolph E.	USV	401-240
Lindenburg, August	SP	401-46
Lindley, C. E.	SR	401-88
Lindley, David	ARM	401-7
Lindley, Jacob	ARM	401-7
Lindon, Ben	TVG	401-203
Lindsay, Ben	TVG	401-203
Lindsay, G. F.	USV	401-240
Lindsay, J. Benton	TVG	401-203
Lindsay, John	NAV	401-20

Index to Texas Adjutant General Service Records—All Service Branches

Name	Branch	Record
Lindsey, A.	TST	401-36
Lindsey, B. D.	FB	401-160
Lindsey, Benjamin D.	USV	401-240
Lindsey, Carl	SR	401-88
Lindsey, Charles E.	TVG	401-203
Lindsey, D. E.	RR	401-58
Lindsey, D. E.	FB	401-160
Lindsey, David	LR	401-129
Lindsey, E. J.	RRR	401-120
Lindsey, G. W.	RRR	401-120
Lindsey, John	ARM	401-7
Lindsey, Josiah L.	RR	401-58
Lindsey, Thomas E.	SR	401-88
Lindsey, W.	FB	401-160
Lindsey, William A.	USV	401-240
Linebarger, Michael Shearman	TVG	401-203
Linecum, L. J.	FB	401-160
Liner, J. A.	SR	401-88
Lingenfelter, George R.	SR	401-88
Lingo, W. M.	TVG	401-203
Link, A. K.	FF	401-136
Link, H. R.	TVG	401-203
Linn, O. M.	LR	401-129
Linscott, Harry	SR	401-88
Linsey, David	SR	401-88
Lintelman, A. H.	SR	401-88
Linthicum, Pearre Jones	USV	401-240
Lion, Elario	FF	401-136
Liorge, F. W.	NAV	401-20
Lipper, F. J.	TVG	401-203
Lipper, O. M.	TVG	401-203
Lipscomb, C. E.	TVG	401-203
Lipscomb, Charles C.	USV	401-240
Lipscomb, J. P.	TVG	401-203
Lipscomb, S. M.	SR	401-88
Lipscomb, W. C.	LR	401-129
Lipscomb, Wade Hampton	USV	401-240
Lipscomb, Walker B.	LR	401-129
Lipscomb, William S.	USV	401-240
Lisle, Claude L.	TVG	401-203
Lisle, Paul W.	TVG	401-203
Lister, John R.	SR	401-88
Lister, Josiah	USV	401-240
Liston, John B.	USV	401-240
Liton, William	FB	401-160
Littell, John M.	TVG	401-203
Litten, M. Francis	ARM	401-7
Little, Augustus	USV	401-240
Little, Dan W.	USV	401-240
Little, E. H.	SR	401-88
Little, Elmer G.	SR	401-88
Little, George M.	TVG	401-203
Little, Harvey	RRR	401-120
Little, Harvey E.	SR	401-88
Little, J. D.	SR	401-88
Little, Jake H.	TVG	401-203
Little, James	LR	401-129
Little, John	NAV	401-20
Little, John J.	SR	401-88
Little, John L	USV	401-240
Little, John L.	USV	401-240
Little, Robert Alex	RRR	401-120
Little, Sam	SR	401-88
Little, Walter W.	USV	401-240
Littlejohn, Walter Glenn	TVG	401-203
Littleton, Alfred	FB	401-160
Littleton, John	RR	401-58
Littleton, W. B.	FB	401-160
Litton, D. S.	TVG	401-203
Litton, Dickson S.	USV	401-240
Litton, William	FF	401-136
Lively, Richard H.	USV	401-240
Lively, Robert T.	USV	401-240
Lively, W. P.	SR	401-88
Livesay, Lester W.	SR	401-88
Living, Thomas H.	NAV	401-20
Livingston, Alonzo W.	RR	401-58
Livingston, Alonzo W.	FB	401-160
Livingston, G. A.	TVG	401-203
Livingston, George W.	USV	401-240
Livingston, Henry L.	SR	401-88
Livingstone, George	ARM	401-7
Lloyd, Daniel	NAV	401-20
Lloyd, George	FB	401-161
Lloyd, Reeves	TVG	401-203
Lloyd, Samuel	FB	401-161
Lloyd, W. H.	SR	401-88
Lloyd, W. W.	FF	401-136
Lloyd, Walter Kenyon	USV	401-240
Lloyd, Wesley	ARM	401-7
Lloyd, William H.	RRR	401-120
Lochabay, William H.	USV	401-240
Lochridge, Tom A.	SR	401-88
Lochwitzky, Alexander M.	RR	401-58
Lochwitzky, Alexander M.	SR	401-88
Lock, A. H.	SR	401-88
Lock, A. P.	RR	401-58
Lock, Edgar A.	SR	401-88
Lock, Henry F.	USV	401-240
Lock, L. C.	SP	401-46
Lock, Sidney J.	USV	401-240
Lock, Toney	SR	401-88
Lockart, A. N.	SR	401-88
Lockart, Joe R.	TVG	401-203
Locke, Henry W.	RRR	401-120
Locke, Henry W.	SR	401-88
Locke, Henry W.	FB	401-161
Locke, Henry W.	USV	401-240
Locke, Joseph	TVG	401-203
Locke, N. F.	FB	401-161
Locke, N. S.	SR	401-88
Locke, Richard	TVG	401-203

Index to Texas Adjutant General Service Records—All Service Branches

Name	Branch	Record
Locke, Victor M.	USV	401-240
Locke, William K.	SP	401-46
Lockett, Lige G.	USV	401-240
Lockett, Reese B.	SR	401-88
Lockett, Samuel C.	FF	401-136
Lockett, W. A.	TVG	401-203
Lockett, Wade Hampton	TVG	401-203
Lockhart, B.	ARM	401-7
Lockhart, Clem C.	USV	401-240
Lockhart, Jesse B.	RRR	401-120
Lockhart, John W.	SR	401-88
Lockhart, Joseph N.	MM	401-32
Lockhart, L. E.	USV	401-240
Lockinore, George	NAV	401-20
Lockling, Levi A.	ARM	401-7
Lockman, J. T.	FB	401-161
Lockmiller, J. F.	SR	401-88
Lockwood, Benjamin H.	USV	401-240
Lockwood, Charles E.	SP	401-46
Lockwood, Thomas S.	SR	401-88
Loden, O. J.	USV	401-240
Loerwald, Frank A.	USV	401-240
Loeser, Robert M.	FB	401-161
Loessin, John	USV	401-240
Loewenstein, C.	ARM	401-7
Loewenstein, Gus	SR	401-88
Loewenstein, James	SR	401-88
Lofland, Charles	TVG	401-203
Lofland, J. W.	TVG	401-203
Loftin, Ruben	SR	401-88
Loftus, Frank	TVG	401-203
Logan, Alonzo T.	TST	401-36
Logan, David L.	SP	401-46
Logan, Eugene	FB	401-161
Logan, Fred A.	TVG	401-203
Logan, John	SP	401-46
Logan, Perry	TVG	401-203
Logan, Vasquez	FB	401-161
Logan, William Stinson	ARM	401-7
Loggins, William D.	SP	401-46
Lokey, Gustavus A.	USV	401-240
Lomax, John H.	USV	401-240
Lombard, Russell H.	TVG	401-203
Long, A. N.	FF	401-136
Long, A. N.	SP	401-46
Long, Alma C.	USV	401-240
Long, C. P.	FB	401-161
Long, C. P.	FB	401-161
Long, Charles	USV	401-240
Long, F. M.	LR	401-129
Long, Fred	SR	401-88
Long, G. W.	CSA	401-39
Long, George	SR	401-88
Long, Harry A.	USV	401-240
Long, Ira	FB	401-161
Long, Iran	FF	401-136
Long, J. F.	LR	401-129
Long, J. H.	RR	401-58
Long, J. L.	SP	401-46
Long, J. S.	TVG	401-203
Long, Jack W.	FB	401-161
Long, James	SR	401-88
Long, James H.	RR	401-58
Long, Jesse	TVG	401-203
Long, John H.	RR	401-58
Long, Lawrence	NAV	401-20
Long, Lee	TVG	401-203
Long, Michael	USV	401-240
Long, Nathan D.	ARM	401-7
Long, Parke C.	USV	401-240
Long, R. A.	USV	401-240
Long, Samuel	FB	401-161
Long, Thomas H.	TVG	401-203
Long, Tobe A.	TST	401-36
Long, Tobe A.	MV	401-30
Long, Wade	USV	401-240
Long, William M.	FB	401-161
Long, William T.	USV	401-240
Longarilla, Francisco	ARM	401-7
Longbotham, R. E., Dr.	SR	401-88
Longley, A. H.	FF	401-136
Longley, Arthur	TVG	401-203
Longley, Campbell	ARM	401-7
Longley, George O.	SR	401-88
Longley, Mack G.	USV	401-240
Longmire, C. C.	FB	401-161
Longmire, M. C.	FB	401-161
Longoria, J. L.	RR	401-58
Longtine, Louis	TVG	401-203
Lonsford, J. B.	LR	401-129
Look, Austin D.	MV	401-30
Look, Park	TVG	401-203
Loomis, Charles H.	FB	401-161
Looney, Guy T.	USV	401-240
Looney, J. E.	TVG	401-203
Looney, John	ARM	401-7
Looney, R. H.	FB	401-161
Looney, Timothy	SP	401-46
Looney, W. E.	TVG	401-203
Looper, M. L.	TVG	401-203
Loper, Charles A.	USV	401-240
Lopez, Evaristo	SP	401-46
Lopez, Guadalupe	FF	401-136
Lopez, Pedro	FF	401-136
Lopez, Placido	FF	401-136
Lord, W. L.	TVG	401-203
Lordan, E. R.	SR	401-88
Lordan, Jerry	FB	401-161
Lorenskjold, Frederick	USV	401-240
Lorenz, J. A.	SP	401-46
Lorenz, R. W.	RR	401-58
Lormond, Jerome	ARM	401-7

Index to Texas Adjutant General Service Records—All Service Branches

Name	Branch	Record
Lothrop, John T. K.	NAV	401-20
Lotspeich, B. W.	TVG	401-203
Lott, A. T.	FB	401-161
Lott, Angier	SR	401-88
Lott, C. G.	RRR	401-120
Lott, J. T.	SR	401-88
Lott, John	FB	401-161
Lott, Martin K.	TVG	401-203
Lott, R. W.	RR	401-58
Lott, R. W.	SR	401-88
Lott, Virgil W.	USV	401-240
Lott, Will T.	RR	401-58
Lotts, William	TST	401-36
Louden, Robert B.	TVG	401-203
Loudon, A. L.	FB	401-161
Loudon, Thomas	FB	401-161
Louis, Joseph C.	MV	401-30
Louthian, Will D.	RR	401-58
Louthian, Will D.	RRR	401-120
Love, Albert L.	USV	401-240
Love, Albert S.	USV	401-240
Love, Andrew C., Jr.	SR	401-88
Love, Andrew P.	USV	401-240
Love, Ben C.	USV	401-240
Love, F. M.	MM	401-32
Love, F. O.	SR	401-88
Love, Francis M.	MV	401-30
Love, H.	ARM	401-7
Love, Henry	SR	401-88
Love, J. W.	TVG	401-203
Love, Jack B.	SR	401-88
Love, James E.	TVG	401-203
Love, Joseph E.	TST	401-36
Love, Mack M.	TVG	401-203
Love, Marvin F.	SR	401-88
Love, Oscar M.	USV	401-240
Love, R. C.	RR	401-58
Love, Richard	USV	401-240
Love, Robert C.	USV	401-240
Love, Thomas H.	RRR	401-120
Love, Thomas H.	SR	401-88
Love, Wallace A.	TVG	401-203
Loveall, J. A.	TVG	401-203
Loveall, J. H.	SP	401-46
Lovejoy, Bonnie Ray	TVG	401-203
Lovejoy, J. H.	USV	401-240
Lovelace, Louie E.	USV	401-240
Loveless, Charles C.	USV	401-240
Loveless, Paul B.	SR	401-88
Lovell, Charles P.	USV	401-240
Lovell, J. A.	TVG	401-203
Lovely, Frank	NAV	401-20
Lovett, Thomas C.	USV	401-240
Lovett, Thomas, Jr.	SR	401-88
Loving, Samuel E.	USV	401-240
Loving, W. M.	USV	401-240
Lovring, Otis R.	NAV	401-20
Low, Gay S.	SR	401-89
Low, H. O.	SR	401-89
Low, Sam D. W.	SR	401-89
Lowe, Arthur E.	TVG	401-203
Lowe, Frank	FB	401-161
Lowe, George H.	USV	401-240
Lowe, John	ARM	401-7
Lowe, John L.	USV	401-240
Lowe, Lee A.	USV	401-240
Lowe, Marcellus	RR	401-59
Lowe, R. G.	TVG	401-203
Lowe, R. G.	TVG	401-203
Lowe, Thomas J.	RR	401-59
Lowe, W. A., Jr.	LR	401-129
Lowe, W. E.	RR	401-59
Lowe, W. W.	TVG	401-203
Lowenbins, F. A.	SP	401-46
Lowenstein, James	RR	401-59
Lowenstein, James	SR	401-89
Lowery, Michael	FF	401-136
Lowery, Michael	SP	401-46
Lowery, O. L.	SR	401-89
Lowrance, William J.	FB	401-161
Lowrey, A. S.	FB	401-161
Lowrey, Albert M.	CSA	401-39
Lowrey, John	FF	401-136
Lowrey, Mark J.	USV	401-240
Lowrie, Edward E.	USV	401-240
Lowrie, Isaac	ARM	401-7
Lowrie, R. B.	TST	401-36
Lowry, A. S.	FB	401-161
Lowry, Bernard	NAV	401-20
Lowry, Daniel L.	USV	401-240
Lowry, Ennis	TVG	401-203
Lowry, Francis A.	USV	401-240
Lowry, Quincy	TVG	401-203
Lowry, Ray	SR	401-89
Loya, Gabino	FF	401-136
Loya, Hijenio	FF	401-136
Loyless, H.	FB	401-161
Lubbock, J. L.	RR	401-59
Lubet, Joseph	NAV	401-20
Lucas, David R.	TVG	401-203
Lucas, Frank	SP	401-46
Lucas, Frank	USV	401-240
Lucas, Frederick J.	TST	401-36
Lucero, Juan	FF	401-136
Lucid, D.	FB	401-161
Luck, Adolphus G.	TST	401-36
Luck, Fred L.	MV	401-30
Luckett, Alfred	RR	401-59
Luckett, Philip N.	CSA	401-39
Luckett, R. F.	MM	401-32
Lucy, J. R.	USV	401-240
Lucy, James E.	FB	401-161

Index to Texas Adjutant General Service Records—All Service Branches

Name	Branch	Page
Luder, E. B.	TVG	401-203
Luderts, Frederick	NAV	401-20
Ludlam, Drew	SR	401-89
Ludlow, Louis L.	USV	401-240
Ludwick, M.	FB	401-161
Ludwick, W. W.	FB	401-161
Ludwig, Amos P.	USV	401-240
Ludwig, J. B.	FB	401-161
Luedecke, A. F.	SR	401-89
Lueders, William	USV	401-240
Luer, Albert	FF	401-136
Luercher, L.	FB	401-161
Lufkin, Joel A.	SP	401-46
Luhn, Fred Ravenel	TVG	401-203
Luke, W. Y.	FB	401-161
Luman, Ed J.	TVG	401-203
Luman, J. W.	SR	401-89
Lumbeck, F. W.	FB	401-161
Lumkin, Fred	SP	401-46
Lummons, William	NAV	401-20
Lumpkin, G. S.	SR	401-89
Lumpkin, Theo	SR	401-89
Lunbeck, F. M.	FB	401-161
Lundel, Collier	ARM	401-7
Luney, Harve	TVG	401-203
Lunn, Sidney	TVG	401-203
Lunsford, Charles W.	USV	401-240
Luscomb, Robert	NAV	401-20
Lusk, Leon	SR	401-89
Lusk, Oscar S.	TVG	401-203
Lusk, Oscar S.	USV	401-240
Lusk, T. C.	SP	401-46
Lustus, Joseph	NAV	401-20
Luth, Lawrence M.	TVG	401-203
Luth, Perry	SR	401-89
Luther, John T.	FB	401-161
Lybrand, Herschel L.	SR	401-89
Lykins, John	USV	401-240
Lyle, Thomas Bibb	RRR	401-120
Lyles, Bob J.	SR	401-89
Lyles, J. K.	SR	401-89
Lynch, Alex	NAV	401-20
Lynch, D. L.	FB	401-161
Lynch, E. B.	RRR	401-120
Lynch, F. K.	FB	401-161
Lynch, H. D.	FB	401-161
Lynch, I. L.	LR	401-129
Lynch, James Henry	RRR	401-120
Lynch, John	NAV	401-20
Lynch, John P.	ARM	401-7
Lynch, L. R.	RR	401-59
Lynch, M.	FF	401-136
Lynch, Michael	FB	401-161
Lynch, William West	RR	401-59
Lynch, William West	SR	401-89
Lynn, Fred C.	USV	401-240
Lynn, George R.	RR	401-59
Lynn, Joseph	TST	401-36
Lynn, Ted E.	SR	401-89
Lyon, Cecil Andrew	TVG	401-203
Lyon, Charles G.	ARM	401-7
Lyon, DuPont B.	USV	401-240
Lyon, F. D.	USV	401-240
Lyon, W. L.	FB	401-161
Lyons, Jacob	TVG	401-203
Lyons, James H.	USV	401-240
Lyons, Leander P.	MV	401-30
Lyons, P. G.	USV	401-240
Lyons, Ransom L.	USV	401-240
Lyons, Thomas	NAV	401-20
Lyons, Thomas	USV	401-240
Lyons, Vade W.	USV	401-240
Lytle, Lewis Francis	SR	401-89
Lytle, Samuel	MV	401-30
Lytton, F. O.	SR	401-89
Maben, Horace	FB	401-163
Mabold, Jacob	ARM	401-7
Mabry, Allen	FB	401-163
Mabry, H. P.	FB	401-163
Mabry, J. Childs	USV	401-242
Mabry, James L.	NAV	401-20
Mabry, James R.	SP	401-46
Mabry, R. E.	MV	401-30
Mabry, W. H.	USV	401-242
Mabry, Wooten	SR	401-89
MacDanniel, George W.	TVG	401-204
MacDonald, A. R.	RRR	401-120
Mace, Albert R.	RR	401-59
Mace, Francis	ARM	401-7
Macha, Robert	USV	401-242
Machen, E. W.	FB	401-163
Machen, E. W.	USV	401-242
Mack, Clay	USV	401-242
Mack, Robert P.	USV	401-242
Macken, Patrick	SP	401-46
Mackey, Dick	SP	401-46
Mackey, Elgin W.	USV	401-242
Mackey, J. D.	SR	401-89
Mackin, John E.	USV	401-242
Macknotte, William	NAV	401-20
Mackrell, W. H.	TVG	401-204
Macmanus, A. F. Watson	TVG	401-204
Macmanus, A. F. Watson	USV	401-242
Macmanus, C. J.	FB	401-163
Macmanus, M. E. Arnold	TVG	401-204
MacNider, V. S.	TVG	401-204
Macomber [McComber], H. A.	SP	401-46
Macon, J. E.	TVG	401-204
Macune, Charles W.	USV	401-242
Madden, A. C.	MV	401-30
Madden, Fred	TVG	401-204
Maddin, Gene	SR	401-89

Index to Texas Adjutant General Service Records—All Service Branches

Name	Branch	Record
Maddow, James A.	TVG	401-204
Maddox, A. P.	TVG	401-204
Maddox, A. R.	FB	401-163
Maddox, Alvin Newton	SR	401-89
Maddox, Arch	SR	401-89
Maddox, Dennis O.	USV	401-242
Maddox, Earnest D.	RRR	401-120
Maddox, Emit C.	RRR	401-120
Maddox, G. O.	RR	401-59
Maddox, H. C.	RRR	401-120
Maddox, Houston	SP	401-46
Maddox, James A.	TVG	401-204
Maddox, M. D.	USV	401-242
Maddox, P. P.	USV	401-242
Maddox, W. T.	TVG	401-204
Maddrey, J. A.	FB	401-163
Maddux, T. M.	USV	401-242
Madeley, Bell	TVG	401-204
Madeley, Fred	SR	401-89
Maese, Crespin	FF	401-137
Maese, Thomas	FF	401-137
Maethe, Michael	ARM	401-8
Magadieu, Gustav T.	USV	401-242
Magary, Maxwell	ARM	401-8
Magears, Jim	USV	401-242
MaGee, Edgar S.	RR	401-59
Magee, Eli E.	MV	401-30
Magee, H.	FB	401-163
MaGee, L. B.	RR	401-59
Magee, Samuel B.	USV	401-242
Magers, Charles A.	USV	401-242
Magerstadt, A. L.	TVG	401-205
Maggard, Harry C.	TVG	401-205
Magill, E. H.	FB	401-163
Magill, George H.	FB	401-163
Magill, James K.	MM	401-32
Magill, W. H.	MM	401-32
Magnon, Antonio	FB	401-163
Magnon, E. C.	USV	401-242
Magrill, Henry D.	USV	401-242
Magruder, Hamilton	SR	401-89
Magruder, J. C.	USV	401-242
Magruder, James L.	USV	401-242
Magruder, R. F.	SR	401-89
Maguenat, Fred L.	TVG	401-205
Maguire, John	ARM	401-8
Maguire, Thomas	ARM	401-8
Mahaffey, Mark	RRR	401-120
Mahaffy, M. B.	RRR	401-120
Maheau, Charles	ARM	401-8
Maher, Robert E.	TVG	401-205
Mahon, Asa M.	USV	401-242
Mahon, J.	FB	401-163
Mahone, John R.	USV	401-242
MaHoney, John	TST	401-36
Mahoney, John P.	TVG	401-205
Mahoney, Laurence	SP	401-46
Mahony, G. M.	SR	401-89
Mahony, G. M.	LR	401-130
Mahood, James	FF	401-137
Mahorner, Louis R.	USV	401-242
Maier, Moses	FB	401-163
Main, Albert	RRR	401-120
Mains, Josiah	RR	401-59
Majia, Pablo	FB	401-164
Majors, Norman Jake	RRR	401-120
Majors, Thomas J.	RR	401-59
Malcolm, James	NAV	401-20
Malcolmson, Alfred N.	USV	401-242
Maldanado, P.	FB	401-163
Malior, T. O.	FB	401-163
Mallard, A. R.	SR	401-89
Mallard, A. R.	LR	401-130
Mallard, T. C.	RRR	401-120
Mallia, Joe L.	SR	401-89
Mallord, C. S.	TVG	401-205
Mallord, J. D.	TVG	401-205
Mallory, George M.	USV	401-242
Malone, Charles A.	SR	401-89
Malone, Dink	USV	401-242
Malone, F. T.	RRR	401-120
Malone, F. T.	SR	401-89
Malone, Fred	TVG	401-205
Malone, Fred B.	FB	401-163
Malone, George Q.	USV	401-242
Malone, J. A.	TVG	401-205
Malone, J. W.	USV	401-242
Malone, James Mack	FB	401-163
Malone, James Nat	RR	401-59
Malone, James Nat	SR	401-89
Malone, John	RR	401-59
Malone, John	SR	401-89
Malone, Matthew	NAV	401-20
Maloney, Ben L., Major	SR	401-89
Maloney, John P.	RR	401-59
Maltimore, C. H.	FB	401-163
Maltimore, Henry	FB	401-163
Maltsberger, J. T.	FB	401-163
Maltsberger, V. G.	FB	401-163
Maltsby, H. A.	FB	401-163
Maltsby, W. J.	FB	401-163
Malty, Thomas	NAV	401-20
Malven, Lee	USV	401-242
Mancha, Jesus	FB	401-163
Mancill, Morris	TVG	401-205
Mandy, S. M.	FB	401-163
Manerrey, H. S.	NAV	401-20
Maness, Edgar A.	USV	401-242
Manger, Michael	FF	401-137
Manger, Philipp	SP	401-46
Mangham, Clarence Edmond	RRR	401-120
Mangold, John	SP	401-46

Index to Texas Adjutant General Service Records—All Service Branches

Name	Branch	Record
Mangrum, F. E.	SR	401-89
Mangum, Aaron S.	ARM	401-8
Manint, Earle M.	SR	401-89
Manios, Lorenzo	TST	401-36
Manis, W. B.	SR	401-89
Maniscalco, Joseph A.	SR	401-89
Mankins, Jeff D.	FB	401-163
Manley, L. B.	SR	401-89
Manley, R. S.	TVG	401-205
Mann, C. M.	FB	401-163
Mann, Charles S.	USV	401-242
Mann, George P.	TVG	401-205
Mann, Henry	ARM	401-8
Mann, James S.	SR	401-89
Mann, James S.	LR	401-130
Mann, John B.	NAV	401-20
Mann, Morgan M.	TVG	401-205
Mann, Percy A.	USV	401-242
Mann, Ralph	USV	401-242
Mann, Walter L.	USV	401-242
Mann, William	MV	401-30
Manning, Charles E.	USV	401-242
Manning, D.	FB	401-163
Manning, E.	TST	401-36
Manning, E. B.	SR	401-89
Manning, Edwin H.	SR	401-89
Manning, Frank	FB	401-163
Manning, J. E.	USV	401-242
Manning, John	ARM	401-8
Manning, Robert	NAV	401-20
Manning, Wentworth	SP	401-46
Manning, William	FF	401-137
Manning, William	FB	401-163
Manning, William E.	FB	401-163
Manry, A. L.	SR	401-89
Mansell, Calvin Lee	SR	401-89
Mansell, W. E., Jr.	SR	401-89
Mansfield, Pat	SR	401-89
Mansfield, Rhea	SR	401-89
Mansinger, Abe	SR	401-89
Manson, John	ARM	401-8
Manton, Charles	TVG	401-205
Mantovanis, C. A.	SR	401-89
Mantte, Andrew	ARM	401-8
Manuel, Marlin C.	USV	401-242
Manville, W. H.	TVG	401-205
Manziel, Bobby	SR	401-89
Manzingo, C. G.	TVG	401-205
Mapel, John	FB	401-163
Maples, Paul	SR	401-89
Marable, Herbert T.	USV	401-242
Marble, George A.	USV	401-242
Marcelino, Peter	MV	401-30
March, George S.	TVG	401-205
March, J. B.	TVG	401-205
March, N. M.	TVG	401-205
Marchal, Ferdinand	SP	401-46
Marcom, James V.	USV	401-242
Marcos, Cortes	FF	401-137
Marcuse, William A.	USV	401-242
Mardtines, Michael	FF	401-137
Marek, F.	TVG	401-205
Marek, Joseph	TVG	401-205
Marett, Thomas	USV	401-242
Margiotta, Tony	SR	401-89
Margozewitz, Gustav F.	USV	401-242
Marichal, John X.	TVG	401-205
Marie, Felipe	FF	401-137
Marines, Rhillip R.	USV	401-242
Marion, George G.	NAV	401-20
Marion, John	FF	401-137
Markey, T. J.	FB	401-163
Markin, Alfred C.	TVG	401-205
Markin, James	NAV	401-20
Marklee, C. H.	TVG	401-205
Markley, B[eneval] H.	FB	401-163
Markowitz, E. J.	SR	401-89
Marks, C. J.	TVG	401-205
Marks, David	TVG	401-205
Marks, Fred E.	RR	401-59
Marks, Fred E.	SR	401-89
Marks, Fred E.	LR	401-130
Marks, Jo. S.	TVG	401-205
Markwell, R.	TVG	401-205
Marlett, William	FF	401-137
Marley, F. J.	RRR	401-120
Marlin, Auge	RR	401-59
Marlin, Ernest	RR	401-59
Marlin, John	ARM	401-8
Marlow, James	ARM	401-8
Marple, B. W.	TVG	401-205
Marple, Raleigh W.	USV	401-242
Marquis, George C.	USV	401-242
Marr, H. F.	TVG	401-205
Marr, W. B.	USV	401-242
Marr, W. T.	FB	401-163
Marritt, Moses	ARM	401-8
Marrs, E. C.	SR	401-89
Mars, J. G.	FB	401-163
Marsden, Crosby	RR	401-59
Marsh, Bryan	FB	401-163
Marsh, Dan S.	TVG	401-205
Marsh, Harold	TVG	401-205
Marsh, Robert C.	USV	401-242
Marsh, T. W.	RRR	401-120
Marsh, William D.	FB	401-163
Marshall, A. J.	FB	401-163
Marshall, A. L.	TVG	401-205
Marshall, Benjamin F.	FF	401-137
Marshall, C. L.	USV	401-242
Marshall, Cassius Clay	TVG	401-205
Marshall, Emmett	SR	401-89

Index to Texas Adjutant General Service Records—All Service Branches

Name	Branch	Page
Marshall, Ferdinand	FF	401-137
Marshall, James W.	TVG	401-205
Marshall, John	RR	401-59
Marshall, John	MV	401-30
Marshall, Thomas E.	FB	401-163
Marshall, W. F.	SR	401-89
Marshall, W. L.	TVG	401-205
Marshall, Walter	SP	401-47
Marshall, William F.	LR	401-130
Marston, Jack	SR	401-89
Marti, Jake	SR	401-89
Martial, W. O.	SR	401-89
Martin, A. H.	FF	401-137
Martin, Andrew H.	SR	401-89
Martin, Andrew J.	USV	401-242
Martin, Arch	SR	401-89
Martin, Arch	LR	401-130
Martin, Ben W.	SR	401-89
Martin, Benjamin D.	CSA	401-39
Martin, C. A.	SP	401-47
Martin, C. L.	SR	401-89
Martin, C. L.	LR	401-130
Martin, Charles E.	FB	401-163
Martin, Charles E.	USV	401-242
Martin, Cyrus R.	FB	401-163
Martin, Donald M.	USV	401-242
Martin, E. A.	RRR	401-120
Martin, E. C.	SR	401-89
Martin, E. C.	LR	401-130
Martin, Edgar	USV	401-242
Martin, Enoch	NAV	401-20
Martin, Frank	SR	401-89
Martin, Frank	USV	401-242
Martin, Frank H.	FB	401-163
Martin, Frank W.	SR	401-89
Martin, G. C.	SR	401-89
Martin, G. C.	LR	401-130
Martin, G. H.	SR	401-89
Martin, George A.	CSA	401-39
Martin, George Estill	RRR	401-120
Martin, George F.	SR	401-89
Martin, George M.	FF	401-137
Martin, H. R.	SR	401-89
Martin, Haywood	USV	401-242
Martin, Horace H.	USV	401-242
Martin, Howard Taylor	RRR	401-120
Martin, Ivan	TVG	401-205
Martin, J. C.	RRR	401-120
Martin, J. C.	SR	401-89
Martin, J. C.	FB	401-163
Martin, J. C.	USV	401-242
Martin, J. F.	SR	401-89
Martin, J. F.	USV	401-242
Martin, J. P.	SP	401-47
Martin, J. T.	RR	401-59
Martin, J. W.	FB	401-163
Martin, J. W. P.	FB	401-163
Martin, Jack	FB	401-163
Martin, James	RR	401-59
Martin, James	ARM	401-8
Martin, James C.	SP	401-47
Martin, James T.	RR	401-59
Martin, Jesse R.	USV	401-242
Martin, Joe A.	SR	401-89
Martin, John	ARM	401-8
Martin, John	FF	401-137
Martin, John G.	SR	401-89
Martin, John H.	USV	401-242
Martin, John S.	USV	401-242
Martin, Joseph L.	SP	401-47
Martin, Kirby E.	USV	401-242
Martin, L. J.	TVG	401-205
Martin, L. K.	SR	401-89
Martin, O. J.	SR	401-89
Martin, Oscar T.	RR	401-59
Martin, Otis Turner	SR	401-89
Martin, Otto	FF	401-137
Martin, R. B.	RRR	401-120
Martin, R. B.	SR	401-89
Martin, R. O.	SR	401-89
Martin, Ralph D.	RRR	401-120
Martin, Rudolph E.	SR	401-89
Martin, S. A.	SR	401-89
Martin, Samuel A.	USV	401-242
Martin, Seth	RRR	401-120
Martin, T.	SR	401-89
Martin, T. G.	FB	401-163
Martin, T. J.	SR	401-89
Martin, T. J.	TVG	401-205
Martin, Thomas	FB	401-163
Martin, Thomas G.	SP	401-47
Martin, Thomas P.	FB	401-163
Martin, W. B.	TVG	401-205
Martin, W. C.	TVG	401-205
Martin, W. D.	FB	401-163
Martin, W. H.	RR	401-59
Martin, W. P.	FB	401-163
Martin, Walter W	RR	401-59
Martin, William	ARM	401-8
Martin, William	SP	401-47
Martin, William	USV	401-242
Martin, William Chaille	TVG	401-205
Martin, William E.	RR	401-59
Martin, William G.	USV	401-242
Martin, William M.	TVG	401-205
Martine, O. R.	RRR	401-120
Martines, Crisanto	FF	401-137
Martinex, Teophilis	RR	401-59
Martinez, Encarnacion	FB	401-163
Martinez, Mercurio	SR	401-89
Martinez, Miguel	FB	401-163
Martinez, Rafael	SP	401-47

Index to Texas Adjutant General Service Records—All Service Branches

Name	Branch	Record
Marton, C. C.	TVG	401-205
Martony, Henry F.	USV	401-242
Marx, A. J.	FB	401-163
Marx, Robert	FF	401-137
Masegee, J. R.	FB	401-163
Maser, Simonle	NAV	401-20
Mason, A. Haydn	SR	401-89
Mason, Arthur	SR	401-89
Mason, B. B.	USV	401-242
Mason, Barney	FB	401-163
Mason, C. A.	FB	401-163
Mason, Clarence H.	USV	401-242
Mason, Claude E.	TVG	401-205
Mason, F. S.	USV	401-242
Mason, George	NAV	401-20
Mason, George H.	SR	401-89
Mason, Henry E.	USV	401-242
Mason, Isaac S.	USV	401-242
Mason, J. N.	SR	401-89
Mason, J. T.	FB	401-163
Mason, Joe	TVG	401-205
Mason, Mack	ARM	401-8
Mason, Silas	TVG	401-205
Mason, Walter	TVG	401-205
Mason, William	ARM	401-8
Mason, Willie	TVG	401-205
Massay, J. M.	SR	401-89
Massegee, J. R.	FB	401-163
Massengale, Bob	SR	401-89
Massey, Charles J.	USV	401-242
Massey, Charles L.	USV	401-242
Massey, D. J.	SR	401-89
Massey, Dixon	RRR	401-120
Massey, George S.	USV	401-242
Massey, Guy D.	SR	401-89
Massey, J. W.	RRR	401-120
Massey, John M., Jr.	SR	401-89
Massey, Orren J.	TVG	401-205
Massey, Walter S.	USV	401-242
Massey, William H.	USV	401-242
Massie, W. A.	RRR	401-120
Massingale, James	USV	401-242
Massingale, Sam C.	USV	401-242
Mast, Eugene Z.	USV	401-242
Mast, Milton	MV	401-30
Masterson, E. M.	TVG	401-205
Masterson, James R.	USV	401-242
Masterson, L. S.	RRR	401-120
Masterson, L. S.	SR	401-90
Masterson, N. T.	SR	401-90
Masterson, R. B.	FB	401-163
Matcik, John A.	USV	401-242
Mateer, Charles T. L.	TVG	401-205
Maten, D. S.	TVG	401-205
Mather, Andrew	FB	401-163
Mather, F. W.	NAV	401-20
Matheson, George W.	USV	401-242
Matheson, William J.	USV	401-242
Mathews, C. C.	SR	401-90
Mathews, Christopher Columbus	RRR	401-120
Mathews, Gus	FB	401-163
Mathews, H. L.	USV	401-242
Mathews, Milo B.	USV	401-242
Mathews, Nathan	CSA	401-39
Mathews, Orville Andrews	TVG	401-205
Mathews, William	FB	401-163
Mathis, C. H.	TVG	401-205
Mathis, John M., III	SR	401-90
Mathis, John M., Jr.	SR	401-90
Mathis, L. W.	TVG	401-205
Mathis, Robert J.	USV	401-242
Mathis, Theodore F.	USV	401-242
Matlock, W. H.	SR	401-90
Matt, J. B.	FB	401-163
Matta, Andres	RR	401-59
Mattern, James J., Lt. Col.	SR	401-90
Matteson, William Henry	FF	401-137
Matthews, Ballard D.	USV	401-242
Matthews, Ben H.	USV	401-242
Matthews, Britt S.	SR	401-90
Matthews, Clarence S.	TVG	401-205
Matthews, D. T.	TVG	401-205
Matthews, Dallas J.	SR	401-90
Matthews, Dallas J., Jr.	SR	401-90
Matthews, E.	TVG	401-205
Matthews, E. E.	TVG	401-205
Matthews, Edward J.	USV	401-242
Matthews, Frank W.	RR	401-59
Matthews, Frank W.	RRR	401-120
Matthews, H. H.	SR	401-90
Matthews, H. O.	FB	401-163
Matthews, Harp	SP	401-47
Matthews, Herbert	FB	401-163
Matthews, J. M.	CSA	401-39
Matthews, J. M.	FB	401-163
Matthews, J. W.	FB	401-163
Matthews, Jack Clarence	RRR	401-120
Matthews, James C.	CSA	401-40
Matthews, John	FB	401-163
Matthews, John L.	SR	401-90
Matthews, John W.	FB	401-163
Matthews, Joseph J.	ARM	401-8
Matthews, Joseph W.	TVG	401-205
Matthews, Kinchen N.	TVG	401-205
Matthews, V. F.	TVG	401-205
Matthews, W. A.	FB	401-163
Matthews, W. H.	TVG	401-205
Matthews, W. T.	FB	401-164
Matthews, Z. Becton	USV	401-242
Matthies, Cleburne H.	SR	401-90
Mattias, Otto	FF	401-137
Matton, Batto	FF	401-137

Index to Texas Adjutant General Service Records—All Service Branches

Name	Branch	Record
Mattox, Louis W.	USV	401-242
Mattox, Swiss T.	SR	401-90
Mauer, Henry Conrad	TVG	401-205
Maul, A. J.	FB	401-164
Maul, Walker	MV	401-30
Maulden, G. Q.	SR	401-90
Mauldin, J. B.	SR	401-90
Maule, J. T.	FB	401-164
Mauntel, John	TVG	401-205
Mauntel, Pror.	TVG	401-205
Maupin, A. W.	TVG	401-205
Maupin, Columbus H.	FB	401-164
Maupin, J. D.	RRR	401-120
Maure, A.	NAV	401-20
Maurer, Leslie D., Dr.	SR	401-90
Maurer, R. R.	SR	401-90
Maury, M. F.	FB	401-164
Maxey, F. L.	SR	401-90
Maxfield, James Robert, Jr.	SR	401-90
Maxfield, Jesse O.	USV	401-242
Maximillian, Joe	RR	401-59
Maxon, Edmond S.	TVG	401-205
Maxwell, E. C.	SR	401-90
Maxwell, Enoch A.	FB	401-164
Maxwell, Harvey	RR	401-59
Maxwell, Henry	RR	401-59
Maxwell, J. A.	TST	401-36
Maxwell, J. B.	TST	401-36
Maxwell, J. M.	TVG	401-205
Maxwell, J. W.	SR	401-90
Maxwell, J. W.	LR	401-130
Maxwell, Richard T.	RRR	401-120
Maxwell, Thomas B.	FB	401-164
May, A. S.	NAV	401-20
May, Alexander S.	ARM	401-8
May, David J., Jr.	SR	401-90
May, Fred	TVG	401-205
May, George B.	FB	401-164
May, H. B., Jr.	SR	401-90
May, Harry H.	TVG	401-205
May, Holmes A.	USV	401-242
May, J. D.	SR	401-90
May, J. D.	LR	401-130
May, John	ARM	401-8
May, John H.	TVG	401-205
May, Nathaniel	NAV	401-20
May, R. E.	SR	401-90
May, R. L.	RRR	401-120
May, R. L.	SR	401-90
May, Sam M.	USV	401-242
May, Thomas J.	TVG	401-205
May, W. B.	SP	401-47
May, W. G.	TVG	401-205
May, W. J.	SR	401-90
May, W. P.	SR	401-90
May, W. P.	FB	401-164
May, Walter B.	SR	401-90
Mayben, John William	TVG	401-205
Mayberry, James E.	TVG	401-205
Mayberry, Walter E.	RR	401-59
Mayberry, Walter E.	SR	401-90
Mayer, John Paul	USV	401-242
Mayer, Joseph	ARM	401-8
Mayers, Edward	FB	401-164
Mayers, Felix J.	RR	401-59
Mayers, John H.	USV	401-242
Mayes, Adolphus B.	CSA	401-40
Mayes, Charlie	SR	401-90
Mayes, J. P.	SR	401-90
Mayes, James H.	TVG	401-205
Mayes, John	TST	401-36
Mayes, Sam C.	RR	401-59
Mayes, W. M.	TVG	401-205
Mayes, Will	SR	401-90
Mayfield, F. J.	TVG	401-205
Mayfield, Jacob	CSA	401-40
Mayfield, James P.	USV	401-242
Mayfield, John	RR	401-59
Mayfield, John C.	FB	401-164
Mayfield, Seth Newton	TVG	401-205
Mayfield, T. S.	LR	401-130
Mayfield, W. N.	USV	401-242
Mayfield, Walter	RR	401-59
Maynard, R. E. L.	SR	401-90
Maynard, W. G.	TST	401-36
Mayniel, Pedro	FB	401-164
Mayo, Frank D.	TVG	401-205
Mayo, R. B.	SR	401-90
Mayo, T. W.	RR	401-60
Mayo, William	MV	401-30
Mayor, Joseph	NAV	401-20
Mays, B.	FB	401-164
Mays, Curtis	RR	401-60
Mays, M. B.	TVG	401-205
Mazzei, Louis	ARM	401-8
McAdams, C. A.	SR	401-90
McAdams, Frank W.	USV	401-240
McAdams, J. P.	SR	401-90
McAdoo, S. L.	USV	401-240
McAfee, A. K.	TVG	401-203
McAfee, D. C.	SR	401-90
McAfee, R. L.	SR	401-90
McAlister, Paul	RR	401-59
McAllister, Alex. William	TVG	401-203
McAllister, Alexander	NAV	401-21
McAllister, Joseph	SP	401-46
McAllister, Rons.	TVG	401-203
McAlpine, A. D.	LR	401-130
McAlpine, Angus	TVG	401-203
McAnally, Fred	TVG	401-203
McAnally, Robert E.	USV	401-240
McArrio, Villeme	FF	401-136

Index to Texas Adjutant General Service Records—All Service Branches

Name	Branch	Record
McAtee, W. L.	TST	401-36
McAugham, C. H.	USV	401-240
McAulay, Sam	SR	401-90
McBath, H. K.	SR	401-90
McBeath, Andrew S.	USV	401-240
McBeath, James K.	USV	401-240
McBee, Charles W.	RR	401-59
McBee, Marion F.	SR	401-90
McBee, S. B.	RRR	401-120
McBrearty, William J.	USV	401-240
McBreaty, Patrick	USV	401-240
McBride, D. A.	FB	401-161
McBride, Earl	SR	401-90
McBride, Edward F.	USV	401-240
McBride, Henry	TVG	401-204
McBride, James L.	USV	401-240
McBride, John E.	FB	401-161
McBride, Martin	SR	401-90
McBride, P.	SR	401-90
McBride, W. E.	FB	401-161
McBride, William C.	USV	401-240
McBride, William W.	TVG	401-204
McCain, James Nash	SR	401-90
McCain, John P.	USV	401-240
McCain, R. D.	SR	401-90
McCain, William	ARM	401-7
McCaleb, Claude	SR	401-90
McCaleb, Claude Howard	TVG	401-204
McCaleb, David C.	SR	401-90
McCaleb, David Courtland	TVG	401-204
McCall, C. D.	FB	401-161
McCall, Edwin Francis	USV	401-240
McCall, James L.	TVG	401-204
McCall, Oliver W.	USV	401-240
McCall, Thomas P.	TST	401-36
McCall, Will A.	TVG	401-204
McCallum, A. N.	FB	401-161
McCallum, Brown	SR	401-90
McCallum, Bryan	SR	401-90
McCallum, E. B.	RR	401-59
McCallum, E. B. C.	RR	401-59
McCallum, Thomas	SR	401-90
McCambridge, Francis	NAV	401-21
McCampbell, Frederick	USV	401-240
McCampbell, J. H.	RR	401-59
McCampbell, J. Howell	SR	401-90
McCampbell, John T.	USV	401-240
McCampbell, W.	TVG	401-204
McCampbell, William B.	TVG	401-204
McCampbell, William S.	TST	401-36
McCamroch, Robert S.	SR	401-90
McCamroch, Robert Sidney	LR	401-130
McCane, James	SR	401-90
McCanless, Eldredge	USV	401-241
McCanless, J. E.	FB	401-161
McCann, G. T.	FB	401-161
McCann, J. B.	SR	401-90
McCann, James	FB	401-161
McCann, Robert L.	FF	401-136
McCann, Robert W.	USV	401-241
McCarley, James P.	FB	401-161
McCarron, Gilbert	USV	401-241
McCarter, J. D. P.	SP	401-46
McCarter, R. A.	SR	401-90
McCarthy, Ed, Jr.	RR	401-59
McCarthy, F. J.	FB	401-161
McCarthy, Joe R.	TVG	401-204
McCarthy, John M.	MV	401-30
McCarthy, Owen	TVG	401-204
McCarthy, Owen T.	USV	401-241
McCarthy, William	FF	401-136
McCarty, Edward M.	USV	401-241
McCarty, F. P.	TVG	401-204
McCarty, James M.	USV	401-241
McCarty, Jerome	USV	401-241
McCarty, Nick	SR	401-90
McCarty, R. H.	TVG	401-204
McCarty, Richard H.	USV	401-241
McCarty, Tim	FB	401-161
McCarvell, Arther	TVG	401-204
McCarvell, Horace	USV	401-241
McCarver, Charles H.	RRR	401-120
McCary, Cecil M.	TVG	401-204
McCary, Richard E.	USV	401-241
McCaskill, Joseph E.	USV	401-241
McCastle, Henry B.	TVG	401-204
McCauless, J. E.	FB	401-161
McCauley, C., Major	SR	401-90
McCauley, E. L.	RRR	401-120
McCauley, E. L.	SR	401-90
McCauley, Henry	TST	401-36
McCauley, Henry	FB	401-161
McCauley, Leake	SR	401-90
McCauley, Matthew	TVG	401-204
McCauley, Sloane	SR	401-90
McCauley, W. J.	RR	401-59
McCauley, William J.	FB	401-161
McCauly, Barny	NAV	401-21
McCaw, William C.	USV	401-241
McCawley, Hilliard F.	USV	401-241
McCawley, John	NAV	401-21
McClain, Alva D.	SR	401-90
McClain, G. V.	SR	401-90
McClain, J. H.	SR	401-90
McClain, J. P.	FB	401-161
McClain, John M.	TVG	401-204
McClain, L. D.	SR	401-90
McClain, S. Y.	RRR	401-120
McClanahan, M. R.	SR	401-90
McClanahan, William E.	USV	401-241
McClarty, Hugh G.	RRR	401-120
McClaskey, James B.	ARM	401-7

Index to Texas Adjutant General Service Records—All Service Branches

Name	Branch	Record
McClellan, C. E.	TVG	401-204
McClellan, Clarence L.	USV	401-241
McClellan, James D.	RR	401-59
McClellan, W. J.	TVG	401-204
McClellan, W. J.	USV	401-241
McClelland, Charles E.	TVG	401-204
McClelland, Charles E.	USV	401-241
McClelland, H. A.	FB	401-161
McClenahan, John	ARM	401-7
McClendon, George Lee	USV	401-241
McClendon, James W.	USV	401-241
McClendon, Robert L.	SP	401-46
McClintock, Robert F.	USV	401-241
McClosky, James	FF	401-136
McClosky, James	FB	401-161
McCloy, J. B.	SR	401-90
McCloy, J. F.	TVG	401-204
McClung, J. E.	TVG	401-204
McClung, Oscar B.	USV	401-241
McClure, C. P.	TVG	401-204
McClure, Charles P.	USV	401-241
McClure, Cornelius E.	USV	401-241
McClure, E. B.	RRR	401-120
McClure, E. B.	SR	401-90
McClure, Elmer B.	RR	401-59
McClure, G. Fred	USV	401-241
McClure, G. H.	TVG	401-204
McClure, J. F.	RRR	401-120
McClure, R. C.	FB	401-161
McClure, R. Q.	TVG	401-204
McClure, Robert B.	FB	401-161
McClyman, John B.	ARM	401-7
McCollough, B. F.	TVG	401-204
McCollough, W. H.	TVG	401-204
McCollum, C. J.	SR	401-90
McCollum, J. W.	FB	401-161
McCollum, J. W.	FB	401-161
McCollum, J. W.	TVG	401-204
McCollum, John W.	USV	401-241
McCollum, Robert M.	USV	401-241
McComb, George	RR	401-59
McComb, William Robert	TVG	401-204
McCombs, D. I.	RR	401-59
McCombs, D. I.	SR	401-90
McCombs, David J.	RR	401-59
McCommas, C. C.	FB	401-161
McCommas, Mike	FB	401-161
McConnell, A.	FF	401-136
McConnell, C. D.	SR	401-90
McConnell, George	TVG	401-204
McConnell, Isaac R.	USV	401-241
McConnell, J. S.	FB	401-161
McConnell, J. V.	SR	401-90
McConnell, Joe F.	USV	401-241
McConnell, W. C.	TVG	401-204
McConnell, W. H.	TVG	401-204
McConnell, W. P.	RR	401-59
McConnell, W. P.	RRR	401-120
McConville, Dennis	ARM	401-7
McCord, A. H.	USV	401-241
McCord, James E.	RR	401-59
McCord, John E.	USV	401-241
McCord, Leon C.	USV	401-241
McCord, R. C.	USV	401-241
McCord, R. P.	USV	401-241
McCord, W. M.	MM	401-32
McCord, William	NAV	401-21
McCord, William	MM	401-32
McCord, William Blount	RRR	401-120
McCormack, Ernest	SR	401-90
McCormack, Thomas Jefferson	RRR	401-120
McCormick, C. R.	SR	401-90
McCormick, Charles H.	USV	401-241
McCormick, George	USV	401-241
McCormick, Harry	SR	401-90
McCormick, J.	TVG	401-204
McCormick, J. W.	RR	401-59
McCormick, J. W.	SR	401-90
McCormick, James	NAV	401-21
McCormick, James	ARM	401-7
McCormick, John	NAV	401-21
McCormick, John M.	RR	401-59
McCormick, John M.	USV	401-241
McCormick, Robert	ARM	401-7
McCormick, T. B.	TVG	401-204
McCormick, W. T.	USV	401-241
McCowen, Adrian	RR	401-59
McCowen, Jesse	USV	401-241
McCown, A. C.	TVG	401-204
McCown, J. H.	TVG	401-204
McCown, L. H.	TVG	401-204
McCoy, A. A.	TVG	401-204
McCoy, Clay	SR	401-90
McCoy, Hugh	TST	401-36
McCoy, J. H.	RRR	401-120
McCoy, James E.	RR	401-59
McCoy, James E.	FB	401-161
McCoy, John	USV	401-241
McCoy, John C.	TST	401-36
McCoy, S. M.	RR	401-59
McCoy, S. M.	RRR	401-120
McCoy, T. N.	FB	401-161
McCoy, William H.	USV	401-241
McCrabb, W. J.	FB	401-161
McCracken, Ewing N.	FB	401-161
McCracken, J.	TST	401-36
McCracken, John W.	FB	401-161
McCracken, S. M.	SR	401-90
McCracken, William Ross	SR	401-90
McCraney, John	ARM	401-7
McCrary, Oliver	TVG	401-204
McCraw, J. F.	USV	401-241

Index to Texas Adjutant General Service Records—All Service Branches

Name	Branch	Record
McCray, William F.	USV	401-241
McCreary, H. S.	USV	401-241
McCrey, Charles	FB	401-161
McCrocklin, John	MV	401-30
McCuaig, Finley Edgar	RRR	401-120
McCue, John	USV	401-241
McCuen, James	TVG	401-204
McCuistion, B. L.	CSA	401-39
McCuistion, George D.	USV	401-241
McCuiston, George D.	TVG	401-204
McCuiston, T. H.	FB	401-161
McCulloch, Ben E.	CSA	401-39
McCulloch, Charley Bruce	SR	401-90
McCulloch, Davis	TVG	401-204
McCulloch, Henry E.	FB	401-162
McCulloch, Stephen	TVG	401-204
McCulloch, William H.	SR	401-90
McCullough, Clarence	SR	401-90
McCullough, Earl D.	SR	401-90
McCullough, George H.	SR	401-90
McCullough, Jesse K.	USV	401-241
McCullough, Ned	SP	401-46
McCullum, Joseph	ARM	401-7
McCully, William Jethro	RRR	401-121
McCune, W. W.	TVG	401-204
McCurdy, Frank B.	SR	401-90
McCurley, H. W.	SR	401-90
McCutchan, Marion S.	USV	401-241
McCutcheon, Gordon A.	USV	401-241
McCutcheon, James W.	USV	401-241
McCutcheon, W. W.	SR	401-90
McDade, C. N.	FB	401-162
McDade, John W.	USV	401-241
McDaniel, B. N.	SR	401-90
McDaniel, Claude	RRR	401-121
McDaniel, Elishy	MV	401-30
McDaniel, Frank	TVG	401-204
McDaniel, Fred L.	RR	401-59
McDaniel, John T.	USV	401-241
McDaniel, Lester C.	RRR	401-121
McDaniel, Thomas	MM	401-32
McDaniel, U. C.	SR	401-90
McDaniel, W. A.	FB	401-162
McDaniel, William L.	USV	401-241
McDavid, J. E.	CSA	401-39
McDermett, Joe	TVG	401-204
McDermit, Donal	FF	401-136
McDermott, John	TVG	401-204
McDermott, M.	TVG	401-204
McDermott, Michael	USV	401-241
McDevitt, Jack P.	SR	401-90
McDonald, A. W.	ARM	401-7
McDonald, Alexander	NAV	401-21
McDonald, Alexander	RR	401-59
McDonald, Alexander	ARM	401-7
McDonald, Arthur	SP	401-46
McDonald, Brown	USV	401-241
McDonald, C. F.	TVG	401-204
McDonald, C. J.	TVG	401-204
McDonald, C. M.	RRR	401-121
McDonald, Cash	FB	401-162
McDonald, Earl S.	SR	401-90
McDonald, Elisha	MV	401-30
McDonald, F. S.	SR	401-90
McDonald, Frank R.	SR	401-90
McDonald, G. E.	USV	401-241
McDonald, G. N.	RR	401-59
McDonald, G. N.	SR	401-91
McDonald, George	SR	401-91
McDonald, George B.	USV	401-241
McDonald, George W.	USV	401-241
McDonald, H. A.	TVG	401-204
McDonald, H. M.	SR	401-91
McDonald, Hugh F.	USV	401-241
McDonald, J. B.	FB	401-162
McDonald, James	FB	401-162
McDonald, James G.	TST	401-36
McDonald, John	NAV	401-21
McDonald, John C.	ARM	401-7
McDonald, John L.	USV	401-241
McDonald, John Thomas	SR	401-91
McDonald, Malory	RRR	401-121
McDonald, Marcus L.	TVG	401-204
McDonald, Marcus L.	USV	401-241
McDonald, Qulus L.	USV	401-241
McDonald, R. L.	USV	401-241
McDonald, Robert L.	RRR	401-121
McDonald, Robert S.	SR	401-91
McDonald, Stephen C.	USV	401-241
McDonald, Thomas P.	USV	401-241
McDonald, W. G.	SR	401-91
McDonald, W. H.	SR	401-91
McDonald, Will H.	USV	401-241
McDonald, William	CSA	401-39
McDonald, William	CSA	401-39
McDonald, William D.	SR	401-91
McDonald, William J.	FB	401-162
McDonald, Zenus R.	USV	401-241
McDonell, A. A.	FB	401-162
McDonnell, Chris	FF	401-136
McDonogh, Thomas	NAV	401-21
McDonough, Thomas	ARM	401-7
McDowell, B. J.	SR	401-91
McDowell, C. L.	RR	401-59
McDowell, H. B.	RRR	401-121
McDowell, H. H.	SR	401-91
McDowell, H. H.	LR	401-130
McDowell, J. D.	RRR	401-121
McDowell, James B.	USV	401-241
McDowell, R. W.	RRR	401-121
McDowell, T. B.	TVG	401-204
McDowell, V. R.	SR	401-91

Index to Texas Adjutant General Service Records—All Service Branches

Name	Branch	Record
McDowell, W. B.	USV	401-241
McDuffie, Dan L.	RR	401-59
McDuffie, Dan L.	RRR	401-121
McDurmitt, William	ARM	401-7
McEachern, John N.	MV	401-30
McEachin, J. S.	TVG	401-204
McElhannon, W. D.	SR	401-91
McElrath, Samuel J.	MV	401-30
McElree, R. R.	RRR	401-121
McElroy, Bill	SR	401-91
McElroy, Edward L.	USV	401-241
McElroy, J. L.	FB	401-162
McElroy, J. W.	RRR	401-121
McElroy, Jno. L.	LR	401-130
McElroy, Joe W.	SR	401-91
McElroy, John L.	SR	401-91
McElroy, John T.	TVG	401-204
McElroy, S. G.	FB	401-162
McElroy, Stephen G.	FB	401-162
McElroy, W. A.	SR	401-91
McElroy, Will A.	SR	401-91
McElvaney, A. W.	FB	401-162
McElvaney, W. Buell	TVG	401-204
McElvy, George	TVG	401-204
McFadden, John P.	RR	401-59
McFarlan, William W.	NAV	401-21
McFarland, David W.	RR	401-59
McFarland, Earl	TVG	401-204
McFarland, G. E.	RR	401-59
McFarland, J. B.	FB	401-162
McFarland, L.	TVG	401-204
McFarland, M. M.	FB	401-162
McFarland, Mancus H.	USV	401-241
McFarland, Marcus H.	TVG	401-204
McFarland, S. E.	SP	401-46
McFarland, S. J.	TVG	401-204
McFarland, T. C.	SR	401-91
McFarland, V. E.	SR	401-91
McFarland, William	RR	401-59
McFarland, William	FB	401-162
McFarland, William T.	RR	401-59
McFarlane, A. D.	SR	401-91
McFarlane, Linn R.	USV	401-241
McFarlane, R. A.	TVG	401-204
McFarlane, S. J.	RR	401-59
McFarlin, J. L.	SR	401-91
McFarlin, J. L.	LR	401-130
McFarling, R. O.	SR	401-91
McGaffey, A. B.	RR	401-59
McGaffey, Alfred B.	USV	401-241
McGahhey, A. C.	SR	401-91
McGar, Paul	FB	401-162
McGarrah, George	USV	401-241
McGarrah, J. A.	FB	401-162
McGarrah, S. G.	FB	401-162
McGarrah, Seburn G. S.	MV	401-30
McGarvin, John	ARM	401-7
McGary, E. A.	USV	401-241
McGary, Marion	USV	401-241
McGaugher, Charles S.	TVG	401-204
McGaughey, George	NAV	401-21
McGee, Charles A.	USV	401-241
McGee, E. S.	RR	401-59
McGee, J. L.	SR	401-91
McGee, James	NAV	401-21
McGee, James	FF	401-136
McGee, Jinks	SR	401-91
McGee, John R.	FF	401-136
McGee, Laurence E.	SR	401-91
McGee, Mark	SR	401-91
McGee, O. L.	SR	401-91
McGee, Orville L.	RRR	401-121
McGee, Pat	RR	401-59
McGee, Pat	SR	401-91
McGee, Phil	SR	401-91
McGee, R. A.	TVG	401-204
McGee, S. W.	SP	401-46
McGee, W. A.	SR	401-91
McGehee, John O.	TST	401-36
McGhee, H. W.	FB	401-162
McGibbony, Charles P.	TVG	401-204
McGibbony, G. D.	TVG	401-204
McGibbony, W. M.	TVG	401-204
McGill, J.	FF	401-136
McGill, O.	SR	401-91
McGill, R.	USV	401-241
McGill, William	ARM	401-7
McGinnis, Daniel R.	USV	401-241
McGinnis, Jesse C.	USV	401-241
McGinnis, John W.	USV	401-241
McGinnis, Rollin J.	SR	401-91
McGinty, John C.	NAV	401-21
McGlincey, M. A.	TVG	401-204
McGloin, George D.	SR	401-91
McGoffin, Thomas	TST	401-36
McGonagill, E. G.	SR	401-91
McGonnegle, Peter	ARM	401-7
McGough, Clarence	TVG	401-204
McGough, W. C.	TST	401-36
McGovern, Matthew	ARM	401-7
McGovern, Thomas N.	FB	401-162
McGowan, James F.	NAV	401-21
McGown, A. H.	SP	401-46
McGown, G. W.	SP	401-46
McGown, James	ARM	401-7
McGown, W. T.	FB	401-162
McGrady, S. J.	TST	401-36
McGrand, Edward	FF	401-136
McGrath, William M.	USV	401-241
McGree, William M.	USV	401-241
McGregor, Ace	TVG	401-204
McGregor, Alex	NAV	401-21

Index to Texas Adjutant General Service Records—All Service Branches

Name	Branch	Record
McGregor, J. D.	RR	401-59
McGregor, J. D.	SR	401-91
McGregor, Malcom	TVG	401-204
McGrew, Charles	FB	401-162
McGrew, F. J.	FB	401-162
McGrew, Robert	TVG	401-204
McGuffin, John H.	TVG	401-204
McGuin, M. V.	FB	401-162
McGuinn, F. P.	FB	401-162
McGuire, James	SP	401-46
McHanks, Horatio	ARM	401-7
McHenry, A.	FB	401-162
McHenry, Jerry	FB	401-162
McHorse, J. W.	ARM	401-7
McIlhany, M. P.	USV	401-241
McIlhenny, Sam A.	USV	401-241
McIlhenny, Sam T.	USV	401-241
McIlroy, John	ARM	401-7
McIlroy, S. D.	SR	401-91
McIlvoy, Charles	MV	401-30
McInhenny, S. M.	TVG	401-204
McInnes, J. W.	FB	401-162
McInnis, Duncan	USV	401-241
McInnis, W. B.	RRR	401-121
McInnis, W. B.	SR	401-91
McIntire, Edgar O.	TVG	401-204
McIntire, James	FB	401-162
McIntosh, Alexander	NAV	401-21
McIntosh, Pike	SR	401-91
McIntosh, Pike	LR	401-130
McIntosh, William J.	USV	401-241
McInturf, William W.	ARM	401-7
McIntyre, George H.	SR	401-91
McIntyre, John	FB	401-162
McIntyre, William A.	USV	401-241
McIver, Alexander W.	TST	401-36
McIver, F. A.	FB	401-162
McIver, S. Woody	RRR	401-121
McKaughan, L. D.	SR	401-91
McKay, A. S.	FB	401-162
McKay, D. D.	USV	401-241
McKay, Daniel	ARM	401-7
McKay, Daniel Albert	RRR	401-121
McKay, Ed	USV	401-241
McKay, Francis	ARM	401-7
McKay, J. O.	SR	401-91
McKay, Jack N.	RRR	401-121
McKay, John J., Jr.	SR	401-91
McKay, Leslie	SR	401-91
McKay, W. T.	RR	401-59
McKay, W. T.	SR	401-91
McKay, William	RR	401-59
McKean, John	NAV	401-21
McKean, Neal	ARM	401-7
McKee, B.	FF	401-136
McKee, Finley	USV	401-241
McKee, Henry	USV	401-241
McKee, James E.	SR	401-91
McKee, John A.	USV	401-241
McKee, R. S.	SR	401-91
McKee, R. W.	RR	401-59
McKeller, J. B.	TVG	401-204
McKelvy, George R.	SP	401-46
McKelvy, Jesse	MV	401-30
McKelvy, Monroe	USV	401-241
McKen, Joseph	SP	401-46
McKenna, Charles	NAV	401-21
McKenna, James	FF	401-136
McKenna, Thomas	ARM	401-8
McKenzie, A.	FB	401-162
McKenzie, G. D.	RRR	401-121
McKenzie, G. W.	MV	401-30
McKenzie, George W.	FB	401-162
McKenzie, James H.	USV	401-241
McKenzie, Sam	RR	401-59
McKenzie, W. C.	SR	401-91
McKeown, J. M.	FB	401-162
McKew, Joseph	FF	401-136
McKidrict, Joe	FB	401-162
McKim, Horrell	RRR	401-121
McKim, Joe	RRR	401-121
McKinely, P. M.	LR	401-130
McKinley, B. K.	TVG	401-204
McKinley, John	USV	401-241
McKinley, William	ARM	401-8
McKinney, Alex	FB	401-162
McKinney, Allen L.	SR	401-91
McKinney, C. S.	SR	401-91
McKinney, Charles B.	FB	401-162
McKinney, Henry	FB	401-162
McKinney, James P.	TST	401-36
McKinney, John A.	FF	401-136
McKinney, John P.	USV	401-241
McKinney, T. F.	FB	401-162
McKinney, T. G.	TST	401-36
McKinney, T. J.	MV	401-30
McKinney, Thomas Jefferson	RRR	401-121
McKinney, Verna	USV	401-241
McKinney, W. W.	FB	401-162
McKinney, William	TVG	401-204
McKinnon, Herbert D.	USV	401-241
McKinzie, A. M.	SR	401-91
McKithan, W. W.	RRR	401-121
McKnight, A. D.	RR	401-59
McKnight, C. A.	TVG	401-204
McKnight, Charles E.	TVG	401-204
McKnight, Charles E.	USV	401-241
McKnight, H.	FB	401-162
McKnight, James W.	SP	401-46
McKnight, W. M.	FF	401-136
McKue, John	ARM	401-8
McLain, R. L.	TVG	401-204

Index to Texas Adjutant General Service Records—All Service Branches

Name	Branch	Record
McLamor, Julian T.	USV	401-241
McLanahan, W. C.	USV	401-241
McLane, David	SR	401-91
McLane, Ray	USV	401-241
McLaughlin, A. D.	SR	401-91
McLaughlin, C. W.	FB	401-162
McLaughlin, Charles	ARM	401-8
McLaughlin, Guy	USV	401-241
McLaughlin, James	ARM	401-8
McLaughlin, James	ARM	401-8
McLaughlin, John	ARM	401-8
McLaughlin, W. P.	SR	401-91
McLaughlin, Wharton B.	TVG	401-204
McLaury, C. A.	SR	401-91
McLean, C. L.	TVG	401-204
McLean, J. M.	FB	401-162
McLean, J. P.	FB	401-162
McLearen, W. T.	FB	401-162
McLeary, Steven A.	ARM	401-8
McLemore, D. E.	SR	401-91
McLemore, J. B.	USV	401-241
McLemore, Victor	TVG	401-204
McLendon, Dennis J.	USV	401-241
McLendon, Martin M.	USV	401-241
McLendon, Ralph	SR	401-91
McLeod, A. E.	SR	401-91
McLeod, D. Herbert	USV	401-241
McLeod, Gilbert	NAV	401-21
McLeod, John	NAV	401-21
McLeod, John W.	USV	401-241
McLeod, Wimberly	SR	401-91
McLeoud, J. B.	USV	401-241
McLeroy, Francis	NAV	401-21
McLeroy, H. H.	TVG	401-204
McLeroy, Richard Ransom	TVG	401-204
McLow, H. L.	SR	401-91
McMahan, Charles B.	USV	401-241
McMahan, F. D.	FB	401-162
McMahan, F. M.	FB	401-162
McMahan, Martin C.	USV	401-241
McMahan, Robert H. F.	TVG	401-204
McMahan, Will	TVG	401-204
McMahan, William H.	USV	401-241
McMahon, Buster	USV	401-241
McMahon, J. D.	USV	401-241
McMahon, M. H.	SR	401-91
McManigle, Charles	USV	401-241
McManus, William	USV	401-241
McMardin, James C.	RR	401-59
McMaster, R. J.	RRR	401-121
McMaster, S. W.	FB	401-162
McMaster, Thomas Robert	MV	401-30
McMeans, Gee	RR	401-59
McMeans, George	RR	401-59
McMeans, T. B.	RR	401-59
McMillan, Archibald	ARM	401-8
McMillan, Arthur	USV	401-241
McMillan, Arthur	USV	401-241
McMillan, C. R.	FB	401-162
McMillan, D.	CSA	401-39
McMillan, Francis	NAV	401-21
McMillan, J. A.	SR	401-91
McMillan, J. A.	LR	401-130
McMillan, J. B.	TVG	401-204
McMillan, J. R.	SR	401-91
McMillan, John R.	RR	401-59
McMillan, Sam J.	SR	401-91
McMillan, Sam J.	LR	401-130
McMillan, T. I.	SR	401-91
McMillan, William R.	USV	401-241
McMillin, N. D.	SR	401-91
McMillin, W. E.	SR	401-91
McMillon, J. R.	SR	401-91
McMindes, Jacob	ARM	401-8
McMordie, Charles E.	SR	401-91
McMordie, E. B.	RR	401-59
McMordie, E. B.	RRR	401-121
McMordie, E. B.	SR	401-91
McMullen, C. E.	SR	401-91
McMullen, Ira G.	USV	401-241
McMullen, James L.	USV	401-241
McMullen, Willie R.	SR	401-91
McMunn, John	TST	401-36
McMurray, Ed	FB	401-162
McMurray, J. M.	FB	401-162
McMurray, J. W.	TVG	401-204
McMurray, Ralph	RRR	401-121
McMurray, Ralph	SR	401-91
McMurray, W. L.	RRR	401-121
McMurray, Will	SR	401-91
McMurrey, W. (Bill)"	RR	401-59
McMurrey, Willie	SR	401-91
McMurry, H. E.	FB	401-162
McMurry, J. T.	MM	401-32
McMurry, John	FB	401-162
McMurry, S. A.	FB	401-162
McMurry, Y. D.	FB	401-162
McMurtry, Horace C.	TVG	401-204
McMurtry, R. L.	SR	401-91
McNabb, Jess	SR	401-91
McNabb, Rufus O.	TVG	401-204
McNabb, W. E.	USV	401-242
McNairy, John F.	MV	401-30
McNairy, Robert D.	MV	401-30
McNally, John	FB	401-162
McNamar, Robert	FB	401-162
McNamara, Dan	FB	401-162
McNamara, Mike	SR	401-91
McNamee, Patrick, Rev.	SR	401-91
McNatt, Wiley	SR	401-91
McNeal, William H.	USV	401-242
McNeel, James S.	FB	401-162

Index to Texas Adjutant General Service Records—All Service Branches

Name	Branch	Page
McNeely, Lee R.	TVG	401-204
McNees, G. S.	SR	401-91
McNeese, Hugh	SR	401-91
McNeil, Charles	USV	401-242
McNeil, James T.	USV	401-242
McNeil, Neil	ARM	401-8
McNeill, C. E.	TVG	401-204
McNeill, M. W.	FB	401-162
McNeill, Marvil E.	TST	401-36
McNeill, Thomas P.	TST	401-36
McNeill, W. D.	RRR	401-121
McNeill, W. D.	FB	401-162
McNelly, Chauncy	FB	401-162
McNelly, John	FB	401-162
McNelly, L. H.	MV	401-30
McNelly, L. H.	SP	401-46
McNew, Charles W.	TVG	401-204
McNulty, Hugh	ARM	401-8
McNutt, R. C.	FB	401-162
McNutty, Michel	NAV	401-21
McPatterson, B.	FB	401-163
McPearson, Charles F.	USV	401-242
McPearson, William A.	USV	401-242
McPhail, Baty R.	USV	401-242
McPhail, Charles W.	SR	401-91
McPhail, John W.	USV	401-242
McPhail, Virgil	SR	401-91
McPhaill, George	FF	401-136
McPhaill, H. A.	CSA	401-39
McPhee, Archibald	NAV	401-21
McPherson, A. F.	USV	401-242
McPherson, Charles	USV	401-242
McPherson, Charles A.	USV	401-242
McPherson, W. S.	FB	401-163
McPherson, William	TVG	401-204
McQuary, R. D.	RRR	401-121
McQueen, J. W.	FB	401-163
McQueen, John C.	RR	401-59
McQuint, Ed	TVG	401-204
McRae, J. J.	SR	401-91
McRae, John S.	USV	401-242
McRae, Walter C.	USV	401-242
McRaynolds, Virg	TVG	401-204
McRee, Felix	USV	401-242
McRee, John L.	TVG	401-204
McReynolds, A. D.	TVG	401-204
McReynolds, Bill	SR	401-91
McReynolds, G. W.	RR	401-59
McRobbie, James	NAV	401-21
McShane, John	ARM	401-8
McSween, Paul Everett	SR	401-91
McTeer, Gilbert S.	TVG	401-204
McVay, Dave	SR	401-91
McVay, Horace C.	SR	401-91
McVey, Williaim	USV	401-242
McWain, D. G.	TVG	401-204
McWhirk, Charles A.	USV	401-242
McWhirter, S. R.	SR	401-92
McWhirter, Wade H.	USV	401-242
McWhirter, Willis J. B.	USV	401-242
McWhorter, John S.	FB	401-163
McWilliams, Charles S.	USV	401-242
McWilliams, Hunter	RRR	401-121
McWilliams, R. E.	RR	401-59
McWilliams, R. E.	SR	401-92
McWilliams, Walter F.	TVG	401-204
McWilliams, William T.	TVG	401-204
Mead, D. E.	TVG	401-205
Mead, David E.	USV	401-242
Mead, E. K.	SR	401-92
Mead, T. H.	FB	401-164
Mead, William	ARM	401-8
Mead, William Henry	SR	401-92
Mead, Willis	TVG	401-205
Meader, W. H.	FB	401-164
Meador, Frank P.	USV	401-242
Meador, N. E.	SR	401-92
Meador, W. F.	FB	401-164
Meadows, F.	TVG	401-205
Meadows, W. D.	SR	401-92
Means, C. W.	SR	401-92
Means, Lafayette M.	RR	401-60
Mears, Alex	TVG	401-205
Mears, C. M.	TVG	401-205
Mebley, James	NAV	401-21
Mechler, R. A.	USV	401-242
Medford, Craig	SR	401-92
Medina, Mateo	FF	401-137
Medlen, A. W.	TVG	401-205
Medlen, A. W.	USV	401-242
Medlenka, Leonard W.	USV	401-242
Medley, Melchesedeck D.	CSA	401-40
Medlock, Isiah	SP	401-47
Meek, J. S.	FB	401-164
Meek, J. W.	RRR	401-121
Meek, Lassie S.	USV	401-242
Meek, Malcolm M.	SR	401-92
Meek, W. E.	SR	401-92
Meeks, James L.	TVG	401-205
Meeks, S. M. "Charles"	RR	401-60
Meeks, Thomas Houston	SR	401-92
Meeks, V. S.	FB	401-164
Meffley, C. F.	SR	401-92
Megarity, C. B.	TVG	401-205
Megee, Robert E.	SR	401-92
Mehl, George P.	TVG	401-205
Meindorff, John H.	USV	401-242
Meinke, E. H.	SR	401-92
Meinke, H. J.	SR	401-92
Meissner, Max	SR	401-92
Meitzen, Otto	TVG	401-205
Mej, Francisco	FF	401-137

Index to Texas Adjutant General Service Records—All Service Branches

Name	Branch	Record
Mejia, Pablo	SP	401-47
Mekuhn, John	ARM	401-8
Melcher, Willie	TVG	401-205
Meldan, Henry F.	USV	401-242
Melder, F. E.	SR	401-92
Mellard, F. C.	SR	401-92
Mellor, Alfred	USV	401-242
Mellus, James	NAV	401-21
Melms, Paul R.	USV	401-242
Melone, Michel	NAV	401-21
Melong, George	NAV	401-21
Melson, Mack	USV	401-242
Melson, R. L.	TVG	401-205
Melton, Arthur M.	USV	401-242
Melton, George W.	SR	401-92
Melton, George W.	LR	401-130
Melton, H. C.	FB	401-164
Melton, H. M.	RRR	401-121
Melton, Harry M.	RRR	401-121
Melton, James T.	TVG	401-205
Melton, Ollie	TVG	401-205
Melton, Robert Lee	RRR	401-121
Melton, Thomas Evert	CSA	401-40
Melton, W. S.	RR	401-60
Melton, W. S.	SR	401-92
Melton, William T.	FB	401-164
Melugin, J. H.	TVG	401-205
Melven, H. S.	TVG	401-205
Melville, A.	SP	401-47
Melvin, John F.	ARM	401-8
Melvin, Thomas	FB	401-164
Mendeke, William F.	USV	401-242
Mendel, C. B.	TVG	401-205
Menefee, T. B.	FB	401-164
Menefee, T. B.	USV	401-242
Menly, A. H.	FB	401-164
Mensir, Henry	NAV	401-21
Mentzel, Robert	RRR	401-121
Menville, Louis William	TVG	401-205
Menzies, Charles G.	USV	401-242
Menzies, Russell	SR	401-92
Menzies, Thomas	ARM	401-8
Mercer, G. H.	SR	401-92
Mercer, Guy Raymond	RRR	401-121
Mercer, J. B.	RR	401-60
Mercer, W. J.	SR	401-92
Mercer, William H.	MM	401-32
Merchant, James R.	USV	401-242
Merchant, R. E.	SR	401-92
Meredith, Carlton	SR	401-92
Meredith, D. F.	FB	401-164
Meredith, Samuel W.	USV	401-242
Meredith, W. B.	USV	401-242
Mergenthaler, Charles S.	USV	401-243
Meriwether, George B.	USV	401-243
Meroney, Albert	USV	401-243
Merrem, Edgar J.	LR	401-130
Merrem, Edgar J.	SR	401-92
Merrick, George W.	RR	401-60
Merrick, J. A.	SR	401-92
Merrick, M. V. B.	MV	401-30
Merrick, Samuel	NAV	401-21
Merrill, Benjamin H.	RR	401-60
Merrill, H. M.	FB	401-164
Merrill, Henry W.	FB	401-164
Merrill, Hiram G.	NAV	401-21
Merrill, W. T.	SR	401-92
Merrill, W. T.	LR	401-130
Merrill, Wiley Hendrix	SR	401-92
Merriman, Byron C.	TVG	401-205
Merritt, A. J.	FB	401-164
Merritt, A. W.	FB	401-164
Merritt, Alexander	FF	401-137
Merritt, Henry J.	USV	401-243
Merritt, Josh	TVG	401-205
Merritt, Luther H.	USV	401-243
Mersfelder, Nicholas	FB	401-164
Mertz, George W.	USV	401-243
Mesley, John	NAV	401-21
Messer, Tom D.	SR	401-92
Messer, William	ARM	401-8
Messinger, Joe F.	USV	401-243
Metcalf, G. M.	RRR	401-121
Metcalf, Herbert L.	USV	401-243
Metcalf, J. A.	SR	401-92
Metcalf, Walter E.	TVG	401-205
Metcalfe, Earl W.	TVG	401-205
Metcalfe, J. S.	USV	401-243
Methvin, E. P.	FB	401-164
Methvin, Henry	USV	401-243
Metz, O. F.	SR	401-92
Metz, R. H., Jr.	SR	401-92
Metzger, Louis	USV	401-243
Meyer, Andrew	SR	401-92
Meyer, E. L.	SR	401-92
Meyer, Edward	FF	401-137
Meyer, Emil	TVG	401-205
Meyer, George D.	USV	401-243
Meyer, Heinrich	NAV	401-21
Meyer, Howard C.	SR	401-92
Meyer, K. R.	SR	401-92
Meyer, O. H.	SR	401-92
Meyer, Theo. P., Jr.	SR	401-92
Meyer, Thos. Henry Bernard	TVG	401-205
Meyer, Victor	SR	401-92
Meyers, Alexander	TVG	401-205
Meyers, John E.	USV	401-243
Meyers, John G.	USV	401-243
Meyers, Robert	USV	401-243
Mezell, D. C.	RRR	401-121
Michael, Jacob	FF	401-137
Michan, J.	FB	401-164

Index to Texas Adjutant General Service Records—All Service Branches

Name	Branch	Record
Michel, E. L.	TVG	401-205
Michel, Earnest L.	USV	401-243
Michel, John	ARM	401-8
Michel, Joseph	USV	401-243
Michel, Lewis	ARM	401-8
Michels, H. E.	TVG	401-205
Michon, J.	FB	401-164
Mico, Theodore	FF	401-137
Middlebrook, R. M.	USV	401-243
Middleton, C. J.	RRR	401-121
Middleton, C. M.	FB	401-164
Middleton, C. P.	SR	401-92
Middleton, Charles O.	TVG	401-205
Middleton, Charles P.	RR	401-60
Middleton, Charles P.	RR	401-60
Middleton, J. T.	TVG	401-205
Middleton, Peyton	NAV	401-21
Middleton, Robert	NAV	401-21
Midkiff, James	FB	401-164
Midkiff, Morris	SR	401-92
Midkiff, Will M.	TVG	401-205
Miers, Robert N.	USV	401-243
Miers, T. M.	TVG	401-205
Migurski, Gus	USV	401-243
Mikel, Louis	NAV	401-21
Mikesell, O.	TVG	401-205
Milam, B. R.	MM	401-32
Milam, Ben R.	RRR	401-121
Milam, J. W.	RR	401-60
Milam, J. W.	RR	401-60
Milam, Robert L.	USV	401-243
Milam, Tom L.	TVG	401-205
Milam, Will	TVG	401-205
Milchers, P. F.	TVG	401-205
Mileham, Walter E.	USV	401-243
Miler, Charles	FB	401-164
Miles, Bassett	TVG	401-205
Miles, Bassett R.	SR	401-92
Miles, C. H. W.	TVG	401-205
Miles, Harrison	TVG	401-205
Miles, J. S.	TVG	401-205
Miles, John H.	ARM	401-8
Miles, Jonathan S.	FB	401-164
Miles, W. A.	RR	401-60
Miles, W. A.	TVG	401-205
Miles, W. T.	SR	401-92
Miles, William T.	RR	401-60
Milhoan, Miles	SR	401-92
Milhoan, Miles	LR	401-130
Millard, George M.	RR	401-60
Millard, Henry	TVG	401-205
Miller, A. H.	TVG	401-205
Miller, A. H.	TVG	401-205
Miller, A. N.	SR	401-92
Miller, A. N.	LR	401-130
Miller, Abner T.	FB	401-164
Miller, Alex	RRR	401-121
Miller, Andrew	NAV	401-21
Miller, Andrew	TVG	401-205
Miller, Antonio	NAV	401-21
Miller, Arch	RRR	401-121
Miller, Arnold E.	USV	401-243
Miller, Barry	SR	401-92
Miller, Burnolia E.	USV	401-243
Miller, C. B.	FF	401-137
Miller, C. E.	RRR	401-121
Miller, C. E.	SR	401-92
Miller, C. H.	USV	401-243
Miller, C. L.	TVG	401-205
Miller, C. M.	SR	401-92
Miller, C. P.	USV	401-243
Miller, C. R.	TVG	401-205
Miller, Charles	NAV	401-21
Miller, Charles E.	RR	401-60
Miller, Charles E.	RRR	401-121
Miller, Charles Edward	SR	401-92
Miller, Charles H.	ARM	401-8
Miller, Charles R.	SR	401-92
Miller, Chauncey	SP	401-47
Miller, Clarence	SR	401-92
Miller, Claude G.	TVG	401-205
Miller, D. A.	RR	401-60
Miller, David	ARM	401-8
Miller, David S.	USV	401-243
Miller, E. B.	RRR	401-121
Miller, E. W.	SR	401-92
Miller, E. W.	USV	401-243
Miller, Ernest D.	TVG	401-205
Miller, Ernest D.	USV	401-243
Miller, F. H.	FB	401-164
Miller, Fred	FF	401-137
Miller, Frederick	FF	401-137
Miller, G. B.	TVG	401-205
Miller, G. D.	FB	401-164
Miller, George	NAV	401-21
Miller, George	ARM	401-8
Miller, George C.	SR	401-92
Miller, George E.	RR	401-60
Miller, George T.	USV	401-243
Miller, George W.	ARM	401-8
Miller, Harry	RRR	401-121
Miller, Harry W.	ARM	401-8
Miller, Henry	TVG	401-205
Miller, Henry	TVG	401-205
Miller, Hugh	RRR	401-121
Miller, Hugh	SR	401-92
Miller, Hugh B.	SR	401-92
Miller, I. L.	SR	401-92
Miller, J. A.	SR	401-92
Miller, J. B.	FB	401-164
Miller, J. C.	TVG	401-205
Miller, J. D.	FF	401-137

Index to Texas Adjutant General Service Records—All Service Branches

Name	Branch	Record
Miller, J. J.	RRR	401-121
Miller, J. P.	FB	401-164
Miller, J. T.	FB	401-164
Miller, J. W.	FB	401-164
Miller, Jackson H.	USV	401-243
Miller, James	NAV	401-21
Miller, James	ARM	401-8
Miller, James M.	USV	401-243
Miller, James R.	USV	401-243
Miller, James T.	TVG	401-205
Miller, Jefferson C.	USV	401-243
Miller, Joe	TVG	401-205
Miller, Joe Henry	RRR	401-121
Miller, John	NAV	401-21
Miller, John	ARM	401-8
Miller, John	TVG	401-205
Miller, John	USV	401-243
Miller, John A.	RR	401-60
Miller, John D.	USV	401-243
Miller, John J.	RR	401-60
Miller, Joseph B.	RR	401-60
Miller, Joseph H.	RR	401-60
Miller, Lee	USV	401-243
Miller, Lee B.	USV	401-243
Miller, Malcolm M.	USV	401-243
Miller, Mark	TST	401-36
Miller, Martin E.	USV	401-243
Miller, Maximillian H.	USV	401-243
Miller, N. J.	SP	401-47
Miller, Oswald	ARM	401-8
Miller, Otto	TVG	401-206
Miller, Philip R.	SR	401-92
Miller, R. L.	TVG	401-206
Miller, R. M.	RR	401-60
Miller, R. M.	SR	401-92
Miller, Ray	SR	401-92
Miller, Ray L.	SR	401-92
Miller, Robert F.	TST	401-36
Miller, Robert L.	FB	401-164
Miller, Robert L.	USV	401-243
Miller, Samuel Dow	TVG	401-206
Miller, T. A.	FB	401-164
Miller, T. J.	TVG	401-206
Miller, Tom	USV	401-243
Miller, W. H.	USV	401-243
Miller, W. L.	SR	401-92
Miller, W. M.	SR	401-92
Miller, W. P.	TVG	401-206
Miller, William	ARM	401-8
Miller, William	SP	401-47
Miller, William A.	CSA	401-40
Miller, William L.	RR	401-60
Miller, William M.	RR	401-60
Miller, William M.	USV	401-243
Miller, William O.	RR	401-60
Miller, William P.	USV	401-243
Miller, Woods S.	RR	401-60
Millett, Paul	USV	401-243
Milley, J. H.	TVG	401-206
Millholland, J. B.	TST	401-36
Millican, Dewitt C.	USV	401-243
Millican, J. W.	FB	401-164
Millican, Leander R.	SR	401-92
Millican, North	SR	401-92
Millican, W. A.	RR	401-60
Milligan, A. L.	TVG	401-206
Milling, H. H.	SR	401-92
Milling, W. N.	FB	401-164
Millroy, John	FF	401-137
Mills, Ignatious P.	USV	401-243
Mills, John	ARM	401-8
Mills, John B.	SR	401-92
Mills, John R.	USV	401-243
Mills, L. C.	SR	401-92
Mills, L. W.	SR	401-92
Mills, Loyd E.	USV	401-243
Mills, Rupert	TVG	401-206
Mills, Ulysses	TVG	401-206
Mills, W. F.	RR	401-60
Mills, Z. R.	USV	401-243
Millsap, Edward D.	USV	401-243
Millum, Bartley B.	FF	401-137
Millum, John B.	FF	401-137
Milo, Daniel	TVG	401-206
Milroy, John	SP	401-47
Milsap, J. V.	SR	401-92
Milsap, J. V.	LR	401-130
Milsap, Jacob	SP	401-47
Milsap, Silas	NAV	401-21
Milsleeve, P. T.	SP	401-47
Milstead, William N.	TVG	401-206
Milstead, William N.	USV	401-243
Milton, Clarence L.	SR	401-92
Milton, J. D.	FB	401-164
Milton, Jeff	FB	401-164
Milton, Neal	FB	401-164
Milton, W. B.	TVG	401-206
Mimough, Samuel W.	USV	401-243
Mims, A. Dow	TVG	401-206
Mims, R. K.	SR	401-92
Mims, Royle K.	USV	401-243
Minder, Emil	FF	401-137
Minear, Joseph William	FF	401-137
Miner, Arthur J.	USV	401-243
Miner, Joel	ARM	401-8
Miner, Wilburn S.	TVG	401-206
Minhinnett, Frank K.	USV	401-243
Minnes, Joe	TVG	401-206
Minnette, Joshua	NAV	401-21
Minnish, Peter	ARM	401-8
Minor, Houston	SR	401-92
Minor, Louis M.	NAV	401-21

Index to Texas Adjutant General Service Records—All Service Branches

Name	Branch	Record
Minot, Stephen W.	TVG	401-206
Minskey, Louis	NAV	401-21
Minter, A. N.	TVG	401-206
Minter, Claude J.	SR	401-92
Minter, Ebenezer M.	TST	401-36
Minter, Eugen P.	USV	401-243
Minter, W. A.	TVG	401-206
Minter, William	TST	401-36
Minton, J. E.	SR	401-92
Minton, W. H.	TVG	401-206
Mires, Thomas A.	USV	401-243
Misener, R. E.	SR	401-92
Mistrot, G. A.	TVG	401-206
Mistrot, Mabry W.	TVG	401-206
Mitchel, Judge Burris	USV	401-243
Mitchell, Ainsley B.	USV	401-243
Mitchell, Alex	TVG	401-206
Mitchell, Allen	SP	401-47
Mitchell, B. W.	SR	401-92
Mitchell, C. J.	TVG	401-206
Mitchell, Charles	FB	401-164
Mitchell, Charles A.	SR	401-92
Mitchell, Charlie S.	USV	401-243
Mitchell, Clyde	TVG	401-206
Mitchell, Francis	NAV	401-21
Mitchell, Frank T.	FB	401-164
Mitchell, Fred	SR	401-92
Mitchell, George M.	TVG	401-206
Mitchell, George M.	USV	401-243
Mitchell, Harvey Lee	TVG	401-206
Mitchell, Homer R.	TVG	401-206
Mitchell, J. O.	SR	401-92
Mitchell, Joe N.	SR	401-92
Mitchell, John	USV	401-243
Mitchell, John G.	ARM	401-8
Mitchell, John T.	NAV	401-21
Mitchell, Judge Burris	TVG	401-206
Mitchell, Lee	USV	401-243
Mitchell, Maxwell	USV	401-243
Mitchell, O. C.	RRR	401-121
Mitchell, R. H.	SR	401-92
Mitchell, R. S.	RRR	401-121
Mitchell, T. T.	SR	401-92
Mitchell, Thomas Dalton	RRR	401-121
Mitchell, Thomas S.	USV	401-243
Mitchell, W. A.	FB	401-164
Mitchell, William	FB	401-164
Mitchell, William H.	USV	401-243
Mitchell, William J.	SP	401-47
Mittendorf, E.	TVG	401-206
Mittenthal, Albert H.	SR	401-92
Mix, Tom	SR	401-92
Mixon, A. W.	FB	401-164
Mixon, Samuel T.	USV	401-243
Mize, J. M.	FB	401-164
Moad, Thomas P.	FB	401-164
Mobley, Alvern C.	USV	401-243
Mobley, E. M.	SR	401-92
Mobley, Norman O.	USV	401-243
Mobley, Richard D.	USV	401-243
Mobley, Thomas B.	USV	401-243
Mobley, W. B.	SR	401-92
Mobley, W. H.	TVG	401-206
Mock, P. L.	SP	401-47
Mockle, Frank	FF	401-137
Mode, T. N.	FB	401-164
Moeller, Charles	FF	401-137
Moers, W. O.	TVG	401-206
Moffett, H. J.	TVG	401-206
Moffett, R. F.	RRR	401-121
Moffitt, Jesse D.	USV	401-243
Mohler, J. P.	RRR	401-121
Mohon, Tom	FB	401-164
Moinatt, William	NAV	401-21
Molesworth, W. M.	SR	401-92
Molesworth, William M.	RR	401-60
Moline, Roy Victor	RRR	401-121
Molino, Luciano	FB	401-164
Moller, Charles	SR	401-92
Molloy, Henry D.	TVG	401-206
Monaghan, William	ARM	401-8
Monaghan, William H.	USV	401-243
Monall, John	ARM	401-8
Monday, S. W.	FB	401-164
Monell, M. E.	NAV	401-21
Money, Herman L.	SR	401-92
Monier, Frank	FB	401-164
Monk, George	FF	401-137
Monk, J. H.	FF	401-137
Monk, Silas	FF	401-137
Monkhouse, G. A.	SR	401-92
Monkhouse, G. A.	LR	401-130
Monnier, Frank	FF	401-137
Monrie, A. T. M.	NAV	401-21
Monroe, Albert S.	TVG	401-206
Monroe, Ben H.	RRR	401-121
Monroe, Claud M.	USV	401-243
Monroe, Gabriel	FF	401-137
Monroe, George W.	SR	401-92
Monroe, H.	TVG	401-206
Monroe, J.	SR	401-92
Monroe, J.	LR	401-130
Monroe, N. O.	SR	401-92
Monroe, Samuel Edward	SR	401-92
Monroe, Thomas	NAV	401-21
Monroe, William M.	TVG	401-206
Montague, J. W.	USV	401-243
Montague, Joe G.	SR	401-93
Montague, Robert H.	USV	401-243
Montes, Severo	MM	401-32
Montes, Telesferro	FF	401-137
Montgomery, A. Walker, Dr.	SR	401-93

Index to Texas Adjutant General Service Records—All Service Branches

Montgomery, C. E. ....SR...........401-93
Montgomery, Henry R.............SP...........401-47
Montgomery, J. D....................SR...........401-93
Montgomery, J. D....................SR...........401-93
Montgomery, J. J.....................SR...........401-93
Montgomery, J. P....................TST.........401-36
Montgomery, James R............USV........401-243
Montgomery, John...................NAV........401-21
Montgomery, John...................SP...........401-47
Montgomery, John W..............RRR........401-121
Montgomery, John W..............SR...........401-93
Montgomery, Louis D.............SR...........401-93
Montgomery, M. D..................SR...........401-93
Montgomery, R. L...................SR...........401-93
Montgomery, W. A..................TST.........401-36
Montgomery, W. D..................SR...........401-93
Montgomery, Will M...............TVG........401-206
Montgomery, William ....NAV........401-21
Montoya, Domingo..................TVG........401-206
Moody, Charles H...................TVG........401-206
Moody, Charles H...................USV........401-243
Moody, D. O............................TVG........401-206
Moody, E. J.............................TVG........401-206
Moody, Henry.........................SP...........401-47
Moody, J. E.............................NAV........401-21
Moody, James.........................NAV........401-21
Moody, John A........................SR...........401-93
Moody, Louis A......................TVG........401-206
Moody, Shearn ....SR...........401-93
Moody, Thomas B...................USV........401-243
Moody, W. L...........................TVG........401-206
Moon, J. L...............................USV........401-243
Moon, R. B..............................SR...........401-93
Mooney, John ....ARM.......401-8
Mooney, Thomas....................SP...........401-47
Moor, Earl T............................SR...........401-93
Moore, A..................................TVG........401-206
Moore, A. C.............................FB............401-164
Moore, A. G.............................FB............401-164
Moore, A. H.............................TVG........401-206
Moore, Abram C.....................RR...........401-60
Moore, Alex.............................USV........401-243
Moore, Alex H........................NAV........401-21
Moore, Andrew.......................ARM.......401-8
Moore, Andrew.......................SR...........401-93
Moore, C. B.............................CSA.........401-40
Moore, C. O.............................RR...........401-60
Moore, C. R.............................RR...........401-60
Moore, Carlton ....SR...........401-93
Moore, Cornelius....................USV........401-243
Moore, D. W............................USV........401-243
Moore, David B......................USV........401-243
Moore, E. W............................NAV........401-21
Moore, Earle A.......................USV........401-243
Moore, Eldridge......................SR...........401-93
Moore, Elmer..........................USV........401-243

Moore, F. D. ....SR...........401-93
Moore, F. M.............................FB............401-164
Moore, F. R. ....SR...........401-93
Moore, Florence ....TVG........401-206
Moore, Franics........................NAV........401-21
Moore, Frank R. ....FB............401-164
Moore, Fred ....SR...........401-93
Moore, G. ....FB............401-164
Moore, G. C.............................FB............401-164
Moore, G. K.............................FB............401-164
Moore, G. R.............................FB............401-164
Moore, G. W............................FB............401-164
Moore, George........................USV........401-243
Moore, George........................USV........401-243
Moore, George G....................TVG........401-206
Moore, H. ....FB............401-164
Moore, H. C.............................FB............401-164
Moore, H. E.............................TVG........401-206
Moore, Henry ....USV........401-243
Moore, Henry S......................SR...........401-93
Moore, Homer ....TVG........401-206
Moore, Howard......................RR...........401-60
Moore, Hughes C...................FB............401-164
Moore, Irving.........................SP...........401-47
Moore, J. B..............................SR...........401-93
Moore, J. B..............................FB............401-164
Moore, J. J...............................FB............401-164
Moore, J. T..............................FB............401-164
Moore, J. T..............................TVG........401-206
Moore, J. W.............................SR...........401-93
Moore, J. W.............................FB............401-164
Moore, J. W.............................LR...........401-130
Moore, Jack ....RR...........401-60
Moore, Jake J. M....................TVG........401-206
Moore, James.........................FF............401-137
Moore, James H.....................FB............401-164
Moore, James W....................NAV........401-21
Moore, Jeff B..........................SR...........401-93
Moore, Jesse T.......................ARM.......401-8
Moore, Jim..............................RR...........401-60
Moore, Jim..............................FB............401-165
Moore, John............................FF............401-137
Moore, John D........................TVG........401-206
Moore, John D........................USV........401-243
Moore, John P........................FB............401-165
Moore, John T........................TVG........401-206
Moore, John W.......................FB............401-165
Moore, John W.......................USV........401-243
Moore, Joseph A....................CSA.........401-40
Moore, Joseph H....................SP...........401-47
Moore, L. A. ....TST.........401-36
Moore, L. P.............................RR...........401-60
Moore, Lee E..........................USV........401-243
Moore, Louis ....SR...........401-93
Moore, M. B. ....FB............401-165
Moore, M. E. ....SR...........401-93

Index to Texas Adjutant General Service Records—All Service Branches

Name	Branch	Record
Moore, M. F.	FB	401-165
Moore, Malcolm G.	USV	401-243
Moore, Minor L.	USV	401-243
Moore, Morris A.	RR	401-60
Moore, N. G.	SR	401-93
Moore, Nathaniel	SP	401-47
Moore, Olin T.	FB	401-165
Moore, Oscar	TVG	401-206
Moore, R. B.	FB	401-165
Moore, R. L.	FB	401-165
Moore, R. S.	CSA	401-40
Moore, Richard B.	FB	401-165
Moore, Robert	USV	401-243
Moore, Robert	USV	401-243
Moore, Robert Joe	SR	401-93
Moore, Robert K.	USV	401-243
Moore, Robert Lee	TVG	401-206
Moore, Rufus A.	SR	401-93
Moore, S.	TVG	401-206
Moore, S. L.	TST	401-36
Moore, Sampson C.	RR	401-60
Moore, Samuel	NAV	401-21
Moore, Samuel	ARM	401-8
Moore, Sidney W.	USV	401-243
Moore, Thomas E.	USV	401-243
Moore, Travis	TVG	401-206
Moore, Uletes	RRR	401-121
Moore, W. A.	FB	401-165
Moore, W. C.	TVG	401-206
Moore, W. H. "Harry"	RR	401-60
Moore, W. R.	FB	401-165
Moore, Walter	FB	401-165
Moore, Walter L.	TVG	401-206
Moore, William A.	USV	401-243
Moore, William H.	ARM	401-8
Moore, William H.	USV	401-243
Moore, William M.	USV	401-243
Moorehead, Charles	NAV	401-21
Mooreland, Harry	TVG	401-206
Mooreland, T. O.	TVG	401-206
Moores, Collier W.	TVG	401-206
Mooring, Arthur Q.	USV	401-243
Mooring, C. E.	SR	401-93
Mooring, C. E.	LR	401-130
Moorman, Cull C.	SR	401-93
Moorman, W. K.	USV	401-243
Mora, Melchor	FB	401-165
Morales, Albert	USV	401-243
Morales, C.	FB	401-165
Morales, Faustin	FF	401-137
Moran, James	ARM	401-8
Moran, John A.	RR	401-60
Moran, Juan	FF	401-137
Moran, Juan	FF	401-137
Moran, Marcelino	FF	401-137
Moran, Mike	USV	401-243
Moran, William B.	FB	401-165
Mordorff	ARM	401-8
More, C. S.	FB	401-165
Moreau, Billie J.	SR	401-93
Morehead, Thornton L.	USV	401-243
Morehouse, J. A.	SR	401-93
Moreland, A. R.	SR	401-93
Moreland, Charlie	TVG	401-206
Moreland, Harry M.	USV	401-243
Moreland, J. C.	FF	401-137
Moreland, J. C.	FB	401-165
Moreland, M. S.	FB	401-165
Moreland, W. T.	TVG	401-206
Moreno, Macario	FF	401-137
Moreno, Thomas	FF	401-137
Morgan, Claude	RRR	401-121
Morgan, David	NAV	401-21
Morgan, F. L.	SR	401-93
Morgan, Frank	SR	401-93
Morgan, Frank J.	FB	401-165
Morgan, G. W.	ARM	401-8
Morgan, George	CSA	401-40
Morgan, George	NAV	401-21
Morgan, Green	TVG	401-206
Morgan, H. L.	TVG	401-206
Morgan, J. B.	FF	401-137
Morgan, J. C.	ARM	401-8
Morgan, J. H.	TVG	401-206
Morgan, J. W.	SR	401-93
Morgan, James G.	FB	401-165
Morgan, Jno. C.	TVG	401-206
Morgan, Martin J.	SR	401-93
Morgan, O. E.	SP	401-47
Morgan, R. M.	SR	401-93
Morgan, Samuel O.	USV	401-243
Morgan, Thomas I.	RR	401-60
Morgan, Tom	SR	401-93
Morgan, W. J.	SP	401-47
Morgan, Warren W.	USV	401-243
Morgan, William M.	MV	401-30
Morgan, William R.	ARM	401-8
Morgan, William W.	ARM	401-8
Morgenstern, George C.	TVG	401-206
Morgett, William H.	USV	401-243
Morley, John L.	RR	401-60
Morphis, G. B.	FB	401-165
Morran, Martin	ARM	401-8
Morreau, Rob.	TVG	401-206
Morrell, Henry	NAV	401-21
Morrell, M. E.	NAV	401-21
Morrill, W. C.	SP	401-47
Morris, A. W.	TST	401-36
Morris, B. M.	TVG	401-206
Morris, B. P.	SR	401-93
Morris, Ben Franklin	RRR	401-121
Morris, C.	CSA	401-40

Index to Texas Adjutant General Service Records—All Service Branches

Name	Branch	Ref
Morris, Charles	NAV	401-21
Morris, Chas.	TVG	401-206
Morris, D. C.	TVG	401-206
Morris, D. W.	SR	401-93
Morris, Dan	USV	401-243
Morris, Dolan Wheeler	RRR	401-121
Morris, Enos	CSA	401-40
Morris, F. M.	FB	401-165
Morris, Frederick E.	USV	401-243
Morris, George E.	USV	401-243
Morris, George G.	NAV	401-21
Morris, George Luther	RRR	401-121
Morris, J. A.	RRR	401-121
Morris, J. M.	FB	401-165
Morris, J. S.	FB	401-165
Morris, J. W.	FB	401-165
Morris, James B.	TVG	401-206
Morris, James C.	SP	401-47
Morris, John A.	USV	401-243
Morris, Larkin B.	MM	401-32
Morris, Lester H.	USV	401-243
Morris, Lucy Jane, Mrs.	SR	401-93
Morris, N. B., Jr.	RRR	401-121
Morris, Patrick	ARM	401-8
Morris, Price	USV	401-243
Morris, R. D.	SR	401-93
Morris, R. E.	SR	401-93
Morris, Richard L.	RR	401-60
Morris, Robert	ARM	401-8
Morris, Robert	ARM	401-8
Morris, Robert L.	USV	401-243
Morris, Roscoe	RR	401-60
Morris, S.	FB	401-165
Morris, S. J.	TVG	401-206
Morris, Sam G.	USV	401-243
Morris, Sam Houston	TVG	401-206
Morris, Thomas A.	USV	401-243
Morris, Tom O.	TVG	401-206
Morris, W. H.	FB	401-165
Morris, W. M.	SR	401-93
Morris, W. T.	FB	401-165
Morris, William A.	MM	401-32
Morris, William C.	USV	401-243
Morris, Y. Z.	TVG	401-206
Morrison, A. H.	RR	401-60
Morrison, A. H.	SR	401-93
Morrison, Alva	USV	401-243
Morrison, Angus W.	SR	401-93
Morrison, Bridges	TVG	401-206
Morrison, D. B.	SR	401-93
Morrison, George B.	USV	401-243
Morrison, J. C.	ARM	401-8
Morrison, J. P., Jr.	TVG	401-206
Morrison, John	NAV	401-21
Morrison, John F.	FB	401-165
Morrison, John W.	USV	401-244
Morrison, T. D.	SR	401-93
Morrison, Will	USV	401-244
Morrison, William	FF	401-137
Morrisset, J. M.	SR	401-93
Morrow, A. G.	TVG	401-206
Morrow, A. W.	TVG	401-206
Morrow, Alf	FB	401-165
Morrow, B. L.	USV	401-244
Morrow, Clarence	TVG	401-206
Morrow, G. McD.	FB	401-165
Morrow, George D.	CSA	401-40
Morrow, J. B.	RRR	401-121
Morrow, J. E.	TVG	401-206
Morrow, J. H.	SP	401-47
Morrow, J. H.	TVG	401-206
Morrow, J. P.	SR	401-93
Morrow, J. T.	TVG	401-206
Morrow, Joe	RR	401-60
Morrow, John H.	TVG	401-206
Morrow, Preston	TVG	401-206
Morrow, Preston	USV	401-244
Morrow, W. C., Dr.	SR	401-93
Morrow, William A.	RRR	401-121
Morrow, William D.	MV	401-30
Mors, Benjamin	NAV	401-21
Morse, H. D., Jr.	SR	401-93
Morse, Henry Dewitt, Jr.	RR	401-60
Morse, Horace A.	FB	401-165
Morse, Seward P.	NAV	401-21
Morse, W. P.	TVG	401-206
Morter, D. I.	TVG	401-206
Mortimer, C. E.	FB	401-165
Mortimer, J. F.	FB	401-165
Morton, Ed C.	TVG	401-206
Morton, Frank J.	USV	401-244
Morton, Henry M.	USV	401-244
Morton, Louis G.	USV	401-244
Morton, Stanley	RR	401-60
Morton, Walter H.	SP	401-47
Morton, William A.	RR	401-60
Mosbach, Jacob	ARM	401-8
Mosby, William O.	NAV	401-21
Moseley, E. B.	CSA	401-40
Moseley, E. E.	FB	401-165
Moseley, Ewing Sevier	SR	401-93
Moseley, H. H.	TVG	401-206
Moseley, John P.	ARM	401-8
Moseley, L. B.	RR	401-60
Moseley, Slater	SR	401-93
Moseley, W. T.	SR	401-93
Mosely, James H.	SP	401-47
Moses, Eugene	USV	401-244
Moses, G. R.	FB	401-165
Moses, H. B.	RRR	401-121
Moses, Ike	USV	401-244
Moses, Isidore W.	TVG	401-206

Index to Texas Adjutant General Service Records—All Service Branches

Name	Branch	Ref
Moses, Ross	USV	401-244
Moses, S. A.	TVG	401-206
Moses, William	FB	401-165
Mosling, Abe D.	USV	401-244
Moss, E. J.	SR	401-93
Moss, E. J.	LR	401-130
Moss, James R.	USV	401-244
Moss, John S.	USV	401-244
Moss, Joseph	FB	401-165
Moss, M. W.	TVG	401-206
Moss, Mark A.	SR	401-93
Moss, S. E.	TVG	401-206
Mossenton, Charles	ARM	401-8
Mossenton, James Lewis	ARM	401-8
Moten, D. S.	TVG	401-206
Motheral, A. S.	TVG	401-206
Mothershead, Andrew	USV	401-244
Motley, Gooch H.	TVG	401-206
Motley, R. A.	SR	401-93
Motley, R. A.	LR	401-130
Motsch, Charles	FF	401-137
Motsch, Rudolph J.	USV	401-244
Mott, Adolphus R.	MV	401-30
Mott, Charles Stewart	SR	401-93
Mott, Joseph L.	FB	401-165
Mott, Joseph W.	NAV	401-21
Mott, Joseph W.	ARM	401-8
Mott, M. F.	TVG	401-206
Mott, Z. H.	RRR	401-121
Mottley, J. M.	SR	401-93
Moulton, Frank M.	SR	401-93
Mount, John H.	USV	401-244
Mount, S. J.	TVG	401-206
Mounts, J. H.	SP	401-47
Mounts, Orian Lessly	RRR	401-121
Moursand, Albert W.	FF	401-137
Moursund, A. N.	TVG	401-206
Moxley, Frank	TVG	401-206
Moye, J. T.	SR	401-93
Moynahan, Thomas	SR	401-93
Muchert, Jules E.	TVG	401-206
Mudd, J. M.	TVG	401-206
Mudd, Thomas	TVG	401-206
Mueller, William	USV	401-244
Muenster, Joe H.	SR	401-93
Muenster, Sam L.	TVG	401-206
Muenster, W. H.	TVG	401-206
Muery, E. E.	TVG	401-206
Muil, Charles G.	SR	401-93
Muil, Charles G.	LR	401-130
Muir, Charlie C.	SR	401-93
Muir, V. E.	TVG	401-206
Mulholland, Patrick	ARM	401-8
Mulkey, L. A.	MV	401-30
Mullane, George W.	USV	401-244
Mullane, T. C.	SR	401-93
Mullen, Edward	NAV	401-22
Mullen, Edward	ARM	401-8
Mullen, Francis	ARM	401-8
Mullens, Albert H.	FB	401-165
Mullens, M. S., Jr.	SR	401-93
Mullenweg, Henry F.	USV	401-244
Mullenweg, William H.	USV	401-244
Muller, A. E.	TVG	401-206
Muller, G. F.	SP	401-47
Muller, Henry	TVG	401-206
Muller, John	TVG	401-206
Muller, John F.	USV	401-244
Muller, Martin H.	TVG	401-206
Mullikin, Thomas W.	TVG	401-206
Mullinax, G. C.	TVG	401-206
Mullins, Henry	MV	401-30
Mullins, J. C.	TVG	401-206
Mullins, J. N.	SR	401-93
Mullins, James	USV	401-244
Mullins, John W.	USV	401-244
Mullins, Richard	USV	401-244
Mullins, William F.	USV	401-244
Mulray, William J.	USV	401-244
Mulroy, James	FB	401-165
Mulvey, William B.	FB	401-165
Mumford, Carl	SR	401-93
Mumford, R. H.	SR	401-93
Mumme, August	FF	401-137
Munal, H. L.	SR	401-93
Munch, Adam	MV	401-30
Mundel, Henry	ARM	401-8
Munden, Clyde	TVG	401-206
Munden, Jose	USV	401-244
Munden, Pope	TVG	401-206
Munden, W. E.	TVG	401-206
Mundine, J. H.	LR	401-130
Mundrick, Lambert	RR	401-60
Munds, Crispin	FF	401-137
Munford, Edward	ARM	401-8
Munn, John	SR	401-93
Munn, John S.	RRR	401-121
Munn, John S.	USV	401-244
Munro, Dave	TVG	401-206
Munro, George A.	USV	401-244
Munroe, John	NAV	401-22
Murchison, Claud	SR	401-93
Murchison, Claud	SR	401-93
Murchison, Eugene A.	USV	401-244
Murchison, Ivan	RR	401-60
Murchison, Ivan	USV	401-244
Murchison, K. B.	SP	401-47
Murchison, W. H.	USV	401-244
Murchison, William M.	SP	401-47
Murdock, Adam	TST	401-36
Murdock, William	RR	401-60
Murphree, William T.	TST	401-36

Index to Texas Adjutant General Service Records—All Service Branches

Murphy, A. .... SR 401-93
Murphy, A. T. .... TVG 401-206
Murphy, D. K. .... SP 401-47
Murphy, E. C. .... RRR 401-121
Murphy, George .... TVG 401-206
Murphy, J. E. .... TVG 401-206
Murphy, J. M. .... FB 401-165
Murphy, J. W. .... FB 401-165
Murphy, James E. .... USV 401-244
Murphy, James E. .... USV 401-244
Murphy, Jay G. .... RR 401-60
Murphy, John .... NAV 401-22
Murphy, John F. .... ARM 401-8
Murphy, Jordan .... SP 401-47
Murphy, Joseph .... FB 401-165
Murphy, Lewis D. .... TVG 401-206
Murphy, M. H. .... FB 401-165
Murphy, Michel .... SP 401-47
Murphy, Miles P. .... USV 401-244
Murphy, R. J. .... TVG 401-206
Murphy, T. A. .... FB 401-165
Murphy, T. B. .... FB 401-165
Murphy, Thomas .... SP 401-47
Murphy, W. A. .... TVG 401-206
Murphy, W. E. .... RRR 401-121
Murphy, William H. .... FF 401-137
Murphy, William H. .... TVG 401-206
Murphy, William H. .... USV 401-244
Murrah, Dan .... SR 401-93
Murrah, J. E. .... SR 401-93
Murrah, Jake R. .... SR 401-93
Murrah, James B. .... SR 401-93
Murrah, James E. .... SR 401-93
Murray, A. A. .... RRR 401-121
Murray, Cam H. .... SR 401-93
Murray, Charles F. .... SR 401-93
Murray, Eugene J. .... RR 401-60
Murray, G. W. .... SR 401-93
Murray, George J. .... SR 401-93
Murray, Irvin B. .... SR 401-94
Murray, J. D. .... TVG 401-206
Murray, J. L. .... RRR 401-121
Murray, J. R. .... RR 401-60
Murray, J. R. .... SR 401-94
Murray, James E. .... RRR 401-121
Murray, John .... ARM 401-8
Murray, John T. .... USV 401-244
Murray, Joseph H. .... SR 401-94
Murray, M. F. .... SR 401-94
Murray, N. H. .... FB 401-165
Murray, N. T. .... USV 401-244
Murray, R. G. .... TVG 401-206
Murray, Richard .... ARM 401-8
Murray, Steven .... TVG 401-206
Murray, T. W. .... ARM 401-8
Murray, Ted .... SR 401-94
Murray, Thomas .... FF 401-137
Murrell, Dan T. .... SR 401-94
Murrell, Earl B. .... RRR 401-121
Murrell, Edgar R. .... TVG 401-206
Murrell, F. E. .... SR 401-94
Murrell, F. E. .... LR 401-130
Murrell, H. J. .... TVG 401-206
Murrell, Robert E. .... USV 401-244
Murrill, James H. .... FB 401-165
Muse, James H. .... USV 401-244
Muse, McKinley .... SR 401-94
Muse, R. L. .... TVG 401-206
Musgrave, Cebe .... USV 401-244
Musgrave, D. L. .... FB 401-165
Musgrave, L. D. .... USV 401-244
Musgrove, Al .... FF 401-137
Musgrove, E. G. .... SP 401-47
Musgrove, J. H. .... SR 401-94
Musgrove, John .... FF 401-137
Mushall, Ed .... USV 401-244
Mushavay, Alden .... TVG 401-207
Mushavay, R. J. .... TVG 401-207
Music, George W. .... TVG 401-207
Muslow, C. J. .... NAV 401-22
Mussett, Finis E. .... RR 401-60
Mussett, John S. .... FF 401-137
Mussey, Hart, Jr. .... SR 401-94
Myer, Hyman .... USV 401-244
Myer, Sewall .... RR 401-60
Myer, Sewall .... SR 401-94
Myers, D. W. .... SP 401-47
Myers, Edwin Clark .... SR 401-94
Myers, Francis .... ARM 401-8
Myers, Graham .... SR 401-94
Myers, Harley W. .... RRR 401-121
Myers, Julius .... TVG 401-207
Myers, L. A. .... TVG 401-207
Myers, Paul .... SR 401-94
Myers, Richard O. .... USV 401-244
Myers, S. D. .... SR 401-94
Myers, T. G. .... RR 401-60
Myers, William .... SP 401-47
Myers, William .... FB 401-165
Mynatt, J. D. .... RR 401-60
Mynatt, Jeff D. .... SR 401-94
Mynatt, Parlon H. .... USV 401-244
Myres, S. D. .... LR 401-130
Myrick, Edwin R. .... RR 401-60
Myrick, John E. .... ARM 401-8
Myzell, E. R. .... SR 401-94
Nabers, Robert .... SR 401-94
Nabers, S. A. .... RR 401-60
Nabors, J. B. .... RR 401-60
Nabors, W. A., Jr. .... SR 401-94
Nabours, William D. .... TVG 401-207
Nachtrab, L. J. .... SR 401-94

Index to Texas Adjutant General Service Records—All Service Branches

Name	Branch	Record
Naegelin, Joseph	FF	401-137
Nafer, Cornelius George W.	ARM	401-8
Nagle, Pierce	SP	401-47
Nagness, Jack	USV	401-244
Nail, Allen	SP	401-47
Nail, Jim	TVG	401-207
Nail, Jules A.	TVG	401-207
Naill, George	ARM	401-8
Nall, John R.	SR	401-94
Nalls, J. B.	RR	401-60
Nalls, L.	CSA	401-40
Nance, Charles L.	USV	401-244
Nance, E.	TST	401-36
Nance, Mack	TVG	401-207
Nance, Mack	USV	401-244
Nance, W. E.	SR	401-94
Nanney, E. T.	TVG	401-207
Nanney, Walter T.	TVG	401-207
Napier, J. S.	FB	401-165
Napier, W. S.	FB	401-165
Nash, David R.	USV	401-244
Nash, Henry	USV	401-244
Nash, Horace C.	USV	401-244
Nash, James T.	USV	401-244
Nash, Jim	FF	401-137
Nash, Jim	SP	401-47
Nash, John	TVG	401-207
Nash, John C.	MM	401-32
Nash, John M.	TVG	401-207
Nash, Olin W.	TVG	401-207
Nash, T. J.	FB	401-165
Nathare, S.	USV	401-244
Nations, E. W.	SR	401-94
Nations, R. B.	FF	401-137
Natus, Joe	FB	401-165
Natus, John	FB	401-165
Nauwlad, Albert E.	USV	401-244
Navarro, J. Antonio G.	ARM	401-8
Nave, F. W.	TVG	401-207
Naveley, Alfred H.	USV	401-244
Navratil, Frank J.	TVG	401-207
Neagle, Albert F.	TST	401-36
Neal, Arther M.	RR	401-60
Neal, C. E.	SR	401-94
Neal, David L.	TVG	401-207
Neal, Edgar	FB	401-165
Neal, Edgar T.	RR	401-60
Neal, Franklin	USV	401-244
Neal, J. A.	RRR	401-121
Neal, Joe P.	SR	401-94
Neal, Lindsley A.	TVG	401-207
Neal, Overton	SR	401-94
Neatherlin, J. M.	SP	401-47
Neathery, Robert Alan	SR	401-94
Neblett, Edward A.	TVG	401-207
Nebo, Charles	FB	401-165
Needham, M. J.	RR	401-60
Neel, James	TST	401-36
Neeley, B. B.	USV	401-244
Neeley, Frank E.	SR	401-94
Neely, A. A.	FB	401-165
Neely, Callie J.	USV	401-244
Neely, Doc	FB	401-165
Neely, Frank	TVG	401-207
Neely, J. B.	SP	401-47
Neely, R. Louis	USV	401-244
Neely, R. O.	FB	401-165
Neely, W. I.	TVG	401-207
Neely, William	FB	401-165
Neer, S. B.	SR	401-94
Neff, John	FF	401-137
Nefler, Alexander	ARM	401-8
Negbaur, S. A.	USV	401-244
Neighbor, R. B.	FB	401-165
Neighbors, B.	RR	401-60
Neil, C. E.	LR	401-130
Neil, John H.	USV	401-244
Neil, Lewis	ARM	401-8
Neil, Thomas	NAV	401-22
Neil, W.	FB	401-165
Neiland, Patrick J.	USV	401-244
Neill, Benjamin F.	MV	401-30
Neill, Charles Fergus	TVG	401-207
Neill, F. T.	MV	401-30
Neill, Frank T.	RR	401-60
Neill, Robert T.	USV	401-244
Neill, S. H.	RR	401-60
Neill, Sam H.	RR	401-60
Neill, T. T.	SR	401-94
Neill, W. J.	USV	401-244
Neilson, George G.	FB	401-165
Nelms, Haywood	SR	401-94
Nelms, Horace	SR	401-94
Nelms, R. C.	TVG	401-207
Nelson, A. G.	TVG	401-207
Nelson, Albert A.	TVG	401-207
Nelson, Alex	USV	401-244
Nelson, Baud E.	SR	401-94
Nelson, C.	FF	401-137
Nelson, C. L.	TVG	401-207
Nelson, Cyrus Randolph	TVG	401-207
Nelson, F. H.	FB	401-165
Nelson, F. W.	FB	401-165
Nelson, Flay D.	RRR	401-121
Nelson, Floyd S.	SR	401-94
Nelson, Floyd S.	SR	401-94
Nelson, H. Lewis	FF	401-137
Nelson, J. B.	SR	401-94
Nelson, J. D.	FB	401-165
Nelson, J. W.	SR	401-94
Nelson, James	USV	401-244
Nelson, James C.	SR	401-94

Index to Texas Adjutant General Service Records—All Service Branches

Nelson, John L. .... USV 401-244
Nelson, Joseph T. .... USV 401-244
Nelson, Norman .... TVG 401-207
Nelson, Oliver C. .... USV 401-244
Nelson, P. E. .... TVG 401-207
Nelson, Richard .... SP 401-47
Nelson, Richard .... USV 401-244
Nelson, Samuel .... ARM 401-8
Nelson, T. E. .... SR 401-94
Nelson, W. C. .... MV 401-30
Nelson, William .... NAV 401-22
Nelson, William .... USV 401-244
Nelson, William T. .... FF 401-137
Nelson, William Verne .... RRR 401-121
Nenney, James P. .... RR 401-60
Nephler, Clarence J. .... USV 401-244
Nerat, Louis .... NAV 401-22
Nesbit, Newton .... FF 401-137
Nesbitt, Edwin .... NAV 401-22
Nesbitt, J. W. .... SR 401-94
Nesbitt, J. W. .... LR 401-130
Nesbitt, Richard M. .... USV 401-244
Nessmith, A. H. .... SR 401-94
Nester, Valentine .... FF 401-137
Nettles, Leonard C. .... TVG 401-207
Nettles, Robert M. .... USV 401-244
Neuhaus, Charles P. .... SR 401-94
Neumann, Paul .... SR 401-94
Neumann, Paul .... LR 401-130
Neumeyer, A. W. .... USV 401-244
Nevette, Louis .... TVG 401-207
Nevill, C. L. .... FB 401-165
Nevill, C. P. .... SR 401-94
Nevill, Frank .... SR 401-94
Nevill, Frank .... LR 401-130
Nevill, Harvey P. .... USV 401-244
Nevill, Michael .... ARM 401-8
Nevill, R. L. .... FB 401-165
Nevils, Edward .... RR 401-60
Newberry, C. H. .... SR 401-94
Newberry, G. W. .... LR 401-130
Newberry, George W. .... SR 401-94
Newberry, J. H. .... SR 401-94
Newberry, Sam H. .... FB 401-165
Newby, Whaley D. .... MV 401-30
Newcomer, Joe Harvey .... SR 401-94
Newell, E. R. .... SR 401-94
Newing, Francis G. .... USV 401-244
Newland, H. P. .... TST 401-36
Newman, Charles L. .... USV 401-244
Newman, Howard .... TVG 401-207
Newman, J. S. .... RRR 401-122
Newman, James W. .... SP 401-47
Newman, Joe E. .... USV 401-244
Newman, John W. .... FB 401-165
Newman, Mark .... TVG 401-207
Newman, Max .... RR 401-60
Newman, Milton .... USV 401-244
Newman, S. J. .... RR 401-60
Newman, S. J. "Jack" .... SR 401-94
Newman, Tom B. .... SR 401-94
Newman, Volney .... USV 401-244
Newman, William M. .... USV 401-244
Newsom, J. G. .... RR 401-60
Newsum, L. B. .... SR 401-94
Newton, D. A. .... TVG 401-207
Newton, Daniel M. .... SR 401-94
Newton, Eddie R. .... TVG 401-207
Newton, George .... FF 401-137
Newton, Gus .... TVG 401-207
Newton, Isaac E. .... USV 401-244
Newton, J. A. .... FB 401-165
Newton, J. P. .... USV 401-244
Newton, James Oscar .... TVG 401-207
Newton, T. M. .... SR 401-94
Newton, W. B. .... FB 401-165
Newton, W. R. .... SR 401-94
Newton, Westly .... TVG 401-207
Ney, A. .... TVG 401-207
Neyland, M. W., Jr. .... SR 401-94
Nicar, Tom W. .... SR 401-94
Nicewanur, T. L. .... FB 401-165
Nicewarner, Charles M. .... USV 401-244
Nicholas, J. C. .... FB 401-165
Nicholas, W. M. .... SP 401-47
Nichols, Bass .... TVG 401-207
Nichols, D. M. .... SR 401-94
Nichols, D. M. .... LR 401-130
Nichols, E. E. .... RR 401-60
Nichols, Falley .... TVG 401-207
Nichols, George .... FB 401-165
Nichols, George W. .... FF 401-137
Nichols, Henry A. .... FB 401-166
Nichols, Henry G. .... ARM 401-8
Nichols, Irving .... USV 401-244
Nichols, J. I. .... TVG 401-207
Nichols, J. R. .... TVG 401-207
Nichols, J. W. .... RRR 401-122
Nichols, J. W. .... FB 401-166
Nichols, Jack L. .... RRR 401-122
Nichols, Jack L. .... USV 401-244
Nichols, James C. .... USV 401-244
Nichols, James R. .... USV 401-244
Nichols, John .... TST 401-36
Nichols, John .... SP 401-47
Nichols, John A. .... FF 401-137
Nichols, Joseph Francis .... TVG 401-207
Nichols, Joseph Francis .... USV 401-244
Nichols, Lewis G. .... TVG 401-207
Nichols, M. W. .... SR 401-94
Nichols, M. W. .... LR 401-130
Nichols, R. .... TVG 401-207

Index to Texas Adjutant General Service Records—All Service Branches

Name	Branch	Record
Nichols, R. C.	SR	401-94
Nichols, Roy C.	RR	401-60
Nichols, S. M.	SP	401-47
Nichols, S. M.	FB	401-166
Nichols, Taylor	SR	401-94
Nichols, Thomas	TVG	401-207
Nichols, Thomas B.	TVG	401-207
Nichols, W. E.	FB	401-166
Nichols, William	SP	401-47
Nichols, William	TVG	401-207
Nichols, William F.	USV	401-244
Nichols, William H.	CSA	401-40
Nichols, William H.	TVG	401-207
Nichols, William H.	USV	401-244
Nicholson, Albert	TVG	401-207
Nicholson, Benedict R.	USV	401-244
Nicholson, Boston	TVG	401-207
Nicholson, J. B.	MM	401-32
Nicholson, J. E.	TVG	401-207
Nicholson, J. L.	TST	401-36
Nicholson, J. M.	SR	401-94
Nicholson, Jackson	TVG	401-207
Nicholson, John	NAV	401-22
Nicholson, John T.	USV	401-244
Nicholson, T. A.	SR	401-94
Nickell, J. W.	FB	401-166
Nickerson, Albert	TVG	401-207
Nicodemus, E. W.	SR	401-94
Nicol, George H.	TVG	401-207
Nicol, William F.	TVG	401-207
Nicolai, Hugo C.	USV	401-244
Niehaus, Henry F.	USV	401-244
Niemann, Henry	FF	401-137
Niggli, F. F.	TVG	401-207
Niggli, Ferdinand	FB	401-166
Niggli, Gus F.	TVG	401-207
Niggli, Oscar	TVG	401-207
Nigh, Thomas P.	FB	401-166
Nimon, Charles W.	SR	401-94
Nimon, Charles William	TVG	401-207
Nimon, Charles William	USV	401-244
Nipper, George A.	USV	401-244
Niveth, Louis	TVG	401-207
Nix, C. M. "Jack"	SR	401-94
Nix, Charles R.	SR	401-94
Nix, Homer	FB	401-166
Nix, J. F.	FB	401-166
Nixon, Richard	ARM	401-8
Nixon, S. M.	TVG	401-207
Noack, O. E.	TVG	401-207
Noble, E. P., Jr.	SR	401-94
Noble, Ed	TVG	401-207
Noble, Edward B.	RR	401-60
Noble, J. P.	NAV	401-22
Noble, John	ARM	401-8
Noble, Oscar E.	USV	401-244
Noel, Henry G.	RR	401-60
Noessel, Vivian	USV	401-244
Noey, W. R.	NAV	401-22
Nolan, John B.	USV	401-244
Nolan, P. B.	TVG	401-207
Nolan, Thomas W.	USV	401-244
Noland, J. A.	TVG	401-207
Noland, John	NAV	401-22
Noland, Pierce	USV	401-244
Nolen, Harry W.	SR	401-94
Nolen, J. B.	SR	401-94
Noling, Sam	FB	401-166
Nolte, Eugene, Jr.	SR	401-94
Noonan, James	ARM	401-8
Nootug, Francis	FB	401-166
Nordhaus, A.	SP	401-47
Nordhues, A. Theodore	MV	401-30
Nordhues, Fadteaddes	MV	401-30
Norfleet, E. L.	RR	401-60
Norfleet, Frank E.	SR	401-94
Norfleet, J. Frank	SR	401-94
Norman, Alonzo L.	SR	401-94
Norman, James	TST	401-36
Norman, V.	SP	401-47
Norman, W. E.	RRR	401-122
Norman, W. E.	SR	401-94
Norodny, Francis	FF	401-137
Norodny, John	FF	401-137
Norrell, John R.	USV	401-244
Norris, Charles E.	FB	401-166
Norris, Dan E.	TVG	401-207
Norris, J. A.	TVG	401-207
Norris, J. T.	SR	401-94
Norris, J. T.	TVG	401-207
Norris, J. W.	TVG	401-207
Norris, Jasper	TST	401-36
Norris, Major A.	TVG	401-207
Norris, O. E.	SR	401-94
Norris, Robert	FB	401-166
Norris, Samuel	ARM	401-8
Norris, Thomas	NAV	401-22
Norris, W. B.	USV	401-244
Norsworthy, B. H.	TVG	401-207
North, J. H.	FF	401-137
North, J. H. M.	FB	401-166
North, John H.	FB	401-166
North, Rodney K.	FB	401-166
Northcott, S. B.	FB	401-166
Northcut, John H.	SR	401-95
Northey, John W.	TVG	401-207
Northington, E. A.	FB	401-166
Northington, Robert M.	TVG	401-207
Northington, V. R.	USV	401-244
Northway, T. H.	FB	401-166
Northy, Martin	ARM	401-8
Norton, A. F.	TVG	401-207

Index to Texas Adjutant General Service Records—All Service Branches

Norton, Bernard............................ARM.......401-8
Norton, C. B. ....FB...........401-166
Norton, C. L.................................SR...........401-95
Norton, Charles M. ....TVG........401-207
Norton, Harris Eugene.................SR...........401-95
Norton, Harry ....TVG........401-207
Norton, Herbert J. ....USV........401-244
Norton, J. M.................................FB...........401-166
Norton, James T...........................USV........401-244
Norton, James W. ....ARM.......401-8
Norton, Marion D. ....FB...........401-166
Norton, W. M...............................CSA........401-40
Norvell, B. R.................................TVG........401-207
Norvell, J. S. ....RR...........401-60
Norvell, Mac R. ....USV........401-244
Norvell, O. E. ....TVG........401-207
Norwood, Ewing..........................TVG........401-207
Norwood, Frederick G. ....USV........401-244
Norwood, Hamman ....USV........401-244
Norwood, Morris ....SP...........401-47
Norwood, Oscar J. ....USV........401-244
Norwood, Shields ....USV........401-244
Nosler, H. C.................................RRR........401-122
Nossell, P.....................................TVG........401-207
Noton, William Dale....................SR...........401-95
Nourse, W. G. ....TVG........401-207
Novy, Jim ....SR...........401-95
Nowery, B. M. ....SR...........401-95
Nowlan, Robert............................NAV.......401-22
Nowlin, D. C. ....FB...........401-166
Nowlin, James C..........................FB...........401-166
Nowlin, Jas. C..............................FB...........401-166
Nowlin, Jesse G. ....TVG........401-207
Nowlin, Oscar..............................FB...........401-166
Nowlin, Peyton D. ....CSA........401-40
Nowlin, Samuel H. ....TST........401-36
Nowotny, Francis ....FB...........401-166
Nowotny, John.............................FB...........401-166
Nuderhill, Morris D. ....NAV.......401-22
Nugent, B. F. ....SR...........401-95
Nugent, J. W................................RRR........401-122
Nugent, T. L. ....SP...........401-47
Numbers, Charlie F. ....TVG........401-207
Nunez, David E. ....USV........401-244
Nunez, John B. ....RR...........401-60
Nunez, Willie M. ....TVG........401-207
Nunn, Henry S. ....USV........401-244
Nunn, Nevacus N.........................USV........401-244
Nunn, W. L..................................SP...........401-47
Nunnery, J. C. ....RR...........401-60
Nussbaum, Gustave G. ....TVG........401-207
Nussbaum, Harry ....USV........401-244
Nutt, J. W....................................SR...........401-95
Nutt, J. W....................................LR...........401-130
Nutt, Jake R. ....TVG........401-207
Nvakjes, A. G. ....TVG........401-207

Oakden, J. N. ....SR...........401-95
Oakley, John S.............................SR...........401-95
Oakley, Luther William Mathias..RRR........401-122
Oakley, Walter H.........................SP...........401-47
Oates, Harvey C..........................USV........401-244
Oates, Henry D. ....USV........401-244
Oats, Jackson ....SP...........401-47
Oats, William J. ....CSA........401-40
Obar, John M. ....TST........401-36
Obenchain, A. T. ....TST........401-36
Oberle, Eugene A. ....TVG........401-207
Oberst, Martin.............................FB...........401-166
Oberste, A. W. ....SR...........401-95
Oberweather, Fred ....TVG........401-207
Oberwether, E. R. ....FB...........401-166
Oberwether, Oscar.......................FB...........401-166
Oberwetter, Emile........................FB...........401-166
Oberwetter, H. ....FB...........401-166
Oberwetter, Oscar........................FB...........401-166
O'Brien, Chanault ....USV........401-244
O'Brien, Daniel............................ARM.......401-8
O'Brien, John J. ....SR...........401-95
O'Brien, John J. ....TVG........401-207
O'Brien, Thomas..........................ARM.......401-8
O'Brien, Thomas Edmund ....SR...........401-95
O'Brien, Thomas Edmund ....LR...........401-130
O'Brien, Weldon..........................SR...........401-95
O'Brien, William G.....................RR...........401-60
O'Bryan, John ....NAV.......401-22
O'Bryan, T. ....SP...........401-47
O'Bryan, Thomas.........................FF...........401-137
O'Bryan, Tom B. ....SR...........401-95
O'Bryant, Wilson ....TST........401-36
Ochoa, Francisco ....FF...........401-137
Ochs, Herman S...........................USV........401-244
Ochse, Robert ....FF...........401-138
O'Connell, T. J. ....RR...........401-60
O'Connell, Thomas F....................USV........401-244
O'Conner, Edward ....ARM.......401-8
O'Conner, Thomas L. ....TVG........401-207
O'Connor, Dan L. ....SR...........401-95
O'Dell, Charles Frank ....SR...........401-95
Odell, Frederick E. ....TVG........401-207
Odell, J. D...................................TVG........401-207
Odell, S. W..................................FB...........401-166
Odem, D. ....SR...........401-95
Odem, D. ....LR...........401-130
Oden, A. V..................................MV.........401-30
Oden, A. V..................................FB...........401-166
Oden, Louis D. ....RR...........401-60
Oden, W. V..................................FB...........401-166
Oden, William L..........................USV........401-244
Oderbolz, George ....USV........401-244
Odineal, William C......................USV........401-244
Odiorn, Jas...................................FB...........401-166
Odiorne, E. H...............................TVG........401-207

Index to Texas Adjutant General Service Records—All Service Branches

Name	Branch	Record
Odiorne, James	FF	401-138
Odiorne, James G.	FB	401-166
Odneal, Harry T.	RR	401-60
Odneal, Harry T.	SR	401-95
Odom, Dorse	SR	401-95
Odom, J. M.	SR	401-95
Odom, J. M.	LR	401-130
Odom, James	FF	401-138
Odom, James A.	USV	401-244
Odom, P. W.	FB	401-166
Odom, Ruffin	USV	401-244
Odom, W. B.	FB	401-166
O'Donnell, Patrick O.	ARM	401-8
O'Donnell, Richard	ARM	401-8
O'Donnell, Thomas	FB	401-166
O'Donohoe, Thomas T.	USV	401-244
Offer, M.	FB	401-166
Ogden, Joe T.	SR	401-95
Ogden, John N.	SR	401-95
Ogden, Ralph R.	SR	401-95
Ogg, John M.	USV	401-244
Ogg, Lester E.	RR	401-60
Ogilvey, C. J.	TVG	401-207
Ogilvie, Cory W.	USV	401-244
Ogilvie, James W.	USV	401-244
Ogle, D. S.	FF	401-138
Ogle, John	ARM	401-8
Oglesby, B. G.	FB	401-166
Oglesby, J. W.	TVG	401-207
Oglesby, Thomas L.	FB	401-166
Oglesby, Ulysses S.	USV	401-244
Oglesby, W. L.	TVG	401-207
Oglesby, Woody	TVG	401-207
Ogliby, Charles	TVG	401-207
O'Gora, Joe	USV	401-244
O'Grady, F. J.	FB	401-166
O'Grady, W. P.	FB	401-166
O'Hare, Thomas M.	FB	401-166
O'Hern, John J.	SR	401-95
Ohlenburger, F.	SP	401-47
Ohlin, Allie A.	TVG	401-207
Ohlin, H. C.	USV	401-244
O'Kane, Barnett	NAV	401-22
O'Keefe, A. H.	TST	401-36
O'Keefe, Marvin	SR	401-95
O'Keefe, Marvin	LR	401-130
O'Keeffe, John	TVG	401-207
Oland, Robert Edward	SR	401-95
Old, A. Y.	FB	401-166
Old, W. A.	FB	401-166
Oldham, C. C.	TVG	401-207
Oldham, Frank	TVG	401-207
Oldham, O. P.	TVG	401-207
Oldright, John	RR	401-60
Olds, Hollowell	TST	401-36
Ole, John	FB	401-166
O'Leary, James	NAV	401-22
Olgine, Bernardo	FB	401-166
Olgine, Domingo	FB	401-166
Olhe, Albert	USV	401-244
Olhe, Theodore J.	TVG	401-207
Oliphant, Boon	RR	401-60
Oliphant, G. C.	RR	401-60
Oliphant, L. E.	TVG	401-207
Oliphint, Hudson	USV	401-244
Oliphint, T. W.	TVG	401-207
Olive, George W.	USV	401-244
Olive, John T.	FB	401-166
Olive, Lee D.	SR	401-95
Olive, William	TVG	401-207
Oliver, Allen	USV	401-244
Oliver, B. Frank	USV	401-245
Oliver, Bruce E.	TVG	401-207
Oliver, Charles O.	USV	401-245
Oliver, Frank	TVG	401-207
Oliver, Frank H.	USV	401-245
Oliver, Frank L.	TVG	401-207
Oliver, J. F.	FB	401-166
Oliver, James A.	USV	401-245
Oliver, James V.	TVG	401-207
Oliver, Jno.	ARM	401-8
Oliver, John Jefferson	SR	401-95
Oliver, Kenneth D.	SR	401-95
Oliver, Nicholas	ARM	401-8
Oliver, R. B.	FF	401-138
Oliver, Robert	NAV	401-22
Oliver, T. F.	TVG	401-207
Oliver, William	NAV	401-22
Olmos, Vincenti	FB	401-166
Olmyer, Dedric	NAV	401-22
Olonzo, Kirkpatrick	USV	401-245
Olsen, Ole M.	RRR	401-122
Olson, Fred C.	SR	401-95
Olson, G. N.	SR	401-95
Olson, O. M.	RRR	401-122
O'Malior, T.	FB	401-166
Omen, Henry	ARM	401-8
Oneal, A. R.	TVG	401-207
O'Neal, E. E.	SR	401-95
O'Neal, H.	FB	401-166
O'Neal, Norman R.	USV	401-245
Oneal, Robert L.	SP	401-47
O'Neal, Timothy	ARM	401-8
O'Neal, W. B.	FB	401-166
O'Neal, William	FB	401-166
O'Neall, Charles	TVG	401-207
O'Neall, J. B.	TVG	401-207
O'Neall, J. B.	USV	401-245
O'Neals, P. G.	NAV	401-22
O'Neil, H. L.	TVG	401-207
O'Neil, Michael	ARM	401-9
O'Neill, C. F. W.	FB	401-166

Index to Texas Adjutant General Service Records—All Service Branches

Name	Branch	Record
O'Neill, James	ARM	401-9
O'Neill, John	NAV	401-22
O'Neill, John	ARM	401-9
O'Neill, Rue	SR	401-95
O'Neill, Russell	RRR	401-122
O'Neill, Thomas	FB	401-166
O'Neill, William	FF	401-138
Onery, John G.	ARM	401-9
Onstott, S. F.	FB	401-166
Openheimer, Louis M.	TVG	401-207
Openheimer, Louis M.	USV	401-245
Opporto, Fermin	FF	401-138
O'Quinn, Thomas J.	SR	401-95
Oram, H. C.	FB	401-166
Orange, Thomas M.	USV	401-245
Orberg, Joe	RR	401-60
Orberg, Joe	SR	401-95
Orchard, Sam C.	TVG	401-207
Orchard, Sam C.	USV	401-245
Ord, Thomas G.	USV	401-245
O'Reilly, J. J.	FB	401-166
O'Reilly, J. J.	FB	401-166
O'Riley, Charles William	USV	401-245
Orenbaun, T. A.	LR	401-130
Ormand, Alex.	FB	401-166
Ormand, G.	SR	401-95
Ormiston, Robert	NAV	401-22
Ormsby, Charles E.	USV	401-245
Ormsby, Fred E.	USV	401-245
Ormsby, John	ARM	401-9
Orndorff, Lee Hickerson	TVG	401-207
Orndorff, SEth B.	SR	401-95
Oroslany, Louis	FF	401-138
Orr, Charles T. M.	TVG	401-207
Orr, Lonnie	SR	401-95
Orr, Walter L.	TVG	401-207
Orr, William P.	USV	401-245
Orrell, J. D.	FF	401-138
Orrell, John A.	TVG	401-207
Orrell, R. P.	FB	401-166
Orrell, S. C.	SR	401-95
Orsay, Henry	SP	401-47
Orsay, Henry	FB	401-166
Orsborn, Max	SR	401-95
Ortega, Perfeto	SP	401-47
Orth, Leonard A.	LR	401-130
Orton, James	SP	401-47
Osborn, J. H.	FB	401-166
Osborn, John W.	USV	401-245
Osborn, Joseph T.	USV	401-245
Osburn, Eugene Bryce	TVG	401-207
Osburn, George R.	SR	401-95
Osgood, Jesse G.	RR	401-60
O'Shaughnessy, Joseph P.	SP	401-47
O'Shaunessy, James	NAV	401-22
Oslin, Jim	TVG	401-207
Osoba, Joseph	SR	401-95
Osoba, Joseph, Sr.	RR	401-60
Osono, Albeno	MV	401-30
Ostebee, Harry I.	TVG	401-207
Osteen, B. W.	SR	401-95
Osteen, D. R.	SR	401-95
O'Steen, Isaac N.	MV	401-30
Otaro, Guadalupe	RR	401-60
O'Toole, Patrick	SP	401-47
Ott, W. E.	TVG	401-207
Otten, Eberhart	USV	401-245
Otting, A.	SR	401-95
Otto, Albert	TVG	401-207
Otto, W. J.	SR	401-95
Outlaw, B. L.	FB	401-166
Outlaw, G. B.	SR	401-95
Ouzts, T. I.	TVG	401-207
Overand, John W.	FB	401-166
Overmeyer, Charles R.	USV	401-245
Overstreet, A. B.	SR	401-95
Overstreet, C. V.	SR	401-95
Owen, A. J.	FB	401-166
Owen, A. N.	SR	401-95
Owen, B. E.	RRR	401-122
Owen, Bates F.	USV	401-245
Owen, Ira D.	RR	401-60
Owen, James	RR	401-60
Owen, John	NAV	401-22
Owen, Thomas A.	FB	401-166
Owen, W. H.	FB	401-167
Owen, W. M.	FF	401-138
Owen, William	RR	401-60
Owens, B. T.	FB	401-167
Owens, B. W.	ARM	401-9
Owens, Ben D.	SR	401-95
Owens, Bevil	SR	401-95
Owens, C. H.	SR	401-95
Owens, Carl V.	SR	401-95
Owens, Evan	NAV	401-22
Owens, G.	TVG	401-208
Owens, George F.	USV	401-245
Owens, Gilbert L.	RRR	401-122
Owens, H. W.	SR	401-95
Owens, H. W.	LR	401-130
Owens, Henry	ARM	401-9
Owens, I. F.	SR	401-95
Owens, J. W.	FB	401-167
Owens, James L.	USV	401-245
Owens, James M.	RR	401-61
Owens, John	FB	401-167
Owens, John S.	TVG	401-208
Owens, Peter W.	TST	401-36
Owens, Robert J.	TST	401-36
Owens, S.	FB	401-167
Owens, S. A.	SP	401-47
Owens, Troy R.	RR	401-61

Index to Texas Adjutant General Service Records—All Service Branches

Name	Branch	Record
Owens, W. G.	TVG	401-208
Owens, W. J.	SP	401-47
Owens, Wiley	TST	401-36
Owens, William A.	SR	401-95
Owens, William A.	USV	401-245
Owens, William P.	TST	401-36
Owensby, N. M.	TVG	401-208
Oyervides, Miguel	RR	401-61
Ozment, R. L.	TVG	401-208
Pace, Charles D.	RR	401-61
Pace, Gideon G.	TST	401-36
Pace, James M.	USV	401-245
Pace, T. T.	FB	401-167
Pace, W. B.	CSA	401-40
Pace, W. W.	FB	401-167
Pack, Leonard M.	SR	401-95
Padgett, F. C.	TVG	401-208
Padgett, J. E.	SR	401-95
Pafford, S. B.	USV	401-245
Page, Charles W.	TVG	401-208
Page, Edward L.	USV	401-245
Page, Evan C.	USV	401-245
Page, George G.	USV	401-245
Page, Holland	SR	401-95
Page, J. Herbert, Dr.	SR	401-95
Page, J. Watt	SR	401-95
Page, James F.	USV	401-245
Page, L. L.	USV	401-245
Page, S.	TVG	401-208
Page, Samuel Q.	NAV	401-22
Pahnvitz, Adolphy	ARM	401-9
Paige, Joseph	ARM	401-9
Paine, Barrington	NAV	401-22
Paine, Guss L.	TVG	401-208
Pains, J. D.	FF	401-138
Painter, W. E.	TVG	401-208
Painter, William G.	USV	401-245
Pais, Doroteo	FF	401-138
Palmer, C. T.	RRR	401-122
Palmer, Edd	FB	401-167
Palmer, Francis H.	USV	401-245
Palmer, Frank M.	USV	401-245
Palmer, Fred W.	USV	401-245
Palmer, Harry	FB	401-167
Palmer, Howell S.	SR	401-95
Palmer, John A.	USV	401-245
Palmer, John C.	RR	401-61
Palmer, Walter	ARM	401-9
Palmie, A. F.	TVG	401-208
Pamplin, W. S.	TVG	401-208
Panders, Ed	TVG	401-208
Pangburn, H.	TVG	401-208
Pangle, Joe L.	SR	401-95
Pankey, James	TST	401-36
Pankey, Luther M.	USV	401-245
Panneel, Hugh G.	TVG	401-208
Pannell, W. H.	SR	401-95
Pannen, Joe	USV	401-245
Pannill, Paine	TVG	401-208
Panter, Samuel C.	RRR	401-122
Pape, G. H.	TVG	401-208
Papot, J. H.	TVG	401-208
Parada, Esteven	FF	401-138
Parchman, James Lemuel	RR	401-61
Parchman, Leo D.	USV	401-245
Parchman, Whitfield M.	USV	401-245
Parham, Guy	TVG	401-208
Paris, E. V.	SP	401-47
Paris, Samuel	NAV	401-22
Parish, A. H.	TST	401-36
Parish, Louis E.	ARM	401-9
Parish, Richard C.	USV	401-245
Parish, Semmes Wilder	TVG	401-208
Parish, Semmes Wilder	USV	401-245
Park, J. A.	TVG	401-208
Parker, A. L.	TVG	401-208
Parker, Abe	USV	401-245
Parker, Abram	SP	401-47
Parker, Albert L.	USV	401-245
Parker, B.	TVG	401-208
Parker, B. B.	RRR	401-122
Parker, B. J.	SR	401-95
Parker, B. J.	LR	401-130
Parker, C. E.	SR	401-95
Parker, Charles	USV	401-245
Parker, Charles B.	RRR	401-122
Parker, Charles B.	SR	401-95
Parker, Charles F.	TVG	401-208
Parker, Charles W.	TVG	401-208
Parker, Clarence Edgar	SR	401-95
Parker, E. B.	TVG	401-208
Parker, Edward	SP	401-47
Parker, F. B.	FB	401-167
Parker, Fagan	SR	401-95
Parker, Foxhall A.	USV	401-245
Parker, Frank	SR	401-95
Parker, Frank	TVG	401-208
Parker, George E.	RRR	401-122
Parker, George H.	NAV	401-22
Parker, George T.	FB	401-167
Parker, H. C.	SR	401-95
Parker, H. C.	LR	401-130
Parker, H. E.	FB	401-167
Parker, H. R.	SR	401-95
Parker, H. R.	LR	401-130
Parker, J. A.	TVG	401-208
Parker, J. C.	RR	401-61
Parker, J. F.	RR	401-61
Parker, J. F.	SP	401-47
Parker, J. L.	RRR	401-122
Parker, J. W.	FB	401-167
Parker, J. W. C.	NAV	401-22

Index to Texas Adjutant General Service Records—All Service Branches

Name	Branch	Record
Parker, Joe	SR	401-95
Parker, John H.	NAV	401-22
Parker, John Henry	RR	401-61
Parker, John R.	TVG	401-208
Parker, John W.	RRR	401-122
Parker, L. J.	SP	401-47
Parker, Leslie C.	USV	401-245
Parker, Mack	SR	401-95
Parker, Orran D.	USV	401-245
Parker, Oscar	RR	401-61
Parker, Oscar	SR	401-95
Parker, R. T. "Bob"	SR	401-95
Parker, Riley V.	FF	401-138
Parker, S. H.	SR	401-95
Parker, Sam H.	TVG	401-208
Parker, T. F.	FB	401-167
Parker, T. S.	RRR	401-122
Parker, Thomas Alfred	RRR	401-122
Parker, Thomas H.	ARM	401-9
Parker, Troy	RRR	401-122
Parker, Walter W.	USV	401-245
Parker, Will	TVG	401-208
Parker, William A.	SR	401-95
Parker, William Cleveland	RRR	401-122
Parkerson, Edward	SP	401-47
Parkerson, Edward	FF	401-138
Parkerson, Millard M.	ARM	401-9
Parkhurst, John H.	NAV	401-22
Parkinson, Don B.	SR	401-95
Parks, B. E.	RR	401-61
Parks, Beverly E.	FB	401-167
Parks, Cullen	ARM	401-9
Parks, E. S.	SR	401-95
Parks, E. S.	LR	401-130
Parks, George W.	MV	401-30
Parks, Hal B.	SR	401-95
Parks, J. M.	FB	401-167
Parks, J. T.	FB	401-167
Parks, J. T.	TVG	401-208
Parks, P. P.	TVG	401-208
Parks, T. C.	SR	401-95
Parmer, Anthony	ARM	401-9
Parks, T. C.	LR	401-130
Parmer, Clint L.	SR	401-95
Parmer, Clint L.	TVG	401-208
Parmewitz, Ed.	USV	401-245
Parnell, Charles M.	USV	401-245
Parnell, Maxwell C.	USV	401-245
Parr, Jack	RR	401-61
Parr, Jack	SR	401-95
Parr, Jack	LR	401-130
Parrent, E. J.	CSA	401-40
Parrent, Everett J.	CSA	401-40
Parris, J. D.	FF	401-138
Parrish, Byron B.	RR	401-61
Parrish, Charles	TVG	401-208
Parrish, Eugene W.	USV	401-245
Parrish, M. C.	SR	401-95
Parrish, M. C., Jr.	SR	401-95
Parrish, R. W.	TVG	401-208
Parrish, William	USV	401-245
Parrish, William S.	FB	401-167
Parrott, A. L.	FB	401-167
Parrott, J. B.	SR	401-95
Parson, E. B.	RRR	401-122
Parson, Robert	MV	401-30
Parsons, F. H.	SR	401-95
Parsons, J. W.	FB	401-167
Parsons, John	FF	401-138
Parsons, R. B.	SR	401-95
Parsons, R. B.	LR	401-130
Paschal, William	SP	401-47
Paschall, Charles A.	USV	401-245
Pasche, Henry M.	TVG	401-208
Pass, E. L.	TVG	401-208
Passmore, R. A.	USV	401-245
Passmore, William R.	ARM	401-9
Passons, Frank	SP	401-47
Passons, James L.	USV	401-245
Pate, Henry Addison	USV	401-245
Pate, Robert H.	USV	401-245
Patino, Miguel O.	TVG	401-208
Patotzka, Frederick B.	USV	401-245
Patrick, A. T.	FB	401-167
Patrick, Alex	TVG	401-208
Patrick, Alonzo O.	USV	401-245
Patrick, C. H.	RRR	401-122
Patrick, J. H.	SP	401-47
Patridge, James B.	NAV	401-22
Patten, Frank A.	SR	401-96
Patten, W. B.	SR	401-96
Patterson, Amos H.	TVG	401-208
Patterson, Amos H.	USV	401-245
Patterson, Andrew G.	MV	401-30
Patterson, Arthur T.	USV	401-245
Patterson, Charlie E.	USV	401-245
Patterson, Clarence K.	TVG	401-208
Patterson, David O.	USV	401-245
Patterson, E. W.	USV	401-245
Patterson, F. M.	SP	401-47
Patterson, Frank	RR	401-61
Patterson, Frank	SR	401-96
Patterson, Geo. B.	SR	401-96
Patterson, George W.	MV	401-30
Patterson, H. W.	RRR	401-122
Patterson, Harloin	RRR	401-122
Patterson, J. C.	MV	401-30
Patterson, J. H.	TVG	401-208
Patterson, J. J.	USV	401-245
Patterson, J. L.	SR	401-96
Patterson, J. W.	FB	401-167
Patterson, Joe E.	TVG	401-208

Index to Texas Adjutant General Service Records—All Service Branches

Patterson, Joel D. .... USV 401-245
Patterson, John B. .... TVG 401-208
Patterson, John C. .... MM 401-32
Patterson, John G. .... SR 401-96
Patterson, Lee .... FB 401-167
Patterson, R. E. .... RRR 401-122
Patterson, Roburt R. .... USV 401-245
Patterson, Roy .... TVG 401-208
Patterson, Samuel A. .... USV 401-245
Patterson, Sherman M. .... RRR 401-122
Patterson, Sherman M. .... SR 401-96
Patterson, William .... TST 401-36
Patterson, William F. .... USV 401-245
Patteson, Daniel A. .... USV 401-245
Pattillo, Carroll J. .... USV 401-245
Patton, Bayard .... USV 401-245
Patton, Ben F. .... RR 401-61
Patton, Bob .... FB 401-167
Patton, Charles A. .... MM 401-32
Patton, Charles A. .... FF 401-138
Patton, Clyde .... TVG 401-208
Patton, Coy .... RRR 401-122
Patton, Eugene Van .... SP 401-47
Patton, George .... FB 401-167
Patton, George W. .... FF 401-138
Patton, H. A. .... TVG 401-208
Patton, Hubbard D. .... TVG 401-208
Patton, J. L. .... SR 401-96
Patton, James .... NAV 401-22
Patton, John .... NAV 401-22
Patton, Louie .... TVG 401-208
Patton, M. O. .... SR 401-96
Patton, O. .... SR 401-96
Patton, O. .... LR 401-130
Patton, Oscar .... RR 401-61
Patton, Pickens .... TST 401-36
Patton, R. M. .... SR 401-96
Patton, Randolph .... RR 401-61
Patton, Samuel .... FB 401-167
Patton, Samuel B. .... FF 401-138
Patton, Samuel J. .... MV 401-30
Patton, Thomas F. .... FB 401-167
Patton, Thomas L. .... SP 401-47
Patton, W. B. .... RR 401-61
Patton, W. B. .... SR 401-96
Patton, W. F. .... SR 401-96
Patton, W. F. .... LR 401-130
Patton, Warren S. .... SR 401-96
Paugh, William L. .... FB 401-167
Paugle, J. C. .... TVG 401-208
Paugle, J. C. .... USV 401-245
Paugle, John H. .... TVG 401-208
Paugle, John H. .... USV 401-245
Paul, Bain .... SR 401-96
Paul, C. D. .... RRR 401-122
Paul, James .... TST 401-36

Paul, John W. .... SP 401-47
Paul, Stonewall J. .... USV 401-245
Pauli, Louis .... FB 401-167
Paulig, August .... USV 401-245
Paulk, James K. .... FB 401-167
Pavlas, Felix .... SR 401-96
Paxton, Everett .... TVG 401-208
Paylor, M. P. .... RRR 401-122
Payne, B. W. .... SR 401-96
Payne, Erven B. .... USV 401-245
Payne, Frank .... FB 401-167
Payne, J. B. .... FB 401-167
Payne, Joel R. .... FF 401-138
Payne, Lawson C. .... RRR 401-122
Payne, Robert G. .... USV 401-245
Payne, Samuel .... ARM 401-9
Payne, W. L. .... FB 401-167
Payne, William D. .... TVG 401-208
Payton, Charles .... RRR 401-122
Payton, Charles Joseph .... TVG 401-208
Payton, Cross .... SR 401-96
Payton, Fred. E. .... USV 401-245
Payton, John L. .... USV 401-245
Payton, L. C. .... TVG 401-208
Payton, W. H. .... SP 401-47
Peabody, Fred D. .... SR 401-96
Peacher, William M. .... USV 401-245
Peacock, Frank M. .... TVG 401-208
Peacock, Lewis H. .... TVG 401-208
Peak, Junius .... FB 401-167
Peak, M. L. .... FB 401-167
Peak, Sam H. .... SR 401-96
Peal, D. A. .... FB 401-167
Pearce, Chester M. .... SR 401-96
Pearce, Clyde H. .... SR 401-96
Pearce, Frank .... FB 401-167
Pearce, Frank S. .... RRR 401-122
Pearce, Fred C. .... SR 401-96
Pearce, George W. .... SR 401-96
Pearce, George W. .... LR 401-130
Pearce, George Washington .... CSA 401-40
Pearce, J. M. .... FB 401-167
Pearce, Lawson W. .... RRR 401-122
Pearce, Thomas .... NAV 401-22
Pearce, William Huston .... FB 401-167
Pearce, William L. .... RRR 401-122
Pearce, William P. .... RR 401-61
Pearcy, A. R. .... TVG 401-208
Pearcy, Porter .... SR 401-96
Peareson, D. R. .... TVG 401-208
Peareson, E. A. .... USV 401-245
Peareson, E. A. .... TVG 401-208
Pearl, E. W. .... TVG 401-208
Pearson, A. M. .... SR 401-96
Pearson, E. A. .... TVG 401-208
Pearson, J. W. .... RR 401-61

Index to Texas Adjutant General Service Records—All Service Branches

Name	Branch	Record
Pearson, J. W.	FB	401-167
Pearson, John W.	MM	401-32
Pearson, Olice Lowell	RRR	401-122
Pearson, W. N.	USV	401-245
Pease, S. Robert	FB	401-167
Peauch, Aristed	NAV	401-22
Peauch, Henry	NAV	401-22
Pechal, Joseph	RRR	401-122
Pechal, W. J.	RRR	401-122
Peck, A. C.	ARM	401-9
Peck, G. W.	SR	401-96
Peck, Hal C.	SR	401-96
Peck, Leonard Ollie	RRR	401-122
Peck, Lon	USV	401-245
Peckring, Thomas	NAV	401-22
Peddy, James H.	USV	401-245
Peden, Andrew Gehring	SR	401-96
Peden, David D.	SR	401-96
Peden, H. D.	USV	401-245
Pedigo, Abram B.	MV	401-30
Pedigo, Eugene R.	USV	401-245
Pedigo, Smith C.	TVG	401-208
Pedrissor, Toribio	FB	401-167
Peebles, D. L.	TVG	401-208
Peebles, David L.	TST	401-36
Peebles, J. J.	RR	401-61
Peebles, J. J.	SR	401-96
Peebles, Thomas	TVG	401-208
Peek, H. F.	SR	401-96
Peek, H. F.	LR	401-130
Peel, B. H.	TVG	401-208
Peel, James	TST	401-36
Peel, Stephen	FF	401-138
Peel, William H.	FF	401-138
Peeler, A. J., Colonel	SR	401-96
Peeler, Graves	SR	401-96
Peeler, J. A.	FB	401-167
Peeler, John Lowery	TVG	401-208
Peeples, Darling Luther	USV	401-245
Peerce, C. E.	USV	401-245
Peerce, John H.	SR	401-96
Peery, William M.	USV	401-245
Peete, Angus	USV	401-245
Peevey, John C.	CSA	401-40
Peevey, L. L.	RR	401-61
Peevey, L. L.	SR	401-96
Peevey, R. O.	TVG	401-208
Peevey, Tom	SR	401-96
Pegues, Oliver T.	USV	401-245
Peirce, C. E.	TVG	401-208
Peirre, Alpheus	TVG	401-208
Peirson, James	ARM	401-9
Pellow, Robert Emmett	SR	401-96
Peltier, H. A.	RRR	401-122
Pemberton, George	NAV	401-22
Pemberton, Henry	NAV	401-22
Pemberton, John A.	RR	401-61
Pemberton, Robin	MV	401-30
Pemberton, Tisdel G.	MV	401-30
Pembroke, J. H.	FB	401-167
Pen, Jack	SR	401-96
Pena, Nasario	FF	401-138
Penado, Clemento	FF	401-138
Penaloza, Jose Ma.	TST	401-36
Pender, J. W.	USV	401-245
Pendergrass, A. W.	FB	401-167
Pendergrass, William	TST	401-36
Pendleton, Edward	USV	401-245
Pendleton, J. F.	FB	401-167
Pendley, Albert D.	USV	401-245
Pendley, Milburn	USV	401-245
Pendorn, Robert W.	USV	401-245
Penick, J. W.	TVG	401-208
Penick, R. E.	SR	401-96
Penick, R. M.	TVG	401-208
Penick, Robert L.	TVG	401-208
Penland, R. L.	SR	401-96
Penland, R. L.	LR	401-130
Penland, S. M.	TVG	401-208
Penn, J. S.	TVG	401-208
Penn, Justo S.	SR	401-96
Penn, Justo S.	USV	401-245
Penn, Justo S.	LR	401-130
Pennewell, Harry L.	USV	401-245
Pennington, B. F.	FB	401-167
Pennington, Ben L.	RR	401-61
Pennington, Elijah	TVG	401-208
Pennington, Harry	TVG	401-208
Pennington, Hugh	SP	401-47
Pennington, John L.	USV	401-245
Penny, Willie	TVG	401-208
Pennyville, Handy	ARM	401-9
Penrod, L. L.	TST	401-36
Pentecost, George	TVG	401-208
Penuel, Robert D.	USV	401-245
Peoples, Clinton	SR	401-96
Peoples, John	NAV	401-22
Pepper, J. M.	RRR	401-122
Peques, Oliver Thomas	USV	401-245
Perales, Antonio	FB	401-167
Percy, C. W.	SR	401-96
Perez, Betro	RR	401-61
Perez, Desiderio	RR	401-61
Perez, Henry	USV	401-245
Perez, Jesse	RR	401-61
Perez, Jesse, Sr.	RR	401-61
Peril, Rufus D.	FF	401-138
Perkin, Joseph	ARM	401-9
Perkins, A. T.	FB	401-167
Perkins, Andrew	SP	401-48
Perkins, C. F. Dee	RR	401-61
Perkins, C. G.	TVG	401-208

Index to Texas Adjutant General Service Records—All Service Branches

Name	Branch	Record
Perkins, Charles	SR	401-96
Perkins, E. H.	RR	401-61
Perkins, Elisha	ARM	401-9
Perkins, Frank D.	USV	401-245
Perkins, Freeman	FF	401-138
Perkins, H. O.	FB	401-167
Perkins, H. W.	USV	401-245
Perkins, Henry Wright	RRR	401-122
Perkins, J. F.	FB	401-167
Perkins, J. P.	RR	401-61
Perkins, James A.	RRR	401-122
Perkins, James Clarke	RR	401-61
Perkins, Jesse H.	USV	401-245
Perkins, Jim	SR	401-96
Perkins, Joe B.	USV	401-245
Perkins, John C.	USV	401-245
Perkins, Lee A.	USV	401-245
Perkins, Lon A.	SR	401-96
Perkins, Lon A.	LR	401-130
Perkins, Norman L.	USV	401-245
Perkins, Paul	FB	401-167
Perkins, Perry W.	SR	401-96
Perkins, R. O.	SR	401-96
Perkins, T. E. P.	RR	401-61
Perkins, Thomas H.	USV	401-245
Perkins, W. A.	SR	401-96
Perkins, W. H.	FB	401-167
Perkins, William	RR	401-61
Perkins, William	SP	401-48
Perl, Leon	USV	401-245
Perlitz, W. E.	USV	401-245
Permenter, Claud O.	SR	401-96
Permenter, G. W.	SR	401-96
Perocheau, Louis H.	NAV	401-22
Perrenot, Earle E.	USV	401-245
Perrin, W. F.	FB	401-167
Perrin, William F.	FB	401-167
Perron, Clovis F.	USV	401-245
Perron, M. R.	TVG	401-208
Perrow, H. C.	RR	401-61
Perry, A. C.	NAV	401-22
Perry, A. E.	FB	401-167
Perry, A. J.	USV	401-245
Perry, Albert	FB	401-167
Perry, C. F.	SR	401-96
Perry, C. R.	FB	401-167
Perry, Clarence A.	USV	401-245
Perry, Eldred	SR	401-96
Perry, Fred	TVG	401-208
Perry, Henry G.	FB	401-167
Perry, Ira	SR	401-96
Perry, J. M.	FB	401-167
Perry, J. T.	TVG	401-208
Perry, John F.	TST	401-36
Perry, L. C.	SR	401-96
Perry, Lon	USV	401-245
Perry, Ollie J.	FB	401-167
Perry, W. H.	TVG	401-208
Perry, William	FB	401-167
Perry, William E.	USV	401-245
Perry, William T.	USV	401-245
Person, John	ARM	401-9
Peters, E. H.	RRR	401-122
Peters, Ernest J.	RRR	401-122
Peters, Henry	CSA	401-40
Peters, Joe	TVG	401-208
Peters, John	NAV	401-22
Peters, Joseph Johnson	RRR	401-122
Peters, Landon C.	RR	401-61
Peters, Nic	SP	401-48
Peters, Nicholas	FF	401-138
Peters, S. R.	FB	401-167
Peters, Samuel	RR	401-61
Peterson, B. F.	FB	401-167
Peterson, Frederick R.	TVG	401-208
Peterson, J. D.	FB	401-167
Peterson, Thomas N.	TVG	401-208
Peterson, Victor	USV	401-245
Peterson, W. S.	SR	401-96
Peterson, William Sanders	RR	401-61
Petit, J. P.	NAV	401-22
Petmecky, Charles	RRR	401-122
Petmecky, Joe G.	FB	401-167
Petree, Luther A.	USV	401-245
Petreswich, F.	ARM	401-9
Petri, Arthur	FF	401-138
Petrich, O. C.	TVG	401-208
Pettis, S. R.	FB	401-167
Pettite, William	MV	401-30
Pettus, Thomas H.	USV	401-245
Petty, Alexander W.	MV	401-30
Petty, Hazel A.	TVG	401-208
Petty, J. W.	FB	401-167
Petty, James E.	SP	401-48
Petty, Joseph R.	RR	401-61
Petty, T. A.	RRR	401-122
Petty, Thornton M.	MV	401-30
Petzel, William	TVG	401-208
Peverler, C. O.	FB	401-167
Peveto, A. B.	SR	401-96
Peveto, Alva B.	LR	401-130
Peveto, J. T.	TVG	401-208
Peyromand, Joseph	ARM	401-9
Peyton, Alex G.	NAV	401-22
Peyton, Charles J.	TVG	401-208
Peyton, George	TVG	401-208
Peyton, Jim H.	SR	401-96
Peyton, Thomas L.	FB	401-167
Peyton, William S.	SR	401-96
Peyton, William S.	LR	401-130
Pfaeffle, Geo. A., Jr.	SR	401-96
Pfarr, Augustus	USV	401-245

Index to Texas Adjutant General Service Records—All Service Branches

Name	Branch	Record
Pfatt, David A.	USV	401-245
Pfeiffer, John W.	TVG	401-208
Pfeiffer, Walter	TVG	401-208
Pfeuffer, Ulrich S.	TVG	401-208
Pflughaupt, Albert	TVG	401-208
Phansteel, Walter B.	USV	401-245
Phares, L. G.	SR	401-96
Phelan, C. D.	TVG	401-208
Phelan, E.	TST	401-36
Phelan, Edward T.	TVG	401-208
Phelan, J. H., Jr.	SR	401-96
Phelan, James	ARM	401-9
Phelon, S. O.	FB	401-167
Phelps, E. M.	FB	401-167
Phelps, Edwin M.	TVG	401-208
Phelps, H. T.	USV	401-245
Phelps, Lucile	RR	401-61
Phelps, Robert Carrol, Jr.	SR	401-96
Phelps, William E.	RR	401-61
Phenix, Leroy	TVG	401-208
Phifer, Forrest	RRR	401-122
Phillip, Adolph	USV	401-245
Phillips, Barron E.	SR	401-96
Phillips, Byron	RRR	401-122
Phillips, Byron	SR	401-96
Phillips, Carl	SR	401-96
Phillips, Charles M.	SR	401-96
Phillips, Charlie	RRR	401-122
Phillips, Edgar	USV	401-245
Phillips, Geo. W.	SR	401-96
Phillips, George P.	USV	401-245
Phillips, George R.	USV	401-245
Phillips, H. L.	SR	401-96
Phillips, J. C.	TVG	401-208
Phillips, J. E.	TVG	401-208
Phillips, J. H.	FB	401-167
Phillips, J. Len	USV	401-245
Phillips, J. T.	TVG	401-208
Phillips, J. T.	USV	401-246
Phillips, J. W.	FB	401-167
Phillips, J. W.	FB	401-167
Phillips, James G.	USV	401-246
Phillips, Joe	RRR	401-122
Phillips, John D.	ARM	401-9
Phillips, John W.	TVG	401-208
Phillips, M. F.	SR	401-96
Phillips, Manfred E.	FB	401-167
Phillips, N. W.	RRR	401-122
Phillips, R. L.	TVG	401-208
Phillips, Reuben S.	USV	401-246
Phillips, T.	FB	401-167
Phillips, W. C.	SP	401-48
Phillips, W. E.	RR	401-61
Phillips, William J.	USV	401-246
Phillips, William John	TVG	401-208
Philpot, T. C.	TVG	401-208
Philpott, H. B.	FB	401-167
Philpott, J. C.	FB	401-167
Phinn, William	TVG	401-208
Phinn, William	USV	401-246
Phinney, C. D.	TVG	401-208
Phinney, Carl L.	SR	401-96
Phinney, Heber	TVG	401-208
Phipp, J.	TVG	401-208
Phipps, E. G.	ARM	401-9
Piatt, Donn	USV	401-246
Pichard, Victor	TVG	401-208
Pickard, Orren T.	TVG	401-208
Pickens, B. D.	FB	401-168
Pickens, J. L.	FB	401-168
Pickens, S. F.	SR	401-96
Pickering, Oren O.	SR	401-96
Pickett, Dewitt C.	USV	401-246
Pickett, G. B.	FB	401-168
Pickett, George B.	CSA	401-40
Pickett, Howell L.	USV	401-246
Pickett, John L.	USV	401-246
Pickett, R. G.	FB	401-168
Pickett, S. R.	FB	401-168
Pickett, Thomas	FB	401-168
Pickett, W. M.	RRR	401-122
Pickett, W. W.	RRR	401-122
Pickle, Charles, Jr.	SR	401-96
Pickle, David J.	SR	401-96
Pickle, M. L.	SR	401-96
Picks, Lawrence C.	RRR	401-122
Piel, Martin	SP	401-48
Pielop, Ernest	TVG	401-208
Pierce, Albert	USV	401-246
Pierce, Clem W.	SR	401-96
Pierce, Frank B.	USV	401-246
Pierce, G. T.	RRR	401-122
Pierce, H. H.	RRR	401-122
Pierce, Hadley M., Jr.	SR	401-96
Pierce, J. M.	FB	401-168
Pierce, Jasper N.	USV	401-246
Pierce, John	MV	401-30
Pierce, Robert	USV	401-246
Pierce, Robert L.	USV	401-246
Pierce, Sam S.	USV	401-246
Pierce, Silas C.	NAV	401-22
Pierce, W. C.	TVG	401-208
Pierpont, William J. D.	NAV	401-22
Pierre, Jean	NAV	401-22
Pierson, A. R.	USV	401-246
Pierson, E.	FB	401-168
Pierson, Homer	SR	401-96
Pierson, J. W.	RR	401-61
Pierson, John W.	USV	401-246
Pierson, Marion B.	RRR	401-122
Pigott, Edward E.	USV	401-246
Pike, G. G.	RRR	401-122

Index to Texas Adjutant General Service Records—All Service Branches

Name	Branch	Record
Pike, J. T.	FB	401-168
Pike, Jack Price	RRR	401-122
Pike, R. L.	RRR	401-122
Piland, George A.	FB	401-168
Piland, J. W.	MM	401-32
Pilkington, Clifford R.	RRR	401-122
Pillot, Camille G.	SR	401-96
Pillot, J. E.	SR	401-96
Pillot, Norman V.	SR	401-96
Pillow, Jesse M.	USV	401-246
Pinchback, William H.	USV	401-246
Pinchin, B.	TVG	401-208
Pinchin, R. P.	TVG	401-208
Pinchin, Richard J.	USV	401-246
Pindus, David	ARM	401-9
Pingenot, Celestine	TST	401-36
Pingenot, Celestine	FF	401-138
Pinkson, Hamilton	ARM	401-9
Pinkston, W. E.	TVG	401-208
Pinner, M. M.	SP	401-48
Pino, Jesus	FF	401-138
Pinson, W. C., Jr.	RRR	401-122
Pinto, Henry	SR	401-96
Pinto, Joe, Jr.	SR	401-96
Piper, Frank Wade	TVG	401-208
Piper, Henry	FB	401-168
Piper, J. M.	FB	401-168
Piper, John Bryan	RRR	401-122
Pipes, C. E.	RRR	401-122
Pippin, Charles L.	TVG	401-208
Pirie, William	FB	401-168
Pirtle, G. D.	FB	401-168
Pirtle, Isaac Hundley	RRR	401-122
Pirtle, J. G.	FB	401-168
Pitcher, Abner	ARM	401-9
Pitchlynn, Eli	USV	401-246
Pitcock, George T.	SR	401-96
Pither, Walter J.	TVG	401-208
Pitrucha, Steban	USV	401-246
Pitschmann, F. W.	FB	401-168
Pittman, C. L.	TVG	401-208
Pittman, James E.	USV	401-246
Pittman, S. C.	TVG	401-208
Pittman, Venley M.	USV	401-246
Pitts, R.	FB	401-168
Pitts, William A.	FB	401-168
Place, Joe T.	SR	401-96
Placke, William	USV	401-246
Plank, O. A.	RRR	401-122
Plant, Quinn	USV	401-246
Platt, Jake	FB	401-168
Platt, John R.	FB	401-168
Platt, S. M.	FB	401-168
Platt, Thomas	FB	401-168
Platte, William J.	TVG	401-208
Pleasant, Dennis	ARM	401-9
Pleasant, Lucky	SR	401-96
Pledger, J. P.	SR	401-96
Plott, C. H.	RR	401-61
Plott, C. H., Jr.	SR	401-96
Plumar, Samuel	FB	401-168
Plumb, J. D.	FB	401-168
Plumber, E. W.	NAV	401-22
Plumlee, C. C.	RRR	401-122
Plumley, L. P.	RRR	401-122
Plummer, Earl	USV	401-246
Plummer, J. A.	FF	401-138
Plummer, Joseph F.	USV	401-246
Plunkett, Walter	USV	401-246
Pluto, John G.	TVG	401-208
Poe, J. A.	RR	401-61
Poe, W. F.	TVG	401-208
Poerner, William	FF	401-138
Pogue, W. C.	RR	401-61
Pogues, Eugene S.	USV	401-246
Poh, George	ARM	401-9
Pohle, H.	TVG	401-208
Poietiger, Lorenzo	FF	401-138
Poindexter, R. G.	TVG	401-208
Pointer, William J.	USV	401-246
Poland, Dan G.	SR	401-97
Poland, E. L.	SR	401-97
Polk, L. J.	SR	401-97
Polk, L. J.	TVG	401-208
Polk, Neal	SR	401-97
Polk, Robert L.	TVG	401-208
Polk, T. T.	SR	401-97
Polk, W. A.	TVG	401-208
Polkinghorn H.	USV	401-246
Pollard, James H.	ARM	401-9
Pollard, Tomas G.	SR	401-97
Polley, J. O.	RRR	401-122
Pollock, Artie	SR	401-97
Pollock, D. D.	RR	401-61
Pomes, Emile	USV	401-246
Pompa, Jesus	FB	401-168
Ponder, J. E.	TVG	401-208
Pool, Arthur	USV	401-246
Pool, C. F. P.	RR	401-61
Pool, C. Y.	FB	401-168
Pool, J. F. P.	SR	401-97
Pool, Lee M.	SR	401-97
Pool, Luther B.	USV	401-246
Pool, R. J.	SR	401-97
Pool, Ray	SR	401-97
Pool, Robert S.	SR	401-97
Poole, G. T.	TVG	401-208
Poole, Garner C.	SR	401-97
Poole, Gus	FF	401-138
Poole, M. J.	RR	401-61
Poole, Milton Raymond	RRR	401-122
Poole, R. E.	RR	401-61

Index to Texas Adjutant General Service Records—All Service Branches

Name	Branch	Record
Poole, R. E.	SR	401-97
Poole, T. H.	FB	401-168
Poole, Tom Reed	SR	401-97
Poole, W. H.	RRR	401-122
Poole, William C., Jr.	SR	401-97
Pope, Ben F.	SR	401-97
Pope, Bowen	TVG	401-208
Pope, Fletcher B.	SR	401-97
Pope, G. B.	SR	401-97
Pope, Grover C.	SR	401-97
Pope, J. T.	FB	401-168
Pope, John T.	FB	401-168
Pope, John Winfred, Jr.	SR	401-97
Pope, S. B.	SR	401-97
Pope, Virgil	SR	401-97
Pope, W. B.	SR	401-97
Pope, W. B.	SR	401-97
Pope, W. J.	SP	401-48
Popejoy, Rufe	SR	401-97
Porr, T. D.	RRR	401-122
Porter, Breckenridge	SR	401-97
Porter, Burford H.	USV	401-246
Porter, C. C.	SR	401-97
Porter, C. D.	RRR	401-122
Porter, Emil	FB	401-168
Porter, G. W.	CSA	401-40
Porter, Gilmore E.	USV	401-246
Porter, H. A.	SR	401-97
Porter, H. A.	LR	401-130
Porter, Horton B.	SR	401-97
Porter, J. C.	SR	401-97
Porter, J. W.	FB	401-168
Porter, James B.	SP	401-48
Porter, John Sharp	MM	401-32
Porter, Josey	CSA	401-40
Porter, Julius	RR	401-61
Porter, L. L.	SR	401-97
Porter, Lon B.	USV	401-246
Porter, M. W.	FB	401-168
Porter, Milby	USV	401-246
Porter, N. Connor	SR	401-97
Porter, R. C.	TST	401-36
Porter, Randon, Jr.	SR	401-97
Porter, Richard L., Jr.	RR	401-61
Porter, Richard L., Jr.	SR	401-97
Porter, Samuel	TST	401-36
Porter, Samuel C.	RRR	401-122
Porter, W. E.	FB	401-168
Porter, W. J., Jr.	FB	401-168
Porter, W. Maynard	SR	401-97
Porter, William	USV	401-246
Portis, W. B.	USV	401-246
Portman, George	RR	401-61
Posey, C. E.	RR	401-61
Post, Calvin	ARM	401-9
Post, Fred Orville	USV	401-246
Post, K. M.	RRR	401-122
Postel, Herrmann	FF	401-138
Postell, J. N.	NAV	401-22
Postell, Joseph	NAV	401-22
Postell, William Ross	NAV	401-22
Postra, Augustin	FF	401-138
Potash, M. L.	TVG	401-208
Poteet, B. R.	USV	401-246
Poteet, W. B.	USV	401-246
Potter, Frank	FB	401-168
Potter, J. E.	FB	401-168
Potter, Luther M.	USV	401-246
Potter, Richard M.	RR	401-61
Potter, Tom	SR	401-97
Pottinger, J. V.	RRR	401-122
Pottorff, W. J.	SR	401-97
Potts, Amos E.	USV	401-246
Potts, H. B.	FB	401-168
Potts, Henry B.	USV	401-246
Potts, John S.	USV	401-246
Potts, Thomas H. D.	NAV	401-22
Potts, William H.	RR	401-61
Poulson, Thomas J.	USV	401-246
Pouncey, J. M.	SR	401-97
Pound, E. J.	FB	401-168
Pounden, James	TST	401-36
Pounds, D. F.	TVG	401-208
Powell, Alley	RR	401-61
Powell, Asa N.	USV	401-246
Powell, B. M.	RRR	401-123
Powell, Benjamin F.	FB	401-168
Powell, Bird	SP	401-48
Powell, Bob	SR	401-97
Powell, Bob	LR	401-130
Powell, Buell H.	SR	401-97
Powell, C. C.	RRR	401-123
Powell, Charles M.	USV	401-246
Powell, Clyde Alvin	RRR	401-123
Powell, E. L.	SR	401-97
Powell, Frank	LR	401-130
Powell, Frank D.	TVG	401-208
Powell, Frank D.	USV	401-246
Powell, Galveston	USV	401-246
Powell, George F.	USV	401-246
Powell, H. M.	TVG	401-209
Powell, J. H.	SR	401-97
Powell, J. L.	TVG	401-209
Powell, James M.	MV	401-30
Powell, John C.	TVG	401-209
Powell, Nathaniel J.	ARM	401-9
Powell, Robert L.	USV	401-246
Powell, Roger M.	SR	401-97
Powell, Ross J.	TVG	401-209
Powell, Walker	USV	401-246
Powell, Warren	USV	401-246
Powell, William	FB	401-168

Index to Texas Adjutant General Service Records—All Service Branches

Powell, William E. ....USV 401-246
Powell, William F. ....USV 401-246
Powell, William M. ....USV 401-246
Power, Charles J. ....USV 401-246
Power, E. C. ....FB 401-168
Power, Jacob B. ....USV 401-246
Powers, Andrew L. ....TST 401-36
Powers, Ben. ....SR 401-97
Powers, C. E. ....RRR 401-123
Powers, Ed. E. T. ....TVG 401-209
Powers, Edmond E. T. ....USV 401-246
Powers, Everett Thornton. ....TVG 401-209
Powers, J. E. ....RRR 401-123
Powers, Joe. ....USV 401-246
Powers, Pat. ....SR 401-97
Powers, W. A. ....SR 401-97
Powers, William E. ....RR 401-61
Powers, William S. ....USV 401-246
Powles, Thomas W. ....FB 401-168
Poynor, Tom. ....SR 401-97
Prather, E. B. ....SR 401-97
Prather, J. H. ....SR 401-97
Prather, J. H. ....FB 401-168
Prather, Raisin. ....SP 401-48
Prather, Robert ....USV 401-246
Pratt, A. W. ....RRR 401-123
Pratt, J. M. ....FF 401-138
Pratt, P. P. ....USV 401-246
Preacher, L. H. ....SR 401-97
Preble, C. H. ....SR 401-97
Preece, Andrew G. ....TVG 401-209
Preece, Edmond D. ....TVG 401-209
Preece, Edward D. ....USV 401-246
Preece, Reuben. ....USV 401-246
Premont, Charles ....SR 401-97
Premont, Charles ....FB 401-168
Prendergast, George P. ....TVG 401-209
Prescott, E. H. ....USV 401-246
Preslar, H. C. ....SR 401-97
Presley, John D. ....USV 401-246
Presley, R. L. ....USV 401-246
Presley, Will W. ....USV 401-246
Presnall, H. H. ....RRR 401-123
Presnall, Owen W. ....SR 401-97
Presnall, P. A. ....SR 401-97
Pressley, Calvin. ....USV 401-246
Prestidge, S. B. ....FB 401-168
Preston, C. W. ....TVG 401-209
Preston, George H. ....SR 401-97
Preston, James S. ....USV 401-246
Preston, John ....RR 401-61
Prestwood, J. T. ....FB 401-168
Prestwood, Peter D. ....ARM 401-9
Preussner, George Harry ....TVG 401-209
Prevost, Paul. ....ARM 401-9
Prewitt, W. B. ....SR 401-97

Prewitt, W. C. ....USV 401-246
Pribble, Luther M. ....TVG 401-209
Price, Andy F. ....SR 401-97
Price, B. F. ....CSA 401-40
Price, Benjamin S. ....USV 401-246
Price, Berry T. ....TVG 401-209
Price, C. W. ....SR 401-97
Price, Caleb A. ....USV 401-246
Price, Charles W. ....RR 401-61
Price, Clay L. ....SR 401-97
Price, David. ....SP 401-48
Price, E. O. ....TVG 401-209
Price, E. P. ....USV 401-246
Price, Elbert H. ....USV 401-246
Price, Frank W. ....TVG 401-209
Price, G. H. ....SR 401-97
Price, George E. ....USV 401-246
Price, George Harley ....SR 401-97
Price, George T. ....FB 401-168
Price, George W. ....TVG 401-209
Price, Herbert J. ....SR 401-97
Price, J. A. ....SR 401-97
Price, James. ....ARM 401-9
Price, James M. ....SR 401-97
Price, James R. ....TVG 401-209
Price, John L. ....USV 401-246
Price, John R. ....RRR 401-123
Price, Joseph R. ....FB 401-168
Price, Leslie S. ....RRR 401-123
Price, Lewis. ....TVG 401-209
Price, R. N. (Bud), Jr. ....SR 401-97
Price, Robert L. ....USV 401-246
Price, Sam G. ....TVG 401-209
Price, Sterling. ....FB 401-168
Price, T. H. ....FB 401-168
Price, Volney N. ....USV 401-246
Price, W. E. ....TVG 401-209
Price, W. S. ....SR 401-97
Price, W. S. ....LR 401-130
Price, W. Y. ....FB 401-168
Price, Watt W. ....USV 401-246
Price, West F. ....TVG 401-209
Price, West F. ....USV 401-246
Price, William B. ....NAV 401-22
Prichard, Leslie A. ....SR 401-97
Priddy, J. B. ....TVG 401-209
Priddy, J. T. ....RR 401-61
Pridgen, Oscar F. ....SR 401-97
Pridgen, Oscar F. ....FB 401-168
Priesmuth, William A. ....USV 401-246
Priess, Charles ....FF 401-138
Priest, Cecil ....SR 401-97
Priester, William G. ....TVG 401-209
Priestley, J. S. ....SP 401-48
Priestley, William P. ....TST 401-36
Priestly, J. H. ....TVG 401-209

Index to Texas Adjutant General Service Records—All Service Branches

Primavesi, Felix ....USV 401-246
Primavesi, Frank J. ....USV 401-246
Prince, Fred E. ....SR............401-97
Prince, Fred E. ....LR 401-130
Prince, George R. ....TVG 401-209
Prince, John H. ....CSA..........401-40
Prince, L. J. ....SR............401-97
Prince, R. E. ....TVG 401-209
Prince, R. P. ....SR............401-97
Prindle, Thomas J. ....RR 401-61
Pring, William ....RR 401-61
Pringle, Robert L. ....USV 401-246
Pritchett, W. T. ....SP............401-48
Procter, W. J. ....FB............401-168
Proctor, George A................TVG 401-209
Proctor, J. C. ....FB............401-168
Proctor, John M. ....USV 401-246
Proctor, Leonard ....SR............401-97
Proctor, Pleasant H. ....USV 401-246
Prosens, Henry....................ARM 401-9
Proseus, H. ....NAV........401-22
Prout, Comfort ....ARM 401-9
Provino, Charles C...............USV 401-246
Provo, Sam ....FB............401-168
Pruett, D. L. L. ....FF 401-138
Pruitt, A. M. ....SR............401-97
Pruitt, John T. ....SP............401-48
Pruitt, Reese E. ....USV 401-246
Pryor, William E. ....USV 401-246
Puckett, A. M. ....USV 401-246
Puckett, C. R. ....TST 401-36
Puckett, Corby O. ....USV 401-246
Puckett, H. H. ....FB............401-168
Puckett, J. A. ....FB............401-168
Puckett, J. B. ....RR 401-61
Puckett, John B. ....SR............401-97
Puckett, R. ....FB............401-168
Puckitt, L. W. ....RR 401-61
Puckitt, L. W. ....SR............401-97
Pue, Arthur ....RR 401-61
Pugh, Carl ....RRR 401-123
Pugh, Carl ....SR............401-97
Pugh, Claude H...................RRR 401-123
Pulaski, John.......................NAV........401-22
Pullen, J. C. ....TVG 401-209
Pulliam, E. P. ....ARM 401-9
Pulliam, George L. ....TVG 401-209
Pulliam, T. W. ....TVG 401-209
Pullin, Louis ....SR............401-97
Pullin, T. N. ....RR 401-61
Pulse, N. B. ....FB............401-168
Pumphrey, Jesse C..............USV 401-246
Pundt, J. G. ....SR............401-97
Pupier, Alexander ....ARM 401-9
Purcell, Benjamin S. ....USV 401-246
Purcell, John ....FB............401-168
Purcell, Wilmer O................RRR 401-123
Purdom, Robert Wilson........TVG 401-209
Purdy, McPherson ....USV 401-246
Purdy, R. S. ....FB............401-168
Purl, B. F. ....RRR 401-123
Purnell, William Fisher ....TVG 401-209
Pursch, Rudolph ....USV 401-246
Pursley, William Lee............TVG 401-209
Purvis, Frank Harris.............RR 401-61
Purvis, H. B. ....SR............401-97
Purvis, Robert ....SP............401-48
Puryera, C. T. ....SR............401-97
Putegnot, Henry S...............FB............401-168
Putman, Amzy ....RR 401-61
Putman, E. ....RR 401-61
Putman, J. G. ....SR............401-97
Putman, J. M. ....FB............401-168
Putnam, Carl ....SR............401-97
Putnam, Roger ....SR............401-97
Putnam, W. G. ....USV 401-246
Putney, R. J. ....TVG 401-209
Putz, Henry ....FB............401-168
Pyant, Basil ....ARM 401-9
Pyle, C. R. ....RR 401-61
Pyle, C. R. ....SR............401-97
Pyle, T. M. ....FB............401-168
Pyle, T. M., Jr. ....SR............401-97
Pyles, F. M. ....TST 401-36
Pyron, R. B. ....FB............401-168
Pyron, Robert A..................USV 401-246
Quaite, S. A. ....RR 401-61
Qualls, Jesse ....TVG 401-209
Quarles, Curtis B. ....USV 401-246
Quarles, W. J. ....CSA.........401-40
Quasso, Henry ....USV 401-246
Quayle, Robert...................NAV........401-22
Quayle, William ....TST 401-36
Quayle, William H..............SP............401-48
Quean, Turner....................SP............401-48
Queen, Beale.....................SR............401-97
Queen, F. L. ....RR 401-61
Queen, John Allen ....USV 401-246
Queen, Lee........................FB............401-168
Queen, R. L. ....FB............401-168
Queensbury, George..........USV 401-246
Query, J. W. ....FB............401-168
Quesenberry, L. M. ....FB............401-168
Quick, William M................SR............401-97
Quimby, John ....ARM 401-9
Quinlan, James W.............RR 401-61
Quinn, D. O. ....TVG 401-209
Quinn, Edmund.................RR 401-61
Quinn, John ....ARM 401-9
Quinn, John Olie................SR............401-98
Quinn, Joseph A................TVG 401-209
Quinn, Matthew.................NAV........401-22

Index to Texas Adjutant General Service Records—All Service Branches

Name	Branch	Record
Quinn, Patrick	MV	401-30
Quinn, S. A.	FB	401-168
Quinn, William J.	USV	401-246
Quirk, John	NAV	401-22
Quisenberry, W. L.	TVG	401-209
Qulligan, Andrew	NAV	401-22
Rabb, A. R.	TVG	401-209
Rabb, Christopher	SP	401-48
Rabb, Frank	SR	401-98
Rabier, Alexander	CSA	401-40
Rabourn, John C.	USV	401-246
Rabun, Howell	MV	401-30
Rabyor, Frederick J.	USV	401-246
Race, Buel J.	TVG	401-209
Race, John	NAV	401-23
Race, O. L.	FB	401-168
Rachal, D. C.	CSA	401-40
Rackley, I. T.	SR	401-98
Rackley, J. T. [Isaac Troy]	RR	401-61
Rackly, Wilson	TST	401-36
Racy, J.	FB	401-168
Radcliff, Robert	FF	401-138
Radford, E. E.	TVG	401-209
Radford, Erle H.	USV	401-246
Radford, John S.	SR	401-98
Radford, John S.	TVG	401-209
Radigan, Patrick J.	USV	401-246
Radley, Henry Dudley	TVG	401-209
Rafferty, Patrick	SP	401-48
Ragan, Floyd	USV	401-246
Ragan, R. H.	SR	401-98
Ragan, W. C.	SR	401-98
Ragland, C. E.	USV	401-246
Ragland, C. M.	TVG	401-209
Ragland, De Soto M.	USV	401-246
Ragland, Eldred	USV	401-246
Ragland, Henry	SP	401-48
Ragland, N. M.	SR	401-98
Ragland, Richard W.	USV	401-246
Ragland, Thomas	FB	401-168
Ragland, V. M.	USV	401-246
Ragsdale, R. A.	RR	401-61
Ragsdale, Sam F.	FF	401-138
Ragsdale, Samuel F.	MV	401-30
Raguet, Charles Henry	TVG	401-209
Railins, C. E.	RR	401-61
Rain, D. W. C.	MM	401-32
Rainbo, Edward A.	USV	401-246
Rainbolt, John W.	USV	401-246
Rainbolt, L. W.	TST	401-36
Rainbolt, Peter A.	MV	401-30
Rainey, Ed	SR	401-98
Rainey, J. L.	FB	401-168
Rains, George Perry	TVG	401-209
Rains, Isaac	SP	401-48
Rains, J. D.	FF	401-138
Rains, J. D.	FB	401-168
Rains, John D.	ARM	401-9
Rains, L. C.	SP	401-48
Rains, L. O.	TVG	401-209
Rains, Mercer G.	TVG	401-209
Rains, Sam F.	SR	401-98
Rains, Thomas R.	TST	401-36
Rains, William	FF	401-138
Rainwater, W. A.	FB	401-168
Ralls, Percy B.	USV	401-246
Ralston, John	USV	401-246
Ralston, John G.	USV	401-246
Ramedis, Serilda	FF	401-138
Ramey, William Neal	CSA	401-40
Ramirez. Luz	FF	401-138
Ramirez, Albert	SR	401-98
Ramirez, Jose	FB	401-168
Ramon, Francisco	FF	401-138
Ramon, Manwell	FB	401-168
Ramos, Tomas	TVG	401-209
Ramsay, Frank H.	USV	401-246
Ramsay, J. W.	TVG	401-209
Ramsay, James S.	USV	401-246
Ramsay, John H.	TVG	401-209
Ramsay, Walter	TVG	401-209
Ramsdell, F. R.	USV	401-246
Ramsdell, Frank M.	USV	401-246
Ramsey, A.	NAV	401-23
Ramsey, E. O.	RRR	401-123
Ramsey, G. W.	TVG	401-209
Ramsey, George	USV	401-246
Ramsey, George F.	USV	401-246
Ramsey, H. H.	RR	401-61
Ramsey, H. H.	SR	401-98
Ramsey, M. T.	RR	401-61
Ramsey, M. T.	SR	401-98
Ramsey, Milton	TVG	401-209
Ramsey, Moody T.	USV	401-246
Ramsey, O. M.	SR	401-98
Ramsey, Pollard	TVG	401-209
Ramsey, R. D.	ARM	401-9
Ramsey, R. J. M.	SP	401-48
Ramsey, S. M.	SR	401-98
Ramsey, Vernon H.	SR	401-98
Ramsey, Wade	TVG	401-209
Ramson, E. D.	SP	401-48
Ranck, George N.	RRR	401-123
Ranck, James E.	TST	401-36
Rand, Amasa	ARM	401-9
Randall, Edward	TVG	401-209
Randall, Ellwood A.	FB	401-168
Randall, J. E.	FB	401-168
Randall, James P.	TST	401-37
Randall, N. K.	NAV	401-23
Randel, W. D.	FF	401-138
Randle, D. E.	USV	401-246

Index to Texas Adjutant General Service Records—All Service Branches

Randle, D. H. ....FB............401-168
Randle, E. L. ....TVG 401-209
Randle, Ernest L. ....USV 401-246
Randle, Henry F. ....USV 401-246
Randle, Joe H. ....SR.............401-98
Randle, Vernon ....RR 401-61
Randle, Vernon S. ....SR.............401-98
Randolph, J. D. ....FB.............401-169
Randolph, J. P. ....RR 401-61
Randolph, R. A. ....TVG 401-209
Randolph, R. B. ....SR.............401-98
Randolph, R. D. ....SR.............401-98
Randolph, Riley ....TVG 401-209
Randolph, Robt. ....ARM 401-9
Randolph, Tom ....TVG 401-209
Randolpoh, Cary ....FB.............401-169
Raney, William L. ....USV 401-246
Rank, H. H. ....SR.............401-98
Rankin, C. H. ....FF.............401-138
Rankin, Carlos P. ....TVG 401-209
Rankin, David ....ARM 401-9
Rankin, John Y. ....TST 401-37
Rankin, Johnny ....TST 401-37
Rankin, Julian ....SR.............401-98
Rankin, Lewis M. ....SR.............401-98
Rankin, W. E. ....USV 401-246
Rankin, Will W. ....USV 401-246
Rankin, William ....ARM 401-9
Rankin, William A. ....USV 401-246
Ransom, Elmore W. ....SR.............401-98
Ransom, Elmore W. ....LR 401-130
Ransom, G. E. ....SR.............401-98
Ransom, Henry L. ....USV 401-247
Ransom, Henry Lee ....RR 401-61
Ransom, R. F. ....USV 401-247
Ransom, W. B. ....SR.............401-98
Ranson, G. E. ....SR.............401-98
Ranspot, William George ....RRR 401-123
Rant, Edward H. ....USV 401-247
Rape, Benjamin F. ....USV 401-247
Rapp, G. A. ....SR.............401-98
Rareshide, Albert M. ....TVG 401-209
Rareshide, Albert M. ....USV 401-247
Rasbury, E. L. ....FB.............401-169
Rasco, S. L. ....SR.............401-98
Rasco, S. L. ....LR 401-130
Rascoe, W. P. ....FB.............401-169
Rascoe, William P. ....SR.............401-98
Rase, J. W. ....FB.............401-169
Rasor, M. L. ....FB.............401-169
Rassmussen, P[eter] ....NAV.........401-23
Rasson, H. E. ....USV 401-247
Ratcliff, Edward B. ....MV 401-30
Ratcliff, R. G. ....SR.............401-98
Ratcliff, Wilton ....USV 401-247
Rather, Charles ....SR.............401-98
Rather, Charles, Jr. ....LR 401-130
Rathman, John ....FF.............401-138
Ratke, William ....FF.............401-138
Ratliff, Samuel R. ....USV 401-247
Rattan, Volney ....SP.............401-48
Ratzel, Charles J. ....USV 401-247
Rau, Willie C. ....USV 401-247
Rausch, Gustav E. ....USV 401-247
Ravell, Tom F. ....FB.............401-169
Raven, H. L. ....SR.............401-98
Ravenscraft, S. A. ....FB.............401-169
Ravenstone, Hubert ....ARM 401-9
Rawles, J. F. ....SR.............401-98
Rawley, Patrick ....SP.............401-48
Rawlings, J. C. ....SR.............401-98
Rawlings, J. C. ....TVG 401-209
Rawlings, Thomas B. ....RR 401-61
Rawlinson, Hardy Elbert ....TVG 401-209
Rawls, J. W. ....SR.............401-98
Rawls, James ....ARM 401-9
Rawls, S. J. ....FB.............401-169
Rawls, T. H. ....SR.............401-98
Rawson, Albert G. ....NAV.........401-23
Ray, A. F. ....SR.............401-98
Ray, A. L. ....SR.............401-98
Ray, A. L. ....LR 401-130
Ray, C. B. ....SR.............401-98
Ray, C. L. ....FB.............401-169
Ray, George ....TVG 401-209
Ray, J. J. ....SR.............401-98
Ray, J. J., Jr. ....LR 401-130
Ray, J. O. ....TVG 401-209
Ray, James E. ....TVG 401-209
Ray, John C. ....SR.............401-98
Ray, Joseph ....ARM 401-9
Ray, Joseph Warren ....FB.............401-169
Ray, Melvin B. ....USV 401-247
Ray, Oscar F. ....RRR 401-123
Ray, Roy Francis ....RRR 401-123
Ray, Samuel B. ....USV 401-247
Ray, T. B. ....TVG 401-209
Ray, Thomas J. ....FB.............401-169
Ray, W. L. ....TVG 401-209
Ray, William K. ....TVG 401-209
Ray, William Q. ....USV 401-247
Ray, Worth S. ....USV 401-247
Rayfield, James ....SR.............401-98
Raymond, G. C. ....FB.............401-169
Raymond, G. C. ....TVG 401-209
Raymond, G. R. ....FB.............401-169
Rayner, Hamilton ....FB.............401-169
Rayner, W. P. ....FB.............401-169
Raysor, Marion C. ....TVG 401-209
Raysor, Marion C. ....USV 401-247
Rea, Edward G. ....MV 401-30
Rea, Jesse D. ....SR.............401-98

Index to Texas Adjutant General Service Records—All Service Branches

Name	Branch	Record
Read, D. B.	SR	401-98
Read, Ezra	NAV	401-23
Read, George	ARM	401-9
Read, J. A.	RRR	401-123
Read, J. B.	ARM	401-9
Read, J. D.	USV	401-247
Read, James G.	ARM	401-9
Read, Levi C.	ARM	401-9
Read, Thomas A.	SR	401-98
Reade, William	ARM	401-9
Reader, R. L.	SR	401-98
Reading, Andrew O.	USV	401-247
Ready, A. K.	SR	401-98
Reagan, Chester H.	SR	401-98
Reagan, Forrest	SR	401-98
Reagan, J. M.	SR	401-98
Reagan, J. M.	TVG	401-209
Reagan, J. M., Jr.	LR	401-130
Reagan, John	USV	401-247
Reagan, Taylor Mills	USV	401-247
Reagan, Thomas R.	USV	401-247
Reagan, William R.	FB	401-169
Reams, J. E.	TVG	401-209
Reasoner, T. J.	FB	401-169
Reasonover, Charley	SR	401-98
Reaves, Gould	TVG	401-209
Reaves, Lewis	ARM	401-9
Reavis, James B.	ARM	401-9
Rebuck, Ed	USV	401-247
Rech, Henry	USV	401-247
Rechy, Robert	TVG	401-209
Record, Rawley Kenndy	TVG	401-209
Rector, Howard G.	FB	401-169
Rector, James Bouldin	TVG	401-209
Rector, Nelson Avery	TVG	401-209
Red, James E.	USV	401-247
Red, R. B.	SR	401-98
Reddell, A. B.	SR	401-98
Redden, C. W.	TVG	401-209
Redden, Reuben L.	CSA	401-40
Reddick, A. Leon	USV	401-247
Reddick, Leo	TVG	401-209
Redding, Al G., Jr.	SR	401-98
Redding, Curtis A.	SR	401-98
Redding, William G.	ARM	401-9
Reddy, R. E. L.	TVG	401-209
Reddy, R. E. L.	USV	401-247
Redfearn, J. B.	SR	401-98
Redfield, Albert	ARM	401-9
Redfield, Henry	ARM	401-9
Redfield, William	ARM	401-9
Redford, Hemming W.	USV	401-247
Redman, William J.	USV	401-247
Redmon, John M.	SP	401-48
Redmon, Lafayett	SP	401-48
Redus, Roscoe	RR	401-61
Redus, Roscoe	USV	401-247
Redwine, Jerry	SP	401-48
Redwood, J. G.	SR	401-98
Reeb, C. H.	TVG	401-209
Reece, Ate	SR	401-98
Reece, John	NAV	401-23
Reece, Thomas	RR	401-61
Reed, A. H.	USV	401-247
Reed, Alex H.	SR	401-98
Reed, Ed E.	TVG	401-209
Reed, Edward H.	USV	401-247
Reed, Elmo D.	RR	401-61
Reed, Elmo D.	SR	401-98
Reed, Frank J.	USV	401-247
Reed, G. W.	FB	401-169
Reed, J. E.	TVG	401-209
Reed, J. H.	SR	401-98
Reed, J. M.	FB	401-169
Reed, Jack F.	SR	401-98
Reed, Jacob	MV	401-30
Reed, James B.	TVG	401-209
Reed, James C.	SR	401-98
Reed, Jefferson	ARM	401-9
Reed, John	NAV	401-23
Reed, John	USV	401-247
Reed, John Clark	USV	401-247
Reed, L. W.	SR	401-98
Reed, M. D.	FB	401-169
Reed, M. T.	USV	401-247
Reed, Samuel	TST	401-37
Reed, W. G.	SR	401-98
Reed, W. M.	FB	401-169
Reed, W. W.	USV	401-247
Reed, William	ARM	401-9
Reed, William Edward	RRR	401-123
Reed, William G.	SR	401-98
Reed, William G.	LR	401-130
Reede, Evan	ARM	401-9
Reeder, Frank	SR	401-98
Reedy, William M. T.	RRR	401-123
Rees, David G.	SR	401-98
Rees, G. T.	RRR	401-123
Rees, George A.	TVG	401-209
Rees, William	ARM	401-9
Reese, D. J.	RRR	401-123
Reese, Henry B.	SP	401-48
Reese, Isaac N.	MV	401-30
Reese, J. H.	SR	401-98
Reese, J. W.	RR	401-61
Reese, James Vinson	TVG	401-209
Reese, Jeff L.	SR	401-98
Reese, John W.	SR	401-98
Reese, Joseph Alfred	TVG	401-209
Reese, M. M.	SR	401-98
Reese, R. L.	TVG	401-209
Reese, Wilson R.	RR	401-61

Index to Texas Adjutant General Service Records—All Service Branches

Name	Branch	Page
Reeser, Mannell	SP	401-48
Reeve, J. H.	TVG	401-209
Reeve, T. W.	TVG	401-209
Reeves, C. J.	RR	401-61
Reeves, Frank	SR	401-98
Reeves, J. E.	TVG	401-209
Reeves, J. L.	RR	401-61
Reeves, James H.	USV	401-247
Reeves, Mills Q.	SR	401-98
Reeves, Van	TVG	401-209
Reeves, William T.	RR	401-61
Regan, J. E.	TVG	401-209
Regan, John T.	USV	401-247
Register, William	FB	401-169
Rehm, J. L. "Chic"	RR	401-61
Rehpemug, Charles G.	USV	401-247
Reich, Henry H.	USV	401-247
Reichel, W. O.	FB	401-169
Reichelt, H. W.	USV	401-247
Reichenstein, Louis	SP	401-48
Reicherzer, Theodore	TST	401-37
Reid, Charles T.	USV	401-247
Reid, E. M.	MV	401-30
Reid, George W.	SR	401-98
Reid, J. W.	MV	401-30
Reid, James	ARM	401-9
Reid, James G.	NAV	401-23
Reid, Lewis V.	USV	401-247
Reid, Nathaniel	ARM	401-9
Reid, Oliver P.	USV	401-247
Reid, Oscar D.	RR	401-61
Reid, S. B.	SP	401-48
Reid, W. S.	TVG	401-209
Reid, Warren	SP	401-48
Reid, William E.	USV	401-247
Reid, William H.	NAV	401-23
Reiharz, Walter	FF	401-138
Reiley, B. J.	RRR	401-123
Reiley, T.	FB	401-169
Reilly, Bernard	ARM	401-9
Reilly, T. F.	FB	401-169
Reilly, Thomas F.	FB	401-169
Reily, George D.	USV	401-247
Reily, John	ARM	401-9
Reily, Joseph	RR	401-61
Reimers, Archie	TVG	401-209
Reinhardt, John	TST	401-37
Reinhart, Jacob	FF	401-138
Reiser, William H.	USV	401-247
Reitz, A. H.	SR	401-98
Reiwald, Renshorn	TVG	401-209
Remeuller, John	NAV	401-23
Remingen, John	NAV	401-23
Remling, John	FF	401-138
Renaud, Henry	USV	401-247
Renaud, James W.	FB	401-169
Renchen, Clarence	USV	401-247
Reneau, Barney	SR	401-98
Reneau, J. D.	SR	401-98
Reneau, J. D.	LR	401-130
Reneau, Nelson Elmo	RRR	401-123
Reneau, T. N.	RR	401-61
Reneau, T. N.	RRR	401-123
Reneau, T. N.	SR	401-98
Renfro, C. F.	USV	401-247
Renfro, Clarence L.	USV	401-247
Renfro, Claude F.	USV	401-247
Renfro, David	ARM	401-9
Renfrow, Peter	ARM	401-9
Renick, G. W.	FB	401-169
Renick, J. H.	FB	401-169
Renick, John M.	TVG	401-209
Renick, R. A.	TVG	401-209
Renick, R. A.	USV	401-247
Rennock, A. R.	TST	401-37
Reno, John M.	USV	401-247
Renter, Louis	ARM	401-9
Resendezes, Jesus	RR	401-62
Reser, S. V.	FB	401-169
Rethke, Rudolph	TVG	401-209
Reuck, Amaziah	ARM	401-9
Reuter, Louis	ARM	401-9
Reuter, Rudolph	FF	401-138
Revis, James G.	USV	401-247
Revis, Perfecto	FF	401-138
Rex, George	ARM	401-9
Reyes, Eugene	FF	401-138
Reynaud, Thomas Preston	TVG	401-209
Reynold, A. G.	TVG	401-209
Reynolds, Dee	TVG	401-209
Reynolds, E. A.	RRR	401-123
Reynolds, E. A.	SR	401-98
Reynolds, F. W.	TST	401-37
Reynolds, Geo.	ARM	401-9
Reynolds, George J.	FB	401-169
Reynolds, Guy W.	SR	401-98
Reynolds, H. M.	USV	401-247
Reynolds, J. B.	TVG	401-209
Reynolds, J. C.	ARM	401-9
Reynolds, J. G.	FB	401-169
Reynolds, Jefferson L.	USV	401-247
Reynolds, Joe	SR	401-98
Reynolds, John R.	RR	401-62
Reynolds, Joshua	RR	401-62
Reynolds, Mark F.	USV	401-247
Reynolds, N. O.	FB	401-169
Reynolds, N. O.	FB	401-169
Reynolds, P. G.	TVG	401-209
Reynolds, Pallace O.	USV	401-247
Reynolds, S. F.	CSA	401-40
Reynolds, Smith P.	SR	401-98
Reynolds, T. H.	USV	401-247

Index to Texas Adjutant General Service Records—All Service Branches

Name	Branch	Page
Reynolds, W. T.	RR	401-62
Reynolds, W. W.	TST	401-37
Reynolds, West M.	USV	401-247
Reynolds, William	FB	401-169
Reynolds, William J.	USV	401-247
Rhame, Joseph B.	ARM	401-9
Rhea, Ansel A.	SR	401-98
Rhea, Boyd	SR	401-98
Rhea, James F.	USV	401-247
Rhea, Joe	TVG	401-209
Rhea, Rodgers	TVG	401-209
Rheiner, J. J., Jr.	SR	401-98
Rhew, Austin	SR	401-98
Rhinehart, Asa	ARM	401-9
Rhodes, B. F.	TVG	401-209
Rhodes, Carl	USV	401-247
Rhodes, Erskine	SR	401-98
Rhodes, Frank	TVG	401-209
Rhodes, Ike H.	FB	401-169
Rhodes, J. B.	SP	401-48
Rhodes, James W.	TVG	401-209
Rhodes, Neil	ARM	401-9
Rhodes, W. T.	FB	401-169
Rhyne, James R.	TVG	401-209
Rice, D.	TVG	401-209
Rice, George	SP	401-48
Rice, H. B.	TVG	401-209
Rice, J. H.	TST	401-37
Rice, James	NAV	401-23
Rice, James H.	SP	401-48
Rice, Jesse H.	USV	401-247
Rice, John	NAV	401-23
Rice, John	SR	401-99
Rice, Joseph Carlisle	USV	401-247
Rice, Lawrence A.	USV	401-247
Rice, Lorenzo	ARM	401-9
Rice, O. C.	SR	401-99
Rice, Pleasant H.	FF	401-138
Rice, Rus	ARM	401-9
Rice, S. G.	SR	401-99
Rice, Sanford	ARM	401-9
Rice, Thomas	FB	401-169
Rice, Walter Alexander	RRR	401-123
Rice, William C.	ARM	401-9
Rich, Bennie	RRR	401-123
Rich, F. M.	FB	401-169
Rich, G. W.	SP	401-48
Rich, J. M.	SR	401-99
Rich, J. T.	FB	401-169
Rich, Newton G.	SR	401-99
Rich, Samuel S.	USV	401-247
Richard, J. B.	NAV	401-23
Richard, J. B.	SR	401-99
Richards, B. C.	SR	401-99
Richards, Bert D.	USV	401-247
Richards, Charles	ARM	401-9
Richards, Charles M.	USV	401-247
Richards, Ed L.	TVG	401-209
Richards, Ed L.	USV	401-247
Richards, Edmund L.	USV	401-247
Richards, George E.	USV	401-247
Richards, Ivy	USV	401-247
Richards, Jefferson	ARM	401-9
Richards, Jesse	ARM	401-9
Richards, John	FB	401-169
Richards, John B.	ARM	401-9
Richards, Melville H.	USV	401-247
Richards, Pat	SR	401-99
Richards, Statford Harrison	SR	401-99
Richards, W. H.	SR	401-99
Richards, William	ARM	401-9
Richards, William Henry	LR	401-130
Richards, William S.	USV	401-247
Richards, Wray	SR	401-99
Richardson, A. H.	SR	401-99
Richardson, A. L.	TVG	401-209
Richardson, Adran	USV	401-247
Richardson, Andrew J.	USV	401-247
Richardson, Ben M.	USV	401-247
Richardson, Bob	TVG	401-209
Richardson, Dan	SP	401-48
Richardson, David O.	RRR	401-123
Richardson, Dennis	RR	401-62
Richardson, Dudley T.	CSA	401-40
Richardson, E. L.	TVG	401-209
Richardson, E. M.	USV	401-247
Richardson, George P.	USV	401-247
Richardson, Henry	SP	401-48
Richardson, J. W.	TVG	401-209
Richardson, James U.	ARM	401-9
Richardson, Jerry William	SR	401-99
Richardson, John	ARM	401-9
Richardson, L. D.	TVG	401-209
Richardson, Lewis	FF	401-138
Richardson, Lewis	SP	401-48
Richardson, Louis	ARM	401-9
Richardson, Martin	SR	401-99
Richardson, R. L.	USV	401-247
Richardson, Robert R.	USV	401-247
Richardson, W. K.	SR	401-99
Richardson, William	NAV	401-23
Richardson, William H., Jr.	SR	401-99
Richarz, H. J.	FF	401-138
Richbourg, John S.	RRR	401-123
Richey, James R.	ARM	401-9
Richey, P. B.	SR	401-99
Richey, R. E. L.	TVG	401-209
Richmond, John	FB	401-169
Richmond, R. W.	SR	401-99
Richter, George A.	TVG	401-209
Richter, John F.	USV	401-247
Richter, Julian A.	RRR	401-123

Index to Texas Adjutant General Service Records—All Service Branches

Name	Branch	Page
Richter, Otto	USV	401-247
Richter, Richard	USV	401-247
Richy, Richard Henry	NAV	401-23
Rick, A. C.	TVG	401-209
Ricke, Charles A.	TVG	401-209
Ricker, Charles C.	TVG	401-209
Ricker, John Romaine	TVG	401-209
Ricker, Nathaniel H.	TVG	401-209
Rickerson, Jesse M.	USV	401-247
Ricketson, Aaron	FF	401-138
Ricketson, Abner	USV	401-247
Ricks, George	ARM	401-9
Ricks, John	TST	401-37
Riddell, W. H.	SR	401-99
Riddermann, Haver	FF	401-138
Riddle, Guy L.	TVG	401-209
Riddle, John M.	RR	401-62
Riddle, Thomas E.	TST	401-37
Riddle, W. E.	SR	401-99
Riddle, William N.	TST	401-37
Riden, J. J.	SR	401-99
Riden, Jesse J.	LR	401-130
Riden, Will	RRR	401-123
Rider, G. W.	FB	401-169
Rider, George J.	RRR	401-123
Ridgeway, H. S.	SR	401-99
Ridley, Mark C.	ARM	401-9
Riebe, Gordon A.	SR	401-99
Rieger, Albert c.	RRR	401-123
Rieger, Albert C.	USV	401-247
Rieger, J. H.	FB	401-169
Rieger, John g.	USV	401-247
Rieger, Walton T.	USV	401-247
Riegger, Frank	SR	401-99
Rieley, Benjamin C.	FB	401-169
Rieves, James	TST	401-37
Riff, Joseph	FF	401-138
Riffe, J.	RRR	401-123
Rigby, Benjamin	ARM	401-9
Rigby, James	USV	401-247
Riggs, Allen T.	USV	401-247
Riggs, Barney K.	MV	401-30
Riggs, H. A.	TVG	401-209
Riggs, K. L.	SR	401-99
Riggs, M. D.	RRR	401-123
Riggs, W. E.	RR	401-62
Riggs, W. H.	RR	401-62
Riggs, William	CSA	401-40
Rigney, Tom	TVG	401-210
Riley, C. T.	FB	401-169
Riley, Charles	CSA	401-40
Riley, G. H.	FF	401-138
Riley, George	NAV	401-23
Riley, J. D.	SP	401-48
Riley, J. E.	TVG	401-210
Riley, J. R.	SR	401-99
Riley, J. R.	TVG	401-210
Riley, J. R.	LR	401-130
Riley, James	ARM	401-9
Riley, John	NAV	401-23
Riley, John	FF	401-138
Riley, John	FB	401-169
Riley, Michael	ARM	401-9
Riley, S. A.	RRR	401-123
Riley, T. W.	CSA	401-40
Riley, Thomas	NAV	401-23
Riley, Thomas	ARM	401-9
Riley, Thomas	ARM	401-9
Riley, W. A.	TVG	401-210
Rilling, J. M.	FF	401-138
Rimassa, George W.	TVG	401-210
Rimchissell, F. L.	FF	401-138
Rine, James	ARM	401-9
Rine, John M.	ARM	401-9
Ringer, J. J.	FB	401-169
Ringer, John	RR	401-62
Ringer, John H.	RR	401-62
Ringo, William	ARM	401-9
Riordan, S. E.	TVG	401-210
Ripley, F. E.	TVG	401-210
Ripley, Phineas	ARM	401-9
Ripley, Roy Stephen	RR	401-62
Ripley, Thomas	ARM	401-9
Ripperton, L. A.	SR	401-99
Rippetoe, H.	TVG	401-210
Rippey, William	RR	401-62
Ripstein, Adolph	FF	401-138
Ripstein, Gottfried	FF	401-138
Ripy, O. P.	TVG	401-210
Risch, Alex	NAV	401-23
Riser, Robert J.	USV	401-247
Riser, W. D.	SR	401-99
Riser, W. D.	LR	401-130
Risien, John T.	USV	401-247
Risinger, Michael M.	USV	401-247
Risley, Zeph L.	USV	401-247
Ristworth, H.	FB	401-169
Ritch, E. L.	TVG	401-210
Ritch, Frank	TVG	401-210
Ritchie, A. T.	FB	401-169
Ritchie, James Taylor	USV	401-247
Ritchison, W. C.	SR	401-99
Rittenburg, D. C.	USV	401-247
Ritter, F. G.	FF	401-138
Ritter, John Q.	USV	401-247
Ritz, Rudolf R.	TVG	401-210
Rivera, T. P.	TVG	401-210
Rivers, Clovis D.	USV	401-247
Rivers, Harry D.	TVG	401-210
Rivers, John	FB	401-169
Rivers, John F. D.	NAV	401-23
Rivers, Thomas E.	TVG	401-210

Index to Texas Adjutant General Service Records—All Service Branches

Name	Branch	Record
Rix, Guy W.	USV	401-247
Rix, R. E.	FB	401-169
Rizer, J. M.	FB	401-169
Rizzo, G[iroconi]	NAV	401-23
Roach, Burton	RRR	401-123
Roach, Emmett D.	USV	401-247
Roach, Erskine H.	TVG	401-210
Roach, Erskine Horton	USV	401-247
Roach, J. D.	TVG	401-210
Roach, John A.	MM	401-32
Roach, Thomas	ARM	401-9
Roach, W. W.	TVG	401-210
Roark, J. F.	SR	401-99
Roark, Jackson	ARM	401-9
Roark, John E.	TVG	401-210
Robar, Lewis A.	RR	401-62
Robard, C. L.	TST	401-37
Robards, Frank F.	USV	401-247
Robb, A. L.	TVG	401-210
Robb, Arthur J.	USV	401-247
Robb, Duncan M.	RRR	401-123
Robb, J. H.	TVG	401-210
Robb, N. L.	TVG	401-210
Robb, Norman K.	USV	401-247
Robb, S. J.	FB	401-169
Robberts, Dick J.	SR	401-99
Robbins, G. W.	TST	401-37
Robbins, J. M.	RR	401-62
Robbins, J. M.	SR	401-99
Robbins, J. P.	SR	401-99
Robbins, James	RR	401-62
Robbins, John	ARM	401-9
Robbins, John M.	FB	401-169
Robbins, Reg. L.	SR	401-99
Robbins, W. H.	SR	401-99
Roberdeau, George M.	TVG	401-210
Roberdeau, Roger C.	USV	401-247
Roberds, G. A.	FB	401-169
Roberson, A. M.	TST	401-37
Roberson, B. F.	SR	401-99
Roberson, C. P.	TVG	401-210
Roberson, Charles M.	TVG	401-210
Roberson, Charles M.	USV	401-247
Roberson, D. S.	SR	401-99
Roberson, D. S.	FB	401-169
Roberson, H. L.	RR	401-62
Roberson, H. L.	SR	401-99
Roberson, James A.	FB	401-169
Roberson, James S.	USV	401-247
Roberson, Jesse	SR	401-99
Roberson, Joseph W.	MV	401-31
Roberson, T. H.	FB	401-169
Roberson, Walter B.	USV	401-247
Robert, A. B.	TVG	401-210
Robert, A. Beale	USV	401-247
Robert, Hadley	FB	401-169
Robert, W. C.	SR	401-99
Roberts, A. G.	SP	401-48
Roberts, A. S.	CSA	401-40
Roberts, A. S.	TVG	401-210
Roberts, Albert F.	USV	401-247
Roberts, Alexander S.	ARM	401-9
Roberts, Allen P.	RR	401-62
Roberts, B. C.	FB	401-169
Roberts, Carrol C.	USV	401-247
Roberts, Charles	NAV	401-23
Roberts, Charles	ARM	401-9
Roberts, Charles	USV	401-247
Roberts, Charles E.	USV	401-247
Roberts, Charlie	TVG	401-210
Roberts, Cliff C.	TVG	401-210
Roberts, Daniel W.	FB	401-169
Roberts, David	ARM	401-9
Roberts, Edward	NAV	401-23
Roberts, Edward P.	USV	401-247
Roberts, Ernest L.	SR	401-99
Roberts, Evan	MM	401-32
Roberts, F. S.	FB	401-169
Roberts, Fenton F.	USV	401-247
Roberts, G. A.	FB	401-169
Roberts, H.	CSA	401-40
Roberts, H. C.	LR	401-130
Roberts, H. L.	TVG	401-210
Roberts, Hardy	SR	401-99
Roberts, Harry	TVG	401-210
Roberts, Harry C.	TVG	401-210
Roberts, Isaac	ARM	401-9
Roberts, Isaac N.	TST	401-37
Roberts, Isham [?] S.	TVG	401-210
Roberts, J.	NAV	401-23
Roberts, J.	SP	401-48
Roberts, J. B.	SR	401-99
Roberts, J. B.	TVG	401-210
Roberts, J. E.	TVG	401-210
Roberts, J. H.	FF	401-138
Roberts, J. H.	SR	401-99
Roberts, J. H.	LR	401-130
Roberts, J. J.	RRR	401-123
Roberts, Jack H.	USV	401-247
Roberts, James H.	ARM	401-9
Roberts, James P.	USV	401-247
Roberts, Jerry	FB	401-169
Roberts, Joe B.	USV	401-247
Roberts, John	NAV	401-23
Roberts, John D.	TVG	401-210
Roberts, John S.	ARM	401-9
Roberts, Joseph E.	USV	401-247
Roberts, Joseph W.	ARM	401-9
Roberts, Josiah	ARM	401-9
Roberts, L. D.	SR	401-99
Roberts, L. D.	LR	401-130
Roberts, Liston C.	USV	401-247

Index to Texas Adjutant General Service Records—All Service Branches

Roberts, Louis C. ....USV 401-247
Roberts, Lynn ....TVG 401-210
Roberts, M. C. ....SR...........401-99
Roberts, M. E. ....SR...........401-99
Roberts, Moses Brown ....FB............401-169
Roberts, N. F. ....SR...........401-99
Roberts, Oscar E. ....SR...........401-99
Roberts, Otto...............................FB............401-169
Roberts, P. L. ....FB............401-169
Roberts, P. P. ....TVG 401-210
Roberts, P. S. ....FB............401-169
Roberts, R. F. ....ARM 401-9
Roberts, R. H. ....NAV........401-23
Roberts, R. L. ....RR 401-62
Roberts, Raymond ....RR 401-62
Roberts, Redding ....ARM 401-9
Roberts, Robert C. ....FB............401-169
Roberts, Robert E. ....USV 401-247
Roberts, Roy ....TVG 401-210
Roberts, S. C. ....FB............401-169
Roberts, Sidney..........................RR 401-62
Roberts, Silvan ....FB............401-169
Roberts, Tom ....FB............401-169
Roberts, W. A. ....RR 401-62
Roberts, W. A. ....FB............401-169
Roberts, W. F., Jr. ....LR 401-130
Roberts, W. H. ....SR...........401-99
Roberts, Walter L. ....TVG 401-210
Roberts, William.........................NAV........401-23
Roberts, William.........................ARM 401-9
Roberts, William.........................TVG 401-210
Roberts, William H. ....FB............401-169
Roberts, William J. L. ....TVG 401-210
Roberts, Wilson ....TVG 401-210
Roberts, Zion ....ARM 401-9
Robertson, A. J. ....RR 401-62
Robertson, Arthur ....NAV........401-23
Robertson, Bee ....USV 401-247
Robertson, C. W. ....USV 401-247
Robertson, Claude ....TVG 401-210
Robertson, Clinton ....ARM 401-9
Robertson, D[] P. ....TVG 401-210
Robertson, Duke H. ....SR...........401-99
Robertson, E. L. ....SR...........401-99
Robertson, E. Sterling C. ....TST 401-37
Robertson, Felix Davis ....TVG 401-210
Robertson, Guy ....USV 401-247
Robertson, H. P., Jr. ....SR...........401-99
Robertson, Harper W. ....SR...........401-99
Robertson, I. N. ....TST 401-37
Robertson, J. C. ....TVG 401-210
Robertson, J. F. ....TVG 401-210
Robertson, J. W. ....FB............401-169
Robertson, J. W. R. ....TVG 401-210
Robertson, Jack..........................RR 401-62
Robertson, Jack..........................FB............401-169
Robertson, John S. ....TVG 401-210
Robertson, Joseph.....................FB............401-169
Robertson, Marion ....FB............401-169
Robertson, Peter ....NAV........401-23
Robertson, Rebel L. ....USV 401-247
Robertson, Robert L. ....SR...........401-99
Robertson, Samuel C. ....TVG 401-210
Robertson, Thomas M. ....USV 401-247
Robertson, W. J. T. ....RRR 401-123
Robertson, W. P. ....SR...........401-99
Robertson, Wade H. ....SR...........401-99
Robertson, Wade H. ....LR 401-130
Robertson, Walter L. ....USV 401-247
Robertson, Walter M. ....FB............401-169
Robertson, William H. ....NAV........401-23
Robertson, William James T. ....RR 401-62
Robeson, John...........................SP...........401-48
Robinette, Varde O. ....SR...........401-99
Robins, Dave ....SR...........401-99
Robins, Early ....ARM 401-9
Robinson, A. F. ....SR...........401-99
Robinson, A. J. ....RR 401-62
Robinson, A. W. ....FB............401-169
Robinson, Alfred ....MV 401-31
Robinson, C. M. ....MV 401-31
Robinson, C. P. ....RR 401-62
Robinson, C. P. ....FF 401-138
Robinson, C. P. ....RRR 401-123
Robinson, C. P. ....TVG 401-210
Robinson, C. T. ....FB............401-169
Robinson, Cecil ....FF 401-138
Robinson, Charles.....................TVG 401-210
Robinson, Charles E. ....FB............401-169
Robinson, Charles P. ....FF 401-138
Robinson, Charley ....TVG 401-210
Robinson, D. G. ....RR 401-62
Robinson, D. L. ....TVG 401-210
Robinson, D. W. ....RR 401-62
Robinson, David ....MV 401-31
Robinson, Edmund ....SP...........401-48
Robinson, Edward ....USV 401-247
Robinson, F. G. ....FB............401-169
Robinson, F. M. ....SR...........401-99
Robinson, Frank ....FB............401-169
Robinson, George.....................MV 401-31
Robinson, George A. ....SR...........401-99
Robinson, George Washington .....RR 401-62
Robinson, H. A. ....FB............401-169
Robinson, H. L. ....RR 401-62
Robinson, Harry H. ....RR 401-62
Robinson, J. A. ....MV 401-31
Robinson, J. F. ....SR...........401-99
Robinson, J. H. ....SP...........401-48
Robinson, J. H. ....USV 401-247
Robinson, J. P. ....SR...........401-99
Robinson, J. T. ....FB............401-169

Index to Texas Adjutant General Service Records—All Service Branches

Robinson, J. W. .... RR 401-62
Robinson, Jack .... FB 401-170
Robinson, James .... MV 401-31
Robinson, James C. .... RRR 401-123
Robinson, James R. .... FB 401-170
Robinson, James W. .... USV 401-247
Robinson, James W. .... USV 401-247
Robinson, John A. .... USV 401-247
Robinson, John C. .... RR 401-62
Robinson, John E. .... TVG 401-210
Robinson, John F. .... SR 401-99
Robinson, John Numa .... USV 401-247
Robinson, John T. .... FB 401-170
Robinson, John W. .... FB 401-170
Robinson, Josiah D. .... MV 401-31
Robinson, Judah .... USV 401-247
Robinson, Lawson .... SP 401-48
Robinson, Maury .... SR 401-99
Robinson, Max's .... TVG 401-210
Robinson, O. M. .... TVG 401-210
Robinson, Peter .... NAV 401-23
Robinson, R. E. .... FB 401-170
Robinson, R. J. .... RRR 401-123
Robinson, Ragland .... TVG 401-210
Robinson, Richard .... NAV 401-23
Robinson, Robert E. .... FF 401-138
Robinson, S. A. .... RR 401-62
Robinson, T. C. .... FB 401-170
Robinson, T. H. .... FB 401-170
Robinson, T. P. .... SR 401-99
Robinson, Thaddeus P. .... RR 401-62
Robinson, Vincent G. .... USV 401-248
Robinson, W. F. .... RR 401-62
Robinson, Wade J. .... USV 401-248
Robinson, William .... SP 401-48
Robinson, William D. .... USV 401-248
Robinson, William F. .... USV 401-248
Robinson, William H. .... NAV 401-23
Robinson, William H. .... FB 401-170
Robinson, William J. .... USV 401-248
Robinson, William M. .... USV 401-248
Robinson, William Spencer .... TVG 401-210
Robison, Columbus .... CSA 401-40
Robison, E. Waid, Dr. .... SR 401-99
Robison, J. T. .... TVG 401-210
Robison, John .... ARM 401-10
Robison, Lemuel P. .... USV 401-248
Robison, W. S. .... TVG 401-210
Roblin, H. B. .... SR 401-99
Robnett, A. H. .... TVG 401-210
Robson, Charles G. .... USV 401-248
Robuck, Robert G. .... SR 401-99
Robuck, Robert G. .... LR 401-130
Robuck, W. E. .... FB 401-170
Rochelle, J. B. .... TVG 401-210
Rochester, E. P. .... RR 401-62

Rockefeller, Winthrop .... SR 401-99
Rockenback, C. C. .... SR 401-99
Rockett, Herman B. .... USV 401-248
Roddy, James A. .... ARM 401-10
Roddy, Louis H., Dr. .... SR 401-99
Roddy, Theodore J. .... USV 401-248
Roden, R. J. .... SR 401-99
Roder, C. A. .... FB 401-170
Rodgers, A. W. .... SR 401-99
Rodgers, B. F. .... RRR 401-123
Rodgers, Hiram B. .... RR 401-62
Rodgers, James Holland .... SR 401-99
Rodgers, Jim .... USV 401-248
Rodgers, Jimmie .... SR 401-99
Rodgers, John D. .... USV 401-248
Rodgers, John M. .... FF 401-138
Rodgers, Leroy .... TVG 401-210
Rodgers, Samuel .... NAV 401-23
Rodgers, Thomas .... USV 401-248
Rodrigers, F. M. .... SR 401-99
Rodrigo, Manuel .... ARM 401-10
Rodriguez, Anastasio .... FF 401-138
Rodriguez, Diego .... FF 401-138
Rodriguez, Francisco .... FF 401-138
Rodriguez, Juan .... FF 401-138
Rodriguez, Simon .... FB 401-170
Rodriguez, Vicente L. .... TVG 401-210
Rodriquez Echalecu, Me. .... ARM 401-10
Rodriquez, Juan .... SR 401-99
Roe, S. T. .... SR 401-99
Roecker, Charles A. .... USV 401-248
Roeper, Alfred .... TVG 401-210
Roescher, C. F. .... TVG 401-210
Roesler, Ernest Louis John .... TVG 401-210
Roessler, John .... TVG 401-210
Roff, R. R. .... TVG 401-210
Rogers, A. C. .... TVG 401-210
Rogers, Austin C. .... USV 401-248
Rogers, C. A. .... SR 401-99
Rogers, C. C. .... FB 401-170
Rogers, C. L. .... SR 401-99
Rogers, C. L. .... SR 401-99
Rogers, C. L. .... FB 401-170
Rogers, C. S. .... USV 401-248
Rogers, Carroll .... USV 401-248
Rogers, Charles W. .... TVG 401-210
Rogers, Clarence Aaron .... LR 401-130
Rogers, Doc .... TVG 401-210
Rogers, Duncan W. .... RRR 401-123
Rogers, Duncan W. .... SR 401-99
Rogers, E. Newt .... USV 401-248
Rogers, E. W. .... RR 401-62
Rogers, Ernest .... FB 401-170
Rogers, Fred B. .... TVG 401-210
Rogers, G. .... TVG 401-210
Rogers, George T. .... USV 401-248

Index to Texas Adjutant General Service Records—All Service Branches

Name	Branch	Record
Rogers, Gilbert T.	USV	401-248
Rogers, H. O.	SP	401-48
Rogers, Hiram	SP	401-48
Rogers, J. A.	FB	401-170
Rogers, J. H.	FB	401-170
Rogers, J. N.	TVG	401-210
Rogers, J. W.	FB	401-170
Rogers, Jacob	ARM	401-10
Rogers, James B.	FB	401-170
Rogers, James H.	TST	401-37
Rogers, James Herman	TVG	401-210
Rogers, James R.	ARM	401-10
Rogers, John	ARM	401-10
Rogers, John C.	TVG	401-210
Rogers, John D.	SR	401-99
Rogers, John E.	SR	401-99
Rogers, John H.	RR	401-62
Rogers, L. P.	TVG	401-210
Rogers, L. T.	SR	401-99
Rogers, L. T.	FB	401-170
Rogers, L. W.	FB	401-170
Rogers, Lovic T.	USV	401-248
Rogers, Lovic T., Col.	SR	401-99
Rogers, Marcus Cullum	TVG	401-210
Rogers, N. N.	FB	401-170
Rogers, Norman N.	FB	401-170
Rogers, O. W.	RR	401-62
Rogers, Offic	USV	401-248
Rogers, P. G.	SR	401-99
Rogers, P. H.	FB	401-170
Rogers, Robert Tilden	TVG	401-210
Rogers, Roy Talbert	SR	401-99
Rogers, Selwyn P.	USV	401-248
Rogers, Starling S.	USV	401-248
Rogers, Stephen	ARM	401-10
Rogers, Thomas J.	CSA	401-40
Rogers, W. G.	SR	401-99
Rogers, Wallace	SP	401-48
Rogers, Walton	USV	401-248
Rogers, Will	SR	401-99
Rogers, William E.	USV	401-248
Rohde, Carl	SR	401-99
Rohde, J. G.	TVG	401-210
Rohde, Louie	TVG	401-210
Roland, Albert R.	USV	401-248
Roland, James T.	RR	401-62
Roland, Lester	RRR	401-123
Roland, Robert E.	USV	401-248
Roles, Frank W.	USV	401-248
Rollens, Thomas B.	RR	401-62
Rollins, C. E.	LR	401-130
Rollins, Clarence A.	USV	401-248
Rollins, Edward T.	USV	401-248
Rollins, H. F.	USV	401-248
Rollins, Henry M.	USV	401-248
Rollins, John A.	USV	401-248
Rollins, Thomas B.	RR	401-62
Rollins, William	CSA	401-40
Rollo, Kent	SR	401-99
Rolsten, J. A.	FB	401-170
Romansky, Alvin S., Lt. Col.	SR	401-99
Rome, Charles	FF	401-138
Romo, Jesus	USV	401-248
Romulus, Raymond	NAV	401-23
Ronaldson, Robert	ARM	401-10
RonQuillo, Jose Ignacio	FF	401-138
Rood, Bert E.	USV	401-248
Roof, George E.	USV	401-248
Rook, C. A.	ARM	401-10
Rooke, Charles	TST	401-37
Rooker, Lorenza B.	SR	401-99
Rooker, Lorenza B.	LR	401-130
Rooney, James G.	SR	401-99
Rooney, John M.	RR	401-62
Rooney, John Monroe	RRR	401-123
Rooney, P. H.	SP	401-48
Roosevelt, Al	FB	401-170
Roosevelt, Elliott	SR	401-99
Root, Elias B.	ARM	401-10
Root, Frank A.	TVG	401-210
Rootes, Thomas R.	MV	401-31
Roper, Arthur	TVG	401-210
Roper, Daniel	ARM	401-10
Roper, E. H.	TVG	401-210
Roper, Elmer H.	USV	401-248
Roper, George C.	TVG	401-210
Roper, H. L.	SR	401-99
Roper, William A.	USV	401-248
Roquemore, G. A.	TVG	401-210
Roquemore, Joe B.	TVG	401-210
Rosale, Sylvestre	SP	401-48
Rose, F. R.	TVG	401-210
Rose, G. C.	RR	401-62
Rose, J. W.	FB	401-170
Rose, John	ARM	401-10
Rose, John	SP	401-48
Rose, John R.	TVG	401-210
Rose, R. A.	SR	401-100
Rose, William P.	USV	401-248
Rose, Wilton Ford	USV	401-248
Rosebrough, Arthur S.	TVG	401-210
Rosebrough, Thomas B.	USV	401-248
Rosen, Harry M.	SR	401-100
Rosenau, Joe	TVG	401-210
Rosenbaum, Morris	USV	401-248
Rosenberg, Henry W.	TVG	401-210
Rosenberg, William von	TVG	401-210
Rosenblum, Abraham Edward	SR	401-100
Rosendal, Frantz	ARM	401-10
Rosendale, Francis	NAV	401-23
Rosendelth, Francis	NAV	401-23
Rosenfeld, Samuel	USV	401-248

Index to Texas Adjutant General Service Records—All Service Branches

Name	Branch	Record
Rosenfield, S. H.	TVG	401-210
Rosenthal, A. J.	TVG	401-210
Rosenthal, David R.	SR	401-100
Rosenthal, Sam	TVG	401-210
Ross, Albert A.	RRR	401-123
Ross, Alexander	RR	401-62
Ross, Charles	NAV	401-23
Ross, Charlie D.	USV	401-248
Ross, Clay E.	SR	401-100
Ross, Clay E.	LR	401-130
Ross, Ed	SR	401-100
Ross, Elmer L.	TVG	401-210
Ross, F. R.	TVG	401-210
Ross, Frank C.	USV	401-248
Ross, Frank R.	TVG	401-210
Ross, Guy G.	SR	401-100
Ross, Guy G.	LR	401-130
Ross, Harry	USV	401-248
Ross, J. B.	TVG	401-210
Ross, J. W.	TVG	401-210
Ross, John	FF	401-138
Ross, Lawrance Elmore	TVG	401-210
Ross, Perry M.	SR	401-100
Ross, Primus	SP	401-48
Ross, Reuben	ARM	401-10
Ross, Richard	ARM	401-10
Ross, Richard M.	ARM	401-10
Ross, Rob C.	FB	401-170
Ross, Robert	FB	401-170
Ross, Thomas H.	ARM	401-10
Ross, Tom	SR	401-100
Ross, Tom M.	RR	401-62
Ross, Tom M.	SR	401-100
Ross, Tom M.	FB	401-170
Ross, Vernon	TVG	401-210
Ross, W. A.	USV	401-248
Ross, W. F. J. W.	MM	401-32
Ross, Walter	USV	401-248
Ross, William	NAV	401-23
Ross, William	TVG	401-210
Ross, William Philip	TVG	401-210
Rossen, J. N.	ARM	401-10
Rosser, Lee	RR	401-62
Rosser, Lee	SR	401-100
Rossignol, Charles	NAV	401-23
Rostell, William Ross	NAV	401-23
Rote, W. P., Jr.	SR	401-100
Roten, Neal	SR	401-100
Roth, Louis	USV	401-248
Rothan, Lee	SR	401-100
Rothrock, W. L.	RRR	401-123
Rouche, Peter	ARM	401-10
Rouff, Leon	TST	401-37
Roughton, A. S.	TVG	401-210
Rounds, Lyman F.	ARM	401-10
Roundtree, James H.	ARM	401-10
Roundtree, M. C.	ARM	401-10
Rounkamp, Charles	TST	401-37
Rountree, E. B.	SR	401-100
Rountree, F. S.	TST	401-138
Rountree, J. T., Dr.	SR	401-100
Rountree, Joseph L.	USV	401-248
Rountree, Lee J.	SR	401-100
Rountree, Mason L.	RR	401-62
Rountree, O. B.	TVG	401-210
Rountree, Oscar J.	FB	401-170
Rountree, Robert	USV	401-248
Rountree, Robert L.	USV	401-248
Rountree, William C.	SR	401-100
Rountree, William H.	USV	401-248
Rourk, James H.	TST	401-37
Rourke, Lawrence	ARM	401-10
Rousseau, E. D.	FB	401-170
Rousseau, Travis	USV	401-248
Roussette, Adlolphe	ARM	401-10
Routch, Jos.	ARM	401-10
Routh, A. M.	MM	401-32
Routt, H. R.	LR	401-130
Routt, W. T.	SP	401-48
Rowan, A. L.	USV	401-248
Rowan, Thomas E.	NAV	401-23
Rowan, Thos. E.	ARM	401-10
Rowe, Charles	FF	401-138
Rowe, Charles E.	USV	401-248
Rowe, D. F.	TVG	401-210
Rowe, E. O.	FB	401-170
Rowe, Judson A.	NAV	401-23
Rowe, Martin M.	USV	401-248
Rowe, R. R.	FB	401-170
Rowe, T. C.	FB	401-170
Rowe, Thomas B.	SP	401-48
Rowe, Walter I.	RR	401-62
Rowe, Walter Ivory	RRR	401-123
Rowell, C. H.	FB	401-170
Rowell, T. D.	TVG	401-210
Rowen, Wilmer A.	SR	401-100
Rowland, C. L.	TVG	401-210
Rowland, Coke	TVG	401-210
Rowland, J. J.	SP	401-48
Rowland, J. R.	RR	401-62
Rowland, James J.	RR	401-62
Rowland, John D.	TVG	401-210
Rowland, John T.	TST	401-37
Rowland, Samuel	ARM	401-10
Rowland, Shiloh E.	USV	401-248
Rowlett, Hal J.	RRR	401-123
Rowls, T. H.	RR	401-62
Rowsey, G. L.	SR	401-100
Roxborough, George	TVG	401-210
Roy, A. L.	SP	401-48
Roy, Alexander	NAV	401-23
Roy, James E.	ARM	401-10

Index to Texas Adjutant General Service Records—All Service Branches

Name	Branch	Record
Roy, W. L.	FB	401-170
Roy, William T.	SR	401-100
Royal, A. J.	RR	401-62
Royal, Isiah	NAV	401-23
Royall, Ben H.	SR	401-100
Royall, Thomas	ARM	401-10
Rozier, John P.	ARM	401-10
Rubarth, Leander L.	RR	401-62
Rubendall, Henry E.	SP	401-48
Ruble, Henry L.	ARM	401-10
Ruby, T. E.	SR	401-100
Rucker, Anthony	SP	401-48
Rucker, Charles B.	USV	401-248
Rucker, Horace P.	USV	401-248
Rucker, James M.	RR	401-62
Rucker, Lee	TVG	401-210
Rucker, Lindsey P.	USV	401-248
Rucker, Robert E.	USV	401-248
Rucker, Robert G.	USV	401-248
Rucker, Thomas F.	USV	401-248
Rucker, William H.	USV	401-248
Rudd, Charles	USV	401-248
Rudd, J. D.	TVG	401-210
Rudd, James B.	USV	401-248
Rudd, Luther	USV	401-248
Rudd, W. L.	FB	401-170
Ruddull, George	ARM	401-10
Ruddull, John	ARM	401-10
Rudge, Frederick	ARM	401-10
Rudisill, Robert	TVG	401-210
Rue, Frank	TVG	401-210
Rueter, Will	RR	401-62
Rueter, Will	SR	401-100
Ruetz, Fritz	TVG	401-210
Ruff, George W.	ARM	401-10
Ruff, John	FF	401-138
Rugeley, Frank L.	FB	401-170
Rugeley, Mushat	TVG	401-210
Rugers, Charles C.	TVG	401-210
Ruhl, Englebert	ARM	401-10
Ruhl, J. H.	TVG	401-210
Ruhlmann, Edwin P.	USV	401-248
Ruland, Thomas D.	SR	401-100
Rulfs, Carl Henry	USV	401-248
Rumage, Horace C.	USV	401-248
Rumley, William	NAV	401-23
Rummegate, John	NAV	401-23
Rummel, Walter	USV	401-248
Rumsey, A.	FF	401-139
Rumsey, Alfred	SP	401-48
Rumsey, Charles Stewart	RR	401-62
Rumsey, John	FF	401-139
Rumsey, Robert	RR	401-62
Runyon, L. G.	RR	401-62
Rusch, Alfred	TVG	401-210
Rusche, R. Conrad	TVG	401-210
Rush, C.	FB	401-170
Rush, H. R.	SP	401-48
Rush, J. Henderson	TVG	401-210
Rush, Oliver E.	ARM	401-10
Rush, Philip	ARM	401-10
Rush, R. L. "Bob"	SR	401-100
Rush, Thomas W.	USV	401-248
Rush, W. M.	SR	401-100
Rush, W. P.	SP	401-48
Rushin, Walter	RR	401-62
Rushing, Emmett Orren, Dr.	SR	401-100
Rushing, F. C.	LR	401-130
Rushing, T. J.	FB	401-170
Rusk, David	ARM	401-10
Ruska, H. V.	SP	401-48
Russek, Henry	SR	401-100
Russell, Avery M.	USV	401-248
Russell, B. W.	RRR	401-123
Russell, Bud	SR	401-100
Russell, C. A.	RR	401-62
Russell, C. A.	SR	401-100
Russell, C. T.	SR	401-100
Russell, Charles	ARM	401-10
Russell, Decatur	RR	401-62
Russell, F. B.	NAV	401-23
Russell, Frank M.	USV	401-248
Russell, G. W.	MV	401-31
Russell, G. W.	USV	401-248
Russell, Grady	SR	401-100
Russell, J. E.	SR	401-100
Russell, J. R.	USV	401-248
Russell, James H.	TVG	401-210
Russell, James W.	USV	401-248
Russell, Jno. T.	ARM	401-10
Russell, John T.	SP	401-48
Russell, John W.	USV	401-248
Russell, L. P.	USV	401-248
Russell, Max	SR	401-100
Russell, R. L.	RR	401-62
Russell, R. R.	FB	401-170
Russell, Robert	FF	401-139
Russell, Robert E.	USV	401-248
Russell, Robert R.	USV	401-248
Russell, Robt.	ARM	401-10
Russell, Roy	SR	401-100
Russell, S. A.	SR	401-100
Russell, Sam M.	RR	401-62
Russell, Scott	RR	401-62
Russell, T. J.	SR	401-100
Russell, Thomas P.	NAV	401-23
Russell, W. A.	SR	401-100
Russell, W. B.	TVG	401-210
Russell, W. C.	SR	401-100
Russell, W. E.	TVG	401-210
Russell, W. H.	SR	401-100
Russell, W. H.	USV	401-248

Index to Texas Adjutant General Service Records—All Service Branches

Name	Branch	Record
Russell, William E.	SR	401-100
Russell, William I.	ARM	401-10
Russell, Wilson B.	USV	401-248
Russett, Charles S.	TST	401-37
Rust, James P.	RRR	401-123
Ruth, Michael	ARM	401-10
Rutherford, Austin	ARM	401-10
Rutherford, L. L.	SR	401-100
Rutherford, L. L.	LR	401-130
Rutherford, L. Munroe	SR	401-100
Rutherford, Patric W.	USV	401-248
Rutherford, Thos. M. C. G.	ARM	401-10
Rutherford, William L.	FB	401-170
Rutherford, Zebulon B.	CSA	401-40
Rutland, James W.	TVG	401-210
Rutland, Joseph B.	USV	401-248
Rutledge, E. S.	FB	401-170
Rutledge, J. E.	SR	401-100
Rutledge, J. F.	FB	401-170
Rutledge, James	RR	401-62
Rutledge, John W.	FB	401-170
Rutledge, L. C.	RRR	401-123
Rutledge, W. O.	RRR	401-123
Rutledge, W. T.	SR	401-100
Rutledge, Will J.	FB	401-170
Ruzen, A. A.	FB	401-170
Ryall, A.	FB	401-170
Ryan, Alvis D.	USV	401-248
Ryan, Ambrose E.	USV	401-248
Ryan, Andrew	ARM	401-10
Ryan, C. T.	RR	401-62
Ryan, C. T.	FB	401-170
Ryan, Dan	TVG	401-210
Ryan, Edward	NAV	401-23
Ryan, George W.	FB	401-170
Ryan, Henry M.	SP	401-48
Ryan, J. W.	SR	401-100
Ryan, James	FF	401-139
Ryan, James	SP	401-48
Ryan, John C.	SP	401-48
Ryan, Joseph William	LR	401-130
Ryan, Michael	USV	401-248
Ryan, Nicholas James	ARM	401-10
Ryan, Pat	USV	401-248
Ryan, T. N.	TVG	401-210
Ryan, Thomas	TVG	401-210
Ryan, Tom	TVG	401-210
Ryan, Walter W.	TVG	401-210
Ryan, William M.	RR	401-62
Ryburn, Clifford W.	TVG	401-210
Ryburn, Clifford W.	USV	401-248
Rye, J. J.	SR	401-100
Ryerson, Peter	NAV	401-23
Rynold, Micheal	FF	401-139
Saathoff, Gansen	FF	401-139
Sabin, Elridge H.	USV	401-248
Sachs, Isidor	TVG	401-210
Sackett, Henry	FF	401-139
Sackman, Ferdinand	ARM	401-10
Sackville, H. A.	SR	401-100
Sackville, H. A.	LR	401-131
Sadler, George W.	RR	401-62
Sadler, George W.	SR	401-100
Sadler, Harley H.	SR	401-100
Sadler, John W.	RR	401-62
Sadler, John W.	SR	401-100
Sadler, L. T.	RR	401-62
Sadler, Robert B.	FB	401-170
Sadler, Tom H.	RR	401-62
Sadler, William	RR	401-62
Sadler, Willis A.	SR	401-100
Saegert, H. H.	RRR	401-123
Saelis, W. F.	RR	401-62
Sage, Harold A.	SR	401-100
Saint Clair, Charles B.	TVG	401-210
Saint Clair, E. B.	TVG	401-210
Saint Clair, John	NAV	401-23
Saint Clear, John	FB	401-170
Saint Clear, Thomas	FB	401-170
Saint Leon, Ernest	FB	401-170
Sais, Antoni	FF	401-139
Salias, Mcario	FF	401-139
Salinas, Antonio	SR	401-100
Salinas, Antonio	FB	401-170
Salinas, Gomecindo	FF	401-139
Salinas, Juan	FF	401-139
Salisbury, A. H.	USV	401-248
Sallas, J. D.	RR	401-62
Sallee, Frank Mackinder	RRR	401-123
Salley, A. J.	TVG	401-210
Sallis, F. M.	USV	401-248
Sallis, W. F.	RR	401-62
Salmon, Jack	SR	401-100
Salmon, R. S.	RR	401-62
Salsido, Cisto	FF	401-139
Salsido, Jesus	FF	401-139
Salten, T.	NAV	401-23
Salter, Arthur Duncan	TVG	401-211
Salter, Joe	USV	401-248
Salters, John	NAV	401-23
Samford, Elmer E.	SR	401-100
Sammon, C. E.	SR	401-100
Sammon, E. W.	SP	401-48
Sammon, J. J.	SP	401-48
Sammons, A. J.	SR	401-100
Sammons, Charles	RR	401-62
Sammons, Charles	SR	401-100
Sammons, John C.	USV	401-248
Sammons, Timothy E.	SR	401-100
Samon, Joseph	FF	401-139
Sample, John R.	TVG	401-211
Sample, T. J.	SR	401-100

Index to Texas Adjutant General Service Records—All Service Branches

Samples, John...............................FB............401-170
Samples, R. S. ....FB............401-170
Sampson, Ernst...........................USV 401-248
Sampson, James..........................TST 401-37
Sampson, Orsby C. ....USV 401-248
Sampson, Oscar B. ....USV 401-248
Samudio, Antonio........................FF 401-139
Samuel, Ira C. ....TVG 401-211
Samuels, G. E. ....TVG 401-211
Samuels, Lawrence M. ....TVG 401-211
Sanchez, Amador.........................TVG 401-211
Sanchez, D. ....SR............401-100
Sanchez, Dario.............................LR 401-131
Sanchez, Francisco ....FF 401-139
Sanchez, L. ....FB............401-170
Sanchez, Outa ....RR 401-62
Sanchez, Romano ....FF 401-139
Sandefer, Gilbert Bryan...............SR............401-100
Sandel, Henry L. ....SR............401-100
Sandel, Henry Luther...................LR 401-131
Sandel, William L. ....TVG 401-211
Sanderford, Ghent.......................SR............401-100
Sanderlin, William T. ....USV 401-248
Sanders, A. F. ....RR 401-62
Sanders, A. F. ....RR 401-62
Sanders, C. A. ....TVG 401-211
Sanders, C. B. ....FB............401-170
Sanders, C. J. ....FB............401-170
Sanders, Cal.................................FB............401-170
Sanders, D. F. ....FB............401-170
Sanders, J. R. ....FB............401-170
Sanders, J. W. ....FB............401-170
Sanders, James............................SR............401-100
Sanders, James E. ....FF 401-139
Sanders, Jesse B..........................USV 401-248
Sanders, Jesse C. ....RR 401-62
Sanders, Jesse C. ....FB............401-170
Sanders, John J. ....RR 401-62
Sanders, John J. ....RRR 401-123
Sanders, John W. ....SR............401-100
Sanders, Oscar Dick ....RRR 401-123
Sanders, Otis D. ....USV 401-248
Sanders, S. W. ....TVG 401-211
Sanders, Samuel S. ....ARM 401-10
Sanders, T. F. ....RRR 401-123
Sanders, Tom...............................SR............401-100
Sanders, W. O..............................TVG 401-211
Sanders, Wade H. ....USV 401-248
Sanders, William ....SP............401-48
Sanders, William J.......................TVG 401-211
Sanders, William T. ....USV 401-248
Sanderson, Thomas J. ....USV 401-248
Sandford, Samuel C....................USV 401-248
Sandherr, Charles ....RR 401-62
Sandherr, Charles ....FB............401-170
Sandifer, W. W. ....SR............401-100
Sandifer, W. W. ....LR 401-131
Sandlin, Charles..........................SR............401-100
Sandlin, Charley ....RR 401-62
Sandlin, Charley ....SR............401-100
Sandlin, James L.........................SR............401-100
Sandlin, James L.........................FB............401-170
Sandoloski, Leo B. ....RRR 401-123
Sandoval, Jesus...........................FB............401-170
Sands, Richard M. ....SR............401-100
Sands, W. B. ....RR 401-62
Sands, William B.........................FB............401-170
Sands, William B.........................FB............401-170
Saner, J. M. ....SR............401-100
Saner, J. M. ....LR 401-131
Saner, Ludwig.............................FF 401-139
Sanford, Alex...............................SR............401-100
Sanford, W. F. ....USV 401-248
Sanford, Wilber E. ....TVG 401-211
Sansom, C. L. ....FB............401-170
Sansom, Charles ....SR............401-100
Sansom, George L. ....FB............401-170
Sansom, J. T. ....FF 401-139
Sansom, John W. ....FF 401-139
Sansom, John W. ....FF 401-139
Sansom, T. J. ....FB............401-170
Santos, Felipe de Los.................FB............401-170
Sapp, Jeff....................................TVG 401-211
Sapp, P. W. ....SP............401-48
Sapp, Wade H. ....USV 401-248
Sapper, Frank..............................SR............401-100
Sappington, Oliver H..................USV 401-248
Sargent, John J. ....SR............401-100
Sartain, Andy R. ....USV 401-248
Sartain, George F. ....USV 401-248
Sarvis, A. O. ....TVG 401-211
Sary, James C. ....RR 401-62
Satchell, Forrest W. ....USV 401-248
Satterwhite, Irby ....USV 401-248
Satterwhite, Thomas L................USV 401-248
Sauer, Edwin J. ....TVG 401-211
Sauer, William G. ....USV 401-248
Sauer, Willis ....SR............401-100
Sauers, Henry ....FF 401-139
Saulman, Malon F. ....USV 401-248
Saulsbery, Lee ....RR 401-62
Saunders, A. ....TVG 401-211
Saunders, D. W. ....TVG 401-211
Saunders, Earnest ....TVG 401-211
Saunders, H. C. ....FB............401-171
Saunders, Ira ....SR............401-100
Saunders, J. C. ....SR............401-100
Saunders, J. W. ....FB............401-171
Saunders, James K. ....SR............401-100
Saunders, James M. ....TVG 401-211
Saunders, John H. ....RRR 401-123
Saunders, L. D. ....SP............401-48

Index to Texas Adjutant General Service Records—All Service Branches

Name	Branch	Record
Saunders, N.	FB	401-171
Saunders, S. D.	TVG	401-211
Saunders, T. B.	TST	401-37
Saunders, Tom Smither	RRR	401-123
Saunders, W. W.	SR	401-100
Saunders, Winfrey B.	RR	401-62
Savage, All	TVG	401-211
Savage, B. R.	TVG	401-211
Savage, George B.	USV	401-248
Savage, J. E.	SR	401-101
Savage, James	ARM	401-10
Savage, John	NAV	401-23
Savage, Robert	MM	401-32
Savage, Russell	SR	401-101
Savage, Russell	LR	401-131
Savage, Samuel G.	USV	401-248
Savell, A. A.	SR	401-101
Savells, W. H.	FB	401-171
Sawyer, E. E.	FB	401-171
Sawyer, M. B.	FB	401-171
Sawyer, Selkerk O.	NAV	401-23
Sawyer, Tom	SR	401-101
Sawyers, Ed	TVG	401-211
Sawyers, F. R.	TVG	401-211
Saxon, A. L.	FB	401-171
Sayer, Quillain	TVG	401-211
Sayers, W. B.	TVG	401-211
Sayers, W. M.	SR	401-101
Sayers, Walter L.	SR	401-101
Sayle, Robert	USV	401-248
Sayles, John	TST	401-37
Scaff, Gordon	USV	401-248
Scaggs, Lee	TVG	401-211
Scales, D.	TVG	401-211
Scales, Dalton	TVG	401-211
Scales, H. L.	TVG	401-211
Scales, John Melrose	TVG	401-211
Scalloru, O. B.	RRR	401-123
Scannell, M. J.	RR	401-62
Scarborough, E. B.	RR	401-62
Scarborough, E. B.	SR	401-101
Scarborough, H. W.	TVG	401-211
Scarborough, J. S., Jr.	SR	401-101
Scarborough, J. S., Sr.	SR	401-101
Scarborough, N. V.	CSA	401-40
Scarborough, O. A.	SR	401-101
Scarborough, Roy R.	TVG	401-211
Scarborough, Tatum	TVG	401-211
Scarborough, W. F.	SR	401-101
Scarborough, W. F.	FB	401-171
Scarborough, W. G.	SR	401-101
Scarbrough, Lawrence P.	TVG	401-211
Scarbrough, Newton H.	USV	401-248
Schaefercater, August	FF	401-139
Schaeffer, E. W.	SR	401-101
Schaff, C. E.	RRR	401-123
Schattel, Adolph	USV	401-248
Schatzkey, A.	TVG	401-211
Schawe, Walter	TVG	401-211
Scheble, E. S.	TVG	401-211
Scheidemantel, Louis W.	USV	401-248
Scheidley, Benjamin A.	TST	401-37
Schelmico, William	ARM	401-10
Schemerhorn, L. J.	SR	401-101
Schentz, Phillip	MV	401-31
Schepler, Charles	FF	401-139
Scherer, W. L.	TVG	401-211
Scherffins, Henry	USV	401-248
Schertz, John E.	SP	401-48
Scherze, Charles R.	USV	401-248
Scheultz, R. Alvin	SR	401-101
Schieffer, Emmett	TVG	401-211
Schieffer, Fred	USV	401-248
Schieffer, O. S.	TVG	401-211
Schill, August	TVG	401-211
Schilling, F. L.	TVG	401-211
Schimacher, Max	TVG	401-211
Schimacher, Theo. Her. Jul.	TVG	401-211
Schimmel, Vernon G.	SR	401-101
Schintzius, T. H.	TVG	401-211
Schiskoski, William	USV	401-248
Schiveley, R. F.	SR	401-101
Schlador, Friedrick	MV	401-31
Schlegel, John O., Dr.	SR	401-101
Schley, R. H.	SR	401-101
Schleyer, Emil	TVG	401-211
Schlittler, Edward A.	USV	401-249
Schlittler, Walter	TVG	401-211
Schluchter, J. G.	TVG	401-211
Schluter, Joseph	ARM	401-10
Schmeltzer, Gustav H.	MV	401-31
Schmerbeck, Robert L.	TVG	401-211
Schmerbeck, Robert L.	USV	401-249
Schmerber, Joseph	SP	401-48
Schmid, B.	TVG	401-211
Schmid, F. L.	FB	401-171
Schmid, R. A. "Smoot"	SR	401-101
Schmidt, Ben	TVG	401-211
Schmidt, Charles	SP	401-48
Schmidt, E. H.	TVG	401-211
Schmidt, Edward	SP	401-48
Schmidt, Erich	TVG	401-211
Schmidt, Gustav	FB	401-171
Schmidt, H.	USV	401-249
Schmidt, Henry	FB	401-171
Schmidt, Henry	USV	401-249
Schmidt, Henry	USV	401-249
Schmidt, Julius	TVG	401-211
Schmidt, Julius F.	TVG	401-211
Schmidt, Louis	SR	401-101
Schmidt, Louis	FB	401-171
Schmidt, William	FB	401-171

Index to Texas Adjutant General Service Records—All Service Branches

Name	Branch	Page
Schmitt, George H.	FB	401-171
Schmitt, Glen Adam	NAV	401-23
Schmitt, William	NAV	401-23
Schmitz, A.	ARM	401-10
Schnaubert, Charles O.	SR	401-101
Schneider, C.	RR	401-62
Schneider, Henry J.	USV	401-249
Schneider, John E.	USV	401-249
Schneider, Otto	USV	401-249
Schneider, Semon	FF	401-139
Schneider, W. H.	TVG	401-211
Schnelle, W. G.	SR	401-101
Schnittker, H. W.	SR	401-101
Schnitzins, Thomas H.	USV	401-249
Schobel, George	SR	401-101
Schobey, George W.	SP	401-48
Schock, Charles George	TVG	401-211
Schoellkopf, J. Fred	SR	401-101
Schofield, Hugh	NAV	401-23
Scholl, Ernst	TVG	401-211
Schonfelder, Julius	TVG	401-211
Schoolcroft, Joe	RR	401-62
Schoonover, Henry A.	TST	401-37
Schoonover, James W.	TST	401-37
Schoonover, Peter	TST	401-37
Schorm, Wenzel	TVG	401-211
Schorre, Edward	FF	401-139
Schott, Augustus V.	ARM	401-10
Schott, Dominick	FF	401-139
Schoultz, R. Alvin	SR	401-101
Schramm, B. L.	USV	401-249
Schramm, Jesse A.	TVG	401-211
Schramm, Max	SR	401-101
Schreiber, John	USV	401-249
Schreiner, Charles	MV	401-31
Schrobe, Charles	FF	401-139
Schrock, John W.	FB	401-171
Schroeder, Arthur H.	TVG	401-211
Schroeder, E.	TVG	401-211
Schroeder, Fritz	USV	401-249
Schroeder, George	ARM	401-10
Schroeder, Henry	FB	401-171
Schubert, Aug. H.	TVG	401-211
Schubert, J.	TVG	401-211
Schubert, John N.	USV	401-249
Schubert, Louis H.	SP	401-48
Schubert, Otto, Jr.	SR	401-101
Schubert, Ottomar	FF	401-139
Schuchardt, Charles F.	TST	401-37
Schuessler, J. H.	SR	401-101
Schuessler, J. H.	LR	401-131
Schuessler, W. W.	SR	401-101
Schuett, Harry C.	SR	401-101
Schuetze, Hugo	USV	401-249
Schulenburg, W. D.	TVG	401-211
Schulte, E. H.	TVG	401-211
Schulten, Alfred	FF	401-139
Schultz, Henry W.	USV	401-249
Schultz, John	TVG	401-211
Schultz, Louis B.	TVG	401-211
Schultz, Philip	MV	401-31
Schultz, William	USV	401-249
Schultze, Alfred	TVG	401-211
Schulz, August W.	TVG	401-211
Schulz, H. R.	TVG	401-211
Schulze, Adolph	TVG	401-211
Schurman, S. F.	RR	401-62
Schuster, Adolph	TVG	401-211
Schuster, Carl E.	USV	401-249
Schuster, Joseph H.	USV	401-249
Schutze, Fred W.	RRR	401-123
Schwab, W. A.	TVG	401-211
Schwartz, Edward	USV	401-249
Schwartz, Henry	SP	401-48
Schwartz, Issy	SR	401-101
Schwartz, J. W.	SR	401-101
Schwartz, Morris S.	SR	401-101
Schwartz, Tom J.	SR	401-101
Schwartz, W. J.	RRR	401-123
Schwartz, William I.	USV	401-249
Schwarz, Reinhard	TST	401-37
Schweir, Frederick	FF	401-139
Schweitzer, George J.	USV	401-249
Schwertner, Herman, Jr.	SR	401-101
Schwinn, F. S.	SR	401-101
Scisson, Charley T.	RR	401-63
Scoggin, Nathan M.	USV	401-249
Scogin, J. L.	USV	401-249
Scollard, H. B.	SR	401-101
Scott, A. H.	ARM	401-10
Scott, Albert P.	USV	401-249
Scott, B. F.	FB	401-171
Scott, Bob	TVG	401-211
Scott, David	FB	401-171
Scott, E. H.	SR	401-101
Scott, Efrion	TVG	401-211
Scott, Elihu W.	FB	401-171
Scott, Felix C.	RR	401-63
Scott, Francis M.	CSA	401-40
Scott, Frank	SR	401-101
Scott, Frank R.	FB	401-171
Scott, Fred	RR	401-63
Scott, G. M.	FB	401-171
Scott, G. M., Jr.	SR	401-101
Scott, G. W.	SR	401-101
Scott, George B.	SR	401-101
Scott, George F.	SR	401-101
Scott, H. B.	TVG	401-211
Scott, H. V.	SR	401-101
Scott, H. V.	LR	401-131
Scott, Harry	USV	401-249
Scott, J. J.	FB	401-171

Index to Texas Adjutant General Service Records—All Service Branches

Name	Branch	Record
Scott, J. W.	SR	401-101
Scott, Jack	SP	401-48
Scott, James	ARM	401-10
Scott, James H.	NAV	401-23
Scott, James L.	USV	401-249
Scott, James M.	USV	401-249
Scott, John	FB	401-171
Scott, John	USV	401-249
Scott, John A.	TVG	401-211
Scott, John R.	FB	401-171
Scott, John W.	NAV	401-23
Scott, John W.	ARM	401-10
Scott, Jordan D.	MV	401-31
Scott, L. F.	USV	401-249
Scott, Patrick	SP	401-48
Scott, Preston	USV	401-249
Scott, R. F., Jr.	SR	401-101
Scott, Richard B. D.	TVG	401-211
Scott, Robert	FB	401-171
Scott, S. J.	SR	401-101
Scott, S. J., Jr.	LR	401-131
Scott, Samuel	FB	401-171
Scott, Samuel C.	ARM	401-10
Scott, Samuel P.	NAV	401-23
Scott, Sidney L.	SR	401-101
Scott, T. M.	TVG	401-211
Scott, Thomas	FB	401-171
Scott, Tully C.	SR	401-101
Scott, Vicinti	FB	401-171
Scott, W. A.	TVG	401-211
Scott, W. H.	SR	401-101
Scott, W. J.	USV	401-249
Scott, W. M.	FF	401-139
Scott, William	RR	401-63
Scott, William	ARM	401-10
Scott, William	FB	401-171
Scott, William A.	NAV	401-23
Scott, William A.	FB	401-171
Scott, William C.	USV	401-249
Scott, William G.	ARM	401-10
Scott, William H.	TST	401-37
Scott, Z. T., Dr.	SR	401-101
Scotten, Ed H.	FB	401-171
Scougale, Ernest R.	TVG	401-211
Scraktier, Martin C.	TVG	401-211
Scrivener, Jack G.	USV	401-249
Scroggins, Henry	TVG	401-211
Scruggs, G. R.	TVG	401-211
Scruggs, J. C.	SR	401-101
Scruggs, J. C.	LR	401-131
Scruggs, J. P.	SP	401-48
Scruggs, William E.	USV	401-249
Scruggs, William R.	USV	401-249
Scudamore, Edwin A.	TVG	401-211
Scudday, W. H.	MM	401-32
Scull, J. Ed.	USV	401-249
Scullin, Harry	RR	401-63
Scullin, Harry	SR	401-101
Scurlock, Marvin	USV	401-249
Scurry, Richard A.	USV	401-249
Scurry, Thomas	TVG	401-211
Scurry, Thomas	USV	401-249
Seaburn, J. W.	FB	401-171
Seago, Wiley	SR	401-101
Seale, Allan	TVG	401-211
Seale, Carrol T.	USV	401-249
Seale, Ed A.	TVG	401-211
Seale, James L.	RR	401-63
Seale, James Lovett	RRR	401-123
Seale, Jim	SR	401-101
Seale, John C.	SR	401-101
Seale, John H.	TVG	401-211
Sealey, Homer T.	SR	401-101
Sealey, Julius W.	RRR	401-123
Seaman, Arthur G.	USV	401-249
Seaman, Claude O.	USV	401-249
Seaman, Harry	TVG	401-211
Searcy, Oliver C.	TST	401-37
Searcy, W. A.	TVG	401-211
Searight, G. A.	SR	401-101
Sears. James E.	RR	401-63
Sears, E. A.	USV	401-249
Sears, J. A.	FB	401-171
Sears, John	RR	401-63
Seary, Daniel	FF	401-139
Seavey, Arthur Clement	SR	401-101
Seawright, Crayton	USV	401-249
Seay, E. S.	FB	401-171
Seay, Edward Sanders	FB	401-171
Seay, Geroge Mabry	SR	401-101
Seay, J. B.	FB	401-171
Seay, J. P.	FB	401-171
Sebalt, Tom D.	RRR	401-123
Sebastian, E. S.	RR	401-63
Sebree, Douglas	RRR	401-123
Sebree, Victor	FB	401-171
Seckman, Frank G.	TVG	401-211
Secrest, F. M.	TVG	401-211
Secrest, R. Y.	RR	401-63
Secrest, R. Y.	SR	401-101
Sedberry, J. M.	FB	401-171
Sedberry, M. A.	FB	401-171
Sedberry, T. D.	CSA	401-40
Sedberry, Tom D.	FB	401-171
Sedgely, M. V.	USV	401-249
Sedgwick, Samuel	NAV	401-24
Seekamp, H.	USV	401-249
Seelhorst, Herman	TVG	401-211
Seelig, James	FB	401-171
Seely, Charles	TVG	401-211
Seemuller, Henry C.	USV	401-249
Segler, E. B.	FF	401-139

Index to Texas Adjutant General Service Records—All Service Branches

Name	Branch	Record
Segler, James T.	FF	401-139
Seguin, Juan N.	ARM	401-10
Seibel, Adam	USV	401-249
Seick, Edmond	FF	401-139
Seifert, Robert	TVG	401-211
Seipp, Henry	FF	401-139
Seitz, H. C.	TVG	401-211
Seitzler, Thomas L.	SR	401-101
Seitzler, Thomas L.	LR	401-131
Seitzler, Zexer	USV	401-249
Seldner, M. O.	RRR	401-124
Self, C. B.	SR	401-101
Self, J. B.	SR	401-101
Selkirk, Wyatt Owen	TVG	401-211
Sellars, Bonnie B.	TVG	401-211
Sellers, James	FB	401-171
Sellers, James	FB	401-171
Sellers, James M.	USV	401-249
Sellers, M. T.	USV	401-249
Sellers, Sam C.	RR	401-63
Sellers, T. F.	FB	401-171
Sellick, Levi	ARM	401-10
Sellman, Charles J.	FB	401-171
Selman, Ben Thomas	RRR	401-124
Selman, H. S.	TVG	401-211
Selvidge, John V.	SR	401-101
Selvidge, John Vernon	RRR	401-124
Selz, H. L.	RRR	401-124
Seman, E. W.	TVG	401-211
Semmelmann, F. H.	TVG	401-211
Sendrey, Hugo	TVG	401-211
Senel, M.	SP	401-48
Sennett, L. M.	FB	401-171
Sennott, Owen	TVG	401-211
Senock, Antonio	NAV	401-24
Sentell, John P.	USV	401-249
Serda, Juan	FF	401-139
Sere, Leon	TVG	401-211
Sergeant, Charles H.	FB	401-171
Serur, William G.	SR	401-101
Service, George	ARM	401-10
Sessions, D. S.	TVG	401-211
Sessions, George M.	USV	401-249
Sessums, John	TVG	401-211
Settegast, Binz J.	SR	401-101
Settegast, Leon R. F.	TVG	401-211
Settle, A. D.	FB	401-171
Settle, O. B.	FB	401-171
Settle, T. B.	USV	401-249
Severns, James P.	TVG	401-211
Sevier, Hal	TVG	401-211
Sewell, Charlie P.	TVG	401-211
Sewell, Houston O.	CSA	401-40
Sewell, John C.	USV	401-249
Sewell, T. E.	USV	401-249
Sewell, Thomas E.	USV	401-249
Sexton, George Samuel	USV	401-249
Sexton, Horatio	MV	401-31
Sexton, J. F.	FB	401-171
Sexton, Thurmond	USV	401-249
Sexton, William	CSA	401-40
Sexton, William Madison	CSA	401-40
Seydler, W. H.	USV	401-249
Seymour, Charles A.	SR	401-101
Seymour, Rogers	USV	401-249
Seyster, Morgan	USV	401-249
Shackelett, B. C.	TVG	401-211
Shackleford, J. D.	TVG	401-211
Shackelford, W. O.	TVG	401-211
Shadbolt, L. M.	SR	401-101
Shady, James	USV	401-249
Shafer, W.	SR	401-101
Shaffer, Lawrence	FB	401-171
Shaffer, Robert L.	TVG	401-211
Shaley, J. L.	TST	401-37
Shanblum, L.	USV	401-249
Shane, Michael	ARM	401-10
Shane, Oscar W.	FB	401-171
Shane, Wesley O.	USV	401-249
Shank, S.	SR	401-101
Shanklin, J. F.	RR	401-63
Shanklin, J. L.	FB	401-171
Shanklin, John William	TVG	401-211
Shanks, Cyrus	SP	401-48
Shanks, E. B.	TVG	401-211
Shannon, Hugh Smith	RRR	401-124
Shannon, J. A.	FF	401-139
Shannon, James B.	USV	401-249
Shannon, John Alonzo	FB	401-171
Shannon, Lee	RR	401-63
Shannon, Lee	RRR	401-124
Shannon, N. C.	TVG	401-211
Shannon, Samuel E.	FB	401-171
Shannon, Solomon A.	USV	401-249
Shannon, Thomas J.	USV	401-249
Shannonhouse, J. G.	FB	401-171
Shapard, H. H.	USV	401-249
Shapard, Howard F.	USV	401-249
Sharman, Robert L.	TVG	401-211
Sharp, A. T.	SR	401-101
Sharp, A. T.	LR	401-131
Sharp, Carl G.	SR	401-101
Sharp, E. H.	RRR	401-124
Sharp, G. W.	FB	401-171
Sharp, J. A.	SR	401-101
Sharp, J. A.	LR	401-131
Sharp, J. E.	FF	401-139
Sharp, J. F.	FB	401-171
Sharp, J. J.	RRR	401-124
Sharp, W. R.	SR	401-101
Sharpe, J. Q.	TVG	401-211
Sharpless, A. G.	NAV	401-24

Index to Texas Adjutant General Service Records—All Service Branches

Name	Branch	Page
Shartzer, Hiram	ARM	401-10
Sharver, A. M.	LR	401-131
Sharver, A. M.	SR	401-101
Shatton, R. S.	SR	401-101
Shaw, Charles	FB	401-171
Shaw, Daniel	TVG	401-211
Shaw, Daniel P.	TVG	401-211
Shaw, Dusk	TVG	401-211
Shaw, E. F.	FB	401-171
Shaw, Edward Nisha	USV	401-249
Shaw, Franklin	TST	401-37
Shaw, Gus	TVG	401-211
Shaw, J. C.	SR	401-101
Shaw, J. M.	SR	401-101
Shaw, J. M.	FB	401-171
Shaw, Jacob	ARM	401-10
Shaw, James C.	USV	401-249
Shaw, Joe	TVG	401-211
Shaw, Joe R.	RR	401-63
Shaw, John	ARM	401-10
Shaw, John	ARM	401-10
Shaw, John F.	FB	401-171
Shaw, Joseph B.	RRR	401-124
Shaw, Joseph B.	USV	401-249
Shaw, Robert C.	USV	401-249
Shaw, Ted	TVG	401-211
Shaw, Tom M.	TVG	401-211
Shaw, W. G.	TST	401-37
Shaw, Wallace Nelson	TVG	401-211
Shaw, Will M.	TVG	401-211
Shaw, William C.	RR	401-63
Shaw, William S.	USV	401-249
Shay, John	ARM	401-10
Shea, Michael	ARM	401-10
Shea, Peter	NAV	401-24
Shearer, H. R.	ARM	401-10
Shearer, Joseph W.	USV	401-249
Shears, J. D.	SP	401-48
Sheedy, Pat	RR	401-63
Sheedy, Pat	SR	401-101
Sheegog, Edward T.	USV	401-249
Sheehan, James M.	USV	401-249
Sheeks, William C.	CSA	401-40
Sheely, A. L.	FB	401-171
Sheely, Joseph	FB	401-171
Sheets, Alexander A.	TVG	401-211
Sheffield, D. N.	FB	401-171
Sheffield, E. C.	FB	401-171
Sheffield, E. C.	FB	401-171
Sheffield, Floy M.	USV	401-249
Sheffield, Mat H.	FB	401-171
Sheffield, W. F.	FB	401-171
Shelby, David	ARM	401-10
Shelby, Harmon C.	SR	401-101
Shelby, Launcelot C.	USV	401-249
Sheldon, J. C.	NAV	401-24
Sheldon, R. G.	SP	401-48
Shelley, B. A.	TVG	401-211
Shelley, Frederick W.	USV	401-249
Shelley, George E.	TVG	401-211
Shelley, S. S.	TVG	401-211
Shelley, T. H.	TST	401-37
Shelley, Tom	SR	401-101
Shells, L. C.	FB	401-171
Shellshear, Charles Edward	TVG	401-211
Shellshear, Joe	TVG	401-211
Shellshear, Walter	TVG	401-212
Shelton, B. R.	TVG	401-212
Shelton, C. B.	RR	401-63
Shelton, Cal	FB	401-171
Shelton, Fred M.	SR	401-101
Shelton, Frederick Victor	TVG	401-212
Shelton, J. C.	SP	401-48
Shelton, J. O.	TVG	401-212
Shelton, James	TVG	401-212
Shelton, M. N.	SR	401-101
Shelton, Matthew	USV	401-249
Shelton, R. S.	SR	401-101
Shelton, Thomas B.	CSA	401-40
Shelton, William R.	TVG	401-212
Shely, A. L.	FB	401-171
Shely, George Rutledge	RR	401-63
Shely, Joseph	FB	401-171
Shely, L. D.	FB	401-171
Shely, W. I.	FB	401-171
Shely, W. W.	FB	401-171
Shely, William	SR	401-101
Shely, William	FB	401-171
Shely, William Almond	RR	401-63
Shepard, J. C.	SR	401-101
Shepard, T. L.	RR	401-63
Shepard, T. L.	SR	401-101
Shepard, Thomas P.	ARM	401-10
Shepherd J.	ARM	401-10
Shepherd, Allen S.	TVG	401-212
Shepherd, C. L.	TVG	401-212
Shepherd, C. M.	SR	401-101
Shepherd, D.	RRR	401-124
Shepherd, Frederick	ARM	401-10
Shepherd, J. V.	TVG	401-212
Shepherd, James L.	TVG	401-212
Shepherd, Robert C.	USV	401-249
Shepherd, Walter D.	TVG	401-212
Shepherd, William Albert	CSA	401-40
Shepherd, William D.	FF	401-139
Sheppard, Clarence	USV	401-249
Sheppard, H. J.	USV	401-249
Sheppard, Jacob H.	ARM	401-10
Sheppard, John William	RRR	401-124
Sheppard, Simeon C.	SR	401-101
Sheppeard, Horace C.	RRR	401-124
Sheppeard, Horace Cleveland	SR	401-101

Index to Texas Adjutant General Service Records—All Service Branches

Name	Branch	Page
Shepperd, Fred	NAV	401-24
Shepperd, Henry T.	USV	401-249
Sheren, T.	TST	401-37
Sherer, William O.	USV	401-249
Shererdon, John	ARM	401-10
Sheriff, Thomas	SP	401-48
Sherles, Louis	TVG	401-212
Sherman, A. B.	FB	401-172
Sherman, F. N.	FB	401-172
Sherman, J. F.	FB	401-172
Sherman, L. A.	SR	401-101
Sherman, S. F.	RRR	401-124
Sherrell, B. F.	TVG	401-212
Sherrill, A.	ARM	401-10
Sherrill, C. J.	TVG	401-212
Sherrill, Louis	TVG	401-212
Sherrill, M. F.	TVG	401-212
Sherum, James D.	ARM	401-10
Sherwood, John P.	NAV	401-24
Shield, G. W.	FB	401-172
Shield, Leon L.	SR	401-101
Shields, Ethol H.	TVG	401-212
Shields, F. T.	FB	401-172
Shields, Jesse	TVG	401-212
Shields, Jonathan	MV	401-31
Shields, Morgan	USV	401-249
Shields, Richard	FB	401-172
Shields, W. S.	USV	401-249
Shields, William J.	ARM	401-10
Shifflette, A. A.	FB	401-172
Shindler, Charles I.	USV	401-249
Shindler, R. T.	USV	401-249
Shine, J. E.	RRR	401-124
Shineman, Fred W.	SR	401-101
Shiner, Walter W.	USV	401-249
Shingle, Charles	ARM	401-10
Ship, W. A.	MV	401-31
Ship, William	ARM	401-10
Shipley, Aubrey	RR	401-63
Shipman, Charles	NAV	401-24
Shipman, Jas. R.	ARM	401-10
Shipman, John M.	ARM	401-10
Shipman, O. L.	FB	401-172
Shipp, Claude S.	SR	401-101
Shipp, J. M.	CSA	401-40
Shipp, L. C.	FF	401-139
Shipp, W. H.	SR	401-101
Shippey, Henry	NAV	401-24
Shirley, Don Le Roy	RRR	401-124
Shirley, George	FB	401-172
Shirley, J. W.	USV	401-249
Shirley, William Bert	TVG	401-212
Shivers, G. O.	FB	401-172
Shockley, B. M.	USV	401-249
Shockley, Glenn	RRR	401-124
Shoemake, Albert B.	SR	401-102
Shoemaker, J. L.	SR	401-102
Shoemaker, J. L.	LR	401-131
Shoemaker, Sam Jr.	TVG	401-212
Shofner, V. B.	SR	401-102
Sholl, J. P.	ARM	401-10
Shook, Clive H.	USV	401-249
Shook, Jeff Davis	USV	401-249
Shook, William M.	MV	401-31
Shores, J. M.	FF	401-139
Shores, W. M.	FF	401-139
Short, F. C.	SR	401-102
Short, Jacob Lindsey	TVG	401-212
Short, John	FB	401-172
Short, Matthew	NAV	401-24
Short, Pete	SR	401-102
Short, Samuel	RR	401-63
Short, T. J.	FB	401-172
Short, W. W.	FB	401-172
Shorter, C. B.	SR	401-102
Shorts, M. A.	ARM	401-10
Shotwell, A. J.	SP	401-48
Shotwell, J. H.	TVG	401-212
Shotwell, Louis	ARM	401-10
Shoults, Gaines T.	SR	401-102
Shouse, Walter L.	USV	401-249
Showman, Frederick	ARM	401-10
Shown, James J.	RR	401-63
Shown, Jim J.	SR	401-102
Shreve, Benjamin F.	FB	401-172
Shrock, J. W.	FB	401-172
Shropshire, Banjaman	USV	401-249
Shryach, E. H.	ARM	401-10
Shuber, J. C.	FF	401-139
Shuler, Ellis M.	RR	401-63
Shuler, James C.	FF	401-139
Shull, W. B.	TVG	401-212
Shults, C. E.	SR	401-102
Shults, Casper	SR	401-102
Shults, J. O.	USV	401-249
Shultz, John	ARM	401-10
Shultz, John	FF	401-139
Shumate, I. E.	RRR	401-124
Shumate, I. T.	RRR	401-124
Shumate, J. W.	RRR	401-124
Shumate, P. O.	RRR	401-124
Shumate, Parker	RRR	401-124
Shumate, R. D.	RR	401-63
Shumate, R. D.	SR	401-102
Shumate, W. M.	RR	401-63
Shumway, George R.	ARM	401-10
Shupak, Frank F.	TVG	401-212
Sibley, Isaac G.	FB	401-172
Sickora, Anton	USV	401-249
Siddal, Vene P.	USV	401-249
Siddon, John A.	USV	401-249
Siders, H. E.	FB	401-172

Index to Texas Adjutant General Service Records—All Service Branches

Name	Branch	Record
Sidney, Robert	TVG	401-212
Siebert, F.	FB	401-172
Siekatz, W. E.	TVG	401-212
Sieker, E. A.	FB	401-172
Sieker, F. E.	FB	401-172
Sieker, L. P.	FB	401-172
Sieker, L. P.	TVG	401-212
Sieker, S. P.	FB	401-172
Sieker, Thomas	FB	401-172
Siekold, Jacob	SP	401-48
Siekski, Henry M.	SR	401-102
Sielski, Edward D.	TVG	401-212
Sielski, John S.	USV	401-249
Sier, James W.	MM	401-32
Sierra, Jose	FF	401-139
Sierra, Pedro	FF	401-139
Sieverts, Hiram A.	USV	401-249
Sigal, Mike	SR	401-102
Sigel, Morris P.	SR	401-102
Sigler, G. W.	RR	401-63
Sikes, Benjamin G.	TVG	401-212
Sikes, Henry	NAV	401-24
Sikes, John F.	USV	401-249
Sikes, Robert E.	USV	401-249
Sikes, Roly F.	USV	401-249
Sikes, Samuel T.	TVG	401-212
Sikora, Joe	USV	401-249
Silcreggs, David	ARM	401-10
Sillery, Charles	ARM	401-10
Silliman, J. H.	TVG	401-212
Silliman, R. B.	TVG	401-212
Sills, Henry	NAV	401-24
Sillski, Henry M.	SR	401-102
Silva, John	TVG	401-212
Silven, Earl H.	SR	401-102
Silven, Earle Henri	SR	401-102
Silvernail, Harry C.	USV	401-249
Silvey, Howard	USV	401-249
Silvey, James Lawrence	RRR	401-124
Simmang, John S.	SR	401-102
Simmonds, Samuel B.	ARM	401-10
Simmons, C. A.	TVG	401-212
Simmons, C. B.	TVG	401-212
Simmons, C. C.	SP	401-48
Simmons, Charles B.	TVG	401-212
Simmons, Clint S.	TVG	401-212
Simmons, E. W.	TVG	401-212
Simmons, Elisha H.	USV	401-249
Simmons, F. B.	FB	401-172
Simmons, F. J.	FB	401-172
Simmons, Flavius J.	FB	401-172
Simmons, Green B.	ARM	401-10
Simmons, Grover C.	TVG	401-212
Simmons, Israel	ARM	401-10
Simmons, J. A.	USV	401-249
Simmons, J. C.	TVG	401-212
Simmons, J. E.	TVG	401-212
Simmons, J. R.	TVG	401-212
Simmons, J. R.	USV	401-249
Simmons, James	ARM	401-10
Simmons, John B.	ARM	401-10
Simmons, L. V.	RRR	401-124
Simmons, Lee	RRR	401-124
Simmons, Lee	SR	401-102
Simmons, M. K.	RRR	401-124
Simmons, M. K.	SR	401-102
Simmons, Marvin C.	USV	401-249
Simmons, Newt. C.	TVG	401-212
Simmons, Obediah	ARM	401-10
Simmons, R. C.	TVG	401-212
Simmons, Robert M.	TVG	401-212
Simmons, Robert M.	USV	401-249
Simmons, Thomas S.	TVG	401-212
Simmons, W. D.	USV	401-249
Simmons, W. H.	TVG	401-212
Simmons, W. M.	TVG	401-212
Simmons, Wellington	USV	401-249
Simmons, William	ARM	401-10
Simmons, William V.	SR	401-102
Simms, Edmund G.	USV	401-249
Simms, George D.	USV	401-249
Simms, James	ARM	401-10
Simms, Robert H.	TVG	401-212
Simms, T. A.	FB	401-172
Simms, William H.	USV	401-249
Simon, Cain W.	USV	401-249
Simon, George V.	TVG	401-212
Simon, Harold C.	SR	401-102
Simon, Louis M.	TVG	401-212
Simonds, Harry P.	USV	401-249
Simons, James	ARM	401-10
Simons, James S.	NAV	401-24
Simonton, C. C.	SR	401-102
Simpson, Albert E.	SR	401-102
Simpson, Alfred R.	RR	401-63
Simpson, Andrew J.	USV	401-249
Simpson, Dee	TVG	401-212
Simpson, Eliah	ARM	401-10
Simpson, Francis	ARM	401-10
Simpson, Harrison	NAV	401-24
Simpson, Harrison	ARM	401-10
Simpson, Hugh H.	USV	401-249
Simpson, J. T.	TVG	401-212
Simpson, J. W.	SR	401-102
Simpson, James	USV	401-249
Simpson, James Robert	USV	401-249
Simpson, John D.	USV	401-249
Simpson, John R.	USV	401-249
Simpson, Oscar	TVG	401-212
Simpson, R.	TVG	401-212
Simpson, Robert L. R.	TVG	401-212
Simpson, Sam	FB	401-172

Index to Texas Adjutant General Service Records—All Service Branches

Name	Branch	Record
Simpson, Sam P.	TVG	401-212
Simpson, Thad C.	RRR	401-124
Simpson, Thomas	ARM	401-10
Simpson, W. A.	SR	401-102
Simpson, William	NAV	401-24
Simpson, William Sloan	TVG	401-212
Sims, Alonzo	USV	401-249
Sims, Burris	ARM	401-10
Sims, C. W.	TVG	401-212
Sims, Dick	SR	401-102
Sims, Ernest B.	USV	401-249
Sims, Harry T.	SR	401-102
Sims, James T.	USV	401-249
Sims, John	TVG	401-212
Sims, Lee C.	USV	401-249
Sims, Manuel B.	USV	401-249
Sinclair, John	TVG	401-212
Singler, Joseph M.	USV	401-250
Singletary, Fritz	TVG	401-212
Singleton, D. A.	TVG	401-212
Singleton, D. E.	RR	401-63
Singleton, Darwin E.	RR	401-63
Singleton, Isaac	TVG	401-212
Singleton, J. L.	FF	401-139
Singleton, J. M.	TVG	401-212
Singleton, Jeremiah	NAV	401-24
Singleton, Jesse	SR	401-102
Singleton, N. A.	FB	401-172
Sinico, Uriah	ARM	401-10
Siros, Earnest A.	USV	401-250
Sisco, Charles N.	USV	401-250
Sisk, Charles M.	USV	401-250
Sisk, E. B.	SR	401-102
Sisk, H. S.	FB	401-172
Sisk, James M.	USV	401-250
Sisk, William B.	USV	401-250
Sisson, Arthur W.	TVG	401-212
Sitter, Joseph R.	FB	401-172
Sittre, John B.	RR	401-63
Sjoberg, C. R.	RRR	401-124
Skaggs, George W.	TVG	401-212
Skaggs, George W.	USV	401-250
Skains, Thomas W.	RRR	401-124
Skeen, Carrol	TVG	401-212
Skeen, Franklin T.	USV	401-250
Skeen, Ira J.	USV	401-250
Skeen, Spencer D.	RRR	401-124
Skeley, J. S.	TVG	401-212
Skelton, Alexander H.	RRR	401-124
Skelton, John E.	TVG	401-212
Skidmore, J. R.	SR	401-102
Skidmore, John	ARM	401-10
Skinell, Samuel	NAV	401-24
Skinner, Derwood U.	RRR	401-124
Skinner, J. F.	SR	401-102
Skinner, Walter	RR	401-63
Skinner, Walter Scott	SR	401-102
Skipper, J.	TST	401-37
Skipper, W. P.	SR	401-102
Skipworth, G. J.	FF	401-139
Slack, F. L.	USV	401-250
Slack, H. C.	SR	401-102
Slack, Harold	RR	401-63
Slack, W. E.	SR	401-102
Slade, W. C.	SP	401-48
Slade, William J.	USV	401-250
Slagle, Walter T.	USV	401-250
Slate, Harry D.	USV	401-250
Slater, Burt A.	SR	401-102
Slaton, C. C.	TVG	401-212
Slator, J. M.	FB	401-172
Slaughter, David L.	USV	401-250
Slaughter, George M.	TVG	401-212
Slaughter, R. L.	FB	401-172
Slaughter, Reuben	MV	401-31
Slaughter, Robert E.	USV	401-250
Slaughter, S. H.	TVG	401-212
Slaughter, W. F.	TVG	401-212
Slaughter, W. F.	USV	401-250
Slaughter, W. W.	TVG	401-212
Slaughter, William S.	NAV	401-24
Slaughter, Wyatt W.	SR	401-102
Slauson, H. A.	SR	401-102
Slayden, O. B.	TVG	401-212
Slaymin, James	NAV	401-24
Slayton, Fred W.	TVG	401-212
Sledge, L. W.	SR	401-102
Sleeper, John E.	RRR	401-124
Slimm, W. N.	USV	401-250
Sloan, Eben C.	USV	401-250
Sloan, Hugh	TVG	401-212
Sloan, J. C.	MM	401-32
Sloan, James	ARM	401-10
Sloan, Lawrence	RRR	401-124
Sloan, M. S.	RRR	401-124
Sloan, W. E.	TVG	401-212
Slough, E. L.	FB	401-172
Slough, John W.	SR	401-102
Slover, J.E.	FF	401-139
Slover, M. F.	SR	401-102
Slover, M. F.	LR	401-131
Sluder, E. A.	RR	401-63
Sluder, E. A.	SR	401-102
Slyman, William E.	USV	401-250
Small, F. J.	SR	401-102
Small, J. J.	SR	401-102
Small, Lycurgis	FB	401-172
Smalley, Jim	SP	401-48
Smallwood, W. H.	USV	401-250
Smally, Edd	TVG	401-212
Smart, William M.	USV	401-250
Smedley, W. T.	TVG	401-212

Index to Texas Adjutant General Service Records—All Service Branches

Name	Branch	Record
Smedt, W.	FB	401-172
Smiley, Sylvanus	RR	401-63
Smith, A. F.	SR	401-102
Smith, A. J.	FB	401-172
Smith, A. M.	SP	401-49
Smith, A. M.	FB	401-172
Smith, A. V.	SR	401-102
Smith, Abb	SR	401-102
Smith, Alfred	SP	401-49
Smith, Alvin	ARM	401-10
Smith, Anthony	MV	401-31
Smith, Arthur A.	USV	401-250
Smith, Arthur D.	USV	401-250
Smith, Arthur O.	USV	401-250
Smith, Asbery F.	TVG	401-212
Smith, August	RR	401-63
Smith, Augustus	FB	401-172
Smith, Austin V.	TVG	401-212
Smith, Austin V.	USV	401-250
Smith, B. F.	MM	401-32
Smith, B. F.	TVG	401-212
Smith, B. L.	SR	401-102
Smith, B. V.	TST	401-37
Smith, Ben S.	TVG	401-212
Smith, Benjamin F.	FB	401-172
Smith, Benjamin F.	USV	401-250
Smith, Bernard E.	TVG	401-212
Smith, Bernard R.	USV	401-250
Smith, Berry C.	USV	401-250
Smith, Boyce	USV	401-250
Smith, Bruce	TVG	401-212
Smith, Burck	SR	401-102
Smith, C.	FB	401-172
Smith, C. B.	SR	401-102
Smith, C. D.	SR	401-102
Smith, C. D.	LR	401-131
Smith, C. L.	FB	401-172
Smith, C. S.	RRR	401-124
Smith, C. S.	FB	401-172
Smith, C. W.	SR	401-102
Smith, Calvert Philpott	RRR	401-124
Smith, Carey J.	TVG	401-212
Smith, Carroll	TVG	401-212
Smith, Chapman J.	RR	401-63
Smith, Charles	NAV	401-24
Smith, Charles	ARM	401-10
Smith, Charles	SR	401-102
Smith, Charles D.	TVG	401-212
Smith, Charles D.	USV	401-250
Smith, Charles E.	SR	401-102
Smith, Charles H.	NAV	401-24
Smith, Charles K.	SR	401-102
Smith, Charles P.	TST	401-37
Smith, Charles R.	FB	401-172
Smith, Charles Russell	SR	401-102
Smith, Charles W.	SR	401-102
Smith, Charlie O.	USV	401-250
Smith, Clarence S.	USV	401-250
Smith, Claude T.	RR	401-63
Smith, Clint	TVG	401-212
Smith, Cyrus R.	SR	401-102
Smith, D. P.	SR	401-102
Smith, D. R.	FB	401-172
Smith, Dan E.	TVG	401-212
Smith, Daniel	ARM	401-10
Smith, Daniel D.	USV	401-250
Smith, Daniel W.	NAV	401-24
Smith, David T.	FF	401-139
Smith, Dean O.	SR	401-102
Smith, Dewitt C.	RR	401-63
Smith, Dick	RRR	401-124
Smith, Dick	SR	401-102
Smith, Dott E.	RR	401-63
Smith, E. H.	RR	401-63
Smith, E. H.	RRR	401-124
Smith, E. H.	SR	401-102
Smith, E. M.	USV	401-250
Smith, E. R.	USV	401-250
Smith, E. S.	TVG	401-212
Smith, E. W.	FB	401-172
Smith, Earl B.	SR	401-102
Smith, Earl W.	SR	401-102
Smith, Earle C.	TVG	401-212
Smith, Ed	SR	401-102
Smith, Ed	SR	401-102
Smith, Edward	ARM	401-10
Smith, Edward E.	USV	401-250
Smith, Edward J.	TVG	401-212
Smith, Edward W.	USV	401-250
Smith, Elijah	ARM	401-10
Smith, Elmer	USV	401-250
Smith, Emmett	RR	401-63
Smith, Emory G.	USV	401-250
Smith, Erastus "Deaf"	ARM	401-10
Smith, Estes	USV	401-250
Smith, Eugene J.	SR	401-102
Smith, F.	TST	401-37
Smith, Felix D.	USV	401-250
Smith, Fenwick	NAV	401-24
Smith, Frank A.	TVG	401-212
Smith, Frank M.	USV	401-250
Smith, Frank S.	FF	401-139
Smith, Fred	TVG	401-212
Smith, Fred G.	TVG	401-212
Smith, Fred R.	TVG	401-212
Smith, Frederick	TST	401-37
Smith, G. A.	SR	401-102
Smith, G. L.	TVG	401-212
Smith, G. P.	SR	401-102
Smith, G. P.	LR	401-131
Smith, G. T.	SR	401-102
Smith, Geary	ARM	401-10

Index to Texas Adjutant General Service Records—All Service Branches

Smith, Geary..........................ARM.......401-10
Smith, Gee R. ....SR...........401-102
Smith, Gene.........................SR...........401-102
Smith, George......................NAV.......401-24
Smith, George A. ....USV.......401-250
Smith, George L. ....USV.......401-250
Smith, George R. ....LR..........401-131
Smith, George W. ....FB..........401-172
Smith, H. B. ....RR..........401-63
Smith, H. B. ....TVG........401-212
Smith, H. C. ....RRR........401-124
Smith, H. C. ....SR...........401-102
Smith, H. E. ....FF...........401-139
Smith, H. E. ....SP...........401-49
Smith, H. E. ....USV.......401-250
Smith, H. M. ....SR...........401-102
Smith, H. M. ....TVG........401-212
Smith, H. M. L......................TST........401-37
Smith, H. O. ....TVG........401-212
Smith, Hal............................TVG........401-212
Smith, Harry M.....................TVG........401-212
Smith, Harvey G. ....USV.......401-250
Smith, Hazell Bee ....USV.......401-250
Smith, Henry........................NAV.......401-24
Smith, Henry........................FB..........401-172
Smith, Henry C.....................USV.......401-250
Smith, Henry J. ....ARM.......401-10
Smith, Hiland R. ....SR...........401-102
Smith, Howard A..................USV.......401-250
Smith, Hugh.........................RR..........401-63
Smith, Hugh.........................RRR........401-124
Smith, Hugh.........................SR...........401-102
Smith, Hugh.........................FB..........401-172
Smith, I. L. ....TVG........401-212
Smith, J. ....ARM.......401-10
Smith, J. A. ....FB..........401-172
Smith, J. Arthur ....FB..........401-172
Smith, J. B. ....TST........401-37
Smith, J. B. ....FB..........401-172
Smith, J. C. ....RR..........401-63
Smith, J. E. ....FB..........401-172
Smith, J. E. ....FB..........401-172
Smith, J. F. ....CSA........401-40
Smith, J. F. ....SR...........401-102
Smith, J. Guy ....FB..........401-172
Smith, J. L. ....CSA........401-40
Smith, J. L. ....TVG........401-212
Smith, J. P. ....TVG........401-212
Smith, J. Sanford ....TVG........401-212
Smith, J. W. ....FB..........401-172
Smith, Jacob ....SP...........401-49
Smith, James ....NAV.......401-24
Smith, James ....ARM.......401-10
Smith, James ....ARM.......401-10
Smith, James ....SP...........401-49
Smith, James ....USV.......401-250

Smith, James A. ....TVG........401-212
Smith, James A. ....USV.......401-250
Smith, James E. ....FB..........401-172
Smith, James H. ....TST........401-37
Smith, James H. ....RR..........401-63
Smith, James K. ....USV.......401-250
Smith, James Marcus...........SR...........401-102
Smith, James Marcus...........LR..........401-131
Smith, James R. ....USV.......401-250
Smith, James S. ....ARM.......401-10
Smith, James W. ....SR...........401-102
Smith, James W. ....USV.......401-250
Smith, James Warren..........RR..........401-63
Smith, James Willie..............RR..........401-63
Smith, Jay...........................TVG........401-212
Smith, Jesse ....TVG........401-212
Smith, Jesse G. ....SR...........401-102
Smith, Jesse Lee ....RR..........401-63
Smith, Jim C. ....TVG........401-212
Smith, Joe H. ....SR...........401-102
Smith, Joe J. ....RRR........401-124
Smith, John........................NAV.......401-24
Smith, John........................NAV.......401-24
Smith, John........................ARM.......401-10
Smith, John........................ARM.......401-10
Smith, John........................ARM.......401-10
Smith, John........................MV..........401-31
Smith, John........................SP...........401-49
Smith, John B. ....CSA........401-40
Smith, John B. ....TST........401-37
Smith, John E.....................SP...........401-49
Smith, John E.....................RRR........401-124
Smith, John F. ....USV.......401-250
Smith, John Gilbert..............USV.......401-250
Smith, John M. ....MV..........401-31
Smith, John M. ....SP...........401-49
Smith, John S. ....RR..........401-63
Smith, John W. ....TVG........401-212
Smith, Joshua....................ARM.......401-10
Smith, Julius G. ....TVG........401-212
Smith, Kathryn Elizabeth ....SR...........401-102
Smith, L. B. ....FB..........401-172
Smith, Landis E. ....SR...........401-102
Smith, Lazarus...................MV..........401-31
Smith, Lee ....TVG........401-212
Smith, Lee ....TVG........401-212
Smith, Leroy H. ....NAV.......401-24
Smith, Levi ....SR...........401-102
Smith, Lonnie ....SR...........401-102
Smith, Louis ....TVG........401-212
Smith, Luther J. ....USV.......401-250
Smith, M. ....FB..........401-172
Smith, M. C. ....SR...........401-102
Smith, M. C. ....TVG........401-212
Smith, M. M., Jr..................SR...........401-102
Smith, M. P. ....FB..........401-172

Index to Texas Adjutant General Service Records—All Service Branches

Name	Branch	Record
Smith, M. R.	SR	401-102
Smith, Mack	USV	401-250
Smith, Michael	ARM	401-10
Smith, Murray	SR	401-102
Smith, Nathain	TVG	401-212
Smith, Nathan S.	CSA	401-40
Smith, Norris F.	SR	401-102
Smith, O. E.	SR	401-102
Smith, O. H., Jr.	SR	401-103
Smith, O. L., Dr.	SR	401-103
Smith, O. W.	RR	401-63
Smith, Olin Welborn	RRR	401-124
Smith, Orsina L.	USV	401-250
Smith, Oscar	TVG	401-212
Smith, Oscar P.	USV	401-250
Smith, P. H.	FB	401-172
Smith, Patrick	TST	401-37
Smith, Patrick	ARM	401-10
Smith, Paul E.	TVG	401-212
Smith, R. E.	RR	401-63
Smith, R. J.	SR	401-103
Smith, R. J.	FB	401-172
Smith, R. L.	SR	401-103
Smith, R. R.	LR	401-131
Smith, R. T.	TVG	401-212
Smith, Reuben	TVG	401-212
Smith, Richard E.	RRR	401-124
Smith, Riley Robert	SR	401-103
Smith, Robert	NAV	401-24
Smith, Robert	RR	401-63
Smith, Robert	SP	401-49
Smith, Robert B.	RR	401-63
Smith, Robert J.	RR	401-63
Smith, Robert L.	USV	401-250
Smith, Rufus H.	USV	401-250
Smith, S. S.	SR	401-103
Smith, S. S.	TVG	401-212
Smith, Sam W.	USV	401-250
Smith, Samuel C.	FB	401-172
Smith, Samuel H.	USV	401-250
Smith, Samuel R.	NAV	401-24
Smith, Schubie	TVG	401-212
Smith, Sidney A.	TVG	401-212
Smith, Singleton	MV	401-31
Smith, Sledge	SR	401-103
Smith, Sledge	LR	401-131
Smith, Sonny W.	TVG	401-213
Smith, Squire	FB	401-172
Smith, Stephen	NAV	401-24
Smith, Steret	ARM	401-10
Smith, Stewart Wiggins	RRR	401-124
Smith, Strother	TST	401-37
Smith, T. B.	TVG	401-213
Smith, T. Frank	TVG	401-213
Smith, T. J.	TVG	401-213
Smith, Thomas	NAV	401-24
Smith, Thomas	FB	401-172
Smith, Thomas	USV	401-250
Smith, Thomas G.	USV	401-250
Smith, Thomas J.	SP	401-49
Smith, Thomas P.	USV	401-250
Smith, Thomas Richard	SR	401-103
Smith, Thos. F.	ARM	401-10
Smith, Tony A.	TVG	401-213
Smith, Ulvin M. [M. U.]	TVG	401-213
Smith, W. A.	RRR	401-124
Smith, W. A.	TVG	401-213
Smith, W. B.	USV	401-250
Smith, W. E.	USV	401-250
Smith, W. G.	RRR	401-124
Smith, W. G.	SR	401-103
Smith, W. H.	ARM	401-10
Smith, W. M.	TVG	401-213
Smith, W. M.	USV	401-250
Smith, W. R.	SR	401-103
Smith, W. R.	TVG	401-213
Smith, W. S.	RRR	401-124
Smith, W. S.	SR	401-103
Smith, W. T.	FB	401-172
Smith, Wade	TVG	401-213
Smith, Walter	TVG	401-213
Smith, Walter	SR	401-103
Smith, Walter	LR	401-131
Smith, Walter B.	SR	401-103
Smith, Walter L.	TVG	401-213
Smith, Walter L.	TVG	401-213
Smith, Walter N.	USV	401-250
Smith, Warren	SR	401-103
Smith, Warren H.	RRR	401-124
Smith, William	NAV	401-24
Smith, William	RR	401-63
Smith, William	ARM	401-10
Smith, William	ARM	401-10
Smith, William	ARM	401-10
Smith, William	USV	401-250
Smith, William	USV	401-250
Smith, William A.	USV	401-250
Smith, William H.	NAV	401-24
Smith, William J.	TVG	401-213
Smith, William R.	RR	401-63
Smith, William T.	USV	401-250
Smith, William T.	USV	401-250
Smith, Willie Lee	TVG	401-213
Smith, Z. B.	SR	401-103
Smitheal, Claude	TVG	401-213
Smither, Allen T.	USV	401-250
Smither, John M.	USV	401-250
Smither, R. F.	USV	401-250
Smithey, Will	TVG	401-213
Smithwick, J. W. A.	FB	401-172
Smoot, Edgar K.	TVG	401-213
Smoot, L. C.	RRR	401-124

Index to Texas Adjutant General Service Records—All Service Branches

Smothers, John O. .... USV 401-250
Smothers, Samuel M. .... USV 401-250
Smothers, W. T. .... FB 401-172
Smyth, Dudley Downman .... TVG 401-213
Smyth, Dudley Downman .... USV 401-250
Smyth, Jot .... SR 401-103
Smyth, R. P. .... TVG 401-213
Smyth, R. P. .... USV 401-250
Smythe, H. .... TVG 401-213
Smythe, M. H. .... TVG 401-213
Smythe, Thomas S. .... USV 401-250
Snearley, W. J. .... FB 401-172
Sneddon, B. H. .... USV 401-250
Sneed, Henry .... SP 401-49
Sneed, Mahlon P. .... TVG 401-213
Sneed, Mahlon P. .... USV 401-250
Sneed, N. .... TVG 401-213
Sneed, Nicholas T. .... CSA 401-40
Sneed, Trice .... RRR 401-124
Sneed, Walter G. .... TVG 401-213
Sneed, Walter G. .... USV 401-250
Snell, James Henry .... TVG 401-213
Snell, Phillip Nathaniel .... TVG 401-213
Snell, Thomas W. .... TVG 401-213
Snelling, Harry F. .... SR 401-103
Snelling, J. H. .... FB 401-172
Snider, John .... ARM 401-10
Snoddy, Charles .... USV 401-250
Snodgrass, Homer Grant .... RRR 401-124
Snodgrass, W. W. .... TVG 401-213
Snody, Walter F. .... SR 401-103
Snody, Walter F. .... LR 401-131
Snow, Charles B. .... NAV 401-24
Snow, Charles I. .... USV 401-250
Snow, J. Burrows .... NAV 401-24
Snow, J. P. .... TVG 401-213
Snow, Luther D. .... SR 401-103
Snow, Wyatt E. .... TVG 401-213
Snowden, J. G. .... SR 401-103
Snowden, J. G. .... LR 401-131
Snowdon, Stuart .... NAV 401-24
Snyder, C. C. .... TVG 401-213
Snyder, Frank .... USV 401-250
Snyder, Gustave .... RR 401-63
Snyder, H. P. .... SR 401-103
Snyder, John C. .... FF 401-139
Snyder, T. W. .... SR 401-103
Snyder, V. L. .... RR 401-63
Soape, Ralph .... SR 401-103
Sobey, Francis J. H. .... USV 401-250
Soikum, William .... NAV 401-24
Soiland, A. .... TVG 401-213
Sokalski, Joseph .... ARM 401-11
Solinsky, Alvin .... SR 401-103
Solms, Gustave .... USV 401-250
Solomon, Albert Peter .... RRR 401-124

Solomon, E. W. .... TVG 401-213
Solomon, Harry .... SR 401-103
Solomon, Solly .... SR 401-103
Solomon, Thomas .... FB 401-172
Solomon, Walter Wightman ..... TVG 401-213
Somervell, James A. .... FB 401-172
Somerville, Charles F. .... RRR 401-124
Somerville, Charles F. .... SR 401-103
Somerville, Chas. .... ARM 401-11
Son, Frank .... USV 401-250
Sonneberg, Christen .... NAV 401-24
Sorce, Frank G. .... SR 401-103
Sorey, Jesse W. .... TVG 401-213
Sorrells, F. M. .... FF 401-139
Sorrells, William R. .... FF 401-139
Sory, Ben W. .... TVG 401-213
Sory, Ben W. .... USV 401-250
Sotillo, Apolonio .... FB 401-172
Sotin, Charles .... NAV 401-24
Soule, Silas S. .... NAV 401-24
Sour, Frederick .... TST 401-37
South, Bester .... SP 401-49
South, C. A. .... SR 401-103
Southard, Charles .... FB 401-172
Southlee, Thomas Ernest .... USV 401-250
Southward, Charles Edward .... RRR 401-124
Southworth, Alvah H. .... USV 401-250
Southworth, John .... SR 401-103
Southworth, John .... LR 401-131
Southworth, W. A. .... SR 401-103
Sowell, A. J. .... RR 401-63
Sowell, A. J. .... FF 401-139
Sowell, Andrew Jackson .... RRR 401-124
Sowell, Earnest .... TVG 401-213
Sowell, G. P. .... SR 401-103
Sowell, Jason B. .... SR 401-103
Sowell, M. C. .... SR 401-103
Sowell, Perry O'Neal .... RRR 401-124
Sowells, Clide .... TVG 401-213
Spain, Hugh M. .... USV 401-250
Spalden, James Madison .... ARM 401-11
Spalding, Clarence F. .... USV 401-250
Spalding, E. C. .... TVG 401-213
Spalding, Frank E. .... TVG 401-213
Spalding, Levi .... ARM 401-11
Spandau, Christian .... USV 401-250
Spang, Frank Armitage .... SR 401-103
Spangler, J. Y. .... SR 401-103
Spangler, Ross A. .... SR 401-103
Spangler, S. H. .... FB 401-172
Spann, T. T. .... RR 401-63
Sparger, John Lanius .... TVG 401-213
Sparkman, F. C. .... SR 401-103
Sparkman, F. C. .... FB 401-172
Sparkman, Louis C. .... USV 401-250
Sparks, Bailey .... SP 401-49

Index to Texas Adjutant General Service Records—All Service Branches

Sparks, Benjamin Warden............RRR........401-124
Sparks, Cliff W..............................TVG........401-213
Sparks, George L..........................USV........401-250
Sparks, H. B.................................SR...........401-103
Sparks, J. B..................................FB............401-172
Sparks, J. C..................................FB............401-172
Sparks, James E...........................RRR........401-124
Sparks, James H...........................ARM.......401-11
Sparks, Lee..................................SR............401-103
Sparks, Otto B.............................TVG........401-213
Sparks, R. G.................................SR...........401-103
Sparks, Richard C........................TVG........401-213
Sparks, Samuel N........................MM.........401-32
Sparks, T. C.................................FB............401-172
Sparks, Thos. M..........................FB............401-173
Sparks, W. W...............................USV........401-250
Sparks, Wade H...........................USV........401-250
Spaulding, Elias S........................USV........401-250
Spaulding, John...........................NAV.......401-24
Speaks, Robert.............................FB............401-173
Spear, Angus Bert, Jr...................SR...........401-103
Spears, Henry..............................TVG........401-213
Spears, J. Franklin.......................SR...........401-103
Spears, James D..........................SP............401-49
Spears, Noa..................................TVG........401-213
Spears, Walter T..........................SR...........401-103
Speary, John L.............................USV........401-250
Speckels, Hugo W.......................USV........401-250
Speckles, H. W............................SR...........401-103
Speed, A. W.................................TVG........401-213
Speed, Eustice H.........................FF............401-139
Speed, G. B..................................TVG........401-213
Speed, J. H...................................USV........401-250
Speed, J. J....................................FB............401-173
Speed, John J...............................FB............401-173
Speed, Robert E...........................RR...........401-63
Speed, Stepehn G.........................TST.........401-37
Speed, W. R.................................RR...........401-63
Speed, William B........................SR...........401-103
Speegle, Elbert M........................USV........401-250
Speer, Cal.....................................SR...........401-103
Speer, R. H...................................TVG........401-213
Speight, Joseph Warren...............TVG........401-213
Speights, J. H. H..........................SP............401-49
Speights, William M...................SP............401-49
Speiser, Christ.............................USV........401-250
Spellings, S. G.............................CSA.........401-40
Spellings, Solomon A..................CSA.........401-40
Spence, A. L................................TVG........401-213
Spence, J. E..................................SR...........401-103
Spence, J. H..................................RRR........401-124
Spence, James A..........................NAV.......401-24
Spence, John................................SR...........401-103
Spence, W. L................................RRR........401-124
Spence, William Frank................RRR........401-124
Spencer, Augustus.......................ARM.......401-11
Spencer, Charles A......................USV........401-250
Spencer, Elbert L.........................SR...........401-103
Spencer, F. A................................SR...........401-103
Spencer, F. L................................TVG........401-213
Spencer, F. M...............................TVG........401-213
Spencer, Flavius..........................USV........401-250
Spencer, George W.....................USV........401-250
Spencer, I. W...............................TVG........401-213
Spencer, J. M...............................USV........401-250
Spencer, John L...........................USV........401-250
Spencer, John P...........................RR...........401-63
Spencer, T. S................................FB............401-173
Spencer, William A.....................USV........401-250
Sperath, Martin...........................FF............401-139
Spicer, John L..............................USV........401-250
Spiers, James...............................NAV.......401-24
Spikes, Samuel L.........................USV........401-250
Spikes, T. J..................................TVG........401-213
Spiller, J. R..................................SR...........401-103
Spiller, Joe L................................SR...........401-103
Spiller, P. H..................................USV........401-250
Spillers, J. W................................CSA.........401-40
Spilman, Joshua..........................NAV.......401-24
Spindle, W. M.............................FB............401-173
Spindle, W. M.............................FB............401-173
Spinelli, H. B...............................TVG........401-213
Spires, V.......................................RRR........401-124
Spitler, W. M...............................TVG........401-213
Spivey, Austin.............................RR...........401-63
Spivey, W. E................................SR...........401-103
Spooner, George W.....................SR...........401-103
Spooner, George W.....................USV........401-250
Spooner, Thomas H.....................ARM.......401-11
Sport, L. C...................................RR...........401-63
Sport, L. C...................................SR...........401-103
Spottswood, Leo D.....................USV........401-250
Spradley, A. J..............................SR...........401-103
Spradley, Arch............................SR...........401-103
Spradley, Bennett........................SR...........401-103
Spradley, C. M............................SR...........401-103
Sprague, George W.....................SR...........401-103
Sprague, W. G.............................TVG........401-213
Spring, Harry...............................TVG........401-213
Spring, John V.............................USV........401-250
Springer, A. W.............................FB............401-173
Springer, E. F...............................FB............401-173
Springer, J. J................................MM.........401-32
Springer, William H....................FB............401-173
Springfield, R. B..........................TVG........401-213
Sproles, Ed..................................SR...........401-103
Sproles, T. A................................SR...........401-103
Sproles, W. C...............................SR...........401-103
Sproul, W. C................................TVG........401-213
Sproule, Ira Frank.......................TVG........401-213
Sproule, Ira Frank.......................USV........401-250
Spruill, A. J..................................SR...........401-103

Index to Texas Adjutant General Service Records—All Service Branches

Name	Branch	Record
Spruill, Andrew J.	RR	401-63
Spurlock, William Josiah	TVG	401-213
Squires, Jasper W.	RRR	401-124
Squires, Sam	TVG	401-213
Srader, Albert	FB	401-173
St. Claire, William K.	SR	401-100
St. Prie, Chas. Francis	ARM	401-10
Staber, Hermann T.	TVG	401-213
Staberg, Emmet E. K.	USV	401-250
Stacey, George	NAV	401-24
Stacy, Tom	RRR	401-124
Stacy, Tom	SR	401-103
Stacy, William Henry	TVG	401-213
Stacy, William Henry	USV	401-250
Stafford, Brook	TVG	401-213
Stafford, Charles B.	USV	401-250
Stafford, E. M.	FB	401-173
Stafford, G. E.	RRR	401-124
Stafford, Jack	RRR	401-124
Stafford, Jack Carl	SR	401-103
Stafford, John	USV	401-250
Stafford, Louis P.	RR	401-63
Stafford, Patrick	USV	401-250
Stafford, W. W.	TVG	401-213
Stafford, William	NAV	401-24
Stagg, Allan	SR	401-103
Stagg, Allen	LR	401-131
Stagner, Robert T.	TVG	401-213
Stagner, Robert T.	USV	401-250
Stagner, W. E.	LR	401-131
Stahl, Moses S.	FF	401-139
Stair, Oscar H.	USV	401-250
Stakes, Ben	FB	401-173
Stakes, E. T.	SP	401-49
Stallcup, C. H.	RRR	401-124
Stallcup, J. F.	USV	401-250
Stallcup, Robert E.	USV	401-250
Stallings, O. J.	TVG	401-213
Stallworth, Frank M.	SR	401-103
Stamper, Flaeger	TVG	401-213
Stamper, George E.	USV	401-250
Stamps, Henry F.	TVG	401-213
Standard, L. T.	SR	401-103
Standard, L. T.	LR	401-131
Standefer, Charles J.	USV	401-250
Standefer, Harold Wilson	SR	401-103
Standefer, I. S.	RR	401-63
Standefer, J. M.	FB	401-173
Standenmier, J. W.	FB	401-173
Standifer, H.	FF	401-139
Standifer, Ike	TVG	401-213
Standifer, J. M.	TVG	401-213
Standifer, S. B.	RRR	401-124
Standridge, J. J.	FB	401-173
Stanfield, John C.	SP	401-49
Stanford, Edgar E.	USV	401-250
Stanford, G. H.	SR	401-103
Stanford, J. W.	TVG	401-213
Stanford, Joseph W.	RR	401-63
Stanford, R. B.	SR	401-103
Stanley, Claude D.	USV	401-250
Stanley, Flem	SP	401-49
Stanley, J. E.	SR	401-103
Stanley, J. E.	LR	401-131
Stanley, James W.	SP	401-49
Stanley, Joseph a.	TST	401-37
Stanley, L. N.	SR	401-103
Stanley, O. P.	SR	401-103
Stanley, S. J.	SP	401-49
Stanley, Sam B.	SR	401-103
Stanley, Stewart	SR	401-103
Stanley, W. G.	SP	401-49
Stanmire, Charles	NAV	401-24
Stansbury, Ephraim	ARM	401-11
Stansell, Ivy, Dr.	SR	401-103
Stansell, Mance	USV	401-250
Stanton, Littleton	MV	401-31
Staples, Pete	FB	401-173
Stapleton, Patrick	SP	401-49
Stapleton, William	FB	401-173
Stapleton, William W.	USV	401-250
Stapp, Arthur G.	TVG	401-213
Stapp, G.	TVG	401-213
Stapp, Walter	SR	401-104
Stapp, William H.	RR	401-63
Stappenbeck, E. B.	USV	401-251
Stappenbeck, George	TVG	401-213
Star, A.	TVG	401-213
Starck, John	ARM	401-11
Stark, Gladwin Harding	SR	401-104
Stark, H. J. Lutcher	SR	401-104
Stark, P. J.	SR	401-104
Stark, Wiley	USV	401-251
Starke, Paul	USV	401-251
Starker, Julius F.	USV	401-251
Starkey, H. B.	SR	401-104
Starkey, Jepthe	USV	401-251
Starks, Anthony	USV	401-251
Starley, James E.	USV	401-251
Starmosky, Henry	FF	401-139
Starnes, C. R.	SR	401-104
Starnes, Charles J., Capt.	SR	401-104
Starnes, Horace L.	USV	401-251
Starr, Harry	TVG	401-213
Starr, J. M.	SR	401-104
Starr, William T.	SR	401-104
Statham, G. W.	SR	401-104
Statham, John F.	USV	401-251
Statler, John	USV	401-251
Stauffer, Clyde E.	RRR	401-125
Stavinoha, Anton	USV	401-251
Stayton, J. Archie	TVG	401-213

Index to Texas Adjutant General Service Records—All Service Branches

Name	Branch	Page
Stayton, J. W.	SR	401-104
Stayton, Robert Weldon	TVG	401-213
Stayton, W. T.	TST	401-37
Steager, A. H.	TVG	401-213
Steanberg, John	ARM	401-11
Steane, Benjamin C.	ARM	401-11
Stedham, G. W.	RR	401-63
Steed, Heartsell H.	TVG	401-213
Steede, Budson	RRR	401-125
Steele, Charles	RR	401-63
Steele, Ernest L.	TVG	401-213
Steele, J. B.	SR	401-104
Steele, J. M.	USV	401-251
Steele, James R.	USV	401-251
Steele, John	ARM	401-11
Steele, John F.	USV	401-251
Steele, Vance R.	TVG	401-213
Steele, William	RR	401-63
Steele, William H.	ARM	401-11
Steele, William O.	USV	401-251
Steen, B. C.	TVG	401-213
Steen, George N.	MV	401-31
Steen, Marvin D., Lt. Col.	SR	401-104
Steen, Robert	SP	401-49
Stefand, Angelo de	USV	401-251
Steffens, Albert	FB	401-173
Steffian, P. A.	USV	401-251
Stegall, John	FB	401-173
Stegall, Leslie	SR	401-104
Stegall, N. R.	FB	401-173
Stegall, N. R. J.	FB	401-173
Stegall, W. C.	RR	401-63
Stegall, W. C.	SR	401-104
Steger, Jack D.	USV	401-251
Stegman, W. B.	USV	401-251
Steiger, John	FF	401-139
Stein, James	ARM	401-11
Stein, John	ARM	401-11
Steinbeck, G. F.	FB	401-173
Steiner, Joe	TVG	401-213
Steiner, John	SR	401-104
Steinfeldt, Fred W.	USV	401-251
Steinhagen, Albert William	TVG	401-213
Steinheil, Thaddeus	SP	401-49
Steinlein, George	TVG	401-213
Steinlein, J. F.	TVG	401-213
Steinlein, S. S.	TVG	401-213
Steinmetz, A. E.	RRR	401-125
Steinmetz, Albert E.	SR	401-104
Stelfox, C. H.	RR	401-63
Stelfox, C. H.	TVG	401-213
Stelfox, John H.	FB	401-173
Stell, Aubrey T.	USV	401-251
Stells, Mack	TVG	401-213
Stengel, John	FB	401-173
Stenger, Lawrence E.	USV	401-251
Stephen, Charles Edgar	USV	401-251
Stephen, Henry	FF	401-139
Stephen, Henry C.	USV	401-251
Stephens, Albert L.	RR	401-63
Stephens, Charles	USV	401-251
Stephens, E. F.	SR	401-104
Stephens, F. H.	TVG	401-213
Stephens, George	SP	401-49
Stephens, George B.	USV	401-251
Stephens, Henry M.	CSA	401-40
Stephens, J. C.	SR	401-104
Stephens, J. D.	FB	401-173
Stephens, J. F.	NAV	401-24
Stephens, James A.	TVG	401-213
Stephens, James Alexander	RRR	401-125
Stephens, James F.	USV	401-251
Stephens, James J.	SR	401-104
Stephens, James M. R.	MV	401-31
Stephens, Jesse	NAV	401-24
Stephens, John	NAV	401-24
Stephens, Joseph W.	USV	401-251
Stephens, Justin	NAV	401-24
Stephens, Robert	MM	401-32
Stephens, Samuel	ARM	401-11
Stephens, T. F.	FB	401-173
Stephens, W. D.	FB	401-173
Stephens, Walter L.	USV	401-251
Stephens, Washington	ARM	401-11
Stephenson, Edward M.	USV	401-251
Stephenson, F. W.	TVG	401-213
Stephenson, J. C.	RR	401-63
Stephenson, J. H.	SR	401-104
Stephenson, J. H., Dr.	SR	401-104
Stephenson, James R.	USV	401-251
Stephenson, Lex	SR	401-104
Stephenson, Robert	ARM	401-11
Stephenson, Thomas E.	USV	401-251
Steppenback, C.	FB	401-173
Stereimann, Louis	FF	401-139
Sterling, Charles M.	FB	401-173
Sterling, Edward A., Jr.	SR	401-104
Sterling, J. N.	RR	401-63
Sterling, William	USV	401-251
Sterling, William Hayden	SR	401-104
Sterling, William W.	RR	401-63
Sterling, William W.	SR	401-104
Stern, D. E.	USV	401-251
Stern, Henry O.	USV	401-251
Stern, Milton	TVG	401-213
Stern, Robert	SR	401-104
Sterne, A. G.	TVG	401-213
Sterne, George F.	USV	401-251
Stessloe, James	NAV	401-24
Stevens, Andrew G.	USV	401-251
Stevens, Andrew M.	SP	401-49
Stevens, Charles F.	RR	401-63

Index to Texas Adjutant General Service Records—All Service Branches

Stevens, D. M. ....USV 401-251
Stevens, E. A. ....RR 401-63
Stevens, E. N. ....FB............401-173
Stevens, Edward ....TVG 401-213
Stevens, George W. ....FB............401-173
Stevens, George W. ....FB............401-173
Stevens, H. P. ....FB............401-173
Stevens, J. A. ....FB............401-173
Stevens, J. King ....TVG 401-213
Stevens, James..................TST 401-37
Stevens, Joe ....FB............401-173
Stevens, John Henry ....TVG 401-213
Stevens, Pierce..................FB............401-173
Stevens, Samuel H. ....USV 401-251
Stevens, W. D. ....FB............401-173
Stevens, Washington ....ARM 401-11
Stevens, Wesley..................FB............401-173
Stevenson, Alexander ....NAV........401-24
Stevenson, Charlie J. ....TVG 401-213
Stevenson, E. M..................SR............401-104
Stevenson, G. B. ....TVG 401-213
Stevenson, Harold..............TVG 401-213
Stevenson, Henry F. ....TVG 401-213
Stevenson, Herbert E. ....TVG 401-213
Stevenson, J. B., Jr............SR............401-104
Stevenson, J. S. ....TVG 401-213
Stevenson, John ....ARM 401-11
Stevenson, Joseph S..........USV 401-251
Stevenson, Mark A. ....SR............401-104
Stevenson, S. A. ....USV 401-251
Stevenson, S. W. ....SR............401-104
Stevenson, Thomas A. ....TVG 401-213
Stevenson, W. C. ....TVG 401-213
Stevenson, William A..........USV 401-251
Steveson, Robert................NAV........401-24
Steward, Charles A. ....FB............401-173
Steward, Robert..................ARM 401-11
Steward, Wiley ....ARM 401-11
Stewart, Alburt R................USV 401-251
Stewart, Alton E. ....SR............401-104
Stewart, Alvin A. ....SR............401-104
Stewart, Andrew J. ....MM 401-32
Stewart, Bill......................SR............401-104
Stewart, Bill......................LR 401-131
Stewart, C. A. ....FB............401-173
Stewart, C. A. ....TVG 401-213
Stewart, Charles R. ....SR............401-104
Stewart, Charlie G. ....USV 401-251
Stewart, Clyde ....SR............401-104
Stewart, E. W. ....TVG 401-213
Stewart, Gene ....SR............401-104
Stewart, I. A. ....RR 401-63
Stewart, Isaac....................ARM 401-11
Stewart, J. A. ....SP 401-49
Stewart, J. G. ....FF 401-139
Stewart, J. W. ....RR 401-63
Stewart, James..................TST 401-37
Stewart, James I................RRR 401-125
Stewart, John ....NAV........401-24
Stewart, John ....ARM 401-11
Stewart, John H..................USV 401-251
Stewart, John William ....TVG 401-213
Stewart, L. G. ....SP 401-49
Stewart, Lee......................USV 401-251
Stewart, Maco, Jr...............SR............401-104
Stewart, O. E. ....FF 401-139
Stewart, Peter Pauls ....SR............401-104
Stewart, Sam......................TST 401-37
Stewart, Samuel L. ....USV 401-251
Stewart, Solon....................TVG 401-213
Stewart, T. W. ....TVG 401-213
Stewart, W. ....USV 401-251
Stewart, Will D. ....USV 401-251
Stewart, Will H. M. ....USV 401-251
Stewart, Will P....................USV 401-251
Stewart, William ....NAV........401-24
Stewart, William ....TST 401-37
Stewart, William ....ARM 401-11
Stewart, William J. ....RR 401-63
Stewart, William T. ....USV 401-251
Stidham, Marsh..................ARM 401-11
Stiefer, Doyle E. ....SR............401-104
Stiff, J. E. ....FB............401-173
Stiff, Oli............................USV 401-251
Stiles, L. M. ....TVG 401-213
Stiles, N. D. ....TVG 401-213
Stiles, Samuel T..................FF 401-139
Stiles, T. J. ....TVG 401-213
Stiles, William B. ....USV 401-251
Still, Calvin M. ....FB............401-173
Stillwell, Andrew................MV 401-31
Stillwell, D. V. ....SR............401-104
Stillwell, Jacob ....NAV........401-24
Stillwell, W. P. ....RR 401-63
Stilwell, Dudley V. ....RR 401-63
Stimson, A. C. ....SR............401-104
Stimson, David ....MV 401-31
Stinchcomb, T. B., Jr...........SR............401-104
Stinebaugh, Jonah D..........USV 401-251
Stinnett, J. W. ....TVG 401-213
Stinnett, John W. ....USV 401-251
Stinson, James P................SR............401-104
Stinson, John E. ....FB............401-173
Stirman, Shug ....SR............401-104
Stites, C. E. ....USV 401-251
Stites, Claude E. ....TVG 401-213
Stith, William B. ....TVG 401-213
Stith, William B. ....USV 401-251
Stockdale, F. S. ....TST 401-37
Stockman, P. F. ....TVG 401-213
Stockridge, Frank A............USV 401-251
Stockton, A. ....CSA........401-40

Index to Texas Adjutant General Service Records—All Service Branches

Name	Branch	Page
Stockton, A.	CSA	401-40
Stockton, Douglas H.	TVG	401-213
Stockton, Hugh	TVG	401-213
Stockton, James Madison	SR	401-104
Stockton, James T.	RR	401-63
Stockton, T. J., Colonel	SR	401-104
Stockton, William T.	USV	401-251
Stockwell, A. E.	FB	401-173
Stockwell, Elmer P.	USV	401-251
Stoddard, Henry B.	TVG	401-213
Stoddard, Jesse W.	ARM	401-11
Stogaugh, J. A.	TVG	401-213
Stogner, W. E.	SR	401-104
Stokes, A. W.	TVG	401-213
Stokes, C. D.	FB	401-173
Stokes, C. E.	TVG	401-214
Stokes, David G.	CSA	401-40
Stokes, J. B.	SR	401-104
Stokes, J. B.	LR	401-131
Stokes, John F.	SP	401-49
Stokes, Thomas J.	MM	401-32
Stokes, William N.	USV	401-251
Stokes, William N., Jr.	SR	401-104
Stollenwerek, John W.	TVG	401-214
Stollings, James A.	FB	401-173
Stone, A. R.	RR	401-63
Stone, Ben	TVG	401-214
Stone, Clifford L.	RR	401-63
Stone, Douglas	TVG	401-214
Stone, G. T.	RR	401-63
Stone, George	FF	401-139
Stone, George	SP	401-49
Stone, J. C.	SP	401-49
Stone, J. G.	FF	401-139
Stone, J. R.	SR	401-104
Stone, J. W.	SR	401-104
Stone, John F.	USV	401-251
Stone, John W.	LR	401-131
Stone, Otho	SR	401-104
Stone, R. D.	FB	401-173
Stone, R. M.	FB	401-173
Stone, Van D., Jr.	SR	401-104
Stone, W. B.	SP	401-49
Stone, W. C.	FB	401-173
Stone, W. Ellis	USV	401-251
Stone, William E.	USV	401-251
Stone, Wilson H.	USV	401-251
Stoneall, John T.	NAV	401-24
Stonebaker, J. P.	FB	401-173
Stonebaker, William B.	FB	401-173
Stonehan, Seaborn A.	USV	401-251
Stoner, Edwin L.	USV	401-251
Stoner, G. O., Jr.	SR	401-104
Stoner, General B.	USV	401-251
Stoner, Robert O.	TVG	401-214
Stoops, Clete	SR	401-104
Storey, Alonzo	ARM	401-11
Storey, Harvey E.	TVG	401-214
Storey, W. R.	TVG	401-214
Storie, John W.	SR	401-104
Stork, Johan	NAV	401-24
Storm, Oliver P.	USV	401-251
Storm, Pleasant	TVG	401-214
Storts, Jefferson D.	USV	401-251
Story, David E.	USV	401-251
Story, James B.	TVG	401-214
Story, Robert F.	TVG	401-214
Story, Sid	TVG	401-214
Stoudenmier, C. S.	SR	401-104
Stout, David W.	USV	401-251
Stout, Lonnie A.	TVG	401-214
Stout, R. H.	TVG	401-214
Stoutenburgh, Abraham	ARM	401-11
Stovall, Elmer J.	RR	401-63
Stovall, Elmer J.	RRR	401-125
Stovall, George W.	USV	401-251
Stovall, R. C., Sr.	SR	401-104
Stover, Charles E.	RR	401-63
Stover, Charley A.	TVG	401-214
Stow, William	ARM	401-11
Stowe, C. A.	USV	401-251
Stowe, Ellwood E.	TVG	401-214
Stowe, John W.	TVG	401-214
Stowe, Thomas B.	RR	401-63
Stowe, W. H.	RRR	401-125
Strahan, Bruce	USV	401-251
Strahan, V. V.	RRR	401-125
Strait, J. S.	SR	401-104
Strait, Y. C.	SR	401-104
Straley, John F.	USV	401-251
Stramler, Arthur Harris	SR	401-104
Strange, Porter A.	USV	401-251
Stratton, James M.	RRR	401-125
Stratton, John M.	FB	401-173
Straus, Samuel C.	USV	401-251
Strawder, William A.	SP	401-49
Streachant, Richard	NAV	401-24
Street, John M.	MV	401-31
Streit, August M.	USV	401-251
Strength, Frank	TVG	401-214
Stresson, W. A.	TVG	401-214
Stribling, Thomas S.	USV	401-251
Stricker, Walter W.	USV	401-251
Strickland, George	SP	401-49
Strickland, George W.	FB	401-173
Strickland, Gideon S.	FB	401-173
Strickland, J. H.	FB	401-173
Strickland, J. J.	SR	401-104
Strickland, Jerome W.	USV	401-251
Strickland, W. A.	FB	401-173
Strickland, W. L.	USV	401-251
Stricklen, Henry	RR	401-64

Index to Texas Adjutant General Service Records—All Service Branches

Name	Branch	Record
Stricklin, Owen R.	USV	401-251
Striegler, Frederic C.	FF	401-139
Stringer, Pleasant W.	USV	401-251
Strittmatter, William	USV	401-251
Stroburg, J. B.	SR	401-104
Stroele, T. V. S.	FF	401-139
Strol, Ernest	ARM	401-11
Strom, John E.	TVG	401-214
Strong, Augustus H.	USV	401-251
Strong, C. W.	USV	401-251
Strong, E. R.	SR	401-104
Strong, Harvey M.	USV	401-251
Strong, Lewis P.	TST	401-37
Strong, Seth	TVG	401-214
Stroud, Charles	ARM	401-11
Stroud, Charles B.	TVG	401-214
Stroud, Charles B.	USV	401-251
Stroud, F. G.	RRR	401-125
Stroud, George W.	RR	401-64
Stroud, J. B.	FB	401-173
Stroud, J. R.	TVG	401-214
Stroud, J. T.	TVG	401-214
Stroud, L. N.	SR	401-104
Stroud, T. M.	RR	401-64
Stroud, T. M.	USV	401-251
Strube, Charles	ARM	401-11
Struck, A. J.	TVG	401-214
Strunk, William	ARM	401-11
Strupper, Joseph M.	USV	401-251
Strutton, W. M.	TVG	401-214
Stuart, Barney	USV	401-251
Stuart, Edward A.	TVG	401-214
Stuart, Edward A.	USV	401-251
Stuart, Elmer	TVG	401-214
Stuart, F. J.	RRR	401-125
Stuart, Ferdinand	ARM	401-11
Stuart, Harry A.	TVG	401-214
Stuart, J. M.	TVG	401-214
Stuart, R. T.	SR	401-104
Stuart, R. W.	TVG	401-214
Stuart, William	ARM	401-11
Stubblefield, J. E.	USV	401-251
Stubblefield, J. R.	TVG	401-214
Stubblefield, Lowry M.	TVG	401-214
Stubblefield, Roy H.	TVG	401-214
Stubbs, S. E.	FB	401-173
Stubbs, T. J.	SR	401-104
Stubbs, T. J.	LR	401-131
Stubbs, William	RRR	401-125
Stuckee, Constantine	ARM	401-11
Stucken, Alfred Vander	SR	401-104
Stuckenholz, Leon De V.	USV	401-251
Stuckers, Frank V. D.	TST	401-37
Stuckler, E. P.	SR	401-104
Stuckler, E. P.	LR	401-131
Stude, A. J.	TVG	401-214
Studemann, John	USV	401-251
Stukes, John	FF	401-139
Stump, W. H.	RRR	401-125
Sturdivant, Edward D.	USV	401-251
Sturdovan, Sam	USV	401-251
Sturges, Theodore T.	USV	401-251
Sturgis, Dawes E.	SR	401-104
Sturgis, Dawes E.	LR	401-131
Stuteville, L. Z.	SR	401-104
Stutzel, Charlie	USV	401-251
Styron, James A.	TVG	401-214
Styron, James A.	USV	401-251
Subira, John	SR	401-104
Sublett, Frank B.	TST	401-37
Sudbury, B. H.	SR	401-104
Sudbury, Buford Henry	RRR	401-125
Sudderth, W. A.	RR	401-64
Sudduth, John T.	FB	401-173
Suderman, A. D.	SR	401-104
Sugden, John	FF	401-139
Sugden, John	SP	401-49
Suggs, George T.	USV	401-251
Suggs, L. H.	SR	401-104
Sullenger, R. G.	SR	401-104
Sullinger, R. G.	RRR	401-125
Sullitt, John B.	FB	401-173
Sullivan, Ance	TVG	401-214
Sullivan, Andrew C.	SR	401-104
Sullivan, C. F.	TVG	401-214
Sullivan, D. H.	SR	401-104
Sullivan, E. L.	TVG	401-214
Sullivan, Eugene	TVG	401-214
Sullivan, George	NAV	401-25
Sullivan, H. E.	SR	401-104
Sullivan, Horace O.	TVG	401-214
Sullivan, Humphrey	ARM	401-11
Sullivan, J. F.	SR	401-104
Sullivan, J. L.	SP	401-49
Sullivan, J. L.	SR	401-104
Sullivan, J. M.	RR	401-64
Sullivan, J. P.	SR	401-104
Sullivan, J. W.	FB	401-173
Sullivan, John	RR	401-64
Sullivan, John	RR	401-64
Sullivan, John	SR	401-104
Sullivan, John	USV	401-251
Sullivan, M. E.	SR	401-104
Sullivan, McKenzie Johnston	TVG	401-214
Sullivan, Michael	ARM	401-11
Sullivan, Michael B.	USV	401-251
Sullivan, Morgan E.	RRR	401-125
Sullivan, Patrick	ARM	401-11
Sullivan, Patrick	SP	401-49
Sullivan, R. H.	SR	401-104
Sullivan, Ray	RR	401-64
Sullivan, Thomas	ARM	401-11

Index to Texas Adjutant General Service Records—All Service Branches

Name	Branch	Record
Sullivan, Thomas	USV	401-251
Sullivan, W. J.	FB	401-173
Sullivan, W. J. L.	FB	401-173
Sullivan, Warren T.	TVG	401-214
Sullivan, William	USV	401-251
Sullivan, William C.	TVG	401-214
Sullivant, Carroll F.	SR	401-104
Sulnon, Max	USV	401-251
Sulzbacher, Laurence I.	RR	401-64
Sulzbacher, Phil	TVG	401-214
Summerrow, Ray E.	SR	401-105
Summers, Charles B.	FB	401-173
Summers, Harry M.	USV	401-251
Summers, Hiram	ARM	401-11
Summers, J. G.	TVG	401-214
Summers, J. W.	SR	401-105
Summers, J. W.	LR	401-131
Summers, Jim	TVG	401-214
Summers, S. H.	TST	401-37
Summers, Samuel Y.	TVG	401-214
Summers, Simon A.	USV	401-251
Summers, Taylor A.	USV	401-251
Summers, W.	TVG	401-214
Summers, W. F.	TVG	401-214
Summers, William	SP	401-49
Summers, William	USV	401-251
Sumner, George	FF	401-139
Sumpter, Guy	FB	401-173
Sumrall, Robert W.	RR	401-64
Sunday, T. J.	SR	401-105
Surber, L. H.	SR	401-105
Surface, Emmerson F.	USV	401-251
Suter, C.	TVG	401-214
Sutherland, Arthur	USV	401-251
Sutherland, George	RR	401-64
Suttle, I. Newton	TVG	401-214
Sutton, C. R.	SR	401-105
Sutton, H. H.	SR	401-105
Sutton, J. B.	FB	401-173
Sutton, J. F.	SR	401-105
Sutton, J. F.	LR	401-131
Sutton, John W.	MV	401-31
Sutton, M. V.	SR	401-105
Sutton, M. V.	LR	401-131
Sutton, Robert Bell	RR	401-64
Swaim, A. P.	RRR	401-125
Swain, Duncan E.	RR	401-64
Swain, Frank K.	TVG	401-214
Swain, M. S.	TVG	401-214
Swales, Frank E.	USV	401-251
Swan, Harry Roswell	SR	401-105
Swan, O. K[inbrek]	TVG	401-214
Swan, S. D.	SR	401-105
Swan, W. E.	SP	401-49
Swan, W. R.	SR	401-105
Swann, L. J.	TVG	401-214
Swann, S. H.	TVG	401-214
Swann, Winsor A.	USV	401-251
Swanson, S. A.	SR	401-105
Swany, John	NAV	401-25
Swartz, Charles B.	FB	401-173
Swartz, Harry O.	TVG	401-214
Swartz, Julius A.	USV	401-251
Sweany, James A.	TVG	401-214
Swearengen, James	FB	401-173
Swearingen, J. B.	TVG	401-214
Swearingen, S. W.	SP	401-49
Swearinger	ARM	401-11
Swearinger, E. E.	TVG	401-214
Sweat, Horace H.	USV	401-251
Sweatt, Stanley E.	SR	401-105
Sweener, William S.	ARM	401-11
Sweeney, Edward A.	USV	401-251
Sweeney, Nathan H.	SR	401-105
Sweeney, Thomas	FB	401-173
Sweeney, William P.	TVG	401-214
Sweeny, Thomas C.	SR	401-105
Sweeten, N. Q.	RRR	401-125
Swenson, August	FF	401-139
Swenson, August	SP	401-49
Swenson, Will	USV	401-251
Sweny, Guy A.	SR	401-105
Sweny, Guy A.	LR	401-131
Swift, Albert	FF	401-139
Swift, George	TVG	401-214
Swift, J. B.	SR	401-105
Swift, L. F., Jr.	SR	401-105
Swift, Luther	SR	401-105
Swift, O. A.	FB	401-173
Swift, O. G.	SR	401-105
Swift, Thomas J.	FB	401-173
Swilling, Thomas W.	FB	401-173
Swindells, A. K.	USV	401-251
Swinden, A. A.	TVG	401-214
Swinford, J. Kenneth	SR	401-105
Swing, M. L.	TST	401-37
Swink, G. M.	FB	401-173
Swinny, John	ARM	401-11
Swisher, Charles	FB	401-173
Swisher, James	FB	401-173
Swisher, James G.	MV	401-31
Swisher, James M.	FF	401-139
Swisher, John M.	NAV	401-25
Switzer, Al	TVG	401-214
Swofford, E. A.	SR	401-105
Swope, Charles A.	USV	401-251
Swope, W. A.	TVG	401-214
Sydnor, Barrel	TVG	401-214
Sykes, Dan T.	TVG	401-214
Syler, Robert	SR	401-105
Syler, Robert	USV	401-251
Syler, Robt.	SR	401-105

Index to Texas Adjutant General Service Records—All Service Branches

Sylvester, V. D. .... SR 401-105
Symonds, George W. .... FB 401-173
Syphrett, Daniel Webster .... USV 401-251
Taber, Alf S. .... TVG 401-214
Taber, Alfred S. .... USV 401-251
Taber, H. .... TVG 401-214
Taber, Samuel H. .... TVG 401-214
Tabor, D. C. .... SR 401-105
Tabor, Horace J. .... SR 401-105
Tabor, Horce J. .... LR 401-131
Tabor, Josiah C. .... USV 401-251
Tabor, Thomas J. .... TVG 401-214
Tabor, William H. .... SP 401-49
Tack, Will .... TVG 401-214
Tackett, Andrew C. .... FB 401-173
Tackett, Louis J. .... SR 401-105
Tackett, M. D. .... MM 401-32
Tackett, S. S. .... MM 401-32
Tackitt, Robert E. .... MM 401-32
Tadlock, J. B. .... TVG 401-214
Tadlock, Malcolm G. .... TVG 401-214
Tadlock, S. .... TST 401-37
Taff, J. A. .... FB 401-173
Taff, Joseph Caswell .... RRR 401-125
Taffier, Lawrence .... USV 401-251
Tafolla, James, Jr. .... SR 401-105
Tagart, W. D. .... TVG 401-214
Taggart, L. J. .... SR 401-105
Tagle, A. P. .... RR 401-64
Talbot, John F. .... CSA 401-40
Talbott, E. L. .... SR 401-105
Talbott, Lee .... TVG 401-214
Talcott, John Belknap .... SR 401-105
Talemantes, Jose Maria .... FF 401-139
Taler, James M. .... USV 401-251
Taliaferro, Edwin M. .... TVG 401-214
Taliaferro, G. C. .... TVG 401-214
Taliaferro, Pat .... SR 401-105
Taliaferro, Weyman T. .... USV 401-251
Talifaro, M. L. .... MM 401-32
Tall, Charles .... NAV 401-25
Talley, C. A. .... SR 401-105
Talley, George W. .... FB 401-173
Talley, Jacob R. .... MV 401-31
Talley, Riley .... SP 401-49
Talley, Samuel L. .... USV 401-251
Talley, W. B. .... FB 401-173
Tallichet, J. H. .... SR 401-105
Tallow, Frank .... USV 401-251
Tandy, Frank A. .... FB 401-173
Tankersley, Albert P. .... USV 401-252
Tankersley, Arthur E. .... USV 401-252
Tankersley, Fayette .... FB 401-173
Tankersley, James H. .... MV 401-31
Tanmir, Charles S. .... NAV 401-25
Tanner, A. Y. .... FB 401-173

Tanner, Isaac .... MV 401-31
Tanner, J. W. .... RRR 401-125
Tanner, Samuel .... MV 401-31
Tanner, Solomon .... MV 401-31
Taplin, Charles V. .... ARM 401-11
Tarble, Edward .... FB 401-173
Tarbox, Jeremiah .... NAV 401-25
Tardy, John T. .... SR 401-105
Tarpley, J. Lee .... TVG 401-214
Tarpley, Sam S. .... SP 401-49
Tarrant, Garland P. .... TVG 401-214
Tarver, Bee G. .... USV 401-252
Tarver, H. B. .... TVG 401-214
Tarver, Hamilton Bee .... USV 401-252
Tarver, Jack .... SR 401-105
Tarver, James M. .... FB 401-173
Tarver, Robert Thomas .... SR 401-105
Tarver, Thad .... RR 401-64
Tarver, William Hugh .... RRR 401-125
Tasker, W. J. .... USV 401-252
Tass, Charles .... ARM 401-11
Tate, Fred .... SR 401-105
Tate, George W. .... TVG 401-214
Tate, H. H. .... TVG 401-214
Tate, J. T. .... TVG 401-214
Tate, J. Waddy .... TVG 401-214
Tate, Thomas .... ARM 401-11
Tate, Tom R. .... RR 401-64
Tate, Tom R. .... SR 401-105
Tate, William B. .... ARM 401-11
Tator, Jacob .... ARM 401-11
Tatum, B. R. .... SP 401-49
Tatum, Dan .... USV 401-252
Tatum, Joseph B. .... ARM 401-11
Tatum, Sam H. .... FB 401-174
Tatum, Thomas .... RR 401-64
Tatum, Thomas S. .... ARM 401-11
Tatum, Walter M. .... MM 401-32
Taulbee, Granville H. .... USV 401-252
Tauzin, E. M. .... USV 401-252
Tax, James .... TVG 401-214
Taxman, Mike .... SR 401-105
Taylor, A. H. .... USV 401-252
Taylor, A. L. .... FB 401-174
Taylor, A. W. .... SR 401-105
Taylor, Albert .... SR 401-105
Taylor, Albert .... LR 401-131
Taylor, Alex .... MM 401-32
Taylor, Andrew .... RR 401-64
Taylor, Andrew L. .... USV 401-252
Taylor, B. Frank .... FB 401-174
Taylor, C. .... FB 401-174
Taylor, C. A. .... SR 401-105
Taylor, C. A. .... LR 401-131
Taylor, C. M. .... SR 401-105
Taylor, C. S. .... TVG 401-214

Index to Texas Adjutant General Service Records—All Service Branches

Name	Branch	Record
Taylor, C. W.	USV	401-252
Taylor, Campbell	ARM	401-11
Taylor, Charles D.	ARM	401-11
Taylor, Chas. S.	ARM	401-11
Taylor, Choice	USV	401-252
Taylor, Collie	FB	401-174
Taylor, Cread E.	USV	401-252
Taylor, Creed	ARM	401-11
Taylor, D. H.	FB	401-174
Taylor, D. K.	RR	401-64
Taylor, D. K.	SR	401-105
Taylor, Dan	SP	401-49
Taylor, Daniel Lewis	USV	401-252
Taylor, David	TVG	401-214
Taylor, David M.	ARM	401-11
Taylor, Drew K.	RR	401-64
Taylor, E. D.	FF	401-139
Taylor, E. M.	USV	401-252
Taylor, E. W.	TVG	401-214
Taylor, Ed M.	TVG	401-214
Taylor, Edward K.	CSA	401-40
Taylor, Edward M.	TVG	401-214
Taylor, Elmer J.	SR	401-105
Taylor, F. H.	USV	401-252
Taylor, Felix	ARM	401-11
Taylor, Frank	USV	401-252
Taylor, Frank C.	MV	401-31
Taylor, Frank C.	USV	401-252
Taylor, Fred W.	TVG	401-214
Taylor, George	RR	401-64
Taylor, George	ARM	401-11
Taylor, George	SR	401-105
Taylor, George M.	MV	401-31
Taylor, H. G.	TST	401-37
Taylor, Harrison C.	ARM	401-11
Taylor, Henry	TVG	401-214
Taylor, Henry C.	USV	401-252
Taylor, Holman	TVG	401-214
Taylor, Homer E.	SR	401-105
Taylor, Horace G.	TVG	401-214
Taylor, I. R.	TVG	401-214
Taylor, J. A.	RR	401-64
Taylor, J. C.	RR	401-64
Taylor, J. E.	SR	401-105
Taylor, J. H.	SP	401-49
Taylor, J. M.	TVG	401-214
Taylor, J. N.	ARM	401-11
Taylor, J. O.	FB	401-174
Taylor, J. P.	FB	401-174
Taylor, J. R.	TVG	401-214
Taylor, J. W.	RRR	401-125
Taylor, Jacob	FF	401-139
Taylor, James A.	USV	401-252
Taylor, James B.	SP	401-49
Taylor, James B.	TVG	401-214
Taylor, James C.	RRR	401-125
Taylor, Jessie	TVG	401-214
Taylor, Joe	SR	401-105
Taylor, John	NAV	401-25
Taylor, John	ARM	401-11
Taylor, John	FB	401-174
Taylor, John B.	USV	401-252
Taylor, John C.	USV	401-252
Taylor, John H.	FB	401-174
Taylor, John Perry	TVG	401-214
Taylor, John W.	NAV	401-25
Taylor, Joseph A.	SR	401-105
Taylor, Joseph F.	USV	401-252
Taylor, Joseph K.	TST	401-37
Taylor, Josiah	ARM	401-11
Taylor, Lee	USV	401-252
Taylor, Leonard	ARM	401-11
Taylor, Lewis	TVG	401-214
Taylor, Lewis H.	FB	401-174
Taylor, M. D. K.	SR	401-105
Taylor, M. D. K.	LR	401-131
Taylor, Marion	SR	401-105
Taylor, Milton	SR	401-105
Taylor, Milton, Jr.	LR	401-131
Taylor, O. G.	RR	401-64
Taylor, O. G.	SR	401-105
Taylor, O. L.	SR	401-105
Taylor, Otto B.	USV	401-252
Taylor, P. C.	SR	401-105
Taylor, P. C.	LR	401-131
Taylor, P. J.	RR	401-64
Taylor, Paul	USV	401-252
Taylor, Paul W.	SR	401-105
Taylor, Pink	FB	401-174
Taylor, R. A.	SR	401-105
Taylor, R. L.	FB	401-174
Taylor, R. R.	SR	401-105
Taylor, R. S.	SR	401-105
Taylor, Robert B.	MV	401-31
Taylor, Robert J.	USV	401-252
Taylor, Robert L.	USV	401-252
Taylor, Rufus H.	USV	401-252
Taylor, S. L.	SR	401-105
Taylor, Samuel E.	USV	401-252
Taylor, Stephen L.	SR	401-105
Taylor, Summerfield	SR	401-105
Taylor, T. C.	SR	401-105
Taylor, T. C.	FB	401-174
Taylor, Theo	TVG	401-214
Taylor, Theo	USV	401-252
Taylor, Thomas	NAV	401-25
Taylor, Thomas	ARM	401-11
Taylor, Thurston M.	NAV	401-25
Taylor, Tom J.	SR	401-105
Taylor, Tom J.	LR	401-131
Taylor, W. A.	RR	401-64
Taylor, W. A.	TVG	401-214

Index to Texas Adjutant General Service Records—All Service Branches

Name	Branch	Record
Taylor, W. A.	USV	401-252
Taylor, W. C.	ARM	401-11
Taylor, W. E.	TVG	401-214
Taylor, W. G.	USV	401-252
Taylor, W. M.	FB	401-174
Taylor, W. R.	SR	401-105
Taylor, W. W.	CSA	401-40
Taylor, W. W.	RR	401-64
Taylor, W. W.	SR	401-105
Taylor, Walter B.	SR	401-105
Taylor, William	NAV	401-25
Taylor, William	ARM	401-11
Taylor, William	TVG	401-214
Taylor, William E.	SR	401-105
Taylor, William H.	FB	401-174
Taylor, William H.	TVG	401-214
Taylor, William J.	USV	401-252
Taylor, William S.	ARM	401-11
Taylor, William W.	ARM	401-11
Taylor, Woodward O.	RR	401-64
Taylor, Yantis H.	RR	401-64
Tays, George H.	FB	401-174
Tays, James A.	SP	401-49
Tays, James A.	FB	401-174
Tays, John B.	FB	401-174
Teague, C. E.	RRR	401-125
Teague, J. L.	RRR	401-125
Teague, Massey	USV	401-252
Teague, Peter	SP	401-49
Tebo, A. E.	FB	401-174
Tecumseh, Charles	NAV	401-25
Tedford, Henry M.	TVG	401-214
Tedford, Robert Oscar	FF	401-139
Teeling, James	USV	401-252
Teeling, Philip	USV	401-252
Teeter, George T.	MV	401-31
Teina, Patrick	NAV	401-25
Telfair, J. S.	FB	401-174
Telford, J. R. "Joe"	SR	401-105
Tellgmann, C.	MV	401-31
Tellgmann, Charles	FB	401-174
Tellgmann, W.	MV	401-31
Telotte, N. L.	FB	401-174
Temple, Abe	FB	401-174
Temple, Bernard Moore	TVG	401-214
Temple, Charles	SP	401-49
Temple, James S.	FF	401-139
Temple, William H.	ARM	401-11
Templeman, William I.	USV	401-252
Templer, Mahlon J.	USV	401-252
Templer, Mahlon S.	TVG	401-214
Templeton, A. S.	SR	401-105
Templeton, C. M.	SR	401-105
Templeton, Clive	SR	401-105
Templeton, D. A.	USV	401-252
Templeton, La J.	SP	401-49
Templeton, W. R.	FB	401-174
Ten Eyck, W. J.	FB	401-174
Tennison, Thomas W.	USV	401-252
Tennison, Will	RRR	401-125
Tennison, William A.	NAV	401-25
Tero, Francisco	RR	401-64
Terrel, J.	FB	401-174
Terrell, A. J.	FB	401-174
Terrell, Arthur	FB	401-174
Terrell, B. G.	RRR	401-125
Terrell, George H.	TVG	401-214
Terrell, George H.	USV	401-252
Terrell, H. O.	FB	401-174
Terrell, J. P.	TVG	401-214
Terrell, Joe J.	SR	401-105
Terrell, John	FF	401-139
Terrell, John L.	TVG	401-214
Terrell, John L.	USV	401-252
Terrell, John N.	USV	401-252
Terrell, Lee R.	RRR	401-125
Terrell, Ray	TVG	401-214
Terrell, Rigdon	FB	401-174
Terrell, Roy L.	USV	401-252
Terrell, Samuel A.	MV	401-31
Terrell, W. A.	TVG	401-214
Terrell, W. H.	FB	401-174
Terrell, Ward	TVG	401-214
Terrell, William E.	USV	401-252
Terry, A. B.	TVG	401-214
Terry, A. L.	SR	401-105
Terry, A. L.	LR	401-131
Terry, D. S.	CSA	401-40
Terry, Daniel	NAV	401-25
Terry, M. J.	TST	401-37
Terry, Nathaniel	MV	401-31
Terry, Stephen P.	ARM	401-11
Terry, Tom P.	RR	401-64
Terry, William	FB	401-174
Terry, William J.	USV	401-252
Test, Clarence L.	TVG	401-214
Tevis, F. F.	TVG	401-214
Tevis, Ira	SR	401-105
Tevis, Reid	SR	401-105
Tevis, Reid	LR	401-131
Tevis, Robert M.	SR	401-105
Tewmey, Arthur T.	USV	401-252
Tewmey, Artur T.	TVG	401-214
Thach, Jess T.	RRR	401-125
Thagard, George F.	SR	401-105
Tharpley, W. C.	FB	401-174
Thatcher, John C.	USV	401-252
Thavonat, E. J.	FB	401-174
Thaxton, H. J.	SR	401-105
Thaxton, John B.	FB	401-174
Thayer, Charles H.	SP	401-49
Theall, J. D.	TVG	401-214

Index to Texas Adjutant General Service Records—All Service Branches

Name	Branch	Record
Thedford, John C.	RRR	401-125
Theis, August	TST	401-37
Thenstedt, Charles N.	ARM	401-11
Theobalds, William P.	ARM	401-11
Theriot, Victor N.	TVG	401-214
Theriot, Victor N.	USV	401-252
Therrell, J. V.	TVG	401-214
Thiel, Louis H.	TVG	401-214
Thiele, Alfred F.	TVG	401-214
Thiele, Alfred F.	USV	401-252
Thiele, O. F.	TVG	401-214
Thiell, William H.	SP	401-49
Thielman, Ernest M.	SR	401-105
Thigpen, Thomas J.	TST	401-37
Thomas, A. B.	RRR	401-125
Thomas, A. L.	RRR	401-125
Thomas, Arthur	FB	401-174
Thomas, Arthur	FB	401-174
Thomas, Asa	ARM	401-11
Thomas, Benjamin	ARM	401-11
Thomas, C. C.	FB	401-174
Thomas, C. E.	USV	401-252
Thomas, Calvin M.	CSA	401-40
Thomas, Claude F.	USV	401-252
Thomas, Clyde	SR	401-105
Thomas, D. Martin	SR	401-105
Thomas, Dave	TVG	401-214
Thomas, David S.	TVG	401-214
Thomas, Edgar O.	USV	401-252
Thomas, Elisha F.	RR	401-64
Thomas, Ernest M.	TVG	401-214
Thomas, Frank	USV	401-252
Thomas, G. A.	USV	401-252
Thomas, G. E.	TVG	401-214
Thomas, George	ARM	401-11
Thomas, George	FF	401-139
Thomas, George	FB	401-174
Thomas, H. J.	SR	401-105
Thomas, H. J.	FB	401-174
Thomas, H. M.	TVG	401-214
Thomas, Henry	FB	401-174
Thomas, Hiram F.	USV	401-252
Thomas, I. F.	TVG	401-214
Thomas, J. A.	SR	401-105
Thomas, J. A.	RRR	401-125
Thomas, J. Bert	SR	401-105
Thomas, J. Covey	FB	401-174
Thomas, J. L.	CSA	401-40
Thomas, J. M.	SP	401-49
Thomas, J. R.	SR	401-105
Thomas, J. R.	TVG	401-214
Thomas, James	NAV	401-25
Thomas, James G.	RR	401-64
Thomas, James G.	USV	401-252
Thomas, James L.	USV	401-252
Thomas, James P.	USV	401-252
Thomas, James T.	TVG	401-214
Thomas, Joe B.	SR	401-105
Thomas, John	NAV	401-25
Thomas, John	FB	401-174
Thomas, John	SR	401-105
Thomas, John C., Dr.	SR	401-105
Thomas, John D.	FB	401-174
Thomas, John J.	RRR	401-125
Thomas, John R.	SR	401-105
Thomas, Leonard A.	USV	401-252
Thomas, Lynn Earl	RRR	401-125
Thomas, Mc	TVG	401-214
Thomas, N. B.	SR	401-105
Thomas, N. P.	RR	401-64
Thomas, Nicholas T.	ARM	401-11
Thomas, R. M.	RRR	401-125
Thomas, Robert P.	USV	401-252
Thomas, S. M.	TVG	401-214
Thomas, Shirley L.	TVG	401-214
Thomas, Sidney	FB	401-174
Thomas, Smith B.	ARM	401-11
Thomas, W.	TVG	401-214
Thomas, W. H.	SR	401-105
Thomas, W. J.	TVG	401-214
Thomas, W. K.	RR	401-64
Thomas, W. L.	TVG	401-214
Thomas, W. P.	RR	401-64
Thomas, W. Tass	USV	401-252
Thomas, Wiley Howard	SR	401-105
Thomas, Will G.	USV	401-252
Thomas, William I.	RRR	401-125
Thomas, William S.	TVG	401-214
Thomas, William W.	TVG	401-215
Thomason, David E.	USV	401-252
Thomason, James H.	USV	401-252
Thomason, John William Jr.	SR	401-105
Thomason, Thomas W.	RR	401-64
Thomason, William	RR	401-64
Thomason, William Edgar	USV	401-252
Thomerson, E. W.	SR	401-105
Thomey, Conrad	FB	401-174
Thompson, Albert L.	USV	401-252
Thompson, Arthur A.	USV	401-252
Thompson, Ben	SR	401-106
Thompson, C. M.	SR	401-106
Thompson, Charles	NAV	401-25
Thompson, Charles	MV	401-31
Thompson, Charles	SP	401-49
Thompson, Charles	FB	401-174
Thompson, Charles E.	USV	401-252
Thompson, Dewey	SR	401-106
Thompson, Edward V.	USV	401-252
Thompson, Eli W.	USV	401-252
Thompson, Eugene M.	TVG	401-215
Thompson, F. E.	SR	401-106
Thompson, Floyd L.	SR	401-106

Index to Texas Adjutant General Service Records—All Service Branches

Name	Branch	Record
Thompson, G. M.	USV	401-252
Thompson, G. P.	TVG	401-215
Thompson, George	SP	401-49
Thompson, George A.	USV	401-252
Thompson, George R.	USV	401-252
Thompson, George W.	TVG	401-215
Thompson, George W.	USV	401-252
Thompson, Gideon H.	USV	401-252
Thompson, Guy	SR	401-106
Thompson, Henry C.	FB	401-174
Thompson, Isaac M.	NAV	401-25
Thompson, J. A.	RRR	401-125
Thompson, J. A.	SR	401-106
Thompson, J. A.	TVG	401-215
Thompson, J. C.	SR	401-106
Thompson, J. P.	FB	401-174
Thompson, J. V.	SR	401-106
Thompson, James	NAV	401-25
Thompson, John	SP	401-49
Thompson, John F.	SR	401-106
Thompson, John H.	USV	401-252
Thompson, John L.	USV	401-252
Thompson, John W.	ARM	401-11
Thompson, Joseph	ARM	401-11
Thompson, Lee	TVG	401-215
Thompson, Lee M.	USV	401-252
Thompson, Lonnie	SR	401-106
Thompson, Lowrie	USV	401-252
Thompson, M. W.	FB	401-174
Thompson, Manlus h.	USV	401-252
Thompson, Nathaniel	MV	401-31
Thompson, Oliver	FF	401-139
Thompson, Oscar	SR	401-106
Thompson, Prince	NAV	401-25
Thompson, R. A.	FB	401-174
Thompson, R. W.	SR	401-106
Thompson, Richard	ARM	401-11
Thompson, Roy C.	TVG	401-215
Thompson, Stephen	SP	401-49
Thompson, T. B.	SR	401-106
Thompson, T. E.	USV	401-252
Thompson, T. H.	FB	401-174
Thompson, Thomas Birdwell	RRR	401-125
Thompson, Thomas M.	NAV	401-25
Thompson, W. D.	TVG	401-215
Thompson, W. E.	TVG	401-215
Thompson, W. G.	FF	401-139
Thompson, W. G.	TVG	401-215
Thompson, W. M.	USV	401-252
Thompson, Wiley G.	USV	401-252
Thompson, William	NAV	401-25
Thompson, William	ARM	401-11
Thompson, William	ARM	401-11
Thompson, William	ARM	401-11
Thompson, William	ARM	401-11
Thompson, William A.	RRR	401-125
Thompson, William H.	TVG	401-215
Thomson, John	NAV	401-25
Thomson, Louie	TVG	401-215
Thomson, P. W.	SR	401-106
Thomson, P. W.	FB	401-174
Thoresen, Oscar	USV	401-252
Thorn, F. W. R.	SP	401-49
Thorn, John S.	ARM	401-11
Thorn, T. W.	FF	401-139
Thorne, Francis	TVG	401-215
Thornhill, W. J.	USV	401-252
Thornton, Edward	ARM	401-11
Thornton, George H.	TVG	401-215
Thornton, George W., Jr.	SR	401-106
Thornton, J. W.	TVG	401-215
Thornton, L. F.	TVG	401-215
Thornton, R. A.	SR	401-106
Thornton, R. A.	LR	401-131
Thornton, R. L.	SR	401-106
Thornton, Thomas	TVG	401-215
Thornton, Thomas C.	SR	401-106
Thornton, Walter V.	USV	401-252
Thornton, Walter Willis	RRR	401-125
Thornton, William H.	MV	401-31
Thorogood, Robert C.	USV	401-252
Thorp, Ben	TVG	401-215
Thorp, Edward Earl	USV	401-252
Thorp, R. D.	SR	401-106
Thorp, Tom	RR	401-64
Thorp, Tom D.	SR	401-106
Thorpe, Henry W.	TVG	401-215
Thorpe, Henry W.	USV	401-252
Thorwald, John	SR	401-106
Thrall, Frank	FB	401-174
Thrasher, Ben O.	USV	401-252
Thrasher, Chester	RRR	401-125
Thrasher, Chester	SR	401-106
Thrasher, Douglas R.	SR	401-106
Thrasher, S. R., Jr.	SR	401-106
Thrasher, T. E., Sr.	SR	401-106
Threadgill, Alexander H.	USV	401-252
Thrift, Lee S.	SR	401-106
Throckmorton, Julian G.	FB	401-174
Thumm, Benjamin F.	USV	401-252
Thurman, A. J.	FF	401-139
Thurman, George	RRR	401-125
Thurman, George	SR	401-106
Thurman, Henry G.	FF	401-139
Thurman, J. O.	FB	401-174
Thurman, Jerry M.	USV	401-252
Thurman, M. J. "Jack"	SR	401-106
Thurman, Roger	SR	401-106
Thurman, Sam	SR	401-106
Thurman, Thomas Edward	FF	401-140
Thurmond, A. P.	USV	401-252
Thurmond, J. M.	RRR	401-125

Index to Texas Adjutant General Service Records—All Service Branches

Thweatt, Algernon S. .... USV 401-252
Thweatt, N. M. .... FF 401-140
Thyne, Thomas............................. RR 401-64
Tibbetts, Edward .... USV 401-252
Tibbs, K. P. .... SR 401-106
Tibbs, K. P. .... LR 401-131
Tibbs, William L. .... USV 401-252
Tidwell, James A. .... RR 401-64
Tidwell, W. P. .... SR 401-106
Tifft, Fred R. .... USV 401-252
Tigner, H. G. .... SR 401-106
Tignor, F. G. .... FB 401-174
Tileston, George .... ARM 401-11
Tilgner, Herrmann......................... FF 401-140
Tilley, G. W. .... SR 401-106
Tilley, S. G. .... SR 401-106
Tilley, St. George .... RRR 401-125
Timberlake, D. .... RR 401-64
Timberlake, D. .... SR 401-106
Timberlake, Delbert .... RR 401-64
Timberlake, Edgar .... RR 401-64
Timbs, Frank .... USV 401-252
Timmins, C. G. .... TVG 401-215
Timmons, James A. .... USV 401-252
Timmons, James G. .... TVG 401-215
Timmons, Joe .... SR 401-106
Timmons, Joe .... LR 401-131
Timmons, R. H. .... SR 401-106
Timmons, R. H. .... LR 401-131
Timmons, William T. .... USV 401-252
Timms, Jack H. .... SR 401-106
Timon, Walter F. .... SR 401-106
Tims, Bowden .... FB 401-174
Tindale, William .... ARM 401-11
Tindall .... ARM 401-11
Tindall, Robert M. .... USV 401-252
Tindill, Robt. H. .... ARM 401-11
Tinker, W. C. .... FB 401-174
Tinkle, Cliff M. .... SR 401-106
Tinney, Griffin .... MV 401-31
Tinney, Sam C. .... USV 401-252
Tinney, Thomas N. .... USV 401-252
Tinnin, W. H. .... FB 401-174
Tinsley, Benjamin .... USV 401-252
Tinsley, Douglas A. .... USV 401-252
Tinsley, Edward H. .... TVG 401-215
Tinsley, William Evendar .... TVG 401-215
Tippen, W. W. .... SR 401-106
Tippen, W. W. .... LR 401-131
Tippett, A. J., Jr. .... SR 401-106
Tippett, H. M. .... TST 401-37
Tippins, James O. .... TVG 401-215
Tippitt, C. E. .... TVG 401-215
Tippitt, Ernest .... TVG 401-215
Tippitt, Ernest .... USV 401-252
Tipple, Harry H. .... TVG 401-215

Tipps, Charles E. .... TVG 401-215
Tipton, Isham .... RR 401-64
Tipton, N. C. .... TVG 401-215
Tisdale, I. M. .... SR 401-106
Tisdale, I. M. .... LR 401-131
Tisdale, Ira .... SR 401-106
Tisdale, Ira .... LR 401-131
Tison, William T. .... CSA 401-40
Titcomb, Ed. .... TVG 401-215
Titcomb, John P. .... NAV 401-25
Tittle, Charles T. .... SR 401-106
Tittle, Charles T. .... LR 401-131
Tittle, Edward L. .... USV 401-252
Toake, J. P. .... TVG 401-215
Toberman, C. E. .... TVG 401-215
Tobin, C. E. .... SR 401-106
Tobin, C. R. .... SR 401-106
Tobin, Charles E. .... USV 401-252
Tobin, Charles Milton .... SR 401-106
Tobin, Cornelius D. .... USV 401-252
Tobin, James P. .... SR 401-106
Tobin, John W. .... FB 401-174
Tobin, John W. .... USV 401-252
Tobin, Ted .... TVG 401-215
Tobin, Thos. .... ARM 401-11
Tobin, William G. .... MV 401-31
Todd, Charles .... TVG 401-215
Todd, Frank .... TVG 401-215
Todd, George W. .... RR 401-64
Todd, Jack .... TVG 401-215
Todd, John D. .... SR 401-106
Todd, John F. .... USV 401-252
Todd, Lawrence C. .... SR 401-106
Todd, V. D. .... TVG 401-215
Todd, W. R. .... SR 401-106
Todd, Winburne Reese .... RR 401-64
Toland, A. W. .... USV 401-252
Toldera, Ramon .... FF 401-140
Toler, Joe .... SR 401-106
Toler, John T. .... FF 401-140
Toler, W. J. .... FB 401-174
Toliver, E. A. .... TVG 401-215
Toliver, John O. .... TST 401-37
Tolman, Stephen W. .... USV 401-252
Tom, John .... SP 401-49
Tom, William .... RR 401-64
Tombs, George A. .... USV 401-252
Tomek, August R. .... USV 401-252
Tomelly, Nicholas .... ARM 401-11
Tomerlin, Martin .... FB 401-174
Tomkins, J. Frank .... TVG 401-215
Tomlin, Jas G. .... SR 401-106
Tomlinson, E. A. .... FB 401-174
Tomlinson [Tumlinson], Joseph .... SP 401-49
Tompkins, George .... TVG 401-215
Tompkins, J. P. .... TVG 401-215

Index to Texas Adjutant General Service Records—All Service Branches

Name	Branch	Record
Tompkins, Sidney C.	SR	401-106
Tompkins, W. O.	FB	401-174
Tonahill, B. J.	SR	401-106
Toncray, A. C.	SR	401-106
Toncray, A. C.	LR	401-131
Tongate, E.	FF	401-140
Toombs, Alfred L.	TVG	401-215
Toomey, D. H.	FB	401-174
Tope, James	MV	401-31
Topperwein, Hermann W.	FF	401-140
Torbron, Jerome F.	USV	401-252
Torrence, C. H.	SR	401-106
Torrence, William C.	SR	401-106
Torres, Edward J.	RRR	401-125
Torres, Louis	USV	401-252
Torres, Pablo	FB	401-174
Torrey, George N.	TVG	401-215
Torrey, R. G.	TVG	401-215
Tosney, Martin	NAV	401-25
Totten, Jesse M.	USV	401-252
Toumey, A. C.	FB	401-174
Tounsley, R. L.	RRR	401-125
Towers, Edward L.	USV	401-252
Towers, Philip O.	SR	401-106
Towers, William M.	TVG	401-215
Towers, William M.	USV	401-252
Towery, Forrest Lee	SR	401-106
Towery, O. A.	SR	401-106
Towles, Churchill	TVG	401-215
Towles, Churchill	USV	401-252
Town, William D.	ARM	401-11
Townes, Charles B.	USV	401-252
Townes, E. D.	TST	401-37
Townes, John C.	SR	401-106
Townsend, A. Web	FB	401-174
Townsend, Alice, Mrs.	SR	401-106
Townsend, E. E.	SR	401-106
Townsend, E. E.	FB	401-174
Townsend, G. L.	FB	401-174
Townsend, H. A.	SR	401-106
Townsend, H. S.	SR	401-106
Townsend, Henry I.	USV	401-252
Townsend, Henry W.	TVG	401-215
Townsend, J. B.	FB	401-174
Townsend, J. P.	FF	401-140
Townsend, James W.	FB	401-174
Townsend, Joseph B.	TVG	401-215
Townsend, Joseph B.	USV	401-252
Townsend, Light	RR	401-64
Townsend, Light	RRR	401-125
Townsend, Percy Clifton	TVG	401-215
Townsend, S. T.	RR	401-64
Townsend, Shep. H.	USV	401-252
Townsend, W. T.	SR	401-106
Townsend, W. T.	LR	401-131
Townsend, William Earl	RRR	401-125
Townsend, Woody	RR	401-64
Townsley, H. F.	FB	401-174
Townsley, R. L.	FB	401-174
Tozer, Charles H.	USV	401-252
Tracy, N. H.	TVG	401-215
Tracy, William H.	TVG	401-215
Trahan, Frank T.	USV	401-252
Trail, Henry C.	USV	401-252
Trainer, Vernon	SR	401-106
Trammel, Merrick	SP	401-49
Trammell, B. F.	USV	401-252
Trammell, F. Winfield	TVG	401-215
Trammell, Giles	SP	401-49
Trammell, J. H.	TVG	401-215
Trammell, J. M.	TVG	401-215
Trammell, Thomas D.	TVG	401-215
Trammell, Thomas D.	USV	401-253
Trammell, William H.	CSA	401-40
Trammell, Wood	SP	401-49
Trask, J. Henry	TST	401-37
Travis, Charles E.	MV	401-31
Travis, Edmunds	SR	401-106
Travis, M. T.	SR	401-106
Travis, M. T.	LR	401-131
Travis, William H.	USV	401-253
Traw, J. A.	TVG	401-215
Traw, John A.	USV	401-253
Traweek, William B.	FB	401-174
Trayler, S. A.	TVG	401-215
Traylor, Frederick	ARM	401-11
Traylor, John D.	USV	401-253
Traynham, John H.	USV	401-253
Traynor, John	FF	401-140
Treadway, Clifford A.	USV	401-253
Treadwell, B. B.	TVG	401-215
Treadwell, Bascom B.	USV	401-253
Treadwell, O. G.	TST	401-37
Treadwell, P. E.	USV	401-253
Treadwell, W. M.	FB	401-174
Treadwell, William	FB	401-174
Trejo, Martin E.	RR	401-64
Tremble, Alex	FB	401-174
Trempe, Jacob	FF	401-140
Trentham, Charles N.	FB	401-174
Trevinia, Juan	FF	401-140
Trevinio, Florencio	FB	401-174
Trevino, Ramon	FF	401-140
Tribble, W. B.	TVG	401-215
Trice, Charles H.	TVG	401-215
Trice, Leroy	TVG	401-215
Tridle, John	RR	401-64
Trigg, Alexander	NAV	401-25
Trigg, O. P.	TVG	401-215
Trimble, B. L.	FB	401-174
Trimble, Charles E.	TVG	401-215
Trimble, George	SP	401-49

Index to Texas Adjutant General Service Records—All Service Branches

Name	Branch	Record
Trimble, James M.	CSA	401-40
Trimble, John M.	TVG	401-215
Trimble, John M.	USV	401-253
Trimble, La Fetra Elisha	SR	401-106
Trimble, LaFetra E.	RR	401-64
Trimble, W. C.	SP	401-49
Triplett, Armstead T. E.	TVG	401-215
Tripps, William R.	USV	401-253
Trollinger, Harris C.	RR	401-64
Trotman, T. B.	TVG	401-215
Trotter, Albert L.	FB	401-174
Trotter, M. T.	TVG	401-215
Trout, W. A.	TVG	401-215
Troutt, Alfred	FB	401-174
Troutt, James	FB	401-174
Trouty, Christophal	ARM	401-11
Troy, Ellis	ARM	401-11
Trube, F. E.	TVG	401-215
Trube, R. C.	TVG	401-215
True, Archie M.	USV	401-253
Truelove, John A.	SP	401-49
Truitt, Charley	SP	401-49
Trujillo, Thomas	FF	401-140
Truly, John W.	SR	401-106
Trumbull, Neil	USV	401-253
Trussell, Andrew J.	MV	401-31
Tschumy, Herman	TVG	401-215
Tubb, Lesser W.	USV	401-253
Tubbs, B. M.	SR	401-106
Tubbs, John W.	USV	401-253
Tucker, Albert	USV	401-253
Tucker, Arthur	USV	401-253
Tucker, B. F.	LR	401-131
Tucker, Charles E.	FB	401-174
Tucker, E.	ARM	401-11
Tucker, E. L.	SR	401-106
Tucker, Frank E.	USV	401-253
Tucker, George H.	FB	401-174
Tucker, Hillory	TST	401-37
Tucker, J. E.	USV	401-253
Tucker, J. S.	SR	401-106
Tucker, J. S.	LR	401-131
Tucker, James	CSA	401-40
Tucker, Jim	TVG	401-215
Tucker, Lee S.	FB	401-175
Tucker, Napoleon B.	CSA	401-40
Tucker, P. P.	NAV	401-25
Tucker, Phil E.	TVG	401-215
Tucker, R. H.	TVG	401-215
Tucker, Ralph J.	FB	401-175
Tucker, Richard J.	SR	401-106
Tucker, Roger V.	USV	401-253
Tucker, T. F.	FB	401-175
Tucker, W. H.	TVG	401-215
Tucker, Walter L.	TVG	401-215
Tucker, Will L.	USV	401-253
Tucker, William H.	USV	401-253
Tucker, William H.	USV	401-253
Tucker, William M.	MV	401-31
Tucker, William R.	USV	401-253
Tudror, B. F.	SR	401-106
Tuggle, James Clark	FB	401-175
Tuley, R. R.	RRR	401-125
Tullis, Dick	SR	401-106
Tullis, O. L.	SR	401-106
Tullis, Thomas W.	FB	401-175
Tullis, W. A.	SR	401-106
Tullis, W. A.	LR	401-131
Tullock, D. D.	RR	401-64
Tullos, Aubrey R.	SR	401-106
Tully, T. L.	RR	401-64
Tully, Walker	FB	401-175
Tumlinson, Absalom T.	MV	401-31
Tumlinson, Benjamin T., Jr.	RR	401-64
Tumlinson, Eugene H.	RR	401-64
Tumlinson, Joseph	MV	401-31
Tumlinson, Lott	RR	401-64
Tumlinson, Peter	MV	401-31
Tumlinson, Peter	FB	401-175
Tumlinson, William O.	RR	401-64
Tummelty, Nicholas	ARM	401-11
Tunstall, William V.	SP	401-49
Tupper, Carl Lee	SR	401-106
Turbett, Frank H.	RRR	401-125
Turck, George V.	USV	401-253
Turck, J. E.	RRR	401-125
Turk, Albert	SR	401-106
Turk, J. E.	SR	401-106
Turlany, Thomas	FB	401-175
Turley, R. L.	FB	401-175
Turman, John C., Jr.	SR	401-106
Turnbo, L. S.	FB	401-175
Turnbow, A. N.	FB	401-175
Turnbow, L. S.	FB	401-175
Turnbow, N.	FB	401-175
Turnbow, W. C.	SR	401-107
Turnbull, Fred	FB	401-175
Turner, Allison N.	USV	401-253
Turner, Alonzo Y.	USV	401-253
Turner, C. W.	USV	401-253
Turner, Claude	USV	401-253
Turner, D. M., Jr.	TVG	401-215
Turner, Ernest H.	TVG	401-215
Turner, F. E.	SR	401-107
Turner, Frank E.	RRR	401-125
Turner, Frank P.	USV	401-253
Turner, Frank W., Jr.	SR	401-107
Turner, H. A.	RR	401-64
Turner, H. A.	SR	401-107
Turner, H. R.	RR	401-64
Turner, H. W.	SR	401-107
Turner, Harold	FB	401-175

Index to Texas Adjutant General Service Records—All Service Branches

Turner, J. C. ....FB............401-175
Turner, James M. ....NAV........401-25
Turner, James R. ....USV 401-253
Turner, Jim Scott ....TVG 401-215
Turner, Joe..................................SR.............401-107
Turner, John................................SR.............401-107
Turner, John A............................NAV........401-25
Turner, John F. ....USV 401-253
Turner, Joseph D. ....USV 401-253
Turner, O. A. ....RR 401-64
Turner, Oliver M. ....USV 401-253
Turner, R. C. ....MM 401-32
Turner, Robert Lee ....USV 401-253
Turner, Roscoe ....SR.............401-107
Turner, Theodore E....................SP.............401-49
Turner, Thomas Oakes ....TVG 401-215
Turner, Thomas Oakes ....USV 401-253
Turner, Van.................................TVG 401-215
Turner, W. H. ....FB............401-175
Turner, W. J. ....TVG 401-215
Turner, W. L. ....SR.............401-107
Turner, W. L. ....LR 401-131
Turner, Will ....USV 401-253
Turner, William ....NAV........401-25
Turney, John...............................RR 401-64
Turney, R. L. ....TVG 401-215
Turney, S. L. ....TVG 401-215
Turpin, Sidney J.........................SR.............401-107
Turrill, Samuel A. ....MV 401-31
Tursky, Constantine...................ARM 401-11
Tutt, Martin................................ARM 401-11
Tuttle, Charles ....USV 401-253
Tuttle, George.............................ARM 401-11
Twaddell, Jacob C. ....RR 401-64
Tweed, James ....NAV........401-25
Tweed, James ....ARM 401-11
Twiggs, Frank C. ....USV 401-253
Twombly, Frank B.....................USV 401-253
Tyler, Gordon ....SR.............401-107
Tyler, John..................................ARM 401-11
Tyler, John H..............................RRR 401-125
Tyler, Richard ....TVG 401-215
Tyler, Robert L...........................USV 401-253
Tynan, John S. ....USV 401-253
Tynan, Patrick............................NAV........401-25
Tyner, Harry T. ....USV 401-253
Tyng, George McA....................USV 401-253
Tynon, William..........................ARM 401-11
Tyrrell, George W. ....USV 401-253
Tyson, John T. ....USV 401-253
Tyson, Jout ....TVG 401-215
Uanderlepper, Levi Otto ....ARM 401-11
Uhr, August ....FF 401-140
Uhrbach, Robert C.....................USV 401-253
Ulillre, Robert L. ....FB............401-175
Ullriak, William.........................NAV........401-26

Ullrich, W. J. ....TVG 401-215
Umscheid, Max..........................SR.............401-107
Underhill, Charles B..................NAV........401-26
Underhill, Morris D. ....NAV........401-26
Underwood, E. T. ....SR.............401-107
Underwood, Thomas B..............USV 401-253
Upchurch, Moses ....TST 401-37
Upshaw, A. M............................MV 401-31
Upton, Brad K. ....USV 401-253
Upton, Monroe ....RR 401-64
Upton, William T.......................FB............401-175
Uranga, Jose ....FF 401-140
Urban, Jesse ....SR.............401-107
Uro, Silbestre.............................FF 401-140
Urteaga, Demetrio ....FF 401-140
Usrey, John W. ....USV 401-253
Ussery, Charles C. ....SR.............401-107
Ussery, Charles C. ....LR 401-131
Ussery, Emmett T. ....USV 401-253
Utecht, R. J. ....SR.............401-107
Utley, C. E. ....USV 401-253
Utley, D. R. ....RRR 401-125
Utley, David J. ....FB............401-175
Utley, R. K. ....RRR 401-125
Utter, S. A. ....FB............401-175
Uzzell, Winter W.......................USV 401-253
Vacek, I. James...........................SR.............401-107
Vaden, Frank S. ....USV 401-253
Vaden, W. J. ....FB............401-175
Vaeck, Chas................................ARM 401-11
Vail, George A...........................NAV........401-26
Valdez, I. M. ....FF 401-140
Valentine, Edward ....ARM 401-11
Valentine, Edward H. ....NAV........401-26
Valentine, John...........................FF 401-140
Valentine, John...........................SP.............401-50
Valentine, L. G. ....TVG 401-215
Valle, Calixto.............................SR.............401-107
Vallins, Thomas N.....................FB............401-175
Van Benthuysen, James A. ....RRR 401-125
Van Buren, Frederick Arthur.....SR.............401-107
Van Cleave, Jack ....SR.............401-107
Van Cleave, William F. ....USV 401-253
Van Cleve, E. C. ....SR.............401-107
Van Cleve, Jack ....SR.............401-107
Van Dell, H. G. ....SR.............401-107
Van Devender, S. C. ....FB............401-175
Van Ende, John..........................USV 401-253
Van Haesen, H. M. ....SR.............401-107
Van Haesen, H. M. ....LR 401-131
Van Lehn, Clarence Wilbur......RRR 401-125
Van Liew, Archie M..................RRR 401-125
Van Norman, S. S. ....SP.............401-50
Van Orden, Pete.........................SR.............401-107
Van Riper, Frank ....FB............401-175
Van Riper, G. P. ....SR.............401-107

Index to Texas Adjutant General Service Records—All Service Branches

Van Riper, J. E. .... FB 401-175
Van Riper, J. F. .... USV 401-253
Van Riper, William H. .... FB 401-175
Van Shaw, W. H. .... SR 401-107
Van Slyck, K. .... RRR 401-125
Van Wey, D. C. .... SP 401-50
Van Zandt, R. C. .... RRR 401-125
Vance, Charles H. .... USV 401-253
Vance, F. J. .... TST 401-37
Vance, F. O. .... SR 401-107
Vance, Hugh I. .... ARM 401-11
Vance, John H. .... USV 401-253
Vance, W. E. .... FB 401-175
Vancleave, W. .... SR 401-107
Vancleve, Jack .... RR 401-64
Vancleve, L. D. .... SR 401-107
Vandagriff, T. L. .... FB 401-175
Vander Stucken, Alfred .... SR 401-107
Vandergrift, W. E. .... SR 401-107
Vanderleppe, Levi Otto .... ARM 401-11
Vanderpool, C. T. .... SR 401-107
Vandersall, Jesse W. .... RRR 401-125
Vandervoort, Robert B. .... TVG 401-215
Vanderweide, Sam G. .... SR 401-107
VanEaton, H. .... TVG 401-215
Vanfleet, H. M. .... FB 401-175
Vanhooser, W. B. .... FB 401-175
VanHorn, Samuel H. .... TVG 401-215
VanLiew, Carl fred .... TVG 401-215
Vanmeter, William C. .... MV 401-31
Vann, Bishop L. .... SR 401-107
Vann, Charles C. .... RR 401-64
Vann, John W. .... SR 401-107
Vannetten, James .... NAV 401-26
Vannoy, J. F. .... RR 401-64
Vannoy, J. F. .... SR 401-107
Vanover, B. C. .... RRR 401-125
VanZandt, K. M. .... TVG 401-215
Vardell, T. W. .... SR 401-107
Vardeman, Arch .... SR 401-107
Varden, George .... TVG 401-215
Varley, Joseph A. .... USV 401-253
Varnell, Ellis A. .... TVG 401-215
Varnell, William R. .... TVG 401-215
Vasburgh, William .... FB 401-175
Vass, William .... TST 401-37
Vastell, W. R. .... NAV 401-26
Vastine, Edward L. .... USV 401-253
Vaughan, Arthur H. .... TVG 401-215
Vaughan, D. R. .... SR 401-107
Vaughan, Everett .... TVG 401-215
Vaughan, J. M. .... SP 401-50
Vaughan, J. R. .... FB 401-175
Vaughan, Jack .... SR 401-107
Vaughan, Jeff E. .... SR 401-107
Vaughan, Jefferson Eagle .... RR 401-64

Vaughan, John G. .... SR 401-107
Vaughan, John H. .... FF 401-140
Vaughan, M. J. .... SP 401-50
Vaughan, R. W. .... RR 401-64
Vaughan, Rufus G. .... RR 401-64
Vaughan, T. D. .... TVG 401-215
Vaughan, W. J. .... SR 401-107
Vaughan, Wilson W. .... SR 401-107
Vaughn, Charles .... TVG 401-215
Vaughn, Henry L. .... USV 401-253
Vaughn, J. B. .... TST 401-37
Vaughn, John H. .... FB 401-175
Vaughn, Pink .... SR 401-107
Vaughn, Robert L. .... USV 401-253
Vaughn, Roy C. .... SR 401-107
Vaughn, Walter C. .... USV 401-253
Vaughn, William D. .... USV 401-253
Vaught, J. R. .... FB 401-175
Veale, Bert Clinton .... RR 401-64
Veale, H. C. .... TST 401-37
Veatch .... ARM 401-11
Veazey, J. L. .... TVG 401-215
Veazey, James M. .... USV 401-253
Veazey, John .... TVG 401-215
Veazey, John L. .... USV 401-253
Veck, Henry B. .... USV 401-253
Vega, George F. B. .... SP 401-50
Vela, Apolonio .... SP 401-50
Vela, Cecilio .... SP 401-50
Vela, Reyes .... FB 401-175
Velder, J. M. .... FF 401-140
Veltmann, Henry .... TVG 401-215
Veltmann, W. A. .... TVG 401-215
Vercoe, James .... FF 401-140
Vergnon, Gilbert .... ARM 401-11
Verhey, Pete .... SR 401-107
Vermillion, R. M. .... SR 401-107
Verner, Bud .... SR 401-107
Verner, Lawrence T. .... SR 401-107
Vernon, George .... TST 401-37
Vernon, T. J. .... SR 401-107
Vernon, W. O. .... SR 401-107
Vernor, H. D. .... RRR 401-125
Verschoyle, Chas. H. .... SR 401-107
Vervatz, John .... ARM 401-11
Via, Walter T. .... USV 401-253
Vick, Frank .... USV 401-253
Vick, G. H. .... TVG 401-215
Vicker, Ben .... TVG 401-215
Vickers, E. C. .... RRR 401-125
Vickers, G. E. .... SR 401-107
Vickers, J. H. .... TVG 401-215
Vickers, Jim .... TVG 401-215
Victory, Sidney Patrick .... RRR 401-125
Vidler, Robert J. .... TVG 401-215
Vidor, W. S. .... TVG 401-215

Index to Texas Adjutant General Service Records—All Service Branches

Name	Branch	Record
Viemark, Swen	ARM	401-11
Vignos, James E.	FB	401-175
Vigon, Francis	ARM	401-11
Vilas, Walter N.	USV	401-253
Villanueva, Mauricio	SP	401-50
Villarreal, E. C.	SR	401-107
Vince, William	ARM	401-11
Vincent, George J.	USV	401-253
Vincent, Henry	NAV	401-26
Vincent, U. S.	USV	401-253
Vincent, William	NAV	401-26
Vines, J. M.	FB	401-175
Vines, J. M.	TVG	401-215
Vines, Joe P.	USV	401-253
Vineyard, B.	TVG	401-215
Vineyard, B. R.	USV	401-253
Vining, A. M.	TVG	401-215
Vining, Charles	TVG	401-215
Vining, George	TVG	401-215
Vinson, E. W.	TVG	401-215
Vinson, J. E.	SR	401-107
Vinson, T. R.	RR	401-64
Vinson, Theodore R.	SR	401-107
Vinson, W. Roy	SR	401-107
Vint, Edward	TVG	401-215
Vinton, Fred W.	FB	401-175
Vinton, Josiah S.	TVG	401-215
Virlon, Thomas	SP	401-50
Vivion, Otho D.	RR	401-64
Vivion, Wesley Tildon	SR	401-107
Vogelsang, A.	TVG	401-215
Vogler, Charley H.	TVG	401-215
Vogler, George	TVG	401-215
Vogtsberger, E. W.	TVG	401-215
Vollantine, James	TST	401-37
Volta, Gitano	ARM	401-11
Von Brixen, Fred	USV	401-253
Von Hagen, Louis	FB	401-175
Von Koenneritz, S. J.	SR	401-107
Von Loopin, Peter	USV	401-253
Von Roeder, G. W.	FB	401-175
Von Schlumbach, Alexander	USV	401-253
VonBrixen, Fred	TVG	401-215
VonGermar, Albert	NAV	401-26
Vosburg, Hulet E.	RRR	401-125
Voss, Albert	TVG	401-215
Wackman, F. J.	TVG	401-215
Waddell, H. P.	FB	401-175
Waddell, Minton P.	USV	401-253
Waddell, William	USV	401-253
Waddill, G. C.	TVG	401-215
Waddill, H. B.	FB	401-175
Waddill, William A.	MV	401-31
Waddle, George L.	USV	401-253
Wade, Alexander	ARM	401-12
Wade, E. B.	MV	401-31
Wade, J. J.	FF	401-140
Wade, James W.	SP	401-50
Wade, John C. N.	TVG	401-215
Wade, John L.	RR	401-64
Wade, Maurice	TVG	401-215
Wade, Robert	TVG	401-215
Wade, S. H.	FB	401-175
Wade, T. A.	FF	401-140
Wade, Telemicus	CSA	401-40
Wade, W.	FB	401-175
Wade, W. A.	TVG	401-215
Wade, Willie	TVG	401-215
Wadsworth, W. B.	SP	401-50
Waechter, Edmund	USV	401-253
Wages, Riley J.	USV	401-253
Waggoner, E. P.	SR	401-107
Waggoner, George	ARM	401-12
Waggoner, Guy L.	SR	401-107
Waggoner, W. B.	USV	401-253
Waggoner, William H.	TVG	401-215
Wagner, A.	FB	401-175
Wagner, Carl	NAV	401-26
Wagner, Charles	FF	401-140
Wagner, G. E.	TVG	401-215
Wagner, Herman	RRR	401-125
Wagner, J.	TVG	401-215
Wagnon, Harvey	USV	401-253
Wagstaff, John	ARM	401-12
Wahatley, Edmond	RR	401-64
Wahnschaffe, Charles	FF	401-140
Wahrmund, Otto	TVG	401-216
Wahrmund, W.	TST	401-37
Waid, W. W.	SR	401-107
Waide, D. H.	FB	401-175
Wainscott, Hiram	FB	401-175
Wait, D. V.	TVG	401-216
Waite, Alfred A.	NAV	401-26
Waite, Irwin R.	SR	401-107
Waite, Robert L.	USV	401-253
Waites, Franklin L.	MV	401-31
Waits, Leroy	FB	401-175
Waits, Pat	SR	401-107
Waits, William	FB	401-175
Wakefield, Paul L.	SR	401-107
Wakefield, U.	ARM	401-12
Walch, Edward	NAV	401-26
Walch, John	SP	401-50
Walde, V. H.	FB	401-175
Walden, Sam A.	USV	401-253
Waldert, Edward	MV	401-31
Waldie, Alexander	TVG	401-216
Waldie, Walter	TVG	401-216
Waldon, James T.	TVG	401-216
Waldon, William W.	RRR	401-125
Waldrep, James A.	TVG	401-216
Waldridge, J. M.	SR	401-107

Index to Texas Adjutant General Service Records—All Service Branches

Name	Branch	Record
Waldron, C. W.	ARM	401-12
Waldrope, F. S.	FB	401-175
Walk, James	ARM	401-12
Walk, Joe A.	SR	401-107
Walke, John	USV	401-253
Walker, Alfred	NAV	401-26
Walker, Alfred	FB	401-175
Walker, Andrew	FB	401-175
Walker, Aruthur L.	TVG	401-216
Walker, C. E.	SR	401-107
Walker, Charles	FB	401-175
Walker, Charles	USV	401-253
Walker, Charles E.	TVG	401-216
Walker, David	NAV	401-26
Walker, David	USV	401-253
Walker, Edgar	SR	401-107
Walker, Edward	FB	401-175
Walker, Euin	SR	401-107
Walker, G. G.	FB	401-175
Walker, G. W.	FB	401-175
Walker, Geo. A.	RRR	401-125
Walker, George F.	FB	401-175
Walker, George H.	SR	401-107
Walker, George W.	TST	401-37
Walker, Gilbert	USV	401-253
Walker, Hartwell	ARM	401-12
Walker, Harvey	USV	401-253
Walker, Henry C.	FB	401-175
Walker, Horace	SR	401-107
Walker, J. A.	FB	401-175
Walker, J. C.	FB	401-175
Walker, J. C.	LR	401-131
Walker, J. F.	SR	401-107
Walker, J. H.	FB	401-175
Walker, J. L.	ARM	401-12
Walker, J. M.	FB	401-175
Walker, Jacob C.	USV	401-253
Walker, James	NAV	401-26
Walker, James	ARM	401-12
Walker, James Knox	TVG	401-216
Walker, James W.	TST	401-37
Walker, James W.	USV	401-253
Walker, Jesse R.	USV	401-253
Walker, John	TST	401-37
Walker, John	ARM	401-12
Walker, John A.	TVG	401-216
Walker, John C.	ARM	401-12
Walker, John F.	LR	401-131
Walker, John H.	ARM	401-12
Walker, John W.	FB	401-175
Walker, Johnson	CSA	401-40
Walker, Joseph	RR	401-64
Walker, Joseph	ARM	401-12
Walker, Joseph S.	ARM	401-12
Walker, Lee A.	TVG	401-216
Walker, Leonard	RR	401-64
Walker, Martin	ARM	401-12
Walker, Merce W.	TVG	401-216
Walker, P. F.	TVG	401-216
Walker, Phillip	ARM	401-12
Walker, R. A.	SR	401-107
Walker, Roy M.	LR	401-131
Walker, Royal	SR	401-107
Walker, S. R.	FB	401-175
Walker, Sam T.	RR	401-64
Walker, Sherrod R.	ARM	401-12
Walker, Stephen W.	MV	401-31
Walker, Swayne	TVG	401-216
Walker, T. S.	USV	401-253
Walker, W. M.	TVG	401-216
Walker, W. P.	TVG	401-216
Walker, W. W.	USV	401-253
Walker, Will T.	TVG	401-216
Walker, William	NAV	401-26
Walker, William	ARM	401-12
Walker, William	ARM	401-12
Walker, William G.	ARM	401-12
Walkins, Robert C.	TVG	401-216
Wall, Alonzo E.	RR	401-64
Wall, C. F.	FB	401-175
Wall, David D.	TST	401-37
Wall, John E.	USV	401-253
Wall, Thomas	ARM	401-12
Wall, Thomas	SR	401-107
Wall, Thomas L.	USV	401-253
Wallace, Alex	FB	401-175
Wallace, B. C.	ARM	401-12
Wallace, B. R.	SP	401-50
Wallace, C. B.	USV	401-253
Wallace, C. M.	FB	401-175
Wallace, Caleb	ARM	401-12
Wallace, Clayton P.	MV	401-31
Wallace, E. H.	FB	401-175
Wallace, Earl	RRR	401-125
Wallace, Homer A.	USV	401-253
Wallace, Huett E.	USV	401-253
Wallace, J. F.	SR	401-107
Wallace, J. H.	USV	401-253
Wallace, Jesse E.	USV	401-253
Wallace, John Henderson	FB	401-175
Wallace, John L.	TST	401-37
Wallace, John W.	FB	401-175
Wallace, Jouett	TVG	401-216
Wallace, Keath	USV	401-253
Wallace, Keity L.	USV	401-253
Wallace, Ralph E.	USV	401-253
Wallace, Sam	NAV	401-26
Wallace, Ted	LR	401-131
Wallace, Tom A.	SR	401-107
Wallace, W. B.	SR	401-107
Wallace, W. H.	LR	401-131
Wallace, Warren	RR	401-64

Index to Texas Adjutant General Service Records—All Service Branches

Wallace, William .... NAV 401-26
Wallace, William .... TVG 401-216
Wallace, William R. .... USV 401-253
Wallace, William T. .... USV 401-253
Wallen, J. A. .... RR 401-64
Waller, Barney .... TVG 401-216
Waller, H. B. .... SP 401-50
Waller, H. W. "Dusty" .... SR 401-107
Waller, James M. .... FB 401-175
Waller, John R. .... FB 401-175
Waller, L. D. .... RRR 401-125
Waller, Thomas M. .... TVG 401-216
Waller, W. R. .... FB 401-175
Wallin, John H. .... TVG 401-216
Walling, H. H. .... FB 401-175
Walling, John C. .... ARM 401-12
Walling, W. A. .... LR 401-131
Wallingford, W. W. .... ARM 401-12
Wallis, G. W. .... RR 401-64
Wallis, Guy .... FB 401-175
Wallis, Harry J. .... FB 401-175
Wallis, Hayes M. .... RR 401-64
Wallis, Hayes M. .... RRR 401-125
Wallis, Hayes M. .... SR 401-107
Wallis, Taylor .... RRR 401-125
Wallridge, J. M. .... SR 401-107
Walls, James E. .... USV 401-253
Walpole, George F. .... USV 401-253
Walpole, William .... TVG 401-216
Walpole, William .... USV 401-253
Walsan, William .... USV 401-253
Walsh, Charles Dennis .... FB 401-175
Walsh, Charles Homer .... USV 401-253
Walsh, Jas. .... ARM 401-12
Walsh, John .... SP 401-50
Walsh, John S. .... USV 401-253
Walsh, Lindsay M. .... USV 401-253
Walsh, Patrick J. .... SP 401-50
Walshe, E. P. .... TVG 401-216
Walter, Henry G. .... TST 401-37
Walter, L. H. .... TVG 401-216
Walter, Peter .... MV 401-31
Walters, Christopher W. .... ARM 401-12
Walters, Ed T. .... USV 401-253
Walters, G. E. .... SR 401-107
Walters, H. M. .... TVG 401-216
Walters, John B. .... ARM 401-12
Walters, O. E. .... RR 401-64
Walters, Sam T. .... SR 401-107
Walterscheid, Henry .... USV 401-253
Walthall, Harris .... TVG 401-216
Walthers, H. H. .... SR 401-107
Waltman, Frank P. .... USV 401-253
Walton, Charles .... USV 401-253
Walton, D. A. T. .... FB 401-175
Walton, J. D. .... FB 401-175
Walton, J. E., Jr. .... SR 401-107
Walton, J. T. .... TVG 401-216
Walton, James A. .... RRR 401-126
Walton, James C. .... USV 401-253
Walton, Richard .... NAV 401-26
Walton, Richard .... ARM 401-12
Walton, W. .... TVG 401-216
Wanen, Thomas .... NAV 401-26
Wanslow, David .... FF 401-140
Wanston, David .... FB 401-175
Wanz, Haver .... FF 401-140
Ward, Art .... RRR 401-126
Ward, Benjamin B. .... USV 401-253
Ward, Charles .... SP 401-50
Ward, Charles C. .... USV 401-253
Ward, Daniel S. .... ARM 401-12
Ward, Eugene B. .... USV 401-253
Ward, F. C. .... FB 401-175
Ward, George .... USV 401-253
Ward, Henry .... TST 401-37
Ward, Henry L. .... FB 401-175
Ward, Henry M. .... USV 401-253
Ward, Henry W. .... ARM 401-12
Ward, Herman G. .... NAV 401-26
Ward, Ignacio .... TVG 401-216
Ward, J. F. .... FB 401-175
Ward, J. L. .... TVG 401-216
Ward, J. L. .... USV 401-253
Ward, James H. .... ARM 401-12
Ward, James Russell .... TVG 401-216
Ward, John E. .... USV 401-253
Ward, John H. .... ARM 401-12
Ward, Nathan P. .... USV 401-253
Ward, Onesimus .... MV 401-31
Ward, Otis B. .... USV 401-253
Ward, Russell .... ARM 401-12
Ward, Samuel .... ARM 401-12
Ward, Thomas D. .... TVG 401-216
Ward, Thomas H. .... USV 401-254
Ward, Thomas W. .... ARM 401-12
Ward, W. Terry .... USV 401-254
Ward, Walter B. .... TVG 401-216
Ward, Walter T. .... USV 401-254
Ward, William F. .... USV 401-254
Ware, A. H. .... SR 401-107
Ware, C. L. .... FB 401-176
Ware, C. M. .... USV 401-254
Ware, Ellis .... RRR 401-126
Ware, G. W. .... RRR 401-126
Ware, George W. .... USV 401-254
Ware, Graydon L. .... RR 401-64
Ware, H. P. .... SR 401-107
Ware, Ira J. .... FB 401-176
Ware, J. H. .... FB 401-176
Ware, J. I. .... FB 401-176
Ware, J. T. .... RRR 401-126

Index to Texas Adjutant General Service Records—All Service Branches

Ware, James Ira................................SR............401-107
Ware, Joe V.......................................SR............401-107
Ware, N...FB............401-176
Ware, N. O...FB............401-176
Ware, Nathaniel M............................RR............401-64
Ware, Nicholas..................................FB............401-176
Ware, Orlando...................................NAV.........401-26
Ware, R. C...FB............401-176
Ware, Richard C................................TVG.........401-216
Ware, Robert W.................................RR............401-64
Ware, W. M..FB............401-176
Ware, William....................................NAV.........401-26
Ware, William L.................................FB............401-176
Waring, F. M......................................FB............401-176
Waring, Frank W................................FB............401-176
Warman, Will E..................................FB............401-176
Warmouth, Isaac................................ARM........401-12
Warner, Andrew.................................FB............401-176
Warner, B. G......................................FB............401-176
Warner, Brady Walker........................TVG.........401-216
Warner, Charles Willis.......................USV.........401-254
Warner, E. R......................................TVG.........401-216
Warner, G. B......................................FB............401-176
Warner, William.................................ARM........401-12
Warnick, W. A....................................FF............401-140
Warnken, Louise Walton, Mrs...........SR............401-108
Warnken, R. S....................................TVG.........401-216
Warren, Bert......................................USV.........401-254
Warren, C. E......................................TVG.........401-216
Warren, C. P......................................FB............401-176
Warren, Claude D..............................TVG.........401-216
Warren, Ed..RR............401-64
Warren, Ed..SR............401-108
Warren, G. G.....................................TVG.........401-216
Warren, George.................................TVG.........401-216
Warren, H..FB............401-176
Warren, Henry c.................................RR............401-64
Warren, Henry R................................USV.........401-254
Warren, J. D......................................FB............401-176
Warren, J. W.....................................FB............401-176
Warren, James..................................ARM........401-12
Warren, James A...............................TST..........401-37
Warren, John.....................................MV...........401-31
Warren, John H.................................NAV.........401-26
Warren, Joseph N..............................MV...........401-31
Warren, V. C......................................SR............401-108
Warren, William.................................TVG.........401-216
Warrington, Lewis W.........................TVG.........401-216
Warsham, Jack D..............................USV.........401-254
Wartenbach, F. C...............................LR............401-131
Warwick, V. V....................................SR............401-108
Wash, Debraugh O............................USV.........401-254
Washam, Oscar F..............................RR............401-65
Washington, Edward.........................TVG.........401-216
Washington, George..........................FF............401-140
Washington, Hardy............................TVG.........401-216
Washington, Isom P..........................TVG.........401-216
Washington, John.............................NAV.........401-26
Wasson, A. L.....................................LR............401-131
Wasson, Charles P............................RRR.........401-126
Wasson, Den.....................................TVG.........401-216
Wasson, Ed.......................................TVG.........401-216
Waters, D. E......................................USV.........401-254
Waters, E...SP............401-50
Waters, J...TVG.........401-216
Waters, J. S......................................TVG.........401-216
Waters, Ray......................................SR............401-108
Waters, Stephen Y............................USV.........401-254
Waties, J. R......................................USV.........401-254
Watkins, Benjamin F.........................TST..........401-37
Watkins, Claud..................................TVG.........401-216
Watkins, G. B....................................RR............401-65
Watkins, H. H....................................TVG.........401-216
Watkins, Henry..................................FF............401-140
Watkins, Homer J..............................TVG.........401-216
Watkins, Jack Hays...........................TVG.........401-216
Watkins, James A.............................TVG.........401-216
Watkins, John A................................SR............401-108
Watkins, Milton P..............................TST..........401-37
Watkins, Percy..................................TVG.........401-216
Watkins, Richard...............................USV.........401-254
Watkins, Richard H...........................NAV.........401-26
Watkins, Robert C.............................TVG.........401-216
Watkins, Robert C.............................USV.........401-254
Watkins, Stanley...............................USV.........401-254
Watkins, Thomas..............................RR............401-65
Watkins, Thomas..............................SR............401-108
Watkins, Thomas N..........................TVG.........401-216
Watkins, Tom....................................TVG.........401-216
Watkins, W. W...................................RR............401-65
Watkins, William M...........................USV.........401-254
Watrous, Charles Perry....................TVG.........401-216
Watson, A. C....................................SR............401-108
Watson, A. Gavin..............................TVG.........401-216
Watson, A. W....................................FB............401-176
Watson, Alexander............................FB............401-176
Watson, Alexander............................FB............401-176
Watson, C. C....................................USV.........401-254
Watson, Cress W..............................USV.........401-254
Watson, Daniel.................................TVG.........401-216
Watson, David R...............................USV.........401-254
Watson, G. B....................................USV.........401-254
Watson, German...............................TVG.........401-216
Watson, Green Bery.........................RRR.........401-126
Watson, Isaac...................................ARM........401-12
Watson, J. A.....................................SR............401-108
Watson, J. A.....................................FB............401-176
Watson, J. A. W................................FF............401-140
Watson, J. C.....................................USV.........401-254
Watson, J. H.....................................FB............401-176
Watson, Jacob B..............................FB............401-176
Watson, James.................................NAV.........401-26

Index to Texas Adjutant General Service Records—All Service Branches

Name	Branch	Record
Watson, James T.	SP	401-50
Watson, Jim M.	TVG	401-216
Watson, John	FF	401-140
Watson, O. S.	FB	401-176
Watson, Oscar J.	USV	401-254
Watson, Paul Luce	USV	401-254
Watson, Phillip	TVG	401-216
Watson, R. E.	SR	401-108
Watson, Robert	RR	401-65
Watson, Robert J.	USV	401-254
Watson, S. L.	RRR	401-126
Watson, T. G.	SR	401-108
Watson, Ted	SR	401-108
Watson, Thomas	TVG	401-216
Watson, Tom	SR	401-108
Watson, W. B.	NAV	401-26
Watson, W. Henry	SR	401-108
Watson, W. S.	SR	401-108
Watson, Will W.	SR	401-108
Watson, William	USV	401-254
Watson, William	USV	401-254
Watson, William M.	FF	401-140
Watson, William Madison	RRR	401-126
Watson, William W.	RRR	401-126
Wattles, Z. T.	FB	401-176
Watts, Albert B.	TVG	401-216
Watts, Archie	USV	401-254
Watts, Arthur P.	SR	401-108
Watts, Arthur P.	TVG	401-216
Watts, Arthur P.	USV	401-254
Watts, C. J.	LR	401-131
Watts, Charles Wesley	RRR	401-126
Watts, Claude De	USV	401-254
Watts, Edwin H.	TVG	401-216
Watts, Edwin H.	USV	401-254
Watts, Henry	SP	401-50
Watts, Herman	TVG	401-216
Watts, John Hill	TVG	401-216
Watts, John Hill	USV	401-254
Watts, R. V.	LR	401-131
Watts, Robert E.	USV	401-254
Watts, Sam T.	TVG	401-216
Watts, Taylor	SP	401-50
Watts, Thomas J.	TVG	401-216
Watts, W. P.	LR	401-131
Watts, Wiltz W.	USV	401-254
Waugh, Andrew M.	SR	401-108
Waugh, Sam	FB	401-176
Waugh, William A.	RR	401-65
Waut, W. J.	TVG	401-216
Wautzloeben, Frederick G.	USV	401-254
Way, J. R.	SR	401-108
Way, W. W.	SR	401-108
Wayborn, W. D.	FB	401-176
Wayborn, W. L.	FB	401-176
Wear, William	NAV	401-26
Wearzy, George	TVG	401-216
Wease, D. C.	SR	401-108
Weatherall, J. G.	RRR	401-126
Weatherall, J. G.	SR	401-108
Weatherby, Harper	SR	401-108
Weatherby, J. S.	SR	401-108
Weatherby, R. W.	SR	401-108
Weathered, Chas. D.	SR	401-108
Weatherford, Ion J.	TVG	401-216
Weatherford, W. W.	SR	401-108
Weatherford, William M.	USV	401-254
Weatherly, Edwin	SP	401-50
Weatherly, Jim	USV	401-254
Weatherred, David F.	TVG	401-216
Weatherred, T. P.	RRR	401-126
Weathers, Hactar J.	USV	401-254
Weathers, James P.	CSA	401-40
Weathers, Jasper M.	USV	401-254
Weathersby, Thomas J.	USV	401-254
Weathersby, W. W.	FB	401-176
Weaver, B. T.	SR	401-108
Weaver, B. W.	TVG	401-216
Weaver, Bud	RR	401-65
Weaver, Bud	RRR	401-126
Weaver, C. M.	SR	401-108
Weaver, Charlie	SR	401-108
Weaver, Claremore M.	RR	401-65
Weaver, David W.	TVG	401-216
Weaver, E. A.	RRR	401-126
Weaver, Frank "Cicero"	SR	401-108
Weaver, George W.	SP	401-50
Weaver, George W. L.	RR	401-65
Weaver, J. C., Sr.	RRR	401-126
Weaver, J. T.	FB	401-176
Weaver, J. W.	MV	401-31
Weaver, James Albert	TVG	401-216
Weaver, John	USV	401-254
Weaver, Leon	SR	401-108
Weaver, Matthew Z.	FB	401-176
Webb, Britain R.	SR	401-108
Webb, David Cornelius	RR	401-65
Webb, E. H.	SP	401-50
Webb, Francis B.	NAV	401-26
Webb, Grover C.	RR	401-65
Webb, Harry	TVG	401-216
Webb, J. C.	SR	401-108
Webb, J. D.	ARM	401-12
Webb, J. R.	LR	401-131
Webb, John	ARM	401-12
Webb, John Everett	SR	401-108
Webb, Lake	RR	401-65
Webb, Lucius A.	TVG	401-216
Webb, O. G.	SR	401-108
Webb, Otto T.	TVG	401-216
Webb, Peter S.	USV	401-254
Webb, Raymond H.	USV	401-254

Index to Texas Adjutant General Service Records—All Service Branches

Webb, Sanford C. .... SR 401-108
Webb, W. H. .... SP 401-50
Webb, W. P. .... SR 401-108
Webb, W. W. .... TVG 401-216
Webb, Walter Prescott .... SR 401-108
Webb, William .... FF 401-140
Webb, William .... USV 401-254
Webber, E. H. .... USV 401-254
Webber, Guy H. .... SR 401-108
Webber, John .... USV 401-254
Weber, Carl .... SR 401-108
Weber, Henry .... ARM 401-12
Weber, Henry V. .... TVG 401-216
Weber, J. W. .... TVG 401-216
Weber, William .... USV 401-254
Webster, A. S. .... CSA 401-40
Webster, C. H. .... RR 401-65
Webster, George W. .... MV 401-31
Webster, I. N. .... TVG 401-216
Webster, James S. .... SR 401-108
Webster, John .... ARM 401-12
Webster, Robert T. .... RRR 401-126
Wedekind, Heine .... NAV 401-26
Weed, Austin E. .... RRR 401-126
Weed, T. A. .... FB 401-176
Weeks, Dan G. .... USV 401-254
Weems, James .... FB 401-176
Weems, W. Z. .... RR 401-65
Weems, W. Z. .... SR 401-108
Weeren, C. .... TVG 401-216
Weeren, Ed. .... TVG 401-216
Weeren, Robert .... TVG 401-216
Weete, Benno .... USV 401-254
Weever, Thomas .... NAV 401-26
Wegemann, Fritz .... USV 401-254
Wegner, Charles .... FF 401-140
Wehmeyer, W. E. .... SR 401-108
Weickersheimmer, James P. .... USV 401-254
Weidenaur, Charles .... CSA 401-40
Weil, Bennie .... TVG 401-216
Weilbacher, J. E. .... TVG 401-216
Weimer, Christoph .... FF 401-140
Weimer, Edward C. .... TVG 401-216
Weimer, Edward C. .... USV 401-254
Weiner, Samuel H. .... FF 401-140
Weiner, Thomas .... USV 401-254
Weinert, Ferd. .... SR 401-108
Weinert, H. H. .... SR 401-108
Weingoff, George .... ARM 401-12
Weintz, John .... ARM 401-12
Weir, A. .... SP 401-50
Weir, T. C. .... RR 401-65
Weir, T. C. .... SR 401-108
Weiss, Charles H. .... USV 401-254
Weiss, Leon .... USV 401-254
Weiss, Ulysses .... TVG 401-216

Welborn, Bowen .... LR 401-131
Welborn, George S. .... TVG 401-216
Welborne, Bumpsia B. .... USV 401-254
Welch, C. H. .... FF 401-140
Welch, E. J. .... SR 401-108
Welch, Jim .... TVG 401-216
Welch, John .... ARM 401-12
Welch, John Randolph .... ARM 401-12
Welch, Joshua .... FF 401-140
Welch, Patrick .... NAV 401-26
Welch, W. T. .... FB 401-176
Welch, William .... NAV 401-26
Welcker, Daniel H. .... FF 401-140
Welcome, Frank .... TVG 401-216
Welder, R. .... FB 401-176
Weldon, A. A. .... SR 401-108
Weldon, C. H. .... TVG 401-216
Welhausen, G. A. .... FB 401-176
Welker, Mike .... USV 401-254
Wellborn, C. V. .... LR 401-131
Wellborn, Caleb .... ARM 401-12
Wellborn, George S. .... USV 401-254
Wellborn, H. F. .... FB 401-176
Wellborn, Marshall C. .... TVG 401-216
Wellbrock, J. J. .... FB 401-176
Welle, Alphonso .... TVG 401-216
Wellhousen, Henry J. .... USV 401-254
Wells, Charles S. .... TVG 401-216
Wells, Earl E. .... SR 401-108
Wells, Edward F. .... NAV 401-26
Wells, Ernest .... USV 401-254
Wells, F. T. .... NAV 401-26
Wells, F. W. .... FB 401-176
Wells, G. W. .... USV 401-254
Wells, H. J. .... FB 401-176
Wells, James B. .... NAV 401-26
Wells, L. B. .... FB 401-176
Wells, L. C. .... TVG 401-216
Wells, M. .... USV 401-254
Wells, Munroe .... RR 401-65
Wells, Norman L. .... USV 401-254
Wells, R. Q. .... USV 401-254
Wells, Rice .... USV 401-254
Wells, W. C. .... RRR 401-126
Wells, Wright C. .... RR 401-65
Welschmeyer, John G. .... ARM 401-12
Welsh, Edward .... NAV 401-26
Welsh, Frank .... FB 401-176
Welsh, Tom .... SR 401-108
Wendler, C. F. .... SP 401-50
Wendler, Kenneth S. .... SR 401-108
Wenz, Jacob .... FF 401-140
Wenz, L. A. .... USV 401-254
Wenzel, J. H. Fred .... TVG 401-216
Werder, J. W. .... USV 401-254
Werking, Jacob .... ARM 401-12

Index to Texas Adjutant General Service Records—All Service Branches

Name	Code	Ref
Werley, Jacob	FF	401-140
Werner, Albert E.	TVG	401-216
Werner, Andrew	FB	401-176
Werner, August	SP	401-50
Werner, Christian	FF	401-140
Werner, John R.	USV	401-254
Werner, John William	RRR	401-126
Werner, Max G.	SR	401-108
Werst, Oliver	USV	401-254
Wertheimer, S.	TVG	401-216
Wesp, Herman	USV	401-254
Wessarges, Adolf	USV	401-254
Wessell, Frederick	TVG	401-216
Wessendorff, T. A.	TVG	401-216
Wesson, Charles P.	USV	401-254
West, A. W.	SR	401-108
West, Albert, Jr.	RR	401-65
West, Anthoney	NAV	401-26
West, Arthur M.	TVG	401-216
West, Benjamin	RR	401-65
West, Buck	SR	401-108
West, C. R.	FB	401-176
West, Duval	TVG	401-216
West, Duval	USV	401-254
West, Eugene	SR	401-108
West, Eugene B.	USV	401-254
West, George F.	USV	401-254
West, George Thornton	TVG	401-216
West, George Thornton	USV	401-254
West, Gustav S.	FF	401-140
West, Harry L.	USV	401-254
West, Henry A.	USV	401-254
West, Ike	SR	401-108
West, J. B.	RRR	401-126
West, J. C.	TVG	401-216
West, J. Marion	SR	401-108
West, J. R.	TVG	401-216
West, James	MV	401-31
West, James M.	SR	401-108
West, L. E.	SR	401-108
West, M. A.	RR	401-65
West, M. C.	SR	401-108
West, M. V.	SR	401-108
West, Milton H.	SR	401-108
West, Milton V.	RR	401-65
West, Paul M.	RR	401-65
West, Pinckney E.	USV	401-254
West, R. S.	LR	401-131
West, Robert	ARM	401-12
West, W. P.	FB	401-176
West, W. R.	SR	401-108
West, Walter E.	USV	401-254
West, William [F.]	USV	401-254
West, William O.	USV	401-254
Westall, A. H.	TVG	401-216
Westall, E. L.	USV	401-254
Westbrook, A. L.	FB	401-176
Westbrook, Ed	SR	401-108
Westbrook, L. C.	RR	401-65
Westbrook, Tom M.	USV	401-254
Westeralt, H.	TVG	401-216
Westergard, Aage	USV	401-254
Westerhouse, John	TVG	401-216
Westerman, Henry	TST	401-38
Westervelt, J. D.	TVG	401-216
Westervelt, W. Deryee	TVG	401-216
Westgate, George V.	TVG	401-216
Westhausen, Herman	TVG	401-216
Westmoreland, Reid T.	TVG	401-216
Weston, A. G.	SR	401-108
Weston, A. G.	LR	401-131
Weston, Parker M.	RR	401-65
Westrope, Frederick N.	USV	401-254
Wetherell, Martie John	TVG	401-216
Wettermark, B. S.	TVG	401-216
Weyman, Edward A.	NAV	401-26
Weymiller, Thomas	FB	401-176
Weynorth, Henry E.	USV	401-254
Whalen, Edward	RR	401-65
Whalen, J. R.	USV	401-254
Whalen, James A.	USV	401-254
Whalen, Thomas	FF	401-140
Whaley, Bert	TVG	401-216
Whaley, Lucelius	USV	401-254
Whaley, T. E.	TVG	401-216
Wharton, E. L.	USV	401-254
Whatley, B. F.	RR	401-65
Whatley, George	LR	401-131
Whatley, H. B.	SR	401-108
Whatten, Howard	TVG	401-217
Whayne, A. T.	SR	401-108
Wheat, Allen	SR	401-108
Wheat, Allen	LR	401-131
Wheat, Edward E.	USV	401-254
Wheat, Eugene	TVG	401-217
Wheat, James	SP	401-50
Wheat, James W.	USV	401-254
Wheat, Mack	USV	401-254
Wheat, W. H.	FB	401-176
Wheatley, George A.	FB	401-176
Wheatley, George A.	TVG	401-217
Wheatley, George A.	USV	401-254
Wheatley, J. B.	RR	401-65
Wheatly, Walter S.	CSA	401-40
Wheeldon, C. H.	TVG	401-217
Wheeler, A. G.	TVG	401-217
Wheeler, A. H.	TVG	401-217
Wheeler, D. A.	SR	401-108
Wheeler, D. C.	SR	401-108
Wheeler, Frank	USV	401-254
Wheeler, Harry H.	USV	401-254
Wheeler, J. L.	SP	401-50

Index to Texas Adjutant General Service Records—All Service Branches

Wheeler, J. R. .... SR 401-108
Wheeler, J. V. .... FB 401-176
Wheeler, J. W. .... RR 401-65
Wheeler, James H. .... NAV 401-27
Wheeler, James Moncrief .... TVG 401-217
Wheeler, James Samuel .... TVG 401-217
Wheeler, Joel Robert .... RRR 401-126
Wheeler, Joel S. .... FB 401-176
Wheeler, John H. .... USV 401-254
Wheeler, M. W. .... TVG 401-217
Wheeler, Peter .... SP 401-50
Wheeler, Richard .... FB 401-176
Wheeler, Royal T. .... TST 401-38
Wheeler, Thomas .... ARM 401-12
Wheeler, William C. .... MM 401-32
Wheeless, John G. .... USV 401-254
Wheeley, J. A. .... USV 401-254
Wheelis, Thos. P. .... RRR 401-126
Wheelock, John .... ARM 401-12
Wheelock, R. L. .... SR 401-108
Wheelwright, George .... NAV 401-27
Whelan, D. M. .... FB 401-176
Whelan, Patrick .... SP 401-50
Whelan, Thomas .... FB 401-176
Whetstone, Marion N. .... USV 401-254
Whickline, George .... FF 401-140
Whipple, A. W. .... SP 401-50
Whisenant, M. .... LR 401-131
Whisnand, Bert .... RR 401-65
Whitacre, John Sylvester .... FB 401-176
Whitaker, A. W. .... TVG 401-217
Whitaker, F. A. .... ARM 401-12
Whitaker, Guest .... USV 401-254
Whitaker, Harrison Morris .... TVG 401-217
Whitaker, Harrison Morris .... USV 401-254
Whitaker, J. C. .... FF 401-140
Whitaker, Larkin M. .... MV 401-31
Whitaker, Willis .... TVG 401-217
Whitburn, Charles .... USV 401-254
Whitcomb, George .... NAV 401-27
Whitcomb, Walter B. .... TVG 401-217
Whitcomb, Walter B. .... USV 401-254
White, A. H. .... ARM 401-12
White, B. F. .... TVG 401-217
White, B. S. .... RR 401-65
White, Ben .... SR 401-108
White, Benj. J. .... ARM 401-12
White, Buck .... SR 401-108
White, C. A. .... SR 401-108
White, C. M. .... TVG 401-217
White, Charles .... ARM 401-12
White, Charles L. .... NAV 401-27
White, Charlie .... SR 401-108
White, Coley C. .... SR 401-108
White, Dabney .... FB 401-176
White, Daniel .... NAV 401-27
White, Daniel .... ARM 401-12
White, David .... ARM 401-12
White, Dudley, Jr. .... SR 401-108
White, E. D. .... TVG 401-217
White, E. L. .... SR 401-108
White, Ebenezer .... NAV 401-27
White, Edward L. .... USV 401-254
White, Emmett .... RR 401-65
White, Ernest H. .... USV 401-254
White, Ezekiel .... RR 401-65
White, F. W. .... TVG 401-217
White, Fountain W. .... USV 401-254
White, Francis W. .... ARM 401-12
White, Fred .... SP 401-50
White, George .... FF 401-140
White, George V. .... USV 401-254
White, George W. .... NAV 401-27
White, Goff .... RR 401-65
White, H. .... FB 401-176
White, H. A. .... TVG 401-217
White, H. L. .... SR 401-108
White, Harold .... RRR 401-126
White, Harry A. .... USV 401-254
White, Homer .... RR 401-65
White, Isaac E. .... USV 401-254
White, J. D. .... RR 401-65
White, J. M. .... CSA 401-40
White, J. Will .... LR 401-131
White, Jack .... USV 401-254
White, James .... ARM 401-12
White, James .... RRR 401-126
White, James .... SR 401-108
White, James .... USV 401-254
White, James C. .... RR 401-65
White, James D. .... USV 401-254
White, James G. .... ARM 401-12
White, James L. .... FB 401-176
White, James S. .... ARM 401-12
White, Jared S. .... USV 401-254
White, Jasper .... RRR 401-126
White, Jesse .... ARM 401-12
White, Jno. M. .... ARM 401-12
White, Joe .... SR 401-108
White, Joe W. .... RR 401-65
White, Joe W. .... SR 401-108
White, John .... ARM 401-12
White, John .... SP 401-50
White, John B. .... MV 401-31
White, John D. .... USV 401-254
White, John L. .... CSA 401-40
White, John L. .... USV 401-254
White, John N. .... USV 401-254
White, John R. .... USV 401-254
White, Karl Kirk .... USV 401-254
White, Leslie G. .... TVG 401-217
White, Levy W. .... ARM 401-12

Index to Texas Adjutant General Service Records—All Service Branches

Name	Branch	Record
White, P. A.	FB	401-176
White, P. J.	SP	401-50
White, Paul	SR	401-108
White, Pleasant L.	FB	401-176
White, R. S.	TVG	401-217
White, Robert H.	TVG	401-217
White, Robert M.	RR	401-65
White, S. F.	FB	401-176
White, Sam'l. A.	ARM	401-12
White, Samuel M.	USV	401-254
White, Stephen	ARM	401-12
White, T. F.	SP	401-50
White, T. J.	TVG	401-217
White, T. J.	FB	401-176
White, Thomas B.	RR	401-65
White, Thomas Bruce	SR	401-108
White, Tom	TVG	401-217
White, V.	TVG	401-217
White, Vandyke	TVG	401-217
White, Vardie C.	USV	401-254
White, W. D.	CSA	401-40
White, W. R.	SR	401-108
White, W. T.	ARM	401-12
White, Wallace W.	TVG	401-217
White, William	NAV	401-27
White, William M.	ARM	401-12
White, William O.	TVG	401-217
White, Willie S.	USV	401-254
Whiteacre, B. M.	SR	401-108
Whiteaker, W. R.	TVG	401-217
Whiteaker, W. R.	USV	401-254
Whitefield, B. W.	LR	401-131
Whitehead, Augustin R.	FB	401-176
Whitehead, Edward P.	ARM	401-12
Whitehead, John P. C.	FB	401-176
Whitehead, L. K.	TVG	401-217
Whitehead, R. L.	TVG	401-217
Whitehorn, T. D.	SR	401-108
Whiteker, B. M.	LR	401-131
Whiteman, J.	CSA	401-40
Whitenton, W. M.	RRR	401-126
Whiteside, J. J.	ARM	401-12
Whiteside, John	FF	401-140
Whiteside, John	SP	401-50
Whitfield, J. D.	USV	401-254
Whitfield, Robert Wilkins	SR	401-108
Whitfield, W.	NAV	401-27
Whitford, Charles	USV	401-254
Whitham, C. E.	RRR	401-126
Whiting, Thomas J.	RR	401-65
Whitis, F. C.	TVG	401-217
Whitley, F. E.	RRR	401-126
Whitley, George O.	USV	401-254
Whitley, Oscar	TVG	401-217
Whitley, Robert S.	USV	401-254
Whitley, Theo J.	FB	401-176
Whitley, Thomas E.	TVG	401-217
Whitley, William E.	RR	401-65
Whitlock, Robert	ARM	401-12
Whitlow, D. W.	TVG	401-217
Whitman, M. C.	RRR	401-126
Whitman, W. B.	TVG	401-217
Whitman, W. J.	SR	401-108
Whitmore, Charles	NAV	401-27
Whitmore, Ed	TVG	401-217
Whitney, Frank	SP	401-50
Whitney, J. F.	SP	401-50
Whitney, Robert G.	ARM	401-12
Whitsett, Taylor	FB	401-176
Whitsitt, Lawton	USV	401-254
Whittaker, Herbert C.	USV	401-254
Whitteberg, Ernst	TVG	401-217
Whitteberg, F. A.	SR	401-108
Whittemore, James W.	NAV	401-27
Whittenberg, J. L.	RR	401-65
Whittington, A. G.	SR	401-108
Whittington, Gabe	SR	401-108
Whittington, John	FB	401-176
Whittington, John W.	USV	401-254
Whittington, Nat	USV	401-254
Whittington, William	TST	401-38
Whittington, William C.	USV	401-254
Whittle, W. D.	FF	401-140
Whitwell, J. O.	SR	401-108
Whitworth, J. B.	FB	401-176
Wiard, Seth	SR	401-108
Wicker, George T.	SR	401-108
Wickes, Percy E.	TVG	401-217
Wickliffe, Joseph	ARM	401-12
Wicks, Charles	FB	401-176
Wicks, Marshall	TVG	401-217
Wicks, Thomas E.	TVG	401-217
Wickson, Dyrun	ARM	401-12
Wickson, M. B.	FB	401-176
Wiedemann, Ernest	TVG	401-217
Wiedmann, Edwd.	ARM	401-12
Wiener, Jake	SR	401-108
Wier, A. S.	SR	401-109
Wier, Frank L.	SR	401-109
Wiese, John	TVG	401-217
Wiess, Chas. T.	SR	401-109
Wiggins, Allen	USV	401-254
Wiggins, Allen T.	USV	401-254
Wiggins, Charlie	TVG	401-217
Wiggins, Earl	TVG	401-217
Wiggins, George W.	USV	401-254
Wiggins, Harbard	ARM	401-12
Wiggins, Hugh L.	SP	401-50
Wiggins, Jasper	USV	401-254
Wiggins, John B.	USV	401-255
Wiggins, Jules A.	USV	401-255
Wiggins, Mason	SR	401-109

Index to Texas Adjutant General Service Records—All Service Branches

Name	Branch	Record
Wiggins, Thomas	ARM	401-12
Wiggins, Tom E.	TVG	401-217
Wight, L. L.	MM	401-32
Wightman, Charles R.	FB	401-176
Wightman, J. S.	TVG	401-217
Wigley, Willard R.	SR	401-109
Wigman, Edward A.	NAV	401-27
Wilbanks, Judson L.	USV	401-255
Wilber, Daniel C.	NAV	401-27
Wilbern, Andrew M.	SR	401-109
Wilborn, Neal	FB	401-176
Wilbourne, William S.	USV	401-255
Wilbur, Walter H.	USV	401-255
Wilburn, Felix G.	MV	401-31
Wilburn, Joel	ARM	401-12
Wilcox, Charles	ARM	401-12
Wilcox, George	SP	401-50
Wilcox, Sanford	ARM	401-12
Wilcox, W.	RR	401-65
Wildenthal, B., Jr.	LR	401-131
Wilder, A. Mac	TVG	401-217
Wilder, Altus	TVG	401-217
Wilder, James M.	USV	401-255
Wilder, Jesse	NAV	401-27
Wilder, W. H.	RRR	401-126
Wilder, W. L.	FB	401-176
Wilder, William	FB	401-176
Wildy, Samuel	ARM	401-12
Wile, Henry	SR	401-109
Wiles, C. S.	SR	401-109
Wiley, Andrew	TVG	401-217
Wiley, Andrew P.	TVG	401-217
Wiley, Clark Johnson	TVG	401-217
Wiley, J. Horatio	USV	401-255
Wiley, John N.	ARM	401-12
Wiley, Samuel	USV	401-255
Wiley, W. W.	FB	401-177
Wilhelm, Clifford T.	USV	401-255
Wilhelm, Frank C.	USV	401-255
Wilhite, Fielding E.	USV	401-255
Wilhoit, A. J.	FF	401-140
Wilhoit, A. J.	FB	401-177
Wilke, W. E.	USV	401-255
Wilkerson, Charles Scott	TVG	401-217
Wilkerson, Charles Scott	USV	401-255
Wilkerson, Dee P.	USV	401-255
Wilkerson, Ed	SP	401-50
Wilkerson, Thomas	TVG	401-217
Wilkerson, W.	TVG	401-217
Wilkerson, W.	FB	401-177
Wilkerson, W. M.	TVG	401-217
Wilkes, C. M.	FB	401-177
Wilkes, Frank	USV	401-255
Wilkes, Frank C.	CSA	401-40
Wilkes, H. M.	FB	401-177
Wilkes, Mark	NAV	401-27
Wilkes, Rex	TVG	401-217
Wilkes, Roy T.	USV	401-255
Wilkins, B. B.	USV	401-255
Wilkins, Charles	TVG	401-217
Wilkins, Charles L.	TVG	401-217
Wilkins, Horace M.	TVG	401-217
Wilkins, J. D.	TVG	401-217
Wilkins, John	TST	401-38
Wilkins, John	RR	401-65
Wilkins, John	ARM	401-12
Wilkins, John B.	TVG	401-217
Wilkins, Simon P.	TVG	401-217
Wilkins, Simon P.	USV	401-255
Wilkins, Tom B.	USV	401-255
Wilkins, Wilhugh	TVG	401-217
Wilkinson, Arthur	TVG	401-217
Wilkinson, C. C.	TVG	401-217
Wilkinson, Calvin B.	USV	401-255
Wilkinson, Calvin B.	USV	401-255
Wilkinson, David	ARM	401-12
Wilkinson, E. C.	TVG	401-217
Wilkinson, H. J.	SR	401-109
Wilkinson, James	ARM	401-12
Wilkinson, James G.	ARM	401-12
Wilkinson, John	ARM	401-12
Wilkinson, Joseph M.	USV	401-255
Wilkinson, Thaddeus A.	USV	401-255
Wilkinson, Wiley	ARM	401-12
Wilkite, J. T.	SR	401-109
Wilks, B. T.	FB	401-177
Wilks, Mark	ARM	401-12
Wilks, U. B. T.	FB	401-177
Willacy, John G.	TVG	401-217
Willand, Charles L.	USV	401-255
Willard, Tim	SR	401-109
Willburn, John D.	MV	401-31
Willcox, Berry J.	USV	401-255
Willeford, C. H.	SR	401-109
Willeford, John W.	TVG	401-217
Willett, Frank	SR	401-109
Williams, A. J.	RRR	401-126
Williams, A. Jackson	USV	401-255
Williams, Alex S.	USV	401-255
Williams, Andrew	SP	401-50
Williams, B. A.	TVG	401-217
Williams, B. E.	SR	401-109
Williams, B. H.	SP	401-50
Williams, Ben	SR	401-109
Williams, Burnet E.	TVG	401-217
Williams, C. A.	SR	401-109
Williams, Caleb T.	RR	401-65
Williams, Caloway	USV	401-255
Williams, Charles	FB	401-177
Williams, Charles	FB	401-177
Williams, Charles	MV	401-31
Williams, Charles	SR	401-109

Index to Texas Adjutant General Service Records—All Service Branches

Williams, Charles	TVG 401-217	Williams, James W.	USV 401-255
Williams, Charles A.	RR 401-65	Williams, Jim M.	RR 401-65
Williams, Charles C.	SP 401-50	Williams, John	NAV 401-27
Williams, David	NAV 401-27	Williams, John	RR 401-65
Williams, E. W.	TVG 401-217	Williams, John	SP 401-50
Williams, Ed	SR 401-109	Williams, John	USV 401-255
Williams, Ed	TVG 401-217	Williams, John	USV 401-255
Williams, Ed	TVG 401-217	Williams, John A.	TVG 401-217
Williams, Edgar W.	USV 401-255	Williams, John A.	USV 401-255
Williams, Elvin W.	RR 401-65	Williams, John D.	TST 401-38
Williams, Eugene	RRR 401-126	Williams, John F.	USV 401-255
Williams, Eugene	TVG 401-217	Williams, John H.	RR 401-65
Williams, Eugene	USV 401-255	Williams, John H.	SP 401-50
Williams, Evan	NAV 401-27	Williams, John R.	RR 401-65
Williams, F. M.	SP 401-50	Williams, John T.	RR 401-65
Williams, F. W.	SR 401-109	Williams, John T.	USV 401-255
Williams, Frank	USV 401-255	Williams, John W.	SP 401-50
Williams, Fred	TVG 401-217	Williams, Jordan B.	USV 401-255
Williams, Fred	USV 401-255	Williams, Joseph D.	USV 401-255
Williams, Fred M.	TVG 401-217	Williams, Larnce	TVG 401-217
Williams, Frederic Lee	TVG 401-217	Williams, Leon Dudley	SR 401-109
Williams, G. R.	SR 401-109	Williams, Morris	TVG 401-217
Williams, George	FB 401-177	Williams, Nat	TVG 401-217
Williams, George	CSA 401-40	Williams, Nathaniel	USV 401-255
Williams, George	NAV 401-27	Williams, Noland G.	RR 401-65
Williams, George	TVG 401-217	Williams, Norton	RR 401-65
Williams, George	TVG 401-217	Williams, Norton	RRR 401-126
Williams, George B.	USV 401-255	Williams, Owen M.	USV 401-255
Williams, George S.	TVG 401-217	Williams, R. C.	RR 401-65
Williams, George T.	TVG 401-217	Williams, R. D.	SR 401-109
Williams, George W.	RR 401-65	Williams, Reid	TVG 401-217
Williams, Gordon	USV 401-255	Williams, Richard	FF 401-140
Williams, H. B.	MV 401-31	Williams, Richard	TVG 401-217
Williams, H. F.	TVG 401-217	Williams, Roy S.	SR 401-109
Williams, H. L.	TVG 401-217	Williams, S. M.	TVG 401-217
Williams, H. P.	TVG 401-217	Williams, S. N.	TVG 401-217
Williams, Harrison P.	TVG 401-217	Williams, Sam	USV 401-255
Williams, Harry Frank	SR 401-109	Williams, Searcy H.	TVG 401-217
Williams, Henry	USV 401-255	Williams, Sim M.	RR 401-65
Williams, Henry R.	TVG 401-217	Williams, T. J.	SP 401-50
Williams, Henry S.	ARM 401-12	Williams, T. S.	SP 401-50
Williams, Henry T.	RR 401-65	Williams, T. V.	RR 401-65
Williams, J. B.	USV 401-255	Williams, T. W.	TVG 401-217
Williams, J. F.	SP 401-50	Williams, T. W.	LR 401-131
Williams, J. G.	TVG 401-217	Williams, Thomas	TST 401-38
Williams, J. H.	RRR 401-126	Williams, Thomas	SP 401-50
Williams, J. H.	TVG 401-217	Williams, Thomas	TVG 401-217
Williams, J. H.	TVG 401-217	Williams, Tom	SR 401-109
Williams, J. J.	LR 401-131	Williams, Tom	TVG 401-217
Williams, J. S.	FB 401-177	Williams, W. C.	TVG 401-217
Williams, James B.	TVG 401-217	Williams, W. E.	TVG 401-217
Williams, James Lee	RRR 401-126	Williams, W. H.	TVG 401-217
Williams, James H.	FB 401-177	Williams, W. L.	SR 401-109
Williams, James P.	FB 401-177	Williams, W. S.	USV 401-255
Williams, James R.	USV 401-255	Williams, Walker	SR 401-109
Williams, James T.	FB 401-177	Williams, Walter	ARM 401-12

Index to Texas Adjutant General Service Records—All Service Branches

Name	Branch	Record
Williams, Walter D.	USV	401-255
Williams, Walter L.	SR	401-109
Williams, Walter T.	USV	401-255
Williams, William	FB	401-177
Williams, William	ARM	401-12
Williams, William	SR	401-109
Williams, William B.	USV	401-255
Williams, William L.	RR	401-65
Williams, William N.	USV	401-255
Williams, Willie	TVG	401-217
Williamson, C. E.	RRR	401-126
Williamson, C. E.	SR	401-109
Williamson, C. E.	TVG	401-217
Williamson, E. R.	SR	401-109
Williamson, Frank	SR	401-109
Williamson, Fred L.	TVG	401-217
Williamson, Fuller	RRR	401-126
Williamson, Fuller	SR	401-109
Williamson, G. H.	SR	401-109
Williamson, J. E.	SR	401-109
Williamson, James R.	TVG	401-217
Williamson, John W.	NAV	401-27
Williamson, Joseph	NAV	401-27
Williamson, Joseph	ARM	401-12
Williamson, L. E.	FB	401-177
Williamson, L. M.	TVG	401-217
Williamson, P. B.	TVG	401-217
Williamson, P. D.	TVG	401-217
Williamson, Silas B.	USV	401-255
Williamson, Thomas	TVG	401-217
Williamson, Vollie F.	USV	401-255
Williamson, William	ARM	401-12
Williamson, William H.	SR	401-109
Williamson, William L.	NAV	401-27
Williford, Frank, Jr.	SR	401-109
Williford, Henry	USV	401-255
Williford, Horace	TVG	401-217
Willingham, O. A.	RRR	401-126
Willingham, Oscar R.	USV	401-255
Willis, Albert E.	USV	401-255
Willis, Benj.	ARM	401-12
Willis, C. C.	RRR	401-126
Willis, C. C.	LR	401-131
Willis, C. E.	LR	401-131
Willis, Charles	FB	401-177
Willis, Charles	NAV	401-27
Willis, Chris C.	RR	401-65
Willis, Claude R.	USV	401-255
Willis, F. D.	SR	401-109
Willis, George R.	SR	401-109
Willis, J. Bradley	SR	401-109
Willis, Lon L.	RR	401-65
Willis, Lon L.	SR	401-109
Willis, M. C.	SR	401-109
Willis, M. D.	TVG	401-217
Willis, M. F.	SR	401-109
Willis, M. P.	SR	401-109
Willis, R. T.	TVG	401-217
Willis, Robert G.	USV	401-255
Willis, Samuel B.	USV	401-255
Willis, William	SP	401-50
Willoughby, Bert Edward	SR	401-109
Willoughby, W. H.	SR	401-109
Willow, Walter C.	ARM	401-12
Willrich, George	USV	401-255
Wills, George W.	NAV	401-27
Wills, William	NAV	401-27
Willson, C. W.	TVG	401-217
Willson, John W.	SP	401-50
Willson, Sam A.	FB	401-177
Willy, Albert S.	USV	401-255
Wilmath, T. J.	RR	401-65
Wilmeth, W. C.	RR	401-65
Wilmore, T. N.	FB	401-177
Wilmoth, John B.	LR	401-131
Wilmoth, John Henry	RRR	401-126
Wilmoth, W. D.	RRR	401-126
Wilson, A. F.	TVG	401-217
Wilson, A. J.	FF	401-140
Wilson, A. J.	TVG	401-217
Wilson, Allee	TVG	401-217
Wilson, Andres	FB	401-177
Wilson, Andrew	FF	401-140
Wilson, Andy E.	TVG	401-217
Wilson, Arthur F.	USV	401-255
Wilson, Asa C.	TVG	401-217
Wilson, C. G.	USV	401-255
Wilson, C. L.	TVG	401-217
Wilson, Charles	FB	401-177
Wilson, Charles	ARM	401-12
Wilson, Charles	TVG	401-217
Wilson, Clarence	TVG	401-217
Wilson, Collie L.	USV	401-255
Wilson, Cyrus M.	SP	401-50
Wilson, D. J.	RRR	401-126
Wilson, D. R.	RRR	401-126
Wilson, E.	FB	401-177
Wilson, E. H.	TVG	401-217
Wilson, E. M.	SR	401-109
Wilson, E. M.	TVG	401-218
Wilson, E. M.	LR	401-131
Wilson, E. S.	FB	401-177
Wilson, Edgar	SR	401-109
Wilson, Elisha	FB	401-177
Wilson, Eugene J.	SR	401-109
Wilson, Francis	NAV	401-27
Wilson, George C.	TVG	401-218
Wilson, George N.	SR	401-109
Wilson, George T.	USV	401-255
Wilson, H. Baylor	USV	401-255
Wilson, H. C.	FB	401-177
Wilson, H. G.	TVG	401-218

Index to Texas Adjutant General Service Records—All Service Branches

Wilson, H. L. ....SR............401-109
Wilson, H. W. ....SR............401-109
Wilson, Harold L. ....RRR 401-126
Wilson, Henry B. ....TVG 401-218
Wilson, Hillsman D. ....LR 401-131
Wilson, Homer K. ....TVG 401-218
Wilson, Homer W. ....RR 401-65
Wilson, J. C. ....NAV 401-27
Wilson, J. C. ....TST 401-38
Wilson, J. C. ....TVG 401-218
Wilson, J. D. ....TVG 401-218
Wilson, J. Frank ....SR............401-109
Wilson, J. M. ....RRR 401-126
Wilson, J. O. ....TVG 401-218
Wilson, J. P. H. ....FB.............401-177
Wilson, J. T. ....FB.............401-177
Wilson, J. T. ....FF 401-140
Wilson, J. W. ....SP 401-50
Wilson, J. W. ....SR............401-109
Wilson, Jace ....MV 401-31
Wilson, James ....NAV 401-27
Wilson, James ....FF 401-140
Wilson, James C. ....USV 401-255
Wilson, James E. ....USV 401-255
Wilson, James M. ....FB.............401-177
Wilson, Jesse ....SR............401-109
Wilson, Jesse C. ....USV 401-255
Wilson, Joe ....SR............401-109
Wilson, John ....NAV 401-27
Wilson, John ....ARM 401-12
Wilson, John Henry ....USV 401-255
Wilson, John M. ....TVG 401-218
Wilson, John W. ....ARM 401-12
Wilson, John W. ....USV 401-255
Wilson, Joseph H. ....TVG 401-218
Wilson, L. C. ....RR 401-65
Wilson, Lee ....FB.............401-177
Wilson, Lenord ....TVG 401-218
Wilson, Leonard ....TVG 401-218
Wilson, Mack ....SP 401-50
Wilson, Maple ....SR............401-109
Wilson, O. J. ....SR............401-109
Wilson, P. A. ....SP 401-50
Wilson, P. H. ....TVG 401-218
Wilson, R. C. ....SR............401-109
Wilson, Robert ....ARM 401-12
Wilson, Robert ....FF 401-140
Wilson, Robert E. ....TVG 401-218
Wilson, Robert E. ....USV 401-255
Wilson, Robert H. ....NAV 401-27
Wilson, Robert Lovel ....RRR 401-126
Wilson, S. N. ....FB.............401-177
Wilson, Samuel ....TVG 401-218
Wilson, Samuel O. ....USV 401-255
Wilson, T. B. ....FB.............401-177
Wilson, T. E. ....TVG 401-218
Wilson, T. J. ....TVG 401-218
Wilson, T. W. ....TVG 401-218
Wilson, Tandy ....USV 401-255
Wilson, Thomas ....NAV 401-27
Wilson, Thomas C. ....RR 401-65
Wilson, Thomas F. ....SR............401-109
Wilson, Thomas G. ....USV 401-255
Wilson, V. C. ....FB.............401-177
Wilson, Van C. ....TVG 401-218
Wilson, W. ....RRR 401-126
Wilson, W. A. ....FB.............401-177
Wilson, W. B. ....SR............401-109
Wilson, W. D. ....FF 401-140
Wilson, W. L. ....FB.............401-177
Wilson, Walter ....SR............401-109
Wilson, Walter ....TVG 401-218
Wilson, Walter B. ....USV 401-255
Wilson, Walter E. ....USV 401-255
Wilson, Will F. ....TVG 401-218
Wilson, William ....NAV 401-27
Wilson, William C. ....RR 401-65
Wilson, William C. ....USV 401-255
Wilson, William W., Jr. ....SR............401-109
Wily, Samuel ....ARM 401-12
Wimberly, J. B. ....FF 401-140
Wimberly, Jules ....USV 401-255
Wimbish, J. A. H. ....FB.............401-177
Winchester, Nelson W. ....ARM 401-12
Winder, M. R. ....SR............401-109
Winder, R. D. ....SR............401-109
Winders, William L. ....USV 401-255
Windham, Page S. ....FB.............401-177
Windham, Warren ....USV 401-255
Windham, William C. ....LR 401-131
Windrow, J. M. ....TVG 401-218
Windrow, Mercer J. ....USV 401-255
Windsor, James B. ....SR............401-109
Winebrenner, John ....SR............401-109
Winfield, J. B. ....SR............401-109
Winfield, M. ....SP 401-50
Winfree, Edwin H. ....LR 401-131
Winfree, Joseph Edwin, Jr. ....SR............401-109
Winfree, Raymond J. ....USV 401-255
Winfrey, Jack ....SR............401-109
Wing, A. ....FB.............401-177
Wing, C. L. ....ARM 401-12
Wing, E. H. ....FB.............401-177
Wingren, E. P. ....TVG 401-218
Wingren, Otto ....TVG 401-218
Winkel, H. ....RR 401-65
Winkle, Henry ....MV 401-31
Winkler, A. J. ....FF 401-140
Winkler, L. B. ....TVG 401-218
Winkler, Walton C. ....USV 401-255
Winn, Claude C. ....USV 401-255
Winn, J. H. ....FB.............401-177

Index to Texas Adjutant General Service Records—All Service Branches

Name	Branch	Record
Winn, Peter B., Jr.	RR	401-65
Winn, Phil A.	RR	401-65
Winnett, George W.	USV	401-255
Winscoatte, W. B.	RR	401-65
Winslow, Frank D.	SR	401-109
Winslow, Henry F.	FB	401-177
Winslow, John J.	USV	401-255
Winston, B. H.	FB	401-177
Winston, E. E.	SR	401-109
Winston, Samuel C.	FB	401-177
Winston, William	USV	401-255
Winter, George W.	TVG	401-218
Winter, George W.	USV	401-255
Winter, L. C.	RRR	401-126
Winter, W. E.	TST	401-38
Winters, Howard	LR	401-131
Winters, James W.	TST	401-38
Winters, Raymond W.	USV	401-255
Winters, Terrell	MM	401-32
Winzeuried, G.	USV	401-255
Wipff, John M.	SP	401-50
Wipprecht, Rudolph	TVG	401-218
Wisby, Ernest E.	SR	401-109
Wisdom, Andrew J.	MV	401-31
Wisdom, J. L.	RR	401-65
Wise, C. W.	USV	401-255
Wise, J. M.	FB	401-177
Wise, W. M.	RRR	401-126
Wisecarve, William H.	USV	401-255
Wiseman, P. M.	USV	401-255
Wisener, J. W.	TVG	401-218
Wisner, Henry B.	USV	401-255
Wissinger, Fred	USV	401-255
Wisterzil, William	TVG	401-218
Withereys, M. L.	SR	401-109
Withers, A.	NAV	401-27
Withers, Lewis V.	SR	401-109
Withers, W. T.	FF	401-140
Withers, W. T.	FB	401-177
Withof, Fredrick	FF	401-140
Withoft, Charles	FF	401-140
Witney, Stanislaus	FF	401-140
Witt, E. B.	SR	401-109
Witt, Frank	TVG	401-218
Witt, J. C.	RR	401-65
Witt, J. W.	FB	401-177
Witt, John C.	FB	401-177
Witt, Sam P.	RR	401-65
Witt, Sam P.	SR	401-109
Witt, William Henry	FB	401-177
Wittat, Robert	NAV	401-27
Witteborg, Edward A.	USV	401-255
Witter, Tully	SR	401-109
Witter, Tully L.	RRR	401-126
Wittig, Joseph	TVG	401-218
Wittrock, Albert W.	USV	401-255
Woelber, A. H.	RR	401-65
Wofford, D. W.	LR	401-131
Wofford, James R.	FB	401-177
Wofford, Joe	SP	401-50
Wofford, John T.	TVG	401-218
Wofford, Joseph H.	USV	401-255
Wofford, William F.	LR	401-131
Wolcott, Reuben	ARM	401-12
Wolf, A. L.	SR	401-109
Wolf, Carl M.	SR	401-109
Wolf, Charles, Jr.	SR	401-109
Wolf, Chas.	SR	401-109
Wolf, E. N.	FB	401-177
Wolf, George	SR	401-109
Wolf, Ike	TVG	401-218
Wolf, J. A.	SR	401-109
Wolf, Jacob	ARM	401-12
Wolf, Joe	TVG	401-218
Wolf, Sam D.	TVG	401-218
Wolf, Saul	SR	401-109
Wolf, W. M.	RR	401-65
Wolfe, Frank	SR	401-110
Wolfe, J. A.	FB	401-177
Wolfe, O. P.	SR	401-110
Wolfe, O. P.	SR	401-110
Wolfe, O. P.	LR	401-131
Wolfe, Paul A.	SR	401-110
Wolfe, Thomas J.	USV	401-255
Wolfe, W. E.	SR	401-110
Wolff, John Jacob	ARM	401-12
Wolford, H. F., Dr.	SR	401-110
Woliuski, Ben	TVG	401-218
Wolten, John	RR	401-65
Wolters, J. F.	USV	401-255
Wolters, Jacob F.	SR	401-110
Womack, C. I.	USV	401-255
Womack, F. B.	TVG	401-218
Womack, Gaston	CSA	401-40
Womack, Henry F.	USV	401-255
Womack, Thomas	USV	401-255
Womack, William	MV	401-31
Womble, Romulo	FB	401-177
Wonsley, David W.	FB	401-177
Wood, C. C.	FB	401-177
Wood, Carl	RR	401-65
Wood, Chester	TVG	401-218
Wood, D. W.	LR	401-131
Wood, Duke	TVG	401-218
Wood, Edd	TVG	401-218
Wood, F. E.	RRR	401-126
Wood, Fred T.	SR	401-110
Wood, George W.	MM	401-32
Wood, Harold Chester	TVG	401-218
Wood, Harold Chester	USV	401-255
Wood, Ira	SR	401-110
Wood, J. B.	SR	401-110

Index to Texas Adjutant General Service Records—All Service Branches

Wood, J. B. ....TVG 401-218
Wood, J. H. ....SP............401-50
Wood, J. T. ....FB............401-177
Wood, James.................................TVG 401-218
Wood, James D..............................USV 401-255
Wood, James Gillam......................RRR 401-126
Wood, James Gilliam ....SR............401-110
Wood, James Henry......................FF 401-140
Wood, James P. ....SP............401-50
Wood, Jim.....................................TST 401-38
Wood, John...................................ARM 401-12
Wood, John M. ....RR............401-65
Wood, Joseph ....FB............401-177
Wood, Joseph S. ....RR............401-65
Wood, Lawrence B........................MV 401-31
Wood, Lewis N..............................USV 401-255
Wood, Lionel B. ....USV 401-255
Wood, M. K. ....USV 401-255
Wood, Mandred............................NAV........401-27
Wood, Nev V. ....USV 401-255
Wood, R. C. ....SP............401-50
Wood, R. H. ....SR............401-110
Wood, Robert Bruce.....................TVG 401-218
Wood, Royce C. ....SR............401-110
Wood, S. J. ....MV 401-31
Wood, S. J. ....SR............401-110
Wood, Samuel ....ARM 401-12
Wood, Samuel Mohon..................SR............401-110
Wood, Spurgeon H. ....RRR 401-126
Wood, T. C. ....SR............401-110
Wood, Thomas ....NAV........401-27
Wood, Thomas J...........................MM 401-32
Wood, Tom...................................USV 401-255
Wood, William W. ....USV 401-255
Woodall, G. M. ....TVG 401-218
Woodall, Robert Henry................RRR 401-126
Woodard, W. L. ....TVG 401-218
Woodard, William H. ....RR............401-65
Woodbridge, J. E. ....FF 401-140
Wooden, John W. ....RRR 401-126
Woodhead, E. S. ....TVG 401-218
Woodhouse, Nathan W................USV 401-255
Woodhull, Frost............................SR............401-110
Woodhull, George S. ....ARM 401-12
Woodland, B. H............................RRR 401-126
Woodland, Ben H. ....RR............401-65
Woodley, John..............................TVG 401-218
Woodley, M. B..............................LR 401-131
Woodlief, M. ....TST 401-38
Woodlief, Wallace ....TVG 401-218
Woodman, James O.....................SR............401-110
Woodridge, Strother ....SP............401-50
Woodrome, T. E. ....USV 401-255
Woodruff, Benjamin F..................NAV........401-27
Woodruff, D. G.............................FF 401-140
Woodruff, E. B. ....FF 401-140
Woodruff, M. Frank ....USV 401-255
Woods, Alva..................................RR............401-65
Woods, Aubrey Travis..................SR............401-110
Woods, C. A. ....TVG 401-218
Woods, Cullen C. ....USV 401-255
Woods, D. R. ....TST 401-38
Woods, H. A. ....USV 401-255
Woods, Henry..............................SR............401-110
Woods, J. E...................................TVG 401-218
Woods, J. W. ....FB............401-177
Woods, James W. ....RRR 401-126
Woods, Joe ....FB............401-177
Woods, John ....FB............401-177
Woods, John D. ....RRR 401-126
Woods, John D. ....SR............401-110
Woods, John N. ....USV 401-255
Woods, Joseph.............................FB............401-177
Woods, Oscar C. ....SR............401-110
Woods, P. C. ....TVG 401-218
Woods, Robert.............................TST 401-38
Woods, Roy J. ....USV 401-255
Woods, S. H. ....TVG 401-218
Woods, Seth.................................SR............401-110
Woods, T. B. ....TVG 401-218
Woods, Tom C..............................USV 401-255
Woods, W. E.................................FB............401-177
Woods, William M. ....RR 401-65
Woodson, W. W. ....USV 401-255
Woodul, Louis E. ....USV 401-255
Woodul, Walter F. ....SR............401-110
Woodward, E. F. ....SR............401-110
Woodward, F. M. ....SR............401-110
Woodward, H. ....TVG 401-218
Woodward, I. G. ....SR............401-110
Woodward, J. F. ....SR............401-110
Woodward, Parker G. ....USV 401-255
Woodward, Ross..........................USV 401-255
Woodward, Samuel W. ....USV 401-255
Woodward, W. ....TVG 401-218
Woodward, W. H. ....TST 401-38
Woodworth, W. W. ....SR............401-110
Woody, J. V. ....SR............401-110
Woody, John E. ....SR............401-110
Woodyard, Edward F...................USV 401-256
Wooldridge, Charles A.................MV 401-31
Wooldridge, John R.....................NAV........401-27
Woolfolk, Joe A ....TST 401-38
Wooliver, John ....RR............401-65
Woolley, M. L. ....SP............401-50
Woolley, T. W. ....USV 401-256
Woolley, Walter T. ....TVG 401-218
Wooten, C. H. ....USV 401-256
Wooten, George H.......................USV 401-256
Worcester, Warren Wesley...........FF 401-140
Worcester, Warren Wesley...........FB............401-177
Word, Arthur ....TVG 401-218

Index to Texas Adjutant General Service Records—All Service Branches

Name	Branch	Record
Word, Arthur	USV	401-256
Word, Thomas Stutsman	SR	401-110
Work, John	MV	401-31
Work, Lea A.	USV	401-256
Work, Philip A.	MV	401-31
Worley, George E.	USV	401-256
Wormser, A. W.	SR	401-110
Wormwood, Henry R.	FB	401-177
Worsham, Dow A.	RRR	401-126
Worsham, Jerrymiah	USV	401-256
Worsham, Joe Boone	SR	401-110
Worthan, Chas. I.	SR	401-110
Worthington, A. M.	SR	401-110
Worthington, N.	FB	401-177
Worthington, Walter	USV	401-256
Worthy, Arthur V.	USV	401-256
Worthy, E. G.	RRR	401-126
Worthy, Paul C.	USV	401-256
Woyeichowsky, Edward	ARM	401-12
Wozencraft, A. P.	TVG	401-218
Wrarzy, George	USV	401-256
Wreford, Thomas	ARM	401-12
Wren, C. C.	RR	401-65
Wren, Clark C.	SR	401-110
Wren, Clark Campbell	TVG	401-218
Wren, James A.	MV	401-31
Wren, John K.	SR	401-110
Wren, W. R.	LR	401-131
Wren, W. W.	TVG	401-218
Wright, A. M.	NAV	401-27
Wright, A. P.	TVG	401-218
Wright, Andrew W. P.	MV	401-31
Wright, Asa	USV	401-256
Wright, Benjamin F.	USV	401-256
Wright, Benjamin T.	MV	401-31
Wright, Charles C.	TST	401-38
Wright, Charles D.	SR	401-110
Wright, Charles E.	USV	401-256
Wright, Charles F.	SR	401-110
Wright, Charlie Hays	RR	401-65
Wright, Dan	SP	401-50
Wright, Duncan S.	RR	401-65
Wright, E. B.	RR	401-65
Wright, E. E.	TVG	401-218
Wright, E. F.	SR	401-110
Wright, E. G.	TVG	401-218
Wright, E. J.	TVG	401-218
Wright, E. R.	RR	401-65
Wright, E. V.	TVG	401-218
Wright, Earl V.	SR	401-110
Wright, Emanuel A.	RR	401-65
Wright, Eugene C.	SR	401-110
Wright, Francis B.	NAV	401-27
Wright, G. M.	FB	401-177
Wright, George H.	TVG	401-218
Wright, Harry L.	FB	401-177
Wright, Henry C.	TST	401-38
Wright, Howell	SR	401-110
Wright, J. B.	FB	401-177
Wright, J. M.	RR	401-65
Wright, J. M.	SP	401-50
Wright, J. M.	FB	401-177
Wright, James B.	SR	401-110
Wright, James C.	USV	401-256
Wright, James Clinton	TVG	401-218
Wright, James Logan	USV	401-256
Wright, James T.	CSA	401-40
Wright, John F.	USV	401-256
Wright, John R.	TST	401-38
Wright, John W.	FB	401-177
Wright, John W.	USV	401-256
Wright, L. B.	FB	401-177
Wright, L. L.	FB	401-177
Wright, Leon A.	USV	401-256
Wright, M. H.	FB	401-178
Wright, Milam	FB	401-178
Wright, Milam H.	RR	401-65
Wright, Pleasant	MV	401-31
Wright, Robert F.	USV	401-256
Wright, Sterling	TVG	401-218
Wright, T. W.	FB	401-178
Wright, Thomas R.	RR	401-65
Wright, W. C.	USV	401-256
Wright, W. J.	RR	401-65
Wright, W. J.	LR	401-131
Wright, W. L.	FB	401-178
Wright, W. L.	TVG	401-218
Wright, W. W.	SP	401-50
Wright, William C.	USV	401-256
Wright, William J.	FB	401-178
Wright, William J.	USV	401-256
Wright, William L.	RR	401-65
Wroe, E. R. L.	SR	401-110
Wroe, H. A.	SR	401-110
Wroten, Charles E.	RRR	401-126
Wuerschmidt, Paul	SR	401-110
Wukasch, Charles G.	USV	401-256
Wukasch, Rudolph	SR	401-110
Wulfing, Robert	SP	401-50
Wurzbach, August	RR	401-65
Wurzbach, George C.	TVG	401-218
Wurzbach, George C.	USV	401-256
Wurzbach, Harry M.	USV	401-256
Wyatt, Clyde	SR	401-110
Wyatt, Harris	USV	401-256
Wyatt, Jackson Hall	TVG	401-218
Wyatt, Jackson Hall	USV	401-256
Wyatt, James S.	SR	401-110
Wyatt, James W.	ARM	401-12
Wyatt, James W.	USV	401-256
Wyatt, Jordon	MM	401-32
Wyatt, Millard F.	USV	401-256

Index to Texas Adjutant General Service Records—All Service Branches

Name	Branch	Record
Xydias, Anthony	TVG	401-218
Yacky, Louis	TVG	401-218
Yadon, Joseph	ARM	401-12
Yaeger, W. H.	SR	401-110
Yale, Sid	SR	401-110
Yancey, C. R.	TVG	401-218
Yancey, Fayette	SP	401-50
Yancey, J. C.	SR	401-110
Yancey, W. E.	SR	401-110
Yandell, W. H.	FB	401-178
Yantis, G. A.	FB	401-178
Yarborough, William H.	MV	401-31
Yarbrough, D.	FB	401-178
Yarbrough, Henry E.	USV	401-256
Yarbrough, J. S.	SR	401-110
Yarbrough, M. T.	SR	401-110
Yarbrough, Robert H.	USV	401-256
Yarbrough, S.	SR	401-110
Yarbrough, W. J.	SP	401-50
Yates, G. H.	SR	401-110
Yates, Green	TVG	401-218
Yates, Ira G., Jr.	SR	401-110
Yates, John E.	TVG	401-218
Yates, Louis A.	SR	401-110
Yates, M. C.	FB	401-178
Yates, Milton F.	USV	401-256
Yates, O. W.	SR	401-110
Yates, Thomas	ARM	401-12
Yates, W. E.	RRR	401-126
Yates, W. H.	TVG	401-218
Yates, W. J.	SR	401-110
Yates, Walter	TVG	401-218
Yates, William	USV	401-256
Yates, William James	USV	401-256
Yaw, Ralph E.	USV	401-256
Yeager, Anson B.	USV	401-256
Yeager, Arthur Chandler	RRR	401-126
Yeager, J. D.	TVG	401-218
Yeargin, John	TVG	401-218
Yeargin, Will	TVG	401-218
Yeary, E. R.	RR	401-65
Yeates, J. C.	FB	401-178
Yeates, John C.	SR	401-110
Yelvington, Henry b.	SR	401-110
Yerby, John H.	ARM	401-12
Yerger, E. M.	FB	401-178
Yergin, Baalam	ARM	401-12
Yerian, Adam	ARM	401-12
Yingling, Jesse F.	USV	401-256
Yoakum, H. J.	SR	401-110
Yocum, Christopher	ARM	401-12
Yolland, P. L.	TVG	401-218
Yolton, Frank Louis	RRR	401-126
Yonce, Sanford J.	USV	401-256
Yonker, John	FF	401-140
Yopp, Horace G.	SR	401-110
York, Chas. F.	SR	401-110
York, Edwin R., Colonel	SR	401-110
York, Edwin Ruth Van	USV	401-256
York, J. A.	FB	401-178
York, James A.	ARM	401-12
York, Johnny G.	TVG	401-218
York, Milton	SP	401-50
York, N. J.	RRR	401-126
York, Thornton	USV	401-256
York, W. J.	SR	401-110
York, W. W.	FB	401-178
York, William KeRR	ARM	401-12
York, William M.	CSA	401-40
Yorston, Charles	NAV	401-27
Younce, Allison L.	USV	401-256
Young, A. B.	FB	401-178
Young, A. S.	ARM	401-12
Young, B. F.	TVG	401-218
Young, C. H.	FB	401-178
Young, Charles C.	FB	401-178
Young, Charles T.	USV	401-256
Young, E. L.	RR	401-65
Young, E. L.	SR	401-110
Young, E. S.	TVG	401-218
Young, E. S.	TVG	401-218
Young, Frank L.	RRR	401-126
Young, Frederick S.	TVG	401-218
Young, Frederick S.	USV	401-256
Young, G. P.	TVG	401-218
Young, H. G.	SR	401-110
Young, Hamilton C.	USV	401-256
Young, Horace G.	CSA	401-40
Young, J. M. H.	SP	401-50
Young, J. T.	TVG	401-218
Young, J. W.	ARM	401-12
Young, J. W.	LR	401-131
Young, James	NAV	401-27
Young, James	ARM	401-12
Young, James W.	USV	401-256
Young, John S.	FB	401-178
Young, John T.	USV	401-256
Young, John T.	USV	401-256
Young, John W.	SR	401-110
Young, Joseph	ARM	401-12
Young, Joseph B.	ARM	401-12
Young, Joseph M.	USV	401-256
Young, M. C.	RR	401-65
Young, Michael C.	USV	401-256
Young, Noble	SR	401-110
Young, Philip	ARM	401-12
Young, Phillip	USV	401-256
Young, R. E.	RRR	401-126
Young, R. R.	FB	401-178
Young, Richard	FB	401-178
Young, Roy	SR	401-110
Young, Sam F.	USV	401-256

Index to Texas Adjutant General Service Records—All Service Branches

Name	Branch	Number
Young, Sharp	RR	401-65
Young, Thomas P.	RR	401-65
Young, W. E.	TVG	401-218
Young, W. H.	SR	401-110
Young, W. H.	FB	401-178
Young, W. J.	SP	401-50
Young, W. J.	TVG	401-218
Young, W. L.	SR	401-110
Young, W. N.	FB	401-178
Young, W. V.	RRR	401-126
Young, W. W.	TVG	401-218
Young, W. W.	USV	401-256
Young, William	SP	401-50
Young, William E.	RR	401-65
Young, William W.	USV	401-256
Youngblood, Bonney	USV	401-256
Youngblood, Harvey H.	USV	401-256
Younger, Louis Henry	TVG	401-218
Younger, Louis Henry	USV	401-256
Younger, Windfield H.	USV	401-256
Youngkin, Frank	USV	401-256
Yozell, Charles G.	USV	401-256
Yregoyen, Cresano	SP	401-50
Yung, Chris	TVG	401-218
Yung, William	TVG	401-218
Zach, Alfons	USV	401-256
Zacharias, Louis	ARM	401-12
Zachary, W. L.	USV	401-256
Zachry, John Henry	TVG	401-218
Zackie, Dave	SR	401-110
Zander, August	FB	401-178
Zanker, E. E.	TVG	401-218
Zapata, Clemente	SP	401-50
Zavala, Aug. De	USV	401-256
Zeanon, A.	RRR	401-126
Zeaze, Herman	USV	401-256
Zeitz, Bennie	TVG	401-218
Zeitz, Charlie	TVG	401-218
Zeitz, Henry	ARM	401-12
Zellner, Francis	ARM	401-12
Zepeda, Vicente	ARM	401-12
Zerwer, Richard E.	USV	401-256
Zickefoose, A. S.	FB	401-178
Zickefoose, Thomas A.	FB	401-178
Zieschang, J. A.	SR	401-110
Zilker, A. J.	SR	401-110
Ziller, R. L.	SR	401-110
Zimmerman, Joseph H.	USV	401-256
Zimmermann, Albin	USV	401-256
Zimmermann, Eugene E.	TVG	401-218
Zingelar, Jacob	ARM	401-12
Zinsmeyer, Emile M.	TVG	401-218
Zinsmeyer, Emile M.	USV	401-256
Zinsmeyer, Stephen	FF	401-140
Zinsmeyer, Stephen	SP	401-50
Zivley, George D.	TVG	401-218
Zivley, John H.	USV	401-256
Zoeller, Joseph	ARM	401-12
Zollicoffer, Oscar	FB	401-178
Zorb, A.	SP	401-50
Zorkowsky, Archie	TVG	401-218
Zorn, F. A.	FB	401-178
Zuberbier, H.	NAV	401-27
Zuberbier, Louis	NAV	401-27
Zubibier, Simon	NAV	401-27
Zucker, Bruno	USV	401-256
Zuercher, Leopold	FB	401-178
Zumwalt, Thomas B.	FB	401-178
Zurcher, Fred C.	TVG	401-218
Zwernemann, E. T.	SR	401-110